William Edward Hartpole Lecky

A history of England In the XVIII. century

Vol. III

William Edward Hartpole Lecky

A history of England In the XVIII. century
Vol. III

ISBN/EAN: 9783742842695

Manufactured in Europe, USA, Canada, Australia, Japa

Cover: Foto ©Andreas Hilbeck / pixelio.de

Manufactured and distributed by brebook publishing software (www.brebook.com)

William Edward Hartpole Lecky

A history of England In the XVIII. century

A HISTORY OF ENGLAND
IN THE
EIGHTEENTH CENTURY

BY

WILLIAM EDWARD HARTPOLE LECKY

VOLUME III.

FOURTH EDITION

LONDON
LONGMANS, GREEN, AND CO.
1890

CONTENTS

OF

THE THIRD VOLUME.

CHAPTER X.

	PAGE
Difficulty of combining in fixed governments security and ability	1
Evils of elective monarchy	1
English type of monarchy	5
Requires the withdrawal of the King from active politics	7
George III. the last English King who greatly influenced politics	10
His early life	10
Enthusiasm at his accession. His virtues	12
Evils produced by his personal policy	14

Circumstances that favoured his power.

Example of foreign monarchies	16
Ecclesiastical and legal tendencies towards despotism	17
Extinction of Jacobitism. Growth of Tory sentiment	18
Scheme for destroying parties. Bolingbroke, Carteret, and Pitt	19
Adopted by the Court. Divided administrations	20
Position of the Cabinet	21
'Seasonable hints of an honest man'	22
Magnificent position of England	23
Divisions in the Government. The King's speech	25
Bute and the Jacobites	26
Supply. Tenure of Judges	27
Changes in the Ministry	28
General election	29
Arguments for peace	30
Alliance of France and Spain. Policy of Pitt	32
Resignation of Pitt and Temple	35
Pitt accepts a pension for himself and a title for his wife	36
Conquest of Martinique and Havannah	39
Other victories	40
Resignation of Newcastle. Bute Prime Minister	41

		PAGE
Negotiations for peace. Bedford	. . . .	42
The Peace of Paris	. . . .	44
Excessive requirements of Pitt	. . . . . .	48
Unpopularity of Bute	. . . .	49
Hatred of the Scotch	. . . .	50
Character and position of Bute .	. . . . . .	55
Henry Fox. Gross intimidation	. . . . . .	56
Literary patronage of Bute	. . . .	58
Parliament approves of the peace .	. . . . .	61
Its unpopularity in the country. Bute and Dashwood resign		62
Quarrel of Fox and Shelburne .	. . . . . .	62
Failure of the Tory Ministry .	. . . . . .	63

Grenville Ministry (April 1763).

Temple and Bedford refuse to join .	. . . . .	68
First contest with Wilkes. No. 45, 'North Briton'	. . .	70
Arrest of Wilkes under a General Warrant	. . .	73
Pronounced to be illegal. Prosecution of the Messengers	. .	74
Wilkes dismissed from the Militia. Prosecuted for libel	. .	75
Parliament orders the 'North Briton' to be burnt	. .	76
The 'Essay on Woman' .	. . . .	76
Martin's duel with Wilkes.	. . . .	78
Popular support of Wilkes	. . . .	78
Parliament votes libels to be not protected by privilege .	. .	80
Wilkes goes to France, is expelled and outlawed	. . .	81
Multiplication of riots and libels	. . . . .	82
The Manilla ransom. Bedford joins the Government .	.	83
Purchase of the Isle of Man .	. . . . . .	83
Party aspect of Grenville's Ministry .	. . . .	84
Relations of the King to Grenville and Bedford .	. .	85
Resignation of Shelburne .	. . . .	87
The Regency Bill .	. . . .	89
Bedford attacked by the mob .	. . . . . .	91
Change of Ministry. The Whigs return under Rockingham, July 1765 .	. . . .	92

The Rockingham Ministry.

Its weakness. Pitt refuses to join it .	. . . .	95
The King undermines it .	. . . .	96
Its dismissal	. . . .	97
Conduct of Pitt towards the Rockingham Whigs .	. .	98
Questions on which he differed from Rockingham	. . .	101
His views about party. Good and evil of party	. . .	102
Degeneracy of parties under George III. Remedies of Burke .	.	110

Ministry of Pitt.

Its heterogeneous character .	. . . . . .	111
Quarrel with Temple .	. . . .	113

	PAGE
Pitt accepts the Earldom of Chatham. Popular indignation	114
Rockingham refuses to see Chatham	115
The 'forty days' tyranny'	116
The Land-tax reduced by the Opposition	117
Resignation of remaining partisans of Rockingham	118
Failure of an attempted northern alliance	119
Project of withdrawing the territorial revenue from the East India Company	119
Growth of the Tory element in the Government	120
Chatham incapacitated by illness	121
Changes in the Ministry	123
Corsica becomes French	124
Plunder of the Duke of Portland	125
Growing ascendency of North. The King favours the Ministry	127

CHAPTER XI.

The Middlesex election.

Wilkes on the Continent	128
Stands unsuccessfully for the City of London. Elected for Middlesex, March 1768	129
Perplexity of the Government. King orders his expulsion	130
Wilkes freed from his outlawry	130
Condemned for the 'North Briton' and 'Essay on Woman'	131
Great riots in London	131
Disturbed condition of the country	135
Resignation of Chatham	138
New provocations by Wilkes	139
His expulsion, February 1769. Opposed by Grenville	140
Wilkes re-elected and pronounced incapable of sitting	141
Third election. Luttrell pronounced to be member	142
Great popularity of Wilkes	143
Arguments on the doctrine of incapacity	144
Petitions from the country in favour of Wilkes	150
Renewed riots	151
Unpopularity of the Government. Corsica. The Falkland Isles	153
The King's debts	154
Unpopularity of Grafton	155
Weakness of Conway	156
And of Camden	157
Dismissal of Camden. New changes	160
Charles Yorke, his tragic end	161
Final resignation of Conway	163
Violent opposition of Chatham	163
Overtures to Rockingham	165
Triumph of the Government	167
Apostacy of Wedderburn	168
Despondency of the Opposition	169

Parliamentary reform.   PAGE

 Extent of corrupt influence 170
 The nabobs 171
 Disfranchisement of Shoreham freemen 173
 Inequalities of representation 173
 Birth of English Radicalism—1769 174
 Public meetings 174
 Society of the Supporters of the Bill of Rights. Horne . 175
 Instructions to members 176
 Whigs compelled to identify themselves with Parliamentary
  reform 176
 Views of Chatham about reform 178
 Edmund Burke. His life, character, and genius . . 181
 Differs from Chatham 192
 His conception of party . . . 195
 Dislike to Chatham's character . . . 198
 Extent to which he supported reform . 201
 His opposition to triennial Parliaments . 202
 To a Place Bill 203
 To instructions to members 203
 To changes in the constitution of Parliament . 204
 Consistency and nature of his Conservatism . 205
 Distinctions between Whig and Radical . . 209
 Objects of representative systems 211
 Criticism of the views of Burke 218

 Dangers to constitutional government in eighteenth and nine-
  teenth centuries 220
 Grenville's Election Act 224
 Unsuccessful attempt to disfranchise revenue officers . . 226
 Curtailment of Parliamentary privileges . . . 226
 Growth of the Democratic spirit 228

The Press.

 Its growing influence 229
 The doctrine of libel 229
 Changed character of newspapers 232
 The 'Letters of Junius' 233
 Problem of their authorship 246
 Parliamentary reporting 256
 Contest with printers 257
 Estimate of the influence of the Press . . . 262
 Defeat of the Tory party due to its influence and to the American
  War 266

CHAPTER XII.

AMERICA, 1763–1776.

	PAGE
Effects of the Peace of Paris on the American colonies	267
Predictions of their separation from England	268
Question of the cession of Canada	269
Impossibility of retaining the colonies by force	271
Strong loyalty of the colonies	272
Their independence of each other	274
New England	276
The Middle States	280
Virginia	285
The other Southern colonies	288
Intellectual and material condition of the colonies	289
Their moral and political condition	292
Their relations to the mother-country	296
And to the Crown	298
Commercial restrictions	299
American smuggling	302
'Writs of assistance'	303
Elements of dissension	304

Policy of Grenville.

Revision of the trade laws	307
Establishment of an army in the colonies	310
Determination to tax the colonies	312
Earlier proposals to tax America	314
Arguments in favour of it	315
Franklin on a colonial army	318
The Stamp Act	319
Speech of Barré	324
Taxation and representation	325
Commercial concessions. Quartering Act	328
General resistance to the Stamp Act	329
Impossibility of enforcing it	332

The Rockingham Ministry.

General indifference to American affairs	332
Distress in the trading towns	333
Meeting of Parliament (December 1765). The Opposition	334
Pitt justifies the Americans	336
Government repeals the Stamp Act, but asserts the right to tax	339
Necessity of the Declaratory Act	341
New revision of the commercial laws	343
Opinion in America	344
Governor Bernard	346
New York refuses to obey the Mutiny Act. 'The Farmer's Letters'	348

The Chatham Ministry.

	PAGE
Irritation in England against America	349
Charles Townshend proposes to tax America	350
Suspends the New York Assembly	352
Establishes a new Board of Customs	353
Imposes new duties for purposes of revenue	353
Review of Townshend's policy	353
Reception of Townshend's measures in America	355
Death of Townshend (September 1767)	356
Changes in the Ministry. Ascendency of North	358
Hillsborough censures the Massachusetts Circular	358
Growing spirit of insurrection	359
Samuel Adams	360
Attitude of Massachusetts	362
Attitude of the English Parliament, 1768 and 1769	363
Revival of a law for trying traitors in England	363
Determination to repeal all the duties except that on tea	365
Recall of Bernard. Submission of New York	365
The Boston massacre	366
Acquittal of the soldiers. American humanity	368
The tea duty	370
Abandonment of the non-importation agreements	372
The destruction of the 'Gaspee'	373
Measure to protect the King's ships. Committees of correspondence	375
Benjamin Franklin	375
Sends Hutchinson's letters to America	380
Wedderburn's invective	385
The Boston tea ships	387
Impeachment of Oliver	388

English opinion on the American Question.

Tucker advocates the cession of America	388
Adam Smith	389
Chatham	392
Burke	393
Parliament in favour of coercion	397
Closing of Boston harbour	397
Suspension of the Charter of Massachusetts	397
Soldiers to be tried in England	398
General Gage made Governor of Massachusetts. Quartering Act.	399
The Quebec Act	399
The other colonies support Boston	403
Numerous riots	405
Proclamation of Gage	407
The Congress at Philadelphia (September 1774)	408
General arming. How far Americans wished for independence	412
Illusions in America and in England	415
Divided opinion in America	417
The loyalists	418

	PAGE
Enrolment of an American army. Capture of Fort William	420
English Parliament meets, November 1774	420
New efforts of conciliation by Chatham	421
By Burke, Hartley, &c.	422
Parliament cuts off the trade of America. Increases the army at Boston	423
Conciliatory measure of North	423
Battle of Lexington, April 19, 1775	425
Battle of Bunker's Hill, June 17, 1775	426
Congress of Philadelphia, 1775	428
Washington appointed commander. His life and character	430
Capture of Ticonderoga. Invasion of Canada	436
Death of Montgomery. American retreat	437
Lord Dunmore in Virginia.	437
Proceedings in the Middle and Southern colonies	438
The negroes and Indians	439
The English party in America	441
Misgivings in America	442
The army of Washington	445
Dilatoriness of Gage	448
Replaced by Howe. Situation of the Americans, December 1775	449
Boston evacuated, March 17, 1776	451
Paine's 'Common Sense'.	451
Motives leading to separation	452
The French alliance	453
Difficulty of England in raising soldiers	455
Enlistment of German mercenaries	458
Produces the Declaration of Independence	459

CHAPTER XIII.

Domestic troubles of the King	461
The Royal Marriage Act	463
Charles Fox	465
His brief separation from North (1772)	472

Affairs of the East India Company.

Despotism exercised by its servants	473
The private trade	474
Displacement of native princes	475
Growing power of the Company in Bengal	476
Administration of Clive (1765)	477
Parliament claims authority over the territorial revenue	481
Regulates the dividends	481
War with Hyder Ali	482
Bankruptcy of the Company (1772)	484
Views of Adam Smith about India	484
Select Committee of 1773. Speeches of Burke	486

	PAGE
Indian Acts of 1773	488
Charges against Clive	490
His acquittal and death	491

Religious legislation.

Great diminution of intolerance	492
Abuses of the Ecclesiastical Courts	493
Nonconformists elected Sheriffs in London	496
Proposed abolition of subscription to the Articles	497
Dissenters freed from the subscription	501
The Quebec Act	502
Propriety of legislating for Catholics. Diminution of Catholic fanaticism	503
Obsolete laws	504
How far the anticatholic laws were enforced	506
Position of Catholics in England	508
Relief Bill of 1778	508
Riots in Scotland	509
The Gordon riots, 1780	510
Trials of rioters	522
Effects of the riots on opinion	523
General popularity of the North Ministry	524
Parliamentary approval of its American policy	525
Secession of Fox	527
English opinion on the American question, 1775 and 1776	528
Scotch opinion	533
Irish opinion	534
Difficulties of enlistment. Impressment	535
Criminals enrolled in the army	539
Party aspects of the American question	541
Grave divisions in the country	545

HISTORY OF ENGLAND

IN

THE EIGHTEENTH CENTURY.

CHAPTER X.

ONE of the most difficult problems which the framers of constitutions are called upon to solve is that of providing that the direction of affairs shall be habitually in the hands of men of very exceptional ability, and at the same time of preventing the instability, insecurity, and alarm which perpetual and radical changes in the Government must produce. Among the many objections to hereditary despotism, one of the most obvious is that it implies that the members of a single family, educated for the most part under circumstances peculiarly fitted to enervate the character, shall, during many generations, be competent to discharge one of the most arduous of human undertakings, the direction of the complicated and often conflicting interests of a nation. Among the many objections to elective monarchy, the most serious is that it condemns the country in which it exists to perpetual conspiracies, tumults, and intrigues, which are fatal to the formation of settled political habits, and derange every part of the national organisation. Considered as a matter of pure theory, no form of government might appear more reasonable than that under which the leading men in the country assemble at each vacancy of the throne to choose the man who appears to them the most fitted for the crown. But no form of government has been more decisively condemned by experience. The elected sovereign is always likely to conspire with the assistance either of his own army or of foreign Powers to perpetuate the sovereignty in his family. The other great powers in the State, through fear of such attempts, are tempted to reduce the military establishments below what is necessary for the security of the nation. Bitter factions, profoundly detrimental to the well-being of the community, are inevitably formed among the great families who are competing to raise their candidates to the throne. Every illness of the sovereign gives rise to intrigues, conspiracies, and insecurity; his death usually leads to disorder, and sometimes to anarchy and civil war. Each new King ascends the throne tainted by the arts of electioneering, deeply pledged to one section of his people, the object of the vehement hostility of another section, and conscious that large classes are looking forward eagerly to his death. Such are the inevitable vices of elective monarchy, and they are so grave that, with the exception of the Papacy, which rests upon conditions wholly unlike those of any other monarchy, this form of government has been long extirpated from Europe. The crowns of Sweden and of Denmark became in the sixteenth and seventeenth centuries strictly hereditary. The German Empire, and the kingdoms of Hungary, Poland, and Bohemia passed away or were absorbed, and they perished mainly by their own incurable weakness.

Several attempts have been made in the way of compromise to obviate these evils, and to combine the advantages of hereditary and of elective monarchy. One theory of government which was widely diffused in antiquity, and which may be traced far into the middle ages, but which has now passed altogether out of the sphere of practical politics, was that royalty was hereditary in a single family, but that the chiefs, tribes, or nations had the power of electing whom they pleased from among its members.

Another theory, which if not openly avowed, has been sometimes practically adopted, is that the King holds his office only during good behaviour. In modern France the sovereign has always been an active power in the State, continually intervening in the direction of affairs, but liable, whenever he showed himself either incompetent or unpopular, to be displaced by a sudden revolution. To men who are firmly convinced that the ecclesiastical notion about the Divine right of kings is a baseless superstition, that the sovereign is but the first magistrate of the State, and that the office he holds is intended for the benefit of his people, such a system appears at first sight very simple. In the natural course of events it must often happen that the sovereign, being selected by no principle of competition and being exposed to more than ordinary temptations, must be contemptible both in intellect and character, and large sections of his subjects come to look upon him as nothing better than an overpaid and inefficient official, who, on the first offence, should be unceremoniously discharged.

But the evils which have resulted from the predominance of such a way of thinking in a community are so great that they have led many who have no personal sympathy with the superstitious estimate of royalty, as a matter of expediency, rather to encourage than oppose it. An hereditary monarchy which subsists only on the condition of the monarch being a superior man must be in a chronic state of insecurity, and the stability of the government is one of the first conditions of national well-being. Every revolution brings to the surface the worst elements in the community, demoralises public life, impairs material interests, and weakens the empire of the law. It is a great calamity for a people when its criminal classes have learnt to take an active part in politics. It is a still greater calamity when the appetite for organic and revolutionary change has taken hold of large classes, when the political enthusiasm of opposition assumes the form of rebellion, and when the prevailing disposition is to undervalue the slow process of constitutional reform, and to look upon force as the natural solution of political questions. This habit of regarding revolution as in itself admirable and desirable, and making, in the words of Burke, the extreme remedy of the State its habitual diet, is perhaps the most fatal of all the diseases which now affect political bodies in Europe. It necessarily throws the rulers into the posture of self-defence, and makes them nervously and constantly jealous of their subjects. It produces reactions in which the most important reforms are endangered, drives from politics the very class whose co-operation is most valuable, and exposes every nation in which it exists to the opposite evils of despotism and anarchy. Political liberty, whether in Parliament or in the press, is only safe and permanently possible when oppositions are content to act within the lines of the Constitution and the limits of the law, and the amount of freedom which any nation can endure is measured much less by its positive civilisation and intelligence, than by the weakness of the element of anarchy that is within it.

There are also other evils, if possible more serious, which follow in the train of revolutions. Every deposed dynasty has its devoted followers, and the nation is thus cursed with the calamity of a disputed succession, which often leads to civil war, and always makes it impossible for the Government to command the whole national energies in great emergencies of the State. No other influence is so fatal to the spirit of patriotism. Through hostility to the Government a large proportion of the heroism, fidelity, and devotion of the nation is permanently alienated from its affairs, and forms a clear deduction from its strength. Subjects learn to look with indifference or complacency upon the disasters of their country, and to throw perpetual obstacles in the course of its policy. Rulers learn to pursue two policies—a national one intended to benefit the nation, and a dynastic one intended to benefit themselves. It was the great merit of the conciliatory policy of Walpole that it saved England during the period of its disputed succession from a large part of these evils; but in France, during the period that has elapsed since the Revolution, they have all been abundantly displayed. A soil once peculiarly fertile in political genius blasted by repeated revolutions; large classes wholly separated from the management of affairs, or animated by an insane passion for anarchy; a Government embarrassed by dynastic and revolutionary Opposition in the most critical moments of its foreign policy, and vainly seeking by wild military adventures to divert to foreign channels the passions that are dangerous at home; an administration, both civil and military, deeply tainted with corruption; a great empire invaded, humiliated and dismembered, and finally all the elements of disorder rising into fierce insurrection against the Government at the very time when a foreign enemy was surrounding the capital; these have been in our own day the fruits of that diseased appetite for organic change and that contempt for all constituted authority which the Great Revolution implanted in the chief cities of France. Blind indeed must be that politician who fails to perceive their significance, who has not learnt from this long train of calamities the danger of tampering with the central pillars of the State, and letting loose those revolutionary torrents which spread such ruin and desolation in their path.

The problem of combining stability, capacity, and political freedom has, in modern constitutional monarchies of the English type, been most fully met by a careful division of powers. The sovereignty is strictly hereditary, surrounded by a very large amount of reverence, and sheltered by constitutional forms from criticism or opposition, but at the same time it is so restricted in its province that it has, or ought to have, no real influence on legislation. The King, according to a fundamental maxim, 'can do no wrong.' The responsibility of every political act rests solely with the minister, and, as he has the whole responsibility, he has a right to claim the whole management. The credit of success and the stigma of failure belong alike to him. The King is placed altogether above the vicissitudes of party and of politics; he is confined to the discharge of certain offices which are universally admitted to be useful and essential, and which at the same time require not more than ordinary abilities. The chief efficient power, on the other hand, in a constitutional monarchy, is virtually, though not avowedly, as truly elective as in a republic, for although the sovereign chooses the minister, he is restricted in his choice to the statesman whom the dominant political party has selected as its leader, and who has obtained the confidence of Parliament.

In this system the direct political power of the sovereign is very small, but yet the position which he occupies is more important than might at first sight be imagined. In the first place, as the head of society, the patron of art, the dispenser of international courtesies, the supreme representative of his country in the council of nations, he discharges social, and so to speak, ornamental functions, both of dignity and value, and in the next place he contributes very largely to foster the patriotic enthusiasm which is the animating principle and moral force of national greatness. The great majority of men in political matters are governed neither by reason nor by knowledge, but by the associations of the imagination, and for such men loyalty is the first and natural form of patriotism. In the thrill of common emotion that passes through the nation when some great sorrow or some great happiness befalls the reigning dynasty, they learn to recognise themselves as members of a single family. The throne is to them the symbol of national unity—the chief object of patriotic interest and emotion. It strikes their imaginations. It elicits their enthusiasm. It is the one rallying cry they will answer and understand. Tens of thousands of men who are entirely indifferent to party distinctions and to ministerial changes, who are too ignorant or too occupied to care for any great political question, and to whom government rarely appears in any other light than as a machinery for taxing them, regard the monarch with a feeling of romantic devotion, and are capable of great efforts of self-sacrifice in his cause. The circle of political feeling is thus extended. The sum of enthusiasm upon which the nation in critical times can count is largely increased, and, however much speculative critics may disparage the form which it assumes, practical statesmen will not disdain any of the tributary rills that swell the great tide of patriotism. Even in the case of more educated men it is extremely conducive to the strength, unity, and purity of the national sentiment, that the supreme ruler of the nation should be above the animosities of party, and that his presence at the head of affairs should not be the result of the defeat of one section of his people.

To these advantages it must be added that the monarchical form of government provides a simple and admirably efficacious machinery for effecting without convulsion the necessary ministerial changes. In no other form of government do profound mutations of men and policy, violent conflicts of opinion, disordered ambitions, and glaring instances of administrative incapacity, affect so slightly the stability of the Constitution. A ministerial crises has no affinity to a revolution. The permanence of the supreme authority, unchallenged and undisturbed amid all the conflicts of parties, calms the imaginations of men. The continuity of affairs is unbroken. The shock is deadened. The changes take place with regularity and in a restricted orbit, and the country is saved from an insecurity which long before it touches the limit of anarchy is disastrous to the prosperity of nations. Indirectly the monarchy has a great political influence, for if it did not exist the aristocracy could hardly subsist as a considerable political power. In the distribution of non-political patronage the sovereign may not unreasonably claim a real voice, and if he be an able man the experience derived from an official connection with many successive ministries, and the peculiar sources of knowledge arising from his relations with foreign Courts, will never be wholly unfelt in the councils of the nation. In a few rare cases of nearly balanced claims he has a real power of deciding to whom he will entrust the task of forming an administration; in a few rare cases, when a ministry commanding a majority in Parliament is pursuing a course which appears plainly repugnant to the feelings of the country, he may justifiably exercise his prerogative to dissolve Parliament, and submit the question to the decision of the country. But in the immense majority of cases he is at once neutral and powerless in party politics. He simply puts in motion a machine the action of which is elsewhere determined, and is no more responsible for the policy to which he assents than a judge for the laws which he administers. The spirit of loyalty, while it remains a powerful adjunct to the spirit of patriotism, has thus ceased to be in any degree prejudicial to liberty. The position of the King in the Constitution resembles that of the Speaker in the House of Commons, and like that dignitary his political neutrality and the deference with which he is regarded contribute largely to his utility.

The extreme importance of freeing the sovereign from all responsibility and withdrawing him from all official influence in politics, wherever the Parliament is a real exponent of the people's will and is at the same time the most powerful body in the State, may be easily proved. In the great majority of cases he must necessarily be a man of very ordinary ability, and even were it otherwise, his exclusion from Parliament and from the common life of his people deprives him of the kind of experience which is most essential for a popular statesman. And no statesman, though he possessed the ability and experience of a Walpole, a Chatham, or a Peel, could conduct the policy of the nation for the period of a long reign without occasionally incurring violent unpopularity and differing from the majority of the legislators. In a purely constitutional country this causes little disturbance, for the minister at once retires and is replaced by a statesman who shares the views of the majority. But in the case of the sovereign no such expedient is possible. He must remain at his post. He must eventually carry out the policy of his Parliament, and select advisers in whom it has confidence. If then he regards himself as personally responsible for the policy of the nation, and if he be a man of strong, conscientious political convictions, his position will soon become intolerable. He cannot resist without danger, or yield without humiliation. He will be in the position of an irremovable Prime Minister, compelled to carry out a policy which he detests, and to select his subordinates from among his opponents. A more painful, a more insecure, a more fatally false position could hardly be conceived, but it must be that of every sovereign who in a constitutional monarchy is an active party in politics. If the collision be public, it may shake the monarchy to its basis. If it be confined to the precincts of the council-room, it is only a little less dangerous. A secret influence habitually exercised is sure to be suspected, to be exaggerated, and to be misrepresented. The national policy will almost inevitably be weakened when the confidence of the sovereign is withheld from the ministers, or when he is perpetually interfering with their conduct. Court intrigues, secret and unofficial advisers, responsible ministers surrendering their real convictions in deference to the wishes of an irresponsible sovereign, are the natural results; and even if the firmness of ministers succeeds in averting them, it is no small evil that the duty of discussing in detail every political step with the sovereign should be added to the almost overwhelming burden which already rests upon parliamentary statesmen. The King may retain a great influence in the management of affairs where

Parliament is altogether a subordinate body, restricted in its functions and authority. He may even retain it, though more precariously, when Parliament has become the strongest body of the State, if the composition of that Parliament is so exclusive or aristocratic that he can sway it by the influences at his disposal. But whenever Parliament has become a direct expression of the people's will, and especially whenever the existence of a free press and the aggregation of a large proportion of the population in great towns has given popular opinion an irresistible volume and momentum, the withdrawal of the sovereign from the arena is equally essential to his security and to his dignity. The only political power he can reasonably be suffered to exercise is that of a suspensory veto, preventing hasty legislation, and above all delaying the decision of Parliament on great questions till they have been brought directly before the constituencies by an election. But this power —which should certainly be lodged somewhere in the Constitution—is exercised as efficiently and much less invidiously by the House of Lords, and the royal veto has accordingly fallen into desuetude and has not been employed since the reign of Anne.

The substantial, though still somewhat imperfect realisation of this ideal of constitutional monarchy, has, since the period of the Act of Settlement, been only slightly due to legislation, or at least to legislation which was intended to affect the position of the Crown. It has resulted partly from a series of historical facts growing out of the accession of the House of Hanover which have been described in a former volume, and partly from the steady subsequent growth of the popular element in the Constitution. The reigning sovereign has exactly the same legal power of vetoing bills passed by both Houses of Parliament as William III. or the Stuarts, but it is a power which it has become impossible to exercise with safety. The Cabinet, which has gradually drawn to itself nearly all the ancient powers of the Privy Council, which sits without the presence of the sovereign, and which determines the policy of the Government, is a body entirely unknown to the law and to the theory of the Constitution; and it is no special enactment, but only the silent strengthening of party government, that has virtually deprived the sovereign of his legally unrestricted power of choosing his ministers. Even the power so largely exercised by the Tudors and by James I. of changing the composition of the representative body by summoning previously unrepresented towns to send members to Parliament, was in theory untouched by the Revolution, and no less a writer than Locke defended the propriety of extinguishing the rotten boroughs and readjusting the proportion of members to electors by a simple exercise of prerogative.[1] Such schemes soon became impossible, but the form which popular government has assumed in England is mainly to be attributed to the Whig party, who, while they have combated steadily the Tory doctrine of the Divine right of kings, and the conception of monarchy that flows from it, and have restricted within very narrow limits the political functions of the sovereign, have at the same time, unlike many continental Liberals, carefully respected his dignity and his office, and made it a main object to place both outside the sphere of controversy. But in the eighteenth century the Whig ideal was still far from its attainment, and George III. is the last instance of an English sovereign endeavouring systematically to impose his individual opinion upon the nation, and in a great degree succeeding in his attempt.

When George II. died, on October 25, 1760, his grandson and successor had but just completed his twenty-second year. The life of the young Prince had hitherto been very unsuitable for the task he was to fulfil. Since his thirteenth year, when his father died, he had lived entirely with his mother, and he exhibited during his whole career the characteristic merits and defects of a female education. His mother was a woman of a somewhat hard, reserved, and tortuous character; with few friendships and several bitter enmities; with a power of concealing her true sentiments which baffled even those who came in closest connection with her; strict in the observance of her religious duties, and in her care of her nine children; eminently discreet in her dealings with a bad husband and a jealous father-in-law; deeply imbued with

---

[1] Locke, *On Government*, Book 2, ch. xiii. See too Hallam's *Const. Hist.* ch. xiii. O'Connell once drew up a legal argument to prove that it was within the prerogative of the Crown to restore the Irish Parliament by its sole action. See O'Neil Daunt's *Personal Recollections of O'Connell*, ch. xvi.

the narrow prejudices of a small German Court, fond of power, unamiable, and somewhat soured by adversity. The early death of her husband had deprived her of the prospect of a crown, and although after his death Leicester House ceased to be a centre of active opposition, the old King looked upon both the Princess and his grandchild with jealousy, and they had in consequence little intercourse with the Court circle, with the Whig ministers, and even with the other members of the royal family. The education of the young Prince was feebly and fitfully conducted; and it is remarkable that among his preceptors Scott had been recommended by Bolingbroke, while Stone had been suspected of Jacobitism. They appear to have discharged their functions very ill; for George III. was always singularly deficient in literary culture. Lord Waldegrave, who was much the ablest of his governors, described him as a boy of respectable abilities, but great constitutional indolence; scrupulous, dutiful, ignorant of evil, and sincerely pious, but neither generous nor frank; harsh in his judgments of others, with strong prejudices, indomitable obstinacy, and great command over his passions, exceedingly tenacious of his resentments, and exhibiting them chiefly by prolonged fits of sullenness. His indolence he succeeded in completely overcoming, but the other lines of this not very pleasing picture continued during his whole life. He mixed very little in the world—scarcely at all with the young nobility. His mother said that their lax manners would probably corrupt her son. Her enemies declared that the real explanation of this strange seclusion was her own insatiable avarice of power, which made her wish beyond all things to establish a complete ascendency over his mind, and to withdraw him from every influence that could rival her own. Like most members of German royal families, she exaggerated the prerogative of monarchy to the highest degree, and her favourite exhortation, 'George, be a king!' is said to have left a deep impression on the mind of her son. The most important figure in the small circle was John, Earl of Bute, a Scotch nobleman who had held an office in the household of Frederick, Prince of Wales, had lived after his death for some years a life of more than common retirement in Scotland, and, on the establishment of the household of the young Prince, had been placed at the head of it as Groom of the Stole. He was a man of some literary and artistic taste, but of very limited talents, entirely inexperienced in public business, arrogant, reserved, and unpopular in his temper, and with extreme views of the legitimate powers of royalty. The very confidential relations of Bute with the Princess gave rise to a scandal which was widely spread and generally believed.[1] He became the chief adviser or instructor of her son, and strengthened in his mind those plans for the emancipation of the royal authority which George III. pursued steadily throughout his whole life.

The new sovereign came to the throne amid an enthusiasm such as England had hardly seen since Charles II. restored the monarchy. By the common consent of all parties the dynastic contest was regarded as closed, and after two generations of foreign and unsympathetic rulers, the nation, which has always been peculiarly intolerant of strangers, accepted with delight an English king. The favourable impression was still further confirmed when the more salient points of the private character of the King became generally understood. Simple, regular, and abstemious in all his tastes and habits, deeply religious without affectation or enthusiasm, a good son, a faithful husband, a kind master, and (except when he had met with gross ingratitude) an affectionate father, he exhibited through his whole reign, and in a rare perfection, that type of decorous and domestic virtue which the English middle classes most highly prize. The proclamation against immorality with which he began his reign; the touching piety with which, at his coronation, he insisted on putting aside his crown when receiving the sacrament; his rebuke to a Court preacher who had praised him in a sermon; his suppression of Sunday levees; his discouragement of gambling at Court; his letter of remonstrance to an Archbishop of Canterbury who had allowed balls in his palace; his constant attendance and reverential manner at religious services; his solemn and pious resignation under great private misfortunes, contrasted admirably with the open immorality of his father, his grandfather, and his great-grand-

---

[1] See *e.g.* Lord Waldegrave's *Memoirs*, p. 53. Walpole's *Memoirs of George II.* ii. 201, 205.

father, and with the outrageous licentiousness of his own brothers and of his own sons. He never sought for popularity; but he had many of the kingly graces, and many of the national tastes that are most fitted to obtain it. He went through public ceremonies with much dignity, and although his manner in private was hurried and confused, it was kind and homely, and not without a certain unaffected grace. Unlike his two predecessors, he was emphatically a gentleman, and he possessed to a rare degree the royal art of enhancing small favours by a gracious manner and a few well-chosen words. His country tastes, his love of field-sports, his keen interest in the great public schools, endeared him to large classes of his subjects; and, though he was neither brilliant nor witty, several of his terse and happy sayings are still remembered. He was also a very brave man. In the Wilkes riots, in 1769, when his palace was attacked; in the Lord George Gordon riots, in 1780, when his presence of mind contributed largely to save London; in 1786, when a poor madwoman attempted to stab him at the entrance of St. James's Palace; in 1795, when he was assailed on his way to Parliament; in 1800, when he was fired at in a theatre, he exhibited the most perfect composure amid danger. His habit in dating his letters, of marking, not only the day, but the hour and the minute in which he wrote, illustrates not unhappily the microscopic attention which he paid to every detail of public business, and which was the more admirable because his natural tendency was towards sloth. In matters that were not connected with his political prejudices, his sincere appreciation of piety and his desire to do good sometimes overcame his religious bigotry and his hatred of change. Thus he always spoke with respect of the Methodists, and especially of Lady Huntingdon; he supported Howard, and subscribed to a statue in his honour; he supported the Lancaster system of education, though Lancaster was a Dissenter, and was looked upon with disfavour by the bishops; he encouraged the movement for Sunday-schools. He was sincerely desirous of doing his duty, and deeply attached to his country, although stronger feelings often interfered both with his conscientiousness and with his patriotism.

It is not surprising that a sovereign of whom all this may

be truly said should have obtained much respect and admiration; and it must be added that, in his hatred of innovation and in his vehement anti-American, anti-Catholic, and anti-Gallican feelings, he represented the sentiments of large sections—perhaps of the majority—of his people. The party which he drew from its depression has naturally revered his memory, and old age, and blindness, and deafness, and deprivation of reason, and the base ingratitude of two sons, have cast a deep pathos over his closing years.

All these things have contributed very naturally to throw a delusive veil over the political errors of a sovereign of whom it may be said without exaggeration, that he inflicted more profound and enduring injuries upon his country than any other modern English king. Ignorant, narrow-minded, and arbitrary, with an unbounded confidence in his own judgment and an extravagant estimate of his prerogative, resolved at all hazards to compel his ministers to adopt his own views, or to undermine them if they refused, he spent a long life in obstinately resisting measures which are now almost universally admitted to have been good, and in supporting measures which are as universally admitted to have been bad. He espoused with passionate eagerness the American quarrel; resisted obstinately the measures of conciliation by which at one time it might easily have been stifled; envenomed it by his glaring partisanship, and protracted it for several years, in opposition to the wish and to the advice even of his own favourite and responsible minister. He took the warmest personal interest in the attempts that were made, in the matter of general warrants, to menace the liberty of the subject, and in the case of the Middlesex election to abridge the electoral rights of constituencies, and in the other paltry, violent, and arbitrary measures by which the country was inflamed and Wilkes was converted into a hero. The last instance of an English officer deprived of his regiment for his vote in Parliament was due to the personal intervention of the King; and the ministers whom he most warmly favoured were guilty of an amount and audacity of corruption which is probably unequalled in the parliamentary history of England. All the measures that were carried or attempted with the object of purifying the representative body

—the publication of debates, the alteration of the mode of trying contested elections, the reduction of sinecures and pensions, the enlargement of the constituencies—were contrary to the wishes of the King. Although his income during the greater part of his reign was little less than a million a year,[1] although his Court was parsimonious to a fault, and his hospitality exceedingly restricted, and although he succeeded to a considerable sum that had been saved by his predecessor, he accumulated in the course of his reign debts to the amount of no less than 3,398,061*l*.;[2] and there can be little doubt that contemporary public opinion was right in attributing a great part of these debts to his expenditure in parliamentary or electoral corruption. Of all the portions of the empire none was so impoverished, distracted, and misgoverned as Ireland, but every attempt to improve its condition found in the King a bitter adversary. He opposed the relaxation of the atrocious laws by which Irish commerce had been crushed, although his own Tory ministers were in favour of it. He opposed Catholic emancipation with a persistent bitterness, although that measure alone could have made the Irish union acceptable to the people, and although his minister had virtually pledged himself to grant it, and by his refusal he consigned the country to a prolonged and disastrous agitation, the effects of which may never disappear. He opposed the endowment of the Catholic clergy, although statesmen of the most various schools concurred in the belief that no other measure would act so beneficially on the social condition of Ireland, or would so effectually tranquillise the minds of its people. He refused to consent to throw open the higher ranks in the army to the Catholics, although that measure had already been conceded to the army in Ireland by the Irish Parliament; and he flung the country into all the agonies of a 'No Popery' dissolution at the very time when a fearful struggle with France was demanding the utmost unanimity, and when thousands of Catholic soldiers were fighting bravely in his cause. In the same spirit he supported the slave trade; he approved of all the various measures by which Pitt in 1794 and 1795 suspended almost

---

[1] See the calculations in Burke's *Causes of the Present Discontents.*
[2] May's *Const. Hist.* i. 206.

every guarantee of the liberty of the subject; he described the Test and Corporation Acts as the palladium of the constitution, and was inexorably opposed to their abolition; he created Tory peers in such lavish numbers, and with such an exclusive view to their political subserviency, that he seriously lowered the character and fundamentally altered the tendencies of the House of Lords, and produced that strong permanent difference between the two Houses which is one of the greatest dangers of the Constitution; and in the last years of his reign, before insanity extinguished his powers of evil, he was fanning the disastrous French war, and opposing every attempt to negotiate a peace. In a word, there is scarcely a field of politics in which the hand of the King may not be traced—sometimes in postponing inevitable measures of justice and reform, sometimes in sowing the seeds of enduring evil.

The root, however, of his great errors lay in his determination to restore the royal power to a position wholly different from that which it occupied in the reign of his predecessor; and this design was in many respects more plausible than is now generally admitted. Every functionary has a natural tendency to magnify his office, and when George III. ascended the throne he found his position as an hereditary constitutional sovereign almost unique in the world. In France, in Spain, in Austria, in the smallest principality in Germany, the sovereign was hardly less absolute than in Russia or Turkey. And the power of the English sovereign had for many years been steadily declining, and the limitations to which he was practically subject went far beyond the mere letter of the law. The time had indeed long passed when Elizabeth directed her Parliaments to abstain from discussing matters of state, and when James I. declared that, 'as it is atheism and blasphemy in a creature to dispute what the Deity may do, so it is presumption and sedition in a subject to dispute what a king may do in the height of his power;' but even after the Revolution, William III. had been a great political power, and Anne, though a weak and foolish woman, had exercised no small amount of personal influence. What the position of the English sovereign was in the eyes of the English Church was sufficiently shown by the long series of theologians who proclaimed in the most emphatic terms that he possessed a Divine right, different, not only in degree but in kind, from that of every other power in the State; that he was the representative or vicegerent of the Deity; that resistance to him was in all cases a sin. The language of English law was less unqualified, but still it painted his authority in very different colours from those which an historian of George I. or of George II. would have used. The 'Commentaries' of Blackstone were not published till George III. had been for some time on the throne; but Bute had obtained a considerable portion of them in manuscript from the author, for the purpose of instructing the Prince in the principles of the Constitution.[1] 'The King of England,' in the words of Blackstone, 'is not only the chief, but properly the sole magistrate of the nation, all others acting by commission from and in due subordination to him.' 'He may reject what bills, may make what treaties . . . . may pardon what offences he pleases, unless when the Constitution hath expressly, or by evident consequence, laid down some exception or boundary.' He has the sole power of regulating fleets and armies, of manning all forts and other places of strength within the realm, of making war and peace, of conferring honours, offices, and privileges. He governs the kingdom: statesmen, who administer affairs, are only his ministers.[2]

It is not surprising that the contrast between such language and the actual position of George II. during the greater part of his reign should have vividly impressed a young sovereign surrounded by Tory followers, and naturally extremely tenacious of power, or that he should have early resolved to bend all his faculties to the task of emancipating his office from the restrictions that surrounded it. The period of his accession was in some respects exceedingly propitious to his design. Among the causes of the depression of royalty one of the most obvious and important had been the long exclusion from office of that great Tory party which naturally exalts most highly the royal prerogative. It had originally been defended, and perhaps justified, by the Jacobitism of Bolingbroke and of his col-

[1] Adolphus, *Hist. of George III.* i. p. 12.
[2] *Blackstone*, Book 1, ch. vii.

leagues; but it had been perpetuated through party motives, and the borough system, assisted by royal favour, had enabled a few great Whig families gradually to command the chief power in the State. But with the extinction of Jacobitism the necessity for this exclusion had ceased. Scotland had been completely pacified by the abolition of hereditary jurisdictions; the English Jacobites were shown by the Rebellion of 1745 to be few and insignificant. The animosity against George II. on account of the severities that followed the Rebellion was not extended to his successor. The dislike to a foreign king, which had hitherto been the strongest support, had now become one of the most formidable difficulties of the Jacobites. George III was English by birth, by education, by character, and by creed. The Pretender was at once a foreigner and a Papist, with few or no English tastes, and sunk, according to common report, in habitual drunkenness.[1] So many years had elapsed since the Act of Settlement that the new dynasty had struck its roots firmly in the soil, and all those large classes who were most attached to the theory of legitimacy were only waiting for the death of George II. to rally around his successor as they had rallied around Anne or around Charles II.

The propriety of breaking down the system of exclusion seemed manifest. The Tory sentiment of the country had long found no adequate expression in the Government. The party which carried with it the genuine sympathies both of the country gentry and of the country clergy had been so discouraged that after the death of Bolingbroke and of the Prince of Wales it was scarcely represented in Parliament, and its political eclipse had been followed by a great increase both of oligarchical influence and of corruption. There was something manifestly unhealthy in the continuance during many years, of a Government like that of Walpole, which was supported chiefly by a majority of members of nomination boroughs in opposition

[1] 'The Pretender continues to be perpetually drunk; the other day he forced a Cordelier to drink with him as long as he possibly could. At last the friar made his escape, which the other resented so much that he fired with ball from the window at him. He missed him, but killed a cow that was passing by.' Mr. Stanley to Pitt. —*Grenville Papers*, i. 366. In another letter Stanley says: 'The Pretender's eldest son is drunk as soon as he rises, and is always senselessly so at night, when his servants carry him to bed. He is not thought of even by the exiles.'—*Chatham Corresp.* ii. 128.

to the large majority of the county votes; and nothing but the wisdom and moderation with which the Whig party used their ascendency could have repressed serious discontent in the country. Bolingbroke, in works which seem to have suggested the policy of George III., had strongly urged the necessity of disregarding the old party distinctions, and building up the royal authority on their decay. Carteret, after the fall of Walpole, had designed a mixed ministry, in which Tories as well as Whigs could be admitted largely to power. Pitt had long chafed bitterly against the system of government by connection, and it was noticed that although the higher offices in the Government were still occupied exclusively by Whigs, the country party, who had remained sullenly indifferent to preceding Governments, rallied warmly around him, and that in his militia appointments he entirely overlooked the distinction of Whig and Tory.[1]

The object of Pitt was to check the corruption that prevailed and to extend the area of patriotic feeling. The object of George III. and of the little group of politicians who surrounded and counselled him was very different, but their means were in some respects the same. In order to estimate their policy it is necessary in the first place to form a clear conception of their aims and methods. It is probable that Burke, in the famous pamphlet in which he described the condition of English politics in the first years of George III., considerably exaggerated the systematic and elaborate character of the plan that was adopted, but its leading features are sufficiently plain. 'Prerogative,' as Horace Walpole said, had once more 'become a fashionable word,'[2] the Divine right of kings was once again continually preached from the pulpit, and the Court party never concealed their conviction that the monarchy in the preceding reign had fallen into an essentially false position, and that it should be the first object of the new sovereign to restore it to

---

[1] After his resignation Pitt said: 'He lay under great obligations to many gentlemen who had been of the denomination of Tories, but who during his share of the administration had supported Government upon the principles of Whiggism and of the Revolution.'—Albemarle's *Life of Rockingham*, i. 150. 'The country gentlemen deserted their hounds and their horses, preferring for once their parliamentary duty ... and displayed their banner for Pitt.'—Glover's *Memoirs*, p. 97; see too p. 115. Walpole speaks of Pitt's 'known design of uniting, that was breaking, all parties.'—*Memoirs of George III.* i. 15.

[2] Ibid. 16.

vigour. They had, however, no wish to restrict or override the authority of Parliament, or to adopt any means which were not legal and parliamentary. Their favourite cries were abolition of government by party or connection, abolition of corruption at elections, emancipation of the sovereign from ministerial tyranny. No class of politicians were to be henceforth absolutely excluded, but at the same time no class or connection were to be allowed to dictate their policy to the King. The aristocracy, it was said, had obtained an exaggerated place in the Constitution. A few great families, who had been the leading supporters of the Revolution, who were closely connected by family relationships, by friendship, by long and systematic political co-operation, had come to form a single coherent body possessing so large an amount of borough patronage and such vast and various ramifications of influence, that they were practically the rulers of the country.[1] This phalanx was beyond all things to be broken up. If a great nobleman consented to detach himself from it and to enter into new combinations; if on a change of ministry subordinate officials were content to abandon their leaders and to retain their places, such conduct was to be warmly encouraged. The system of divided administrations which had existed under William and Anne was to be revived. The ministers were to be as much as possible confined to their several departments; they were to be drawn from many different connections and schools of policy, and they were not to be suffered to form a coherent and homogeneous whole. The relations of the Crown to the ministry were to be changed. For a considerable time the Treasury, the Ecclesiastical patronage, the Cornish boroughs, and all the other sources of influence which belonged nominally to the Crown had been, with few exceptions, at the disposal of the minister, and were employed to strengthen his administration. They were now to be in a great degree withdrawn from his influence, and to be employed in maintaining in Parliament a body of men whose political at-

[1] 'During the last two reigns a set of undertakers have farmed the power of the Crown at a price certain; and under colour of making themselves responsible for the whole have taken the sole direction of the royal interest and influence into their own hands and applied it to their own creatures without consulting the Crown or leaving any room for the royal nomination or direction.' — Lord Melcombe to Bute. *Adolphus*, i. 21.

tachment centred in the King alone, who looked to him alone for promotion, who, though often holding places in the Government, were expected rather to control than to support it, and, if it diverged from the policy which was personally acceptable to the King, to conspire against it and overthrow it. A Crown influence was thus to be established in Parliament as well as a ministerial influence, and it was hoped that it would turn the balance of parties and accelerate the downfall of any administration which was not favoured by the King.

There were many sources from which 'the King's friends,' as this interest was very invidiously called,[1] might be recruited. Crown and Court patronage was extravagantly redundant, and it was certain in the corrupt condition of Parliament that many politicians would prefer to attach themselves to the permanent source of power rather than to transitory administrations. The popularity of the King strengthened the party. The Tories, who resented their long exclusion from power, and who recognised in the young sovereign a Tory king, supported it in a body; the divisions and jealousies among the Whig nobles made it tolerably certain that some would be soon detached from their old connections and would gather round the new standard, and the personal influence of the sovereign over the leading politicians was sufficient to secure in most ministries at least one member who was content to draw his inspiration from him alone.

It must be remembered, too, that the conception of the Cabinet as a body of statesmen who were in thorough political agreement, and were jointly responsible for all the measures they proposed, was still in its early stage, and was by no means fully or universally recognised. A great step had been taken towards its attainment on the accession of George I., when the principle was adopted of admitting only the members of a single party into the Government. The administration of Walpole, in unity, discipline, and power, was surpassed by few of the present century. After the downfall of that administration the Whigs defeated the attempt of the King's favourite

---

[1] The term 'King's friends,' as a distinction for a particular class of politicians, if not invented, was at least adopted by Bute. See a letter from him (March 25, 1763).—*Grenville Papers*, ii. 32, 33

statesman to mix the Government with Tories, and a joint resignation of the Government in 1746 obliged the King to break finally with Bath and Granville, and admit Pitt to his councils. But on the other hand, the lax policy of Pelham and the personal weakness of Newcastle had led to great latitude and violent divergences of policy in the Cabinet which they formed. Fox and Hardwicke, in the debates on the Marriage Act, inveighed against one another with the utmost bitterness, though the one was Secretary of State and the other Chancellor in the same Government. Fox and Pitt made their colleagues, Murray, Newcastle, and Robinson, the objects of their constant attacks, and these examples rendered it more easy for the King to carry out his favourite policy of a divided Cabinet.

A very remarkable pamphlet, called 'Seasonable Hints from an Honest Man on the new Reign and the new Parliament,' appeared in 1761, defending the new system of government, and it soon attracted much attention from the fact that it was understood to be the composition of no less a person than Lord Bath, the old rival of Walpole and the old colleague of Carteret.[1] The question, the writer said, for the sovereign to determine was, 'Whether he is to content himself with the shadow of royalty while a set of undertakers for his business intercept his immediate communication with his people, and make use of the legal prerogatives of their master to establish the illegal claims of factitious oligarchy.' He complains that 'a cabal of ministers had been allowed to erect themselves into a fourth estate, to check, to control, to influence, nay, to enslave the others;' that it had become usual 'to urge the necessity of the King submitting to give up the management of his affairs and the exclusive disposal of all his employments to some ministers, or set of ministers, who, by uniting together, and backed by their numerous dependents, may be able to carry on the measures of Government;' that 'minis-

---

[1] Walpole's *George III.* i. 54. Wilkes in private conversations said that the 'distinction which has been supposed to exist between the friends of the King and the friends of the minister originated in the councils of Lord Bath.'—Butler's *Reminiscences*, i. p. 74. 'This project,' said Burke, 'I have heard was first conceived by some persons in the Court of Frederick Prince of Wales.'—*Thoughts on the Present Discontents.*

terial combinations to engross power and invade the closet,' were nothing less than a 'scheme of putting the sovereign in leading-strings,' and that their result had been the monstrous corruption of Parliament and the strange spectacle of 'a King of England unable to confer the smallest employment unless on the recommendation and with the consent of his ministers.' He trusts that the new King will put an end to this system by showing 'his resolution to break all factious connections and confederacies.' Already he has 'placed in the most honourable stations near his own person, some who have not surely owed their place to ministerial importunity, because they have always opposed ministerial influence,' and by steadily pursuing this course, the true ideal of the Constitution will be attained, 'in which the ministers will depend on the Crown, not the Crown on the ministers.' But to attain this end it was necessary that the basis of the Government should be widened, the proscription of the Tories abolished, and the sovereign enabled to select his servants from all sections of politicians. 'Does any candid and intelligent man seriously believe that at this time there subsists any party distinction amongst us that is not merely nominal? Are not the Tories friends of the royal family? Have they not long ago laid aside their aversion to the Dissenters? Do they not think the Toleration and Establishment both necessary parts of the Constitution? and can a Whig distinguish these from his own principles?' One glorious result of the new system of government the writer confidently predicts. With the destruction of oligarchical power the reign of corruption would terminate, and undue influence in Parliament was never likely to be revived.

The young King came to the throne when rather more than three years of almost uninterrupted victory had raised England to an ascendency which she had scarcely attained since the great days of Henry V. The French flag had nearly disappeared from the sea. Except Louisiana, all the French possessions in North America, except St. Domingo, all the French islands in the West Indies, had been taken, and the last French settlements in Hindostan were just tottering to their fall. The wave of invasion which threatened to submerge Hanover had been triumphantly rolled back, and the nation, intoxicated by victory, and roused from its long lethargy by the genius of its great statesman, displayed an energy and a daring which made it a wonder to its neighbours and to itself. No sacrifice seemed too great to demand, yet in spite of every sacrifice, commerce was flourishing and national prosperity advancing. The sudden growth of the colonial empire of England, and the destruction of her most formidable rival on the sea, had an immediate effect, and it was computed that in 1761 English commerce was a fifth greater than in the last year of the preceding peace.[1]

A ministry which had achieved such triumphs, and which was supported by such a tide of popular favour, would have been able, had it been cordially united, to defy any attempt to subvert it. But it was divided by deep fissures, distracted by bitter jealousies and animosities. Its war policy had hitherto been directed absolutely by Pitt, who almost monopolised the popular enthusiasm, and who could count in the Cabinet upon the firm alliance of his brother-in-law Lord Temple, the head of the Grenvilles. The great wealth and position of Temple had given him some political weight, and he was usually entrusted with the defence of the policy of Pitt in the Lords; but his character, at once grasping, arrogant, and intriguing, seldom failed to alienate those with whom he co-operated. With this exception, Pitt had scarcely a cordial friend in the Cabinet. Personal jealousies and rivalry, real differences of opinion, but above all the unbounded arrogance with which Pitt treated his colleagues, had raised against him a weight of animosity which it needed all his genius, popularity, and success to repress. In the council the other ministers cowered like timid schoolboys before him. More than once, when doubts were expressed whether the Treasury would be able to furnish with sufficient celerity or in sufficient quantity the necessary supplies for the expeditions that were prepared, Pitt cut short the debate by declaring that in case of the smallest failure he would at once impeach the Commissioners of Treasury, or Newcastle himself, before Parliament. He compelled no less a man than Anson to sign orders as First Lord of the Admiralty which he was not allowed even to read, and he constantly gave

---

[1] Burke, *Observations on the State of the Nation*.

orders relating to the war, in different departments without even informing the responsible heads of those departments of his intentions.[1] Newcastle lived in a continual state of mingled terror and resentment. Fox could not forget that he had been once deemed the equal of Pitt, and that his lucrative post of Paymaster of the Forces was in truth purely subordinate. Lord Granville, the old President of the Council, who had stood in the foremost rank of English politics before Pitt had even entered the House of Commons, could hardly brook the imperious tone of his younger colleague, and a powerful section of the ministry looked with great alarm upon the rapidly increasing debt, and desired at all hazards to bring the war to a speedy conclusion. The Duke of Bedford, who had a large number of personal adherents, strongly maintained this opinion, and predicted nothing but calamities, and his view was warmly supported by the Duke of Devonshire, by Lord Hardwicke, and above all by George Grenville, who, though he had not yet obtained a seat in the Cabinet, was already looked upon as the best man of business in the Government.

The change which had taken place in the spirit of the Court appeared from the very beginning. Bute at once obtained the dignity of Privy Councillor, to which, however, as an old servant of the new sovereign, he had an undoubted right;[2] and the first royal speech to the Council was composed by the King and Bute without any communication with the responsible ministers of the Crown. The sentences in which it spoke of 'a bloody and expensive war,' and of 'obtaining an honourable and lasting peace,' were justly interpreted as a covert censure upon the great minister who was conducting the war; and it was only after an altercation which lasted for two or three hours that Pitt induced Bute to consent that in the printed copy the former sentence should be changed into 'an expensive, but just and necessary war,' and that the words 'in con-

---

[1] See the curious account of Sir G. Colebrooke. Walpole's *Memoirs of George III.* i. 80–82.

[2] Walpole says Bute was admitted into the Cabinet (i. p. 8), but it is, I think, evident that he only means the Privy Council. The same distinction was given at the same time to the Duke of York. Compare Walpole's Letters to Montagu and to Mann, October 28, 1760. *Hist. of the late Minority*, pp. 10, 11. *Adolphus*, i. 11. *Annual Register*, 1760, p. 142.

cert with our allies' should be inserted after the latter. It was speedily spread abroad from lip to lip that, although the King for the present retained his old ministers, he would not be governed by them as his grandfather was. Bute became the medium of most private communications between the King and the more prominent statesmen, and he was generally understood to be the real centre of power. The necessity of drawing together the divided elements of the ministry was very manifest, and it is said that Pitt invited Newcastle to join with him in a closer union;[1] but the old statesman, who, though he sometimes spoke of resigning office, was in truth as wedded to it as ever, had already turned towards the rising star. Both the King and Bute skilfully flattered Newcastle and aggravated the jealousy with which he regarded Pitt, and Newcastle, though one of the oldest and most experienced statesmen in England, actually offered to serve under Bute.[2]

It was noticed in the first days of the new reign that the great Jacobite families who had long been absent from Court now crowded the antechamber. Horace Walpole, who was present at the first levee, was favourably struck with the affable behaviour of the King, and its contrast to the half-shy, half-sullen manners of his predecessor.[3] Much scandal, however, was caused by the warm reception given to Lord G Sackville, who was an intimate friend of Bute, but whose conduct at Minden had deeply tarnished his reputation;[4] and much criticism was provoked by a sentence which the King himself inserted in his first speech to Parliament. Queen Anne was believed to have reflected on her predecessor when she de-

---

[1] Walpole's *George III.* i. 10, 12.
[2] According to Lo d Hardwicke, Bute 'availed himself with much art and finesse of the dissensions between the Duke of Newcastle and Mr. Pitt, and played off one against the other occasionally till he had got rid of the popular minister.'—Rockingham's *Memoirs*, i. 6, 7. See too pp. 8–10, and Dodington's *Diary*, Dec. 27, 1760.
[3] 'For the King himself, he seems all goodnature and wishing to satisfy everybody; all his speeches are obliging; I was surprised to find the levee room had lost so entirely the air of the lion's den. This sovereign don't stand in one spot with his eyes fixed royally on the ground and dropping bits of German news; he walks about and speaks to everybody. I saw him afterwards on the throne, where he is graceful and genteel, sits with dignity and reads his answers to addresses well.'—Walpole to Montagu, Nov. 13, 1760. See too the *Letters of the first Earl of Malmesbury*, i. 82.
[4] Pitt seems to have especially resented it, and it is said to have been the first cause of his enmity to Bute.—Fitzmaurice's *Life of Shelburne*, i. 232.

scribed herself, on a similar occasion, as 'entirely English' at heart, and George III. indicated a somewhat similar spirit in the sentence, 'Born and educated in this country, I glory in the name of Briton.' 'What a lustre,' replied the House of Lords, in a strain of almost Oriental servility, 'does it cast upon the name of Briton, when you, Sir, are pleased to esteem it among your glories!'[1] In a different spirit, but with almost equal absurdity, the King was afterwards accused of insulting his English subjects by 'melting down the English name' into that of Briton.[2]

The chief business of the first short session of Parliament was to regulate the civil list and the supplies. The first was fixed at 800,000l., and the second at a little less than twenty millions, and in order to supply what was defective a new duty of 3d. a barrel was imposed on beer and ale. One act, however, was accomplished in this session at the recommendation of the King, by which, at the cost of a very small diminution of the prerogative of his successors, he acquired great popularity for himself. The Act of William III. making the judges irremovable, except by the intervention of Parliament, during the lifetime of the King, had effectually checked the gross sycophancy and subserviency that had long disgraced the judicial bench, but it still left it in the power of a new sovereign to remove the judges who had been appointed by his predecessor. Such a power could hardly be defended by any valid argument; it was inconsistent with the spirit of the Act; its legality had been disputed on the death of William by Sir J. Jekyll, and it had been very sparingly exercised.[3] On the accession of George I., Lord Trevor, who was a notorious Jacobite, was removed from the chief justiceship of the King's Bench, and a few minor changes had been recommended by the Chancellor.[4] A judge named Aland was removed by George II., but no change was made by his successor, and the young King recommended the Parliament to provide that the commissions of the judges should no longer expire on the demise of the

---

[1] *Parl. Hist.* xv. 982–986.
[2] Stephen's *Life of Horne Tooke*, i. 61. Junius talks of the King having 'affectedly renounced the name of Englishman.'—*Letter to the King.*
[3] See Townsend's *Hist. of the House of Commons*, ii. 51.
[4] Campbell's *Lives of the Chancellors*, v. 295, 296.

sovereign. The measure was a wise and liberal, though not a very important one, and, although the concession was made entirely at the expense of his successors, it was accepted in the then state of men's minds as if it were an act of heroic self-sacrifice.

A general election was necessary, by Act of Parliament, within six months of the accession, but before that time several changes were effected. George Grenville, who was known to be conspicuously opposed to the prosecution of the war, obtained a place in the Cabinet. Lord Henley, afterwards Earl of Northington, exchanged the position of Lord Keeper for the fuller dignity of Chancellor. He was a coarse, drunken, and unprincipled lawyer, of no very extraordinary abilities, who had early attached himself to the Leicester House faction, and who, partly through a desire to conciliate that faction, and partly through jealousy of Lord Hardwicke, had been appointed Lord Keeper in the Coalition ministry of Pitt and Newcastle; but George II. refused to raise him to the House of Lords until the trial of Lord Ferrers, when there was a difficulty in finding a lawyer who would preside as Lord Steward.[1] In the new reign he became one of the most docile and useful agents of the policy of the King. The enterprise of giving Bute high political office was found somewhat difficult, but a characteristic method was adopted. Lord Holdernesse, who, though a man of very insignificant abilities, was a Secretary of State, agreed with Bute, as early as November 1760, to quarrel with his colleagues, and throw up his office in seeming anger.[2] The resignation was for a time deferred; but it was accomplished in March 1761. Lord Holdernesse obtained a pension of 4,000*l*. a year for life, and a reversion of the Cinque Ports, and his place was filled by the favourite. Nearly at the same time, Legge, the Chancellor of the Exchequer, who had some time before quarrelled with Bute about a Hampshire election, was dismissed with circumstances of great discourtesy, and his place was filled by Lord Barrington—an honest man, but one who adopted and avowed the principle that it was his duty always, except in case

---

[1] He was accused of taking money in private causes from both sides, and availing himself of the information communicated on one side in advocating the opposite. See Walpole's *George III.* i. 240. Junius's *Letters*, 39.

[2] Dodington's *Diary*, Nov. 1760.

of the gravest possible causes of difference, to support the
ministers selected by the King, whatever party or connection
they belonged to, and whatever might be his opinion of the
men and of their measures.[1] He was thus completely identified
with the King's friends, and by the wish of the King was
kept in office through several successive administrations. The
brilliant but versatile and unprincipled Charles Townshend
filled his place, and a few other changes were made which,
though unimportant in themselves, showed that Tory tendencies, and especially personal devotion to the sovereign,
had become the passports of favour. Notwithstanding the professions of purity that were made by the King's friends, it was
noticed that the general election which now took place was one
of the most corrupt ever known in England, that large sums
were issued by the Treasury, that the King took an active part
in naming the candidates, and that the boroughs attached to
the Duchy of Cornwall, which had hitherto been at the disposal
of the ministry, were now treated as solely at the disposal of the
Crown.[2]

It was evident that it was intended, in the first place, to
strike down Pitt;[3] and an opportunity soon occurred. The
great question now impending was the negotiation for peace.
The arguments in favour of terminating a war are always
strong, but in this case they had a more than common force.
The debt was rapidly increasing, and the estimates had arisen
to a most alarming extent. The total sum granted by Parliament for 1761 was more than nineteen millions. The British
forces in different parts of the world amounted to no less
than 110,000 soldiers and 70,000 seamen, besides 60,000 German auxiliaries in British pay.[4] The success of England had
hitherto been almost unparalleled, but there was now but
little left for her to gain, and she had many dangers to fear.
She had hitherto been very successful in Germany, but a

---

[1] See the very curious letters published in the *Life of Barrington* by
his brother the Bishop of Durham,
pp. 79, 99, 103–105.

[2] Albemarle's *Life of Rockingham*,
i. 61–64. Walpole's *Memoirs of George
III.* i. 41, 42. *Dodington's Diary*,
Feb. 2, 1761.

[3] See on the feeling of Bute towards Pitt a letter of the Duke of
Newcastle.—*Bedford Correspondence*,
iii. 19.

[4] *Parl. Hist.* xv. 1000–1006.

German war could not fail to be extremely bloody and expensive. The interests of England in it were very subordinate, and as the colonial empire of France was passing away, it was certain that the war would be concentrated chiefly in this quarter. In a Continental war the normal strength of France was so great that the chances were much in her favour, and, in the opinion of some good judges, there was much danger lest the King's German dominions should be ultimately absorbed.[1] The Tory party had always looked with great aversion on Continental wars, and, as we have seen, there was a strong minority in the Cabinet, including Newcastle and Hardwicke, who were prepared to sacrifice much for a peace.[2] A very able pamphlet, called 'Considerations on the German War,' appeared about this time, and exercised an influence which was probably greater than that of any other English pamphlet since Swift's 'Conduct of the Allies.' Its author was an obscure writer named Mauduit, and it was said to have been published under the countenance of Lord Hardwicke. The writer fully approved of the capture of the French islands, and of the destruction of the naval power of France; but he argued with much force, that no policy could be more manifestly suicidal than to squander larger sums than were expended for the whole land and sea service during the Duke of Marlborough's campaigns, in a German war waged between two great German Powers, for the possession of a remote German province which might belong to either without affecting in any way the real interests of England. The burden of the war was beginning to be seriously felt. In March 1761, when there were rumours of an approaching peace under the superintendence of Pitt, the funds rose four per cent. When the three years' term of service in the militia expired, and a new ballot was about to take place, there were riots in several of the Northern counties. At Hexham, in Northumberland, a body of Yorkshire militia were attacked by six or seven thousand rioters armed with clubs,

---

[1] See *Bedford Correspondence*, iii. 22-29.

[2] In Dodington's *Diary*, Jan. 2, 1761, there is a report of a conversation he had with Bute on the prospects of the peace. Bute said 'the ministry neither were nor could be united; that the Duke of Newcastle most sincerely wished for peace, and would go any length to obtain it; that Mr. Pitt meditated a retreat and would stay in no longer than the war.'

and a serious struggle ensued, in which forty-two persons were killed and forty-eight others wounded.¹ The expedition against Belleisle caused many murmurs, for it cost much bloodshed, and the island was little more than a barren rock, of no value to England, and at the same time so near the French coast that it was tolerably certain that it would be restored at the peace. The unhealthy quarters to which English conquests had recently extended, made the mortality among the troops very great. Bounties rose to an unexampled height, and there were fears that if the war continued it would be a matter of great difficulty to fill the ranks.²

Negotiations for peace had taken place as early as November 1759, and they were resumed in the spring of 1761, but neither party appears to have entered very keenly into them. Pitt had just sent out his expedition against Belleisle, and he was anxious that nothing should be done until it succeeded. He told the King that he by no means thought ill of the state of the war in Germany; that he thought the total destruction of the French power in the East Indies, the probability of taking Martinique as well as Belleisle, and the probable results of the next German campaign, would enable us to secure all Canada, Cape Breton, the neighbouring islands, and the exclusive fishery of Newfoundland, and that he would sign no peace on lower terms. It was quite certain that the French were not prepared to accede to such terms, and both the King and Newcastle strongly remonstrated against the determination of Pitt to lay them down as indispensable at the very outset of the negotiations.³ On the French side, also, new prospects were opening out which produced an equal hesitation. Charles III., who had very recently exchanged the throne of Naples for that of Spain, still remembered with bitterness how the English had threatened to bombard Naples in 1742. He looked forward with great dread to the complete naval supremacy which England was rapidly attaining; he inherited the old Spanish grievances against England about Gibraltar and the trade of the Indies;

---

¹ *Annual Register*, 1761, p 83. *Chatham Correspondence*, ii. 100, 101. Walpole to Montagu, March 19, 1761. See too Adolphus's *Hist. of England*, i. 571, 572.

² *Adolphus*, i. 100.
³ See the letter of Newcastle to Lord Hardwicke, April 15, 1761. Albemarle's *Life of Rockingham*, i. 23, 24.

he was closely connected with the French sovereign, and he also saw a prospect of obtaining in Portugal conquests of great value at little cost. These various considerations were rapidly drawing him into closer alliance with France.[1] Belleisle was captured by the English on June 7, 1761. On the 15th of the following month, the French negotiator took the very significant and very startling step of presenting a memorial in behalf of Spain, claiming the restitution of some prizes bearing the Spanish flag which had been taken by the English, the right of the Spaniards to fish upon the banks of Newfoundland, and the demolition of the English settlements on the disputed territory in the Bay of Honduras.[2]

Such demands, made by a Power with which England was at perfect peace, through the intervention of a Power with which England was at war, could have but one meaning, and Pitt loftily expressed to the French agent his opinion of the transaction. 'His Majesty,' he answered, 'will not suffer the dispute with Spain to be blended in any manner whatever in the negotiations of peace between the two Crowns, and it will be considered as an affront to his Majesty's dignity, and as a thing incompatible with the sincerity of the negotiations, to make further mention of such a circumstance. Moreover, it is expected that France will not at any time presume a right of intermeddling with such disputes between England and Spain.' The rupture of the negotiations between France and England soon followed. It is not necessary to examine the proceedings in great detail; it is sufficient to say that Pitt was prepared to purchase the restitution of Minorca by restoring Belleisle, Guadaloupe, and Marie-Galante to the French, and that he consented to a partition of the Antilla Isles; but he maintained that England should retain all the other conquests. He refused the French demands for a participation in the fisheries of Newfoundland, for the cession of Cape Breton in America, for the restoration of either Goree or Senegal as a depôt for the French slave trade in the West Indies, and for the re-establishment in

---

[1] The earlier stages of this negotiation may be traced in the letters between Grimaldi and Fuentes, the Spanish ambassadors at Paris and London, in Jan., Feb. and March 1761.

Chatham Correspondence, vol. ii.
[2] See the official documents on the subject in *Parl. Hist.* xv. There is a good epitome in De Flassan's *Hist. de la Diplomatie Française*.

Hindostan of the frontier of 1755. He refused equally the demand for the restoration of prizes made before the declaration of war, and he insisted, in the interest of the King of Prussia, that the French should withdraw their armies from Germany, while England still retained her right of assisting her ally.[1] The spell of success which had so long hung over the British arms was still unbroken. The capture of Belleisle in June 1761; the capture of Dominica, by Lord Rollo, in the same month; the tidings of new successes in Hindostan, and a victory of Prince Ferdinand at Vellinghausen in July, contributed to raise the spirits of the country, and formed the best defence of the demands of Pitt. Nor is there any reason to doubt that he sincerely desired peace, if he could have obtained it on terms which he deemed adequate.[2] The alliance, however, between France and Spain was rapidly consummated. On August 15, 1761, the family compact between the French and Spanish kings was signed, binding the two countries in a strict offensive and defensive alliance, and making each country guarantee the possessions of the other. Mr. Stanley, the vigilant English agent who had been negotiating in Paris, obtained secret knowledge of one of the articles, and confidential communications from other quarters corroborated the account.[3] Pitt, who had for some time watched with great suspicion the armaments of Spain, perceived clearly that the declaration of war was only delayed till the naval preparations of Spain were completed and the treasure ships which were expected from Mexico and Peru had arrived safely in port. He acted with characteristic promptitude and decision. Spain had committed no overt act which could be reasonably taken as a pretext for war. The evidence of the family compact was somewhat doubtful, and, being derived exclusively from secret information, it could not be publicly

---

[1] *Adolphus*, i. 36–40. *De Flassan*, v. 382–388. A curious picture of the debates in the Cabinet, and of the imperative manner in which Pitt silenced all opposition, will be found in the letters of Newcastle to Hardwicke in Albemarle's *Life of Rockingham*, vol. i.

[2] It is remarkable that Jenkinson, who was one of the most uncompromising adherents of Bute, had no doubt of this. He wrote (Aug. 6, 1761): 'The Duke of Newcastle has already been with Lord Bute to beg that we may not lose sight of peace; and take my word for it, Mr. Pitt is almost as unwilling, though he is too wise to show it.'—*Grenville Papers*, i. p. 382.

[3] Compare Walpole's *George III.* i. 123, 124. *Adolphus*, i. 41–45. *Chatham Correspondence*, ii. 140, 141.

produced   The Spanish Government loudly disclaimed all
hostile intentions, and asserted that the ships of war which were
building in the Spanish arsenals were only such as were required
for convoying merchant vessels from Naples to Spain and re-
pressing the Barbary pirates. Pitt, however, was prepared to
take the responsibility of a war which it was very difficult to
justify to the world, and he resolved to strike, and to strike at
once. Expeditions were speedily planned against the most as-
sailable parts of the Spanish dominions, and on September 18 a
cabinet council was held in which Pitt proposed to his colleagues
the immediate withdrawal of the English ambassador from
Madrid, and a declaration of war against Spain based upon the
warlike demands she had made through the intervention of the
French negotiator in the preceding July.[1]

Frederick the Great afterwards expressed in warm terms his
admiration for the sagacity and enterprise displayed by Pitt in
this conjuncture, and the event showed that the policy of the
great minister was as wise as it was daring. It must be owned,
however, that modern public opinion would have seldom acquiesced in a war the avowed and known reasons of which were
so plainly inadequate, and it was probably by no means only a
desire to expel Pitt from the ministry that actuated those who
rejected his advice. The King was strongly opposed to the
policy of Pitt and much irritated by his conduct.[2] ' In three
successive cabinet councils the question was debated, and in
the last Pitt, finding himself supported by no one but Lord
Temple, rose with great warmth, declaring that 'he was called
to the ministry by the voice of the people, to whom he considered himself accountable for his conduct, and he would not
remain in a situation which made him responsible for measures
he was no longer allowed to guide.' He was answered by old Lord
Granville, the President of the Council, who made himself the
representative of the majority, and who exhibited on this
occasion one last flash of his old fire. 'I can hardly,' he said,

---

[1]. See *Grenville Papers*, i. 386-7. *Chatham Correspondence*, ii. 140-143. *Bedford Correspondence*, iii. 46-49.

[2] Sept. 23, 1761. Newcastle wrote to Hardwicke: 'The King seemed so provoked and so weary that his Majesty was inclined to put an end at all events to the uncertainty about Mr. Pitt.' Sept. 26, he writes: 'The King seems every day more offended with Mr. Pitt, and plainly wants to get rid of him at all events.'—Albemarle's *Life of Rockingham*, i. 42, 44. See too *Bedford Corresp.* iii. 48.

'regret the right honourable gentleman's determination to leave us, as he would otherwise have compelled us to leave him; but if he be resolved to assume the right of advising his Majesty and directing the operations of the war, to what purpose are we called to this council? When he talks of being responsible to the people, he talks the language of the House of Commons and forgets that at this board he is only responsible to the King. However, though he may possibly have convinced himself of his infallibility, still it remains that we should be equally convinced before we can resign our understandings to his direction and join with him in the measures he proposes.' Pitt and Temple persisted in their determination, and on October 5, 1761, they placed their resignations in the hands of the King.[1]

So ended an administration which had found England in a condition of the lowest depression, and by the efforts of a single man had raised her to a height of glory scarcely equalled in her annals. It is true indeed that with the exception of James Grenville, who resigned the insignificant post of Cofferer, no other official accompanied Pitt and Temple into retirement, but with Pitt the soul of the administration had passed away. As Burke truly said, 'No man was ever better fitted to be the minister of a great and powerful nation, or better qualified to carry that power and greatness to their utmost limits... With very little parliamentary, and with less Court influence, he swayed both at Court and in Parliament with an authority unknown before, and under him for the first time, administration and popularity were united.' The seals of Secretary of State were offered to George Grenville, but he refused them, though accepting the leadership of the House of Commons, and they were then given to Lord Egremont, an avowed Tory, and son of Sir W. Windham, the Tory leader in the last reign.[2] The Duke of Bedford soon after replaced Temple as Privy Seal.

So far the policy of the secret counsellors of the young King had been brilliantly successful. In less than twelve months, and in the midst of the war, the greatest war minister England had ever produced was overthrown, and the party with

---

[1] *Adolphus,* i. 43, 44. *Hist. of the late Minority,* pp. 33–37. *Annual Register,* 1761.
[2] *Grenville Papers,* i. 411, 412.

Pitt had no wish to enter into permanent opposition, and had he refused all favours from the Crown, such an intention would have been undoubtedly ascribed to him. No rewards were ever more amply earned, and the pension was smaller in amount than that which had just been bestowed upon Lord Holdernesse for his resignation. In English public life it is scarcely possible for anyone who does not possess independent means to take a prominent part out of office, and Pitt had not yet received the legacy of Sir William Pynsent which raised him to comparative wealth. He had however been accustomed to use a language about pensioners, and to talk in a strain of high-flown and heroic disinterestedness, not quite in harmony with his conduct, and a storm of indignation and obloquy was easily aroused. Writers connected with the Court party were the foremost in lampooning him, and the extreme bitterness with which Horace Walpole and Gray spoke of his conduct [1] is sufficient to show that the feeling was not confined to the mob. Pitt also exhibited at this time one of those strange fits of humility and extravagant deference to royalty to which he was liable. He burst into tears at a few civil words from the young King, exclaiming, 'I confess, Sir, I had but too much reason to expect your Majesty's displeasure; I did not come prepared for this exceeding goodness. Pardon me, Sir; it overpowers, it oppresses me.' [2] His letters to Bute acknowledging the kindness of the King were couched in a strain of florid, fulsome, almost servile humility, lamentably unworthy of a great statesman.[3]

For a short time it appeared as if the popularity of Pitt were eclipsed, and as if the torrent of popular indignation which was so greatly feared had been turned against the fallen statesman. It was also a fortunate circumstance for the Court party that the resignation took place at a time when the recent marriage of the King with the Princess of Mecklenburg Strelitz, and the gorgeous ceremonies of the wedding and of the coro-

---

[1] See for Walpole's opinions his letters to the Countess of Ailesbury, Oct. 10, 1761, and to Conway, Oct. 12, 1761. Gray wrote at the same time: 'Oh that foolishest of great men, that sold his inestimable diamond for a paltry peerage and pension! The very night it happened was I swearing it was a d——d lie and never would be; but it was for want of reading Thomas à Kempis, who knew mankind so much better than I.'—*Works*, iii. p. 265.

[2] *Chatham Correspondence* ii. 147.

[3] Ibid. ii. 149-152.

nation, had to some extent stimulated anew that sentiment of loyalty which was already beginning to fade.¹

But the exultation of the ministers was very shortlived. A few days of reflection and a brief and dignified letter written to the Town Clerk of London restored the popularity of Pitt, and a speedy reaction set in. Addresses congratulating him on his conduct poured in from many of the chief towns. The City of London, which had long been his chief supporter, after a momentary hesitation remained firm to its allegiance. The Common Council passed a vote of thanks to him five weeks after his resignation. On the occasion of the Lord Mayor's day, the King and Queen went in state to dine at the Guildhall, and Temple induced Pitt to take the injudicious and unbecoming step of joining the procession. The result was what had probably been predicted. The populace received the King and Queen with contemptuous indifference, Bute with an outburst of insult, and Pitt with the most enthusiastic applause. In Parliament he was assailed with disgraceful virulence by Colonel Barré, a partisan of Shelburne who was then 'devoted to Lord Bute,'² but although it was noticed that Barré was immediately after received with special favour at Court,³ both Parliament and the public were disgusted with the ferocity and the scurrility he displayed. Events soon justified the sagacity of Pitt. No sooner had he retired from office than the Spanish Court threw aside the mask, and the conciliatory language they had hitherto employed was exchanged for a tone of haughty menace. The treasure ships which Pitt had wished to intercept arrived safely in Spain. Military preparations were pressed on without disguise. The alliance between France and Spain was

---

¹ 'Mr. Pitt himself,' wrote Walpole, Sept. 9, 1761, 'would be mobbed if he talked of anything but clothes and diamonds and bridesmaids.'—Walpole to Mann.

² This was Shelburne's own expression. See Fitzmaurice's *Life of Shelburne,* i. 120.

³ See the statement of Barré himself in a letter to Shelburne.—Fitzmaurice's *Life of Shelburne,* i. 126. Walpole's *George III.* i. 122. Barré had served with Wolfe, and he had written to Pitt shortly before his attack upon him, in a strain of warm admiration, asking for a promotion. Pitt had refused the request on the ground that senior officers would be injured by the promotion, and Barré in a letter to Pitt described himself as 'bound in the highest gratitude for the attention he had received.'—Chatham's *Corresp.* ii. 41–43, 171. A graphic account of the manner in which Pitt was attacked in this debate will be found in a letter of Mr. Noel Milbanke to Rockingham.—*Life of Rockingham,* i. 79–83.

openly avowed, but the Spanish Government haughtily refused to state its character and its conditions. Wall propounded a long series of grievances against England, and declared that Spain would no longer suffer France 'to run the risk of receiving such rigid laws as were prescribed by an insulting victor.' On December 10, 1761, the English Government, having vainly demanded a promise that the Spanish king would not join in hostilities against England, recalled their ambassador from Madrid. On the 31st war was declared against Spain, and very soon after, one of the secret motives of the Spanish policy was disclosed. Portugal was on friendly terms with England, but she had been perfectly neutral during the struggle, and had given no kind of provocation to her neighbours. Without even a colourable pretext for hostility, Spanish armies were now massed on the Portuguese frontier, and in March the Spanish ambassador and the French plenipotentiary presented a joint and peremptory memorial to the Portuguese King, ordering him at once to break off all correspondence and commerce with England, and to join France and Spain in the war that was waging. The insolent demand was refused. War was declared, and a Spanish army was soon desolating the plains of Portugal.

But the hand of the great English minister, though withdrawn from the helm, was still felt in every department of the war. The perfection to which he had brought every branch of the military and naval service, the spirit of emulation and enterprise he had breathed into them, the discernment with which he had selected the commanders for the most arduous posts, were all still felt, and victory after victory crowned the British arms. In February 1762, the important island of Martinique was taken from the French, and the conquest was followed by that of the dependent isles of Grenada, St. Lucia, and St. Vincent, leaving the English sole possessors of all the Caribbean Islands, extending from the eastern point of Hispaniola nearly to the continent of South America. Another and still greater conquest speedily followed. Among the designs of Pitt one of the most important was the conquest of Havannah, the richest and most important town in Cuba. Its harbour was one of the best in the world. It was the centre of the whole trade of the Spanish West Indies, and it was defended by strong fortifications and by a powerful fleet. The siege—which was conducted with signal skill and daring—lasted for two months and eight days. On August 14, 1762, Havannah fell, nine noble ships of the line and four frigates were taken, five others were destroyed during the siege or in the docks, and the treasure taken is said to have amounted to not less than three millions sterling.[1] On September 21 a formidable French attack on Brückenmühle was repelled with great loss to the assailants by a German and English army under Prince Ferdinand and the Marquis of Granby. On October 6 Manilla, with the Philippine Islands, was conquered by Sir W. Draper, and among the Spanish galleons taken at sea was one which contained a treasure valued at little less than a million. In Portugal the Spanish army was at first successful, but it was soon checked by the assistance of English and Hanoverians under General Burgoyne, and the Spanish were compelled to evacuate Estramadura. The only serious reverses were the capture by the Spaniards of the Portuguese settlement of Sacramento, on the Rio de la Plata, and the capture by the French of Fort St. John, in Newfoundland, from which, however, three months later they were easily expelled.

A campaign which was on the whole so brilliant would naturally have raised the reputation of the ministry that conducted it; but in this case every success was mainly attributed to Pitt, and was regarded as a justification of his wisdom and as a condemnation of his enemies. It was known that the war with Spain was his policy; that he had sent out the expedition against Martinique; that its success was mainly due to the troops his victories had liberated in America; that he had planned the conquest of Havannah; that if his counsels had been adopted, the number of rich Spanish prizes that were brought into English harbours would have been greatly increased. Without the ministry, discontent was gathering fast, and within there was jealousy or division. Grenville, though still acting with docility the part of leader of the House of Commons, was not suffered to take any part in the secret corruption which was one of the most important functions usually attached to his post.[2] Newcastle, in the first exultation that

---

[1] *Annual Register*, 1762. See too *Bedford Correspondence*, iii. 130.

[2] See his complaint of the difficulty he had 'to carry on the business

followed the resignation of Pitt, had anticipated a renewal of his ascendency, but he soon learned how greatly he had miscalculated. Although First Lord of the Treasury, he found that he was powerless in the Government. Even his own subordinates at the Treasury Bench are said to have been instructed to slight him. The most important political steps were taken without consulting him. Cabinet councils were summoned without any notice of the subject for discussion being given him. The King made no less than seven peers without even informing Newcastle of his intention. Neither his age, his rank, his position in the ministry, nor his eminent services to the dynasty, could save him from marked coldness on the part of the King, from contemptuous discourtesy and studied insults on the part of the favourite.[1] The situation soon became intolerable, and when Bute announced his intention of withdrawing the subsidy which England paid to the King of Prussia, Newcastle refused to consent. In May 1762 the old statesman resigned, refusing with some dignity a pension that was offered him for the purpose of recruiting a fortune which had been wrecked in the public service.[2] Bute then became in name, what since the resignation of Pitt he had been in reality, the head of the ministry, and Grenville became Secretary of State in his stead.

The Whig party which had so long been in power was now put to the test, and the weakness of many of its members was exposed. George Grenville, one of the most rising of its statesmen, and the Duke of Bedford, the head of one of its greatest families, had already gone over to Bute, and a long train of the personal adherents of Newcastle soon followed the example. The bishops led the way. Newcastle had always been especially careful to monopolise the ecclesiastical patronage, and it was said that there was not a single bishop on the bench whom he had not either appointed or translated. In

---

of the House of Commons without being authorised to talk to the members of that House upon their several claims and pretensions.'— *Grenville Papers*, i. p. 483.

[1] See the letters of Newcastle to Hardwicke, Albemarle's *Life of Rockingham*, i. 102–112; and his letter to Bedford, *Bedford Correspondence*,
iii. 79, 80. Walpole's *Memoirs of George III.* i. 156. Harris's *Life of Lord Hardwicke*, iii. 230, 273, 274.

[2] His private fortune is said to have been reduced from 25,000l. to 6,000l. a year by his long tenure of office.— Harris's *Life of Hardwicke*, iii. 280.

the season of his prosperity they had thronged his hall with an assiduity that sometimes provoked a smile, but it was observed that only a single bishop was present at his farewell levee.[1] But the most important of all the accessions to the party of Bute was Fox, the old rival of Pitt, in whose favour Grenville was displaced from the leadership of the Commons, who, in consideration of the promise of a peerage, undertook to carry the peace, and who, having vainly attempted to draw the Duke of Cumberland and other great Whig peers into the same connection, threw himself, with all the impetuosity of his fearless and unscrupulous nature, into the service of the Court.

The main object of the party since the downfall of Pitt had been to press on the peace. For many months Bute, without the knowledge of any of the responsible ministers of the Crown, carried on a secret negotiation through the mediation of the Sardinian ambassador, Count Viri,[2] and when it had arrived at some maturity it was finally entrusted to the Duke of Bedford, who had for a long time identified himself with the extreme peace party. His letters give a vivid picture of the feelings of a section of the Government. Thus in June 1761, while Pitt was still minister, we find him deploring bitterly the expedition against Belleisle, and urging that 'if we retain the greatest part of our conquests out of Europe we shall be in danger of over-colonising and undoing ourselves by them as the Spaniards have done.'[3] In July he predicted the failure of the projected expedition against Martinique and the speedy conquest of the King's electoral dominions by the French.[4] He argued that to deprive the French of the Newfoundland

---

[1] Cornwallis, Bishop of Lichfield. The Bishop of Norwich, however, who was then absent from London, remained staunch to his benefactor. See on the ingratitude of the bishops, Harris's *Life of Hardwicke*, iii. 334. Walpole's *Memoirs of George III.* i. 169, 170. Walpole to Montagu, May 25, 1762. Newcastle is said on this occasion to have made a very happy witticism which is often ascribed to Lord Melbourne. Mrs. Montagu writes: 'The Duke of Newcastle after his resignation had a very numerous levee, but somebody observed to him that there were but two bishops present. He is said to have replied that bishops, like other men, were too apt to forget their maker. I think this has been said for him, or the resignation of power has much brightened his understanding; for of whatever he was accused, the crime of wit was never laid to his charge.'—Doran's *Life of Mrs. Montagu*, p. 120.

[2] See Fitzmaurice's *Life of Shelburne*, i. p. 137.

[3] *Bedford Correspondence*, iii. 17.

[4] Ibid. pp. 23–29.

fishery would be to ruin their naval power, and would unite all the other naval powers against us, as aiming at a naval monopoly ' at least as dangerous to the liberties of Europe as that of Lewis XIV.;'[1] and with the exception of a slight reservation on the article of Dunkirk, he advocated the unqualified acceptance of every one of the French demands in the abortive negotiation I have described.[2] It is remarkable that Bute at this time remonstrated strongly against this spirit of absolute concession, and enumerated conditions very little different from those of Pitt, as essential to the honour and safety of England.[3] In August Rigby, the confidential follower of Bedford, wrote to him: 'While we succeed ... the fire is kept constantly fanned. For my own part I am so convinced of the destruction which must follow the continuance of the war, that I should not be sorry to hear that Martinico or the next windmill you attack should get the better of you.'[4] Lord Shelburne, who was deeply mixed with the intrigues of this evil time, advocated in December 1761, in the House of Lords, the withdrawal of all English troops from Germany, and the complete abandonment of Frederick; and at the beginning of February 1762, Bedford, though now Privy Seal and an active member of the Cabinet, brought forward in the House of Lords a resolution to the same effect, without the consent of any of his colleagues, and he was defeated by Bute, who carried the previous question by 105 to 16.[5]

It is obvious that such a statesman was peculiarly unfit to carry on the negotiation, and he was a man of very little ability, and of a very haughty and unaccommodating temper. His personal honour, which was afterwards malignantly attacked, appears to have been quite unblemished, and on one important question that was raised, relating to the frontier in Hindostan, he asserted the British claims with energy and effect;[6] but he entered upon the negotiation with the strongest desire to succeed at any sacrifice; he showed this spirit so clearly that the ministers thought it necessary to impose considerable

---

[1] *Bedford Correspondence*, p. 26.
[2] Ibid. p. 28.
[3] Ibid. pp. 30–34. *Grenville Papers*, i. 376.
[4] *Bedford Correspondence*, iii. 43.

[5] *Cavendish Debates*, i. 568–575. *Parl. Hist.* xv. 1217–1221. *Bedford Correspondence*, iii. 73. Fitzmaurice's *Life of Shelburne*, i. 123, 124.
[6] *Bedford Correspondence*, iii. xxiii.

restrictions on his powers;[1] and it may easily be gathered from his correspondence that he desired Havannah, though perhaps the richest of all the conquests of the war, to be restored to Spain without any substantial compensation being exacted.[2]

The points of resemblance between the Peace of Paris and the Peace of Utrecht are so many and so obvious that it is impossible to overlook them. In both cases a war of extraordinary success was ended by a peace which was very advantageous, but which in many of its terms was greatly inferior to what might reasonably have been demanded. In both cases the peace was forced through Parliament amid a storm of unpopularity and by corruption and intimidation of the worst kind. In both cases the strange spectacle was exhibited of English ministers looking with positive alarm or dismay on some of the greatest successes that crowned their arms, and in both cases the extreme longing for peace was mainly due to party motives, and especially to the desire of excluding from power a great man who was pre-eminently fitted to conduct a war. It cannot, however, be justly said of the Peace of Paris that England purchased, as she had done under Queen Anne, great advantages for herself at the cost of her allies. Portugal was restored to everything she had lost by the war, and although Frederick the Great had some real reason to complain of England, her conduct to him was far short of the desertion which has been alleged. The wars between Prussia and Austria, and the wars between England and France, were in their origin entirely distinct, and although it afterwards suited the purpose of England to assist Frederick, as France was assisting Austria, the connection was of a purely casual and interested character. No stipulation bound England to continue indefinitely her subsidy to Prussia, and in April 1762, when the Government announced their intention of withdrawing it, they were perfectly justified in doing so.[3] England had just entered into a new war with Spain, and the

---

[1] *Bedford Correspondence*, iii. Ibid. pp. 114–119, 126–129.
[2] Ibid. pp. 118–119, 136–138. Lord Barrington, also, was of opinion that no compensation should be asked for the restoration of Havannah.—Barrington's *Life of Barrington*, p. 82.
[3] See Bute's own defence in a despatch to Mitchell, the English Minister to Frederick (May 26, 1762). Bisset's *Life of Sir A. Mitchell*, ii. 294–302.

necessity of repelling the Spanish invasion of Portugal rendered it peculiarly costly. On the other hand, the death of the Czarina Elizabeth on January 5, 1762, had placed on the throne of Russia a passionate admirer of Frederick. Peace between the two crowns at once ensued. For the few months during which Peter the Third reigned, there was even an alliance between Russia and Prussia, and an armistice and then a peace between Prussia and Sweden speedily followed. The great confederation against Prussia was in this manner dissolved. France and Austria alone remained opposed to her; and although England by the Peace of Paris engaged no longer to assist her ally, she stipulated that France should also withdraw from the war, and should evacuate the territory and strong places she had occupied. It is true, however, that in the course of the negotiations there were some things of which Frederick had real reason to complain. By a strange and significant omission, the article compelling the French to cede the territory and strong places they had taken, did not specify the Power to which they were to be ceded.[1] Bute is said to have even declared in Parliament that they were 'to be scrambled for;'[2] and but for the promptitude of the Prussian king, they would have fallen into Austrian hands. It is certain that in January 1762 some secret overtures were made by Bute to the Queen of Hungary without the knowledge of Frederick, and two charges of bad faith of the worst description were brought against the English minister. It was alleged that in order to induce Austria to consent to an early peace, he held out hopes that England would use her influence to obtain for Austria territorial compensations from Prussia, and that with the same view, after the death of the Czarina, Bute had urged upon Prince Galitzin, the Russian ambassador in London, the necessity of Russia remaining firm to the Austrian alliance, maintaining her army in the Prussian territory, and thus compelling Frederick to make large concessions to Vienna. These charges were fully believed by Frederick, and the latter rests on the authority of Prince Galitzin himself; but Bute positively asserted that they were untrue, and

---

[1] Carlyle's *Frederick*, book xx. ch. 13. Thackeray's *Life of* Chatham, ii. 22.

[2] *Anecdotes of Chatham*, i. 401.

that his language in conversation had been grossly misunderstood or misrepresented.[1]

As far as England was concerned, the provisions of the treaty with France differed but little from those which had been rejected by Pitt in 1761. Minorca was restored by the French, and England retained possession of all Canada, Nova Scotia, and Cape Breton, of Senegal, Grenada, and the Grenadines, and of the three neutral islands, St. Vincent, Dominica, and Tobago. The French, however, secured the right of fishing on the coast of Newfoundland and also in the Gulf of St. Lawrence at a distance of three leagues from the shore, and two small islands were ceded to them as a shelter for their fishermen. England restored Goree, which was deemed essential to the French slave trade. She restored the islands of Guadaloupe, Marie-Galante, De la Désirade, Martinique, Belleisle, and San Lucia, and in Hindostan there was a mutual restoration of conquests made since 1749. The French were, however, forbidden to erect fortifications or to keep troops in Bengal; they were compelled to acknowledge the English candidates as Nabob of the Carnatic and Surbah of the Deccan, and they undertook to reduce Dunkirk to the same condition as before the Peace of Aix-la-Chapelle.

Spain by the treaty of Paris ceded to England the province of Florida, with some adjoining territory to the east and southeast of the Mississippi, but she was partly indemnified by receiving from France New Orleans and all Louisiana west of the Mississippi. She renounced all right to participation in the fishery of Newfoundland. She consented that the adjudication of the prizes made by English cruisers on the coast of Spain should be referred to the English Court of Admiralty, and she acknowledged the long-disputed right of the English to cut logwood in Honduras Bay provided the English destroyed the fortifications they had erected there. In return for these great concessions she received again Havannah and the other ports of Cuba which had been conquered. The news of the conquest of Manilla and the other Philippine Islands did not arrive until

---

[1] Compare Frederick, *Œuvres Posthumes*, iv. 290-292. Bisset's *Memoirs of Sir Andrew Mitchell*, ii. 206-302. *History of the late Minority*, pp. 52-54. Adolphus' *Hist. of England*, i. 76-81; and especially the letters in the appendix, pp. 579-589.

after the preliminaries had been signed, and these valuable possessions were in consequence restored without any equivalent. When Manilla was captured, the private property of the inhabitants was saved from plunder on the condition of a payment of a ransom of a million sterling, one-half of which was paid in money and the other half in bills upon the Spanish Treasury. These bills the Spaniards afterwards refused to honour, and the English Government was never able to obtain their payment.

There can be no doubt that this peace was extremely advantageous to England, but there was hardly a clause in it which was not below what she might reasonably have expected. Every new acquisition which she obtained, and every conquest which she relinquished, was actually in her hands before the peace was signed. Minorca, which was the one great French conquest, would probably have been retaken if the war had continued, and its value did not amount to more than a small fraction of that of the territory which England, after a long series of almost uninterrupted victories, consented to abandon. The terms of the peace were little, if at all, more favourable than might have been obtained in the preceding year, though the war had been since then uniformly and splendidly successful. In the former negotiations France had consented to cede Goree as well as Senegal to England, but Goree, and with it the French slave trade, was now restored. Guadaloupe had been for more than three years an English possession. During that time the importation of a multitude of negroes, and a rapid increase of commerce, had enormously added to its value;[1] and in the impartial and very competent judgment of Chesterfield it might easily have been retained.[2] George Grenville insisted upon its retention, but Bute was so anxious to hurry on the peace that he availed himself of a temporary illness which prevented Grenville from attending to public business, to summon a council by which it was surrendered.[3] St. Lucia, which was selected from the neutral islands for surrender, was alone much more valuable than the three neutral islands that were retained. Martinique, from its

---

[1] See the description of the island by Admiral Rodney.—*Grenville Papers*, ii. 11-13.
[2] Chesterfield's *Letters*, iv. 353.
[3] *Grenville Papers*, i. 450.

situation and its strong fortifications, was extremely important as a military post for the protection of the neighbouring islands [1] and its conquest, which was one of the most arduous and brilliant enterprises of the war, seemed a needless sacrifice of blood and treasure if this rich island was to be restored a few months later without any equivalent. Even Havannah, which was perhaps the richest of all the conquests of the war, would have been restored by Bute without any territorial equivalent, and it was only the resolution of Grenville, and the strong pressure of public opinion, that obliged him to exact in return for it the poor and barren province of Florida.[2] The uncompensated surrender of Manilla was due to the shameful omission of any provision relating to conquests that had been made, though they were not known, before the preliminaries had been signed.

In all these respects the peace was deserving of censure, but we can hardly, I think, regret the abandonment by the ministry of the schemes of Pitt for destroying the whole commercial and naval greatness of France. The war had for the present given England an almost complete monopoly in many fields, and Pitt imagined that it was both possible, and desirable and just, to prevent France, in spite of her vast seaboard and her great resources, from ever reviving as a naval power. He maintained that the whole American fishery should be denied her. He had himself in the preceding negotiations consented, on certain conditions, to leave her a part of it; but he asserted that on this, as on many other points, his opinion had been overruled by his colleagues; that the fisheries of Newfoundland and St. Lawrence formed the great nursery of the French navy, and that they should in consequence be reserved exclusively for England. In the same spirit he desired to obtain for England a strict monopoly of the slave trade, of the sugar trade, of the trade with India, and he protested against any cession which enabled France to carry on any of these branches of commerce. Such a policy could hardly fail to make national animosities indelible. It is probable that France would have resisted it to the uttermost; and it rested not only on exaggerated feelings of national jealousy, but also on very narrow and erroneous views

---

[1] *Grenville Papers*, ii. 12, 13.
[2] Ibid. i. 450, 476, 483. *Life of Shelburne*, i. 154.

of the nature of commerce. No English statesman maintained more persistently than Pitt the advantages of commercial monopoly, or believed more firmly that the commercial interests of different nations were necessarily antagonistic.[1]

If the peace had been made in a different spirit and by other statesmen, it would probably have been favourably received. The Court party, who observed the many signs of weariness in the nation, and who remembered that during the last two reigns the disposition of the sovereign to involve the country in German disputes had been the chief source of disaffection, hoped, not altogether unreasonably, that the young king, by putting an end to the German war and by showing decisively that he was governed by no German sympathies, would have reaped an abundant harvest of popularity.[2] But all such expectations were soon falsified by the event. No character in England is more detested than that of a Court favourite, and the scandal about the relations of Bute and the mother of the King was eagerly accepted. In the very beginning of the new reign a paper was affixed to the Royal Exchange with the words, 'No petticoat government, no Scotch Minister, no Lord George Sackville,'[3] and after the displacement of Pitt the popular indignation rapidly increased. The City gave instructions to its members to promote a strict inquiry into the disposal of the money that was voted, and to refuse their consent to any peace which did not secure to England all or nearly all the conquests she had made. The example was widely followed. The unpopularity of Bute was such that he could not appear unattended or undisguised in the streets, and he was compelled to

---

[1] See the striking statement of his views on this matter, *Parl. Hist.* xv. 1265. 'The trade with these conquests [Martinique and Guadaloupe] is of the utmost lucrative nature and of the most considerable extent. The number of ships employed by it are a great resource to our maritime power; and, what is of equal weight, all that we gain on this system is made fourfold to us by the loss which ensues to France. But, our conquests in North America are of very little detriment to the commerce of France.'

[2] Thus in Jan. 1761, Lord Melcombe wrote to Bute: 'If the intelligence they bring me be true Mr. Pitt goes down fast in the City, and faster at this end of the town. They add you rise daily. . . . Should not a measure so extremely popular as the sacrificing that country [Hanover] to this, for a time, to secure an honourable and advantageous peace. . . . come immediately from the King, and by his order be carried into execution by the hands in which he places his whole confidence?'—*Adolphus*, i. 571, 572.

[3] Walpole to Montagu, Nov. 13 1760.

enroll a bodyguard of butchers and boxers for his protection. He was insulted as he went to Parliament. On one occasion his chair was attacked by so fierce a mob that his life was in serious danger. The jack boot, which by a pun upon his name was chosen as his popular emblem, was paraded ignominiously through the streets, hung up on a gallows, or thrown into the flames,[1] together with a bonnet or a petticoat symbolising the Princess. The declaration of war against Spain, which signally vindicated the foresight of Pitt, the splendid victories that followed, which were universally accepted as the direct results of his policy, the formal resignation of Newcastle which brought the favourite into clear relief as the responsible leader of the ministry, all added to the flame. Never perhaps in English history were libels so bitter or so scurrilous, and the influence of Frederick the Great was employed to foment them.[2] The story of Earl Mortimer, who was united by an illicit love to the mother of Edward III., and who by her means for a time governed the country and the King, became the favourite subject of the satirists. Among the papers left by Ben Jonson were the plot and the first scene of an intended play on the subject, and these were now republished with a dedication to Bute from the pen of Wilkes.

But perhaps the most popular topic in the invectives against Bute was his Scotch nationality. In addition to the strong national antipathy of Englishmen to all foreigners, many reasons had made the Scotch peculiarly unpopular. They had for centuries been regarded as natural enemies. The Union had been almost equally disliked by both nations, and closer contact had as yet done very little to soften the animosity. The Scotch were chiefly known in London as eager place-hunters, entering into keen competition with the natives for minor offices. They were poor, proud, sensitive, and pertinacious. Their strange pronunciation, the barrenness of their country, the contrast between the pride of their old nobility and the wretched shifts to which their poverty compelled them

---

[1] Walpole to Conway, Oct. 26, 1761. Walpole's *Memoirs of George III.* i. 85. *Grenville Papers,* i. 452.

[2] See the very curious letter of Frederick to his Ministers Knyphausen and Micheil urging them to use all their influence to stir up writers and agitators against Bute.—*Grenville Papers,* i. 467, 168.

to resort, furnished endless themes of illiberal ridicule. During more than half a century that followed the Union, only a single Englishman had been elected by a Scotch constituency;[1] and there were bitter complaints that a people so exclusive at home should be suffered to descend upon the rich fields of English patronage. Yet the very unpopularity of the Scotch drew them more closely together, and their tenacity of purpose enabled them in the race of ambition to distance many competitors. The contempt for poverty which is one of the most conspicuous signs of the deep vein of vulgarity that mingles with the many noble elements of the English character, and a more than common disposition to judge all foreigners by their own standard of manners, combined with other and somewhat more serious reasons to make the English look down upon the Scotch. As we have already seen, the Scotch members were as yet an unhealthy and a somewhat inferior element in English political life. They had been the last members who received wages for their services. They were still exempt from the property qualification which was required from most English members.[2] They had very little interest in English affairs. They usually voted together, and their venality was notorious.[3]

The rebellion of 1745 raised the national antipathy to fever heat. The Highland march to Derby and the disgraceful panic it produced in London, were remembered with a bitterness that was all the more intense because it was largely mixed with shame. And now, when a Scotch representative peer of the name and lineage of the Stuarts had become almost omnipotent at the Court, when Jacobite Scotchmen were received with marked favour by the Sovereign; when Scotch birth was believed to be one of the best passports to English promotion,

---

[1] Chauncy Townsend, the Member for Wigtown, who died in 1770.—*Annual Register*, 1770, p. 114.

[2] University members and sons of peers were in England exempt. Townshend's *History of the House of Commons*, ii. 406.

[3] Their subservience had been very bitterly noticed by Jekyll in the last reign. When Walpole's special tax on Papists and Nonjurors was imposed, the Scotch were exempted. Jekyll said: 'I know not why the Scotch should be excused from paying their proportion of this extraordinary tax, unless it was because forty-five Scotch representatives in that House always voted as they were directed.' Townshend's *Hist. of the House of Commons*, ii. 52, 53. Montesquieu, in his *Notes sur l'Angleterre*, which were written in 1730, had said, 'Il y a des membres écossois qui n'ont que deux cents livres sterling pour leur voix et la vendent à ce prix.'

there arose a cry of hatred and indignation which rang through the length and breadth of the land. Churchill, in his 'Prophecy of Famine,' and Wilkes, in his 'North Briton,' were its most powerful exponents. The former, in lines of savage vigour, depicted Scotland as a treeless, flowerless land formed out of the refuse of the universe, and inhabited by the very bastards of creation; where famine had fixed her chosen throne, where a scanty population, gaunt with hunger, and hideous with dirt and with the itch, spent their wretched days in brooding over the fallen fortunes of their native dynasty, and in watching with mingled envy and hatred the mighty nation that had subdued them. At last their greed and their hatred were alike gratified. What Force could not accomplish had been done by Fraud. The land flowing with milk and honey was thrown open to them. Already the most important places were at their disposal, and soon, through the influence of their great fellow-countrymen, they would descend upon every centre of English power to divide, weaken, plunder, and betray. With less genius, but with even greater effect, Wilkes collected in his weekly libels, every topic that could inflame the national hatred against the Scotch. He contended that 'a Scot had no more right to preferment in England than a Hanoverian or a Hottentot;' and he pointed out with bitter emphasis how the Scotchman Mansfield was Chief Justice of England, how the Scotchman Loudon commanded the British forces in Portugal, how the Scots Sir Gilbert Elliot and James Oswald were at the Treasury Board, how the Scotchman Ramsay was Court painter, and the Scotchman Adam Court architect; how a crowd of obscure Scotchmen had obtained pensions or small preferments paid for from the earnings of Englishmen. Buckingham Palace was nicknamed Holyrood on account of the number of Scotchmen who entered it.[1] The Duke of Cumberland had long been one of the most unpopular men in the kingdom, partly on account of the severities that followed Culloden, but these severities were now not only forgiven, but applauded; and as he was in opposition to Bute, he speedily became a hero, and was extolled as the second deliverer of England. The distinction between the two nations was so deep

[1] Walpole to Montagu, June 8, 1762.

and marked that Horace Walpole gave the Scotch birth of Sir Gilbert Elliot as a conclusive reason why he should not lead the House of Commons, and the Duke of Bedford assigned the same reason as one of the objections to the appointment of Forrester to the Speakership.[1] Junius himself never wrote with a more savage hatred than when he reminded the King of the treachery of the Scotch to Charles I., and dilated on the folly of any sovereign of any race who should hereafter rest upon their honour.

These instances are sufficient to show how far the great work of uniting the two nations was from its accomplishment. The dislike of the Scotch continued for many years unchecked, and among the Whigs it was greatly strengthened by the strong vein of Toryism, if not of Jacobitism, which was at this time conspicuous in Scotch writers. In the volumes of his history published in 1754 and 1756, Hume had devoted a grace of style, a skill of narration, and a subtlety of thought, which no English historian had yet equalled, to an elaborate apology for the conduct of the Stuarts. Smollett was one of the most conspicuous and most violent of the writers in defence of the Court. The 'Memoirs of Great Britain,' by Sir John Dalrymple, which appeared in 1771 and 1773, for the first time revealed the damaging fact that Algernon Sidney, whose memory had been almost canonised by his party, had received money from the French ambassador, and in 1775 the 'Original Papers' published by Macpherson gave an almost equal shock to the Whig tradition by proving the later communications of Marlborough with the Stuarts. The writings of Horace Walpole sufficiently show the indignation with which these books were regarded by Whig politicians, while the popular dislike was incessantly displayed. Macklin painted the Scotch in the most odious and despicable light in the character of Sir Pertinax MacSycophant in the 'Man of the World.' Hume wrote in 1765 that the English rage against the Scotch was daily increasing, and he added that it was such that he had frequently resolved never to set his foot on English soil.[2] At a time when the passion for representing plays of Shake-

---

[1] *Bedford Correspondence*, iii. xxxiii.
[2] Burton's *Life of Hume*, ii. 665.

speare with dresses that were historically correct was at its height, it was suggested that Macbeth should wear tartan instead of the modern military dress, but Garrick rejected the proposal, not because it was historically incorrect, but because the appearance of the Scotch national dress would infallibly damn the piece.[1] When Home, the famous author of 'Douglas,' produced his 'Fatal Discovery' in 1769, Garrick, in spite of the success of the earlier play, did not venture to reveal the name of the Scotch author, and induced a young Oxford gentleman to father the piece. The play was successful till the true author having then imprudently disclosed himself, its popularity speedily waned.[2] As late as 1771, when Smollett published 'Humphry Clinker,' the last and perhaps the greatest of his novels, it was assailed with a storm of obloquy on the ground that it was written to defend the Scotch.[3]

It is a remarkable proof of the change that in a few years had passed over English politics, of the disintegration of the Whig party and of the increasing force of corrupt influence in Parliament, that Bute should have been able, in spite of all his disadvantages, by the assistance of royal favour, to carry his measures triumphantly through Parliament. In the preceding reign Carteret had for a short time occupied a somewhat similar position; but notwithstanding his brilliant talents and his long and varied experience, he soon found his task an impossible one. Bute was a man of very ordinary intellect, and he came to office with no previous experience of public business, with no practice of debate, with no skill in managing men. His speech in defence of the Preliminaries of the Peace is said to have exhibited some power both of reasoning and language, but it appears to have been a mere elaborate essay, probably learned by heart, and much impaired by a very formal delivery. Charles Townshend compared the slow monotonous succession of its sentences to the firing of minute-guns.

---

[1] Doran's *Jacobite London*, ii. p. 350.

[2] Scott's *Essay on the Life and Works of John Home*.

[3] See Walpole's *Memoirs of George III.* iv. 328. We have a curious illustration of the change that may take place in national judgments in the Autobiography of Lord Shelburne. 'Like the generality of Scotch,' he says, 'Lord Mansfield had no regard to truth whatever.'—Fitzmaurice's *Life of Shelburne*, i. 89. Among the many admirable qualities of the Scotch there is probably none which a modern observer would regard as so conspicuous and so uncontested as their eminent truthfulness.

There have been statesmen with very little political ability, who have maintained a high place in politics by the personal confidence they inspired, by a frankness and simplicity of character which disarmed enmities and attached friends. But of these qualities, to which the success of Lord Althorp in the present century was mainly due, Bute was wholly destitute. His honour, though it was probably unstained, was certainly not unsuspected. His relations with the Princess Dowager, and the negotiations with Prince Galitzin, left a cloud of suspicion upon it. The publication in 1756 of the 'Memoirs of Torcy' had for the first time disclosed to the English public the startling fact that, in the negotiations between the English and French in 1709, a large bribe had been offered to Marlborough to induce him to favour the French cause, and a charge of having accepted a bribe from France to carry the Peace of Paris was brought publicly against Bute in 1765. Parliament, it is true, a few years later, after a careful investigation, pronounced it wholly frivolous,[1] but it is a remarkable illustration of the low estimate in which Bute was held, that Lord Camden, long afterwards, expressed his firm belief that it was substantially true.[2] A natural turn for tortuous methods and secret intrigues, combined with great moroseness and haughtiness of manner, had made Bute disliked and distrusted by all with whom he had to deal. Even the Duke of Bedford, with whom he chiefly shares the praise or blame of the peace, came to regard him with hatred when he found that during the negotiations, he was secretly corresponding with the French. Of administrative ability he had absolutely nothing. The peace, bad as it was, would have been much worse but for the intervention of his colleagues, and especially of George Grenville, and the financial administration of this ministry was one of the worst ever known in England. Sir Francis Dashwood, who had been made Chancellor of the Exchequer, was honourably distinguished in the last reign by his strenuous opposition to the execution of Byng, but he was better known as the President of the Medmenham Brotherhood or Franciscan Club, a well-known society famous for its debaucheries, and for its blasphemous parodies of the rites of the

---

[1] *Parliamentary Hist.* xvi. 763-785.
[2] See Lord Stanhope's *History of England,* iv. 273.

Catholic religion. Of financial knowledge he did not possess the rudiments, and his ignorance was all the more conspicuous from the great financial ability of his predecessor Legge. His budget speech was so confused and incapable that it was received with shouts of laughter. An excise of 4s. in the hogshead, to be paid by the grower, which he imposed on cyder and perry, raised a resistance through the cyder counties hardly less furious than that which had been directed against the excise scheme of Walpole.[1]

One man, however, of real ability and of indomitable courage stood by Bute. Henry Fox, soured by disappointment and unpopularity, at last saw the possibility, by a bold act of apostasy, of recovering his ascendency, and he fearlessly confronted the tempest of opposition. Of the feeling of the country he had no illusion. Just before he took the lead of the Commons he wrote to his confidant Shelburne: 'Does not your Lordship begin to fear that there are few left of any sort, of our friends even, who are for the peace? I own I do.'[2]

Then came a period of intimidation and corruption compared with which the worst days of the Walpole administration appeared pure. Bribes ranging from 200l. and upwards were given almost publicly at the pay office. Martin, the Secretary of the Treasury, afterwards acknowledged that no less than 25,000l. were expended in a single morning in purchasing votes. Large sums are said to have been given to corporations to petition for the peace. Urgent letters were written to the lord-lieutenants of the counties calling on them to procure addresses with the same object. From the very beginning of the ascendency of Bute, patronage had been extended and employed with extravagant profusion for the purpose of increasing the political power of the Crown, and this process was rapidly extended. Bute did not venture, like Harley, to create simultaneously twelve peers, but sixteen were made in the space of two years. The number of Lords of the Bedchamber was increased from twelve to twenty-two, each with a salary of 500l. a year, and they were

---

[1] *Parl. Hist.* xv. 1307–1316. This tax was said to have been proposed 'because Sir Francis Dashwood could not be made to understand a tax on linen which was first intended, sufficiently to explain it to the House.'— Fitzmaurice's *Life of Shelburne*, i. 186
[2] Ibid. i. 157.

selected exclusively from among the members of Parliament. It was found necessary to raise 3,500,000*l*., and this was done partly by two lotteries, and partly by a loan which was not thrown open to public competition, and which was issued on terms so shamefully improvident that the shares at once rose 10 per cent. A very large proportion of these shares were distributed among the friends of the Government, and thus a new and most wasteful form of bribery was introduced into English politics.[1]

Intimidation of the grossest kind was at the same time practised. All the partisans of Newcastle were at once driven from office, and some of the most prominent men in the country were treated with an arrogance that recalled the worst days of the Stuarts. The Duke of Devonshire was expelled from the office of Chamberlain with circumstances of the grossest insult. The King refused even to see him on the occasion, and with his own hand struck his name from the list of Privy Councillors. The Dukes of Newcastle and Grafton, and the Marquis of Rockingham, were deprived of the Lord-Lieutenancies of their counties.[2] It has always been one of the most healthy features of English political life that the public offices are filled with permanent officials, who are unaffected by party fluctuations, who instruct alike Whig and Tory ministers, preserve unbroken the steady tendencies of government, and from the stability of their position acquire a knowledge of administrative details and an independence and impartiality of judgment which could never be reasonably expected from men whose tenure of office was dependent on the ascendency of a party. This system Fox and Bute resolved to break down. They determined that every servant of the Government, even to the very lowest, should be of their own nomination.[3] A persecu-

---

[1] Walpole's *George III.* i. 199. *Hist. of the Late Minority*, pp. 69, 83, 93–102. *Anecdotes of Chatham*, i. 282. *North Briton.* p. 234.

[2] *Adolphus*, i. 119. Albemarle's *Life of Rockingham*, i. 158, 159. Harris, *Life of Hardwicke*, iii. 320, 333–335.

[3] 'The impertinence of our conquered enemies last night was great, but will not continue so if his Majesty shows no lenity. But, my Lord, with regard to their numerous dependants in Crown employments, it behoves your Lordship in particular to leave none of them. Their connections spread very wide, and every one of their relatives and friends is in his heart your enemy.... Turn the tables and you will immediately have thousands who will think the safety of themselves depends upon your Lordship, and will therefore be sincere and active friends.'—Fox to Bute, Nov. 1762. *Shelburne's Life*, i. 180.

tion as foolish as it was harsh was directed by Fox against the humblest officials who had been appointed or recommended by Whig statesmen, or were in any way connected with them. Clerks, tidewaiters, and excisemen were included in the proscription. The widow of an admiral who was distantly connected with the Duke of Devonshire, a poor man who had been rewarded for bravery against smugglers at the recommendation of the Duke of Grafton, a schoolboy who was a nephew of Legge, were among those who were deprived of places, pensions, or reversions. There was even a design of depriving the members of the Opposition of the great patent places they held, although the terms of the patents distinctly asserted that the places were for life. Fox wished to submit to the twelve judges the question whether it was not in the power of the King to annul the patents; but the Chancellor, Lord Northington, declared that it would be as reasonable to ask them to pronounce upon the validity of the Great Charter. It was the aim of the Court party to crush to the very dust the great Whig connection, by showing that no person, however humble, who had received favours from it could escape the vengeance of the Crown, while every resource of patronage and place was employed for the purpose of consolidating the new interest. One official, who for seven years had been of the King's bedchamber, was turned out solely because he had no seat in Parliament, and could therefore be of no use there.[1]

Among the few merits of Bute must be reckoned his strong literary tastes; and his patronage, though rarely or never extended to any writers except those of his party, was sometimes judiciously bestowed. Johnson owed to him his pension of 300*l.* a year. Sir James Stuart, the Jacobite political economist who had been obliged to fly from England on account of his participation in the rebellion of 1745, was pardoned through his instrumentality.[2] That invaluable collection of about 30,000 pamphlets published at the time of the Commonwealth, which

---

[1] Walpole's *Memoirs of George III.* i. 233–240.

[2] *Burke's Correspondence*, i. 130. Colman's play, *The English Merchant* was written to grace his pardon. An exceedingly favourable account of the literary acquirements and of the conversation of Lord Bute will be found in Dutens' *Mémoires d'un Voyageur qui se repose*, ii. 299–306. The author had been employed by Bute in some negotiations preparatory to the Peace of Paris.

forms one of the most precious treasures of the British Museum had been purchased by Bute for his own library, and it was bought from him for presentation to the nation, by the King.[1] Prosecutions for libel during this ministry were exceedingly rare; it was one of the first objects of Bute to set up a paper to defend the peace, and a crowd of writers were soon induced by pensions or places to support the ministry. It was said, though probably on no very sure authority, that more than 30,000l. were expended on the press in the first two years of the reign.[2] Pitt became the incessant object of the most virulent attacks. Smollett assailed him, in a paper called 'The Briton,' with disgraceful violence, and with very little of the ability he showed in other fields. Dr. Shebbeare, who in 1758 had been sentenced to imprisonment and to the pillory for a virulent libel against the House of Hanover, was pensioned by Bute in order that he should defend the peace, and Dr. Francis, Murphy, Mallet, and several other obscure writers, were employed in the same cause. Hogarth, who was sergeant-painter to the King, powerfully assisted them by his clever print of the 'Times,' which appeared in 1762. Europe was represented in flames, which were rapidly extending to Great Britain, and Pitt, with a pair of bellows, was stimulating the conflagration. Around his neck hung a Cheshire cheese with 3,000l. written on it, alluding to his pension and to an expression in one of his speeches that he would rather live on Cheshire cheese than submit to the enemies of England. The aldermen of London were humbly worshipping him. Newcastle fed the flames with 'Monitors' and 'North Britons,' the chief papers of the Opposition; the King of Prussia, like Nero, was fiddling amid the conflagration; while Bute, assisted by English soldiers and sailors, and by Highlanders, was endeavouring to extinguish it. A man, representing Temple, was squirting at Bute from the window of the Temple Coffee-house. A waggon was bearing off the treasures taken from the Spanish ship *Hermione*. In the distance, the Newcastle arms were being taken down and replaced by the patriotic ones.

---

[1] *Annual Register*, 1763, p. 117. Adolphus, *Hist. George III.* i. 115, 121.
[2] *Anecdotes of Chatham*, i. 203. 1760. Dodington's *Diary*, Dec 20,

The success which attended the measures of Bute was, for a time at least, very great. Parliament was now thoroughly amenable to corrupt influence. In addition to the nucleus of genuine Tories, the Government could count upon the Bedford connection, upon a portion of the Grenville connection, upon the small group of politicians who followed the fortunes of Fox, and upon nearly all the bishops. Newcastle was old and thoroughly discredited, and most of his adherents had gone over to Bute;[1] and Pitt, though incomparably the greatest figure in English politics, had alienated from himself most of his former colleagues, had little Parliamentary influence, and was prostrated during a great part of this critical period by the gout. His appearance at the Guildhall in the procession of the King was much blamed, and was afterwards regretted by himself; but with this exception his conduct was singularly stainless. He had been struck down in the very zenith of his great career and when his popularity was at its height, and in the necessity which compelled Bute to declare war against Spain his policy had received the most complete vindication. But his language was equally free from irritation, recrimination, and triumph. His attitude was that of a great citizen conscious that his country was passing through a great crisis, and resolved at every sacrifice of personal considerations to support the Government in carrying the war to a triumphant issue, and securing an adequate and honourable peace. Violent and impetuous as he often was, no statesman felt more strongly that foreign politics were not the field in which party triumphs might be legitimately sought, and that in time of war internal division should be as much as possible suspended. During the war in Portugal he strongly supported the Government, recommending the strictest union, and declaring against all 'altercation, which was no way to carry on the public business.'[2] The fear of him was very great, and it was doubtless in order to neutralise the effects of his eloquence that the exclusion of strangers from the gallery of the House of Commons was at this time enforced with special rigour.[3] Burke, who was in general by no means one of his greatest admirers, said with truth that the

---

[1] Rockingham's *Memoirs*, i. 152.   [2] *Thackeray*, ii 7.
[3] *Parl. Hist.* xv. 1227.

manner in which after his fall he 'made his own justification, without impeaching the conduct of any of his colleagues, or taking one measure that might seem to arise from disgust or opposition, set a seal upon his character.'[1] No one ever understood better the true dignity of statesmanship. He met the storm of scurrility that raged around him with a majestic and somewhat disdainful silence, and calmly watched the tide of popular favour which was rising higher and higher. At the same time he stooped to no demagogue art. The favourite topic of the opponents of the Government was abuse of the Scotch; but Pitt never lost an opportunity of rebuking the national prejudice, extolling the valour which had been shown by the Highland regiments during the war, and censuring the conduct of those who were trying to sow animosity between the two nations.

The Preliminaries were approved in the House of Lords without a division, in the House of Commons by 319 to 65. The Duke of Newcastle, seeing opposition to be hopeless, induced his friends to retire before the division. Pitt spoke against the terms for three and a half hours; but he was so broken by painful illness that he was obliged to speak sitting, and although his speech contained passages of great beauty and power, his voice often sank into an inaudible murmur. The exultation of the Court was unbounded. 'Now,' said the Princess Dowager, when the news of the decisive vote arrived, 'my son *is* King of England.' But outside the House the feeling was very different, and the Ministers who made the Peace of Paris were scarcely more popular than those who had made the Peace of Utrecht. The City of London and the great county of York refused all solicitations to address. The animosity against Bute grew daily stronger, and Bedford was hissed in the streets.[2] The cyder counties, which had hitherto been the warmest supporters of Toryism, were thrown into a blaze of agitation by the cyder tax; and although it was carried by overwhelming majorities in both Houses, this is said to have been the first occasion on which the House of Lords divided on a money Bill.[3] Probably never since the days of the Revolution

[1] *Annual Register*, 1761, p. 481.   [2] Walpole's *Memoirs of George III.*
[3] *Parl. Hist.* xv. 1316.

had the ministers of the Crown been the objects of such execration in the country. Bute quailed before the storm. He had very little experience in the agitations of public life; he was constitutionally a man of no great resolution of character; he had lately inherited a gigantic fortune, and had obtained from the Crown the Garter and the Rangership of Richmond Park for himself, and an English peerage for his son. He had little left to aspire to, and many dangers to fear. In the Cabinet he found himself isolated, and his Chief Justice, Lord Mansfield, more than once voted against him. He was sincerely attached to the King, and could not but be sensible that he was ruining his popularity. His health was weak, and he hoped under a new Ministry to wield with greatly diminished obloquy the same powers as in the beginning of the reign. These were probably the real reasons of his resignation, which took place, somewhat unexpectedly, on April 8, 1763. Dashwood retired with him, receiving a sinecure and the title of Lord De Spencer. Fox claimed his peerage, but was thrown into transports of fury by hearing that the King and Bute expected him, when receiving it, to resign his enormously lucrative office of Paymaster. The bargain for the peerage had been made through the intervention of Shelburne, and Fox accused Shelburne of having shamefully duped him. It is certain that Shelburne, when engaging the services of Fox to carry the peace, never told him that on receiving the promised peerage he must resign his office. It is equally certain that Fox, when accepting the offers of the Government, had made no such promise, and that nevertheless Shelburne, without his knowledge or authority, had spoken of his resignation as a settled thing. It was said, on the other side, that public opinion would have been greatly scandalised if Fox retained such an office with a peerage, that Fox had at one time been himself of that opinion, and that Shelburne had only given in conversation his own opinion on the subject, and had not professed to be communicating the words of Fox. The contention was long and vehement, and Fox lost no opportunity of describing Shelburne as 'a perfidious and infamous liar;' but he at last succeeded in retaining the office, though entering the Upper House as Lord Holland. He kept it till

1765, but without taking any further part in active politics.[1] The character of the ministers was shown to the very last; not less than 52,000*l.* a year out of the public money was granted in reversions to the followers of Bute.[2]

The history of this ministry is peculiarly shameful. During two reigns the Tory party had been excluded from office, and during all that time they had constituted themselves the special champions of Parliamentary purity. In the writings of Bolingbroke, in the speeches of the Tory leaders, in the place Bills they had repeatedly advocated, the necessity of putting an end to political corruption was given the foremost place. This had been their favourite cry at every election, the battle-ground they continually selected in their contests with the Whig ministers of the first two Georges; and in the beginning of the new reign the purification of Parliament and of administration had been continually represented as the great benefit that might be expected from the downfall of the Whigs.[3] At last the party had risen to power, and in ten months of office they far surpassed the corruption of their predecessors. They had long protested against the monopoly of office by a single party; but when they came to power they had driven out the humblest officials who were connected with their opponents with a severity unparalleled in English history. They had delighted in expatiating upon the administrative incapacity of the great Whig families, and upon the contrast between the scandalous Courts of the first two Georges and the unchallenged purity of the Tory King; but the financial policy of the administration of Bute displayed a grosser incapacity than had been exhibited by any previous Government, and the appoint-

---

[1] Compare Walpole's *George III.* i. 257, 258, with Lord E. Fitzmaurice's elaborate defence of Shelburne.—*Shelburne's Life,* i. 199-229.

[2] Walpole to Montagu, April 14, 1763.

[3] Walpole says: 'It was given out that the King would suffer no money to be spent on elections,' that 'he had forbidden any money [at the general election] to be issued from the Treasury.'—Walpole's *George III.* i. 19, 41. 'Every one,' said Burke, 'must remember that the Cabal set out with the most astonishing prudery, both moral and political. Those who in a few months after soused over head and ears into the deepest and dirtiest pits of corruption, cried out violently against the indirect practices in the electing and managing of Parliaments which had formerly prevailed. . . . . Corruption was to be cast down from Court as Atè was from Heaven.'—*Thoughts on the Causes of the Present Discontents.* See too the *Seasonable Hints from an Honest Man on the present Crisis.*

ment of Dashwood and the policy of Fox produced a scandal at least equal to any in the former reigns. The fame of the country was lowered by the peace; an enthusiastic loyalty was dimmed. The ill-feeling between England and Scotland, which had been rapidly subsiding, was revived, and the whole country was filled with riot and discontent.

After a short negotiation, George Grenville was placed at the head of the Treasury. A remarkable letter, written by Bute to the Duke of Bedford a few days before the resignation of the former, sums up the principles on which the King was resolved that his government should be conducted. The first and most important was, 'never upon any account to suffer those ministers of the late reign who have attempted to fetter and enslave him, ever to come into his service while he lives to hold the sceptre;'[1] in other words, he was determined that the group of Whig noblemen who were accustomed to act together in politics, and who during the last reign had acquired a preponderating power, were, at all hazards and under all circumstances, to be absolutely disqualified from acting as ministers of the Crown. In order to maintain this disqualification, the King was resolved 'to collect every other force, and especially the followers of the Duke of Bedford and of Mr. Fox, to his councils and support,' and to give every encouragement to those Whig country gentlemen who, without abandoning any political principles, would consent to support his Government. It was hoped that in this manner a Government might be formed which would command a secure majority in both Houses, but in which no set of statesmen would be able to dictate to the King. It was hoped, at the same time, that with the retirement of Bute the feeling of loyalty to the Crown would revive, and that the storm of popular agitation would subside. 'I am firmly of opinion,' wrote Bute, 'that my retirement will remove the only unpopular part of Government.'

The character of George Grenville, who for the next two years was the strongest influence in the English Government, has been admirably portrayed by the greatest political writer of his own generation and by the greatest English historian of the present century, and there is little to be added to the

[1] *Bedford Corresp.* iii. 223–226.

pictures they have drawn. Unlike Bute, and unlike a large number of the most prominent Whig statesmen, Grenville was an undoubtedly able man, but only as possessing very ordinary qualities to an extraordinary degree. He was a conspicuous example of a class of men very common in public life, who combine considerable administrative powers with an almost complete absence of the political sense—who have mastered the details of public business with an admirable competence and skill, but who have scarcely anything of the tact, the judgment, or the persuasiveness that are essential for the government of men. Educated as a lawyer, and afterwards designated for the post of Speaker of the House of Commons, he surpassed all his leading contemporaries in his knowledge of parliamentary precedents, of constitutional law, and of administrative details; and he brought to the Government an untiring industry, a rare business faculty, a courage that flinched from no opponent, and an obstinacy that was only strengthened by disaster. Few men were more sincerely respected by their friends, and, though he never attained any general popularity, few men had a greater weight in the House of Commons. His admirers were able to allege with truth that he was one of the most frugal of ministers at a time when economy was peculiarly unpopular;[1] that, though his fortune was far below that of most of his competitors, and though he was by no means indifferent to money, he lived strictly within his private means, and was free from all suspicion of personal corruption; and that he more than once sacrificed the favour of the King, of the people, and of his own family, to what he believed to be right. His enemies maintained with equal truth that he was hard, narrow, formal, and self-sufficient, without extended views or generous sympathies, signally destitute of the tact of statesmanship which averts or conciliates opposition, prone on every occasion to strain authority to the utmost limit which precedent or the strict letter of the law would admit. Being a younger brother of Lord Temple, and brother-in-law of Pitt and of Lord Egremont, he had the assistance of considerable family influence in his career; but he had himself neither high

---

[1] He boasted that the secret service money was lower in his ministry than in any other recent administration.—*Grenville Papers*, ii. 519, iii. 143.

rank nor great wealth; his talents were not shining; he was peculiarly deficient in the qualities that win popularity either with the nation or in the closet, and the success with which he slowly emerged through many subordinate offices to the foremost place was chiefly due to his solid application and indomitable will. In the early part of his life he was closely connected with Pitt. Like him he began his career among the 'Patriots,' who were opposed to Walpole, and as early as 1754, Pitt had pronounced him second only to the great party leaders in his knowledge of the business of the House of Commons.[1] He was dismissed from office by Newcastle, with Pitt, in 1755; held office under Pitt during the German war; but, after many transient differences, at last openly quarrelled with him, and then inveighed against the extravagance of the war of which he had been an official though a subordinate and a reluctant supporter. Apart, indeed, from all questions of personal ambition, the characters of the two brothers-in-law were so opposed that their rupture was almost inevitable. Except in matters of military administration, Pitt had very little knowledge of public business, and he was singularly ignorant of finance. He excelled in flashes of splendid but irregular genius; in daring, comprehensive, and far-seeing schemes of policy; in the power of commanding the sympathies and evoking the energies of great bodies of men. He was pre-eminently a war minister, 'pleased with the tempest when the waves ran high,' continually seeking to extend the power and increase the influence of his nation, too ready to plunge into every European complication, and too indifferent to the calamities of war and to the accumulations of debt. Grenville, on the other hand, was minute, accurate, methodical, parsimonious, and pacific, delighting in detail, anxious above all things to establish a sound system of finance and a safe and moderate system of foreign policy, desponding to a fault in his judgment of events, clear and powerful, indeed, but very tedious in debate, and little accustomed to look beyond the walls of the House and the strict letter of the law. During the last years of George II. he had some connection with the Leicester House party of Bute and the Princess of Wales; and when Pitt retired from office in 1761, Grenville,

---

[1] See *Grenville Papers*, i. pp. ix, x.

as we have seen, became leader of the House of Commons. His sincere desire for peace may excuse, or at least palliate, his acceptance of office under Bute, and his silent acquiescence in the corrupt and arbitrary measures of that unhappy administration; and he at this time did good service to the country by compelling Bute to exact compensation from Spain for the cession of Havannah. He was, however, so discontented with the details of the peace that he refused to take any part in defending it, and was accordingly removed from the leadership of the House, and exchanged his position of Secretary of State for the less prominent and somewhat less dignified office of First Lord of the Admiralty, where he appears to have confined himself chiefly to the duties of his department.[1] Bute recommended him as his successor, apparently under the belief that he was a mere official drudge, and would yield readily to the inspiration of a master.

He became the head of the Government on April 8, 1763, holding the two offices of First Lord of the Treasury and Chancellor of the Exchequer, which had not been united since the death of Pelham. Lord Egremont, whose influence among the Tories was very great, and Lord Halifax, who was a man of popular manners and character, but of no great ability or power, were made Secretaries of State, and were intended to share the chief power; but the early death of the first and the insignificance of the latter left Grenville almost without a rival.

His natural ally would have been his elder brother, Lord Temple, a man of very great wealth and position, of no remarkable talent or acquirement, but in a high degree ambitious, arrogant, violent, jealous, and vindictive. Temple, however, was closely allied with Pitt, who in the early part of his career was in a great degree dependent on the Grenville influence, and had even been under pecuniary obligations to his brother-in-law, and who repaid the boon by giving Temple a very disproportionate influence in his counsels and his combinations. He had been First Lord of the Admiralty in the administration of Pitt and Devonshire, Lord Privy Seal in the far greater administration of Pitt and Newcastle, and, although he was

---

[1] See an interesting autobiographical sketch in the *Grenville Papers*, i. 422-430, 482-485.

extremely disliked by George II., Pitt succeeded in obtaining for him the Garter, which was the great object of his ambition. In spite of several explosions of personal jealousy, he steadily supported the German policy of Pitt, joined him in recommending war with Spain in 1761, retired with him from office, and became from that time one of the most violent and factious of politicians. He is reported to have said of himself, very frankly, that 'he loved faction, and had a great deal of money to spare,'[1] and the saying, whether it be true or false, describes very faithfully the character of his policy. Indifferent to the emoluments of office, and unconscious of any remarkable administrative powers, he delighted in the subterranean and more ignoble works of faction, in forming intrigues, inciting mobs, and inspiring libels. He was the special friend and patron of Wilkes, and he was more closely connected than any other leading politician of his time with the vast literature of scurrilous and anonymous political libels. He assisted many of the writers with money or with information, and he was believed to have suggested, inspired, or in part composed some of the most venomous of their productions. He was accused of having 'worked in the mines of successive factions for near thirty years together,' of 'whispering to others where they might obtain torches, though he was never seen to light them himself;' and although his personal friends ascribed to him considerable private virtues, his honour as a public man was rated very low. His influence upon Pitt, as we shall see in the sequel, was very disastrous, and at the time when Grenville assumed the first place he was bitterly opposed to his brother.

Being deprived of assistance in this quarter, Grenville might naturally have expected his chief support from the Duke of Bedford, who had so lately been his colleague, and who was at the head of a considerable section of the Whigs. The importance of this nobleman, like that of Lord Temple, depended altogether upon the accident of birth which made him the head of one of the greatest of the Whig houses, and it is not, I think, easy to find any consistent principle in his strangely intricate career, except a desire to aggrandise his family influence. The

[1] *Grenville Papers*, iii. p. xxxvii.

great inclination towards wealth which has usually prevailed in English politics has always been justified, among other reasons, by the consideration that a rich man, to whom the emoluments of office are a matter of indifference, is much less likely than a poor man to be bribed or to be guilty of political sycophancy or apostasy; but it is worthy of notice that this presumption hardly applies to the heads of great houses, who, under the system of government that preceded the Reform Bill, were exposed to special corrupting influences scarcely less powerful than those which act upon needy men. The desire of obtaining garters, ribands, and promotions for themselves, and especially the imperious necessity of providing for a long train of rapacious followers on whose support their influence mainly depended, has not unfrequently made great noblemen of splendid fortune and position the most inveterate of place-hunters. The Duke of Bedford does not appear personally to have cared much for office; but his followers were among the most unprincipled politicians in England, and the faction he directed amalgamated cordially with no party, but made overtures in turn to each, entered into temporary alliances with each, deserted each, and formed and dissolved its connections chiefly on personal grounds. The Duke himself was violent, harsh, and fearless, and was noted as the only man who ventured to oppose Pitt in the Cabinet when that imperious statesman was in the zenith of his power.[1] He began his career in opposition to Walpole, and exerted all his powers to produce a Spanish war. In the earlier years of the Pelham ministry, he showed considerable administrative abilities as First Lord of the Admiralty from 1744 to 1748, and he afterwards had the rare fortune of taking a leading part in the negotiation of two peaces, each of which was probably on the whole beneficial to the country, but neither of which was at all glorious or popular. As Secretary of State under Pelham, he in a great degree dictated the Peace of Aix-la-Chapelle, which concluded the Spanish war, without obtaining any object for which that war was undertaken. As Ambassador to France, under Bute, he negotiated the Peace of Paris, which made him

---

[1] See *Bedford Corresp.* iii. 56.

so unpopular that for some time he could not show himself publicly in the streets of London. In the intervening Devonshire administration he was Lord-Lieutenant of Ireland, where he took some measures to mitigate the penal laws against the Catholics, but where his attempts to restrict the rights of the Irish Parliament excited violent riots, and led to the ignominious defeat of his Government. He was closely connected with Fox, with whom he joined the ministry of Bute, and whose harshest and most tyrannical acts received the warm approbation of his confidential follower Rigby. The dissatisfaction of Grenville at some portions of the peace had, however, produced a coldness between Bedford and Grenville, which for some time prevented their cordial co-operation. When Bute retired from office he implored Bedford to accept the position of President of the Council in order to carry on with Grenville a system of government substantially the same as that of the favourite; but Bedford declined the offer on the ground that such a ministry could not stand. He recommended the King and Bute to send for the great Whig families; and, though some of his followers took offices under Grenville, his position towards him in the beginning of his ministry was one of neutrality, if not of secret hostility.

The Government, under these circumstances, was not strong, and at first it appeared probable that the wishes of the Court would be fulfilled, and that Bute would be its real though unofficial director. For some time most important negotiations relating to its composition were conducted by him, and the Speech, which closed Parliament on April 19, 1763, identified its foreign policy with that of the preceding ministry; for the King was made to speak of the peace as having been concluded 'upon conditions so honourable to my Crown, and so beneficial to my people,' and to suggest that England had been the means of securing a satisfactory peace for the King of Prussia. Wilkes, who for a few days had suspended the publication of the 'North Briton' to watch the course of events, now broke silence; and on April 23 the famous 45th number appeared, attacking the King's Speech with great asperity. The writer dilated especially upon the abandonment of the King of Prussia, the inadequate terms of the peace, the Cyder

Act, the frequent promotion of Scotchmen and Jacobites, and he asserted that 'the King is only the first magistrate of this country, . . . responsible to his people for the due exercise of the royal functions in the choice of ministers, &c.' 'The personal character,' he added, 'of our present amiable sovereign makes us easy and happy that so great a power is lodged in such hands; but the favourite has given too just cause for him to escape the general odium.' The King's Speech is, and has always been regarded as, the speech of the ministers, and, judging it in that light, Wilkes pronounced the last speech from the throne to be 'the most abandoned instance of ministerial effrontery ever attempted to be imposed upon mankind.' 'Every friend of his country,' he continued, 'must lament that a prince of so many great and amiable qualities, whom England truly reveres, can be brought to give the sanction of his sacred name to the most odious measures, and to the most unjustifiable public declarations, from a throne ever renowned for truth, honour, and unsullied virtue.' 'The ministers' speech of last Tuesday is not to be paralleled in the annals of this country.'

The blow was a very skilful one. The King's Speech, as Wilkes truly asserted, had long been regarded as simply the composition of the ministers, and as such it was fully open to criticism. Even Fox, the leading minister in carrying the peace, had very recently asserted this doctrine in the plainest terms.[1] Considering the Speech in this light, the criticisms of Wilkes, though severe, were not excessive, and were certainly less violent than some in previous numbers of his paper. It had become, however, a main object of the Court party to draw a broad distinction between the King and his ministers, and to arrest what was regarded as the absorption of Crown influence by the administration. The paper of Wilkes, in the eyes of the Court party, was a direct attack upon the personal veracity of the Sovereign; and although Wilkes was now member for Aylesbury, and therefore protected by the vague and formidable panoply of Parliamentary privilege, it was determined at all hazards to crush him. The King himself

---

[1] Walpole's *George III.* i. 121.

gave orders to prosecute him,[1] and for several years the ruin of one very insignificant individual was a main object of the Executive.

John Wilkes, who now became one of the most prominent figures in English politics, was at this time in his thirty-sixth year. The son of a rich trader and of a Presbyterian mother, he had been educated at a Presbyterian school at Hertford, and in the house of a Presbyterian tutor, and he afterwards studied at the University of Leyden. When only twenty-two he married a rich heiress, ten years older than himself, and of strict Methodistical principles, from whom he was soon after separated and whom he treated with great baseness. His countenance was repulsively ugly. His life was scandalously and notoriously profligate, and he was sometimes guilty of profanity which exceeded even that of the vicious circle in which he lived, but he possessed some qualities which were well fitted to secure success in life. He had a brilliant and ever ready wit, unflagging spirits, unfailing good humour, great personal courage, much shrewdness of judgment, much charm of manner. The social gifts must have been indeed of no common order which half-conquered the austere Toryism of Johnson, extorted a warm tribute of admiration from Gibbon, secured the friendship of Reynolds, and made the son of a London distiller a conspicuous member of the Medmenham Brotherhood, and the favourite companion of the more dissipated members of the aristocracy. It is not probable that he had any serious political convictions, but like most ambitious men he threw himself into politics as the easiest method of acquiring notoriety and position, and he expended many thousands of pounds in the venture. He contested Berwick unsuccessfully, but became member for Aylesbury in 1757, and connected himself by a close personal friendship and political alliance with Lord Temple. Having

---

[1] This is stated in the Journal of the Duke of Grafton.—See Campbell's *Chancellors*, vi. 327; and also *Grenville Papers*, ii. 192. See too, on the warm personal interest which the King took in pushing on the measures against Wilkes, Walpole's *George III.* ii. 296. According to Almon (who is not a very good authority), No. 45 was in a great measure based upon a conversation about the King's Speech between Pitt and Temple which took place at the house of the latter when Wilkes happened to be calling there.

speedily dissipated his own fortune and as much of the fortune of his wife as it was possible by any means to get into his hands, he began to look to office as a means of recruiting his finances, and he had hopes of becoming ambassador at Constantinople, or obtaining the governorship of Canada, but his prospects were blasted by the downfall of the Whigs, and in the beginning of the new reign Bute himself is said to have interfered to defeat one of his applications. He took a prominent part in censuring the King's Speech in 1761, but his speaking was cold and commonplace, and made no impression on the House. The 'North Briton,' however, which he founded in the following year, raised him at once to importance. It had little literary merit beyond a clear and easy style, but it skilfully reflected and aggravated the popular hatred of the Scotch; it attacked the Court party with an audacity that had been rarely paralleled, and it introduced for the first time into political discussions the practice of printing the names of the chief persons in the State at full length instead of indicating them merely by initials.[1] It soon distanced or silenced all competitors, but no prosecution was directed against it till the accession of Grenville and the publication of No. 45.

The first measure of the Government was to issue a general warrant, signed by Lord Halifax, which, without specifying the names of the persons accused, directed the apprehension of 'the authors, printers, and publishers' of the incriminated number and the seizure of their papers. Under this warrant no less than forty-nine persons were arrested, and the publisher having acknowledged that Wilkes was the author of the paper, he was seized and carried before Lord Halifax, while his drawers were burst open and his papers carried away. He refused to answer any question, protested against the illegality of a warrant in which no name was given, and claimed the privilege of Parliament against arrest, but in spite of every protest he was confined a close prisoner in the Tower, and denied all opportunity of consulting with his friends or even with his solicitor.

Such proceedings at once raised legal and constitutional questions of the gravest kind, and Lord Temple warmly supported

---

[1] Walpole's *Memoirs of George III.* iii. 164.

Wilkes in vindicating his rights. The attitude of the demagogue was defiant and irritating in the extreme. One of the Secretaries of State was Lord Egremont, whose father had been imprisoned on suspicion of Jacobitism in the last reign. On his committal to the Tower, Wilkes asked to be lodged in the room in which Windham had been confined, or at all events in a room in which no Scotchman had been lodged, if such a room could be found in the Tower. He wrote a letter to his daughter, who was then in a French convent, congratulating her on living in a free country, and sent it open, according to rule, to Lord Halifax. He applied to the Court of Common Pleas for a writ of Habeas Corpus, and when he succeeded in obtaining it, he addressed the court in a speech in which he complained that he had been 'worse treated than any rebel Scot.' The question of his arrest was fully argued before the Court of Common Pleas, and Chief Justice Pratt and the other judges unanimously pronounced it to be illegal on the ground that Parliamentary privilege secured a member of Parliament from arrest in all cases except treason, felony, and actual breach of the peace, and that a libel, though it might tend to produce the latter offence, could not be regarded as itself a breach of the peace. Numerous actions had been brought against the messengers who executed the general warrant by the persons who were arrested, and damages for various amounts were obtained, and two other constitutional points of great importance were decided. Chief Justice Pratt authoritatively, and with something more than judicial emphasis, determined that 'warrants to search for, seize, and carry away papers,' on a charge of libel, were contrary to law. He also expressed his opinion that general warrants issued by the Secretary of State without specifying the name of the person to be arrested were illegal, and this opinion was a few years later confirmed by Lord Mansfield.[1]

When these decisions were announced the triumph of the people was unbounded. Wilkes was not only released from im-

---

[1] Compare *Adolphus*, i. 136, 137. Campbell's *Chancellors*, vi. 370. The legality of general warrants was brought before Mansfield in November 1765. He gave an opinion similar to that of Pratt. In order to avoid a judgment against the Crown on the merits of the case, the Attorney-General admitted a formal objection, and so contrived to be defeated.—Campbell's *Life of Mansfield*, p. 462.

prisonment, but a special jury at Guildhall awarded him 1,000*l*. damages against Mr. Wood, the Under-Secretary of State; and Lord Halifax himself, against whom an action was brought, was compelled to resort to the most contemptible legal subterfuges to delay the proceedings. Three great constitutional questions had been decided, and in each case in favour of Wilkes, and the triumph was all the greater because both search warrants and general warrants, which were now pronounced to be illegal, had been undoubtedly frequently made use of since the Revolution. Passions on both sides were aroused to the utmost, and neither party was prepared to desist from the contest. Wilkes reprinted all the numbers of the 'North Briton' in a single volume, with notes establishing in the most conclusive manner the constitutional doctrine that the King's Speech should be regarded simply as the speech of the ministers. He showed that this doctrine had been unequivocally laid down in the two preceding reigns by such statesmen as the Duke of Argyle, Carteret, Shippen, and Pulteney, and that in 1715 the House of Commons had impeached Oxford among other grounds 'for having corrupted the sacred fountain of truth and put falsehoods into the mouth of his Majesty in several speeches made to Parliament.' Lord Egremont died on August 21, 1763, but Wilkes pressed on eagerly his action against Lord Halifax. He wrote to him in a strain of great insolence, accusing him of having robbed his house, and he even made a vain attempt to obtain a warrant to search for the missing documents. The King, on the other hand, dismissed Wilkes from the colonelcy of the Buckinghamshire Militia. It was the duty of Temple, as Lord-Lieutenant of the county, to announce to him the fact, and he did so in a letter couched in the most complimentary language. Temple was at once deprived of his Lord-Lieutenancy, and his name was struck off the list of Privy Councillors. The Attorney-General instituted a regular prosecution for libel against Wilkes. He was surrounded by spies, who tracked his every movement and reported to the ministers the names of all who had intercourse with him, and his correspondence was systematically opened in the Post Office.[1]

[1] See much curious evidence of this, *Grenville Papers*, ii. 8, 71, 130, 155–160. In one of his letters to Wilkes, Temple said: 'I am so used

The struggle was speedily transferred to another sphere. On November 15, 1763, Parliament met, and it soon appeared that a majority of both Houses were determined to pursue Wilkes with the most vindictive perseverance. On the first day of the session he rose to complain of the breach of privilege in his person, but he was anticipated by Grenville, who produced a royal message recapitulating the steps that had been taken and calling the attention of the House to the alleged libel. The House at once responded to the demand, and although the question was at this very time pending before the law courts, it proceeded to adjudicate upon it, voted the forty-fifth number of the 'North Briton' 'a false, scandalous, and seditious libel,' and ordered it to be burnt by the common hangman.[1] Wilkes vainly endeavoured to avert the sentence by declaring that if his privilege was asserted, he was quite ready to waive it and to stand his trial before a jury.

At the same time another weapon for ruining him had been discovered. Wilkes, after his release from the Tower, had set up a private printing press in his own house, and among other documents had printed a parody of the 'Essay on Man' called 'An Essay on Woman,' and also a paraphrase of the 'Veni Creator.' They were anonymous, but the former at least appears to have been partly, if not wholly, composed by Potter, the son of the Archbishop of Canterbury, and one of the colleagues of Wilkes in the Medmenham Brotherhood. Bishop Warburton having recently published Pope's poems with illustrative notes, the parody contained some burlesque notes attributed to the same prelate. Both the 'Essay on Woman' and the imitation of the 'Veni Creator' were in a high degree blasphemous and obscene. Both of them would have been most proper subjects for prosecution had they been published or widely circulated. As a matter of fact, however, the little volume had not been published. Wilkes had not intended to publish it. Its existence was a profound secret, and only thirteen copies had been privately struck off for a few of his most intimate friends. Either by the examination of papers that were seized under

---

to things of this sort at the Post Office, and am so sure that every line I write must be seen, that I never put anything in black and white that might not be read at Charing Cross for all I care.'—*Grenville Papers*, i. 489.

[1] *Parl. Hist.* xv. 1354–1360.

the illegal search warrant or by the treachery of some of Wilkes's old associates who were now connected with the Government, the ministers obtained information of its existence, and one of their agents succeeded, by bribing a printer employed by Wilkes, in obtaining the proof sheets, which on the first night of the session were brought before the House of Lords. As if to mark in the clearest light the nature of the proceeding, the task was entrusted to Lord Sandwich, who had been the intimate friend of Wilkes, who had been like him a member of the Medmenham Brotherhood, and who was notorious as one of the most profligate noblemen of his time. Whatever may have been the demerits of the 'Essay on Woman,' no human being could believe in the purity of the motives of Sandwich,[1] and Wilkes afterwards even asserted that he was one of the two persons to whom the poem had been originally read.[2] He discharged his task in a long speech, descanting upon the profligacy of Wilkes in terms which elicited from their common friend Lord De Spencer the pithy comment that he had never before heard the devil preaching. Warburton then rose to complain of a breach of privilege on account of the appearance of his name in the notes, and in language in which the courtier was at least as apparent as the saint, he declared that the blackest fiends in hell would not keep company with Wilkes, and apologised to Satan for comparing Wilkes to him. The House of Lords at once voted the poems a breach of privilege, and a 'scandalous, obscene, and impious libel,' and two days later presented an address to the King demanding the prosecution of Wilkes for blasphemy.[3]

Before this time, however, Wilkes was no longer able to answer for himself. Among the many persons who had been attacked in the 'North Briton' was Martin, a former Secretary to the Treasury, whose corrupt practices at the time of the Peace of Paris have been already noticed. In the debate on November 15

---

[1] A description of the *Essay on Woman* will be found in a contemporary pamphlet denouncing it by a clergyman named Killidge. No genuine copy of the poem is known to exist, though some spurious versions were circulated. The manuscript poem bearing the name which is among the Wilkes papers in the British Museum is certainly not genuine. An elaborate discussion about the authorship and the true version of the poem will be found in Dilke's *Papers of a Critic*.

[2] Walpole to Mann, Nov. 17, 1763. Lord De Spencer was said to have been the other.

[3] Walpole's *George III.* i. 309–312

he got up and denounced the writer in the 'North Briton' as 'a coward and a malignant scoundrel,' and on the following day, Wilkes having acknowledged the authorship of the paper, Martin left at his house a challenge to meet him in Hyde Park with pistols within an hour. Wilkes, among whose faults want of courage cannot be reckoned, at once accepted the challenge. Martin, though the challenger, selected the weapon, and it was afterwards stated that during the whole of the eight months that had elapsed since the provocation was given, he had been assiduously practising at firing at a target. Wilkes fell dangerously, it was at first thought mortally, wounded, and he showed an anxiety to shield his adversary from the consequences of the duel, which was a strong proof of the genuine kindness of his nature, and added not a little to his popularity.[1]

It is not surprising that under these circumstances the angry feeling prevailing through the country should have risen higher and higher. Bute was still regarded as the real director of affairs, and the animosity against the Scotch and against the Court was as far as possible from being appeased. In the cyder counties, a crowned ass was led about by a figure attired in a Scotch plaid and decorated with a blue riband.[2] At Exeter an effigy of Bute was hung on a gibbet at one of the principal gates, and the mob was so fierce that for a whole fortnight the authorities did not venture to cut it down.[3] When, in obedience to the vote of the House of Commons, an attempt was made to burn the 'North Briton,' the high sheriff and constables were attacked, the obnoxious paper was snatched from the flames, and that evening a jack-boot and petticoat were publicly burnt in a great bonfire at Temple Bar.[4] The Common Council of London voted thanks to the City members for asserting the liberties of their country in the question of general warrants. The decisions of Chief Justice Pratt in favour of Wilkes raised that judge to the highest point of popularity. The Corporation of Dublin presented him with its freedom, and the example was speedily followed by the City of London and by a great number of

---

[1] *Parl. Hist.* xv. 1357–1359.
[2] Walpole's *Memoirs of George III.* i. 260.
[3] Campbell's *Chancellors,* vi. 289.
[4] Walpole's *George III.* i. 330. *Annual Register* 1763, p. 144.

other corporations in England. His portrait became the favourite sign of public-houses throughout the country. By the direction of the Corporation of London it was painted by Sir Joshua Reynolds and placed in the Guildhall with an inscription 'in honour of the jealous assertor of English liberty by law.'[1] The blasphemy and obscenity of the poems printed by Wilkes could not be questioned, but the people very reasonably asked whether the private character of Wilkes was at all worse than that of Sandwich, who was the most prominent of his persecutors; and whether there was the least probability that Wilkes would have been prosecuted for immorality if he had not by his defence of liberty become obnoxious to the Court. 'I am convinced,' he himself wrote to the electors of Aylesbury, 'that there is not a man in England who believes that if the "North Briton" had not appeared the "Essay on Woman" would ever have been called in question.' The hypocrisy, the impudence, the folly of the part taken by Lord Sandwich excited universal derision. The 'Beggar's Opera' was soon after represented at Covent Garden, and in the speech in which Macheath exclaims 'that Jemmy Twitcher should peach me I own surprises me,' the whole audience, by a burst of applause, recognised the application, and the name—which has been perpetuated in the well-known lampoon of Gray—ever after clung to Lord Sandwich, as Horace Walpole says, 'almost to the disuse of his title.'[2] The circumstances of the duel with Martin were such that it was commonly regarded as little less than a deliberate conspiracy by the ministry to murder Wilkes, and Churchill embodied the popular sentiment in 'The Duellist,' one of the most powerful of his satires.

Wilkes recovered slowly, but in the mean time the Parliament, rejecting his petition that further proceedings might be delayed till his recovery, pushed on its measures with vindictive energy, and its first step was one of very considerable constitutional importance. Hitherto it had been the steady and invariable policy of the House of Commons to extend as

---

[1] *Annual Register* 1764, p. 51. Campbell, vi. 372.
[2] Walpole's *George III.* i. 314. 'It is a mercy,' wrote Chesterfield, 'that Wilkes, the intrepid defender of our rights and liberties, is out of danger; and it is no less a mercy that God hath raised up the Earl of Sandwich to vindicate and promote true religion and morality. These two blessings will justly make an epocha in the annals of this country.'

far as possible the domain of Privilege. The doctrine that no member of Parliament could be arrested or prosecuted without the express permission of the House, except for treason, felony, or actual breach of the peace, or for refusal to pay obedience to a writ of Habeas Corpus, had hitherto been fully acknowledged, and had, as we have seen, been very recently admitted by the law courts. In spite of the opposition of Pitt and of a powerful protest signed by seventeen peers, a resolution was now carried through both Houses 'that privilege of Parliament does not extend to the case of writing and publishing seditious libels, nor ought to be allowed to obstruct the ordinary course of the laws in the speedy and effectual prosecution of so heinous and dangerous an offence.' As the resolution was given a retrospective application, the proceeding of the House in this as in most other points was grossly and transparently unjust; but considered in itself it had a great value, as making a serious breach in that formidable edifice of Parliamentary privilege which was threatening to become almost as prejudicial to the liberty of the subject as the royal prerogative. It is a singularly curious fact that at a time when Parliamentary privilege was becoming a chief subject of popular complaint, this great concession was made, not in consequence of any pressure of opinion from without, but by the free will of Parliament itself, for the purpose of crushing a popular hero. It is hardly less curious that nearly at the same time the City of London, which had placed itself at the head of the democratic movement, should more than once, through its dislike to particular measures, have petitioned the King to exercise his dormant power of veto, and refuse his assent to Bills which had passed through both Houses of Parliament.[1]

Wilkes was unable to attend Parliament before the Christmas vacation, and during the recess he went over to France. Whether he really intended to return is doubtful. The Crown, the ministers, and the majority in both Houses of Parliament, were all leagued against him, and it was tolerably clear that they were determined to ruin him. A trial for seditious libel and a trial for blasphemy were hanging over his head, and

---

[1] It presented petitions to this effect against both the Cyder Bill and the Quebec Bill.

Parliament had already passed resolutions prejudging his case. His life was by no means safe. He had offended large classes, and he was surrounded by vindictive enemies. One of the earliest numbers of the 'North Briton' had obliged him to fight a duel with Lord Talbot, who had officiated as High Constable at the Coronation. On a former visit to Paris he had been challenged by a Scotchman named Forbes, who was in the French service, on account of his attacks upon Scotland. The duel with Martin bore all the signs of a deliberate and premeditated attempt to destroy him; and when he was lying wounded and helpless on his sick bed, a mad Scotchman named Dun had tried to penetrate into his house to assassinate him. When the time came at which he was summoned to appear before Parliament, he sent a certificate signed by two French doctors, stating that he was unable to travel. The House of Commons, however, made no allowance for his state. On the 19th of January, 1764, he was expelled from the House for having written 'a scandalous and seditious libel,' and on the 21st of February he was tried and found guilty in the Court of King's Bench for reprinting No. 45, and also for printing the 'Essay on Woman;' and as he did not appear to receive sentence, he was at once outlawed. The most important of the actions brought by Wilkes had been that against Lord Halifax. By availing himself of every possible legal technicality, Halifax had hitherto postponed the decision, and now by pleading the outlawry of Wilkes he terminated the affair.

The Court had triumphed; but no one who knew the English people could doubt that the manifest desire of those in power to hunt down an obnoxious politician, would rouse a fierce spirit of opposition in the country. No minister, indeed, was ever more destitute than George Grenville of that which in a free country is the most essential quality of a successful statesman—the power of calculating the effect of measures upon opinion. Every step which had been taken in the Wilkes controversy was ill-advised, vindictive, and substantially unjust. The Government had been formally convicted, on broad legal issues, of illegal conduct. They had resorted to the most disreputable artifices of legal chicanery in order to avert the consequences of the decision, and they had carried with them a great majority of Parliament, in usurping the functions and defying the sentences of the law courts. The Executive and the Legislature were alike discredited, and a most alarming spirit had been raised. For Wilkes personally there was not much genuine sympathy, and he was still far from the height of popularity which he subsequently attained. Churchill, indeed, predicted that—

> An everlasting crown shall twine
> To make a Wilkes and Sidney join.[1]

But Pitt, who represented far more truly the best liberal sentiments of the country, while taking a foremost part in opposition to the unconstitutional proceedings of the Government, denounced his character and his writings in the strongest terms, and it is remarkable that an attempt to raise a public subscription for him was a failure,[2] and that Kearsley, the publisher of the 'North Briton,' became bankrupt in 1764.[3] A Devonshire farmer in that year left Wilkes 5,000*l.* as a testimony of his admiration;[4] and he was always received with abundance of mob applause, but as yet the general public appear to have given him little support except by riots. His law expenses were chiefly paid by Temple, and he afterwards obtained an annuity of 1,000*l.* from the Rockingham Whigs, who supported him in much the same spirit as the Tories under Queen Anne had supported Sacheverell. But the spirit of riot and insubordination was very strong in the country, and it was noticed after the Wilkes case that it was ominously and rapidly extending. Libels attacking in the grossest manner the King, the Princess Dowager, and the ministry, were extremely common, and they were fiercely resented. In 1764 no less than 200 informations were filed against printers. In the whole thirty-three years of the preceding reign there had not been so many prosecutions of the Press.[5] Hitherto, when the author of a libel was known, he alone was prosecuted; but the custom was now introduced, for the first time since the Revolution, of involving in these cases the printers also in the pro-

---

[1] *The Duellist.*
[2] *Grenville Papers,* ii. 138, 142. See, too, Mr. Rae's *Wilkes, Sheridan, and Fox,* p. 69.
[3] *Annual Register,* 1764, p. 113.
[4] Ibid. p. 91.
[5] Walpole's *Memoirs of George III.* ii. 15.

secution.[1] The finances of the country were managed with an increased economy, and corruption had somewhat diminished; but Shelburne and Barré were deprived of their military posts, and Generals Conway and A'Court of their regiments on account of their votes in Parliament. No such act had been perpetrated since Walpole had dismissed Lords Westmoreland and Cobham from the commands of their regiments; and it was remembered that at that time Grenville had been one of the most prominent members in denouncing the act in the House of Commons, while Bedford had signed a protest against it in the House of Lords.

Nor were the other proceedings of the Government fitted to add to their popularity. Their tame acquiescence in the Spanish refusal to pay the Manilla ransom offended bitterly the national pride. The Stamp Act, which was imposed on America in 1765, in order to obtain 100,000*l*. of revenue, though it passed almost unnoticed in England, produced an immediate explosion in America, and led in a few years to the dismemberment of the empire. Bedford, who joined the ministry in the autumn of 1763 as President of the Council, brought with him a great weight of personal unpopularity which his subsequent conduct had no tendency to diminish. Perhaps the only valuable measure that can be ascribed to this ministry is the annexation to the English Crown of the Isle of Man. Its sovereignty had long been vested in the House of Derby, who did honorary service for it by presenting two falcons to the kings and queens of England on their coronation. It passed by marriage to the Dukes of Athol, and the island had been the centre of a great smuggling trade to England and Ireland, which it was found impossible to repress till the Grenville ministry in 1765 purchased the sovereignty for 70,000*l*.[2]

The party aspect of the ministry of Grenville and Bedford was somewhat ambiguous. Bedford, who was one of its leading members, was the head of a great Whig house. Grenville had begun public life as an undoubted Whig; he had never abjured the name, and he always exhibited that high sense of the

---

[1] See a remarkable letter 'Concerning libels, warrants, and the seizure of papers,' ascribed to Dunning, in Almon's *Scarce and Rare Tracts*, i. 102.

[2] *Annual Register* 1764, p. 92; 1765, pp. 96, 97, 262.

prerogative and power of the House of Commons which usually accompanied Whig politics. He felt towards it as men feel towards the sphere in which they are most fitted to excel; and in different periods of his career he maintained its authority with equal energy against the Crown, against the colonies, and against the people. At the same time there was some undoubted truth in the assertion of Pitt, that this Government 'was not founded on true Revolution principles, but was a Tory administration.'[1] It was not simply that Grenville had seceded from the great body of the Whig party, that he had supported the ascendency of the Tory Bute, that he advocated with the Tory party the speedy termination of the French war, that his leaning on almost every question was strongly towards the assertion of authority. It is also certain that he came into office with the definite object of carrying into action the Tory principle of government. The real and essential distinction between the two parties at this period of their history lay in the different degrees of authority they were prepared to concede to the sovereign. According to the Whigs, a connected group of political leaders acting in concert and commanding a majority in both Houses of Parliament, ought virtually to dictate and direct the government of the country. According to the opposite party, the supreme directing power should reside with the Sovereign, and no political organisation should be suffered to impose its will upon the Crown. According to the Whigs, the system of government which prevailed in the last years of George II., whatever might have been the defects of particular statesmen or of particular measures, was on the whole the normal and legitimate outcome of parliamentary government. According to the Tories, it was essentially an usurpation, and it should be the great object of a loyal minister to prevent the possibility of its recurrence. Both parties recognised the necessity of establishing some strong and permanent system of government, but the one party sought it in the connection of agreeing politicians, commanding parliamentary influence; the other party sought it in the creation of a powerful parliamentary interest attached personally to the Sovereign, reinforced by disconnected politicians, and by small groups

[1] *Grenville Papers*, ii. 199.

drawn from the most various quarters, and directed by a statesman who was personally pleasing to the King. Other questions were for the most part casual and incidental, but this lay at the root of the division of parties, and it is the key to the language which was constantly used about breaking up parties, removing disqualifications, admitting politicians of all kinds to the service of the King. Grenville avowedly came into office to secure the King from falling into the hands of the Whig organisation and losing the power of political guidance.[1]

He was in many respects peculiarly pleasing to the King. His official connection with Bute, his separation from the great Whig families, his unblemished private character, his eminent business faculties, his industry, his methodical habits, his economy, his freedom alike from the fire and the vagaries of genius, his dogged obstinacy, his contempt for popularity, were all points of affinity. Again and again during the first months of the ministry the King spoke of him with the warmest affection, and he declared that 'he never could have anybody else at the head of his Treasury who would fill that office so much to his satisfaction.'[2] In the chief lines of their policy King and ministers cordially agreed. The King had himself, as we have seen, directed the prosecution of Wilkes; he warmly supported the Stamp Act, and the disastrous project of coercing the colonies; he both approved of and counselled the unconstitutional measure of depriving officers of their military rank on account of their votes in Parliament.[3] But Grenville was placed in office to act the part of a pliant and convenient tool, and nature had given him the character of the most despotic and obstinate of masters. Whatever might be his principles or his professions, his Sovereign soon discovered that no one was constitutionally more fond of power, less disposed to yield to pressure from without, less capable of making harsh decisions palatable to others. There is something at once whimsical and

---

[1] 'We entered into the King's service . . . to hinder the law from being indecently and unconstitutionally given to him.'—*Grenville Papers*, ii. 86. 'I told his Majesty that I came into his service to preserve the constitution of my country and to prevent any undue and unwarrantable force being put upon the Crown. (Ibid. p. 106. See too a remarkable letter of Sir John Phillips to Grenville, ibid. p. 118.)

[2] Ibid. ii. 192. See too pp. 205, 493, 495, 500.

[3] Ibid. pp. 162, 166, 223, 224.

pathetic in the efforts of the young King to free himself from the yoke. In April, 1763, Grenville became Prime Minister. In July we already find the King and Bute consulting on the possibility of displacing him. A negotiation was accordingly opened with Lord Hardwicke, but he refused to take any part without the co-operation of Pitt and of the Whigs. In August, when the death of Lord Egremont had weakened the Tory element in the Cabinet, and strengthened the ascendency of Grenville, the King and Bute at once renewed their designs, and on the return of Grenville from a brief excursion in the country he found the King closeted with Pitt. The negotiation, however, again failed. Pitt insisted on the expulsion from office of those who had taken a leading part in negotiating the peace, and the restoration to office of the great Whig families, and the King, who dreaded this consummation above all others, was compelled to ask Grenville to continue in office. He did so on the assurance that Bute was no longer to exercise any secret influence; and he was bitterly indignant when he learnt that two or three days after the King had given this assurance, Bute had made through the instrumentality of Beckford a new attempt to obtain more favourable terms from Pitt. The King then considering the Grenville ministry the sole barrier against the Whig families, changed his policy, determined to support it, and resolved to strengthen it by a junction with the Bedford faction. The unpopularity of Bedford in the country was only second to that of Bute, and his blunt manner and domineering character were sure to bring him into conflict with the King, but he had at least quarrelled with the main body of the Whigs, and he could bring some votes and some administrative skill to the support of the Government. Bute accordingly applied to Bedford, who contented himself with recommending the King to apply to Pitt. The advice was taken; but Pitt, who was not informed of the intervention of Bedford, again urged the formation of a Whig ministry and the exclusion of the chief negotiators of the peace, and especially of Bedford. The King at once made a skilful but most dishonourable use of the incautious frankness of Pitt in the closet to sow dissensions among the Whig nobles, reporting to each such expressions as were most likely to offend them, and especially instructing Lord Sandwich to inform Bedford that Pitt had made his exclusion from all offices an essential condition. Bedford, who had himself advised the King to apply to Pitt, and who was probably perfectly unaware that Pitt was ignorant of that fact, was naturally greatly incensed, and through resentment he was induced to join the ministry as President of the Council, while Lord Sandwich, who was his oldest follower, became Secretary of State, Lord Hillsborough President of the Board of Trade, and Lord Egmont First Lord of the Admiralty.[1]

The junction of the Bedford faction with the ministry took place in September, 1763. In the same month Lord Shelburne had resigned his position as President of the Board of Trade. Shelburne had hitherto been the most devoted follower of Bute; he entered the Grenville ministry by the favour and as the warmest friend of Bute,[2] and he had thoroughly identified himself with his theory of government. It was the object of Bute to reduce each minister as much as possible to his own department, and to absolve him from allegiance to his colleagues, in order that the King should have full power to modify the composition of his Cabinet. In the summer of 1763, when the King was resolved to displace Grenville, he had at once applied to Bute, and under the instructions of the favourite, the President of the Board of Trade took a prominent part in the secret negotiations both with Bedford and with Pitt for the purpose of displacing and overthrowing the Prime Minister.[3] Such services showed how fully Shelburne entered into the spirit of the designs of Bute; but he was himself rapidly becoming discontented. He appears to have disliked both his office and his colleagues; he doubted or more than doubted the legality of the measures that were taken against Wilkes, and he seems to have thought that his own influence and importance were not sufficiently recognised. How far his motives were of a public and how far they were of a private nature it is impossible to say, but on September 3 he resigned his post, and he afterwards voted with his followers Barré, Fitzmaurice, and Calcraft

---

[1] See Harris's *Life of Hardwicke*, vol. iii. *Grenville Papers*, ii. 83-97, 104-107, 191-206. *Bedford Correspondence*, vol. iii. *Walpole's George III.*

[2] See the correspondence between Bute and Shelburne.—Fitzmaurice's *Life of Shelburne*, i. 273-278.
[3] Ibid. pp. 281-289.

against the Court and the ministry. The King in bitter anger deprived him of his post of aide-de-camp, and Barré of the posts of Adjutant-General of the Forces and Governor of Stirling Castle; and from this time Shelburne severed himself from Bute and attached himself to what seemed to be the rising fortunes of Pitt.[1]

The junction of Bedford had, however, given some strength to the ministry, and although Bedford complained that he had not a sufficient share in the disposition of places, the year 1764, during which the country was convulsed by the Wilkes riots, was a year of comparative peace in the closet. The King, however, detested the hard and overbearing character of Bedford; he disliked the notorious profligacy of Sandwich,[2] and although for some months he appeared reconciled to Grenville and often expressed warm esteem for him, he soon began to hate him as intensely as the last king had hated Lord Temple. In truth, Grenville was in the closet the most tedious, prolix, and obstinate of men, and his domineering and overbearing temper was shown in the smallest matters. 'When he has wearied me for two hours,' said the King on one occasion, 'he looks at his watch to see if he may not tire me for one hour more.' He refused a grant of 20,000*l*. for the purchase of some grounds adjoining Buckingham Palace, which the King was very anxious to secure in order to prevent buildings that would overlook him in his walks. He adopted so imperious a tone that the King complained that 'when he had anything proposed to him, it was no longer as counsel, but what he was to obey.'[3] His

---

[1] See the detailed account of this event in Lord E. Fitzmaurice's *Life of Shelburne*. Walpole said: 'Many reasons are given [for the resignation], but the only one that people choose to take is, that thinking Pitt must be minister soon, and finding himself tolerably obnoxious to him, he is seeking to make his peace at any rate.'—Walpole to Mann, Sept. 13, 1763.

[2] 'The King speaks daily with more and more averseness to Lord Sandwich, and appears to have a settled dislike to his character.'— *Grenville Papers*, ii. 496. The King would have deserved more credit for his feelings about Sandwich if he had ever shown reluctance to employ bad men who were subservient to his views. When remonstrated with for employing such a man as Fox, his answer was, 'We must call in bad men to govern bad men.'—Ibid. i. 452. In 1778, when North was very anxious to resign and when there was a question of reconstructing the administration on a Whig basis, the King declared he would accept no ministry in which some politicians he mentioned had not seats in the Cabinet, and among these politicians was Sandwich.—*Letters of George III. to Lord North*, ii. 158.

[3] *Grenville Papers*, iii. 213.

management of the Regency Bill was a much graver offence, and it wounded the King in his most sensitive points. In April, 1765, the King was attacked with an alarming illness, and it was afterwards known that symptoms then for the first time appeared of that mental derangement which clouded the latter years of his reign. On his recovery it was thought right to provide against the confusion which might result from the death or illness of the King while his children were still young, and a Regency Bill was accordingly introduced in which it was proposed to restrict the right of becoming regent to the queen and the royal family then residing in England; but when in the course of the discussion in the House of Lords the question arose who constituted the royal family, it appeared that the Cabinet had not agreed upon or even considered the subject. Bedford and Halifax, actuated probably by antipathy to Bute, maintained, in opposition to their own colleague the Chancellor, that the term Royal Family did not include the Princess Dowager. Bedford opposed and threw out a resolution inserting the name of the princess, and Halifax and Sandwich succeeded in extorting from the King his consent to a clause limiting the regency to the Queen and the descendants of the late King usually resident in England, and thus pointedly excluding his mother.

Much obscurity hangs over the motives which induced the King to consent to this insult to a parent to whom he was tenderly attached, but it appears that the affair was transacted in great haste, that the King hardly understood or realised what he was doing, and that he was persuaded by Halifax that if the princess were not indirectly excluded in the Bill, the House of Commons would take the still stronger and more insulting step of excluding her by name. At all events, he soon bitterly repented, and even implored Grenville as a personal favour to himself to include the princess in the Bill, and the matter became still worse when the House of Commons, instead of displaying the spirit which Halifax had predicted, inserted her name on the ground that the omission was a direct insult offered by the King's servants to the King's mother. The King was driven to the verge of madness by the false position in which he was placed.¹ In April, when the Regency question was still pending, he had been negotiating with his uncle the Duke of Cumberland, and also with Bute, about a possible change of government, and on May 6 he implored Cumberland to save him from a ministry which had become intolerable to him.² He had no truer or more loyal subject, but because Cumberland had lately been in opposition to Bute all his services to the dynasty had been forgotten, and the King had looked on him with the most vindictive hatred. A few months before, the Duke had been struck down by apoplexy, and his life was in imminent danger; but the King, though perfectly aware of the condition of his uncle, refused even to send to inquire after him, 'because,' as he explained to Grenville, 'after the Duke's behaviour, no one could suppose he would inquire out of regard to him.'³ Yet it was to this prince that the King now resorted in his distress. The ministers had been for some time aware that the King had lost confidence in them, and that some change of government was contemplated, and on May 9 the Duke of Bedford remonstrated in no measured terms with his master on the treachery of his conduct.⁴ Cumberland was authorised to negotiate with Pitt and with the old Whig families whose exclusion the King had so ardently desired, but who probably appeared less dangerous when allied with a statesman who was in many respects hostile to their system. Pitt

---

¹ Burke—who had not yet entered Parliament—wrote at this time to Flood: 'The Regency Bill has shown such want of concert and want of capacity in the ministers, such inattention to the honour of the Crown, if not such a design against it, such imposition and surprise upon the King, and such a misrepresentation of the disposition of Parliament to the Sovereign, that there is no doubt that there is a fixed resolution to get rid of them all (except perhaps Grenville), but principally of the Duke of Bedford.'—*Burke Correspondence*, i. 79, 80. The best account of the management of the Regency Bill is in the *Grenville Papers*, iii., especially the very interesting Diary of G. Grenville, pp. 112-222. The interview at which the King consented to the exclusion of his mother was on May 3. He immediately after felt that he had committed an impropriety, and his opinion was strengthened by the Chancellor, who assured him that many people were offended at it, and that a motion against it would be made by the Opposition. On the 5th, the King 'in the utmost degree of agitation and emotion, even to tears,' implored Grenville to alter the Bill, but he was unable to prevail.—Ibid. pp. 152-155.

² See Cumberland's own statement.—Albemarle's *Life of Rockingham*, i. 185-203. On the 27th of April the King had an interview with Bute at Richmond.—*Grenville Papers*, iii. 134.

³ Ibid. ii. 490.

⁴ *Grenville Papers*, iii. 159, 160. *Bedford Correspondence*, iii. 279-281.

seemed ready to assume office, and the Whig families to co-operate with him; but Temple, who had lately been reconciled to Grenville, and who probably desired a purely family ministry, declined the office of First Lord of the Treasury, and persuaded Pitt to break off the negotiation. Pitt did so chiefly on the ground that the influence of Bute was as strong as ever, and overrode that of the responsible ministers of the Crown.[1] An attempt was then made to induce Lord Lyttleton to form a government, but this, too, speedily failed.

A serious riot about this time complicated the situation. The silk weavers being in great distress, had petitioned for the exclusion of all French silks from England, and they resented bitterly the terms in which Bedford opposed the measure. On May 15 a great body of them bearing black flags followed the King to the House of Lords, broke the chariot of the Duke of Bedford, wounded him on the hand and on the temple, and two days later attacked Bedford House with such fury that a large body of soldiers was required to save it from destruction. The episode was peculiarly unfortunate, for it gave the impending change of ministry the appearance of a concession to mob violence. Bedford absurdly ascribed the riot to the instigation of Bute, and lost no opportunity of showing his anger.[2]

In the meantime the King had intimated clearly to his ministers his determination to dispense with their services, and they held office only till their places were filled; but Cumberland was soon obliged to recommend his nephew to recall them.[3] The humiliation was almost intolerable, but it was undergone. Grenville insisted on a solemn promise from the King that he would never again have a private interview with Bute. He insisted upon the dismissal of Stewart Mackenzie, the brother of Bute, from the sinecure office of Privy Seal in Scotland, though the King had distinctly pledged his honour that he

---

[1] See the letter of the Duke of Cumberland, May 21, 1765.—Albemarle's *Life of Rockingham*, i. 211.

[2] Walpole's *Memoirs of George III.* ii. 155–159. *Grenville Papers*, iii. 171.

[3] I have compiled this account from the memorial of the Duke of Cumberland describing the negotiations with which he was entrusted, which is printed in Albemarle's *Life of Rockingham*, the 'Diary' of George Grenville in the *Grenville Papers*, and the account given by Walpole. These three accounts are not in all points quite coincident, and some of the dates in the Duke of Cumberland's memorial appear to be wrongly given.

should retain it. He lectured the King again and again on the duplicity he had shown. His Majesty, on the other hand, was at no pains to conceal his sentiments. He displayed the most marked courtesy towards the leaders of the Opposition, listened with a dark and sullen countenance to the expostulations of his ministers, and when they ventured to express a hope that he would accord them his confidence he preserved a blank and significant silence without even the courtesy of a civil evasion. When an appointment was to be made he studiously neglected their wishes, and often filled it up without even informing them of his choice. Bedford, three weeks after the Government had been restored, demanded an audience, and calmly read to the King a paper formally accusing him of acting towards his ministers with a want of confidence and sincerity utterly incompatible with constitutional monarchy. 'If I had not broken into a profuse sweat,' the King afterwards said, 'I should have been suffocated with indignation.' Once more he resorted to Cumberland and empowered him to offer the most liberal terms to Pitt. A ministry directed by that great statesman would have been beyond all comparison the most advantageous to the country; it had no serious difficulty to encounter, and Pitt himself was now ready to undertake the task, but the evil genius of Lord Temple again prevailed. Without his cooperation Pitt could not or would not proceed, and Temple absolutely refused to take office even in the foremost place. The King, however, would not fall back on Grenville. Yielding for a time what had long been the main object of his policy, he authorised the Duke of Cumberland to enter into negotiations with the great Whig families.[1] A communication was made to the old Duke of Newcastle, and in July 1765, after about seven weeks of almost complete administrative anarchy, the main body of the Whigs returned to office under their new leader Lord Rockingham. Of Grenville, the King in after years sometimes spoke with regret and appreciation, but he never forgot or forgave the last months of his ministry. 'I would sooner meet Mr. Grenville,' he is reported to have said, 'at the point of my sword than let him into my Cabinet.' 'I

---

[1] See the *Bedford Correspondence*, iii. 283, 284, 286–290, 293–295. Walpole's *George III*. *Grenville Papers*, iii. Albemarle's *Life of Rockingham*.

had rather see the devil in my closet than George Grenville.'[1]

Of Rockingham, the new minister, there is little to be said. A young nobleman of very large fortune and unblemished character, he had been for some time only remarkable for his passion for horseracing, but had obtained a faint glimmer of notoriety when he resigned his office of First Lord of the Bedchamber and was dismissed from the Lord-Lieutenancy of his county for his opposition to the peace, and he was selected by the Whigs as their leader mainly on account of his property and connections, but partly on account of his conciliatory manners and high character. He was almost absolutely destitute of the ordinary power of expressing his opinions in debate, but his letters show a clear, moderate, and sound judgment, and he had considerable tact in smoothing difficulties and managing men. He carried out a steadily liberal policy with great good sense, a perfectly single mind, and uniform courtesy to opponents. He had the advantage of following one of the most unpopular of ministers, and the genius of Burke, who was his private secretary, and who was brought into Parliament by his influence, has cast a flood of light upon his administration and imparted a somewhat deceptive splendour to his memory. Few English statesmen of the highest rank have been more destitute of all superiority of intellect or knowledge. Few English ministries have been more feeble than that which he directed, yet it carried several measures of capital importance. It obtained from Parliament—what the former ministry had steadily resisted—a formal condemnation of general warrants. By restoring to their posts the officers who had been deprived of their military rank for their votes in Parliament, it affixed such a stigma to that practice that it never was repeated. It allayed the discontent and even disloyalty of large classes of the English people by abolishing or at least profoundly modifying the obnoxious Cyder Act, and by the more doubtful measure of prohibiting the importation of French silks. It negotiated a beneficial commercial treaty with Russia; it was the first ministry since that of Walpole which took serious measures to relax the commercial restrictions which were the true cause of the

[1] Albemarle's *Life of Rockingham*, ii. 50.

alienation of the colonies; and above all, by repealing the Stamp Act, it for a time averted the struggle which soon afterwards brought about the disruption of the empire. It did all this in the short space of one year and twenty days, in spite of every kind of opposition from within and from without, and as far as can be ascertained without resorting to any of the corrupt practices that had been so common among its predecessors. It was essentially a ministry of great families. The Duke of Newcastle brought to it his vast experience, his industry, and influence, and he exerted himself with laudable zeal for the repeal of the Stamp Act. It was characteristic of the habits of the old minister that the Church patronage was at his desire specially attached to the office of Privy Seal which he held, and it is scarcely less characteristic of another side of his character that he anxiously warned Rockingham against Burke, whom he suspected of being a Jacobite and a Papist in disguise.[1] In party politics the leading idea of Newcastle at this time was dread of Pitt, and the great object at which he ineffectually aimed was a junction between the followers of Rockingham and Bedford. The great family connection of the Cavendishes, and many other Whig nobles distinguished only for their wealth and position, joined the ministry, which represented all that remained unbroken and unchanged of the powerful party which in the last two reigns had governed the country.

But in spite of aristocratic support the ministry had no real strength, and it soon perished by the combination of many enemies. Death had greatly thinned the ranks of Whig administrators, and the secession of Grenville and Bedford, the alienation of Pitt and of Temple, had thrown the management of the party into the hands of young men altogether inexperienced in government, mixed with two or three worn-out veterans: Rockingham, who should have led the party in the House of Lords, rarely opened his mouth in debate; Conway, who led the party in the Commons, was a brave and popular soldier, who had served with distinction at Culloden, Fontenoy, and Laffeldt, and had commanded a corps under Prince Ferdinand in 1761, but as a parliamentary leader he had neither resolution, knowledge, nor eloquence; Dowdeswell, the Chancellor of the Ex-

[1] Prior's *Life of Burke*, i. 135.

chequer, was a good financier, but nothing more. Charles Townshend, though he clung to the rich office of Paymaster of the Forces, treated his colleagues with undisguised contempt, described the Government of which he was a member as a 'lutestring administration fit only for summer wear,' and ostentatiously abstained from defending its measures. Northington, the Chancellor, and Barrington, the Secretary for War, were kept in office to please the King, and were completely at his service. They were prepared at any moment to turn against their colleagues, and they were strongly committed to views hostile to those of the Government to which they belonged on the two capital questions of American taxation and the legality of general warrants. Chesterfield very justly described the ministry as an arch which wanted its keystone, and the true keystone was evidently Pitt.[1]

Rockingham had done everything in his power to draw Pitt to his side, but he wholly failed. Pitt remained persistently isolated from all other politicians. While admitting that the characters of the new ministers were good, he openly declared in Parliament that he could not give them his confidence, and he countenanced a charge which is now known to have been completely groundless, but which was believed by both Temple and Bedford,[2] that Bute was exercising a controlling influence upon their counsels. While Pitt maintained this attitude the ministry could have no genuine popularity; and the Duke of Cumberland, who had called it into power, and who warmly supported it, died at the end of October, about three months before the Old Pretender, the son of James II., whose prospects he had ruined at Culloden.

To a truly constitutional sovereign there was no reason why the Rockingham ministry should not have been acceptable. It consisted to an exaggerated extent of members of those great families who are naturally brought into closest contact with the Throne. It was studiously moderate in its policy, and none of its members were ever accused of the

---

[1] Lord Lyttleton wrote at this time (Jan. 28, 1765): 'The desire of Mr. Pitt in the public is inexpressibly strong, and nothing will satisfy them without him. I believe he is also much desired in the Court.'—Phillimore's *Life of Lyttleton*, ii. 683.

[2] *Bedford Correspondence*, iii. 304, 305, 312.

slightest disrespect. But to George III. its very existence was an intolerable humiliation to be endured only from extreme necessity. Only two years had elapsed since the King had authorised Bute to declare that he would never again during his whole reign admit the great Whig connection to power. The Duke of Devonshire, who was one of the chief supporters of the Government, was the son of the very statesman who had so lately been dismissed from office by the King in a manner which amounted to little less than personal insult. The King had been the first man to suggest the dismissal of Conway from his civil and military posts. He was now obliged to restore Conway to his regiment, and to accept him as Secretary of State and leader of the House of Commons. He had vehemently supported the most violent measures against Wilkes, but he now saw general warrants and the seizure of the papers of supposed libellers formally condemned in Parliament by resolutions introduced under the auspices of his ministers, and he was obliged to raise Chief Justice Pratt to the peerage as Lord Camden. The repeal of the American Stamp Act was contrary to the strongest wishes of the King. In order to make it possible it was accompanied by a declaratory Act asserting the abstract right of the Imperial Parliament to tax the colonies. Grenville, Bedford, and the whole party of Bute bitterly opposed the repeal, while Pitt denounced the declaration that accompanied it. The debates were long and vehement, and they were especially noteworthy on account of two speeches in defence of the Government, which extorted warm eulogy from Pitt, and in the words of Dr. Johnson 'filled the town with wonder.' They were the first parliamentary speeches of Edmund Burke.

The King soon made no secret of his hostility to the measures of his ministers. He assured those who held offices in his household that they were at full liberty to vote against the minister, and Lord Strange was authorised to spread about the report that the King was opposed to the repeal of the Stamp Act. Rockingham, who understood the character of his Sovereign, heard of it, and at once insisted upon obtaining in writing the consent of the King, which he showed to those who desired it; but place-hunters knew only too well the real wishes of the King and the weakness of the Government.

It was the evil custom of the time to treat the adjudication of disputed elections as party questions, to be decided according to the majority in the House and not according to the merits of the case. On a question of a Scotch election in February 1766, the ministers only carried their candidate by eleven votes, and on the following day they were beaten in the Lords by a majority of three.[1] Many attempts were made to induce isolated politicians to join the ministry, but they uniformly failed, and it was generally felt that its days were numbered.[2] A motion of Grenville to enforce the Stamp Act was rejected by 274 to 134, but it was remarkable that the minority included not only the friends of Bute, but also nearly a dozen of the King's household.[3] The Chancellor and the Secretary of War both voted against the repeal of the Stamp Act.[4] Rockingham wished to restore some vigour and discipline to the ministry by removing Jeremiah Dyson, one of the under treasurers, who had been in conspicuous opposition to his chief, but the King positively refused. He had indeed two measures. When a ministry represented his personal views, Walpole himself was not more strenuous in enforcing unanimity among its members. When it diverged from his views, Pelham was not more indulgent of dissent. In the same spirit the King refused to create a single peer at the desire of his ministers. The King's friends, who filled the subordinate places in the Government, plotted incessantly and voted fearlessly against their chief. At last, in May 1766, the Duke of Grafton struck the death-blow by resigning the seals of Secretary of State. 'He had no objection,' he said, 'to the persons or the measures of the ministers, but he thought they wanted strength and efficiency to carry on proper measures with success, and that Pitt alone could give them solidity.' In July, the Chancellor, Lord Northington, who had very persistently thwarted and opposed his colleagues in the Cabinet, openly revolted, and informed the King that the ministry could not go on. The ministers were dismissed, and on July 7, 1766, the King once more sent for Pitt.

---

[1] Albemarle's *Life of Rockingham* i. 296.
[2] Thackeray's *Life of Chatham*, ii. 75. *Grenville Papers. Bedford Correspondence, Chatham Correspondence.*
[3] Walpole's *Memoirs of George III.* ii. 287, 288.
[4] Albemarle's *Life of Rockingham*, i. 321. Barrington's *Life of Barrington*, p. 108.

The conduct of Pitt in refusing to join the Rockingham Government, if not the worst, was certainly the most disastrous incident of his career. He had no ground of complaint because Rockingham had taken office, for he had again and again been appealed to during the Grenville ministry to form a government, and he had absolutely refused. Two months before the Grenville ministry fell, Rockingham had visited him at Hayes, with the object of effecting a junction with him; and when the new ministry was formed, and during the whole period of its existence, every possible effort was made to obtain his alliance. At least three separate applications were made to him by Rockingham. His advice was asked with a marked deference. The restoration of the officers who had been removed from their military posts on account of their votes in Parliament, a formal condemnation of general warrants, and the bestowal of some special honour on Chief Justice Pratt, had been three conditions on which Pitt specially insisted in his abortive negotiations with the King before the fall of the Grenville administration. All of these were carried out by Rockingham. In order still further to conciliate him, Grafton, who was his most devoted follower, was made Secretary of State. His brother-in-law, James Grenville, was offered one of the Vice-Treasurerships of Ireland. Nuthall, who was his confidential lawyer, and one of his most intimate friends, was made Solicitor of the Treasury. It was clearly intimated to Pitt that Rockingham and his colleagues 'were most ready to be disposed of as he pleased' and he was expressly asked to place himself at their head.[1] He could have entered the Government on what terms he wished, and could without difficulty have converted the Whig party from a struggling minority into the dominant power of the State. The importance of doing so was self-evident. As Pitt himself declared, 'Faction was shaking and corruption sapping the country to its foundations.' The utter disintegration of parties, and the influence of the Crown, now steadily employed in dissolving connections and sowing dissensions, had threatened the very ruin of parliamentary government, had created both at home and in the colonies a mass of disaffection which had hardly

---

[1] Albemarle's *Life of Rockingham*, i. 312. *Adolphus*, i. 227-230 Fitz- maurice's *Life of Shelburne*, i. 364-371.

been equalled since the accession of the House of Brunswick, had brought Parliament into contempt, and was likely, if any great foreign complication arose, to lead the country to overwhelming disaster.

It has often been said that the democratic character which Parliament has in the present century assumed has weakened the Executive, and produced an excessive number of feeble ministries, but in no period of English history was this evil more conspicuous than in the first years of George III. In less than six years England had been ruled by the united ministry of Pitt and Newcastle, by the ministry of Newcastle alone, by the ministry of Bute, by the ministry of Grenville, and afterwards of Grenville and Bedford, and lastly by that of Rockingham. It was of vital importance to establish once more a system of firm and settled government, resting on an undisputed parliamentary ascendency, and secure from the intrigues of royalty and of faction. This could only be done by a coalition of parties, and the natural lines of combination were very clear. On most important points the followers of Grenville and Bedford agreed with the Tories, and the followers of Pitt with the Whigs. Though Grenville and Bedford had lately proscribed Bute, the political affinity was so strong that they actually made overtures to him in 1766, which he rejected with much contempt. On the other hand, the junction of Pitt and his followers with the genuine Whigs would have given that party a decisively popular bias, and would have brought to it all the weight, ability, and popularity that were required to give it a commanding power in the State. Its leaders were for the most part men of upright character and of liberal views, and unusually free from the taint of Parliamentary corruption. There was little ability in the party, but Charles Townshend only wanted firm guidance to rise very high, and in the still obscure private secretary of Lord Rockingham the ministry could count upon a follower whose genius never indeed exhibited the meteoric brilliancy or the magnetic and commanding power of that of Pitt, but who far surpassed Pitt and all other English politicians in the range of his knowledge, in the depth and comprehensiveness of his judgment, in the sustained and exuberant splendour of his imagination. On nearly all the great questions that were impending, Pitt agreed with Rockingham; he agreed with him about the cyder tax, about general warrants, about the seizure of papers, about the restoration of the military officers who had been removed from their posts for their votes in Parliament, about the necessity of repealing the Stamp Act. The most serious point of difference was the Declaratory Act asserting the right of the English to tax America. But whatever opinion may be held about its abstract truth, it was the only condition on which the great practical measure of the repeal of the Stamp Act could be carried. The Tories, the Grenvilles, the Bedfords, and the King were all bitterly hostile to the Americans. In the ministry itself the Chancellor, Charles Townshend, and Barrington shared their opinion. Lord Mansfield had privately asserted that as a matter of law the English Parliament had an undoubted right to tax the colonies. Lord Hardwicke was strongly of the same opinion. Public opinion in the country and in Parliament was exasperated by the resistance of America. Considered abstractedly, it would no doubt have been better if the Stamp Act had been simply and unconditionally repealed, but it is doubtful if any ministry could have carried such a measure; it is quite certain that a weak one could not. The Rockingham Ministry was very weak, and it was weak chiefly through the abstinence of Pitt.

He not only repelled on repeated occasions the overtures of the Whig leaders, but he also shook the ministry to its basis. On some questions, it is true, he cordially supported it. He seconded the resolution of Dowdeswell for remodelling the cyder tax, and he spoke with extraordinary force in favour of repealing the Stamp Act. The ministers, with their usual deference, had carefully consulted his wishes about the repeal,[1] but he openly declared his want of confidence in them. 'Confidence,' he said in a characteristic phrase, 'is a plant of slow growth in an aged bosom; youth is the season of credulity.'

The reasons for his conduct were probably very various. Much must be allowed for a natural character which was morbidly irritable and impracticable, and peculiarly unfit for co-operation with others. 'Nothing,' wrote Burke in May 1765, 'but

[1] Albemarle's *Life of Rockingham*, i. 269.

an intractable temper in your friend Pitt can prevent a most admirable and lasting system from being put together; and this crisis will show whether pride or patriotism be predominant in his character, for you may be assured that he has it now in his power to come into the service of his country upon any plan of politics he may choose to dictate, with great and honourable terms to himself and to every friend he has in the world, and with such a stretch of power as will be equal to everything but absolute despotism over the King and kingdom. A few days will probably show whether he will take this part or that of continuing on his back at Hayes talking fustian.'[1] But Pitt, as Lord Hardwicke once said, would 'neither lead nor be driven.'[2] Constant attacks of gout had prostrated his strength, irritated his nerves to an extraordinary degree, and perhaps produced in him a secret desire to postpone as much as possible a return to office. He was courted on all sides, and personal friendships or antipathies greatly governed him. His friendship with Temple was now rapidly dissolving, but Temple had still a great influence over his mind, and it had for some time been steadily employed in alienating him from the great body of the Whigs. The old dislike to Newcastle was also still living, and Pitt declared peremptorily that he could never have 'any confidence in a system where the Duke of Newcastle has influence.'[3] The fear was very unreasonable, for the influence of the old duke was nearly gone, and he professed himself ready to take whatever course Pitt required.

There were, however, a few real differences between Pitt and the Rockingham Ministry. On the capital point of American taxation they differed on the question of right, though they agreed on the question of policy. Pitt disliked the free-trade views of Burke, and the more aristocratic Whigs disliked the City agitation which Pitt encouraged. It must be added that the impending dissolution of the Rockingham Ministry would

---

[1] *Burke's Correspondence*, i. 80.
[2] Albemarle's *Life of Rockingham*, i. 177.
[3] *Chatham Correspondence*, ii. 360. See too p. 322. The final rupture seems to have been in Oct. 1764 (ibid. pp. 293-298.) On January 9, 1766, the Duke of Newcastle wrote a letter to Rockingham which does the writer very great credit, urging that a junction with Pitt was absolutely indispensable to the Government, and that he was himself perfectly ready to resign office in order to facilitate it.— Albemarle's *Life of Rockingham*, i. 264, 265.

almost necessarily throw the chief power into the hands of Pitt, and he probably miscalculated greatly his power of forming a strong ministry.

He was, however, also actuated by another reason, which drew him closer to the King. As we have already seen,[1] from an early period of his career he had rebelled much against the system of party government, and in this respect he sympathised strongly with the doctrines which George III. had imbibed from Bolingbroke. Many expressions in his letters show that his real desire was to remain isolated and unconnected, that he wished to form an administration of able men drawn from every quarter, and that he looked with great dread and irritation to the prospect of family or party influence narrowing ministries as they had been narrowed in the days of Walpole. The cry of the abolition of parties was one which had been raised by the followers of the King at the very beginning of the reign, and it is remarkable that Burke himself, though he became the greatest and most earnest of all the advocates of party government, appears to have listened to it with some momentary favour.[2] That Pitt should have felt such sentiments was very natural. Party government in the latter days of George II. had assumed some of its worst forms. The opponents of the dominant party were regarded as the opponents of the dynasty, and disaffection was thus unnaturally and unnecessarily prolonged. In the absence of strong popular influence corrupt family influence had been inordinately increased, and the amount of ability at the disposal of the Crown very unduly limited. It was natural that a statesman who was conscious of unrivalled genius and of unrivalled popularity, and who had at the same time little family influence and but few personal adherents, should have revolted against the constraints imposed by the organisation of the great Whig families. 'As for my single self,' he wrote to Newcastle in October 1764, 'I purpose to continue acting through life upon the

---

[1] See p. 19.
[2] See a very curious passage in the historical section of the *Annual Register* for 1762. 'From the beginning of this reign it had been professed, with the general applause of all good men, to abolish those odious party distinctions [Whig and Tory] and to extend the royal favour and protection equally to all his Majesty's subjects.'—*Annual Register* 1762, p. [147].

best convictions I am able to form, and under the obligation of principles, not by the force of any particular bargains. . . . I shall go to the House free from stipulations about every question under consideration. . . . Whatever I think it my duty to oppose or to promote, I shall do it independent of the sentiments of others. . . . I have little thoughts of beginning the world again upon a new centre of union. . . . I have no disposition to quit the free condition of a man standing single, and daring to appeal to his country at large upon the soundness of his principles and the rectitude of his conduct.'[1] 'The King's pleasure,' he wrote towards the end of the Rockingham ministry, ' and gracious commands alone shall be a call to me. I am deaf to every other thing.'[2] 'As to my future conduct,' wrote his follower Shelburne to Rockingham, 'your lordship will pardon me if I say " measures, not men," will be the rule of it.'[3]

The propriety of discouraging party distinctions, and endeavouring on every occasion to select in a judicial spirit the best man and the wisest measure irrespective of all other considerations, has so plausible a sound that it will appear to many little less than a truism. No reasonable man will question that party government is at best a highly artificial system —so artificial indeed that it is scarcely possible that it can be the final or permanent type of government in civilised nations

---

[1] *Chatham Correspondence*, ii. 296, 297. On Feb. 24, 1766, when Rockingham had been making a new indirect overture to Pitt, the latter wrote to Shelburne: 'Lord Rockingham's plan appears to me to be such as can never bring things to a satisfactory conclusion; his tone being that of a minister, master of the Court and of the public, making openings to men who are seekers of offices and candidates for ministry. . . . In one word, my dear lord [he continued], I shall never set my foot in the closet but in the hope of rendering the King's personal situation not unhappy, as well as his business not unprosperous; nor will I owe my coming thither to any Court cabal or ministerial connection.'— *Chatham Correspondence*, iii. 11, 12. In April 1766, Rigby wrote to the Duke of Bedford that Pitt had made a kind of farewell speech,' in which he said 'that he wished for the sake of his dear country that all our factions might cease; that there might be a ministry fixed such as the King should appoint and the public approve . . . that if ever he was again admitted as he had been into the royal presence, it should be independent of any personal connections whatsoever.' —*Bedford Correspondence*, iii. 333. 'Lord Chatham,' wrote Mitchell in Dec. 1766, 'declares to all the world that his great point is to destroy faction, and he told the House of Lords the other day "that he could look the proudest connection in the face."' —*Chatham Correspondence*, iii. 138.

[2] Fitzmaurice's *Life of Shelburne*, i. 382. See too his very similar declaration in 1762.—Albemarle's *Life of Rockingham*, i. 151.

[3] *Shelburne's Life*, i. 334.

—and that it has many evils and many dangers. It is a great evil that political questions should be decided by the Legislature on a double or a false issue, each member speaking of their intrinsic merits while he is thinking largely of their relation to the well-being of his party. It is a great evil that politicians should be obliged to conceal, or attenuate, or even deny their genuine convictions when on some particular occasion the course which appears to them the wisest is not that which has been adopted by the leaders of their party. It is a great evil in a country in which at least nine out of ten questions have no real connection with party divisions, that men of the greatest administrative ability should for years be excluded absolutely from the management of affairs, because the organisation to which they have attached themselves is politically the weakest. Party interests often run counter to national interests, and there is then much danger lest party spirit should weaken national affection. It is not easy for an Opposition, in the full ardour of conflict, to look with unmixed pleasure upon national triumphs that are due to the policy of their opponents, or to deplore very bitterly national calamities that may lead themselves speedily to power. The mixture of party with foreign politics has sometimes led to the gravest calamities, and the deep division which party introduces into the councils of a nation has often weakened it seriously in the hour of danger, diminished the amount of talent and energy available for its service, and induced its enemies to underrate greatly its patriotism and its strength. In a perfect government the management of affairs would be placed in the hands of men who were not only eminent for their ability and their integrity, but who also made it their sole object to do what they thought best for their country. No one can fail to observe how widely party government diverges from this ideal by the inevitable introduction of other and lower motives of political action. Even apart from the necessities of co-operation, and from the desire for place and power, the keen competition of parties generates a kind of sporting interest like fox-hunting or horse-racing, which becomes to many the strongest and most absorbing of political passions. Those who are nearest to the arena, those who are brought into closest contact with the chief actors, are naturally the most susceptible to it, and they are very apt to regard politics as little more than a game played by rival leaders, and every measure as merely a good or bad move in the race for power. Party government thus never fails to introduce a large amount of insincerity and unreality into politics. When there are two plausible courses to be pursued, the Government takes the one and the Opposition is almost bound to defend the other. The Government have the advantage of the first choice and the most authentic information. The Opposition have the advantage of a somewhat later experience. Whenever any considerable amount of discontent against the conduct of the Government exists in the country, whether it be reasonable or unreasonable, the Opposition is usually practically obliged to constitute itself its representative and exponent.

The gravity of these evils cannot easily be over-estimated. A close observer of English political life can hardly fail to feel how rarely even the greatest intellects can preserve their full sanity of judgment in the fierce excitement of a party conflict, and how dangerous it is that public affairs should in critical moments be administered by men in whom that sanity is in any degree impaired. The transition, too, from opposition to power is, under the system of party government, surrounded with some peculiar difficulties. When a party is in opposition the party element in its policy is usually strongly accentuated. Its leaders must maintain specially, keenly, and vividly the interests and opinions of the particular classes that support it. But once it arrives at power its point of view is widely changed. It inherits and must carry out lines of conduct which it had stubbornly opposed; it must preserve the essential continuity of the national policy; it becomes the representative not merely of one section but of all sections of the people, and while it retains the organisation, it must discard or subdue many of the characteristics of a party. The true spirit in which a statesman should guide the government of his country is not that of a missionary or an advocate, or an avenger, or an experimentalist, but of a trustee. It is his business to adapt institutions to the wants of men with opinions or in stages of civilisation widely different from his own; to provide for the well-being of systems with which he has no personal sympathy;

to protect interests which he never would have created; to carry out engagements into which he never would have entered. Personal and even party ideals can have only a faint and casual influence upon his policy. The spirit of conflict and the sectional habits of thought which party opposition especially develops must be lowered or must disappear. He must cultivate above all things that form of imagination which reproduces habits of thought and feeling widely different from his own, and realises the conditions of the happiness of men in many different circumstances, of many different types and classes, and with many different beliefs.

At the same time, as I have endeavoured to show in a former chapter, party divisions, though in a large degree artificial, have some real or natural basis, and are in some form or measure the inevitable and almost spontaneous products of representative government. Each party usually represents a special theory of government or doctrine or ideal, which more or less colours a great part of political judgments. Each party is the special representative of different class interests, and reflects with some degree of fidelity different types of character and intellect. As long as these differences exist the system of party must grow up; and its political advantages are very great. No other method has ever been devised which is equally efficacious in securing the fidelity of representatives. A man who would have little scruple in changing his opinions if he were an isolated individual, or in yielding to the blandishments or the temptations of power, will be much less likely to abandon an organised body of men to whom he has pledged his allegiance, and to enter formally into new connections or alliances. By pledging successive generations to the advocacy of particular measures or to the attainment of some political ideal, the system of party organisation greatly increases the probability of their ultimate triumph, and it also secures the representation in an organised form of the different opinions and class interests of the nation.

But its chief advantages, and those which make it indispensable in parliamentary government, are that it gives administrations some measure of permanence and stability, and that it places the habitual direction of affairs in the hands of competent leaders. A Government depending for its existence on the isolated and unbiassed judgment of some 600 individuals would be an impossibility. It could never count for a week upon its tenure of office. It could never make an engagement for the future. It could never enter into any course of sustained and continuous policy. In order that a government should faithfully discharge its functions it must have sufficient stability to surmount difficulties, to brave transient unpopularity, to survive occasional blunders. Even if the House of Commons consisted of the six hundred wisest men, a ministry dependent on so many unconnected judgments would be absolutely unfit to conduct the business of the nation; and the more the actual composition of the House is considered the stronger becomes the argument for disciplined political action. The House of Commons usually contains four or five men of extraordinary statesmanlike genius. It contains, perhaps, eighty or ninety others who, from long parliamentary experience, from the education of county or municipal government, or from natural ability improved by reading, are eminently sound judges in politics, and count among their number many men quite capable of conducting departments of government and defending their policy in Parliament. It contains, also, a few men who, without any general legislative knowledge or capacity, are able, from the circumstances of their lives, to throw great light on special subjects, such as agriculture, military organisation, navigation, the money market, or the condition of India or the colonies. There are also a large number of lawyers who are authorities on technical questions of law, but whose general habits of thought and reasoning are essentially unpolitical, whose time and studies are mainly devoted to another sphere, who usually regard the House of Commons simply as a stepping-stone to professional promotion, but who, on account of their practice in speaking, and of that freedom from diffidence which is a characteristic of their profession, are thrown into an unfortunate prominence. But the great majority of members are perfectly incompetent to conduct independently legislative business, or to form opinions of any value on the many intricate and momentous questions submitted to them. There are landlords or sons of landlords brought into the House on account of the importance of their properties or of their local popularity, who have never made the smallest study of the political conditions of the country, or of the general principles that underlie political questions, who value the House as a pleasant club, and their legislative functions as giving them an honorary leadership in their counties. There are manufacturers the spring and summer of whose days have been wholly spent in amassing wealth, and who, having succeeded in business and obtained the influence which naturally belongs to great employers of labour, aspire in their old age to such social consequence as Parliament can afford. There are placehunters, demagogues and intriguers whose sole object is to push their fortunes, and who are ready to spread their sails to any breeze, and to adopt any cause which is conducive to their interests. And this strangely composite assembly has to decide not only questions of home and domestic policy, but also questions of foreign policy of the most delicate description, questions on which accurate and extensive knowledge of circumstances and conditions wholly unlike those of England is imperatively necessary, questions on which the promptest and most decisive action is often required. To suppose that a government dependent on this great mass of unguided, incompetent, and sometimes dishonest judgments, can act under such circumstances with the requisite intelligence and firmness, or can command the respect and confidence of foreign governments, is absurd. The sole way of enabling a popular assembly to exercise supreme power with safety is to divide it into great, coherent, disciplined party organisations. When such organisations exist, they will necessarily be directed by the ablest men, who become responsible for their guidance, who can count upon the habitual support of a large body of followers, and who therefore represent a permanent calculable force in the political world.

These considerations apply to every case in which a Parliament is the most powerful body in the State, though it must be acknowledged that they have a still greater force in our own day than they had under George III. Parliament is now a much larger body. The Irish union added 105 members, and the average attendance of English and Scotch has also been greatly increased. Under the old system so many members had small constituencies completely under their control, and even in large constituencies the means of supervision were so scanty, that a very large proportion of members were usually absent, and public business was practically conducted by a comparatively small body. At the same time, while the average parliamentary attendance has been greatly raised, there has been no corresponding elevation of the average of parliamentary ability. Besides this, under the old system, members who were elected were at least free to exercise their judgments. Now great bodies of uneducated constituents, newspaper writers, demagogues, local agitators, are perpetually interfering with each question as it arises, and putting pressure on the judgment of the representatives. Questions of the most difficult foreign policy, involving consequences of the most various, intricate, and far-reaching nature, are treated in great popular agitations by multitudes who have no real feeling of political responsibility, and no detailed and minute knowledge of the subjects on which they are pronouncing. If the domestic and still more the foreign policy of the country is to be at the mercy of these violent gusts of ignorant, irresponsible, interested agitation, nothing but ruin can be predicted; and it is only the firm coherence of party organisation that gives statesmen the power of resisting them. It must be added, too, that Parliament encroaches much more than formerly on the province of the Executive, and meddles much more habitually in the details of measures. For these reasons parties appear to me not merely expedient but absolutely necessary, if the House of Commons is to retain its present position in the State. A House of Commons without clearly defined parties might exist, but it could not be safely entrusted with the virtual government of the country.

It is easy to maintain the discipline of party organisations when they represent a clear division of principles and measures. It is much more difficult in periods of political languor, when there is no pressing question at issue, when the old grounds of controversy have been exhausted and new ones have not yet arisen, and when the keenest observers of political conflicts can detect but little real difference of principle or even of tendency. At such times the true function of the party in opposition is to restrain the Government from isolated mistakes, to expose such mistakes when they are committed; and if through blunders or personal unpopularity the Government has fallen into discredit, to be prepared to take its place and to carry on the administration on the same general lines, but with greater dexterity of management. This is the contingency for which under such circumstances an Opposition should wait. The great majority of the mistakes of governments are at all times unconnected with party principles, and a body whose function is to criticise and prevent them is discharging a duty of the first importance. No doctrine in modern politics is more mischievous than that an Opposition is bound to justify its separate existence by showing that it differs on broad questions of principle and policy from the party in power. Among the greatest dangers of modern constitutional governments is the temptation presented to Oppositions to go about looking for a cry, seeking for party purposes to force on changes for which there is no real and spontaneous demand.

Although public opinion was quite ripe for some measures of reform, the lines of political division in the first years of George III. were strangely confused, and party had in a great degree degenerated into faction. There was little of the natural union of politicians through community of political principles and aims; but there were several distinct groups united through purely personal motives—through attachment to a particular nobleman, or a desire to secure for particular families a monopoly of power. As long as a very large proportion both of the county and borough votes were at the command of a few great noblemen, who were closely connected by relationship or friendship, it was inevitable that this form of influence should prevail in Parliament; and the evil lay not in the existence but in the great multiplication of these groups, and in the purely personal motives that usually actuated them. The first great object should have been to draw a distinct line of policy according to which these scattered fragments might be combined. The temptation of politicians in popular governments is to outrun, but in oligarchical governments to lag behind, genuine public opinion; and there were questions of the gravest and most pressing kind which had long been calling for the attention of the legislators. Such were the inadequacy of the popular element and the gross and notorious corruption in Parliament, and the appearance within its walls of an organised Court party distinct from the party of administration. By pressing these questions, all statesmen would soon be obliged to take a side, and it was probable that the excessive subdivision of parties would speedily disappear.

This was very much the policy which was advocated by Burke as the spokesman of the Rockingham Whigs. He maintained that the habit of systematic co-operation between politicians was to be encouraged rather than discouraged; that the personal attachments and connections which cemented it were very useful in government, but that it was necessary, in the face of the mass of discontent which was smouldering in the nation, and of the growing corruption and inefficiency of Parliament, that each party should have a distinct line of policy. As time went on, these lines, as we shall see, became clearer and clearer; and the writings of Burke probably contributed more than any other single influence to define them. Pitt, on the other hand, while loudly proclaiming the necessity of strengthening the popular element in Parliament, imagined it to be both possible and useful to break up absolutely the small bodies which had grown up around the great families. He regarded with some reason the selfishness, the incapacity, the intrigues, and the jealousies of the great nobles as the main cause of the weakness, anarchy, and corruption of recent English politics. He imagined that by selecting subordinate ministers from men of the most various factions he might, with the assistance of the King, dissolve these factions, subdue all serious opposition, and by the ascendency of his own genius, character, and popularity, give a firm and consistent movement to the administration.[1]

In accordance with these principles, the new ministry was formed of politicians drawn from the most opposite quarters and encumbered by the most opposite antecedents. Some of them were men of great ability and position; but they were men who in the divisions that had grown out of the Wilkes case, and out

---

[1] The judgment of Walpole when the ministry was first formed is a remarkable instance of his political sagacity. 'The plan will probably be

of the Stamp Act, had recently pursued the most divergent courses, and who in many instances had shown a strange vacillation of character and opinion. The King's friends mustered strongly in the lower offices, and they also held several posts of commanding importance. Lord Northington exchanged the Chancellorship for the post of President of the Council, and as the new office was somewhat less lucrative than the former one he obtained in addition the grant of a pension of 4,000*l.* a year, from the time he quitted office, as well as a reversion of Clerk of the Hanaper for two lives. Lord Barrington was still Secretary of War. Charles Townshend, whose support of the policy of taxing America was no secret, was Chancellor of the Exchequer. Lord North, who had for some time been rising to notice as one of the ablest defenders of the Court policy about Wilkes and about America, was made Joint Paymaster of the Forces. His colleague, George Cooke, is said never to have even spoken to him till they were united in the same office. Side by side with them sat the new Chancellor, Lord Camden, who in the Wilkes case and in the case of America had identified himself with the most popular opinions. Conway, who in the last ministry had introduced and carried the repeal of the Stamp Act, was induced to abandon the Rockingham party, and retain his old office of Secretary of State. Shelburne and Barré, who were now closely attached to Pitt, and who had distinguished themselves by their uncompromising opposition to American taxation, were both in the ministry, the first as Secretary of State, the second as a Vice-Treasurer of Ireland. Lord Granby was made Commander-in-Chief. The head of the Treasury would naturally have fallen to Pitt, but he emphatically refused it. He felt, as the result showed with too good reason, that his health made him wholly unfit for a post of great official duty, and, though the real head of the Government, he held only the almost sinecure office of Privy Seal. The Duke of Grafton, who had so recently revolted against Rockingham, was made First Lord of the Treasury. When only twenty-four, Grafton had been Groom

to pick and cull from all quarters, and break all parties as much as possible. From this moment I date the wane of Mr. Pitt's glory; he will want the thorough-bass of drums and trumpets, and is not made for peace.'— To Montagu, July 10, 1766.

of the Stole to George III. when he was the Prince of Wales, and his courtly manners, as well as a certain ductility of principles, had made him peculiarly acceptable to the King, but had not secured him from being deprived of the Lord-Lieutenancy of his county for his opposition to the peace. His great position, his very considerable powers of speech, and the unbounded admiration he professed for Pitt, explained his promotion; but he hated business, he was passionately devoted to field sports, and he had neither the industry nor the firmness that were required for the head of a Government.

In this strangely incoherent ministry Temple had no place. His influence over his brother-in-law had during the last few months been most disastrously displayed; but the relations between them had been rapidly becoming strained. They differed about the Stamp Act; for Temple on this question agreed with his brother George Grenville. They differed about Wilkes; for Pitt, though condemning the legal proceedings of which he was the object, never concealed his contempt for that demagogue. They differed in party politics; for Temple was now steadily gravitating towards Grenville. At the same time, the popularity which he had lately enjoyed on account of his connection with Wilkes had raised his pretensions to the highest point. Pitt offered to place him at the head of the Treasury; but refused to grant him an equal share in nominating to the other posts. Temple was bitterly offended, broke off the conference in anger, and began to inspire virulent libels against his brother-in-law. In an anonymous pamphlet on the other side there occurred a phrase which was much noticed for its happiness of expression, and in which critics imagined that they could trace the hand of Pitt: 'Had Lord Temple not fastened himself upon Mr. Pitt's train, he might have crept out of life with as little notice as he crept in, and gone off with no other degree of credit than that of adding a single unit to the bills of mortality.' The secession of Temple contributed, indeed, to make the Government more popular with the King; it relieved Pitt from one of his worst advisers, but the whole Grenville connection were now united in opposition.

Much more fatal to the ministry was the news that Pitt was resolved to abandon the House of Commons, and, as Earl of Chatham, to take his seat among the Lords. His promotion to the peerage was the necessary consequence of his acceptance of the post of Privy Seal, as that office was always held by a peer,[1] and it was probably due to a well-founded conviction that his health was so broken and his nervous system so shattered that it was simply impossible for him to conduct public business in the House of Commons. But he soon found, as Pulteney had found before, how ruinous such an honour may be to a popular statesman. The main secret of his unrivalled influence over the people was the conviction that he owed his power to their favour; that in the midst of the corruption of an essentially aristocratic Government he was the great representative of the democracy of England. His pension had for a time obscured his popularity; but it soon returned, and his unrivalled influence in the House of Commons was unshaken. But now, at last, the spell was broken. The revulsion of feeling was immediate and irrevocable. The City, where he had lately been idolised, refused to present an address. The lamps which had already been placed around the Monument, for an illumination in honour of his return to office, were at once removed. Shorn of the popularity which had been the chief element of his power, he passed into an assembly which was eminently uncongenial to his eloquence, while in the House of Commons Charles Townshend alone was able to encounter Grenville and Burke; and Townshend, in spite of his extraordinary abilities, had all the vanity of a woman and all the levity of a child. 'The City,' wrote Sir Robert Wilmot, 'have brought in their verdict of *felo de se* against William, Earl of Chatham.'[2] 'I wish,' wrote Chesterfield to his son, 'I could send you all the pamphlets and half-sheets that swarm here upon the occasion; but that is impossible, for every week would make a ship's cargo. It is certain that Mr. Pitt has by his dignity of Earl lost the greater part of his popularity, especially in the City; and I believe the Opposition will be very strong, and perhaps prevail next session in the House of Commons, there being now nobody there

[1] Thackeray's *Life of Chatham*, ii. 84. [2] *Chatham Correspondence*, iii. 28.

who has the authority and ascendency over them that Pitt had.'¹

At every step the difficulties of Chatham increased. He had at all times remarkably few personal adherents. In one of his conversations in 1762 he represented himself as so isolated in Parliament that he had no one except the Clerk to speak to; and just before his second ministry he described himself, with the gross bad taste into which he occasionally fell, as 'standing like our first parents, naked, but not ashamed.' The politicians whose opinions in general agreed the best with his own were those who were attached to Rockingham, and he wished, while breaking up the Rockingham organisation, to retain the services of the chief members of the party. Rockingham appears to have acted with great moderation. He advised those of his followers who were not removed by Chatham to remain in office, and many great noblemen of the connection accordingly remained in posts which were chiefly honorary. But after the conduct of Chatham during the late ministry cordial co-operation was impossible. Chatham visited Rockingham; but the latter positively refused to see him.² Dowdeswell, whose financial capacity was very considerable, and who was much respected in the House of Commons, was strongly pressed to join the Government, either as President of the Board of Trade or as Joint Paymaster, but he absolutely refused.³ Edmund Burke, whose splendid genius was rising rapidly above the horizon, might have had a seat at the Board of Trade; but he remained faithful to his leader and to his party.⁴

It was unfortunate, too, that the ministry was formed at a period of great and general distress. The harvest had been unusually bad; the price of corn rose with ominous rapidity. In every part of England bread riots took place. Flour mills were destroyed; corn, bread, and other necessaries were in many places seized by the populace and sold at low prices, and several lives were lost in the western counties in collisions between the soldiers and the mob. The jails were filled with prisoners, and discontent was wide and bitter. The Govern-

---

¹ *Chatham Correspondence*, iii. 21.
² *Grenville Papers*, iii. 283.
³ *Chatham Correspondence*, iii. 22, 23.
⁴ Ibid. p. 111. Prior's *Life of Burke*, i. 163.

ment, according to the unwise custom of the time, issued a proclamation in September 1766 for putting in force an old statute against forestallers, regraters, and engrossers of corn; and this measure proving ineffectual, they thought it necessary to prohibit the export of corn. By an Act of Charles II. corn might be legally exported from England as long as the home price was under 53s. 4d. a quarter, and this limit had not yet been attained; but as the price was rapidly rising, and as famine was approaching, the ministers thought it necessary to anticipate the legal period of prohibition. The proper machinery for effecting this was, of course, an Act of Parliament. But Parliament was not sitting, and there were serious objections to summoning it as quickly as might be required. Under these circumstances, an order of Council was issued laying an embargo on corn. The act was obviously beyond the law; but under ordinary circumstances it would probably have excited no comment, for it was called forth by a grave, pressing, and acknowledged necessity, and Parliament was perfectly ready to ratify what was done. Chatham, in a very reasonable and moderate speech, and in language which was perfectly constitutional, defended it as 'an act of power justifiable before Parliament on the ground of necessity;' but Northington contended that under such circumstances the proclamation was legally as well as morally justifiable, and Camden added that, at worst, the measure was 'but a forty days' tyranny.' Mansfield at once saw his advantage, and, assuming the position of the champion of law against prerogative, he answered with crushing force.

In the Commons the debates were even more damaging to the ministry. Beckford, who was one of the most intimate friends of Chatham, and who was sometimes put forward to speak in his name, declared that 'if the public was in danger, the King has a dispensing power, with the advice of the Council, whenever the *salus populi* requires it.' It is not probable that he meant anything very different from what would now be generally acknowledged, that extreme cases sometimes arise in which it is the duty, and therefore the right, of ministers, at their own peril, and subject to the subsequent judgment of Parliament, to set aside the law; but his expressions were plainly inaccurate, and they might be easily construed into a revival of the dispensing doctrine of the Stuarts. Grenville moved that the words should be taken down, and Beckford was ultimately obliged to retract them. A Bill was brought in by Conway to indemnify those who acted under the proclamation; but Grenville maintained that the act of indemnity must include the ministers who advised as well as the officials who acted under the proclamation. The ministers accepted this correction, and Chatham especially recommended that the Act should be 'made as strong as possible;' but the whole transaction raised a great deal of angry and exaggerated outcry against his administration.[1]

It was evidently necessary to strengthen it, but no minister was ever less fitted than Chatham to conciliate opponents or to perform the delicate functions of party management. His colleagues complained that he consulted no one in his nominations, that he took the most important steps without their knowledge, that they were often wholly ignorant of the policy he designed. The letters of his opponents were full of complaints of ' the *hauteur* with which Lord Chatham treats all mankind;' of 'the disgust which extended very wide among the principal families of the kingdom;' of ' the insolent behaviour of the minister to the first nobility of the kingdom.' Continually harassed by the conflicting pretensions of titled beggars, whose sole merit lay in their properties and their names, he met them with a pride which was beyond the pride of birth or wealth, and he made personal enemies at every step. In the House of Commons the Government was especially weak. When Charles Townshend brought forward his first budget, Grenville and Dowdeswell combined to reduce the land-tax from 4s. to 3s. in the pound, and by the assistance of the county members they carried their motion by a majority of 18. This is said to have been the first instance since the Revolution of a minister being defeated on a money Bill, and it is a significant illustration of the declining popularity of Chatham, that on this occasion 'most of those

---

[1] 7 *George III.* cap. vii. See an account of the whole transaction in a letter from Grenville himself, *Grenville Papers*, iii. 341-343, and in a letter from Flood to Charlemont (*Flood's Letters*, ix.). See too *Chatham Correspondence*, iii. 125-128.

who had county or popular elections' were united against him.'[1]

The attempt to withdraw single politicians from their several connections signally failed. Overtures were made to the Bedford faction, but the Duke, whom Chatham had recently endeavoured to drive out of all active politics, would only join if he had the disposal of so many places that he would have become virtually the director of the Government, and the negotiation, to the great delight of the King, accordingly failed. In the course of it, Chatham wished to appoint a partisan of the Duke of Bedford Treasurer of the Council, and Lord Mount Edgcumbe, who held that post, was asked to exchange it for the post of Lord of the Bedchamber. He refused, and was summarily dismissed, and the Government thus lost the support of the patron of four boroughs not long before a general election, and once more mortally affronted the whole Rockingham connection. In November and December 1766, the administration seemed in a state of complete dissolution. The Duke of Portland, the Earls of Besborough and Scarborough, Lord Monson, Sir C. Saunders, Sir W. Meredith, and Admiral Keppel, resigned, and Conway was only prevented with extreme difficulty from following their example. A few scattered politicians—the most remarkable being Sir E. Hawke— were induced to fill the void, but a new negotiation with the Duke of Bedford ended only in a violent altercation. The ministry had neither the strength which grows out of popularity nor the strength which grows out of interest. 'There is still a little twilight of popularity,' wrote Burke, 'remaining round the great peer, but it fades away every moment.'[2] 'One thing,' wrote Charlemont to Flood, ' appears very extraordinary, if not indecent—no member of the Opposition speaks without directly abusing Lord Chatham, and no friend ever rises to take his part. . . . . Never was known such disunion, such a want of concert as visibly appears on both sides. How it will end Heaven only knows.'[3] ' Such a state of affairs,' wrote Chesterfield, after the resignation of the Rockingham section of the ministry, ' was never before seen in this or any other country.

---

[1] *Parl. Hist.* xvi. 362-364. *Chatham Correspondence,* iii. 224.

[2] *Burke's Correspondence,* i. 106.
[3] *Chatham Correspondence,* iii.

When this ministry shall be settled, it will be the sixth in six years' time.'¹

Alarming intelligence had been received of renewed war preparations in France, and Chatham resolved to guard against the danger that was still apprehended from the Family Compact, by a great northern alliance of England, Prussia, and Russia. Frederick, however, resented bitterly the desertion of England in the last war, and he utterly refused the alliance. Of Chatham personally he spoke with respect and admiration, but professed himself entirely sceptical about the continuance of his power and popularity since he had accepted a peerage. Frederick had now entered into a close and separate connection with Russia, and was wholly alienated from England, while Russia would only accept the alliance if it were made to extend to a Turkish war.² 'One thing I feel,' wrote that experienced diplomatist, Sir Andrew Mitchell, 'that the late frequent changes in England have created a degree of diffidence in foreign Powers which renders all negotiation with them difficult and disagreeable.'³

The Government could thus point to no great triumph of policy to counterbalance its internal weakness. A project was indeed entertained of withdrawing the great dominions which had been conquered in Hindostan from the control of a mere mercantile company, placing them under the direct dominion of the Crown, and diverting to the public treasury the territorial as distinguished from the mercantile revenues. Clive had at one time suggested this measure, though he afterwards appears to have opposed it.⁴ Chatham attached very great importance to it, and Shelburne entered cordially into his views, but a parliamentary inquiry into the affairs of the Company was the only step of importance that was taken before Chatham was hopelessly incapacitated by illness. It was moved in the Commons in November 1766, and it was characteristic of Chatham that he entrusted the

---

210. 'There are four parties,' Lord Northington said about this time, 'Butes, Bedfords, Rockinghams, Chathams, and we (the last) are the weakest of the four.'—Albemarle's *Life of Rockingham*, ii. 34.

¹ *Chatham Correspondence*, iii. 136.
² Ibid. iii. 6-9, 84-86.
³ Ibid. iii. 80.
⁴ Ibid. iii. 62. Fitzmaurice's *Life of Shelburne*, ii. 16-18.

motion, not to any of the responsible ministers of the Crown, but to Beckford, one of the vainest and most hot-headed of the City politicians. The inquiry was ordered by a large majority, in spite of the opposition of the Grenvilles and the Rockinghams; but Charles Townshend, while supporting it, took occasion to say, in direct opposition to the leading principle of Chatham, that 'he believed the Company had a right to territorial revenue.'[1] Townshend was already intriguing against his chief, speaking openly against him in private circles, and probably aspiring to the position of Prime Minister, and he soon after more openly raised the standard of revolt by declaring his full sympathy with the policy of taxing America.

The Government was steadily becoming a Tory Government. Separated from the Grenville connection, from the Bedford connection, and from the Rockingham connection, the King's friends were necessarily its chief support. The King was gratified by the restoration of Mr. Stuart Mackenzie, the brother of Bute, to the post from which Grenville had so imperiously thrust him, subject however to the condition that he was to exercise no political power.[2] Lord Northumberland, the brother-in-law of Bute, was thrown into paroxysms of fury because another nobleman had been preferred to him as Master of the Horse, but he was pacified by a dukedom;[3] and, to the astonishment and indignation of many of the old followers of Chatham, most of the vacant places were filled up by Tories. The power of the Government rested upon the extreme division of its opponents, and upon the firm union which was again established between the ministry and the Court. Each of these possessed so great an influence over elections and over members of Parliament that they could seldom fail when united to command a majority. The defeat of the Government on the land-tax was chiefly due to a surprise and to the selfish interests of the county members, but in most cases the Government, even when much divided, discredited, and outdebated, could count upon large majorities in the House of Commons. In critical divisions abstentions were very nume-

---

[1] Fitzmaurice's *Life of Shelburne*, ii. 22.
[2] *Chatham Correspondence*, iii. 58.
[3] *Grenville Papers*, iii. 384, 385.

rous, and one or other section of the Opposition usually left the House.[1]

The clouds darkened more and more. The health of Chatham, which was now of such capital importance, rapidly gave way. In the very first month of his administration he had been prostrated with fever,[2] and it soon became evident that he could exercise no steady direction over affairs. From October 1766 till the following March he was at Bath, but was able to keep up some correspondence with his colleagues, but immediately on his return his disease appeared to settle mainly on his nerves. For some time it had been evident to close observers that his mind was gravely disordered. In public this was shown by the extraordinary and ungovernable arrogance with which he treated almost every leading politician with whom he came in contact; by the strange outbursts of wild rhodomontade that defaced some of his noblest speeches; by the unbridled fury with which he often resented the slightest opposition. In private the symptoms were still more unequivocal. The legacy of Sir W. Pynsent had made him a rich man, but it was wholly insufficient for the extravagant expenses into which he now plunged. He bought up all the residences around Hayes and around his London house in order to free himself from neighbours. He ordered great plantations at Hayes, and pushed on the works with such feverish haste that it was necessary to continue them by torchlight throughout the night. He could not bear to have his children under the same roof, and could not tolerate the slightest noise. He sold Hayes and removed to Pynsent, where he insisted on covering a barren hill with cedars and cypresses, which were brought at enormous expense from London. A constant succession of chickens were boiling or roasting in his kitchen at every hour of the day, as his appetite was altogether uncertain, and when he desired to gratify it his temper could not brook the smallest delay. He soon grew tired of Pynsent, began to pine after Hayes, and at last, with great difficulty, Lady Chatham succeeded in repurchasing it for him. About nine months after he came to power his health wholly gave way. A gloomy and myste-

---

[1] The following were the numbers in several of the chief party divisions in 1766. 129 to 76, 166 to 48, 140 to 56, 131 to 67, 106 to 35, 180 to 147.—Walpole's *George III.* vol. ii.
[2] *Grenville Papers,* iii. 279.

rious malady affecting his nerves and his mind, rendered him incapable of any mental exertion, of any political intercourse, of enduring even the faintest noise, of transacting the most ordinary business, and in this state he continued with little intermission from March 1767 for more than two years.[1]

The Government fell at once into complete anarchy. The spell of the name of Chatham was still so great that he was kept at the head of affairs, but he was unable to take the smallest part in counsel or debate. Sometimes in the height of his malady he was seen taking exercise out of doors,[2] but he could bear no discussion, he could make no mental effort. The King vainly asked an interview of but a quarter of an hour. He wrote letter after letter full of the kindest consideration, imploring him to see Grafton, if it were but for five minutes. He represented to him that the Government majority in the Lords was one day only six, and another only three; that Shelburne was plotting against his colleagues; that Townshend was in open enmity with Grafton; that Conway had already announced his intention of resigning; that the Grenvilles, the Rockinghams, and the Bedfords were united in their efforts to storm the closet, while they confessed that they were far too divided to form an administration. The answers received by the hand of Lady Chatham were always in substance the same. 'Such was the state of Lord Chatham's health that his Majesty must not expect from him any further advice or assistance.' 'He is overwhelmed with affliction still to find that the continuance in extreme weakness of nerves renders it impossible for him to flatter himself with being able soon to present himself before his Majesty. He is as yet utterly incapable of the smallest

---

[1] See Walpole's *Memoirs of George III.* iii. 41-44. *Chatham Correspondence.* Whately wrote (July 30, 1767), 'Lord Chatham's state of health (I was told authentically yesterday) is certainly the lowest dejection and debility that mind or body can be in. He sits all the day leaning on his hands, which he supports on the table; does not permit any person to remain in the room; knocks when he wants anything, and having made his wants known, gives a signal without speaking, to the person who answered his call to return.'—Phillimore's *Life of Lyttleton,* p. 729.

[2] 'Here [at Bath] Lord Chatham is, and goes out every day on horseback when the weather lets him, and looks rather thin and pallid; but otherwise very well in appearance; he sees no one.'—Mr. Augustus Hervey to Mr. Grenville, Nov. 3, 1767. *Grenville Papers,* iv. 180. On May 5, 1767, Chesterfield wrote, 'Lord Chatham is still ill, and only goes abroad for an hour a day to take the air in his coach.'—*Chatham Corresp.* iii. 253.

effort.' He had no wish to continue in a post the duties of which he was unable to discharge, and he again and again implored the King to accept his resignation; but broken and in some respects discredited as he was, his name was still the one support of the Government. The King implored him to remain; Grafton, Camden, and Shelburne wrote urgently to the same effect. On one occasion Grafton obtained an interview with him, but he found him completely prostrated with nervous weakness and depression, and was able to extract from him little more than an entreaty to remain at his post, and the general advice to strengthen the ministry by some coalition; if possible, by a junction with the Bedford party.[1]

That ministry was now indeed the strangest spectacle of confusion. As Charlemont said, it 'was divided into as many parties as there were men in it.' During the latter part of 1767 and some months of 1768 it continued in a condition of chronic fluctuation, perpetual negotiations and intrigues going on between the different fractions of the ministry and the different sections of the Opposition. Every leading Whig statesman took part in them, and in the course of them we for the last time find in public affairs the names of the old Duke of Newcastle and of Lord Holland. Without describing them in detail, it may be sufficient to relate the most important changes. In September 1767 Charles Townshend, the Chancellor of the Exchequer and leader of the House of Commons, died, and Lord North became Chancellor of the Exchequer. A few months later the Bedford faction effected a junction with the Government. The Duke indeed declined office, but Gower, Sandwich, Weymouth, and Rigby were introduced into the ministry, while Northington and Conway retired.[2]

---

[1] See the interesting passage from the Duke of Grafton's autobiography quoted in Walpole's *George III.* iii. 51, 52.

[2] In one of Lord Lyttleton's letters (Nov. 25, 1767) there is a very curious account of a conversation of Lord Mansfield with the writer on the condition and prospects of the ministry. Mansfield said that 'no opposition would signify anything if the ministers held together, that the King mediated between them and kept them from breaking; that he was the most efficient man among them, that he made each of them believe he was in love with them (*sic*) and fooled them all; that unless that madman, Lord Chatham, should come and throw a fireball in the midst of them he thought they would stand their ground, but what *that* might do he could not tell; that Lord Bute alone could make a ministry which could last; that if he was dead, no other man could do it so well. . . . He

In January 1768 Lord Hillsborough, whose sympathies were with the Tory party, was appointed Secretary of State for the Colonies, and in October Shelburne, who was now one of the most trusted adherents of Chatham, was almost forced to resign. Shelburne had become obnoxious both to the King, the Bedford faction, and the Duke of Grafton. He utterly differed from the pacific policy of the Government, and he would have resisted by force the acquisition of Corsica by France. He now went with his follower Colonel Barré into opposition. Lord Camden, the Chancellor, was at variance with all the other members of the Cabinet, and remained for long periods absent from its meetings. The Duke of Grafton, the nominal Prime Minister, was outvoted on some of the most important questions, and desired only to resign. In July 1767 he had told the King that he could not continue at the head of the Treasury under existing circumstances, that he had accepted the foremost place merely for the sake of acting under Chatham, and not with any intention of being First Minister himself, and that unless Chatham was able and willing to grasp the helm he was resolved to retire.[1] He was persuaded with difficulty to continue in office if Conway remained, and then again to continue when Conway resigned, but he was fully conscious that he was unfit for his post, and incapable of controlling the discordant elements of the Government. He gave full rein to his feelings of disgust and of indolence, and remained for long periods in the country, only going once a week to London to discharge his duties as First Minister of the Crown.[2]

On every important question it touched, the ministry which was formed by Chatham pursued a course opposed to the policy of its chief. Beyond all other English statesmen Chatham had been jealous of French power, conspicuous in denouncing the attempt to tax America, and fearless in the assertion of popular rights. His colleagues during the season of his prostration permitted France to obtain possession of Corsica, revived the disloyalty of America by imposing duties on certain goods im-

then dwelt a good deal on the certainty of a fixed resolution in the King not to change his army but only the generals of that army.'—Philli- more's *Life of Lyttleton*, pp. 736–738.
[1] *Grenville Papers*, iv. 27, 31.
[2] Walpole's *George III.* iii. 391, 392. *Grenville Papers*, iv. 268.

ported into the colonies, and flung the country into a paroxysm of agitation by maintaining that the simple vote of the House of Commons was sufficient to disqualify Wilkes. They also justly aroused great indignation by a measure which was regarded as a flagrant violation of personal property for political purposes. Sir James Lowther, the son-in-law of Bute, a man of immense wealth and political influence in Cumberland and Westmoreland, but whose violence, arrogance, despotism, and caprice rose almost to the point of madness,[1] was engaged in a fierce political contest in those counties with the Duke of Portland, the head of the most important family of the Opposition. The property of Portland had been granted by the Crown, and Sir James Lowther discovered that a certain district containing many freemen, which had been for two generations in the undisputed possession of the Portland family, was not distinctly specified in the grant. Availing himself of the legal maxim that no lapse of time can destroy the rights of the Crown or of the Church, Lowther disputed the title of the Duke to this portion of his property, and obtained from the Crown a lease of the lands for himself. The notorious object of this transaction was the transfer of a few votes from the Opposition to the Government, and it appeared peculiarly iniquitous, for the latter refused to give the Duke of Portland access to the collection of grants in the office of the Surveyor-General, which might have enabled him to defend his rights.[2] Even among the supporters of the ministry it produced grave discontent, and it led to the Nullum Tempus Bill, which, though thrown out by the influence of Lord North in 1768, was carried without opposition in the following year, and secured landowners from all dormant claims on the part of the Crown after an undisputed possession of sixty years.

The ministry of Chatham had been warmly supported by the King, for Chatham had thrown himself cordially into the King's great object, the destruction of the previous system of government by party or by connection. 'I know,' wrote the King on the day he signed the warrant creating his minister an earl, 'the Earl of Chatham will zealously give his aid towards

[1] Some very curious anecdotes of this singular personage will be found in Albemarle's *Life of Rockingham*, ii. 70-72.

[2] Walpole's *George III.* iii. 143-146.

destroying all party distinctions and restoring that subordination to government which can alone preserve that inestimable blessing, liberty, from degenerating into licentiousness;'[1] and in another letter he described 'the very end proposed at the formation of the present administration' as being 'to root out the present method of parties banding together.'[2] The patience and consideration with which the King acted towards Chatham during his illness forms one of the brightest pages of his reign, and for some time there was a cordial union between the Court and the Executive. The introduction of the Bedford faction into the Government was contrary to the wishes of the King, but he appears to have recognised the necessity. His objections to this faction were rather personal than political, and the condition of the Government was at this time extremely favourable to his designs. A feeble, uncertain, and wavering ministry, without any efficient head, and paralysed by the dissensions of its most important members, gave rare facilities for the exercise of his influence. Several of the ministers were personally attached to him. The discipline and unity of action of the King's friends gave them an overwhelming power amid the disintegration of parties. Bute, whose personal unpopularity and incapacity had greatly weakened the royal cause, was now wholly removed from politics,[3] and in the new Chancellor of the Exchequer, Lord North, the King had found a parliamentary leader who was prepared to accept office under the conditions he required, and who was in almost every respect pre-eminently fitted to represent his views.

The son of the Earl of Guilford, Lord North had entered Parliament in 1754, had accepted a lordship of the Treasury under Pitt in 1759, had been removed from office by Rockingham in 1765, and had again come into office

---

[1] *Chatham Correspondence*, iii. 21.
[2] Ibid. iii. 137.
[3] In 1778 Bute authorised his son to write to the papers, 'that he declares upon his solemn word of honour that he has not had the honour of waiting upon his Majesty but at his levee or drawing-room; nor has he presumed to offer any advice or opinion concerning the disposition of offices or the conduct of measures either directly or indirectly, by himself or any other, from the time when the late Duke of Cumberland was consulted in the arrangement of a ministry in 1765 to the present hour.'—See the *Correspondence of George III. and Lord North*, i. p. xxi.

with Pitt as Joint Paymaster of the Forces. He belonged, however, to none of the Whig parties, and he possessed in the highest degree that natural leaning towards authority which was most pleasing to the King. Since the beginning of the reign there had been no arbitrary or unpopular measure which he had not defended. He supported the Cyder Act of Bute and opposed its repeal. He moved the expulsion of Wilkes. He was one of the foremost advocates of general warrants in every stage of the controversy. He defended the Stamp Act. He bitterly resisted its repeal. He defeated for a time the attempt to secure the property of the subject from the dormant claims of the Crown. Most of the measures which he advocated in the long course of his ministry were proved by the event to be disastrous and foolish, but he possessed an admirable good sense in the management of details, and he had many of the qualities that lead to eminence both in the closet and in Parliament. His ungainly form, his harsh tones, his slow and laboured utterance, his undisguised indolence, furnished a ready theme for ridicule, but his private character was wholly unblemished. No statesman ever encountered the storms of political life with a temper which it was more difficult to ruffle or more impossible to embitter. His almost unfailing tact, his singularly quick and happy wit, and his great knowledge of business, and especially of finance,[1] made him most formidable as a debater, while his sweet and amiable disposition gave him some personal popularity even in the most disastrous moments of his career. Partly through political principle and partly through weakness of character he continually subordinated his own judgment to that of the King, and carried out with greatly superior abilities a policy not very different from that of Bute. The growing power of North drew the King more closely to his ministers, and he cordially adopted their views on the two great questions on which English politics were now chiefly concentrated. These questions were the Middlesex election and the renewed taxation of America.

---

[1] See a very striking account of his budget speech in 1767, in a letter of Rigby.—*Bedford Correspondence*, iii. 408.

CHAPTER XI.

WHEN we last encountered Wilkes in this narrative he had retired to Paris after his duel with Martin, and had a few months later been outlawed on account of his refusal to appear to take his trial in England. He soon recovered his old health and spirits; but his political enthusiasm seems for a time to have died away in his admiration for 'the matchless charms' of an Italian courtesan named Corradini, with whom he was now violently enamoured. He projected a journey to Italy with her and with Churchill, and in the autumn of 1764 he met Churchill at Boulogne; but a great catastrophe interfered with their plan. Churchill was seized with a malignant fever, and died in a few days, at the early age of thirty-three, leaving a sadly stained and shameful memory, and a few volumes, which were once supposed to rival the poetry of Pope, but which have now almost wholly dropped out of the notice of the world. Wilkes soon after went on with his mistress to Italy. He spent several months between Bologna, Florence, Rome, and Naples; saw much of Winckelmann; was present at Naples at the miracle of St. Januarius, and kissed the phial on his knees; projected a history of England, a biography and annotated edition of the poems of Churchill, but soon found that extended literary undertakings were wholly unsuited to his tastes; and at length, having quarrelled with Corradini, he returned alone to France.[1] He visited Voltaire at Ferney, and the old patriarch was much struck with his liveliness and wit. The Rockinghams had now come to power, and as they had been strongly opposed to the measures which had driven him from England, he expected much from their assistance.

---

[1] The details of his journey through Italy will be found in a curious manuscript fragment of autobiography in the British Museum.

He paid a secret visit to London in 1766 in hopes of obtaining a pardon and a pension, and perhaps the embassy of Constantinople;[1] but he soon found that the ministers, though they raised among themselves a large private subscription for him, could not, or would not, do anything more.[2] On the change of Government he renewed his overtures, trusting to his former friendship with Grafton; but he was told that without Chatham nothing could be done. After the language of Chatham, a personal application would have been a humiliation too great for Wilkes to endure; and he returned, full of indignation, to the Continent, and published an angry account of the transaction. In March 1768, however, on the eve of the general election, he again appeared—this time without any concealment—in London, forwarded a petition for pardon to the King, but at the same time announced himself as a candidate for the representation of the City of London. The spectacle of a penniless adventurer of notoriously infamous character, and lying at this very time under a sentence of outlawry, and under a condemnation for blasphemy and libel, standing against a popular alderman in the metropolis of England, was a very strange one; and although Wilkes was at the bottom of the poll, he obtained more than 1,200 votes, and in the opinion of Franklin, who was then living in England, he would probably have succeeded had he appeared earlier in the field. He at once stood for Middlesex. He had powerful supporters. Temple contributed the freehold qualification which was necessary; the Duke of Portland was on his side; Horne, the rector of Brentford, who was already known as a man of great energy, ability, and local influence, threw all his power into the scale. The election took place at Brentford on March 28, and its result was that Wilkes was at the head of the poll.

The triumph of Wilkes was wholly unexpected by the Government,[3] and they had great doubts about the course they should

---

[1] *Grenville Papers,* iii. 95. Prior's *Life of Burke,* i. 153.
[2] 'The ministers are embarrassed to the last degree how to act with regard to Wilkes. It seems they are afraid to press the King for his pardon, as that is a subject his Majesty will not easily hear the least mention of; and they are apprehensive if he has it not, that the mob of London will rise in his favour.'—The Bishop of Carlisle to Grenville (May 27, 1776), *Grenville Papers,* iii. 241.
[3] See the letters of Lord Camden, Campbell's *Chancellors,* vi. 390-392.

pursue. As a Member of Parliament he was already known, and he was as far as possible from being formidable; nothing, indeed, was more likely to terminate his popularity than a parliamentary career. 'I do not fear firebrands in this House,' Canning once said, with great good sense: 'as soon as they touch its floor they hiss and are extinguished;' and with the single exception of O'Connell, who possessed to a very high degree the talents both of a debater and of a party leader, the truth of this saying has been always verified in England. In the weak, divided, and headless ministry of Grafton there were not wanting voices to urge that in the face of the fierce storm of popular excitement that was rising, and after the many mistakes that had been made in the earlier encounters between Wilkes and the Government, the wisest course was to grant the new member a free pardon, and to allow him to take his seat in the House and sink gradually to his natural level. But the King took a warm and personal interest in the matter, and his firm will dictated the policy of his Government. He complained bitterly that the Duke of Grafton had proposed to him to pardon Wilkes, and he wrote to Lord North a peremptory injunction that the whole power of the Government must be exerted to expel the demagogue from Parliament.[1]

In the meantime two important events had occurred. In order to avoid arrest in the course of the election, Wilkes had written to the solicitor of the Treasury pledging himself to surrender on his outlawry at the Court of King's Bench on the first day of the succeeding term. He accordingly appeared before Lord Mansfield on April 20, and again, after the rectification of some legal informalities, on the 27th. The question of the legality of the outlawry was argued at great length, and Lord Mansfield postponed the decision to the following term, but in the meantime refused to admit Wilkes to bail. He accordingly remained in prison till June 8, when Mansfield, on a purely technical point of law, pronounced the outlawry to be illegal. Wilkes was thus restored to his full rights as a British subject; but the condemnation which had been pronounced against him during his absence for seditious libel and for blasphemy still

---

[1] *Correspondence of George III. with Lord North*, i. 2. Walpole's *George III.* iii. 200.

remained. On June 18 he appeared to receive his sentence. There were the strongest reasons both of justice and policy why the court should deal leniently with him, for he had already suffered much, and he had suffered in defiance of the law. It had been decided that the general warrant by which he had been originally arrested was illegal; that the search warrant by which his papers were seized was illegal; that the outlawry pronounced against him was illegal. It was as certain as any proposition in history could be that the King's Speech had, at least since the accession of the House of Brunswick, been uniformly discussed as the speech of the ministers; and regarding it in that light there was nothing exceptionally violent in the incriminated number of the 'North Briton.' However culpable might be the 'Essay on Woman,' it was an outrage upon common-sense to condemn Wilkes for 'publishing' a pamphlet of which he had only struck off twelve or thirteen copies, with the most profound secrecy, for distribution among his intimate friends; and no human being could believe that the prosecution of the essay had been really undertaken in the interests of public morals. Wilkes, however, was sentenced to be imprisoned for twenty-two months, to be fined 1,000*l*., and to obtain security for good behaviour for seven years after his imprisonment had terminated. One usual element in sentences for libels was omitted. The judges knew too well the feelings of the populace to confer upon Wilkes the popular triumph which would have inevitably ensued had he been sentenced to stand in the pillory.

While these events were taking place, the riotous spirit which had for some years been growing stronger and stronger in England increased almost to the point of revolution. At the opening of the Middlesex election, the mob at break of day took possession of every avenue and turnpike leading to the place of voting, and would suffer no one to pass who did not wear a blue cockade with the name of Wilkes and No. 45; and during the two days of the election the whole town was almost at their mercy. The windows of the Mansion House were demolished. The houses of Lord Bute, Lord Egmont, the Duke of Northumberland, and the Duchess of Hamilton were attacked. The City Marshal and many of the principal opponents of Wilkes were assaulted as they drove through Hyde Park. The coach-glasses of all who refused to huzza for 'Wilkes and Liberty' were broken, and even ladies were taken out of their chairs and compelled to join in the popular cry. The Austrian Ambassador, one of the most stately and ceremonious of men, was dragged from his coach and '45' chalked on the soles of his shoes. The same popular number was inscribed on every carriage that drove through the streets, and on every door along the roads far beyond the precincts of the City. Franklin noticed that there was hardly a house within fifteen miles of London unmarked, and the inscription might be seen from time to time the whole way from London to Winchester.

'For two nights,' wrote the same accurate observer, 'London was illuminated at the command of the mob.... The second night exceeded anything of the kind ever seen here on the greatest occasions of rejoicing, as even the small cross streets, lanes, courts, and other out-of-the-way places, were all in a blaze with lights, and the principal streets all night long, as the mobs went round again after two o'clock and obliged people who had extinguished their candles to light them again. Those who refused had all their windows destroyed.'[1] When Wilkes appeared at the King's Bench to receive judgment as an outlaw, the whole neighbourhood of the Court was thronged by his partisans; and when the Court, refusing to accept bail, committed him to prison, he was rescued on Westminster Bridge; the horses were taken off the carriage in which he was conveyed; he was dragged in triumph by the crowd through the Strand and through Fleet Street, and it was with much difficulty that he at last succeeded in escaping from his admirers and surrendering to the authorities.[2] The sentence that was passed on him exasperated the people to the highest degree, but they assumed that when Parliament met he would be released and allowed to take his seat. It assembled at length on May 10 in the midst of a fierce tumult, great crowds shouting 'Wilkes and Liberty!' about the House. But the chief excitement was in St. George's Fields, around the King's Bench

[1] *Franklin's Works* (Spark's ed.) vii. 399, 400.
[2] *Annual Register*, 1768, p. 100.

prison, where Wilkes was confined. The Government anticipated a dangerous riot, and either because they feared lest the contagion should gain the English troops, or in a spirit of mere bravado, they selected a detachment from a Scotch regiment to keep the peace, and Lord Weymouth, the Secretary of State, wrote to the magistrate of the district urging him not to scruple to employ the soldiers in case of riot. The mob, finding that their hero was not released, began to threaten the prison, and to assail the soldiers with stones and brickbats, and in the course of a confused scuffle which ensued, some soldiers, pursuing into a private house a man who had assaulted them, encountered and killed a young man of very respectable position, named Allen, who is said to have been entirely unconnected with the riot. Soon after, the Riot Act was read. The troops fired; five or six persons were killed and fifteen wounded, and among the latter there were two women, one of whom died soon after. The coroner's inquest held upon Allen found a Scotch soldier, named Donald Maclean, guilty of his murder, and another soldier, as well as the commanding officer, guilty of aiding and abetting it. The Grand Jury, a few months later, threw out the bills against the two latter; but the former was put on his trial and acquitted. It was with difficulty that the mob were restrained from tearing him to pieces; and the indignation became still greater when the colonel of the regiment publicly presented him, after his acquittal, with thirty guineas on the part of the Government; and when Lord Barrington, the Secretary of War, issued a general order conveying special thanks to the soldiers for their behaviour, and promising that 'if any disagreeable circumstances should happen in the execution of their duty,' they should have 'every protection that the law can authorise and their officers can give.' The only sister of Allen survived but a few months the shock she had received in her brother's death, and they were laid together in the churchyard of Newington, in Surrey. The inscription on their tombstone described William Allen as 'an Englishman of unspotted life and amiable disposition, who was inhumanly murdered by Scottish detachments from the army,' and two significant texts adjured the earth to refuse to cover his blood, and the Almighty 'to take away the wicked from before the King.'[1]

The exceeding weakness of the civil power was very evident, and there were great fears that all the bulwarks of order would yield to the strain. The neglect of the ministers to arrest Wilkes as an outlaw when he first appeared in England, and the complete impunity of those who in broad daylight had rescued him from the officers of justice, and conducted him in triumph through London and Westminster, emboldened the mob as much as the tragedy of St. George's Fields exasperated them. The City constables were so few that in the course of the election London was almost unprotected, nearly the whole available force being collected at Brentford. It was doubtful whether even the soldiers could be fully trusted. Some regimental drummers were said to have beaten their drums for Wilkes. A soldier was heard exclaiming in the very Court of King's Bench that he at least would never fire upon his fellow-countrymen; and it was rumoured that if Wilkes were suffered to take his seat in Parliament, his first measure would be to move that, on account of the increased price of provisions, the pay of the soldiers should be raised. Lord Mansfield may have listened too much to his constitutional timidity when he said that unless some vigorous measures were promptly taken, there would be a rebellion in ten days; and Franklin no doubt exaggerated when he said that if Wilkes had possessed a good character and the King a bad one, Wilkes would have driven George III. from the throne; but it is at least certain that the state of England was very alarming. From the beginning of the reign the growing violence of the mobs and the growing weakness of the law had been ominously displayed. Thus in 1763, when an attempt was made to abolish the system of admitting to the theatres at half-price after the third act, the great theatres of Drury Lane and Covent Garden were completely wrecked; every seat and ornament within them was destroyed; the rioters even tried to cut down the pillars on which the gallery of Covent Garden Theatre rested, and they did all this with complete impunity.[2] In two successive

---

[1] *Annual Register*, 1769, p. 116.
[2] *Annual Register*, 1763, pp. 52-58. It is remarkable that the Drury Lane riots were instigated and in part de-

years we find a man who was exposed on the pillory killed by the ill-treatment of the mob.¹ An attempt to rescue a criminal who, in 1763, was condemned for rape, was so formidable that, in spite of the intervention of the military, it was not till near eight in the evening that the authorities could carry out the sentence;² and it was rarely thought safe to execute a criminal at Tyburn without the protection of a military force.³ The number of disbanded soldiers and sailors without any means of subsistence after the peace, greatly added to the evil, and the watchmen were so utterly helpless that Parliament in despair offered a reward of 40*l.* for the apprehension of every robber. The result was a revival of a practice which had appeared in England in the last reign. A confederation of five men employed themselves partly in inducing impoverished wretches to commit robberies, in order to obtain the reward for their conviction, and partly in falsely accusing innocent persons. In a few months they in this manner obtained more that 960*l.*, and most of their victims were in the grave when the hideous crime was discovered.⁴

The Middlesex election took place at a time of great distress and commercial depression. I have already noticed the bad harvest of 1767, the disturbances it produced, and the embargo which was imposed on the export of corn. The following winter was extremely rigorous, and the distress among the workmen in London was so great that the King, at the petition of the City of London, agreed to shorten the Court mourning for the Duke of York.⁵ Strikes were very numerous, and London was full of poor, idle, reckless men prepared for the most desperate enterprise. Six thousand weavers were the most active agents in the Wilkes riots. Four thousand sailors

---

fended by anonymous writings of Philip Francis—his first known compositions in print.—Parkes and Merivale's *Life of Francis*, i. 68, 69.

¹ *Annual Register*, 1762, p. 75; 1763, p. 67; for another instance of a culprit being killed by ill-usage in the pillory, see *Annual Register*, 1780, p. 207.

² *Grenville Papers*, ii. 193. *Annual Register*, 1763, p. 96.

³ *Annual Register*, 1765, p. 58.

⁴ This case is briefly noticed in the *Annual Register* of 1762, p. 75: for a further account see a remarkable essay on capital punishments in England in the *Anthologia Hibernica*, iv. 172. It is a curious illustration of the absurdity of British law that it was found that none of these criminals could be executed, as their offence only amounted to perjury. One of them was killed by the mob on the pillory.

⁵ Holt's *George III.* i. 149, 156.

on board the merchant ships in the Thames mutinied for higher wages, and stopped by force all outward-bound ships which were preparing to sail.¹ The watermen of the Thames, the journeymen hatters, the journeymen tailors, the glass-grinders, were soon on strike, and during two or three years London witnessed scenes of riot that could hardly have been surpassed in Connaught or the Highlands. At Wapping and Stepney the coalheavers, who were chiefly Irish, were for more than a year at war with the masters of the coal ships. They boarded the ships and compelled the sailors to cease from work. They kept guard at every landing-place to prevent them from receiving supplies of provisions; they obliged them to keep watches as if they were in an enemy's country, and fought bloody battles with the sailors in the streets. A man named Green, who was agent of one of the London aldermen, was especially obnoxious to them, and one evening at eight o'clock his house was besieged by a party provided with fire-arms. Green having barricaded his door, defended himself, with the assistance of a sailor and of a maid-servant, for no less than nine hours. Eighteen of the assailants were shot; two hundred bullets were lodged in one of the rooms of the house. At last, when his ammunition was expended, Green succeeded in escaping, but it was not until five in the morning that the Guards appeared upon the scene. A few days later the sister of Green was attacked in her house, dragged into the street, and murdered.² Riots not less serious and still more persistent were caused by the Spitalfields weavers, who were accustomed during 1767 and the three following years to range through the streets disguised and armed, breaking into the shops of weavers who refused to strike, destroying their looms, and cutting their work in pieces. Many were killed or wounded in conflicts with the soldiers. A law was passed making the offence capital; but soon after, more than a hundred and fifty looms were destroyed in two nights. Two 'cutters' were hanged under the new law, but a man named Clarke, who had been a chief witness against them, afterwards fell into the hands of a mob of more than two thousand persons, and in the full daylight, in one of the fields near Bethnal Green,

¹ *Annual Register*, 1768, p. 105.
² Walpole's *Memoirs of George III.* iii. 219-221. *Annual Register*, 1768, pp. 99, 114, 119, 129.

he was deliberately stoned to death. The tragedy lasted for two hours, during which the wretched man vainly implored his murderers to shoot him and put him out of his agonies.[1]

These were but the more conspicuous instances of a spirit of insubordination and of violence which was shown in many forms and in many parts of the country, and was everywhere encouraged by the manifest impotence of authority. Ordinary crime had greatly increased. 'Housebreaking in London,' it was said, 'was never known to be so frequent; seldom a night passing but some house or other was entered and robbed.'[2] The tone of manners was very savage, and several crimes occurred about this time which, though they can only be regarded as instances of extreme individual depravity, and had no real connection with the general disturbance of society, heightened the impression, and sent a thrill of horror through the country. Thus, in 1767, a journeyman shoemaker named Williamson, who had married a half-witted girl for her money, was proved to have bound her daily to a post in her room, handcuffed her, hung her at times so tightly that only her toes could touch the ground, and thus slowly starved her to death. Eighty thousand persons are said to have been present at his execution, and it was with great difficulty that he could be kept out of the hands of the crowd, who desired to tear him limb from limb.[3] In Fetter Lane—one of the most crowded thoroughfares of London—Mrs. Brownrigg and her son, for the space of two years, subjected their apprentices to ill-usage so horrible that after the lapse of a century it is still popularly remembered. The wretched girls were stripped naked, scourged for the slightest offence till the blood streamed from their wounds, tied to a staple in the wall, beaten on the head till every feature was disfigured, flung into a coal-hole to sleep, famished till they could

---

[1] *Annual Register*, 1767, pp. 139, 140, 152, 158; 1768, pp. 139, 157; 1769, pp. 111, 124, 132, 136, 138; 1771, p. 96.

[2] *Annual Register*, 1770, p. 78. Accurate statistics of the crime of housebreaking in London and Westminster may be found in *Parl. Hist.* xvi. 930. Between Michaelmas 1769 and March 14, 1770, no less than 104 houses were broken open and robbed. In 1772 a writer in the *Annual Regis-ter* (p. 80) emphatically said, 'Villany is now arrived at such a height in London that no man is safe in his own house.' And it was noticed that in 1759 and 1760, two years of war, the number of criminals condemned at the Old Bailey was only 29; while during the two last years of peace, 1770 and 1771, the number had risen to 151. *Annual Register*, 1772, pp. 144, 145.

[3] *Annual Register*, 1767, pp. 48, 49.

scarcely stand. One of them after two months of suffering succeeded in escaping; another, covered with wounds and attenuated by hunger, at last gave evidence against her tormentors; the third died in agonies from ill-treatment. The chief culprit was executed amid the wild delight of the mob, who, as she was driven to the gallows, ran by the side of the coach shouting to the chaplain to pray for her damnation.[1] In 1771, an informer fell into the hands of a gang of criminals, who tied a red-hot pair of tongs around his neck, put burning coals into his clothes, and then thrust his head into a fire. In the same year a woman was scourged through the most crowded part of London as far as Temple Bar for having decoyed young children from their parents, blinded them, and then employed them as beggars.[2]

The general election of 1768 made very little change in the strength and disposition of parties, and the interest of the nation was almost wholly concentrated on the contest in Middlesex. To later generations, however, this interest is less exclusive, for it was at this election that Charles Fox first entered the House of Commons, and that Horace Walpole, to whom we have hitherto been indebted for our fullest accounts of parliamentary proceedings, to the great loss of subsequent historians, gave up his seat

Several months elapsed, during which Wilkes lay in prison, and it was hoped that the popular excitement would die away. The Government had become more and more disorganised. The removal of Sir Jeffrey Amherst from the Governorship of Virginia was intended to replace, in a time of great colonial difficulty, a non-resident by a resident governor, but it excited much notice because Amherst had been appointed by Chatham, and was one of his favourite officers, and because he was succeeded by Lord Bottetort, one of the avowed followers of Bute. The resignation—it might almost be called the expulsion—of Shelburne in October 1768 was still more significant, and a few days later Chatham himself resigned. His health and nerves seemed hopelessly disordered. Though incapable of giving any continuous attention to public affairs, he was able to perceive

---

[1] *Annual Register*, 1767, pp. 117–121, 190–197.

[2] Ibid. 1771, p. 65. *Gentleman's Magazine*, 1771, p. 232.

that the ministry were diverging greatly from his policy, and he resented the removal of Amherst and Shelburne. He accordingly wrote to the King in a strain that admitted of no refusal, and he was succeeded as Lord Privy Seal by Lord Bristol. The King's friends were continually becoming more powerful. In the ministry Grafton, sick of his positio , careless of politics, and panting only for freedom, was chiefly occupied in obtaining a divorce from his wife. The King was resolved upon the expulsion of Wilkes, and Lord North, as his representative, urged it upon the ministry; but although he soon induced Grafton to consent, the opposition of Conway, Granby, Hawke, and Camden, during the first session, delayed the decision.[1] In December, Cooke, who was the other member for Middlesex, died; Serjeant Glynn, who had recently distinguished himself as the defender of Wilkes, was set up as the popular candidate, and in spite of all the efforts of the Court and of the ministry, he won the seat. The election, like the preceding one, was very riotous; a man named Clarke, who was on the popular side, lost his life, and two men who belonged to the Court faction were tried for murder and found guilty. The verdict was received by the assembled crowd with an explosion of brutal joy, but it was afterwards shown conclusively that Clarke had been suffering from a disease which might have caused his death, and to the great indignation of the populace, the condemned men were pardoned. Wilkes did everything in his power to fan the flame. He accused Mansfield, in a petition to the House of Commons, of a gross irregularity in his trial in 1763. He accused Webb, the preceding Secretary of the Treasury, of having bribed a printer to give evidence against him; and having obtained a copy of the official letter of Lord Weymouth to the magistrates before the riot in St. George's Fields, he at once sent it to the 'St. James's Chronicle,' with a brief but violent note charging the ministry with having deliberately 'planned and determined upon' 'the horrid massacre of St. George's Fields,' and shown 'how long a hellish project can be brooded over by some infernal spirits without one moment's remorse.' The Government resolved to

---

[1] Walpole's *Memoirs of George III.* iii. 200, 277, 316.

take notice of this letter. The natural course would have been to bring it before the law courts, and if this was not done it was then for the House of Lords alone to resent an insult directed against one of its members. Lord Barrington, however, brought the letter before the House of Commons, which, assuming the functions of a law court, at once voted it a libel. Wilkes, upon being summoned, immediately acknowledged the authorship, claimed the thanks of the country for having exposed 'that bloody scroll,' and calmly remarked that 'he was only sorry he had not expressed himself upon that subject in stronger terms, and that he would certainly do so whenever a similar occasion should present itself.'[1] The Government then resolved to take the step about which they had so long hesitated, and on February 3, 1769, on the motion of Lord Barrington, Wilkes was expelled from Parliament on the ground of his three offences: the forty-fifth number of the 'North Briton,' the volume of obscene poetry, and the preface to the letter of Lord Weymouth.

George Grenville, who had taken so prominent a part in the early measures against Wilkes, but whose profound knowledge of constitutional law was seldom at fault, opposed this expulsion in a speech which was afterwards published at length, and which is the most favourable remaining specimen of his talents. He had no difficulty in showing that the resolution of the House was equally unconstitutional and impolitic. Three distinct charges were combined in one resolution, and it was quite possible that if the House had voted upon them separately, it would have pronounced each of them insufficient to justify the expulsion. For the forty-fifth number of the 'North Briton' Wilkes had been expelled by a previous Parliament, and there was nothing more certain in parliamentary law than that expulsion by one Parliament did not exclude a politician from the next When Walpole was expelled from Parliament for alleged corruption, though he was not allowed again to sit in that Parliament, his election after the next dissolution was not only unopposed but unquestioned. The obscene poems had been written five years

---

[1] The words—which are not in the abstract of Wilkes' speech in the Parliamentary debates—were quoted by G. Grenville in the very remarkable speech he afterwards made and corrected on the subject of the expulsion.—See Almon's *Collection of Scarce and Interesting Tracts*, iii. 31, 32.

before. Wilkes was already expiating the offence in prison. They were in no respect an offence against the House, and a former House of Commons, violently hostile to Wilkes, had not thought fit to make them a ground of expulsion. The preface to Lord Weymouth's letter had been voted a libel, but it was not an offence against a member of the Lower House; it had not been brought before the law courts, and Blackstone, who was the chief legal defender of the ministerial policy, acknowledged that by itself it was no adequate reason for expulsion. The imprisonment of Wilkes would, it is true, incapacitate him for many months from discharging his duties in Parliament, but this imprisonment could not be regarded as a fresh crime, and it was quite certain that a mere inability to discharge parliamentary duties did not justify expulsion. Windham, while still a Member of Parliament, had been for more than two years in the Tower when the Habeas Corpus Act was suspended, and other members had been sent for long periods from London in the army or navy. It was added, too, that it was tolerably clear that the contest would not end with the expulsion of Wilkes. He would at once be re-elected, and the House would be thus confronted with a constitutional question of the gravest kind.

The warning was disregarded. The expulsion was carried by 219 to 137. On February 16 Wilkes was unanimously re-elected, and on the 17th the House, on the motion of Lord Strange, voted that having been expelled he was incapable of sitting in that Parliament.

It is now generally acknowledged that this step was a distinct breach of the law. Whatever might be the injustice, whatever might be the impolicy of the first expulsion, the legal right of the House of Commons to expel an offending member was indisputable. But it was one thing to expel. It was quite another thing to disqualify. The first lay within the province of the House of Commons alone. The second could only be done by Act of Parliament. It was indeed true that the power of expulsion might be reduced to insignificance if the expelled person were immediately sent back by his constituents to the House. It was true that the incapacity the House pretended to create extended only to the existing House of Commons and would be terminated by a dissolution. It was true that it might be very reasonably argued that it was a great evil if the House of Commons should have no means of excluding from its walls a man who had outraged decency or systematically obstructed business, if his constituents approved of his conduct or if he happened to be the proprietor of a nomination borough. In the quiet days of George II. the constituencies would probably have acquiesced in the Wilkes decision as placidly as they acquiesced in the far graver usurpation of a House of Commons which systematically decided disputed elections by party votes, and thus after every dissolution brought into Parliament many men who were certainly not the real choice of the constituencies. But the days of this tolerance were now over, and a spirit had arisen in the country which watched the proceedings of the House with a jealous scrutiny unknown in the previous reign. Immediately on the declaration of incapacity a large body of the Middlesex gentlemen formed themselves into a society for defending the cause of the constituencies. On March 16 there was a new election at Brentford, and Wilkes was again put forward and again unanimously elected. A merchant named Dingley desired to oppose him, but could find no freeholder to second him, and was driven by violence from the hustings. Next day the House again pronounced the election void. Colonel Luttrell, the son of Lord Irnham, was then induced to vacate his seat in Parliament and to stand in opposition to the popular favourite. He was a young officer of the Guards, in no way connected with Middlesex, and his chief recommendation was his courage. The interference was indeed deemed so dangerous that his life was insured at Lloyd's Coffee-house, and the chances of his surviving the contest became a favourite subject of bets. The election, however, contrary to expectation, was a very orderly one, the popular party being resolved to show that without any violence they could command an immense majority. Wilkes obtained 1,143 votes, Luttrell 296, and a lawyer named Whitaker, who had thrust himself into the contest, 5. After the poll a number of horsemen with colours flying and music playing, attended by several thousand people, went through St. James's Street and the Strand and over London Bridge to congratulate Wilkes, and that night London was illuminated. On the 14th the election of Wilkes was again pronounced void. On the 16th, after a long debate and by a majority of only 197 to 143, Luttrell was declared duly elected. A petition against the return was speedily signed, and it was argued in the House on May 8. After a debate of great power the election was confirmed by 221 to 152. Next day, amid a storm of popular insult, the King drove to Westminster to close the session.[1]

Wilkes had lost his seat, but he had no reason to regret the issue of the struggle. Few of the most illustrious English statesmen have enjoyed a greater or a more enduring popularity or have exercised a more commanding power. When in April 1770 he was released from prison London was illuminated for joy, and the word 'liberty' in letters three feet high, blazed on the front of the Mansion House. In spite of all the efforts of the Court he was elected successively alderman and sheriff, and after a fierce struggle which lasted for three years, Lord Mayor, and then once more member of Parliament, and he governed with an almost absolute sway that City influence which was still one of the great forces in English politics. His old action against Lord Halifax, which had been suspended by his outlawry, was resumed. He obtained 4,000*l.* damages, and would probably have obtained more had it not been discovered during the trial that Grenville had in the earlier stages of the action promised Lord Halifax that in case of defeat his expenses should be paid by the Treasury. In addition to the cost of the election, a sum of about 20,000*l.* was raised by subscription to pay his debts, and provide him with a competence; and gifts, legacies, and testimonials poured in upon him from many quarters. He had also done more than any other single man to unite a divided and powerless Opposition, and to mark out the lines of political parties. The doctrine that a resolution of the House of Commons can neither 'make, alter, suspend, abrogate, nor annihilate the law of the land,' became the rallying cry of the party. Grenville on this question cordially concurred with Rockingham. Temple and Chatham were reconciled in 1769, and in the May of that year Temple wrote to Lady Chatham,

[1] Walpole's *Memoirs of George III.* iii. *Annual Register*, 1769. *Parl. Hist.* xvi.

'Things tend apace to coalition among us.'[1] A violent attack of gout at last restored the troubled nerves of Chatham. In September 1769 he appeared unexpectedly at the King's levee; and when Parliament met in the following January, he took his place among the peers, and with an eloquence as powerful as that of his early days he denounced the unconstitutional measure that had taken place, and endeavoured to lead the House of Lords to the rescue of the constitution.

The debates that took place during several years on the Middlesex election brought into clear relief the conflicting doctrines about the relations between members and their constituencies, and, notwithstanding the great length to which they were protracted, the really essential arguments may be condensed in a small space. Blackstone, who was a member of the House, was put forward to defend the Government. He maintained that while a general incapacity to sit in the House of Commons can only be created by Act of Parliament, an incapacity limited to a single Parliament may be created by the House of Commons alone. This, it was said, is involved in the power of expulsion which it was admitted that the House possessed, and which without this addition would be absolutely nugatory, and it was established by the case of Walpole, who was expelled for alleged corruption, re-elected, and then declared incapable of sitting in that Parliament. It is remarkable that while Walpole and his friends complained bitterly that this expulsion was due to a purely factious combination, there is not the smallest reason to believe that they ever questioned the doctrine that it incapacitated the expelled member from sitting till after the dissolution. If indeed that doctrine were discarded, the right of expulsion would only expose the House to perpetual degradation and insult, for a large number of the members were as completely masters of their boroughs as of their estates, and they might, therefore, safely set the House at defiance. Several precedents, more or less applicable, might be discovered in the stormy period between 1642 and 1660, but the case of Walpole was the one undoubted instance since the Revolution of an expelled member being at once re-

[1] *Chatham Correspondence,* iii. 358.

elected, and Walpole was pronounced, on account of his expulsion, incapable of sitting in that Parliament.[1]

The Opposition, on the other hand, maintained that to be eligible as member of Parliament was the common right of all British subjects; that incapacities annulling, suspending, or abridging this common right can only be created by Act of Parliament; that, as a matter of fact, they had been so created, for the law enumerated and defined the several kinds of incapacity, and that it was completely beyond the competence of one branch of the Legislature by its sole action to change the law. Sir Edward Coke and other authorities had, it is true, laid down that as every court of justice has laws and customs for its direction, so there is a *lex et consuetudo parliamenti* which must be gathered out of the records and precedents of the two Houses and which forms part of the unwritten law of the land. But this 'law and custom of Parliament' can only exist when, in the absence of any provision of the statute law, it is possible to point to a long, uniform, and unchallenged series of parliamentary precedents. Were it otherwise the consequences would be of the most dangerous description, for it is certain that in the course of its long and turbulent history each House had often and in many directions transgressed its just limits. It was surely absurd to go to the anarchy of the Great Rebellion for legal precedents, and the case of Walpole could be of little real service to the ministry. The resolution incapacitating him alleged 'that having been expelled this House for a high breach of trust in the execution of his office and notorious corruption when Secretary of War, he was incapable of being re-elected a member to serve in the present

---

[1] In 1698 Mr. Wollaston being a collector of duties was 'expelled' from the House in obedience to a law which had recently disqualified those who held that office from sitting, and having given up the office he was re-elected and allowed to sit. The partisans of Wilkes maintained that this was a valid precedent, while his opponents thought the word 'expelled' was in this case improperly used by the Commons. The case was at least not one of penal expulsion. See a long discussion of it in 'A Fair Trial of the Important Question,' Almon's *Scarce and Interesting Tracts*, vol. iii. In 1715 Sergeant Comyns having refused to take the oath of qualification, the House determined that the votes given to him were lost, and gave the seat to the candidate who stood next on the poll; and in 1727 they adopted a similar course in a case where the elected person being a Commissioner of Customs was disqualified. In both of these cases however, there was a statutory disqualification.—See Belsham's *Hist. of George III.* i. 242-243.

Parliament.' The cause of the expulsion was thus cited, and it was a cause which might possibly justify the exclusion. The resolution incapacitating Wilkes assigned no reason except his expulsion by the House. The resolution incapacitating Walpole was passed at the petition of the rival candidate, but the House refused to give that candidate the seat, and no member sat for the borough of Lynn till after the dissolution. The House of Commons of George III. pronounced the candidate who had the smaller number of votes to be member for Middlesex. It was added that the Whig doctrine that the resolution of one House cannot create a disability, was maintained by no one more clearly than by Blackstone himself, who in his own 'Commentaries' had declared that to be capable of election to Parliament was the common right of all British subjects, and who had given a full enumeration of the legal incapacities which alone could bar this right.[1]

When the subject passed into the House of Lords, however, it was argued on somewhat different grounds, and the Government rallied chiefly upon a doctrine which was propounded by Lord Mansfield in a speech of extraordinary subtlety and power. He began by positively refusing to express any opinion about the legality of the decision which had been arrived at by the House of Commons. 'My sentiments about it,' he said, 'are locked in my own breast and shall die with me.' He would only say that 'whenever the statute law is silent he knew not where to look for the law of Parliament except in the proceedings and decisions of each House respectively.' He added that declarations of law made by either House of Parliament had always bad effects, for they had the semblance of legislative acts whereas they had no real legal force or validity. If either House as a legislative body thought fit to declare a particular doctrine to be law, he as a judge would pay no attention whatever to its declaration. But though the House of Commons had no power of laying down authoritatively general principles of law, it had a legal right of trying and deciding particular cases without appeal. Each House was not only a legislative assembly, it was also a judicial body, supreme in its own pro-

---

[1] The passage was altered in later editions.

vince, and all questions touching the seats of the Lower House could be decided by that House alone. Its decision was final, for there was no other court in which they could be tried. The judges might be corrupt, the sentences might be erroneous, but the determination must be received and submitted to as the law of the land, for no existing body was competent to question or reverse it. The law might no doubt be changed by an Act of Parliament, in which of course the Lower House must concur, but as long as it was not changed, the judicial decision of the Commons on a question touching elections to their House was absolute and final. 'If they determined wilfully wrong it was iniquitous indeed, and in the highest degree detestable; but it was a crime of which no human tribunal could take cognisance, and it lay between God and their conscience.' By the constitution of the country the House of Lords had no right to offer any advice to the Sovereign on the subject or in any way to discuss, question, or impugn the judgment of the House of Commons on a matter which lay within the proper judicial province of that body.

The speech of Chatham in reply to these arguments was one of his greatest efforts, and considering the subtlety and delicacy of the distinctions discussed it gives a very high idea of his power, not only as an orator, but also as a political thinker and as a debater. The danger, indeed, of the doctrine of Mansfield was of the gravest kind. What limit could be put to the usurpations of a body which was itself the sole judge of its own privileges, which, by asserting in a judicial proceeding a power beyond the law, could establish that power without appeal, and was thus able under pretence of declaring the law to make the law? Every judicial body must indeed be vested with the powers and privileges necessary for performing the office for which it is appointed, but no court of justice can have a power inconsistent with or paramount to the known laws of the land. The representatives of the people were the trustees of the people, receiving from the people certain defined powers, and they could not abuse those powers more grossly than when they extended them beyond the limits of the law for the purpose of invading the rights of those from whom they were derived. That which distinguishes constitutional government from blank despotism is that no individual or corporation within it is above the law. This was the meaning of the great conflict of the Revolution, when the doctrine of passive obedience was exploded, when our kings were obliged to confess that their title to the throne and the rule of their government had no other foundation than the known law of the land. But now this doctrine of passive obedience and of a power beyond the law was revived in favour of what was called the popular branch of the Legislature. 'What is this mysterious power undefined by law, unknown to the subject, which we must not approach without awe or speak of without reverence, which no man may question, but which all men must obey?' It is evident that it contained a germ of tyranny fatal to the very idea of constitutional government, and that it would make the House of Commons much less the representative than the ruler of the people. It was said that the Lords had no right to interfere even by the expression of an opinion. On the contrary, to do so was their bounden duty. As mediators between the King and the people it was for them to submit to the King the causes of the discontents of his people. As one of the three powers whose concurrence was necessary to every change of law, it was for them to protest when the law had been virtually changed without their assent. As hereditary guardians of the British constitution, descendants of the barons who had extorted the Great Charter, it was for them to sound the warning when the constitution was invaded. 'Where law ends, tyranny begins.' The attempt of one branch of the Legislature to pass beyond the limits that were assigned to it, and to place itself in the discharge of any of its functions above the law of the land, is an act of revolution, an act of treason against the constitution. The House of Commons, by confusing the province of jurisdiction with that of legislation, by asserting what was virtually a sole power of altering or making the law, by invading the chartered rights which lay at the very heart of British liberty, had been guilty of such an act. The particular instance might appear to some of little moment, but the claim which was advanced extended to a complete subversion of the Constitution. If no other power might even protest against the decision of the House of Commons on any matter relating to elections, that House might by an arbitrary declaration transfer or extinguish the franchises of great bodies of their constituents, change the whole law of election, and annul Acts of Parliament that had been carried for the express purpose of securing the rights of electors. Rather than that such a claim should be acquiesced in, extreme remedies should be resorted to; but it was one of the great advantages of a mixed Government that it did much to make such remedies unnecessary, for each part had a great power of restraining the aberrations of the others. The balance of the constitution was now disturbed, and it was the duty of the House of Lords to aid in restoring it. They were asked to affirm by a solemn resolution the true doctrine of electoral rights, to petition for the dissolution of a House of Commons which had violated the constitution, and to lead the way in a struggle for such a measure of parliamentary reform as would place the representative body in harmony with its constituents.

In addition to these arguments, another doctrine of a very extreme and indeed revolutionary kind was propounded by the popular party. They contended that the introduction of a single illegitimate element into the representative body was sufficient to invalidate all its proceedings, even in cases where the withdrawal or transfer of one vote would make no difference in the decision. In the words of Junius, 'If any part of the representative body be not chosen by the people, that part vitiates and corrupts the whole.' 'The arbitrary appointment of Mr. Luttrell invades the foundations of the laws themselves, as it manifestly transfers the right of legislation from those whom the people have chosen to those whom they have rejected.' The authority of Locke, who was generally regarded as the almost classical exponent of the principles of parliamentary government as established at the Revolution, was cited in favour of this doctrine. 'Governments,' he wrote, ' are dissolved from within when the Legislative is altered. The constitution of the Legislative is the first and fundamental act of society. . . . When any one or more shall take upon them to make laws whom the people have not appointed so to do, they make laws without authority, which the people are not therefore bound to obey.'[1] Neither Chatham nor Burke appears to have asserted this doctrine, but it was strongly maintained in one House by Shelburne, who was usually in alliance with Chatham, and in the other by Sir George Savile, who was one of the most respected members of the Rockingham party, and it formed the burden of numerous addresses and petitions.[2] To a practical politician it may perhaps be sufficient to say that if it were rigidly applied it would have invalidated every Act of Parliament upon the Statute Book.

Independently of the question immediately at issue, the Middlesex election was extremely important from the impulse it gave to political agitation outside the House of Commons. There was at first some slight hesitation as to the form which the pressure of public opinion on the members should assume, and in a few cases instructions were sent by constituencies to their members, but it was soon agreed, in accordance with the urgent representations of Burke,[3] that petitions to the King were likely to be most efficacious. About seventeen counties,[4] and many cities and boroughs, sent up addresses to the Throne, complaining that the rights of freeholders had been violated, and in most cases petitioning for a dissolution. Great efforts were made to procure counter addresses, but only the universities, four counties, and three or four cities responded, and the preponderance of opinion against the Government appeared enormous. A meeting summoned in the City to support the Government was attended by not more than thirty persons, and was soon broken up in confusion by the mob. Some of the merchants signed an address of confidence to the King, and went in a cavalcade to present it, but they were attacked on their way, and it was only after a struggle of some hours that a small remnant succeeded in reaching the palace. In the meantime a hearse with four horses, followed by a long tumultuous procession, and bearing escutcheons representing the murder of Allen and the murder of Clarke, was drawn

---

[1] Locke on *Government*, book ii. ch. xix.
[2] Fitzmaurice's *Life of Shelburne*, ii. 205.
[3] *Burke's Correspondence*, i. 169, 176, 177, 184, 189, 235.
[4] *Annual Register*, 1770, pp. 56– 58. Chatham says fifteen counties petitioned, and that 'these fifteen petitioning counties contain more people than all the rest of the kingdom, as they pay infinitely more land tax.'— *Chatham Correspondence*, iv. 169.

through the Strand to St. James's Palace, to Carlton House, to Cumberland House, and to the residence of Lord Weymouth. The railings of the palace were defended with difficulty; many conspicuous persons were insulted, and the white staff of Lord Talbot was broken in his hand. Five rioters taken in the act were reserved for prosecution, but the grand jury refused to find a true bill against them.[1] The manifest partiality of juries was one of the most alarming symptoms of the time, and one of the chief encouragements to the prevailing violence.[2] For months Luttrell was unable to appear in the streets.[3] A man was arrested in the act of posting up a supposed speech of Oliver Cromwell when he drove the members of the Long Parliament out of their House.[4] In July 1769 the Duke of Bedford having imprudently gone to Exeter to receive some local honours, was attacked in the cathedral, and obliged to escape by a private way into the bishop's palace. At Honiton he was assailed with stones, bull-dogs were let loose at him, and his life was in serious danger.[5] Language breathing all the violence of revolution had become habitual. Barré said in Parliament that disregard to petitions 'might teach the people to think of assassination.'[6] A silver goblet was presented to Wilkes by the Court of Common Council when he was elected sheriff, and he chose as the subject of ornamentation the death of Cæsar, with an inscription from Churchill,

> May every tyrant feel
> The keen deep searchings of a patriot steel.

Alderman Townsend, one of the most active of the City politicians, refused to pay the land tax on the ground that the

---

[1] *Annual Register*, 1769, pp. 84, 87. Walpole's *Memoirs of George III.* iii. 350–353.

[2] The King writing to Lord North complained bitterly of 'the factious and partial conduct of the grand jury,' and added, ' if there be no means by law to quell riots, and if juries forget they are on their oath to be guided by facts not faction, this constitution must be overthrown, and anarchy (the most terrible of all evils) must ensue.'— *Correspondence of George III. and Lord North*, i. 8. The ministers described ' the unhappy disposition of the people to be such that juries, under the influence of the general infatuation, could hardly be got to do justice to soldiers under prosecution.'—*Annual Register*, 1769, p. 62. According to Walpole, ' In the hands of a Middlesex jury at that time no man's life was safe.'—*Memoirs of George III.* iii. 312.

[3] Ibid. iii. 359.

[4] See Cavendish, *Debates*, i. 101.

[5] Walpole, p. 378. *Annual Register*, 1769, pp. 117, 118.

[6] Walpole, iv. 37.

Parliament which imposed it was an illegal one, and he actually brought the case before the Court of King's Bench.

In July 1769 the Lord Mayor and Livery of London presented an address to the King arraigning the whole conduct of his ministers as subversive of the Constitution, on which alone the relation between the House of Brunswick and its subjects depends; and in the following March they presented a new remonstrance, couched in language such as had perhaps never before been used by a public body to its sovereign, except in the course or upon the eve of a revolution. 'Under the same secret and malign influence,' they said, 'which through each successive administration has defeated every good and suggested every bad intention, the majority of the House of Commons have deprived your people of their dearest rights. They have done a deed more ruinous in its consequences than the levying of ship-money by Charles I., or the dispensing power assumed by James II., a deed which must vitiate all the future proceedings of this Parliament, for the acts of the Legislature itself can no more be valid without a legal House of Commons than without a legal prince upon the throne. . . . Parliament,' they continued, 'is corruptly subservient to the designs of your Majesty's ministers. Had the Parliament of James II. been as submissive to his commands as the Parliament is at this day to the dictates of a minister, instead of clamours for its meeting, the nation would have rung as now with outcries for its dissolution.'[1] It is a remarkable fact that Chatham himself was suspected of having drawn up this document, and that he regarded it with unqualified approbation. The King in his answer described it—surely with great justice—as disrespectful to himself and injurious to his Parliament; but this answer was treated by Chatham and others as a violation of the article of the Bill of Rights which secured to subjects the liberty of petition. The London Livery, undeterred by the rebuff, presented another and scarcely less insolent address, and when the King received it with a few words of disapprobation, the Lord Mayor, Beckford, contrary to all precedent, delivered a long rejoinder, which was composed for him by Horne, and which was afterwards engraven on his statue in the Guildhall, declar-

[1] *Parl. Hist.* xvi. 893, 891.

ing that whoever had alienated his Majesty's affections from his loyal subjects in general and from London in particular was an enemy to his Majesty's person and family, and a betrayer of the constitution 'as it was established at the glorious and necessary Revolution.' On the other hand, both Houses of Parliament supported by large majorities the most violent proceedings and doctrines of the ministers. Lord North was accused of having declared that petitions for a dissolution of Parliament were unconstitutional if not illegal,[1] and the King, laying his hand on his sword, exclaimed, 'Sooner than yield to a dissolution I will have recourse to this.'[2]

There was little or nothing to counterbalance the unpopularity of the Government. In America discontent and disaffection were becoming continually more formidable, and in Europe the authority of England had visibly declined. The heroic struggle which the Corsicans under Paoli had for many years waged against their Genoese oppressors had excited only a languid interest, and in December 1763 a proclamation was issued, forbidding English subjects to assist the 'Corsican rebels;' but when the French purchased the island from Genoa in 1768, disregarded the strong protest of the English ambassador, and crushed all resistance by overwhelming forces, the national jealousy of England became actively sensitive. The well-known book of Boswell greatly added to the interest, and the Duke of Devonshire and some other leading persons subscribed large sums to assist the insurgents. The value of the new acquisition of France was enormously exaggerated by Burke[3] and by many other politicians, and it was absurdly represented as sufficient to turn the balance of power in the Mediterranean. By a strange chance which no human sagacity could have predicted, it proved in truth even more important than was feared, for it made Napoleon Buonaparte a French subject.

Nearly at the same time the question of the Falkland Islands brought England to the verge of a war with Spain.

---

[1] *Parl. Hist.* xvi. 578. He afterwards is said to have explained away his meaning, and it is very probable that he was not quite accurately reported. Lord Egmont in the House of Lords described the petitions as 'treasonable.'—*Chatham Correspondence*, iii. 419.

[2] Walpole's *George III.* iv. 60.

[3] Fitzmaurice's *Life of Shelburne*, ii. 119–124. Burke said, 'Corsica, a French province, was terrible to him.' Cavendish, *Debates*, i. 40.

These islands appear to have been first seen by Davis in 1592, and by Hawkins in 1594, but their present name was only given to them in the reign of William, and no attempt was made to colonise them till Anson described them in his 'Voyage' as valuable in themselves, and especially valuable on account of their nearness to Chili in the event of a Spanish war. In 1748 an English expedition to the Falkland Islands was planned, but Wall, the Spanish ambassador, represented in such strong terms that the Spaniards possessed the exclusive dominion of the South Sea, and would treat any intrusion as an act of war, that the design was relinquished. In 1765, however, it was resumed. Lord Egmont instructed Captain Byron to take formal possession of the Islands in the name of his Britannic Majesty, and in the following year a garrison was established and a small wooden fort erected. The transaction appears to have been at first almost unnoticed, but in 1769 the Spaniards demanded the immediate abandonment of the island which had been occupied, and their demand being disregarded, they next year sent out a powerful expedition, which captured the entire garrison, detained a British frigate for twenty days, and summarily expelled the British from the South Sea. Such an act of violence and insult, following as it did the obstinate refusal of Spain to pay the Manilla ransom, seemed to make war inevitable. At last, however, after much not very dignified negotiation, the Spanish king agreed to disavow the act of his servant and to restore the garrison, maintaining, however, his old claim of right, and receiving, it is said, a verbal assurance that the English would speedily evacuate the island.

These events were not fitted to strengthen an unpopular Government, and a few months after the general election the ministers were compelled to ask for the sum of 513,000*l.* in payment of the debts of the King. In the last reign, certain funds, which were intended to produce 800,000*l.* a year, were appropriated to the Civil List, with the understanding that if they fell below that amount Parliament would supply the deficiency. In the present reign, it was determined to abolish the element of uncertainty, and a fixed annual sum of 800,000*l.* was voted for the Civil List. Besides this, the King possessed considerable revenues which were not within the cognisance of Parliament.

He had inherited a large sum from his economical predecessor, he had the hereditary revenues derived from the Principality of Wales and the Duchy of Cornwall, and he derived something from duties which had been recently imposed by royal prerogative in the new West Indian Islands. It was believed—probably with much truth—that these revenues were amply sufficient for the purposes for which they were intended, and that the debt was due to an expenditure which could not be openly avowed. It was the first of a long series which extended during the whole reign. All parties were prepared to pay it, but the Opposition contended that Parliament should at least receive a detailed account of the manner in which it was incurred, and attempts were unsuccessfully made in both Houses to obtain an inquiry into the state and expenditure of the Civil List.[1]

The personal unpopularity of the Government was also very great, and the weakness of the Prime Minister was especially conspicuous. Grafton, though he is now chiefly remembered as the object of the most savage of all the invectives of Junius, was certainly not destitute of the qualities of a statesman, and he was judged very favourably by some of the ablest of his contemporaries. Chatham, for a time, gave him an unreserved confidence. Conway, in 1770, refused to serve under any other leader. Camden assured him that he would 'rather see him at the head of the Government then than any other man in the kingdom;' and a letter of Charles Fox has been preserved in which that great statesman declared that there was no other chief he would more willingly follow. But his better qualities were all marred and clouded by faults very natural to a young man of great position, strong passions, weak character, and moderate ambition, who, without any of the long apprenticeship of office, and contrary to his own wishes, found himself at the age of thirty-two Prime Minister of England. Had Chatham been able to remain at the helm, Grafton, under his guidance, would probably have won an honourable place in English history; but at the head of a divided Cabinet, surrounded by uncongenial colleagues, outvoted in his Cabinet on important questions, and exposed in

[1] *Annual Register*, 1769, p. 63. *Parl. Hist.* xvi. 813-852.

turn to the outrages of the populace and to the blandishments of the Court, his character and his convictions utterly failed. His notorious indolence, vacillation, and indifference, the contrast between his old friendship with Wilkes and his recent policy, and the careless and undisguised profligacy which led him, on one occasion, when still Prime Minister, to appear publicly at the opera with a well-known courtesan, were all sources of scandal or of weakness. In private life he was esteemed an honourable man, and he had but little of the ambition which is the chief cause of political treachery, but he had abandoned Rockingham, he had abandoned Wilkes, and he was now rapidly abandoning Chatham.

The conduct of two of the most important of his colleagues was scarcely more respectable. One of the most remarkable characteristics of the ministry of Chatham was that it exactly reproduced the old type of divided administrations which prevailed in England immediately after the Revolution. The very idea of a consistent Government policy to which all its members were pledged had almost disappeared, and each minister restricted himself mainly to his own department. This was the inevitable consequence of the manner in which the administration had been formed, and of the withdrawal of the great statesman who alone could have given it a steady and consistent direction. General Conway had been persuaded by Horace Walpole to abandon the Rockingham connection, and to retain under Chatham the position not only of Secretary of War, but even of leader of the House of Commons, in order to exclude Grenville from that post;[1] but already, at a time when Chatham was not yet incapacitated by illness, Horace Walpole assures us that Conway, being offended at the dismissal of Lord Mount Edgecumbe, 'dropped all intercourse with Lord Chatham, and though he continued to conduct the King's business in the House of Commons, he would neither receive nor pay any deference to the minister's orders, acting for or against as he approved or disliked his measures.'[2] It was quite consistent with this beginning that he should still have remained in office when Townshend, by reviving the

---

[1] Walpole's *George III.* ii. 339–341. [2] Ibid. ii. 385.

scheme of American taxation, reversed the policy which, in the Rockingham administration, Conway had done so much to carry into effect. In January 1768, however, four months after the death of Townshend, Conway, partly in consequence of his disapproval of the conduct of the Government towards the Duke of Portland, and partly in consequence of the growing influence of the Bedford faction, resigned the seals of office, but he was actually persuaded by the King to continue 'Minister of the House of Commons,' and member of the Cabinet in the ministry with which, on most points, he was both personally and politically at variance.[1] It was soon made a matter of complaint by the Bedford section of the Government that 'there was no acting with Conway, who always in the House adhered to his own opinion, and would not acquiesce in what was determined in council.'[2] Yet, in spite of all this, he remained Cabinet minister and apparent leader of the House of Commons, and he still retained this position when Chatham returned to active politics, although he entirely agreed with Chatham on the main questions that were in dispute. He appears to have supposed that his personal friendship for Grafton, and the fact that he was drawing no salary, justified his position.

The failure of the Chancellor was equally conspicuous. As a lawyer, Camden was surpassed by no contemporary except Mansfield. In Parliament, some good judges preferred the simple, colloquial, and unstrained lucidity of his style to the subtle and elaborate rhetoric of his great rival,[3] and the strong passion for popularity which sometimes showed itself, if not in the substance at least in the expression of his judgments, gave him a bias in favour of liberty at a time when it was gravely endangered. But Camden, like Grafton, was unfit to stand alone, and on the eclipse of Chatham he sank into insignificance. He saw the whole character of the ministry changed by the growing predominance of that Bedford faction which was most hostile to the policy of Chatham. He saw the Government of which he was a member, pursuing, on the two great questions of American taxation and of the Middlesex

[1] Walpole's *George III.* iii. 118–150.
[2] Ibid. p. 311.
[3] Nicholls' *Recollections of George III.* ii. 128.

election, a course which was directly opposed to his opinions, yet he still remained at his post. He was full of difficulties and irresolution. He did not wish by resigning to throw the Government of the country into confusion, or into hands still more hostile to Chatham and to his policy. He expected the return of Chatham, and till his recovery everything seemed provisional and unsettled. He was attached to Grafton, and a strong personal interest bound him to office. He had risen to the first rank in his profession, and had held the great office of Chief Justice of Common Pleas before he accepted his Chancellorship; but if he now resigned, he sank at once into comparative poverty. There was then no regular retiring pension for an ex-Chancellor, and Camden had nothing to fall back upon but a pension of 1,500*l.* a year, which had been procured for him by Chatham. At one time he appears to have disbelieved in the reality of the illness of Chatham, and he spoke of his former leader with much bitterness.[1] He abandoned London during the Middlesex riots. He withdrew more and more from ministerial business. He was thrown into an agony of distress by the libels which described him as ungrateful to Chatham. He was silent in debate, and often absent from the Cabinet councils. He wished to resign on the resignation of Chatham, but suffered himself to be dissuaded by Grafton. Yet he never protested or even distinctly intimated his opinion. In confidential letters to Grafton he urged the grave political danger of the course which was being pursued about the Middlesex election; but when the question was debated in the Cabinet he withdrew, and Grafton afterwards asserted

---

[1] William Gerard Hamilton wrote to Temple (July 20, 1767), 'The idea of continuing Lord Camden as a friend of Lord Chatham's is extremely entertaining if the accounts which I hear are true, and my authority is such that I have not a doubt of them; and they are that, in all places, the most violent man against Lord Chatham, and the harshest interpreter of his long sickness and of his late conduct in every particular, is Lord Camden.'—*Grenville Papers*, iv. 64. In his private letter to Chatham, written January 2, 1768, Junius said, 'The Chancellor on whom you had particular reasons to rely has played a sort of fast and loose game, and spoken of your lordship with submission or indifference according to the reports he heard of your health, nor has he altered his language until he found you were really returning to town.'—*Chatham Correspondence*, iii. 303. This coincidence has been justly pointed out as one of the many slight indications that Junius was well acquainted with the information then current in Lord Temple's circle.

that the Chancellor had never informed him that the vote of incapacity was contrary to law. Their difference about the policy of the measure had produced a coldness between them, and in the summer of 1769 they appear to have had little intercourse. Finding himself in a minority in the ministry, incapable of influencing its decisions, and unwilling at this time to destroy it by resigning, Camden abstained from giving any opinion to his colleagues, and confined himself to his judicial business. Yet it is certain that he communicated his opinion to Chatham when Chatham had resigned office and was preparing for opposition,[1] and at last, when his old leader reappeared in the House, and denounced the ministerial policy as a violation of the Constitution, the Chancellor, who should naturally have been its foremost defender, arose to express his full concurrence with the attack. 'For some time,' he said, 'I have beheld with silent indignation the arbitrary measures of the ministers. I have drooped and hung down my head in council, and disapproved by my looks those steps which I knew my avowed opposition could not prevent. . . . I now proclaim to the world that I entirely coincide in the opinion expressed by my noble friend, whose presence again reanimates us, respecting the unconstitutional and illegal vote of the House of Commons. . . . By their violent and tyrannical conduct ministers have alienated the minds of the people from his Majesty's Government. . . . A spirit of discontent has spread into every corner of the kingdom, and is every day increasing. If some methods are not devised to appease the clamours so universally prevalent, I know not whether the people, in despair, may not become their own avengers, and take the redress of grievances into their own hands.'

It was impossible that any ministry could permit a Chancellor to continue in office who denounced in such terms the main line of policy of the Cabinet of which he was a member, and nothing could be more uncandid than the language of the Opposition, who described the dismissal of Camden as an unwarrantable interference with judicial liberty, the dismissal of an upright and independent judge, because he had given an

---

[1] See *Grenville Papers,* iv. 402, 405. *Parl. Hist.* xvi. 825. *Adolphus,* i. 410.

opinion in accordance with the law. The whole episode was discreditable in the extreme, and it ought to have been followed by an immediate resignation. It was probably thought, however, that a dismissal would have more effect upon public opinion than a resignation, and Chatham strongly supported the Chancellor in remaining at his post.[1] He was dismissed on January 17, 1770, about a week after his speech.[2] Lord Granby, the popular Commander-in-Chief, took the first opportunity in the House of Commons of declaring that he would always lament the vote he had given in favour of the incapacity of Wilkes as the greatest misfortune of his life, and a few days after he resigned his office. In the minor or ornamental departments of the Administration there were several resignations, which implied a considerable loss of Parliamentary influence. The Dukes of Beaufort and Manchester, the Earls of Coventry and of Huntingdon, gave up their places at the Court. James Grenville, ever faithful to Chatham, resigned his office as Vice-Treasurer of Ireland, and Dunning that of Solicitor-General. On January 28 another and much more important resignation was very unexpectedly announced. Grafton had recanted nothing and modified nothing, and he defended the policy of his Government boldly and ably in the House of Lords,[3] but he was disgusted with his position and with the storm of obloquy around him; he disdainfully threw up his post, refusing to give any specific reason,[4] and retired for a time into private life. Lord North, who was already Chancellor of the Exchequer, was his successor.

The post which was most difficult to fill was that of Chancellor. Mansfield positively refused to exchange his Chief Justiceship for a dignity which was so perilous and so precarious, and Sir

---

[1] *Chatham Correspondence*, iii. 389.

[2] Lord Temple described this episode as 'the dismissal of the virtuous and independent lord who sat on the woolsack, in order to supply his place by some obsequious lawyer who would do as he was commanded.' Lord Shelburne 'hoped there would not be found in the kingdom a wretch so base and mean-spirited as to accept the Seals on the conditions on which they were offered.'—Albemarle's *Life of Rockingham*, ii. 157.

[3] Rigby wrote (May 14, 1770), 'I think the very best speech I ever heard in my life was the Duke of Grafton's reply to Chatham, a very memorable part of which was the most solemn declaration that a man can make in public, never to act again in public business with Lord Chatham.'—*Bedford Correspondence*, iii. 412.

[4] Walpole's *George III.* iv. 87.

Eardley Wilmot, the Chief Justice of Common Pleas, who detested and despised party politics, was equally peremptory in his refusal. The Court had at this moment very little legal ability at its disposal, and the candidate who appeared most suitable was Charles Yorke, a younger son of the great Lord Hardwicke, and brother of one of the most intimate friends of Rockingham. As a very young man, he had gained a considerable literary reputation by a once popular, though now forgotten, book called 'Athenian Letters,' and he had become Solicitor-General before the death of George II., and Attorney-General in the troubled ministry that succeeded. He resigned at last, but only after the proceedings against Wilkes. He then separated himself completely from the party of Bute, but still maintained a somewhat independent line. In the debates that grew out of the Wilkes prosecutions he condemned the principle of general warrants, though contending that they had been frequently employed; but he maintained in opposition to Pitt, and in a speech which extorted the highest eulogy from Walpole, that parliamentary privilege does not extend to cases of libel. In the Rockingham Ministry he was again Attorney-General, and he appeared now completely identified with that party, and resigned his post on the accession of Pitt. With something more than the usual keenness of professional ambition, he combined a very unprofessional sensitiveness of character, and though still in the prime of life, and on the whole an exceedingly prosperous man, he was restless, discontented, morbid, nervous, and vacillating, and the natural infirmities of his temperament were at this time aggravated by ill-health. He had been thought of as Chancellor by Charles Townshend, when that statesman contemplated a secession from Chatham, but on the whole he had remained firmly attached to the Rockingham connection, and had pledged himself to Rockingham and to his brother to decline the post which the Duke of Grafton had offered him. He at first honourably fulfilled his promise; but the King, who was passionately interested in maintaining his Ministry, resolved to interpose, and he exerted all his personal influence to gain his point. His efforts in a private interview were in vain; Yorke, though restless and agitated through disappointed ambition, adhered to his pledge and refused to desert his party, and the negotiation appeared to have terminated. On the next day, however, when he was attending a levee, he was again called into the closet of the King, who renewed with intense earnestness his entreaties. Of the particulars of the interview, we only know that the King appealed to his loyalty as a subject not to abandon him in his distress, that he appealed to his self-interest as a lawyer, intimating to him that if he now refused them, the Seals, which were the highest object of his ambition, would under no possible circumstances be again offered to him, and that he at length succeeded by long persistence in over-bearing his opposition, and, in the words of Lord Hardwicke, 'compelling him' to accept the post. The unhappy man went from the royal cabinet to his brother's house, where he met the leaders of the Opposition. He felt at once the full enormity of what he had done, and fled broken-hearted to his own house. In three days he was a dead man. According to the version circulated by his family, his death was due to natural disease, accelerated by excitement and mental anguish. According to another and more probable account, he died by his own hand. The patent which raised him to the peerage had been made out, and awaited only the impression of the Great Seal. When he was dying, he was asked to authorise that impression, but he refused, and added, with a shudder, that he hoped the Seal was no longer in his custody.[1]

It might have been supposed that by this time, at least, Conway, who still shared most of the sentiments of the Rockingham Whigs, would have perceived that it was his duty to sever himself from the Ministry, but he still for some time continued in the Cabinet. In January 1770, shortly after the death of Yorke, the King offered him the Mastership of the Ordnance, which was vacant by the resignation of Granby. The office was a military, not a political one, but to accept it at this critical moment was evidently to involve himself still further in his connection with the Court. After infinite hesitation he at last arrived at a characteristic compromise, and agreed to discharge the duties of the office without accepting

[1] Harris' *Life of Hardwicke*, iii. 465-479. Campbell's *Chancellors*, vii. 96-112.

the salary. As long as Grafton remained he determined to remain in the Cabinet, and he did his utmost to induce Grafton to remain. The resignation of Grafton at last brought this strange and discreditable scene to an end, and Conway then detached himself from the Administration.[1]

The opposition of Chatham to the Government was at this time of the most violent description, and his language recalls that which he was accustomed to employ in his early contests with Walpole and Carteret. He repeatedly, in different forms, endeavoured to obtain from the Lords a resolution affirming the unconstitutional character of the decision of the Commons about Wilkes. He brought forward a resolution asking for the dissolution of Parliament, and even a Bill for reversing the decision of the Lower House. He denounced the conduct of the Commons in language little less vehement than that of the City remonstrance, and intimated not obscurely that if persisted in it would justify rebellion. Of the conduct of the King, of the King's ministers, and especially of the King's friends, he spoke with scarcely an affectation of reserve. 'These measures,' he said in one of his speeches, 'made a part of that unhappy system which had been formed in the present reign with a view to new model the Constitution as well as the Government. . . . The Commons had slavishly obeyed the commands of his Majesty's servants, and had proved to the conviction of every man, what might have been only matter of suspicion before, that ministers held a corrupt influence in Parliament. It was demonstrable, it was indisputable.'[2] Speaking of his own experience as a minister, he said, in words which read like an echo of those of Grenville and Rockingham: 'I was duped, I was deceived. I soon found that there was no original administration to be suffered in this country. The same secret influence still prevailed which had put an end to all the successive administrations as soon as they opposed or declined to act under it. . . . The obstacles and difficulties which attended every great and public measure did not arise from those out of government. They were suggested, nourished,

---

[1] Walpole's *George III.* iv. 55, 56, 60, 61, 193.

[2] *Chatham Correspondence,* iii. 418.

and supported by that secret influence I have mentioned, and by the industry of those very dependants; first by secret treachery, then by official influence, afterwards in public councils. A long train of these practices has at length unwillingly convinced me that there is something behind the throne greater than the King himself.'[1] In Grafton he expressed himself completely deceived. 'There was in his conduct from the time of my being taken ill, a gradual deviation from everything that had been settled and solemnly agreed to by his Grace both as to measures and men, till at last there were not left two planks together of the ship which had been originally launched.'[2] He strenuously supported an inquiry into the expenditure which had caused the King's debts, intimating very clearly that in his judgment the debts had been incurred in corrupting the representatives, and he asked whether the Sovereign 'means, by drawing the purse-strings of his subjects, to spread corruption through the people, to procure a Parliament like a packed jury, ready to acquit his ministers at all adventures?'[3] When the King made his famous answer rebuking the Corporation of London for the disrespectful language of their petition, Chatham moved a resolution censuring those who had advised the King to give such an answer, on the ground that the legal right of the subject to petition for redress of grievances had been indiscriminately checked and reprimanded.[4] Quoting from Robertson, he reminded the House of Lords how Charles V. had once 'cajoled and seduced' the peers of Castile to join him in overturning that part of the Cortes which represented the people; how 'they were weak enough to adopt, and base enough to be flattered with an expectation that by assisting their master in this iniquitous purpose they would increase their own strength and importance,' and how, as a just and natural consequence, they soon 'exchanged the constitutional authority of peers for the titular vanity of grandees.'[5] He reprobated with the utmost vehemence the patient attitude of the Ministry towards Spain; spoke of that Power in language which could only have been used on the supposition that war with her was inevitable

---

[1] *Chatham Correspondence,* iii. 422.
[2] Ibid. pp. 423, 425
[3] Ibid. pp. 424, 426.
[4] Ibid. p. 453.
[5] Ibid. p. 372.

and desirable, blamed the ministers severely for the neglect into which they had suffered the naval and military services to fall, enumerated in a speech of great power and knowledge the different measures that were required to restore them to efficiency, and at the same time, with his usual independence, denounced the conduct of Wilkes and of the popular party, who by raising an outcry against the system of pressgangs were crippling the strength of the nation.[1]

Chatham at this time took great pains to effect an union with the other Whigs, and especially with Rockingham, and he appears to have become at last sensible of the error he had made in so often discarding or repudiating their assistance. His old distinctive doctrine of the necessity of breaking up parties now disappears. 'There are men who, if their own services were forgotten, ought to have an hereditary merit with the House of Hanover.... I would not wish the favours of the Crown to flow invariably in one channel. But there are some distinctions which are inherent in the nature of things. There is a distinction between right and wrong—between Whig and Tory.... An administration must be popular that it may begin with reputation. It must be strong within itself that it may proceed with vigour and decision.'[2] No sound ministry could be maintained by fraud or even by exclusive systems of family connections or powerful friendships, but at the same time he was careful to add that no one valued more 'that honourable connection which arises from a disinterested concurrence in opinion upon public measures, or from the sacred bond of private friendship and esteem.' Of Rockingham himself, both in public and private, he spoke with deep respect. 'As for Lord Rockingham,' he wrote to Calcraft, 'I have a firm reliance on his zeal for liberty, and will not separate from him.'[3] 'His whole language,' he wrote, in another letter, after an interview with Rockingham, 'was as I expected, honourable, just, and sensible. My esteem and con-

---

[1] *Chatham Correspondence*, iv. 2-18.

[2] Ibid. iv. 17, 18.

[3] Ibid. iii. 439. In one of the last speeches Chatham made (Dec. 5, 1777), there is a remarkable passage which can be construed into little less than a confession that the line which he had adopted about party government in the first years of the reign was a mistake. 'For fifteen years,' he said, 'there had been a system at St. James's of breaking all connections, of extinguishing all principle. A few men had got an ascendency where no man should

fidence in his lordship's upright intentions grow from every conversation with him.'¹ In seconding a motion of Rockingham he took occasion to say that he wished this to be considered as a public demonstration of his cordial union with that statesman. 'There has been a time, my lords,' he added, 'when those who wished well to neither of us, who wished to see us separated for ever, found a sufficient gratification for their malignity against us both. But that time is happily at an end. The friends of this country will, I doubt not, hear with pleasure that the noble lord and his friends are now united with me and mine, upon a principle which, I trust, will make our union indissoluble. . . . No ministerial artifices, no private offers, no secret seduction, can divide us.'²

The picture was somewhat overcoloured. The correspondence of Chatham himself, and the correspondence of Burke, who was the most confidential as he was by far the ablest friend of Rockingham, suffice to show that the jealousy that once divided the two parties was by no means extinct. On the Rockingham side there was some very natural personal resentment, and also a constant fear lest Chatham should resume his old policy of breaking up that strong party organisation which in the opinion of Burke was the sole method of putting an end to the impotence of successive administrations and restraining the influence of the Crown. On the side of Chatham, there was a stronger sympathy with the democratic element in the country, and a proneness to employ stronger language and to resort to more energetic measures than the Rockinghams desired. 'The Marquis,' he wrote in one of his letters, 'is an honest and honourable man, but "moderation, moderation," is

have a personal ascendency; by the executive powers of the State being at their command they had been furnished with the means of creating divisions. This brought pliable men, not capable men, into the highest and most responsible situations, and to such men was the government of this once glorious empire now entrusted.'— Thackeray's *Life of Chatham*, ii. 343.

¹ *Chatham Correspondence*, iii. 481.
² Ibid. p. 408. Lord Fitzwilliam reported to Rockingham, November 1769, a conversation in which Chatham said: 'For my own part I am grown old, and find myself unable to fill any office of business; but this I am resolved upon, that I will not even sit at council but to meet the friends of Lord Rockingham; whatever differences may have been between us they must be forgotten. The state of the nation is such that all private animosities must subside. He, and he alone, has a knot of spotless friends such as ought to govern this kingdom.' See too a similar conversation reported by the Duke of Portland.—Albemarle's *Life of Rockingham*, ii. 142, 143

the burden of the song among the body. For myself I am resolved to be in earnest for the public, and shall be a scarecrow of violence to the gentle warblers of the grove, the moderate Whigs and temperate statesmen.'[1] Still in public the two parties were agreed, and a coalition was formed against the Government which once would have been invincible. As Philip Francis afterwards wrote, 'North succeeded to what I believe he himself and every man in the kingdom at that time thought a forlorn hope.'[2] Chatham, Rockingham, Grenville, and Temple were united under the same banner, while a fever of public opinion had been excited in the country by the Middlesex election which had never been paralleled since the fall of Walpole.

The result was the complete triumph of the Government. The influence of the Court was now so great, and its attractive power so irresistible, that in both Houses it commanded a steady and unflinching majority. The House of Lords, which in the case of the Aylesbury electors under Queen Anne, had obtained a most legitimate popularity by its defence of the rights of electors against the usurpations of the Commons, now carried every resolution of the Ministers by a large majority. It abdicated one of its most important functions by formally declining to take any step in the Middlesex election, on the ground that its interference would be unconstitutional; and for some time, in order to diminish as much as possible the effects of the eloquence of Chatham, it carefully excluded all strangers from its debates. In spite of the coalition of the scattered fragments of the Whig party; in spite of the petitions which poured in from every part of the country against the Government; in spite of America, of Corsica, and of the Falkland Islands; in spite of the manifest decline of the reputation of England, which had recently been so great, and of the naval and military services, which had recently been so efficient, the majority of the Government was unbroken. In Lord North the King had found a servant of admirable tact, ability, and knowledge, and new recruits were speedily obtained. The Great Seal having been placed for

---

[1] *Chatham Correspondence*, iii. 468.
[2] See the autobiographical sketch in Parkes and Merivale's *Life of Francis*, i. 362.

about a year in Commission, was bestowed on Bathurst, who, though an undistinguished lawyer and insignificant politician, held it for more than seven years. Lord Granby, who was the most popular of the recent seceders from the ministry, died in October 1770. George Grenville died in the following month, and three months later, Lord Suffolk, who pretended to lead the Grenville party, abandoned all his former principles, and joined the ministry as Privy Seal. Whately, the most confidential friend of Grenville, took the same course. The chief members of the Bedford faction had already gone over, and the Duke, who had for some time been excluded from public life by blindness and ill-health, died in the beginning of 1771. Sir Edward Hawke was replaced at the Admiralty by Lord Sandwich. Grafton, who had once professed to be the most devoted follower of Chatham, solemnly pledged himself, in a speech in May 1770, never again to act with him in public business,[1] and a year later, when Lord Suffolk, on the death of Halifax, exchanged the office of Privy Seal for that of Secretary of State, he accepted the vacant post, though with the characteristic condition that he should not be required to attend the Cabinet.[2] Thurlow, who was advanced to the position of Attorney-General, showed an amount of legal and debating power which restored the strength of the ministry in the department where it was most weak, and, to the astonishment and scandal even of the corrupt assembly at St. Stephen's, he was soon joined by Wedderburn. This very able Scotchman—one of the ablest and most corrupt of the many able and corrupt lawyers who in the eighteenth century were conspicuous in English politics—though he first entered Parliament under the patronage of Bute, had for some time been one of the most conspicuous of the opponents of the Court. His repeated and eloquent denunciations of the American policy of the Government, his magnificent defence of the rights of electors in the case of the Middlesex election, and his resignation of his borough seat because its patron was opposed to the popular cause, had made him one of the idols of the people. Clive, who was at this time in opposition, at once provided him with a new seat. His name was a favourite toast at the popular banquets. The City of London voted him

[1] *Bedford Correspondence*, iii. 412. [2] *Chatham Correspondence*, iv. 179.

its freedom; Chatham spoke of him with warm admiration, and the Whig party imagined that another Camden had arisen in their ranks. Wedderburn, however, was only working with great shrewdness and more than common effrontery to raise his price, and in January 1771 he concluded a secret negotiation with North by becoming Solicitor-General, justifying himself on the ground that he belonged to the Grenville connection. The Tory party, who in the earlier stages of the Government had given it only a partial and hesitating support,[1] rallied in all their strength around Lord North, while the furious quarrels of the City demagogues divided, weakened, and discredited the popular cause. Though the grievance of the Middlesex election was unredressed, the excitement which had blazed so high in 1768, 1769, and 1770, gradually subsided, and it was followed by a long period of ignoble apathy.

The confidential letters of the leaders of the Opposition are full of complaints of the change that had taken place. 'England at this day,' wrote Chatham in January 1771, 'is no more like Old England or England forty years ago, than the Monsignori of modern Rome are like the Decii, the Gracchi, or the Catos.'[2] 'I do not see,' he afterwards wrote, 'that the smallest good can result to the public from my coming up to the meeting of Parliament. A headlong, self-willed spirit has sunk the City into nothing. . . . The narrow genius of old-corps connection has weakened the Whigs, and rendered national union on revolution principles impossible.'[3] 'The public has slept quietly upon the violation of electors' rights and the tyranny of the House of Commons.'[4] '*Fuit Ilium!* the whole constitution is a shadow.'[5] 'After a violent ferment in the nation,' wrote Burke, 'as remarkable a deadness and vapidity has succeeded.' 'The people have fallen into a total indifference to any matters of public concern. I do not suppose that there was ever anything like

---

[1] See a remarkable passage in one of Dr. Johnson's pamphlets in favour of the Government. 'Every honest man must lament that it [the Government] has been regarded with fixed neutrality by the Tories, who, being long accustomed to signalise their principles by opposition to the Court, do not yet consider that they have at last a king who knows not the name of party, and who wishes to be the common father of all his people.'—*The False Alarm.*

[2] *Chatham Correspondence,* iv. 89.
[3] Ibid. iv. 187.
[4] Ibid. p. 204.
[5] Ibid. p. 259.

this stupor in any period of our history.'[1] 'In the present state of things,' wrote Junius in the last letter he addressed to Woodfall, 'if I were to write again, I must be as silly as any of the horned cattle that run mad through the City, or as any of your wise aldermen. I meant the cause and the public Both are given up. I feel for the honour of this country when I see that there are not ten men in it who will unite and stand together upon any one question. But it is all alike, vile and contemptible.'[2]

Yet the consequences of the struggle that has been recounted were by no means so transient as might be supposed. New questions, new lines of party division, new political forces were called into being, and the condition of the representative body assumed a prominence in English politics which had never before been equalled. At the time of the Revolution the question at issue lay mainly between the Crown and the Parliament, and it was the great effort of Whig statesmen and of the Whig party to check the encroachments of prerogative and to strengthen the popular branch of the Legislature. It was not yet foreseen that Parliament could itself become the oppressor of the people, and that in and through the representative body the Crown could regain a great part of the power which it had lost. 'The power of the Crown,' wrote the great Whig statesman in 1770, 'almost dead and rotten as prerogative, has grown up anew, with much more strength and far less odium, under the name of influence. An influence which operated without noise and without violence, an influence which converted the very antagonist into the instrument of power; which contained in itself a perpetual principle of growth and renovation, and which the distresses and the prosperity of the country equally tended to augment, was an admirable substitute for a prerogative that, being only the offspring of antiquated prejudice, had moulded in its original stamina irresistible principles of decay and dissolution.'[3] We have seen the appalling extent to which parliamentary corruption rose under the first two Georges, but the Whig Government usually succeeded so well

---

[1] Burke's *Correspondence*, i. 256, 316.
[2] Woodfall's *Junius*, i. 255.
[3] Burke's *Thoughts on the Present Discontents*.

in avoiding collisions with public opinion that the outbursts against it were rare, transient, and feeble. The most formidable was at the close of the ministry of Walpole; but the evil, though for a time seriously diminished by the legislation of 1743, soon displayed a renewed vigour. It was aggravated by the growing wealth of the country, which made the struggle for seats more keen; by the disorganised and fluctuating condition of parties, which in many constituencies disturbed and unsettled the balance of political power; by the appearance of the Court in the field as a new and active competitor for parliamentary interest. The enormous corruption employed to carry the Peace of Paris, the new system of issuing Government loans at extravagant terms and distributing the shares among partisans of the Government, the profligate multiplication of Court places, all stimulated the evil. It appeared by the list in the 'Court Calendar,' that in 1770, 192 members of the House of Commons held places under the Government, and it was stated that the number of places had doubled since 1740.[1] Another very important source of corruption arose from the great increase of the National Debt resulting from the war. The excise and customs revenue had risen to about six millions sterling, and the numerous officials who were employed to collect it were, for the most part, docile servants of the Government. In 1782 Lord Rockingham declared that as many as 11,500 revenue officers were employed, and that no less than 70 elections were controlled by their votes.[2]

In the first decade of George III. also, the nabobs, or Indian adventurers, who had returned in great numbers laden with the spoils of Hindostan, began to appear prominently in English political life. At the end of 1767, Chesterfield being desirous of bringing his son into Parliament at the approaching election, offered a borough-jobber 2,500*l*. for a secure seat, but was told 'that there was no such thing as a borough to be had now, for that the rich East and West Indians had secured them all at the rate of 3,000*l*. at least, but many at 4,000*l*., and two or three that he knew at 5,000*l*.'[3] 'For some years past,' said Chatham, in one of his speeches in 1770,

---

[1] *Annual Register*, 1770, p. 72.
[2] *Parl. History*, xxiii. 101.
[3] Chesterfield's *Letters to his Son*, December 19, 1767.

'there has been an influx of wealth into this country which has been attended with many fatal consequences, because it has not been the regular, natural produce of labour and industry. The riches of Asia have been poured in upon us, and have brought with them not only Asiatic luxury, but, I fear, Asiatic principles of government. Without connections, without any natural interest in the soil, the importers of foreign gold have forced their way into Parliament by such a torrent of private corruption as no private hereditary fortune could resist.'[1] It was very natural that a class of men who were for the most part utterly ignorant of English politics and indifferent to English liberty, whose habits of thought had been formed in scenes of unbridled violence and despotism, and who had obtained their seats for purely personal ends and by the most lavish corruption, should have been ready to support every attempt to encroach upon the Constitution. They usually attached themselves to the King's friends. Clive himself at one time brought no less than five members into Parliament, and we find him, in 1767, bargaining for an English peerage as the reward of his services against Wilkes.[2] The sums that were lavished in parliamentary contests at this time had probably never before been equalled. In spite of the scandalous spoliation of the Duke of Portland by Sir James Lowther, Portland succeeded in wresting Westmoreland and Cumberland from Lowther in the elections of 1768, but each party is said to have expended 40,000*l.* in the contests.[3] The contest for the town of Northampton at the same election cost each party at least 30,000*l.*[4] 'The immense wealth,' said Walpole, 'that had flowed into the country from the war and the East Indies bore down all barriers of economy, and introduced a luxury of expense unknown to empires of vaster extent.'[5]

There were some cases of corruption so flagrant that Parliament was obliged to take notice of them. In 1761, the borough of Sudbury openly advertised itself for sale.[6] At the

---

[1] *Chatham Correspondence,* iii. 405.
[2] *Grenville Papers,* iv. 14. Walpole's *George III.* i. 330.
[3] Walpole's *George III.* iii. 197.
[4] Chesterfield's *Letters to his Son,* April 12, 1768.
[5] Walpole's *Memoirs of George III.* iii. 198.
[6] Ibid. i. 42.

next election the magistrates of the city of Oxford wrote a formal letter to their late representatives offering to secure their re-election on condition of their paying the Corporation debt. The offending magistrates were summoned before the House, reprimanded for their conduct, and confined for five days in Newgate, but the House refused to authorise their prosecution, and they are said to have completed their bargain with their members during the short period of their detention.[1] A few borough-brokers whose too open proceedings had been brought under the unwilling notice of Parliament after the election of 1768, were thrown for a short time into Newgate;[2] and Judge Willes, in trying an aggravated case of bribery by the mayor of a Cornish borough, took occasion to say that 'the crime had got to such a pitch that it threatened the utter ruin of the nation.'[3] At Shoreham it was discovered that the majority of the freemen had formed themselves into a permanent society called the 'Christian Club,' for the purpose of selling the seat to the highest bidder, and of monopolising the purchase-money to the prejudice of the other electors. After long discussions eighty-one of the offending freemen were disfranchised, and an important precedent was created by a measure extending the right of voting for members of that borough to all 40s. freeholders in the adjoining rape of Bramber.[4]

The constitution of the House of Commons was, indeed, such that even if there had not been systematic corruption in the constituencies and among the members, it would have had but little claim to be regarded as a true representative of the nation. In a book published in 1774 it was shown by very careful computations that out of the 513 members who sat for England and Wales, as many as 254 represented less than 11,500 voters, and as many as 56 about 700 voters. Of these 56 members no one had a constituency of 38 electors, and 6 had constituencies of not more than 3. The county of Middlesex, including London and Westminster, returned only 8 members, while Cornwall returned 44.[5] And yet, taken as a whole, the representation of England and Wales was far more

---

[1] *Parl. Hist.* xvi. 397–402. Walpole's *George III.* iii. 153, 154.
[2] Walpole's *George III.* iii. 157. *Annual Register*, 1769, p. 93.
[4] *Annual Register*, 1771, pp. 54, 56. *Adolphus*, i. 479.
[5] De Burgh's *Political Dissertations*, i. 40–48.

real and more independent than that of Scotland.[1] As long as the House of Commons abstained from violently opposing the popular wishes these anomalies were acquiesced in; but the Middlesex election for the first time brought it into open opposition to public opinion.

The year 1769 is very memorable in political history, for it witnessed the birth of English Radicalism, and the first serious attempts to reform and control Parliament by a pressure from without, making its members habitually subservient to their constituents. Small extra-parliamentary meetings of active politicians, usually members of Parliament, for the purpose of supporting or opposing particular measures or statesmen, were already well known in English public life. The famous meeting at the 'Fountain,' where Pulteney harangued against the policy of Walpole, and the meeting of the followers of Walpole to discuss the propriety of persevering with the Excise Bill, are well-known examples. In the great agitations of 1641 and 1642 there had been many instances of great assemblies for the purpose of subscribing or presenting petitions to the King or to the Parliament,[2] and a movement of the same kind was created in opposition to the Excise Bill of Walpole.[3] But it was only in the agitation of 1769 and 1770 that open, popular meetings, for the purpose of giving expression to public opinion on great political questions became a normal and important element in English public life.[4] The innovation rapidly spread. At one meeting which was held in Westminster Hall in the August of 1769, 7,000 persons are said to have been present;[5] and there were soon few counties in which large bodies of freeholders did not assemble to protest against the conduct of the Parliament, to draw up instructions for their members, or to petition the King for redress of grievances. A multitude of small political societies, under the guidance of local politicians, were accustomed to meet at different taverns in the City; but they were soon

---

[1] On the extraordinary condition of the Scotch representation before the Reform Bill of 1832, see May's *Constitutional History*, i. 301–304.

[2] See Clarendon's *History*, i. 403, 404, 412, 413; iii. 61.

[3] Tindal's *History*, iv. 219.

[4] Cooke's *Hist. of Party*, vol. iii. 187. May's *Constitutional History*, ii. 121. Buckle's *Hist. of Civilisation*, i. 394, 395.

[5] *Annual Register*, 1769, pp. 125, 126.

absorbed or eclipsed by a great democratic association called the Society of the Supporters of the Bill of Rights, which was founded in 1769 for the purpose of assisting Wilkes in his struggle with the Court, and of advocating political changes of the most drastic character. The man who appears to have contributed most largely to its formation was Horne, the Vicar of Brentford, afterwards better known as Horne Tooke, who had now thrown aside the clerical profession, for which he was utterly unsuited, and flung himself unreservedly into political agitation. The great contributions to grammar and the science of language which have given him a permanent place in English literature belong to a later period of his life, and at this time he was known chiefly as one of the most violent agitators among the City politicians. He possessed some literary and still greater forensic ability, and was a man of undoubted energy, courage, honesty, and independence, but at the same time turbulent, vain, and quarrelsome, and very unscrupulous about the means he employed. In the cause which was raised by the Middlesex election, he once said that he was prepared to dye his black coat red; and he was very active in canvassing, organising public meetings, writing libels, and endeavouring to hunt to death those unfortunate men who were accused of having committed murder in the riots that grew out of the election. Wilkes himself, and also Glynn, Sawbridge, Oliver, and Townshend, who represented the City party in Parliament, were among the original members of the society, and a long series of tests were prepared to be offered to candidates at elections. Every candidate was required to aim at a full and equal representation of the people in Parliament, annual Parliaments, the exclusion from the House of Commons of every member who accepted any place, pension, contract, lottery ticket, or other form of emolument from the Crown; the exaction of an oath against bribery; the impeachment of the ministers who had violated the rights of the Middlesex freeholders, and instigated the 'massacre' of St. George's Fields; the redress of the grievances of Ireland, and the restoration of the sole right of self-taxation to America. Horne, and a large section of the more respectable members, soon after retired from the society in consequence of the quarrel between Wilkes and Horne; but the seceders formed a new and very similar club, called the 'Constitutional Society,' which was the parent of many later societies, such as the 'Whig Club,' the 'Friends of the People,' and the 'London Corresponding Society.'[1]

It was a leading doctrine of the new party that a member of Parliament should be simply a delegate, who must regulate his political career entirely according to the wishes of his constituents. In a great meeting which was held in February 1769, Beckford declared that if he received instructions from his constituents directing him to take a course opposed to his convictions, he would consider himself bound to do so, and 'would not oppose his judgment to that of 6,000 of his fellow-citizens.' The habit of sending instructions from constituencies to members was warmly encouraged, and in the course of 1769 it had become common. The Radical party, however, was very weak in Parliament and not strong in the country. It included a few speculative republicans, the most prominent of whom were Mrs. Macaulay, the historian, who was sister to Alderman Sawbridge, and a wealthy and very excellent private gentleman named Hollis, whose passion for printing and collecting magnificent editions of English seventeenth century works in defence of liberty made him well known to students, and whose donations may be traced in several foreign libraries.[2]

One of the results of this movement was, that the Whigs were compelled, though slowly and timidly, to identify themselves with the question of parliamentary reform. Hitherto the question had not been fully appropriated by either party, and it was by no means clear to which party its advocacy would ultimately fall. The Whigs represented especially the mobile and progressive classes in the community; and as they owed their origin to a great struggle for political liberty, they were the natural guardians of the popular element in the Constitution. But, on the other hand, for half a century after the accession of the House of Brunswick, they kept the Revolution Settlement intact mainly by a parliamentary majority derived

---

[1] Stephen's *Life of Horne Tooke*, i. 163-175. See too a remarkable letter of Junius to Wilkes severely criticising the resolutions of the society of 'the supporters of the Bill of Rights.' —Woodfall's *Junius*, i. 275-296.

[2] *Annual Register*, 1769, p. 73. Walpole's *George III*. iii. 331.

from Whig nomination boroughs at a time when the popular sentiment was usually sullen, hostile, or indifferent. During all that time they were the party of the Government, and had therefore the conservative instincts which power naturally produces, and they included the commercial classes, who were much more disposed and tempted to bribe than the country gentry. The Tories, as we have seen, were long the habitual advocates of short parliaments, place Bills, and pension Bills; and one of the strongest sentiments of the country gentry was dislike to that corruption by which merchants, and at a later period Indian nabobs, so often succeeded in defeating them among their tenants. This appears very clearly in the writings of Bolingbroke. 'As to Parliaments,' wrote Swift to Pope in 1721, 'I adored the wisdom of that Gothic institution which made them annual; and I was confident our liberty could never be placed upon a firm foundation until that ancient law were restored among us. For who sees not that while such assemblies are permitted to have a longer duration, there groweth up a commerce of corruption between the ministry and the deputies . . . which traffic would neither answer the design nor expense if Parliaments met once a year.' Among the posthumous works of Swift, there is a short but very remarkable 'Essay on Public Absurdities,' in which that great Tory writer enumerated what he deemed the chief political evils of his time. It is imbued with the strongest prejudices of his party. He speaks of the folly of giving votes to any who did not belong to the established religion of the country. He condemns absolutely standing armies. He deplores that persons without landed property could by means of the boroughs obtain an entrance into Parliament. But side by side with these views we find him blaming the custom of throwing the expense of an election upon a candidate, the custom of making forty-shilling freeholders in order to give votes to landlords, and the immunity of members and their servants from civil suits. 'It is likewise,' he adds, 'absurd that boroughs decayed are not absolutely extinguished because the returned members do in reality represent nobody at all; and that several large towns are not represented though full of industrious townsmen.'[1] But the

---

[1] Scott's *Swift*, x. 362-366.

hopes of reform which had been raised on the accession of George III. soon proved vain; corruption under a Tory ministry advanced in new forms and with an accelerated rapidity, and it was no longer the Court but the people who looked with jealousy on the House of Commons, and desired to limit its authority. The changed attitude of parties was remarkably shown when Chatham, in 1770, brought the Middlesex election before the House of Lords. A motion was introduced by Lord Marchmont, and warmly supported by Lord Mansfield, and by the whole party which was the especial exponent of the views of the Court, deprecating any interference of the House of Lords with that great constitutional question, on the ground that a resolution ' directly or indirectly impeaching a judgment of the House of Commons in a matter wherein their jurisdiction is competent, final, and conclusive, would be a violation of the constitutional rights of the Commons, tends to make a breach between the two Houses of Parliament, and leads to a general confusion.' It was left for the Whigs to maintain the limitations which the Constitution imposed upon the Commons, and above all, to vindicate the rights of the people to a fuller representation within it.

The attitude of the Whigs towards the question of parliamentary reform differed widely from that of the new Radical party. In order to understand it, we must discriminate carefully between the policy of Chatham and that of the followers of Rockingham. The great service of Chatham to the cause is that he was the first statesman who openly maintained the necessity of an extended system of reform, and who brought in a definite plan for accomplishing this end. He never proposed any lowering of the parliamentary suffrage, and he had no sympathy with the doctrine of personal representation which was implied in the resolutions of the Society of the Supporters of the Bill of Rights, and which, a few years later, was clearly formulated by Stanhope, Cartwright, and Jebb. 'The share of the national burdens,' he once said, 'which any part of the kingdom bears, is the only rule by which we can judge of the weight that it ought to have in the political balance.'[1] In a

---

[1] *Chatham Correspondence,* iv. 169. According to Lord Charlemont, Chat- ham, in one of his speeches on the Stamp Act in 1766, said, 'If England

very remarkable speech, delivered in January 1770, he stated clearly the principles that governed him. 'The Constitution,' he said, 'intended that there should be a permanent relation between the constituent and representative body of the people. Will any man affirm that as the House of Commons is now formed, that relation is in any degree preserved? It is not preserved, but destroyed. Let us be cautious, however, how we have recourse to violent expedients.' The representation of the counties and of the great cities and trading towns, he maintained, was still real and independent, but the small boroughs were 'the rotten parts of the Constitution.' These rotten parts, however, he deemed it not possible or not prudent to destroy. 'The limb is mortified, but the amputation might be death.'[1] 'Let us try then,' he continued, 'whether some gentler remedies may not be discovered. Since we cannot cure the disorder, let us endeavour to infuse such a portion of new health into the Constitution as may enable it to support its more inveterate diseases.' This might be done by giving one more member to every county. In this way, the amount of honesty and public spirit in the House would be largely increased; the influence of the mercenary boroughs would be diminished, and the change would be effected in complete accordance with the true spirit of the Constitution for 'the knights of the shire approach nearest to the constitutional representation of the country, because they represent the soil.'[2]

On the subject of shortening the duration of parliaments, Chatham had much hesitation. The cry for annual parliaments in a great degree disappeared among the more moderate members of the Radical party, and triennial parliaments, which had existed for some time after the Revolution, became their

were not properly represented, the representation ought to be amended. The safe advice of Machiavel must one day be pursued, and the Constitution brought back to its first principles. People, however, are apt to mistake the nature of representation, which is not of person but of property, and in this light there is scarcely a blade of grass which is not represented.'—*Original Letters to Henry Flood*, pp. 14, 15.

[1] In another speech, if rightly reported, he spoke with more hesitation of 'the corrupt and venal boroughs which perhaps could not be lopped off entirely without the hazard of a public convulsion.'—*Chatham Corresp.* iii. 457.

[2] Ibid. iii. 406, 407.

object. In 1770, however, when the City of London addressed Chatham on the subject, he distinctly repudiated the notion that triennial parliaments would prove an efficient remedy for the evils of the State.[1] As late as April 1771, he wrote to Shelburne that he had been endeavouring to collect opinions on the question, and found that there was a very real dislike to any proposal for shortening the duration of Parliament. 'The dread of the more frequent returns of corruption, together with every dissoluteness which elections spread through the country, strongly indisposes families of all descriptions to such an alteration. As I am persuaded that this opinion is genuine, and very widely extended, I should think it totally unadvisable for me to stir it.' 'As to additional knights of the shire,' he added, 'I collect little encouragement. At best, the thing in theory is not quite disapproved, but the execution not much desired by any; probably arising from the present conduct of representatives of counties, not the most enlightened or spirited part of the House.'[2] Very soon, however, the manifest impossibility of inducing the existing Parliament to yield to the wishes of the nation on the question of the Middlesex election changed the opinion of Chatham, and on May 1, 1771, he announced his conversion to short parliaments. 'The influence of the Crown is become so enormous that some stronger bulwark must be erected for the defence of the Constitution. The Act for constituting septennial parliaments must be repealed. Formerly the inconveniences attaching to short parliaments had great weight with me, but now we are not debating upon a question of convenience. Our all is at stake. Our whole Constitution is giving way, and therefore, with the most deliberate and solemn conviction, I declare myself a convert to triennial parliaments.'[3] The necessity for some serious change in the constitution of Parliament he strongly felt. He urged Lord Rockingham in 1770 to aim at the strengthening of the democratic part of the Constitution,[4] and he once predicted to Lord Buchan that before the end of the century either the Parliament would reform itself from within or be reformed with a vengeance from without.

[1] *Chatham Correspondence*, iii. 464.
[2] Ibid. iv. 156, 157.
[3] Ibid. iv. 174.
[4] Walpole's *George III.* iv. 57, 58.

These views cannot be regarded as exaggerated, but they were less timid than those of the Rockingham section of the Whigs. The views of this party were chiefly defended by, and may, I believe, be very largely attributed to, a great man who had now appeared among them, and whose writings, even to the present day, have coloured all that is best in English political thinking.

There is no political figure of the eighteenth century which retains so enduring an interest, or which repays so amply a careful study, as Edmund Burke. All other statesmen seem to belong wholly to the past; for though many of their achievements remain, the profound changes that have taken place in the conditions of English political life have destroyed the significance of their policy and their example. A few fine flashes of rhetoric, a few happy epigrams, a few laboured speeches which now seem cold, lifeless, and commonplace, are all that remain of the eloquence of the Pitts, of Fox, of Sheridan, or of Plunket. But of Burke it may be truly said, that there is scarcely any serious political thinker in England who has not learnt much from his writings, and whom he has not profoundly influenced either in the way of attraction or in the way of repulsion. As an orator, he has been surpassed by some, as a practical politician he has been surpassed by many, and his judgments of men and things were often deflected by violent passions, by strong antipathies, by party spirit, by exaggerated sensibility, by a strength of imagination and of affection, which continually invested particular objects with a halo of superstitious reverence. But no other politician or writer has thrown the light of so penetrating a genius on the nature and working of the British Constitution, has impressed his principles so deeply on both of the great parties in the State, and has left behind him a richer treasure of political wisdom applicable to all countries and to all times. He had a peculiar gift of introducing into transient party conflicts observations drawn from the most profound knowledge of human nature, of the first principles of government and legislation, and of the more subtle and remote consequences of political institutions, and there is perhaps no English prose writer since

Bacon whose works are so thickly starred with thought. The time may come when they will be no longer read. The time will never come in which men would not grow the wiser by reading them.

He is one of the very few instances of a conspicuous statesman who took no part in English politics till he had attained the mature age of thirty-six. The second son of an Irish attorney, who was for some time at the head of his profession in Dublin, and of a Catholic lady of good family, he had received an excellent education in a Quaker school at Ballitore, in the county of Kildare, and passed from thence to Dublin University, where he soon after obtained a scholarship, and where he appears to have found an amount of intellectual activity considerably greater than that which Gibbon a few years later found at Oxford.[1] Burke had, however, little or no college ambition. His favourite studies lay outside the regular course; and although he brought from the University a singularly wide, accurate, and intelligent knowledge of the ideas and sentiments of the classical writers, and of the laws and conditions of ancient societies, he never attained, or perhaps aspired to, that fastidious delicacy and polish of scholarship which is the pride of the great English schools. He spoke and wrote much for a college debating society. He assiduously attended the great college library, and he there laid the foundation of that vast and multifarious knowledge which distinguished him from all the statesmen of his time. Had his intellect been less powerful and comprehensive, had his capacity for assimilating knowledge been less extraordinary, the immense variety of his tastes and pursuits would have infallibly dissipated his energies and destroyed that power of concentration without which no great thing can be done, and it is curious to observe how long his mind vibrated doubtfully between different careers. He was called to the Bar, but he disliked the profession and never practised, though he acquired a knowledge of the principles of jurisprudence which has obtained the admiration of great lawyers. He was probably an unsuccessful candidate for the Chair of Logic at

---

[1] See Burke's correspondence with Richard Shackleton, the son of his schoolmaster, in that singularly charming book, the *Leadbeater Papers*, written by the daughter of Richard Shackleton.

Glasgow University.[1] He thought, at one time, under the pressure of straitened circumstances, of emigrating to the American colonies. In 1756 he emerged into notice by his admirable imitation of Bolingbroke, and in the same year he published his well-known treatise on the 'Sublime and Beautiful,' which appeared in a greatly enlarged form in the following year. This class of studies, which Hutcheson had recently made very popular, had always a great fascination to his mind, and it was united in Burke with a delicacy of taste in his judgment of art which was warmly recognised by both Reynolds and Barry. History, at the same time, occupied a large share of his attention. He began, but never finished, a work on early English history. He wrote wholly or in part an anonymous 'Account of the European Settlements in America,' and the historical sketches of the 'Annual Register,' which was founded in 1758, were, for many years, from his pen. His writings are full of admirable examples of that highest kind of historical insight which illuminates the present by the experience of the past, and detects and discriminates amid the great multitude of indifferent facts the true causes and principles of national greatness or decay. In 1759 we find him applying for a consulship at Madrid,[2] and he was afterwards, for a short time, private secretary to Gerard Hamilton, by whose favour he obtained an Irish pension of 300*l.* He soon, however, disagreed with Hamilton, threw up his pension at the end of a year, and resumed his old life, writing much for the booksellers, haunting the gallery of the House of Commons, and mixing largely with the best literary and artistic society of his time.

There are few men whose depth and versatility have been both so fully recognised by their contemporaries, and whose pre-eminence in many widely different spheres is so amply attested. Adam Smith declared that he had found no other man who, without communication, had thought out the same conclusions on political economy as himself. Winstanley, the Camden Professor of Ancient History, bore witness to his great

---

[1] There is some controversy on this point. See Prior's *Life of Burke,* i. 44, 45.

[2] *Chatham Correspondence,* i. 430-433.

knowledge of the 'philosophy, history, and filiation of languages, and of the principles of etymological deduction.' Arthur Young, the first living authority on agriculture, acknowledged his obligations to him for much information about his special pursuits, and it was in a great degree his passion for agriculture which induced Burke, when the death of his elder brother had improved his circumstances, to encumber himself with a heavy debt by purchasing that Beaconsfield estate where some of his happiest days were spent.[1] His conversational powers were only equalled, and probably not surpassed, by those of Johnson. Goldsmith described him as 'winding into his subject, like a serpent.' 'Like the fabled object of the fairy's favours,' said Wilberforce, 'whenever he opened his mouth pearls and diamonds dropped from him.' Grattan pronounced him the best talker he had ever known. Johnson, in spite of their violent political differences, always spoke of him with generous admiration. 'Burke is an extraordinary man. His stream of mind is perpetual.' 'His talk is the ebullition of his mind. He does not talk for a desire of distinction, but because his mind is full.' 'He is the only man whose common conversation corresponds with the general fame which he has in the world. Take up what topic you please, he is ready to meet you.' 'No man of sense could meet Mr. Burke by accident under a gateway to avoid a shower without being convinced that he was the first man in England.' It is not surprising that 'he is the first man in the House of Commons, for he is the first man everywhere.' He once declared that 'he knew but two men who had risen considerably

---

[1] No less than 14,000*l.* (out of 20,000*l.* required to buy the estate) was raised on a mortgage which was still outstanding when the estate was sold in 1812. Mr. (now Sir Joseph) Napier has investigated with great care the circumstances relating to the Beaconsfield estate and to a small property at Clogher, which was also in the Burke family, in a lecture on Edmund Burke delivered in Dublin in 1862 to the Young Men's Christian Association. This lecture contains several particulars about Burke's private life which will not be found elsewhere, and a very complete answer to some obscure slanders on the subject which had been exhumed and elaborated by the late Mr. Dilke, and which have since been reprinted. It was natural that in an age of unsparing calumny a high-minded and very sensitive public man should have endeavoured as much as possible to withdraw his private concerns and domestic relations from the public gaze. It was equally natural that a critic of the stamp of Mr. Dilke should regard such a reticence as profoundly suspicious, and should make it the endless theme of dishonourable insinuations.

above the common standard—Lord Chatham and Edmund Burke.'[1]

The admirable proportion which subsisted between his different powers, both moral and intellectual, is especially remarkable. Genius is often, like the pearl, the offspring or the accompaniment of disease, and an extraordinary development of one class of faculties is too frequently balanced by an extraordinary deficiency of others. But nothing of this kind can be found in Burke. His intellectual energy was fully commensurate with his knowledge, and he had rare powers of bringing illustrations and methods of reasoning derived from many spheres to bear on any subject he touched, and of combining an extraordinary natural facility with the most untiring and fastidious labour. In debate, images, illustrations, and arguments rose to his lips with a spontaneous redundance that astonished his hearers;[2] but no writer elaborated his compositions more carefully, and his printers were often aghast at the multitude of his corrections and alterations. Nor did his intellectual powers in any degree dry up or dwarf his moral nature. There is no public man whose character is more clearly reflected in his life and in his intimate correspondence; and it may be confidently said that there is no other public man whose character was in all essential re-

---

[1] See the different testimonies on the subject collected in Prior and Macknight's Lives of Burke, and also the masterly sketch in Buckle's *Hist. of Civilisation*, i. 414–423. Charles Butler says that 'Burke's conversation was rambling, but splendid, rich and instructive beyond comparison.' —Butler's *Reminiscences*, i. 168. Some interesting fragments which were reported by Mrs. Crewe have been printed by Lord Houghton in the *Philobiblion Society* and in Rogers' *Recollections*.

[2] Sir Gilbert Elliot, after a very interesting description of the eloquence of Sheridan, says, 'Burke also abounds with these fine passages, and he soars also as much out of the lower regions of discourse and infinitely further into those of imagination and fancy; but no man could ever perceive in him the least trace of preparation, and he never appears more incontestably inspired by the moment and transported with the fury of the god within him than in those finished passages which it would cost Shakespeare long study and labour to produce.'—Lady Minto's *Life of Sir G. Elliot*, i. 215. Walpole, on the other hand, while speaking of the 'inexhaustible fertility' with which Burke 'poured out new ideas, metaphors, and allusions which came forth ready dressed in the most ornamental and yet the most correct language,' complained that even when he 'replied extempore, his very answers, that sprang from what had been said by others, were so painted and artfully arranged, that they wore the appearance of study and preparation.' —Walpole's *George III.* ii. 273, 275. Gibbon bears witness to the correctness of those printed speeches which he had himself heard delivered.—*Miscellaneous Works*, i. 235.

spects more transparently pure. Weak health, deep and fervent religious principles, and studious habits, saved him from the temptations of youth; and amid all the vicissitudes and corruption of politics his heart never lost its warmth, or his conscience its sensitiveness. There were faults indeed which were only too apparent in his character as in his intellect—an excessive violence and irritability of temper; personal antipathies, which were sometimes carried beyond all the bounds of reason; party spirit, which was too often suffered to obscure his judgment, and to hurry him into great intemperance and exaggeration of language. But he was emphatically a good man; and in the higher moral qualities of public as of private life, he has not often been surpassed. That loyal affection with which he clung through his whole life to the friends of his early youth; that genuine kindness which made him, when still a poor man, the munificent patron of Barry and Crabbe, and which showed itself in innumerable acts of unobtrusive benevolence; that stainless purity and retiring modesty of nature which made his domestic life so different from that of some of the greatest of his contemporaries; that depth of feeling which made the loss of his only son the death-knell of the whole happiness of his life, may be traced in every stage of his public career. 'I know the map of England,' he once said, 'as well as the noble lord, or as any other person, and I know that the way I take is not the road to preferment.' Fidelity to his engagements, a disinterested pursuit of what he believed to be right, in spite of all the allurements of interest and of popularity; a deep and ardent hatred of oppression and cruelty in every form; a readiness at all times to sacrifice personal pretensions to party interests; a capacity of devoting long years of thankless labour to the service of those whom he had never seen, and who could never reward him, were the great characteristics of his life, and they may well make us pardon many faults of temper, judgment, and taste.

It was in July 1765 that Lord Rockingham, having just become Prime Minister, made Burke his private secretary, and almost immediately afterwards by the influence of Lord Verney he was returned to Parliament for the small borough of Wendover. From this time he became one of the warmest friends and most intimate counsellors of Rockingham, and the chief defender of his policy, both in Parliament and in the press. In Parliament he had great obstacles to contend with. An Irishman unconnected with any of the great governing families, and without any of the influence derived from property and rank, he entered Parliament late in life and with habits fully formed, and during the greater part of his career he spoke as a member of a small minority in opposition to the strong feeling of the House. He was too old and too rigid to catch its tone, and he never acquired that subtle instinct or tact which enables some speakers to follow its fleeting moods and to strike with unfailing accuracy the precise key which is most in harmony with its prevailing temper. 'Of all politicians of talent I ever knew,' wrote Horace Walpole, 'Burke has least political art,' and his defects so increased with age that the time came when he was often listened to with undisguised impatience. He spoke too often, too vehemently, and much too long; and his eloquence, though in the highest degree intellectual, powerful, various, and original, was not well adapted to a popular audience.[1] He had little or nothing of that fire and majesty of declamation with which Chatham thrilled his hearers, and often almost overawed opposition, and as a parliamentary debater he was far inferior to Charles Fox. That great master of persuasive reasoning never failed to make every sentence tell upon his hearers, to employ precisely and invariably the kind of arguments that were most level with their understandings, to subordinate every other consideration to the single end of convincing and impressing those who were before him. Burke was not inferior to Fox in readiness and in the power of clear and cogent reasoning. His wit, though not of the highest

[1] There is an excellent criticism of the merits and defects of Burke as a speaker in a letter of Flood to Charlemont, describing one of Burke's great speeches on conciliation with America. 'His performance was the best I have heard from him in the whole winter. He is always brilliant to an uncommon degree, and yet I believe it would be better he were less so. I don't mean to join with the cry which will always run against shining parts, when I say that I sincerely think it interrupts him so much in argument that the House are never sensible that he argues as well as he does. Fox gives a strong proof of this, for he makes use of Burke's speech as a repertory, and by stating crabbedly two or three of those ideas which Burke has buried under flowers, he is thought almost always to have had more argument.' — *Charlemont MSS.* Erskine used to say that the grand fault of Burke's speaking was that he was too episodical. — Prior's *Life of Burke*, ii. 473.

order, was only equalled by that of Townshend, Sheridan, and perhaps North, and it rarely failed in its effect upon the House. He far surpassed every other speaker in the copiousness and correctness of his diction, in the range of knowledge he brought to bear on every subject of debate, in the richness and variety of his imagination, in the gorgeous beauty of his descriptive passages, in the depth of the philosophical reflections and the felicity of the personal sketches which he delighted in scattering over his speeches. But these gifts were frequently marred by a strange want of judgment, measure, and self-control. His speeches were full of episodes and digressions, of excessive ornamentation and illustration, of dissertations on general principles of politics, which were invaluable in themselves, but very unpalatable to a tired or excited House waiting eagerly for a division. As Grattan once said, 'they were far better suited to a patient reader than an impatient hearer.' Passionately in earnest in the midst of a careless or half-hearted assembly, seeking in all measures their essential and permanent tendencies, while his hearers thought chiefly of their transient and personal aspects, discussing first principles and remote consequences, among men whose minds were concentrated on the struggle of the hour, constantly led away by the endless stream of ideas and images which were for ever surging from his brain, he was often interrupted by his impatient hearers. There is scarcely a perceptible difference between the style of his essays and the style of his published speeches; and if the reader selects from his works the few passages which possess to an eminent degree the flash and movement of spoken rhetoric, he will be quite as likely to find them in the former as in the latter.[1]

Like most men of great imaginative power, he possessed a highly strung and over-sensitive nervous organisation, and the incessant conflicts of parliamentary life brought it at last into a condition of irritability that was wholly morbid and abnormal. Though eminently courteous and amenable to reason in private life, in public he was often petulant, intractable, and ungovernably violent. His friends sometimes held him down by the skirts of his coat to restrain the outbursts of his anger. He spoke with a burning brain and with quivering nerves. The rapid, ve-

---

[1] See e.g. the magnificent declamatory passage on the justice of the French war in the first letter on the Regicidal Peace.

hement, impetuous torrent of his eloquence, kindling as it flowed, and the nervous motions of his countenance reflected the ungovernable excitement under which he laboured; and while Fox could cast off without an effort the cares of public life and pass at once from Parliament to a night of dissipation at Brooks's, Burke returned from debate jaded, irritated, and soured. With an intellect capable of the very highest efforts of judicial wisdom he combined the passions of the most violent partisan, and in the excitement of debate these too often obtained the ascendancy. Few things are more curious than the contrast between the feverish and passionate excitement with which he threw himself into party debates, and the admirably calm, exhaustive, and impartial summaries of the rival arguments which he afterwards drew up for the 'Annual Register.' Though a most skilful and penetrating critic, and though his English style is one of the very finest in the language, his taste was not pure. Even his best writings are sometimes disfigured by strangely coarse and repulsive images, and gross violations of taste appear to have been frequent in his speeches. It is probable that in his case the hasty reports in the 'Parliamentary History' and in the 'Cavendish Debates' are more than commonly defective, for Burke was a very rapid speaker, and his language had the strongly marked individuality which reporters rarely succeed in conveying;[1] but no one who judged by these reports would place his speeches in the first rank, and some of them are wild and tawdry almost to insanity. Nor does he appear to have possessed any histrionic power. His voice had little charm. He had a strong Irish accent, and Erskine described his delivery as 'execrable,' and declared that in some of his finest speeches he emptied the House.[2]

---

[1] It is related of Coleridge that a very experienced shorthand writer was employed to take down his lectures on Shakespeare, and that his manuscript proved almost unintelligible. The reporter afterwards said that from long experience he had, with every other speaker he had ever heard, been almost always able to guess the form of the latter part of each sentence by the form of the beginning, but that the conclusion of every one of Coleridge's sentences was a surprise to him.

[2] There are excellent descriptions of Burke's speaking in Wraxall's *Memoirs*, ii. 35–38; Walpole's *Memoirs of George III.* ii. 273, 274; *Last Journals*, i. 84, 85, 443; and in the letters in Lady Minto's *Life of Sir G. Elliot.* See too Butler's *Reminiscences*, pp. 166–168. Erskine's very unfavourable description of his manner is given in Campbell's *Chancellors*, ix. 68, 69. Lord Brougham, in his sketch of Burke (*Statesmen of George III.*), has collected several instances of his glaring bad taste. Another, too gross for quotation, will be found in Jesse's *Life of Selwyn*, iv. 130, 131.

Gerard Hamilton once said that while everywhere else Burke seemed the first man, in the House of Commons he appeared only the second. At the same time there is ample evidence that with all his defects he was from the first a great power in the House, and that in the early part of his career, and almost always on occasions of great importance, his eloquence had a wonderful power upon his hearers. Pitt passed into the House of Lords almost immediately after Burke had entered the Commons. Fox was then a boy. Sheridan had not yet become a member; and his fellow-countryman, Barré, though a rhetorician of great if somewhat coarse power, was completely eclipsed by the splendour and the variety of the talents of Burke. Charles Townshend alone, who shone for a few years with a meteoric brilliancy in English politics, was regarded as his worthy rival. Johnson wrote to Langton with great delight that Burke by his first speeches in the House had 'gained more reputation than perhaps any man at his first appearance ever gained before.'[1] 'An Irishman, Mr. Burke, is sprung up,' wrote the American General Lee, who was then watching London politics with great care, 'who has astonished everybody with the power of his eloquence and his comprehensive knowledge in all our exterior and internal politics and commercial interests. He wants nothing but that sort of dignity annexed to rank and property in England to make him the most considerable man in the Lower House.'[2] Grattan, who on a question of oratory was one of the most competent of judges, wrote in 1769, 'Burke is unquestionably the first orator among the Commons of England, boundless in knowledge, instantaneous in his apprehensions, and abundant in his language. He speaks with profound attention and acknowledged superiority, notwithstanding the want of energy, the want of grace, and the want of elegance in his manner.'[3] Horace Walpole, who hated Burke, acknowledged that he was 'versed in every branch of eloquence,' that he possessed 'the quickest conception,

---

Wilkes said that the Venus of Burke 'was sometimes the Venus of whisky.' 'What will they think,' Sheridan once said, 'of the public speaking of this age in after times when they read Mr. Burke's speeches and are told that in his day he was not accounted either the first or second speaker?'— Rogers' *Recollections*, p. 89.

[1] Boswell's *Johnson* (Croker's ed.), p. 177.
[2] *Chatham Correspondence*, iii. 111.
[3] Grattan's *Life*, i. 142.

amazing facility of elocution, great strength of argumentation, all the power of imagination and memory,' that even his unpremeditated speeches displayed ' a choice and variety of language, a profusion of metaphors, and a correctness of diction that was surprising,' and that in public though not in private life his wit was of the highest order, 'luminous, striking, and abundant.' He complained, however, with good reason that he 'often lost himself in a torrent of images and copiousness,' that 'he dealt abundantly too much in establishing general positions,' that he had 'no address or insinuation;' that his speeches often showed a great want of sobriety and judgment, and 'the still greater want of art to touch the passions.'[1]

But though their length, their excursiveness, and their didactic character did undoubtedly on many occasions weary and even empty the House, there were others in which Burke showed a power both of fascinating and of moving such as very few speakers have attained. Gibbon, whose sinecure place was swept away by the Economical Reform Bill of 1782, bears testimony to the ' delight with which that diffusive and ingenious orator, Mr. Burke, was heard by all sides of the House, and even by those whose existence he proscribed.'[2] Walpole has himself repeatedly noticed the effect which the speeches of Burke produced upon the hearers. Describing one of those against the American war, he says that the wit of one part ' excited the warmest and most continued bursts of laughter even from Lord North, Rigby, and the ministers themselves,' while the pathos of another part ' drew iron tears down Barré's cheek,' and Governor Johnston exclaimed that 'he was now glad that strangers were excluded, as if they had been admitted Burke's speech would have excited them to tear ministers to pieces as they went out of the House.'[3] Sir Gilbert Elliot, describing one of Burke's speeches on the Warren Hastings' impeachment, says: ' He did not, I believe, leave a dry eye in the whole assembly.'[4] Making every allowance for the enthusiasm of a French Royalist for the author of the ' Reflections on the French Revolution,' the graphic description by the Duke de Levis of one of Burke's latest speeches

---

[1] Walpole's *Last Journals*, i. 84–85, 438, 443, 513; ii. 26.
[2] Gibbon's *Miscellaneous Works*, i. 235.
[3] Walpole's *Last Journals*, ii. 194. Walpole's *Letters*, vii. 29, 30.
[4] Lady Minto's *Life of Sir Gilbert Elliot*, i. 195.

on that subject is sufficient to show the magnetism of his eloquence even at the end of his career. 'He made the whole House pass in an instant from the tenderest emotions of feeling to bursts of laughter; never was the electric power of eloquence more imperiously felt. This extraordinary man seemed to raise and quell the passions of his auditors with as much ease and as rapidly as a skilful musician passes into the various modulations of his harpsichord. I have witnessed many, too many, political assemblages and striking scenes where eloquence performed a noble part, but the whole of them appear insipid when compared with this amazing effort.'[1]

There are few things, I think, more melancholy in English history than that Chatham and Burke should never have been cordially united. They were incomparably the ablest men then living in English politics. Both of them were men of high honour, of stainless morals, of pure and disinterested patriotism, but though often approaching there was always something that kept them asunder. The conduct of Pitt towards the first Rockingham Ministry, and the opposition of the Rockingham party to the Ministry of Grafton, sowed dissensions between them, and they were profoundly different in their characters and their intellects. Burke, whose leaning was always to the side of caution, and usually to the side of authority, was very deficient in that power of popular sympathy which Chatham so eminently possessed; and his nature, at once proud, simple, retiring, and sensitive, shrank from the imperious and impracticable arrogance, and from the elaborate and theatrical ostentation of Chatham. In public he sometimes spoke of him with warm eulogy. Even when he censured his policy, as, for example, in his famous and most admirable description of the ill-assorted and heterogeneous character of his second ministry, his language was studiously deferential and moderate; and on the death of Chatham, Burke was one of the first to pay a generous tribute to his memory, but it is quite evident from his private correspondence, extending over many years, that his admiration for him was largely mixed with dislike. On almost every important question we find some serious divergence of opinion. On the great question of America, they were agreed

[1] Prior's *Burke*, ii. 472.

in reprobating the Stamp Act and in desiring its repeal; but they differed in principle about the Declaratory Act, and they differed in policy about the commercial restrictions. In October 1766 Grafton, in his own name and in that of Conway, urged upon Chatham the necessity of securing the services of Burke, 'the readiest man upon all points, perhaps, in the whole House.' 'The gentleman you have pointed out as a necessary recruit,' replied Chatham, 'I think a man of parts and an ingenious speaker. As to his notions and maxims of trade they never can be mine.'[1]

On the constitutional questions arising from the Middlesex election both sections of the party were agreed, but the Rockinghams would have been content without a dissolution, and they looked with much more reserve and hesitation than Chatham on the democratic agitation which was raised against the Parliament.

On the question of the East India Company they were violently opposed. Chatham desired that the territorial possessions of the Company should be gradually taken under the direct dominion of the Crown; that the immense revenues derived from the treaties of Clive in Bengal should accrue to the national exchequer; and that the Crown should interfere to put an end to the scandalous oppression of the natives. 'India,' he wrote, 'teems with iniquities so rank as to smell to earth and heaven. The reformation of them, if pursued in a pure spirit of justice, might exalt the nation and endear the English name through the world. . . . The putting under circumscription and control the high and dangerous prerogative of war and alliances, so abused in India, I cannot but approve, as it shuts the door against such insatiable rapine and detestable enormities as have on some occasions stained the English name and disgraced human nature.'[2] The subject gave rise to long and intricate discussions in 1766 and the three following years, and considerable restrictions were imposed on the powers of the Company. In 1767 an Act was passed which, among other provisions, restrained it from making a dividend of more than ten per cent., and two years later an Act guaranteed the Com-

---

[1] *Chatham Correspondence*, iii. 110, 111. Lord Stanhope's *Hist. of England*, v. app. p. x.

[2] See the *Chatham Correspondence*, especially iii. 61, 199, 200, 216, 269; iv. 276, 277.

pany the territorial revenues of India for five years longer on several conditions, the most important being an annual payment of 400,000*l.* to the Imperial exchequer.[1] In 1773 Burgoyne carried resolutions embodying the views of Chatham, that all acquisitions made under the influence of a military force, or by treaty with foreign Powers, do of right belong to the State, and that to appropriate such acquisitions to private use is illegal; while Lord North carried a Bill restricting and modifying the constitution of the East India Company. It is a remarkable fact when viewed in the light of his later Indian policy, that Burke was strenuously and even passionately opposed to these proceedings as a violation of the charter of the Company and a spoliation of private individuals. He denied that the Government had any right to territorial revenues acquired by the efforts of a private corporation. He denied that the direct power of the Crown was likely in any way to ameliorate the condition of the natives, and he predicted that if Indian patronage passed into the hands of the Crown it would be 'a beginning of such a scene of frauds, impositions, and Treasury jobbing of all sorts, both here and in India, as would soon destroy all the little honesty and public spirit we have left.'[2]

The next great constitutional question was raised by the doctrine of Mansfield, that in prosecutions for libel the jury must only pronounce on the fact of the publication and the meaning of the innuendos, leaving it to the judge to say whether the document is legally a libel. Both Chatham and Burke agreed in denouncing this doctrine as fatal to the liberty of the press and in desiring its overthrow, but they differed wholly as to the means. The Rockingham party attempted without success to carry an enacting Bill stating in its preamble that doubts had arisen on the subject, and establishing that henceforth the jury should have a right to decide whether the paper submitted to it was a libel. Chatham and his followers, on the other hand, vehemently maintained that Mansfield had been guilty of an infringement of the law which would justify im-

---

[1] 7 George III. c. 57. 9 George III. c. 24.
[2] See *Chatham Correspondence*, iv.
254, 255, 283. *Burke's Correspondence*, i. 210, 211, 389, 390. Walpole's *Last Journals*, i. 169, 207, 210, 242–246.

peachment, that there was no real doubt upon the question, and that the proper way of dealing with it was by a declaratory law. On both sides the irritation was very great. 'If you yield now,' wrote Burke to Dowdeswell, 'the horseman [Chatham] will stick to you while you live. . . . Not an iota should be yielded of the principle of the Bill, or the principle of the preamble.'[1]

Another grave question which threatened to divide the two sections of the Opposition, was the tax upon absentees, which was proposed by the Irish Parliament in 1774, and which caused much agitation among the great Whig nobles who possessed estates in Ireland. Chatham, as we shall hereafter see, contended that if the Irish Parliament voted this tax no other body should interfere with it, for on a question of Irish taxation it was supreme. Burke and the Rockingham party were prepared to resort to all measures in England to overthrow the decision.[2]

The main differences, however, between Burke and Chatham lay in their methods of remedying the abuses of Parliament and the disorganised condition of parties. We have already seen the measures of Chatham, and the views of Burke on the subject are well deserving of careful study. The magnitude of the evil he fully recognised. 'The distempers of monarchy,' he wrote, 'were the great subjects of apprehension and redress in the last century; in this, the distempers of Parliament.' But according to him, the first condition of improvement was that 'the whole scheme of weak, divided, and dependent administrations' should be changed, and especially that 'the King's men should be utterly destroyed as a corps.'[3] His great objects were to build up a party interest independent of Court influence, and sufficiently powerful to decide the course of English politics, to put an end to the system of mere casual and temporary unions of discordant politicians, and to revive a high sense of party discipline. 'Party,' he said in a very striking passage, 'is a body of men united for promoting by their joint endeavours the national interest upon some particular principle

---

[1] *Burke's Correspondence*, i. 251. See on the other side *Chatham Correspondence*, iv. 101-104, 109-114.

[2] *Chatham Correspondence*, iv. 296-307, 318-321. Albemarle's *Life of Rockingham*, ii. 226-234.

[3] *Burke's Correspondence*, i. 170, 216.

in which they are all agreed. For my part I find it impossible to conceive that any one believes in his own politics, or thinks them to be of any weight, who refuses to adopt the means of having them reduced into practice. . . . Every honourable connection will avow it is their first purpose to pursue every just method to put the men who hold their opinions into such a condition as may enable them to carry their common plans into execution with all the power and authority of the State. As this power is attached to certain situations, it is their duty to contend for these situations. Without a proscription of others, they are bound to give to their own party the preference in all things, and by no means for private considerations to accept any offers of power in which the whole body is not included. . . . Men thinking freely will in particular instances think differently. But still as the greater part of the measures which arise in the course of public business are related to, or dependent on, some great leading general principles in government, a man must be peculiarly unfortunate in the choice of his political company if he does not agree with them at least nine times in ten. . . . When the question is in its nature doubtful or not very material, the modesty which becomes an individual, and (in spite of our Court moralists) that partiality which becomes a well-chosen friendship, will frequently bring on an acquiescence in the general sentiment. Thus the disagreement will naturally be rare; it will be only enough to indulge freedom without violating concord or disturbing arrangements. And this is all that ever was required for a character of the greatest uniformity and steadiness in connection. How men can proceed without any connection at all is to me utterly incomprehensible.'[1]

In consolidating this party organisation few things are more important than the services of great historical families who have from generation to generation attached themselves to the same political party; who supply that party with conspicuous and universally recognised leaders, and with a great weight of connection and borough influence, and who devote their leading members from early life to a political career. Much was said about 'the growth of an aristocratic power prejudicial to the rights of the Crown and the balance of the Constitution.' An oligarchical

[1] *Thoughts on the Cause of the Present Discontents.*

despotism like that of Venice might indeed be easily conceived, and in the opinion of Burke it was beyond all other despotisms to be detested. 'But,' he added, 'whatever my dislikes may be, my fears are not upon that quarter. The question on the influence of a Court and of a peerage is not which of the two dangers is the most eligible, but which is the most imminent. He is but a poor observer who has not seen that the generality of the peers, far from supporting themselves in a state of independent greatness, are but too apt to fall into an oblivion of their dignity and to run headlong into an abject servitude. . . . These gentlemen, so jealous of aristocracy, make no complaints of those peers (neither few nor inconsiderable), who are always in the train of a court, and whose whole weight must be considered as a portion of the settled influence of the Crown.' It is only when some peers forming a political interest, separate from the Court and set themselves 'against a back-stairs influence and clandestine government,' that the alarm is sounded and the Constitution pronounced in danger of being forced into an aristocracy. All this was but part of the system that was being steadily pursued 'of sowing jealousies amongst the different orders of the State, and of disjointing the natural strength of the kingdom, that it may be rendered incapable of resisting the sinister designs of wicked men who have engrossed the royal power.'[1]

---

[1] *Thoughts on the Cause of the Present Discontents.* Fox in the same spirit, in two very remarkable letters written in 1794, defended the maintenance of party government as 'the only mode or plan in this country by which a rational man can hope to stem the power and influence of the Crown;' and he says, 'I am convinced that this system, and this alone, has prevented Great Britain from falling into what Hume calls its euthanasia of absolute monarchy.'—Lord Russell's *Life of Fox,* iii. 68-72. I may add a few sentences describing the political condition of England in 1772, from a very able anonymous book published in that year. 'No regular party existing, the breath of the day has formed, dissolved, and changed oppositions; no tie or connection being formed among any set of men, they have fallen into the most unnatural unions imaginable. . . . Every set of men, nay almost every man, has been in and out, with or without any other set of men, so that nothing like the principle of a party is left in the nation. This revolution must in the end have great consequences; the present miserable disconnection among all the great men and their dependants in the kingdom has thrown a greater power into the hands of the Crown, than an augmentation in the army of 10,000 men. . . . At present we have in the nation only one set of men that can pretend to the appearance of a party, which are those who adhere to the Court on every question. . . . These men, who are strictly united and under the ministerial banner, having a principle of union wanted by every other set, are an over-match for all.'—*Letters on the Present State of England,* pp. 202-204.

The influence of the great families if rightly used is a strong barrier against the undue influence of the Court, and it gives a healthy permanence, unity, and consistency to party organisations. In one of his letters to the Duke of Richmond, Burke noticed as a fact very applicable to English history that 'there were two eminent families at Rome that for several ages were distinguished uniformly by opposite characters and principles, the Claudian and Valerian,' and that 'any one who looks attentively to their history will see that the balance of that famous constitution was kept up for some ages by the politics of certain families as much as by anything in the laws and orders of the State.' 'I do not look upon your time or lives as lost,' he added, 'if in this sliding away from the genuine spirit of the country certain parties if possible, if not the heads of certain families, should make it their business by the whole course of their lives, principally by their example, to mould into the very vital stamina of their descendants those principles which ought to be transmitted pure and unmixed to posterity.'[1]

To a statesman of these views it is obvious that the career of Chatham must have been extremely obnoxious. His avowed design of breaking up parties, his incapacity of acting steadily with any connection, his preference for ministries formed out of isolated politicians detached from different connections, the extreme and obsequious reverence he repeatedly showed for the Sovereign, his manifest wish in at least one period of his life to employ the political influence of the Court to destroy the cohesion of aristocratic factions, were all in the highest degree offensive to Burke. The maxim 'not men but measures,' which was current among the followers of Chatham, he described as a kind of charm by which many politicians were enabled 'to get loose from every honourable engagement,'[2] and in more than one passage of splendid eloquence he painted the anarchy into which the ministry of Chatham had fallen on account of the political method employed by its creator.[3] But it is only in his

---

[1] *Burke's Correspondence*, i. 382, 383.

[2] *Thoughts on the Cause of the Present Discontents.*

[3] See, e.g., that noble passage in his speech on American taxation. 'If ever Lord Chatham fell into a fit of the gout, or if any other cause withdrew him from public cares, principles directly the contrary to his own were sure to predominate.... When his face was hid but for a moment, his whole system was on a wide sea without chart or compass.... De-

private correspondence that the extent of his dislike becomes fully apparent. 'The Court,' he wrote to Lord Rockingham in 1769, 'alone can profit by any movements of Lord Chatham, and he is always their resource when they are run hard.' 'By sending for Lord Chatham,' the King's friends can 'mean nothing else than to patch a shred or two of one or more of the other parties upon the old Bute garment, since their last piecing is worn out. If they had been dissatisfied with the last botching of Lord Chatham, they would not have thought again of the same workman.' 'The style of Lord Chatham's politics is to keep hovering in air over all parties and to souse down where the prey may prove best.' 'The character of their party [that of Chatham] is to be very ready to plunge into difficult business—ours is to go through with it.' The Tory Ministry of North, he wrote in 1774, 'has three great securities—the actual possession of power, chapter of accidents, and the Earl of Chatham. This last is the *sacra anchora*.' 'Lord Chatham,' he wrote to Rockingham in the same year, 'shows a disposition to come near you, but with those reserves which he never fails to have as long as he thinks that the closet-door stands ajar to receive him. The least peep into that closet intoxicates him, and will to the end of his life.' 'Lord Chatham is, in a manner, out of the question, and the Court have lost in him a sure instrument of division in every public contest.' 'Acquainted as I am with the astonishing changes of Lord Chatham's constitution (whether natural or political), I am surprised to find that he is again perfectly recovered. But so it is. He will probably play more tricks.' 'Lord Chatham's coming out is always a critical thing to your lordship.'[1] In a letter written after the death of Chatham by Burke to his old schoolmaster, Shackleton, with whom he was accustomed to keep up an exceedingly intimate, affectionate, and unreserved correspondence, there is a character of Chatham which probably reflects

prived of his guiding influence his colleagues were whirled about, the sport of every gust and easily driven into any port; and as those who joined with them in manning the vessel were the most directly opposite to his opinions, measures and character, and far the most artful and most powerful of the set, they easily prevailed so as to seize upon the vacant, unoccupied, and derelict minds of his friends, and instantly they turned the vessel wholly out of the course of his policy.'

[1] *Burke's Correspondence*, i. 179, 204, 206, 252, 475, 506; ii. 55, 63, 78.

the views of the writer much more faithfully than anything which was intended for the public. Shackleton had apparently written something about the moral dangers of party warfare. Burke answered that parties in politics were absolutely inevitable, and that he had only known three classes of men who kept free from them. There were a few country gentlemen who took no considerable part in public business; there were place-hunters, whose sole object was the pursuit of their private interest; and there were 'ambitious men of light or no principles, who in their turns make use of all parties, and therefore avoid entering into what may be construed into an engagement with any.' 'Such,' he added, 'was in a great measure the late Earl of Chatham, who expected a very blind submission of men to him without considering himself as having any reciprocal obligation to them. It is true that he very often rewarded such submission in a very splendid manner, but with very little marks of respect or regard to the objects of his favour; and as he put confidence in no man he had very few feelings of resentment against those who the most bitterly opposed or most basely betrayed him.'[1]

These passages will be sufficient to show the nature and extent of the dislike which Burke felt towards Chatham, and the chief reasons on which it was based. 'The Thoughts on the Cause of the Present Discontents,' which was written by Burke in answer to a pamphlet by a follower of Grenville, exhibited in the most masterly manner the whole system of Rockingham's politics. In its original draught it contained a direct attack upon Chatham, which it was deemed politic to suppress,[2] and it is impossible to read it with attention without perceiving that it implied a severe censure upon his whole past policy. Though one of the most valuable permanent contributions ever made to English political philosophy, its appearance at a time when Grenville, Chatham, and Rockingham were united on the questions growing out of the Middlesex election, was regarded with much reason as of very doubtful expediency.[3] Chatham, in a letter to Rockingham, complained that it had done much hurt

[1] *Burke's Correspondence*, ii. 276, 277.
[2] Ibid. i. 200.
[3] See the remarks of Walpole, *Memoirs of George III.* iv. 129–135.

to the cause, and had dangerously narrowed the basis of opposition. 'In the wide and extensive public, the whole alone can save the whole against the desperate designs of the Court. Let us for God's sake employ our efforts to remove all just obstacles to a true public-spirited union of all who will not be slaves.'[1]

On the subject of parliamentary reform also, Burke differed widely from Chatham, and he manifested a far greater distrust of popular politics. In many respects, indeed, he may be justly regarded as a reformer. No one asserted more strongly that 'to give a direction, a form, a technical dress and a specific sanction to the general sense of the community is the true end of the Legislature;' that the Sovereign and the House of Lords, as well as the Commons, must be regarded as only trustees of the people; that the Lower House was not intended to be a control upon them, but a control for them. He quoted with full approval the saying of Sully that popular revolts never spring from a desire to attack, but always from an impatience of suffering, a saying which has lost much of its truth since the democratic agencies of modern times have begun to act powerfully, systematically, and habitually upon classes which were once wholly untouched by political agitations. In all disputes between the people and their rulers, he contended, the presumption is at least on a par in favour of the people, for they have no interest in disorder, while the governing classes

---

[1] Rockingham's *Memoirs*, ii. 193–195. This letter bears the following strange and very melancholy endorsement written by Burke more than twenty years later amid the excitement of the French Revolution. 'July 13, 1792. Looking over poor Lord Rockingham's papers, I find this letter from a man wholly unlike him. It concerns my pamphlet (*The Cause of the Discontents*). I remember to have seen this knavish letter at the time. The pamphlet is itself by anticipation an answer to that grand artificer of fraud. *He* would not like it. It is pleasant to hear *him* talk of the *great extensive public* who never conversed but with a parcel of low toad-eaters. Alas! alas! how different the *real* from the ostensible public man! Must all this theatrical stuffing and raised heels be necessary for the character of a great man? Edmund Burke. Oh! but this does not derogate from his great, splendid side, God forbid!—E. B.' In Mrs. Crewe's Memoranda of Burke's Conversation there is the following more favourable character of Chatham. 'Lord Chatham was a great minister and bold in his undertakings. He inspired the people with warlike ardour when it was necessary. He considered mobs in the light of a raw material which might be manufactured to a proper stuff for their own happiness in the end.'—Rogers's *Recollections*, p. 82.

have many sinister influences to determine their policy.[1] No statesman defended more ably the rights of electors in the case of the Middlesex election. He supported Grenville's Bill for terminating the scandalously partial decisions of disputed elections. He was perhaps the first statesman who urged that lists of the voters in every important division should be published, in order that the people might be able to judge the conduct of their representatives. He advocated parliamentary reporting. He strenuously defended the right of free criticism in the debates upon the Libel Bill. He supported the disfranchisement of revenue officers. He was the author of one of the most comprehensive measures ever carried through Parliament for diminishing the number of those superfluous places which were a chief source of the corruption of Parliament, and when in opposition he advocated a much larger reduction than he was able in his short period of official life to effect.

All these were great measures of reform, but beyond these he refused to move. To the demand for short Parliaments he offered a strenuous opposition. He urged with great weight and truth the horrible disorder and corruption which constantly recurring elections would produce, as well as the inevitable deterioration of the character, influence, and competence of Parliaments that would arise from frequent breaches in the continuity of public business, and frequent changes in the men who conducted it; and he maintained that the remedy would rather aggravate than diminish the great evil of Court influence. Triennial Parliaments meant triennial contests of independent gentlemen with only their private fortunes to support them, with Court candidates supported by the money and influence of the Treasury; and members who felt their seats tottering beneath them, were at least as likely to lean for support upon the ministry as upon the people. It was noticed by every experienced politician that the influence of the ministry was much greater in the first and last sessions of a Parliament than in the intermediate sessions when members sat a little more firmly on their seats.[2]

---

[1] *Thoughts on the Cause of the Present Discontents. Letter to the Sheriffs of Bristol. Letter on the Duration of Parliament.*

[2] Speech on the Duration of Parliaments. It is curious to contrast this with the statement of Junius that 'the last session of a septennial Par-

A Place Bill, which was another favourite remedy, he almost equally disliked. It was quite right to prune the scandalous redundancy of sinecures and Court places which supplied the minister with such inordinate means of influencing votes. But to remove the responsible heads of the great civil departments and of the army and navy from Parliament, and to disconnect the greater part of those who hold civil employments from all parliamentary interest, could not fail to lower the position of the Legislature, and to endanger the safety of the Constitution.[1]

He was not less hostile to the doctrine, which was rapidly spreading over England, that representatives are simply delegates, and must accept, even against their own judgments, imperative instructions from their constituents. On his election for Bristol in 1774 his colleague spoke in favour of the coercive force of instructions, while Burke at once denounced them as resting upon an essential misconception of the nature of representative government. 'Your representative owes you,' he said, 'not his industry only, but his judgment, and he betrays instead of serving you if he sacrifices it to your opinion. . . . Parliament is not a congress of ambassadors from different and hostile interests. . . . It is a deliberative assembly of one nation with one interest, that of the whole; where not local purposes nor local prejudices ought to guide, but the general good. . . . You choose a member indeed, but when you have chosen him he is not member of Bristol, but a member of Parliament.' Electors are competent to select a man of judgment and knowledge to send into the great council of the nation; but they are not competent to determine the details of legislation, and an attempt to usurp this function would inevitably lower the character of Parliament. 'Government and legislation are matters of reason and judgment.' Every member is bound to decide upon the arguments that are placed before him what course is best for the whole community, and 'what

liament is usually employed in courting the favour of the people.'— Dedication to the English People. Charles I. thought long Parliaments specially hostile to royal influence. He wrote to Wentworth (January 22, 1634-5), 'Parliaments are of the nature of cats. They ever grow curst with age; so that if you will have good of them, put them off handsomely when they come to any age, for young ones are ever most tractable.'

[1] *Thoughts on the Cause of the Present Discontents.*

sort of reason is that in which one set of men deliberate and another decide, and where those who form the conclusion are perhaps 300 miles distant from those who hear the arguments?' These views were generally adopted by the Whig party, and it appears to have been mainly due to the influence of Burke that the fashion of authoritative instructions, which after the Middlesex election threatened to become universal in popular constituencies, in a few years almost passed away.

But Burke went much further than this. He protested against any change in the essential constitution of Parliament, and he looked with a disgust and an indignation, which he was at no pains to conceal, upon the levelling doctrines and the sweeping changes that were advocated by the society of the supporters of the Bill of Rights. 'The bane of the Whigs,' he once wrote, 'has been the admission among them of the corps of schemers who in reality and at bottom mean little more than to indulge themselves with speculations, but who do us infinite mischief by persuading many sober and well-meaning people that we have designs inconsistent with the Constitution left us by our forefathers. . . . Would to God it were in our power to keep things as they are in point of form, provided we were able to improve them in point of substance. The machine itself is well enough to answer any good purpose, provided the materials were sound.'[1] In accordance with these views he opposed all attempts to lower the suffrage, to abolish the rotten boroughs, to add to the county representation, or in any way

---

[1] *Burke's Correspondence*, ii. 383. So again he speaks of 'a rotten subdivision of a faction amongst ourselves who have done us infinite mischief by the violence, rashness, and often wickedness of their measures. I mean the Bill of Rights people;' and he adds, 'If no remedy can be found in the disposition of capital people, in the temper, spirit (and docility too) of the lower, and in the thorough union of both, nothing can be done by any alteration in forms.' Ibid. i. 229, 231. In a later letter he says, 'If the nation at large has disposition enough to oppose all bad principles and bad men, its form of government is in my opinion fully sufficient for it; but if the general disposition be against a virtuous and manly line of public conduct, there is no form into which it can be thrown that will improve its nature or add to its energy.' Ibid. ii. 384. Speaking of the assertion 'that we are not happy enough to enjoy a sufficient number of voters in England,' he says, 'I believe that most sober thinkers on this subject are rather of opinion that our fault is on the other side, and that it would be more in the spirit of our Constitution and more agreeable to the pattern of our best laws, by lessening the number to add to the weight and independency of our voters. And truly, considering the immense and dangerous charge of

to modify the framework of Parliament. In the face of the glaring and monstrous abuses of the representative system he deprecated all change, and even all discussion of the Constitution. 'However much,' he said, 'a change might improve the platform, it could add nothing to the authority of the Legislature.' 'Authority depending on opinion at least as much as on duty, an idea circulated among the people that our Constitution is not so perfect as it ought to be, before you are sure of mending it, is a certain method of lessening it in the public opinion.' 'There is a difference between a moral and political exposure of a public evil relative to the administration of government, whether of men or systems, and a declaration of defects real or supposed in the fundamental constitution of your country.' 'When the frame and constitution of the State is disgraced, patriotism is destroyed in its very source. . . . Our first, our dearest, most comprehensive relation, our country is gone.' He deplored as a great evil 'the irreverent opinion of Parliament which had grown up.' He complained 'that we are grown out of humour with the English Constitution itself,' 'that it is never to have a quietus, but is continually vilified and attacked,' and he quoted with evident sympathy the opinion of those who believed 'that neither now nor at any time is it prudent or safe to be meddling with the fundamental principles and ancient tried usages of our Constitution, that our representation is as nearly perfect as the necessary imperfection of human affairs and of human creatures will suffer it to be, and that it is a subject of prudent and honest use and thankful enjoyment, and not of captious criticism or rash experiment.'[1]

These views he held with consistent earnestness through every portion of his life. They appeared in the 'Observations on the State of the Nation,' and in the 'Thoughts on the Cause of the Present Discontents,' which were written amid the agitation that followed the Middlesex election. In 1780 he seriously thought of retiring from politics on account of the seces-

---

elections, the prostitute and daring venality, the corruption of manners, the idleness and profligacy of the lower sort of voters, no prudent man would propose to increase such an evil.'—*Observations on the State of the Nation.*

[1] See especially his speech on the Reform of Parliament. Burke's *Works,* x. 92–108.

sion of a portion of his party to the Radical views.[1] In 1782, when the younger Pitt introduced the question of parliamentary reform, Burke was his most vehement and most formidable opponent, and he never varied on the question till the sympathy of his party with the democratic aspects of the French Revolution finally severed him from the Whigs. His imagination, which seldom failed to intensify the conclusions of his reason, transfigured the British Constitution into a work of almost superhuman wisdom, and he made it the object of an almost adoring reverence. To unfold its matchless beauties, to trace its far-reaching consequences, to describe the evils that would flow from any attempt to tamper with it, to guard it from captious and irreverent criticism, became a constant object of his life. He possessed to an extraordinary degree that 'retrospective imagination' which Moore has, I think, truly described as a characteristic of his countrymen, and he clung with an instinctive affection to every institution which represented the labours and the experiences, which was interwoven with the habits, associations, and sympathies of many generations, and was supported not only by deliberate judgments but by prescription, custom, unconscious and unreasoning prejudice. It cost him much to eradicate anything that was deeply planted in the habits of a nation, to sap or relax any organism which derived its strength from the long traditions of the past. His writings after the outburst of the French Revolution contain the most powerful apology in all literature for these modes of thinking and feeling, but it is a complete misconception to suppose that his conduct after the Revolution was an apostasy, was anything but the natural and indeed inevitable development of his career. The evil of those levelling, speculative, and metaphysical theories of politics which triumphed at the Revolution was one of his earliest and deepest convictions. It may be traced in every important political work which proceeded from his pen, and it was clearly visible to his contemporaries. Mrs. Macaulay, who was the ablest writer of the New Radical School, at once recognised in Burke the most formidable antagonist of her ways of thinking, and she wrote a reply to his 'Thoughts on the Cause of the Present

[1] *Correspondence,* ii. 385, 386.

Discontents,' in which she described that pamphlet as containing 'a poison sufficient to destroy all the little virtue and understanding of sound policy which is left in the nation,' and as peculiarly fitted to divert the nation from 'organic and truly useful reforms,' to a revival of 'aristocratic faction.' Walpole in 1772 wrote, 'Burke was certainly in his principles no moderate man, and when his party did not interfere generally leaned towards the arbitrary side, as appeared in the debates on the Church.'[1] Bishop Watson declared that long before the French Revolution he had come to regard Burke as 'a High Churchman in religion,' and 'a Tory, perhaps indeed an aristocratic Tory, in the State.'[2] During the Warren Hastings trial his colleagues noticed as a curious characteristic of his mind, the special vehemence with which he dilated on any outrage done to an ancient dynasty, to the worship and the sanctity even of a pagan creed.[3]

It will probably now appear to most persons that on the subject of Parliamentary Reform Chatham exhibited a far greater wisdom than Burke, and that the reverence with which Burke looked upon the Constitution as it existed in his day was exaggerated even to extravagance. The corruption and indeed absurdity of the representative system could hardly be overstated; and experience, which is the one sure test in politics, has decisively shown that it was possible to reform the abuses of Parliament and to allay the deep discontent of the nation without impairing, for any good purpose, the efficiency of government. With Burke an extreme dread of organic change co-existed with a great disposition to administrative reform. The Tory party, which prevailed after the French Revolution, adopted one side of his teaching, but wholly discarded the other, and they made the indiscriminate defence of every abuse, and the repression or restriction of every kind of political liberty, the great end of government. At last in Canning and his followers a school of statesmen arose on whom Burke might have looked with favour,

---

[1] *Last Journals*, i. 84.
[2] Watson's *Anecdotes of his Own Time*, i. 132.
[3] Lord Holland writes: 'Mr. Fox has more than once assured me that in his [Burke's] invectives against Mr Hastings's indignities to the Indian priesthood, he spoke of the piety of the Hindoos with admiration, and of their holy religion and sacred functions with an awe bordering on devotion.'—Lord Holland's *Memoirs of the Whig Party*, i. 5, 6. See too Moore's *Life of Sheridan*, ii. 94, 95.

who were bitterly opposed to any considerable change in the constitution of the House of Commons, but who were at the same time ardent advocates of religious and commercial freedom, of a liberal foreign policy, and of administrative reform. But the abuses of the representative system, which had long been increasing, soon became intolerable, and in 1832 an irresistible wave of public opinion swept away the more corrupt portions of the borough system, and with it the deep English prejudice against parliamentary reform.

It is well worth trying, at a time when very different modes of political thought are prevailing, to realise the reasons which underlie the opinions of Burke. Even the errors of so great a thinker are often more instructive than the wisdom of lesser men, for they spring not from poverty of thought, or want of insight or sagacity, but merely from imperfections of mental balance. No politician ever saw more clearly than Burke the remote, subtle, and indirect, as well as the more immediate consequences of institutions and measures. It was in comparing the good and evil, the advantages and the dangers, that his judgment was often refracted by his passions or his imaginations.

It must be observed, in the first place, that he never adopted some of the favourite arguments of the opponents of reform. The opinion that nomination boroughs were a legitimate form of private property, which cannot be touched without confiscation, was expressed by no less a writer than Junius, and was countenanced by the younger Pitt; but no traces of it will, I believe, be found in the writings of Burke. Nor did he ever hold the favourite Tory doctrine that all right of representation rests ultimately in the owners of the soil. Divine right, whether of kings, or nobles, or freeholders, had no place in his political philosophy. On one occasion when a county member maintained this doctrine, Burke took great pains to refute it, showing by the antiquity of the boroughs, and by the early presence of lawyers in the House, that in the theory of the Constitution the commercial interest and the professions had as much right to representation as the landed interest.[1] 'The virtue, spirit, and essence,' he once said, 'of a House of

[1] *Parl. Hist.* xvi. 920, 921.

Commons consists in its being the express image of the feelings of the nation.'[1]

His first and most important objection to the Radical school of politicians was the method of their reasoning. Nine-tenths of the reformers of his time, as he truly said, argued on the ground of natural right, and treated representation not as a question of expediency, but as a question of morals.[2] Inequalities in their view were equivalent to injustices. All men are naturally equal, all had an equal right to self-government, and therefore to an equal share in the representation. It is evident that if this principle were admitted it would lead to a complete subversion of that whole system of complex, balanced, prescriptive, and heterogeneous government which is known under the name of the British Constitution. It would lead by a logical necessity to universal suffrage, to equal electoral districts, to the destruction of a monarchy and a political aristocracy which did not emanate directly from the people. Nor were these the only dangers to be apprehended. A mode of reasoning which described the House of Commons as neither actually nor virtually representative, and persuaded the people that their natural rights were violated by each branch of the Legislature, could not fail to destroy all feeling of affection for the country and for its Government.

In opposition to these views it was the first principle of Burke and of the school of Whig politicians who took their politics from his writings, that Government rests wholly on expediency, that its end is the good of the community, and that it must be judged exclusively by the degree in which it fulfils this end. The Whig in this respect stood equally apart from the Tory and from the Radical of the eighteenth century. The Tory maintained a theological doctrine of the Divine right of kings as the corner-stone of his politics. The Radical rested upon metaphysical doctrines about natural rights and the natural equality of men, and anomalies, inequalities, inequitable dispositions of political power were the chief subjects

---

[1] *Thoughts on the Present Discontents.* So again, 'To govern according to the sense and agreeably to the interests of the people, is a great and glorious object of government' (Speech on the Duration of Parliaments). *Works,* x. 73.

[2] Speech on the Reform of Parliament (1782). Ibid. x. 95.

of his complaints. In the judgment of Burke this mode of reasoning is essentially and fundamentally false. Government is a matter of experience, and not a matter of theory. The sole question to be asked about an institution is, how it works. That it is an anomaly, that it is formed on other principles from other parts of the Government, that it is what is falsely called 'illogical,' or, in other words, in dissonance with the general tendency of the institutions of the country, is no valid argument against it. The term 'logic' is rightly applied to trains of reasoning, but not to political institutions; for the object of these is neither truth nor consistency nor symmetry, but utility. It may indeed be truly said that no Government which is simple and symmetrical can be a good one, and that the anomalies which are often regarded as the chief blemishes are in truth among the chief excellences of the Constitution. For Government is obliged to discharge the most various functions, to aim at many distinct and sometimes inconsistent ends. It is the trustee and the guardian of the multifarious, complicated, fluctuating, and often conflicting interests of a highly composite and artificial society. The principle that tends towards one set of advantages impairs another. The remedies which apply to one set of dangers would, if not partially counteracted, produce another. The institutions which are admirably adapted to protect one class of interests, may be detrimental to another. It is only by constant adjustments, by checks and counterchecks, by various contrivances adapted to various needs, by compromises between competing interests, by continual modifications applied to changing circumstances, that a system is slowly formed which corresponds to the requirements and conditions of the country, discharges the greatest number of useful functions, and favours in their due proportion and degree the greatest number of distinct and often diverging interests. The comparative prominence of different interests, tendencies, and dangers, must continually occupy the legislator, and he will often have to provide limitations and obstacles to the very tendency which he wishes to make the strongest in his legislation. In the words of Burke, 'There is not, there never was, a principle of government under heaven that does not, in the very pursuit of the good it proposes, naturally and inevitably lead into some inconvenience which makes it absolutely necessary to counterwork and weaken the application of that first principle itself, and to abandon something of the extent of the advantage you proposed by it, in order to prevent also the inconveniences which have arisen from the instrument of all the good you had in view.'[1] The legitimate place of abstract reasoning in politics is therefore a very small one. In political theories, 'the major makes a pompous figure in the battle, but the victory of truth depends upon the little minor of circumstances.' 'Circumstances give in reality to every political principle its distinguishing colour and discriminating effect. The circumstances are what render every civil and political scheme beneficial or obnoxious to mankind.'

To make these views more clear, let us consider for a short time what are the objects which a representative system in England in our own century is expected to attain. It must, in the first place, bring together a Parliament so distinguished for its ability, its political knowledge, and its integrity, that it may be safely entrusted with the chief voice in the Government of the Empire. No task can be conceived more serious or more responsible than that which is imposed on it. The welfare of at least a fifth part of the human race, the relations of this great multitude to the remainder of their kind, the future of millions who are yet unborn, is largely dependent on its decisions. Races, religions, interests, social conditions the most various and the most hostile, pass under its control, and a single false step may be traced in blood over the history of centuries. It is not expected or required that every Member of Parliament should be competent to discharge the high and difficult functions of a statesman, but Parliament must at least include many such men; it must discover, support, and restrain them; and it must exercise a general supervision over the vast and complex field of imperial interests. This is necessary for the welfare and even for the existence of the Empire. It is equally necessary to the popular character of the Government; for if the House of Commons is manifestly inefficient and corrupt, it will inevitably decay. It becomes, then, a matter

---

[1] Speech on the Duration of Parliaments. *Works*, x. 73.

of the most vital importance to consider by what classes a body which is entrusted with these momentous functions is to be elected. Politics would be unlike any other product of the human mind if it were not true that a high average of intelligence among the electors was necessary for a high average of intelligence among the representatives. If the predominating power of election be placed in the hands of the poorest and the most ignorant classes of the community; if it be entrusted mainly to those who have no political knowledge, no real political opinions, no sense of political responsibility; if this great mass of elective incompetence be carefully sheltered from the influence of the more instructed classes, what can possibly be expected except the degradation of Parliament and the decay of the Empire? Nothing in the whole history of superstition is more grotesque than the doctrine that the panacea for parliamentary evils is to be found in lowering the suffrage, as though by some amazing process of political alchemy the ability and intelligence of the representative body were likely to increase in direct proportion to the ignorance and incapacity of the elective body. And the difficulty of the problem is greatly aggravated by the fact that it is necessary to the efficiency of Parliament that it should not only maintain a high average of ability, but also that it should include many young men capable of devoting their lives to the work of statesmanship.

These are among the results which a good elective system is required to accomplish; but it is not true that the sole object of parliamentary government is to secure the best men for the management of the State. It is also required to secure a representation of the people, and under this term many distinct considerations are comprised. Parliament is in the first place a representative of the property of the country. After the maintenance of personal security, the very first object for which all government is created is to secure to every member of the community the possession and enjoyment of that which he has honestly earned or honestly received from others. In practical as in theoretical politics, taxation and representation are very closely connected, and one of the first signs of the undue preponderance or depression of a class is usually to be found in partial and unfair adjustments of taxation. In an ideal system every taxpayer should have some political weight; but it should be a weight proportioned to the amount of his contributions. A bad representative system may easily become an instrument of legal confiscation, one class voting the taxes which another class is obliged to pay, one class plunging the Government into a career of extravagance under the conviction that the burden of the expense will be thrown upon another. Besides this, the possession of property, but especially of property which is moderate in its amount and somewhat precarious in its character, is the chief steadying and restraining influence in politics. Experience shows that the diffusion through the bulk of a community of a fair measure of education and enlightenment is no real guarantee against the pursuit of Utopias, against the contagion of wild, dangerous, or malignant enthusiasms, against the introduction into political life of that spirit of speculation and experiment, of gambling and of adventure, which always leads nations to disaster if not to ruin. It is of capital importance to all nations, but especially to free nations, that they should attain a large measure of stability in their affairs, and that the spirit of caution should predominate in their councils. In no other way can these ends be so adequately reached as by placing the chief political power in the hands of the classes whose material interests are most immediately and most obviously affected by anarchy or by war.

Parliament is, again, a representative of the opinions of the nation. The various ideas, aspirations, and discontents which are circulating in the community should find an expression within its walls, and an expression in some degree proportionate to their weight in the country. To effect this is very difficult, and no simple and symmetrical system of election can attain it; for the divisions of opinion do not correspond with any accuracy to the divisions of classes. Great multitudes can hardly be said to contribute anything to public opinion; and there is much danger of only two or three broad lines being represented, while the intermediate, minor, and rising schools of political thought are suppressed. There are also grave and opposite evils connected with the representation of opinions to be guarded against. It is right that the different forms of political opinion which exist in the nation should be represented; but it is also right that they should hold a due subordination to the great leading principles of party divisions. When Parliament is disintegrated into numerous small fractions acting independently of party organisations, the Executive, being unable to count upon steady majorities, loses all power, and the policy of the country all firmness, consistency, and continuity. On the other hand, it is a great evil when party discipline is too perfect, and when party outlines are too sharply defined. A minister commanding a majority is then able to defy any preponderance of argument against his measures in Parliament, and to neglect great outbursts of discontent in the country; and all those intermediate shades of opinion which produce compromises, soften transitions, and prepare coalitions, disappear. Parliament at different times has been subject to each of these diseases, and their remedy is to be found much more in public opinion than in mere political machinery. It is of the utmost importance, both to the efficiency of a representative body and to its moral influence in the country, that it should reflect as far as possible the various modes of political thought subsisting among the people. Most great truths which have arisen among mankind have been long peculiar to small minorities, and it is a grave calamity if the voice of those minorities should be long unheard in the councils of the nation. Even if an opinion be wholly or partially erroneous, it is well that Parliament should come into direct contact with its representatives. One of the greatest dangers to parliamentary government, one of the surest causes of the decay of loyalty and patriotism, is the growth of great masses of unrepresented opinion. The pacifying influence of Parliament arises chiefly from the fact that it is the safety-valve of the nation; that it gives a voice to its wants, discontents, suspicions, and aspirations; brings them under the direct cognisance of the Government, and submits them to a full and serious examination.

Parliament, again, is the representative of classes and of interests. Every class has its own interests, which should be protected; its own habits of thought, which should be represented; its own special knowledge to contribute to the government of the country. It is necessary that the views of all should be represented. It is also necessary that no one should swamp or overwhelm the others. All government must be carried on by tradition, in regular grooves, according to a formed system; and it is practically impossible that such a system can continue through several generations under the control of a single section of the community without being unduly directed towards the promotion of its special interests. When one class possesses a monopoly or an overwhelming preponderance of power, it is almost certain to abuse it; and even apart from the temptation to a consciously selfish policy, a mixture of classes is very essential to soundness of political judgment. Experience shows how little this is attained by placing political power exclusively in the hands of a small and restricted class, even when as a whole it is incontestably the most enlightened. Class bias often does more to distort than education to expand the intellect, and rectitude of moral judgment is by no means proportioned to intellectual development. It is those who from their position are brought into closest personal contact with the chief actors in the fray, who are most liable to treat politics as a game, and to care more for the party bearing of measures than for their real or intrinsic merit. A small wealthy class is much less quickly and seriously injured by the consequences of misgovernment than the great industrial community. It may even be benefited by a policy which is very injurious to the country at large, and it is liable to many special distorting influences. The close social connection which binds the English upper classes to the Established Church, to the army, to the Indian and diplomatic services, has often had a very perceptible influence upon their policy, and they have always been prone to the spirit of ' clique and of coterie,' to a certain over-refinement of reasoning which is peculiarly misleading in practical politics, to the habit of judging great questions on personal grounds or on side issues. No other constituencies represent so exclusively the highly educated classes as the Universities, and the political influence of the Universities has been almost uniformly hostile to political progress. It is very necessary that opinions which have been formed in the drawing-room or the study should be brought in contact with that shrewd middle-class intellect which judges questions on broader issues and sometimes with larger sympathies.¹ There are, it is true, great sections of the community who are quite incapable of forming any reasonable or competent judgment on political questions; but they, too, have their interests, which may be injured, and it is right that their sufferings and their real or fancied grievances should find a voice in the Legislature. In politics, the evils that spring from monopoly are sometimes even graver than the evils which spring from incompetence. To maintain a proper balance of class representation is a task of no small delicacy; and as the most ignorant and most incompetent portion of the community is necessarily the most numerous, it is evident that an elective system which was at once perfectly simple and perfectly democratic would establish an overwhelming preponderance in favour of the classes least fitted to exercise it.

It must be remembered, too, that the ostensible effects of changes in class representation are often very different from the real effects. The pursuit of equality sometimes leads to the creation of a new aristocracy, to new concentrations of political power. When votes were given in the eighteenth century to the 40s. freeholders in Ireland, the measure was apparently a very democratic one, and it was the more remarkable because the new electors were chiefly Catholic. In reality its effect was to increase greatly the landlord power. For many years the landlord could count upon the votes of the 40s. freeholders on his estate with the most absolute certainty. At last, on one memorable occasion of vital interest to their religion, they presumed to act for themselves. At the Clare election they opposed and defeated their landlords, returned O'Connell to Parliament, and compelled a reluctant Government to concede Catholic Emancipation. It was their first act of independence, and Parliament at once interposed to disfranchise them. When a large class

---

¹ 'One may generally observe that the body of a people has juster views for the public good, and pursues them with greater uprightness, than the nobility and gentry, who have so many private expectations and particular interests, which hang like a false bias upon their judgments, and may possibly dispose them to sacrifice the good of their country to the advancement of their own fortunes, whereas the gross of the people can have no other prospect in changes and revolutions than of public blessings, that are to diffuse themselves through the whole State in general.'—Addison's *Remarks on Italy.*

of voters are perfectly ignorant and dependent, they must necessarily either sell their votes or bestow them according to the directions of a leader. The landlord, the manufacturer, the Catholic priest, the Anglican clergyman, the Dissenting minister, the public-house keeper, the secretary of the trades-union, acquire under such circumstances an extraordinary importance. In purely democratic countries, where the natural social influences are comparatively weak, adventurers frequently arise, who make it their aim, by obtaining the direction of the most ignorant voters, to organise and accumulate great masses of political power, and thus to acquire a preponderating power in the State.

We have here, then, a number of distinct advantages and dangers which must be considered in every good system of representative government. No one of the ends I have enumerated can be neglected without impairing the efficiency of the machine. Yet no one of them can be fully and perfectly attained without a sacrifice of one or more of the others. The question is one of proportion and of degree, of balance and of adjustment. The evils of government lie sometimes in defects of representation and sometimes in vices of administration; and that is on the whole the best which produces fewest evils and discharges the greatest variety of useful functions. Organic legislative changes are scarcely ever unqualified benefits. The statesman has usually to ask himself whether a proposed change removes greater evils than it produces; whether the evils which are now greater do not tend naturally to diminish, and those which are now less, to increase; whether, even if the immediate change be an incontestable good, it may not lead to other changes, or produce remote consequences which alter the balance. It is a dangerous thing to arrest the growth of a living organism; it is a fatal thing to disturb the foundations of an ancient building; and there are lines of policy to which each of these metaphors may be justly applied. The problem of legislation is a practical problem of great difficulty, to be solved by a simultaneous attention to many distinct and often conflicting considerations, and not by any short method of logic or equalisation. A representative system may, no doubt, be framed by this latter method, but it would be essentially different from the English constitution, destitute of its distinctive merits, and at variance with the whole course of its traditions. This was the lesson which Burke was never tired of inculcating, and his dislike to the methods and reasoning of the reformers lay at the root of his dislike to the measures they advocated. 'That man,' he said, 'thinks much too highly, and therefore he thinks weakly and delusively, of any contrivance of human wisdom, who believes that it can make any sort of approach to perfection.' Taking this maxim as a guide, he entirely denied that Parliament exhibited any evils which could not be sufficiently met by secondary remedies, leaving its organic framework untouched. The Constitution as it existed was 'made by the peculiar circumstances, occasions, tempers, dispositions, and moral, civil, and social habitudes of the people, which disclose themselves only in a long space of time. It was a vestment which accommodates itself to the body.' What evil or grievance, he asked, can be distinctly referred 'to the representative not following the opinion of his constituents?' Was it not a fact that under the Constitution which it had become the fashion to decry, the country had enjoyed 'a growing liberty and a growing prosperity for 500 years?' Is it true that the local interests of Cornwall and Wiltshire, where the representation is enormously exaggerated, are less attended to than those of Yorkshire or Warwickshire? Warwick has members—is it more opulent, happy, and free than Birmingham, which is unrepresented?[1]

It is quite possible to recognise the full justice of the general principles laid down by Burke without accepting the consequences he drew from them. It is true that representation is not a matter of speculation but a matter of expediency, but it is also true that the English representative system had become so corrupt and so imperfect, that as a matter of the merest expediency its reform was imperatively demanded. The extreme venality of the representative body, the fact that Crown influence and aristocratic influence were much more powerful within it than the influence of the people whom it was supposed to represent, its opposition during the whole of the Wilkes case to the sentiments of the people, and its con-

[1] Burke's *Works*, x. 97-102.

stant tendency to infringe upon the province of the law, could not reasonably be denied. It may be true that the local interests of the unrepresented portions of the country were not neglected, but it is very certain that the monopoly of power which a small class possessed was reflected very clearly in the strong class bias of the law, and that the education, the sanitary condition, and the material well-being of the great unrepresented masses of the nation were shamefully neglected. No one who contrasts English legislation since it has acquired a more popular character with that of the eighteenth century can be insensible to this fact. Nor is it true that a modification of the representative system was equivalent to a subversion of the Constitution. It was never intended that this system should remain stereotyped and unaltered while great centres of population rose and decayed, and while the relative importance of different classes and of different portions of the country was entirely altered. The Crown had long exercised a power of calling constituencies into existence as the condition of the country required. As might, however, have been expected, this prerogative was shamefully abused: under the Stuarts it was employed solely or mainly for corrupt purposes, and the feeling against it was so strong that the enfranchisement of Newark-on-Trent by Charles II. was the last instance of its exercise. This branch of the prerogative having fallen into desuetude, it was for the whole Legislature to replace it; but the peculiar condition of public opinion at the Revolution, and the long period of disputed succession and aristocratical predominance which followed, adjourned the question. Had the task of parliamentary reform been begun in the eighteenth century, had the seats of small boroughs, which were proved to be corrupt, been systematically transferred to the great towns, or to those portions of the country which were most inadequately represented, it is probable that far larger portions of the old inequalities that existed would have even now continued.

In judging, however, the opinions of Burke, there are some considerations to be remembered which are too often forgotten. Public opinion on the subject was very immature, and Burke continually affirmed that there was no strong or real demand for parliamentary reform, and that if such a demand were general, he would be ready to concede it.[1] Almost the only very active advocates of Reform were the City politicians, who were certainly not generally supported throughout the nation. The abolition of the rotten boroughs, which alone would have been a serious remedy, was demanded by no responsible politician, and in the existing state of parties and of public opinion it was manifestly impracticable. Triennial parliaments would probably have aggravated more evils than they palliated; and a large addition to the county representation, which was the favourite remedy of Chatham, found, as he himself acknowledged, but few and doubtful supporters. The lowering of the suffrage had scarcely any advocates of weight, and in the face of the utter ignorance and extreme lawlessness of the lower sections of society, and of the scenes of riot that had so lately been enacted, it would have required no small courage to attempt it.

It must be added, too, that the future of parliamentary government seemed much more doubtful than at present. The difficulties of maintaining this form of government continually appear in the writings of Burke. 'Our Constitution,' he writes, ' stands on a nice equipoise with steep precipices and deep waters upon all sides of it. In removing it from a dangerous leaning towards one side, there may be risk of oversetting it on the other.' He speaks of ' the extreme difficulty of reconciling liberty under a monarchical government with external strength and with internal tranquillity,'[2] and, like most of the leading Liberal statesmen of the time, he appears to have been continually haunted by a fear of the destruction of British liberty. In modern times

---

[1] Thus in his speech against reform in 1782, he says, 'I went through most of the northern parts—the Yorkshire election was then raging; the year before, through most of the western counties — Bath, Bristol, Gloucester—not one word either in the towns or country on the subject of representation.'—*Burke's Works*, x. 101. In a remarkable letter on the same subject to the chairman of a Buckinghamshire meeting in 1780, he says, ' I most heartily wish that the deliberate sense of the kingdom on this great subject should be known. When it is known it must be prevalent. It would be dreadful indeed if there were any power in the nation capable of resisting its unanimous desire, or even the desire of any great and decided majority of the people. The people may be deceived in their choice of an object, but I can scarcely conceive any choice they can make to be so very mischievous as the existence of any human force capable of resisting it.'—Ibid. ix. 319, 320.

[2] *Thoughts on the Present Discontents*

such fears would hardly be seriously expressed by the gloomiest of prophets. The dangers hanging over parliamentary government are indeed grave and manifest; but they are of another kind. It is but too probable that parliament may decline in ability and efficiency, that it may cease to attract the highest intellect and the highest social eminence of the country, that it may cease to include any considerable number of young men capable of devoting their lives to political duties, that the variety of opinions and interests existing within the country may no longer be represented within its walls. The increasingly democratic character and the increasing strength of the House of Commons may make it impossible for it to co-operate with the other branches of the Legislature; and the constant intervention of the House in the proceedings of the Executive, and of the constituencies in the proceedings of the House, may profoundly alter its character as a legislative body. Governments living from day to day, looking only for immediate popularity, and depending on the fluctuating and capricious favour of great multitudes who have no settled political opinions, may gradually lose all firmness and tenacity, and all power of muscular contraction, all power of restraining, controlling, or resisting, may thus pass out of the body politic. The habit of sacrificing present advantages for the attainment of a distant object, or for the benefit of generations who are yet unborn, which is the essence of true national greatness, may decline. When every question is submitted directly to the popular verdict, it becomes more and more difficult to pursue any long-continued course of prescient policy, to guard against remote dangers, to preserve that amount of secrecy which in foreign policy is often indispensably necessary, to carry any measure which is not level with the average intelligence of the most uninstructed classes of the community.

The dangers resulting from this state of things are very real and serious. There are a few countries, among which the great American republic is the most conspicuous, which are so happily situated that it is scarcely possible for political follies seriously to injure them. There are others which are so situated that any considerable relaxation of their vigour, caution, and sagacity exposes them to absolute ruin. The insular situation of England makes many political follies, which might ruin a continental country, comparatively harmless; but, on the other hand, England is the centre of a vast, complex, and highly artificial empire, which can only be maintained by the constant exertion of a very large amount of political wisdom and virtue. The remote and indirect consequences of a political measure are often more important than its immediate effects, but they have seldom much weight in popular judgments. It is even possible that so great a preponderance of votes may be placed in the hands of men who have no political opinions whatever, that statesmen may come to look upon the opinion and intelligence of the country as little more than one of the minor subdivisions of power, and may almost neglect it in their calculations if they can appeal successfully to the passions, the prejudices, or the fancied interests of the most ignorant masses of the population.

But serious as are the dangers that may threaten the efficiency of parliamentary government, this form of liberty has taken such deep root in European manners that its total destruction seems almost impossible. The degrees of power possessed by representative bodies differ widely, but there are very few countries in Europe, however backward, in which, in some form, they do not subsist. The public opinion which maintains them is no longer merely national. It is European, and it is supported by the great power of the European press. But in the early years of George III. representative institutions were the rare exception, and the influence of foreign example and opinion was almost wholly on the side of despotism. Europe was strewn with the wrecks of the liberties of the past. The Cortes of Spain, the States-General of France, the republics of Central Italy, the greater part of the free institutions of the towns of Flanders, of Germany, and along the Baltic, had passed away. All the greatest States, all the most rising and vigorous Powers on the Continent, were despotic, and the few remaining sparks of liberty seemed flickering in the socket. In 1766 the French King issued an edict declaring that he held his crown from God alone, and that he was the sole fountain of legislative power; and in 1771 the local parliaments, which formed the last feeble barrier to regal power, were abolished. In

Sweden the royal authority was greatly aggrandised by the Revolution of 1772. In Switzerland, if Geneva had made some steps in the direction of democracy, in Berne, Fribourg, Soleure, Zurich, and Lucerne the government had degenerated into the narrowest oligarchy. In Holland, where the House of Orange had recovered a quasi-royal position in 1747, the growing corruption of the States-General and of the administration, the scandalous delays of the law, and the rapid decadence of the nation in Europe, were manifest to all.[1] Poland was already struggling in the throes of anarchy, and in 1772 she underwent her first partition. The freedom of Corsica was crushed by a foreign invader; Genoa had sunk into a corrupt oligarchy; Venice, though she still retained her republican government, and though she had enjoyed an unbroken calm since the peace of Passerowitz in 1718 had deprived her of the Morea and Cerigo, had fallen into complete insignificance, and her ancient liberties were ready to fall at the first touch of an invader's hand.

The prospects of liberty—and especially of monarchical liberty—were very gloomy; and during the American War it was the strong belief of the chief Whig politicians that the defeat of the Americans would be probably followed by a subversion of the Constitution of England. This fear acted in different ways upon different minds. With Burke it showed itself most clearly in an extreme caution in touching that Constitution which alone in Europe still maintained the union of political liberty with political greatness. He felt, as most profound thinkers have felt, that an appetite for organic change is one of the worst diseases that can affect a nation; that essential stability and the formation of settled political habits are the conditions of all good government; that amid the infinite variety and fluctuation of human circumstances, fashions, and opinions, institutions can never obtain a real strength or produce their full benefits till they have taken root in the habits of a nation, and have gathered around them a large amount of unreasoning and traditional support. He was keenly sensible

---

[1] See a striking letter by Rousseau to a Dutch gentleman 'On the Present State of Liberty in Europe.' in the *American Remembrancer* for 1776, part ii. pp. 292-295.

how rapidly fabrics which have taken centuries to build may be destroyed—how easily the poise and balance of a mixed constitution may be irrevocably disturbed—how strong are the temptations drawing active and ambitious minds from the slow, laborious, and obscure process of administrative reform to the more stirring fields of revolutionary change. To oppose this tendency was one of the great objects of his life; and the dislike to fundamental changes, the attachment to traditional forms, and the indifference to theoretical anomalies, which had always been conspicuous in English political life, found their best expression and defence in his writings.

But if no great organic changes were attempted, a number of secondary reforms were accomplished which greatly improved the representative system. Perhaps the most important was George Grenville's measure for reforming the method of deciding disputed elections. I have described in a former chapter [1] the scandalous manner in which election petitions were adjudicated upon by a party vote of the whole House, how the proceedings had lost almost all semblance of a judicial act, how through the systematic disregard of evidence a large number of members owed their seats not to their constituents but to the House. Grenville predicted that 'the abominable prostitution of the House of Commons in elections by voting for whoever has the support of the ministers, must end in the ruin of public liberty if it be not checked,' and he asked the members whether they would not rather entrust their property to a jury drawn from the very dregs of the population than to such a tribunal. The scandal had long been wide and general, but the proceedings of the Middlesex election made it intolerable. It was generally felt that at a time when the outside public had begun to watch with a severe and jealous scrutiny the proceedings of the Commons, it was impossible that so glaring an abuse should be suffered to continue. It was too palpably absurd that the whole country should be convulsed with agitation, that the Constitution should be represented as outraged, and all the proceedings of Parliament as invalidated, because Luttrell had been substituted for Wilkes as member for Middlesex, while every Parliament probably contained twenty or

[1] See Vol. I., pp. 440-442.

thirty members who in reality owed their seats to a party vote in the House of Commons.

The measure of George Grenville remedying this evil was the last public service of that statesman. It transferred the decision of disputed elections from the whole House to a committee of fifteen members, thirteen of whom were elected by ballot, and the remaining two by the rival candidates. They were bound to examine all witnesses on oath, and they were themselves sworn to decide according to evidence. Lord North, who had just become Prime Minister, disliked the Bill, and endeavoured to postpone it, but it was supported by all the sections of the Whig party; it was advocated by Burke in one House and by Chatham in the other, and it found some support even in the Tory ranks. The more honourable members of the party could not be insensible to the enormity of the scandal.[1] Sir W. Bagott, who was conspicuous among the county members, warmly supported the measure, and Mansfield prevented all serious opposition in the Lords by declaring himself in its favour. The Attorney-General, De Grey, vainly adjured the House to bear the present evils rather than 'fly to others which we know not of;'[2] and the measure which was introduced in February 1770, received the royal assent in the following April. It was at first limited to seven years, but it proved so popular and so successful that in 1774 it was made perpetual.[3]

The Opposition were less successful in an attempt to disfranchise the revenue officers, whose numerous votes formed

---

[1] Thus Dr. Johnson in a pamphlet called *The Patriot*, describing the old mode of trying elections, says, 'The claim of a candidate and the right of electors are said scarcely to have been, even in appearance, referred to conscience, but to have been decided by party, by passion, by prejudice, or by frolic. To have friends in the borough was of little use to him who wanted friends in the House; a pretence was easily found to evade a majority, and the seat was at last his that was chosen, not by his electors, but by his fellow-senators.' Since Grenville's Bill, he says, 'a disputed election is tried with the same scrupulousness and solemnity as any other title.'

[2] These were the last words of his speech. Wedderburn began his reply by continuing the quotation:
'And thus the native hue of resolution
Is sicklied o'er with the pale cast of thought,
And enterprises of great pith and moment
With this regard their currents turn awry,
And lose the name of action.'
Parl. Hist. xvi. 921.

[3] Ibid. xvi. 902–923; xvii. 1062–1074. *Annual Register*, 1770, pp. 77, 78, 226, 227. Walpole's *George III.* iv. 111, 112. *Grenville Papers*, iv. 515, 516. Walpole's *Last Journals*, i. 314–325.

one of the great sources of the illegitimate power of the Crown. A motion to this effect was brought forward by Dowdeswell in February 1770, and it gave rise to a long and animated debate. It was contended, probably with some truth, that if Charles I. had possessed as extensive means as the reigning sovereign, of influencing and managing the constituencies, he might have succeeded in his design of enslaving the country, and the rapidly increasing importance of this evil was abundantly displayed. The Tory party had formerly complained of it, but they were now cordially united with the Ministry and with the King's friends, and Dowdeswell was defeated by 263 to 188.[1]

The pretensions of each House of Parliament to place itself outside the law were next dealt with. One of the most obnoxious of parliamentary privileges was the immunity from arrest for debt and for misdemeanor, and from civil suits, which was enjoyed not only by the members of both Houses, but also by their servants, during the Session of Parliament, and for forty days before and after. An enormous amount of fraud was thus sheltered, and tradesmen complained bitterly that, in the case of a large class of their customers, they had no legal method of enforcing their debts. At one time Members of Parliament are said to have issued protections to persons who were not in their service, enabling them to secure the privilege of Parliament; but this practice was condemned by a Standing Order, and in 1677 a member named Wanklyn was expelled for granting a protection to a person, who was not his servant, in order to hinder the execution of a writ.[2] Two statutes, passed under William and Anne, very slightly abridged parliamentary privileges;[3] but, though several attempts had been made to abolish those of the servants of Members, they always miscarried in the Commons till the Middlesex election brought the whole question into the foreground. In 1770 a very important measure was carried, which enacted that any suit might at any time be brought against persons entitled to the privilege of Parliament; and though the immunity of members

---

[1] *Parl. Hist.* xvi. 834–841. *Annual Register*, 1770, pp. 69–71.
[2] *Commons Journals*, vol. ix. 431. Burgh's *Political Disquisitions*, i 212. See too 4 Geo. III. c. 33.
[3] 12 and 13 W. III. c. 3; 2 and 3 Anne, c. 18; see too 11 Geo. II. c. 24.

of the House of Commons from arrest was expressly reserved, no such privilege was any longer granted to their servants. By this measure the worst forms of parliamentary privilege were abolished, and a great step was taken towards the universal ascendency of law.[1]

At the same time the claim of the House of Commons to constitute itself a tribunal for the trial and punishment of private injuries done to its members was suffered totally to fall into desuetude. This power was altogether unknown to the law of England, and it was as inequitable as it was anomalous. During the two preceding reigns it had very frequently been exercised, but the last case appears to have been in 1767, when Mr. Luttrell complained to the House of a breach of privilege because some individuals had entered his fishery and taken fish.[2] The House referred the case to the Committee of Privileges, who examined witnesses without oaths, and who acquitted the prisoners. Proceedings of this kind had never been recognised by the law courts; but the victims were usually poor men, and the public were so indifferent to the matter that the House was enabled, without opposition, continually to try and imprison offenders by a process which was perfectly illegal. The Middlesex election, for the first time, aroused a strong public opinion on the subject; and, though no formal step was taken, the illegal power ceased from this time to be exercised.[3]

Another change, which, though much less important than the foregoing, was also significant of the altered relations of the Commons to the public, was the abolition of the rule which compelled all who were censured by the House for breach of privilege, to receive the censure upon their knees. The ceremony is said to have been brought into some ridicule in 1751 by a culprit who, on rising from the floor, exclaimed in a tone that was audible to all, while ostentatiously dusting his dress, that this was in truth 'the dirtiest house he had ever been in;' and in the same year a Scotch Jacobite named Alexander

---

[1] 10 Geo. III. c. 50. See too Blackstone, Book I. ch. ii. May's *Law of Parliament*, ch. v. Mansfield spoke powerfully in favour of this measure. *Parl. Hist.* xvi. 974-978.

[2] *Commons Journals*, vol. xxxi. p. 540.

[3] For a full history of parliamentary privilege, see Pemberton's *Letter to Lord Langdale on Parliamentary Privilege.*

Murray, on being ordered to kneel, informed the indignant House that he never knelt except to God alone. It was found impossible to make him yield, and he was imprisoned in Newgate for four months, and was then released by a prorogation.[1] A few printers appear to have been subsequently censured in the usual form;[2] but in 1772, when the question of privilege was at its height, the Commons very judiciously resolved to prevent a repetition of the scandal, and the practice of kneeling was abolished by a standing order.

These measures are sufficient to show that, although both Houses of Parliament obstinately supported the Ministry in their contests with Wilkes, they were not insensible to the great change that had passed over the spirit of the country, and were prepared to allay the discontent by very considerable concessions. The immense progress the democratic spirit had made outside the walls was, indeed, too manifest to be overlooked. The institution of public meetings, the creation of great political organisations, the marked change in the attitude of constituents to their members, and the severe scrutiny with which the legal proceedings of Parliament were watched, were all signs of the growing ascendency of opinion. Writing at the end of 1769, Horace Walpole noticed that in the last reign the House of Lords had obtained an ascendency in the State, in the beginning of the present reign the Crown, at this time the people.[3] The victory was, it is true, very far from attained, and the dangers before the Constitution were of the gravest kind; but still the arena of the contest was changed and was enlarged. A new force had begun to enter powerfully into political calculations; and with the growth of public opinion, its organ, the press, naturally acquired an increased importance.

We have already traced the early stages of its progress. We have seen how, in spite of the stamp and of the advertisement duty which had been imposed under Anne and increased under George II., and in spite of the numerous prosecutions instituted under the Grenville Ministry, its importance had been steadily growing. The increase of the number of papers was, indeed,

---

[1] Walpole's *George II.* i. 17, 21, 29, 31.
[2] Andrews' *Hist. of British Journalism*, i. 208.
[3] Walpole's *George III.* iv. 1.

not very rapid, but it appears to have been continuous. According to some statistics which were published, the number of stamps issued in the United Kingdom in 1753 was 7,411,757; in 1760, 9,464,790; in 1774, 12,300,000.[1] No less than seven new magazines were published in England between 1769 and 1771.[2]

The legal position of newspapers was one of considerable danger and perplexity. The conduct of the House of Commons in excepting libels from the offences that were covered by parliamentary privilege, shows the spirit of the legislators, and there was a great desire to withdraw press cases, as far as possible, from the cognisance of juries. By the old method of *ex officio* informations, which was now very frequently employed, the Attorney-General was able to send them to trial without the previous assent of a grand jury, and when the trials took place the judges laid down a doctrine on the subject of libels which almost transferred the decision from the juries to themselves.[3]

I have already referred to this doctrine. Lord Mansfield and those who agreed with him contended that, in all libel cases, there was a question of fact, which was altogether for the jury, and a question of law, which was altogether for the judge. The question of fact was, whether the incriminated person had written or published the alleged libel, and what was the meaning of its several clauses and expressions. The question of law was, whether the document bearing this meaning had or had not the character of a libel, and on this question the jury were bound to follow absolutely the direction of the judge. As the latter question, in the great majority of cases, was the sole real subject of dispute, the decision was virtually removed from the jury-box to the Bench.

To a mind unversed in the subtleties of law, such a position was not a little extraordinary. It was a strange thing to call upon twelve men to determine upon oath whether a man was guilty of the publication of a libel, and at the same time to forbid them to consider whether the document was a libel, and whether its publication involved guilt. It was a strange

---

[1] Andrews' *Hist. of Journalism*, i. 211.
[2] Wright's *House of Hanover*, ii. 373.
[3] See May's *Constitutional History*, ii. 107 116.

thing to introduce the words 'false and malicious' into the information laid before the jury, and then to say that 'these being mere formal words,'[1] the jury had no right to consider them, or to enter into any examination of the intentions of the writer. As Junius truly said, 'In other criminal prosecutions, the malice of the design is confessedly as much a subject of consideration to a jury as the certainty of the fact.' In a trial for homicide, the jury had not to consider only whether the dead man met his death by the hand of the prisoner; they had also to estimate the intentions, motives, and provocations, and to decide whether the act was murder or manslaughter, or neither. It is not easy to see why a different rule should be applied to libels.

It is, however, quite certain that the doctrine as laid down by Mansfield was that of a long succession of the most eminent English lawyers. It was confessedly that of Holt, one of the greatest and most constitutional of judges.[2] Under George II. the question had been raised in the prosecutions which were directed against the 'Craftsman.' Sir Philip Yorke, afterwards the great Lord Hardwicke, while conducting the prosecution, asserted this doctrine in the strongest terms, and though the jury on one occasion refused to give him a verdict, the Chief Justice Raymond fully sanctioned his description of the law.[3] Mansfield himself declared that for fourteen years he had uniformly laid down this doctrine from the Bench without question, and he was supported by the unanimous opinion of the judges who sat with him.[4] The one great authority on the other side, as yet, was Lord Camden, who strenuously, and at every period of his life, maintained that the decision of the

---

[1] See Lord Mansfield's statement of this view in Lord Campbell's *Lives of the Chief Justices*, ii. 478–480.
[2] *Parl. Hist.* xvi. 1267.
[3] Campbell's *Lord Chancellors*, vi. 176. It was on occasion of the acquittal of the *Craftsman* that Pulteney wrote his ballad called *The Honest Jury*, with the well-known stanza:

'For Sir Philip well knows
That his innuendoes
Will serve him no longer
In verse or in prose,
For twelve honest men have decided the cause,
Who are judges alike of the facts and the laws.'

Lord Mansfield, in the case of the Dean of Asaph, is said, by a strange lapse of memory, to have stated that Pulteney had admitted that 'libel or no libel' was a question for the Court, by saying in his ballad—

'For twelve honest men have decided the cause,
Who are judges of facts, though not judges of laws.'

[4] Campbell's *Chief Justices*, ii. 481, 485.

whole question belonged legally to the jury. In the last reign when prosecuting a libel as Attorney-General, he attended so little to the authority of the judges, that in arguing the character of the libel, he turned his back upon them, directing his words exclusively to the jury; and in the House of Lords he made this question especially his own. He had the rare triumph of living to see his doctrine finally established in 1792, and that not by an enacting, but by a declaratory law, which asserted that his version of the law had always been the true one.[1]

To amend or determine the law of libel so as to bring the question of motive and of intention under the jurisdiction of the jury, became one of the great objects of the Whig party, although, as we have seen, they unfortunately differed upon the question whether the law should be made declaratory or enacting. The enacting Bill of Dowdeswell appears to have been chiefly due to Burke, and it was first introduced and defeated in 1771. It may be questioned, however, whether the judicial doctrine about libel was not on the whole rather favourable to libellers than the reverse. When the opinion is widely diffused that men in high political or judicial authority are acting partially, oppressively, or illegally, to some particular class of culprits, it will almost always be found that juries take a strong bias in the opposite direction. The Wilkes case and the excessive multiplication of press trials under Grenville had already done very much to produce such a bias, and the violent discussions on the legal doctrine of libel greatly increased it. In political cases it was scarcely possible to obtain a verdict from a London jury against libellers, and the knowledge of this fact greatly encouraged them.[2]

There was also at this time a great change passing over the

---

[1] Campbell's *Chancellors*, vii. 45–47. Thurlow, Bathurst, and Kenyon protested strongly against the measure. Considering the long chain of authorities who agreed with Lord Mansfield, and the scorn which was so abundantly poured on mere laymen who discussed the question on the grounds of common sense, justice, and analogy, it is amusing to read Lord Campbell's commentary upon the Act. 'Now that the mist of prejudice has cleared away, I believe that English lawyers almost unanimously think that Lord Camden's view of the question was correct on strict legal principles; and that the Act was properly made to *declare* the right of the jury to determine upon the character of the alleged libel, instead of *enacting* it as an innovation' (p. 47).

[2] See some acute observations on this point in the *Annual Register*, 1771, p. 60.

press. In the beginning of the eighteenth century the newspaper was intended for little more than to collect and circulate current news, and to make known the wants of the community by advertisements. Political discussions were conducted in other quarters, by pamphlets, by broadsides, or by periodical papers which were wholly devoted to that purpose. The political papers to which Swift, Addison, Steele, Defoe, and many other writers under Queen Anne contributed, were entirely occupied with party warfare, and made no pretensions to fulfil the functions of regular newspapers. 'Cato's Letters,' which appeared under George I. at the time of the South Sea Bubble, and which were written by Trenchard and Gordon; the 'Craftsman,' in which Bolingbroke, Pulteney, and Amhurst assailed during many years the Government of Walpole; the 'North Briton,' which was the chief organ of opposition in the beginning of the reign of George III., were all of the same nature. It was, however, inevitable that these two classes of periodicals should be eventually amalgamated, and that the amalgamation should greatly add to the importance of each. An editor who combined in a single paper the interest derived from the circulation of news and the interest derived from political discussions, and who selected and recorded in his columns the facts upon which he based his political disquisitions, had a manifest advantage over his neighbours. The political element may sometimes, though rarely, be found in the newspapers of the Revolution; it became more prominent in the reign of Anne,[1] but until the reign of George III. most of the political writing which exercised a powerful influence upon opinion is to be found either in pamphlets, or in periodical papers which were exclusively devoted to political controversy. In the first decade of George III., however, the character of newspapers was gradually changing. Walpole has noticed that before this time political abuse was generally confined to Saturday essays, but that about 1768 the daily and evening newspapers, stimulated by the example of Wilkes, had begun to print every outrageous libel that was sent to them.[2] The great development of magazines and newspapers put an end to

---

[1] Hallam's *Hist. of England.* ch. xvi.

[2] Walpole's *Memoirs of George III.* iii. 164, 165

or absorbed that literature of detached, periodical essays, which during three reigns had been so considerable. It was a significant thing that while the 'Rambler' and the 'Adventurer' were published in a separate form like the 'Spectator' and the 'Tatler,' Dr. Johnson published the 'Idler' every Saturday in a newspaper called the 'Universal Chronicle,' and this kind of writing was now so popular that he complained bitterly that his essays were immediately reproduced by rival papers. Goldsmith's 'Citizen of the World' first appeared in the columns of the 'Public Ledger.' In the same way the best political writing began gradually to find its way into the newspapers.[1]

Newspaper political controversy was then entirely different from what it now is. The leading article in which a modern newspaper asserts its own views with a prominence of type and of position that adds not a little to their authority, had not yet appeared. As a regular feature of newspapers it cannot, I believe, be traced farther back than the French Revolution.[2] The political bias was shown in scattered comments, in a partial and significant selection of news, and especially in letters, written, for the most part, under assumed names. The importance and amount of this correspondence had of late years greatly increased, and in the beginning of 1769 a writer appeared who soon riveted the attention of England, and whose letters have become a classic in English literature.

Under many other signatures Junius had for some time been before the public. He himself asserted that nearly everything that had attracted attention for more than two years before the appearance of the first letters under that name was from his pen, and two of the signatures he has specifically recognised as his own.[3] Whether all the miscellaneous letters which were published by Woodfall are rightly attributed to him may, however, be doubted.[4] Though containing occasional passages of weighty invective and of brilliant

---

[1] This change is noticed in Miller's *Retrospect of the Eighteenth Century*, iii. 93. On the absorption of the old essay writing by newspapers, see Timperley's *Encyclopedia of Literary Anecdote*, p. 702.

[2] Andrews' *History of British Journals*, i. 274. Grant's *History of the Newspaper Press*, i. 430, 431.

[3] See his anonymous letter to G. Grenville, *Grenville Papers*, iv. 381, dated October 20, 1768. See too pp. 355, 356.

[4] See the elaborate argument against the genuineness of these letters in Dilke's *Papers of a Critic*.

epigram, these early letters are, I think, of very little value, and it was only by slow degrees that the writer learnt the secret of true dignity of style, and exchanged the tone of simple scurrility for that measured malignity of slander in which he afterwards excelled. The first letter under the signature of Junius appeared on November 21, 1768, but it was of no considerable importance, and was not republished in the collection of letters that was authorised by the writer. On January 21, 1769, a much abler and more elaborate letter appeared under the same signature, reviewing the whole political condition of the country, and attacking with great virulence the Duke of Grafton, Lord North, Lord Hillsborough, Lord Weymouth, Lord Granby, and Lord Mansfield. In an evil hour Sir William Draper, the distinguished officer who had commanded the expedition which captured the Manilla Islands, entered the lists on behalf of the Commander-in-Chief. The appearance in the field of an officer of such high position and well-known reputation, and the great literary superiority of his opponent, attracted attention to the controversy, while the extraordinary fierceness and ability with which the unknown writer in the succeeding letters assailed the Sovereign and the foremost ministers of the Crown, soon moved public curiosity to the highest point. The interest in them is not to be fairly measured by the increase of the circulation of the 'Public Advertiser,' in which they appeared, for they were copied into many other papers. They were imitated by almost every public writer, and even by a large number of the most eminent speakers. The excitement culminated in the letter to the King which was published on December 19, 1769, but the letters under the signature of Junius continued, with occasional intermissions, till January 21, 1772.

They appeared at a time which was pre-eminently favourable to their success. The Chatham Ministry, on which so many hopes had been built, had been paralysed by the illness of its chief, and a period of administrative anarchy had ensued such as England had rarely witnessed. Chatham at last resigned, and soon after returned full of indignation to public life, to find every principle of his policy abandoned by his former colleagues. Wherever the eye was turned the political horizon was darkly clouded. In the American colonies the flood of discontent rose higher and higher. Abroad, England was humiliated by the refusal of Spain to pay the Manilla ransom, by the acquisition of Corsica by the French, and soon after by the expulsion of the English from the Falkland Islands. At home, the encroachments on the rights of electors had raised popular indignation almost to the point of revolution. Blood had been shed; Parliament and the law courts were alike discredited, and the popularity of the Sovereign was gone. The ministers were strong in their purchased majorities, but they were divided among themselves, without credit or popularity in the country, and for the most part notoriously destitute of administrative capacity. A misgovernment relieved by no gleam of success at home or abroad, and equally fatal to constitutional liberty and to imperial greatness, had reduced the nation which had lately been the arbiter of Europe to a condition of the most humiliating, the most disgraceful impotence. The press and the jury-box alone remained for opposition. The former, which was looked upon as the one still unfettered organ of opinion, was becoming more and more powerful, and Burke noticed as a special characteristic of the time the favour with which the public looked upon the most ferocious libels.[1] The classes from which the London juries were drawn fully shared the feeling, and the belief that the judges were illegally endeavouring in press cases to abridge their authority had irritated them to the highest point.

In order to understand fully the success of Junius, in order to judge fairly the intense virulence which he imported into political controversy, these things must be duly weighed. He had abilities that would command admiration at any time, but at this period everything seemed conspiring in his favour. The mystery that surrounded him added to the effect. As he wrote to Wilkes: 'At present there is something oracular in the delivery of my opinions. I speak from a recess which no human curiosity can penetrate; and darkness, we are told, is one source of the sublime. The mystery of Junius increases his importance.'

The merit of Junius is almost exclusively literary. His letters contain no original views, no large generalisations, no

[1] *Cavendish Debates*, ii. 106.

proofs of political prescience, no great depth or power of thought. He was in no respect before his age, and, unlike Burke, who delighted in arguing questions upon the highest grounds, Junius usually dealt with them mainly in their personal aspects. On the great question of American taxation he avowed himself the partisan of Grenville, and bitterly lamented the repeal of the Stamp Act. On the question of parliamentary reform he maintained the wholly untenable positions that a nomination borough is of the nature of a freehold, that the whole Legislature is incompetent to abolish it, and that the question of parliamentary reform should be decided by the Commons alone. Considering the letters merely in their literary aspect, it must be acknowledged that they are very unequal in their merits. They are sometimes stilted, always too manifestly artificial, and not unfrequently overcharged with epigram and antithesis. They have, however, literary merits of the highest order, and their style is entirely different from that of any of the great models of the time. It bears no resemblance to the style of Swift, of Addison, of Bolingbroke, of Johnson, or of Burke, yet in some respects it is not inferior to any of these. No writer ever excelled Junius in condensed and virulent invective, rendered all the more malignant by the studied and controlled deliberation of the language, in envenomed and highly elaborated sarcasm, in clear and vivid statement; in the art of assuming, though an unknown individual, an attitude of great moral and political superiority; in the art of evading difficulties, insinuating unproved charges, imputing unworthy motives. His letters are perfectly adapted to the purposes for which they were intended. There is nothing in them superfluous or obscure, and nothing that fails to tell. He had to the highest degree the gift of saying things that are remembered, and his epigrams are often barbed with the keenest wit. Like most writing which is at once very good and very laboured, Junius appears to most advantage in quotation. Read continuously, there is a certain monotony of glitter and of rhythm, but passages embedded in the style of another writer seldom fail to shine with the brilliancy of a diamond. Very happy metaphors and phrases of high imaginative beauty may be found in his pages. His rare eulogies are usually intended for the injury of some third person, but the few lines which, in his letter against Horne, he devotes to the praise of Chatham, though their central image is by no means irreproachable,[1] have all that peculiar charm, beyond analysis or definition, which belongs only to the very best writing. As a popular political reasoner he was truly admirable. He introduced, indeed, little or nothing new or original into controversy, but he possessed to supreme perfection the art of giving the arguments on his side their simplest, clearest, and strongest expression; disengaging them from all extraneous matter, making them transparently evident to the most cursory reader. In this, as in most other respects, he is a curious contrast to Burke, who is always redundant, and who delights in episodes, illustrations, ramifications, general reflections, various lights, remote and indirect consequences. Junius never for a moment loses sight of the immediate issue, and he flies swift and direct as an arrow to its heart. The rapid march of the eighteenth century is apparent in his style, and it is admirably suited for a class of literature which, if it impresses at all, must impress at a glance.

He possessed the easy air of good society, and his letters, if not those of a great statesman, are at least unquestionably those of a man who had a real and experimental knowledge of public business, who had mixed with active politicians, who knew the anecdotes which circulated in political society. In the present century the great development of parliamentary reporting, and of a press which is largely written by men who are closely connected with political life, has brought the public into very intimate contact with their rulers, and has diffused the habits of political thought over a wide area. Yet, even now, a few nights spent in the gallery of the House of Commons, and some free social intercourse with political leaders of different parties, will teach much to the most careful student of written politics. But in the eighteenth century the chasm between the mere literary politician and the practical statesman was much wider, and even so great a man as Dr. Johnson altogether failed to

---

[1] 'Recorded honours shall gather round his monument and thicken over him. It is a solid fabric, and will support the laurels that adorn it.' It is no great eulogy of a monument that it is not crushed by laurel wreaths.

bridge it. The letters of Junius are eminently the writings of a man who understood the conditions of public life and the characters of public men—who wrote not simply for public applause or for the gratification of private spite, but for the attainment of definite political ends. He showed an intimate acquaintance with the business and with the staff of the War Office, and much knowledge of the characters and positions of the City politicians. He had a clear view of the distinction between what is practically attainable and what is simply desirable, and of the frequent necessity of waiving general principles for the attainment of definite ends. No one can read his letters to Wilkes without being struck with the eminently practical cast of his judgment—with the rare political sagacity with which he could judge an immediate issue. On broad political questions his judgments, as I have said, are very worthless, but they are at least not those of a mere demagogue. I have already referred to his opinions about American taxation and about nomination boroughs. It may be added that he objected strongly to giving members to the great trading towns; that, while advocating triennial, he opposed annual Parliaments; that he supported against the City politicians the legality of press warrants; that, in spite of his furious hatred of the King, he argued strongly for the superiority of monarchical over republican government. He received no money for his writings, and could have no selfish object to gain, while he had grave dangers to fear. There is little doubt that he had some real public spirit, and a very sincere desire to drag down men whose public lives were scandalously bad. He was evidently one of those men to whose nature hatred is an imperious necessity, and who, without any personal provocation or private interest, are only too glad to gratify it.

It is true that this is not always the character of his writing. No plausible explanation based on mere public grounds has been given of the ungovernable, the almost frantic fury with which, in the spring of 1772, chiefly under the signature of Veteran, and with earnest injunctions to Woodfall to conceal the identity of that signature with Junius,[1] he inveighed against an obscure change at the War Office, which led to the removal

[1] See Woodfall, i. 247, 248.

of D'Oyly, to the resignation of his brother clerk, Philip Francis, and to the appointment by Lord Barrington of Chamier to the higher post of Deputy-Secretary at War. Barrington, though he was one of the most conspicuous of the King's friends, had hitherto been barely mentioned in the attacks of Junius. He is now 'the bloody Barrington, that silken, fawning courtier at St. James's,' whose 'very name' 'implies everything that is mean, cruel, false, and contemptible,' 'a wretch,' 'who wants nothing in his office but ignorance, impudence, pertness, and servility,' next to the Duke of Grafton, 'the blackest heart in the kingdom.' Chamier is assailed in letter after letter in a strain of the coarsest and most vulgar insolence. This gentleman, who was descended from a distinguished refugee French minister, was already at the time of his appointment, one of the ten original members of Dr. Johnson's famous club, and he appears to have been a man of much more than ordinary acquirements, and of a perfectly stainless character and reputation. The sole definite charge indeed which Veteran could bring against him was that in his youth he had been on the Stock Exchange, and this very innocent fact is the chief theme of the witticisms of his assailant. He describes him with wearisome iteration as 'Tony Shammy,' 'a little gambling broker,' 'little Three per Cent. Reduced,' 'a mere scrip of a Secretary,' 'with the activity of a broker and the politeness of a hairdresser,' 'a little Frenchified broker from Change Alley.' It is probable that all this was due to the meanest personal motives, and if Philip Francis was indeed the writer it is very explicable.

Even apart from its moral aspects, the outrageous violence of his language was a grave literary fault. We find in Junius nothing of that relief and variety of colouring, that delicacy of touch, that measured and discriminating severity which has made the immortal letters of Pascal permanent models in controversy. Junius probably never drew a portrait which even approximated to truth. His enemies are all villains of the deepest dye, and his chief task is to diversify and intensify the epithets of hatred. Thus, to give but a few examples, the Sovereign is called by implication 'the basest and meanest fellow in the kingdom.' His mother is 'the demon of discord,' 'the original creating cause of the shameful and deplorable condition of this country,' a being 'who watches with a kind of providential malignity over the work of her hands.'[1] The Duke of Grafton is 'a black and cowardly tyrant,' 'degraded below the condition of a man,' 'who had passed through every possible change and contradiction of conduct, without the momentary imputation or colour of a virtue,' 'the friend of every villain in the kingdom,' though at the same time 'there is not a man in either House, whose character, however flagitious, would not be ruined by mixing with his reputation.' The Duke of Bedford is described as destitute of all natural affection, as having sold his country for money to France, as hated with equal intensity though on different grounds by every honest Englishman and by every honest Scotchman, as having hitherto escaped by a special providence from the detestation of the populace in order that he might be reserved for the public justice of his country. Lord Mansfield is declared 'with the most solemn appeal to God,' to be 'the very worst and most dangerous man in the kingdom.' 'The whole race of the Conways' are 'the meanest of the human species.' Colonel Luttrell 'had discovered a new line in the human character. He has degraded even the name of Luttrell.' Horne is actuated by 'the solitary vindictive malice of a monk brooding over the infirmities of his friend . . . and feasting with a rancorous rapture upon the sordid catalogue of his distresses.' Garrick, who was suspected of the unpardonable crime of having taken some pains to discover the authorship of these letters, was 'a rascal' and a 'vagabond.'

The malignity of Junius was indeed truly fiendish, and it was utterly uncurbed by any restraints of truth, or decency, or honour. In few writers is a delight in the contemplation and infliction of pain more keen and more evident, and he has a peculiar pleasure in directing his sarcasms to those circumstances or moments of private sorrow which are sacred to every honourable disputant. When the Princess Dowager was dying of cancer we find him gloating over her condition, and upon the

---

[1] The passages about the Princess Dowager are from the letters signed Domitian, but Junius in one of his private letters acknowledged that signature. The other passages I have quoted are from the letters signed Junius.

loathsome remedy that was employed to alleviate her suffering.[1] He taunted the King with the imputed frailty of his mother and with the undutiful conduct of his child. He jested with the Duke of Grafton on the infidelity of his wife. In his correspondence with the Duke of Bedford he points with savage pleasure to the death of his only son, and because the Duke had shortly after that event voted on an important public question he falsely and basely charged him with the want of all natural affection.[2] Even his own gallery of monsters scarcely contains a more unlovely picture than that which Junius has unconsciously drawn of himself. We see him full of the most nervous alarm at the prospect of detection, and at the dangers that menaced him,[3] but at the same time thrilling with a keen and undisguised enjoyment at the thought of the pain he was inflicting. At one time he advises Wilkes about the course of conduct 'which will in the end

---

[1] An atrocious note which Woodfall refused to print has been given for the first time by Mr. Twisleton in his great work on the handwriting of Junius, plate 103. In the text of a letter, Junius had written: 'When all hopes of peace are lost, his Majesty tells his Parliament that he is preparing, not for barbarous war, but (with all his mother's softness) *for a different situation*;' and he adds, as a note, 'The lady herself is now preparing for a different situation. Nothing keeps her alive but the horrible suction of toads. Such an instance of Divine justice would convert an atheist.' On this remedy, which was supposed in the 18th century to be useful in cases of cancer, see Twisleton, p. xxv., and compare one of the private letters of Junius to Woodfall, 'What do you mean by affirming that the Dowager is better? I tell you she suckles toads from morning to night.'—Woodfall's *Junius*, i. 241. In a letter signed Domitian, Junius wrote, 'Few nations are in the predicament that we are, to have nothing to complain of but the filial virtues of our Sovereign. Charles I. had the same implicit attachment to his spouse, but his worthy parent was in her grave. It were to be wished that the parallel held good in all the circumstances.'

[2] The infamous falsehoods of Junius about the Duke of Bedford are fully exposed in Lord Brougham's *Statesmen of George III.* art. 'Bedford,' and in Lord J. Russell's Introduction to the third volume of the *Bedford Correspondence*. Among other charges the Duke and Duchess were accused of having sold the clothes and trinkets of their son. The truth was that 'these effects were given, as was the practice, to the immediate servants of Lord and Lady Tavistock, and sold by them for their own benefit.' Bedford's despair at the death of his son was such that, as Hume said, 'nobody believed when it happened that he would have survived the loss.'

[3] 'I must be more cautious than ever. I am sure I should not survive a discovery three days, or if I did they would attaint me by bill. Change to the Somerset Coffee House, and let no mortal know the alteration. I am persuaded you are too honest a man to contribute in any way to my destruction.'—Woodfall's *Junius*, i. 231, 232. 'When you consider to what excessive enmities I may be exposed, you will not wonder at my cautions.' Ibid. i. 208. 'Though you would fight,' he wrote to Draper, 'there are others who would assassinate.'

break the heart of Mr. Horne.' At another he announces his intention, 'having nothing better to do,' to entertain himself and the public with 'torturing Lord Barrington.' The Duke of Grafton he describes by an expressive image of satisfaction as, 'the pillow upon which I am determined to rest all my resentments.' 'Our language,' he writes to Lord Mansfield, 'has no term of reproach, the mind has no idea of detestation, which has not already been happily applied to you and exhausted. Ample justice has been done by abler pens than mine to the separate merits of your life and character. Let it be my humble office to collect the scattered sweets till their united virtue tortures the sense.' He has a manifest pleasure in dragging women into his letters, and he is perfectly regardless of truth if he can only wound an opponent. Thus without a shadow of evidence he accused the Duke of Bedford of having been bribed by the French to sign the Peace of Paris. A certain Dr. Musgrave had, it is true, brought a similar accusation against the Princess Dowager, Lord Bute, and Lord Holland, but Bedford was not included in the charge, which rested only on the gossip of a coffee-house, and which was afterwards unanimously voted by the House of Commons to be frivolous and untrue. Sir W. Draper challenged Junius to produce the evidence of his charge. But the effrontery of the slanderer was quite unshaken. He answered that a bribe had under similar circumstances been offered to Marlborough, and 'only not accepted,' that he judged the proceedings of Bedford by internal evidence, and that 'a religious man might have remembered upon what foundation some truths most interesting to mankind have been received and established. If it were not for the internal evidence which the purest of religions carries with it, what would become of the Decalogue and of Christianity?' In a letter under the signature of Vindex, which Woodfall refused to print as a whole, he accused the King of cowardice. The charge was without truth and without plausibility, for both in moral and in physical courage George III. considerably exceeded the high average of English gentlemen. But a private letter to Woodfall abundantly explains the motives of the attack. 'I must tell you (and with positive certainty) that our gracious * * * * is as callous as a stockfish to everything but the reproach of cowardice. That alone is able to set the humours afloat. After a paper of that kind he won't eat meat for a week.'[1]

The hatred with which Junius regarded the ministers of the King, violent as it was, paled before that with which he regarded their master. 'It lowers me to myself,' he wrote to Wilkes, 'to draw another into a hazardous situation which I cannot partake of with him. This consideration will account for my abstaining from the King so long. . . . I know my ground thoroughly when I affirm that *he alone* is the mark. It is not Bute nor even the Princess Dowager. It is the odious hypocrite himself whom every honest man should detest and every brave man should attack.'[2] He watched with keen delight the domestic sorrows that wrung his heart, and was always ready to pour fresh poison into the wound. 'Since my note of this morning,' he wrote privately to Wilkes, 'I know for certain that the Duke of Cumberland is married to Luttrell's sister. The Princess Dowager and the Duke of Gloucester cannot live, and the odious hypocrite is *in profundis*. Now is your time to torment him with some demonstration from the City. Suppose an address from some proper number of Liverymen to the Mayor for a common hall to consider of an address of congratulation—then have it debated in Common Council—think of something—you see you need not appear yourself.'[3]

The great success of Junius is a striking proof of the low condition of the political writing of the time, of the partiality of juries, and of the exasperated state of public opinion. Among its minor causes was a well-known passage in one of the speeches of Burke, in which for party purposes that great orator not a little exaggerated his merits. It must be remembered too that contemporary writers did not possess the knowledge of Junius derived from his private letters, which both furnish many clues to his character and enable us to trace to him many most discreditable letters published under other sig-

---

[1] Woodfall's *Junius*, i. 221. Compare George Grenville's Journal of May 1765, written at the time of the silk weaver riots. 'Mr. Grenville went in next. The King spoke to him first upon the state of the rioters. He seemed in great disorder and agitation; hurt with people thinking he had kept out of the way from fear, said he would put himself at the head of his army or do anything to save his country.'—*Grenville Papers*, iii. 177.

[2] Junius to Wilkes, Oct. 21, 1771. Wilkes' MSS British Museum. Woodfall, in his published edition, suppressed part of this letter.

[3] Ibid. This letter was received Nov. 7, 1771.

natures. A reader who knows Junius as we know him now, must indeed have an extraordinary estimate of the value of a brilliant style if he can regard him with the smallest respect. He wisely attacked for the most part men whose rank and position prevented them from descending into the arena, and who were at the same time intensely and often deservedly unpopular. His encounter with Horne was the one instance in which he met a really able and practised writer; and although the character of Horne was a very vulnerable one, he appears to me to have had in this controversy a great advantage over his opponent. There was indeed something strangely imprudent, as well as strangely impudent, in an anonymous newspaper libeller assuring a skilful controversialist that 'he could not descend with him to an altercation in the newspapers,' and that for his part 'he measured the integrity of men by their conduct and not by their professions.' The great literary superiority of Junius to Sir W. Draper is incontestable, but the most important charge which he urged against that officer has no real weight. Draper, who had commanded the expedition against the Manilla Islands, and who would have been entitled to no less than 25,000*l.* out of the ransom money which the Spaniards refused to pay, had repeatedly urged upon the Government the duty of prosecuting the claim. At last, when it was plainly useless, he desisted, and he soon after obtained some professional advancement to which his past services amply entitled him. A skilful writer might represent this as the conduct of a man who had betrayed and sold his 'companions at arms for a riband and a regiment,' but there was nothing in it which was not compatible with the most scrupulous honour. The elaborate legal arguments of Junius against Lord Mansfield for admitting a felon named Eyre to bail, and on account of his directions to the jury in an obscure trespass case, are pronounced by lawyers to be so grossly wrong that they are sufficient to prove that the writer cannot have been of their profession.[1] The detailed charge of peculation against the Duke of Grafton about the oaks in Whittlebury forest appears to have been equally false.[2] On the great con-

---

[1] See Campbell's *Life of Mansfield.* Brougham's *Statesmen of George III.* art. 'Mansfield.'

[2] See Almon's *Biographical Anecdotes,* i. 12-15.

stitutional questions of the day Junius did little more than reproduce common arguments with much more than common ability, and with the exception of the abandonment of the Falkland Islands,[1] no foreign question is treated by him with any prominence. He is far more at home in dilating upon such subjects as the Scotch birth of Mansfield, the connection of his family with the Pretender, the matrimonial infelicities and amatory vagaries of Grafton, the descent of that nobleman from an illegitimate son of Charles II., the parsimony of Bedford, his conduct on the death of his son, and an assault which was made upon him on a country racecourse.[2]

For nearly a year under the signature of Junius he continued his libels entirely without restraint; but when the letter to the King appeared, the Attorney-General very properly prosecuted Woodfall who had published it, and Almon and Miller who had reprinted it. The trial of Almon took place first, and he was ultimately found guilty of publishing, and sentenced to pay a fine of ten marks and to find sureties for his good behaviour for two years. Woodfall, who was the chief offender, was next arraigned, and Mansfield, who tried the case, laid down very clearly his doctrine that the libellous character of the document was for the judge and not for the jury. The jury responded by a special and irregular verdict of 'guilty of printing and publishing only.' After long discussion it was ordered that this verdict should be set aside, and that there should be a new trial. But before this decision was carried into effect, Miller had been tried at Guildhall, and in spite of the clearest evidence of the republication he was acquitted amid the enthusiastic applause of a great multitude. The temper of the London juries was sufficiently evident, and no attempt was made to renew the prosecution of Woodfall.[3] Mansfield refused to permit the prosecution of the scandalous libels against himself, and Grafton and Bedford

---

[1] In a letter to Mackrabie, Philip Francis writes, 'The approach of a war loads me with business, as by-and-by I hope it will with money' (Dec. 11, 1770), and in his autobiography he says, 'We thought a Spanish war inevitable, and that Chatham must be employed. Lord Weymouth on that conviction resigned the Secretary of State's office, and I lost 500*l.* in the Stocks.'—Parkes and Merivale's *Life of Francis,* i. 251, 363.

[2] In one of his private letters he begged Woodfall to find out the exact day on which this important event took place.—Woodfall, i. 227, 578.

[3] *Chatham Correspondence,* iv. 35, 36. Campbell's *Chief Justices,* ii. 476–480.

took the same course. The torrent of libel flowed on unchecked and unrestrained, and the writings of Junius became for some time the favourite model of political writers, who, though they could not rival him in ability, often equalled and sometimes even exceeded him in scurrility and falsehood.

The writings of Junius have a great importance in the history of the growing influence of newspapers, and they perhaps contributed something to the resignation of Grafton. They have, however, very little permanent value, and would probably have been almost forgotten, had it not been for the problem of their authorship, which appears to possess to some minds an inexhaustible attraction. Burke, Gerard Hamilton, Boyd, and Dunning seem to have been most suspected at the time, and answers were even published addressed to 'Junius, *alias* Edmund, the Jesuit of St. Omer's.'[1] The publication, however, by Woodfall of the private and miscellaneous letters of Junius, greatly changed the conditions of the inquiry; and the very elaborate work of Taylor, identifying Junius with Philip Francis,[2] gave a renewed impulse to the discussion. Probably no English book, except the plays of Shakespeare, has been submitted to such a minute and exhaustive criticism as the 'Letters of Junius;' and although the sufficiency of the evidence tracing them to Francis is still much disputed, it may, I think, be truly said that rival candidates have almost disappeared from the field. I do not propose to examine in detail a question on which I have nothing new to offer, and which appears to me to have already occupied much more attention than it deserves; but a brief abstract of the arguments in favour of the claim of Francis can in a work like the present hardly be avoided.

The great and evident knowledge shown by the anonymous

---

[1] This, e.g., was the address of a very able letter signed Zeno in defence of Mansfield.—*Public Advertiser*, Oct. 15, 1771. Burke complained bitterly that Lord Mansfield 'had not thought proper to discountenance the blending a vindication of his character with the most scurrilous attacks upon mine; and that he has permitted the first regular defence that I have ever seen made for him to be addressed to me, without the least proof, presumption, or ground for the slightest suspicion that I had any share whatsoever in that controversy.'—*Burke's Correspondence*, i. 270, 271. He again and again distinctly and upon his honour denied that he was the author of Junius.—Ibid. pp. 275, 282. Boswell's *Johnson*, p. 625.

[2] *Junius Identified with a Distinguished Living Character.* (London, 1816.)

writer, of the business and of the officials of the War Office; his furious resentment at the appointment of Chamier, which was in no respect either improper or important, but which was followed by the resignation of Francis; his adoption, while expressing that resentment, of other signatures; and his anxiety to disconnect his letters on this subject from the letters of Junius, as if he feared that they might furnish a clue to the authorship of the latter, first directed suspicion to the former chief clerk of the War Office; and a great number of independent lines of evidence converge to the same conclusion. The handwriting of Junius has been submitted to the most minute, patient, and elaborate examination by one of the first professional authorities on the subject, and has been pronounced by him to be unquestionably the disguised handwriting of Francis, and the argument is greatly strengthened by the fact that Francis had once sent a copy of verses, with an anonymous note in a disguised hand, to a young lady at Bath, and this disguised writing appears identical with that of Junius.[1] The movements of Francis during the Junian period have been minutely traced, and the periods of his absence from London and of his illness have been found to correspond with striking accuracy to the periods in which the letters of Junius were suspended.[2] Junius mentions some speeches of Chatham which he had himself heard, and adopts or imitates many of their phrases. The same speeches were actually published from notes that were taken by Francis.[3] Among the miscellaneous letters is one under the signature of 'Bifrons,' in which the author mentions casually that he had seen the works of the Jesuit Casuists burned at Paris. This event took place in August 1761; and as the war

---

[1] See Twisleton and Chabot's *Handwriting of Junius* — probably the most complete investigation ever made into the handwriting of an author. The facts relating to the copy of verses will be found, pp. 219-244. The verses seem to be in the handwriting of Tilghman, the cousin and intimate friend of Francis.

[2] Parkes and Merivale's *Life of Francis*.

[3] This fact rests on the distinct assertion of the publishers of the *Parl. Hist.* in which the reports appeared. See Stanhope's *History of England*, v. pp. xxxiv., xxxvi. Taylor's *Junius Identified*, pp. 257-313. It was once believed that the reports of those speeches did not appear till long after the letters of Junius. Dilke, however, who has examined the Junius question with great minuteness, has shown that reports may be found in the earlier newspapers. (*Papers of a Critic*, ii. 109-121.) This no doubt weakens the argument from the coincidence of expression, but it leaves the fact that Francis heard and took notes of speeches which Junius heard and imitated.

was raging, the only British subjects who could have seen the transaction were either prisoners of war or those who were attached to the suite of Hans Stanley, who was then in Paris negotiating for peace. Francis was at this time Assistant Treasury Clerk to Pitt at the Foreign Office. He had shortly before been sent to Portugal on the mission of Lord Kinnoul. He was especially recommended for the Foreign Office on account of his perfect knowledge of French; and if it could be proved that he was one of the few persons despatched with, or to, Hans Stanley, this fact would go far towards settling the controversy. Unfortunately, no evidence which is at all decisive has been produced. Lady Francis, who was extremely inaccurate and untrustworthy in her recollections, stated indeed that ' her husband was at the Court of France when Madame de Pompadour drove out the Jesuits;' and that he 'allowed to his family that he had seen the Jesuit books burnt by the hangman.' A letter from a lady with whom Francis was in love proves that when the mission of Hans Stanley was organised, Francis had asked to accompany it as secretary, but had not obtained the post; and it has been noticed that no despatches in the handwriting of Francis exist between July 24 and August 20, 1761. This interval would give ample time for a journey to Paris and back, and it was during this time that the Jesuit books were burnt. But although it has never been proved that Francis was at this time in Paris, it is certain that the letters of Hans Stanley to Pitt passed through his hands, and it is a remarkable fact that one of those letters gives a detailed account of the burning of the Jesuit books.[1]

Evidence of another kind tends not less clearly to identify Francis with Junius. Junius maintains the somewhat unusual combination of Court opinions on the subject of American taxation with popular opinions about the Middlesex election. Francis on both points agreed with him.[2] The character of Francis and

---

[1] This argument was, I believe, first brought forward in an admirable essay in Herman Merivale's *Historical Studies*—a book of great interest and beauty. See too Parkes and Merivale's *Life of Francis*, i. 192-196.

[2] Francis, in a speech made in 1796, said that on the American question he adopted 'the principles and the language of Lord Chatham,' and rejoiced that America had resisted. This has been urged as a strong argument against the Franciscan

the apparent character of Junius were strikingly similar. Mixed with some real public spirit, we find in both the same disposition to carry into political warfare the most rancorous, inveterate, and ungovernable personal hatred, the same vein of profaneness and coarseness,[1] the same passion for concealment and disguise. Francis from very early years was an anonymous writer in the press, and it is certain that in the period immediately preceding the Junius Letters he made Woodfall's 'Public Advertiser' one of the receptacles of his productions.[2] As he had been in both the Foreign Office and the War Office, and was on intimate terms with Calcraft, who was one of the closest advisers of Pitt, he had access to means of information denied to the outer world. His intellectual qualities, like his moral qualities, bore a manifest resemblance to those of Junius. He was one of the most fastidious and accurate masters of English of his time,[3] and was even called by Burke 'the prince of pamphleteers.'[4] His style, like that of Junius, was terse, vivid, and incisive, abounding in sarcasm and in invective, full of energy and brilliancy. He had the peculiar gift of directness, which was so conspicuous in Junius. 'Few men,' said Fox of him, 'say so much in so few words.' 'Ay, sir,' rejoined Burke; 'his style has no gummy flesh about it.'[5] A great part of his undoubted writing appears to me fully equal to the bulk of Junius, and much

---

theory (*Grenville Papers*, iii. p. xx.), but it has been completely overthrown by the *Life of Francis*, which proves that at the time when the letters of Junius appeared, Francis, like Junius, adopted the views of Grenville, though he appears to have abandoned them as early as 1776. In a letter written from India in that year to his friend D'Oyly, he speaks strongly of the folly of carrying on the war against America, and adds, 'There was a time when I could reason as logically and passionately as anybody against the Americans, but since I have been obliged to study the book of wisdom, I have dismissed logic out of my library.'—Parkes and Merivale, i. 104–108, 250.

[1] The great coarseness with which Junius writes about women has been often noticed, and it gave rise to a very characteristic episode. A letter appeared in the *Public Advertiser* in September 1769, directed against Junius and signed Junia. Junius at once answered in a tone of coarse raillery, urging that 'since Junia has adopted my name, she cannot in common matrimonial decency refuse to make me a tender of her person,' &c. Two or three days later, it struck him that this letter was 'idle and improper,' so he wrote to Woodfall to insert a paragraph to the effect that he had 'some reason to suspect that the last letter signed Junius in this paper was not written by the real Junius.'—Woodfall's *Junius*, i. 199; iii. 218, 219.

[2] Parkes and Merivale, i. 211, 212.

[3] See Lord Brougham's sketch of Francis in his *Statesmen of George III.*

[4] Parkes and Merivale, ii. 206.

[5] Ibid. ii. 257.

superior to the miscellaneous letters, though it perhaps never rises to the excellence of the best passages in the former. If Francis was not Junius, few critics will deny that he was one of the best of his imitators. He was still alive when the volume of Taylor was published, and his conduct with reference to it was very remarkable. A few words of direct denial would have gone a long way towards silencing inquiry; but if Francis ever appeared to deny the authorship, it was always in terms that were carefully equivocal. His first gift to his wife after his second marriage was an edition of Junius; and he left her as a posthumous present, a copy of 'Junius Identified,' which was found sealed up and directed to her in his bureau. Whether truly or falsely, it is quite evident, from his whole conduct, that he desired, without committing himself to any positive assertion, to convey to her mind that he was the author of 'Junius.' Many men might have amused themselves with giving their wives falsely such an impression during their lifetime; very few would have taken measures to prolong the comedy after their death.[1]

No one of these considerations can, I think, be regarded as absolutely conclusive; but their combined force is very great. Some others of minor importance have been adduced. Such are, the numerous peculiarities of phrase or spelling that have been found in both Francis and Junius; the apparent regard and even tenderness of Junius for Woodfall, who had been a schoolfellow of Francis, and his anxious inquiry whether he did not suspect the authorship; the very curious excisions in the fragmentary autobiography of Francis, which seem as though the author were anxiously endeavouring to erase every clue to some great secret. It has been noticed that Junius never attacked Lord Holland, who had been so closely connected with Bute, and who was one of the most unpopular men in England. In one of his private letters he said, 'I wish Lord Holland may acquit himself with honour.' In another letter he speaks of himself as having 'designedly spared Lord Holland and his family;' and this forbearance has been explained by the fact that the father of Francis was domestic chaplain to Lord

---

[1] See the curious letter of Lady Francis to Lord Campbell, in Campbell's *Chancellors*, viii 211–214; and a few additional reminiscences of Lady Francis in Parkes and Merivale.

Holland, and that Philip Francis obtained his first appointment by his influence. Too much stress, however, appears to me to have been laid on this argument, for Holland had retired from active politics before Junius began to write. Francis, if he was indeed Junius, had certainly no hesitation in attacking his benefactors; and the autobiography of Francis shows that before the appearance of the Letters of Junius both father and son resented bitterly what they considered the inadequacy of the rewards they had received from Lord Holland.[1] Another common argument, which is, I think, absolutely worthless, is derived from the fact that Francis was by birth and parentage an Irishman. The interest and sympathy which Junius showed in Irish affairs, and also a few expressions which are of Irish origin, have been assumed to point to an Irish writer.[2] Francis may have derived these expressions from his father, who had lived long in Ireland; but he himself left his native country when he was not ten years old, and did not revisit it till long after the period of the letters of Junius.

Still the cumulative weight of the evidence pointing to Francis is extremely great, though it is, perhaps, too much to say that it places the case beyond all reasonable doubt. His life has been minutely investigated without discovering a single fact which is absolutely incompatible with his claim, while the most decisive evidence can be adduced against the chief rival claimants who have been named. All legal authorities seem agreed that Junius was not a lawyer; and if this be true, one large class of competitors is at once removed.[3] The number of

---

[1] Parkes and Merivale, i. 360, 361. Hayward's *More about Junius*.

[2] The most remarkable is his employment of the term 'collegian,' which is used at Dublin University (where Dr. Francis received his education). A few other expressions have been collected in Prior's *Life of Burke*, and in Coventry's *Junius*, but they are not very decisive. Great stress has been laid upon the language in which Junius spoke of Luttrell. 'He has degraded even the name of Luttrell.' 'A family on which nature seems to have entailed a hereditary baseness of disposition.' Macaulay says that to the great majority of English readers such language must have been unintelligible, and he explains it by the fact that 'Philip Francis was born and passed the first ten years of his life within a walk of Luttrellstown' (*Hist. of England*, ch. xvii.). I quite agree with Mr. Hayward (*More about Junius*, pp. 57, 58) that this argument is worthless. Residence in a great town like Dublin is not likely to give much knowledge of families living seven miles away. Francis left Dublin when he was a child, and in a fiercely contested election every family scandal that could be raked up against the unpopular candidate was sure to become known.

[3] Several writers on the subject are very confident that they can also prove (chiefly by Junius's great anxiety that the galleries of the House

persons who possessed the kind of official knowledge which he exhibited was not large, and every rival claim has either been met by some insuperable objection, or has fallen from want of positive support. The evidence pointing to Francis has been continually growing, and it may be safely affirmed that no material or intellectual objection to the theory of his authorship can be sustained.

The moral objections, however, to the Franciscan theory are real and serious; and anyone who adopts that theory must be prepared to admit that Junius was a much less honourable man than some writers have supposed. He must be prepared to admit that he was capable, under the impulse of personal or political resentment, of attacking with savage ferocity men who had been his benefactors or the benefactors of his family, and with whom he had lived on terms of friendship. He must be prepared to admit that he was equally capable of accepting great favours from men whom as an anonymous writer he had been holding up to the execration of the nation, and of associating with them on terms of intimate friendship. The father of Philip Francis had been one of the writers in the service of Bute, and the King had given him a living, a chaplaincy, an English and an Irish pension. Sir William Draper was an intimate friend of the family, and was in close correspondence with the elder Francis at the time when Junius was pursuing him with his most cutting attacks. Garrick was also a friend of his father, who had dedicated to him a play. It may, indeed, be said in extenuation that Francis had adopted opposite politics from his father; that he was only drawn reluctantly and in self-defence into a controversy with Draper; that he suspected Garrick of making inquiries into a secret which it was of vital importance to him to preserve. But what can be said of his wanton attack upon Welbore Ellis, to whom Francis partly owed his situation in the War Office, with whom he was long after on terms of intimate friendship, and whom Junius described as ‘the most contemptible little piece of machinery in the whole

of Parliament should be opened to strangers on particular nights) that he was not a member of either House of Parliament, but I confess that to my own mind there appears no evidence of any real value on the matter. See, however, *Junius Identified*, pp. 130–133. Parkes and Merivale, ii. 532, 533.

kingdom'? What, above all, can be said of his attack upon Calcraft, of whom Junius writes that he 'riots in the plunder of the army, and has only determined to be a patriot when he could not be a peer'? Nearly two years before this attack the elder Francis had described Calcraft to his son as 'the man to whom I am indebted for all your happiness, and for almost all I myself enjoy.' He was the warmest, the most intimate friend of Philip Francis, and he had laboured strenuously to secure his promotion at the War Office. Until the death of Calcraft in 1772, Francis continued in close friendship with him. By a codicil to his will Calcraft left him a legacy of 1,000l., with an annuity of 250l. for his wife, and charged his executors to bring Francis into Parliament.[1] The case of Lord Barrington is little less striking. We have seen the unmeasured ferocity with which Junius, under other names, assailed that nobleman at the time of the appointment of Chamier; and it is certain, on the Franciscan theory, that Francis then considered himself bitterly aggrieved, though it appears from his letters that he parted from Barrington on terms of perfect civility, and that he professed to his friends that he left the War Office at his own wish. He appears, however, soon to have found that Barrington had no real ill-will towards him. A little more than two years after the letters of Veteran had appeared, Francis solicited an Indian appointment of 10,000l. a year from Lord North, the favourite minister of the King, and he obtained it at the special recommendation of Lord Barrington,[2] with whom he ever after was on terms of warm friendship.[3] It may be added that when, in 1787, he was accused of acting dishonourably in accepting the position of manager in the impeachment of his personal enemy Warren Hastings, he publicly defended himself by declaring that he had consulted and obtained the approval of Sir W. Draper, than whom 'there could not be a stricter or more scrupulous judge of points of honour.'[4]

[1] See on the relations of Francis to Calcraft, Parkes and Merivale, i. 282-288.
[2] In his fragment of autobiography he says, speaking of his Indian appointment, 'Barrington was gone to Court. I saw him the next morning. As soon as I had explained everything to him, he wrote the handsomest and strongest letter imaginable in my favour to Lord North. Other interests contributed, but I owe my success to Lord Barrington.'—Parkes and Merivale, i. 324, 325.
[3] Ibid. pp. 328-330.
[4] Ibid. p. 227.

The picture is not an edifying, some have contended that it is not a possible, one. With this view I cannot concur. Of all the professions that have grown up under the conditions of modern society, anonymous writing is perhaps that in which it is most difficult to maintain a high standard of honour, for it is that in which dishonourable acts may be committed with the greatest impunity. The organ which throws the blaze of publicity on all around may be itself an asylum of impenetrable secrecy, and the power of writing without fear of detection attracts many who would once have found a congenial sphere for their talents in the baser forms of political conspiracy and intrigue. An anonymous press enables such men to strike in the dark without fear and without shame, to gratify private malice under the mask of public duty, to spread abroad calumnious falsehoods and venomous insinuations without incurring the risk or the discredit of exposure, to follow the impulses, passions, or interests of the hour without regard either to their past or to their future. It does not appear to me that there was anything in the character either of Junius or of Francis to render it impossible that they should abuse this power to the utmost. If the letters of Poplicola and of Antisejanus have been rightly attributed to Junius, we must believe that in 1767, when he suspected Chatham of subservience to Bute, he denounced him as 'a man purely and perfectly bad,' 'a traitor,' and 'a villain,' worthy of the Tarpeian Rock or of a gibbet ;[1] that a few months later, for the purpose of attaining a political end, he wrote privately to him expressing the 'sentiment of respect and veneration' he had 'always' entertained for his character,[2] and that he afterwards made him the subject of his warmest public eulogy. Even apart from this episode the facts which have been stated in the last few pages are surely sufficient to show how little Junius can be regarded as a man of scruples, truthfulness,

[1] Woodfall's *Junius*, ii. 451–467. The following passage in a letter of Antisejanus is eminently in the style of Junius. 'I will not censure him for the avarice of a pension, nor the melancholy ambition of a title. These were objects which he perhaps looked up to, though the rest of the world thought them far beneath his acceptance. But to become the stalking-horse of a stallion; to shake hands with a Scotchman at the hazard of catching all his infamy; to fight under his auspices against the Constitution, and to receive the word from him, prerogative, and a thistle (by the once respected name of Pitt); it is even below contempt.'—P. 467.

[2] *Chatham Correspondence*, iii. 302–305.

or honour. And if we turn to the acknowledged writings of Francis the probability is greatly strengthened. No single fact is more conspicuous in the character of Francis than the manner in which he continually quarrelled with those from whom he had received benefits, and his writings are full of disparaging and injurious remarks about men with whom he had lived on terms of the closest intimacy, and to whom he should have been bound by strong ties of gratitude.[1] The most powerful moral objection to the Franciscan authorship of Junius is the attack upon Calcraft. At the time it was penned Francis was in close intimacy with Calcraft, but he could not yet know that touching proof of the fidelity of his friendship which was furnished by his will. But long after Calcraft was in his grave Francis wrote the fragment of autobiography which has been discovered among his papers, and the following are the terms in which he speaks of the man who was his constant benefactor, and who was supposed to have been his warmest friend. 'Calcraft undoubtedly owed his rapid fortune to Mr. Fox's patronage. He was the son of an attorney at Grantham, and went to London literally to seek his fortune. At the age of six and forty he had a landed estate, the rent-roll of which was above 10,000l. a year. In his quarrel with Lord Holland I think he had as much reason on his side as an interested man can have for deserting an old friend and benefactor. There was not virtue in either of them to justify their quarrelling. If either of them had had common honesty he could never have been the friend of the other.'[2]

The great progress of the Press, both in literary merit and in political importance, is one of the most remarkable characteristics of the period we are reviewing. Within ten years of the publication of the letters of Junius, three newspapers which played a considerable political part long after the Reform Bill

---

[1] The following is the testimony of Merivale on this subject. 'One friend, supporter, patron, and colleague after another—Kinnoul, Chatham, Robert Wood, Calcraft, D'Oyly, Clavering, Fowke, Coote, Fox, the Prince of Wales - those who had wished well to him, defended him, showered benefits on him, appear at last in his written records branded with some unfriendly or contemptuous notice, some insinuated or pronounced aspersion, ungrateful at best, but treacherous also, if, as has been already conjectured, he meant those records to be known some day to the world.'—Parkes and Merivale, ii. 415, 416.

[2] Parkes and Merivale, i. 359.

of 1832 were called into existence. The 'Morning Chronicle' was established in 1770, the 'Morning Post' in 1772, and the 'Morning Herald' in 1780.[1] The great interest excited by the judgments of Mansfield, and by the Press cases which he decided, is said to have first led to the publication in newspapers of full legal reports.[2] Soon after, John Bell, the proprietor of the 'World' and of the 'Morning Post,' introduced newspaper dramatic criticism, and newspapers began to send their regular reporters to the pit.[3] In 1776 Lord North raised the stamp from 1d. to 1½d., but the measure does not appear to have seriously impeded the progress of the Press. In 1777 there were no less than seventeen papers published in London, seven of which were daily, and in the following year appeared Johnson's 'Sunday Monitor,' the first Sunday paper in England.[4]

But the most important fact in this period of newspaper history was the virtual conquest of the right of parliamentary reporting. William Woodfall, a relative of the printer of the 'Public Advertiser,' had paid great attention to the subject of reporting, and full reports of the more important speeches were becoming common in the newspapers. These reports were distinctly contrary to a standing order of the House. As might be expected from the manner in which they were composed they were very inaccurate and very partial, and they were in some respects much more audacious than those which had excited so much parliamentary indignation in the last reign. They were no longer confined to the recess of Parliament, but appeared when the members were still sitting. The names were sometimes given without disguise, and often indicated by grossly scurrilous nicknames. At the same time the irritation of the country against the House and the desire to make the proceedings of the representatives amenable to criticism were so great that it was dangerous to interfere with them. The City politicians resolved to make this the next subject of dispute, and for the last time Horne and Wilkes co-operated in the struggle.

---

[1] Wright's *House of Hanover*, ii. 373.
[2] Campbell's *Life of Mansfield*.
[3] Foote's *Works*, i. xlv–xlvi. See too Foote's *Bankrupt*; Andrews' *Hist. of Journalism*, i. 193.
[4] Andrews, i. 220.

It was in February 1771 that Colonel George Onslow brought before the House a complaint that two printers had misrepresented the speeches and reflected on several members of the House. The case was very flagrant, for Onslow himself had been designated as 'little cocking George,' 'the little scoundrel,' and 'that paltry, insignificant insect,' but the dangers of a new conflict at this time were so great that even the King, though violently opposed to all parliamentary reporting, recommended great caution,[1] and the same language was held by several leaders of the Opposition. The House, however, ordered the offending printers to be taken into custody; and as the Sergeant proved unable to execute the order, the House addressed the King to issue a proclamation offering a reward of 50l. for the capture of either of the delinquents.

The offence, however, still continued, and on the 12th of March Onslow brought in a new motion for proceeding against six other printers who had been guilty of it. It was determined to put down absolutely the practice of parliamentary reporting, and to declare open war with the Press. A few members, however, of the Rockingham and Chatham connections argued strenuously against this course, and although they were soon shown to be an inconsiderable minority they refused to desist. Probably for the first time in English parliamentary history the forms of the House were employed for the purpose of systematic obstruction. By repeated amendments and motions of adjournment the debate was protracted till past four in the morning, and the House was compelled to divide twenty-three times.[2] At last the majority triumphed. The six printers were ordered to attend, and the House was committed to a struggle with the Press.

Of the eight printers who were now under the ban of the House, one was already in custody by order of the House of Lords. A property case in which Lord Pomfret was defendant had recently been carried on appeal before that House, and owing probably to the social position of the defendant, the lay lords, instead of leaving the matter to the legal members, had

---

[1] *Correspondence of George III. and Lord North*, i. 57, 58.
[2] *Annual Register*, 1771, pp. 62, 63. The minorities ranged from 55 to 10, and the majorities from 143 to 70.

very scandalously taken part in the division. Lord Pomfret was in high favour at Court, and accordingly the Lords of the Bedchamber had voted in his favour. Woodfall and another printer had censured their conduct, and for this offence had been thrown into prison.[1] Of the other printers four appeared when summoned by the Commons, but Thompson and Wheble, who were the two printers first incriminated, and Miller, who was one of the others, resolved to defy the jurisdiction of the House. Wilkes and Horne, though now at enmity, appear to have independently instigated this resistance. On March 14 Wheble addressed a letter to the Speaker inclosing an opinion of counsel, and declaring that he was resolved to 'yield no obedience but to the laws of the land,' and next day both Wheble and Thompson were collusively arrested by fellow-printers and brought before two aldermen who were sitting separately to try cases. One of these aldermen was Wilkes himself; the other was his brother politician Oliver. Wilkes and Oliver at once discharged the prisoners as guilty of no legal offence, and Wilkes bound over Wheble to prosecute his captors for assault and false imprisonment, and he also wrote to the Secretary of State informing him that a man who was charged with no offence against the law of the land had been illegally arrested by virtue of a royal proclamation, in violation of the common rights of Englishmen as well as of the chartered privileges of the City of London. The two men who had made the arrest claimed the reward offered in the proclamation, but the Government being convinced that they had acted on an understanding with the culprits, refused to pay it.

Nearly at the same time a messenger of the House of Commons attempted to arrest Miller in his own house, but Miller at once sent for a constable and gave the messenger into custody. Both parties were taken to the Mansion House, where Crosby, the Lord Mayor, accompanied by Wilkes and Oliver, proceeded to try the case. The Deputy-Sergeant-at-arms attended on the part of the Speaker, and in the name of the House of Commons peremptorily ordered that both messenger and printer should be delivered up to him. The Lord Mayor, in reply, asked whether the Speaker's warrant by which Miller had been arrested had been backed by a City magistrate.

[1] Walpole's *George III.* iv. 284-286.

As the answer was in the negative he decided that it was illegal, for the charters of the City provided that no warrant, attachment, or process could be executed within it except by its own magistrates. The demand of the Deputy-Sergeant was refused. Miller was discharged from custody, and the messenger of the House of Commons was committed to prison, but admitted to bail on his own application.

It was quite evident that another conflict of the most embarrassing nature had arisen. The royal proclamation which was issued to support a standing order of the House of Commons, was of very doubtful legality, and a serious conflict had sprung up between the jurisdiction of the House and the jurisdiction of the City. The right of the House of Commons to enforce its own standing order against reporting by committing those who refused to obey it, cannot reasonably be disputed, but it had unexpectedly come into collision with another jurisdiction, which the Lord Mayor was bound by his oath of office to protect. The excitement produced by the Middlesex election had not yet subsided, and the House of Commons found itself again confronted by an agitator of whose singular audacity and address it had already ample experience. At the same time it was now impossible to recede. The printers whose arrest had been ordered were at large, and the 'Society for the Support of the Bill of Rights' voted each of them 100*l*. for having 'appealed to the law of the land, and not betrayed by submission the rights of Englishmen.' The messenger of the House of Commons was threatened with prosecution for having obeyed the orders of the House, and he would have been in prison had he not reluctantly consented to give bail. The King wrote indignantly to Lord North that the 'authority of the House of Commons is totally annihilated if it is not in an exemplary manner supported to-morrow by instantly committing the Lord Mayor and Alderman Oliver to the Tower.' 'As to Wilkes,' he added, 'he is below the notice of the House,' and he showed an amusingly significant and sagacious wish to separate him, if possible, from the proceedings against his coadjutors.[1]

---

[1] *Letters of George III. to Lord North*, i 64-67. He said very shrewdly that Wilkes must soon get into prison for debt, if some measure was not speedily taken to revive his popularity.

The Lord Mayor and Oliver, who were members of the House, were successively ordered to attend in their places, and Wilkes at the Bar of the House. Wilkes at once wrote a reply, declaring that he was the legitimate member for Middlesex, that he was ready to attend in his place in Parliament, but that he absolutely refused to appear at the Bar. The Lord Mayor and Oliver duly attended, and the former defended himself with great dignity and simplicity, alleging his oath of office which obliged him to preserve inviolate the franchises of the City, the charters of the City which secured the citizens from any law process being served upon them except by their own officers, and the confirmation of those charters by Act of Parliament. The House, as usual, speedily put itself in the wrong. The arrest and bailing of the messenger was the grievance which was most sensibly felt, and the Lord Mayor's clerk was accordingly commanded to attend with the book of minutes, and by order of the House the recognizance of the messenger of the House was erased. The conduct of the House of Commons in thus expunging by its sole authority a judicial record for the purpose of arresting the ordinary course of the law, was justly designated by Chatham as 'the act of a mob and not of a senate,' and most of the members of the Opposition protested against it by leaving the House. The House at the same time ordered that the threatened prosecution of the messenger should not be proceeded with. It had no right or power to take such a course, and accordingly the messenger was duly indicted, and only saved by the *nolle prosequi* of the Attorney-General. The House granted, after long discussion and vacillation, the demand of the Lord Mayor to be heard by counsel, but added the condition that nothing must be said against the privileges of the House, which, as the sole question at issue was the extent of these privileges, rendered the concession a palpable mockery.

Junius lost no time in summing up the proceedings of the Commons with his usual felicitous terseness. 'In their first resolutions [against the printers] it is possible that they might have been deceived by ill-considered precedents. For the rest there is no colour of palliation or excuse. They have advised the King to resume a power of dispensing with the laws by royal proclamation, and kings, we see, are ready enough to follow such advice. By mere violence, and without the shadow of right, they have expunged the record of a judicial proceeding. Nothing remained but to attribute to their own vote a power of stopping the whole distribution of criminal and civil justice.'[1] The illness of the Lord Mayor caused some delay in the proceedings of the House, and in the meantime the strong popular feeling was clearly shown. The horses of the Lord Mayor's carriage were again and again taken off, and his carriage was drawn by an enthusiastic populace who thronged the streets wherever he passed, invaded the lobbies of the House of Commons, and repeated all the scenes of riot which had so lately followed the Middlesex election. The carriages of several of the leading supporters of the Ministry were attacked and broken; Lord North very narrowly escaped with his life, and the King was hissed in the streets. The Lord Mayor and Oliver were at length committed to the Tower, but their residence there was one continued triumph. Addresses expressing admiration for their conduct poured in from every side. The leading members of the Opposition, in a procession of sixteen carriages, went to the Tower to visit them. A great mob, attended by a hearse, beheaded and burnt on Tower Hill figures representing the Princess Dowager, Lord Bute, and the leading opponents of the printers in both Houses; and when at length, after six weeks' detention, the Lord Mayor and Oliver were released by the prorogation, they were saluted by twenty-one cannon belonging to the Artillery Company, and escorted to the Mansion House by an immense crowd of enthusiastic admirers. That night London was illuminated, and the windows of the Speaker of the House of Commons were broken by the mob.

The most significant part, however, of the transaction was the manner in which the House of Commons cowered before Wilkes. He had lost no opportunity of defying it, and he was the soul of the whole movement of opposition. Three times the House summoned him to appear at the Bar, and three times he disobeyed. At last the House put an ignominious end to the contest by ordering him to attend on a day when

[1] Woodfall's *Junius*, ii. 219, 220.

it was itself adjourned.[1] The printers meanwhile remained at liberty, and from this time reports of the proceedings of the House of Commons were tacitly permitted. In the Lords the prohibition was maintained a little longer, but the example of the Commons was soon silently followed. The nation was thus enabled systematically to study and to judge the proceedings of its representatives, and the Press made another gigantic stride in political importance.

The growth of the Press as a great power in English politics is perhaps the most momentous of all the events of the period we are considering. It is not too much to say that it has modified the political life as profoundly as steam in the present century has altered the economical condition of England. Side by side with the recognised Constitution another representative system has grown up, in which the various wants, aspirations, and opinions of the nation are reflected with at least equal accuracy; another debating organ in which political questions are so fully discussed that the debates of Parliament are frequently little more than its echo. On great occasions parliamentary discussion is usually more searching and complete than discussion in the newspapers, but on most minor questions the palm of superiority must, I think, be conceded to the latter. Of all the instruments which human wisdom has devised, a free Press is the most efficacious in putting an end to jobs, abuses, political malversation and corruption. A public writer has strong motives to expose these things, and except in very rare cases he has no motive to conceal them. They wither beneath the blaze of publicity which is thrown on all the details of administration, on the discontents and grievances of every class of the community. The newspaper press not only reflects the many phases and modifications of public opinion, it also gives it an irresistible volume and momentum. Organising, directing, intensifying, and sometimes creating it, bringing the ablest leaders speedily to the surface, adding immensely to the facilities of co-operation, diffusing the popular arguments with unparalleled rapidity and over an enormous area, repeating them day by day till they have become familiar to all classes, and

[1] *Parl. Hist.* xvii. 164.

watching with an unceasing vigilance the smallest encroachment of power, it has strengthened immeasurably the spirit and resources of liberty, and has made dangers which once appeared very imminent wholly chimerical. It at the same time makes it impossible for any man of ordinary intelligence to live exclusively the life of a class or of a province. It brings before him with some degree of vividness the modes of life and thought and reasoning of all classes of his countrymen, and on great occasions it arouses the national passions with a strange velocity and power. It is the most efficacious of all means of political education. Thousands who would scarcely read anything else find in it a source of perpetual interest. The highest special knowledge is poured into its columns, and it raises enormously the average of political information, intelligence, and capacity.

It is difficult to over-estimate these services, and few persons will deny that, in England at least, they outweigh the evils which the abuses of the Press have produced. Whether they do so everywhere is less certain, and the magnitude of those evils is usually underrated by those who judge exclusively from English experience. Nowhere else in free governments do we find so large an amount of power divorced from responsibility. A very few men, who are altogether unconnected with the official business of the State, who are personally unknown to the nation, whose position is entirely self-constituted and peculiarly exposed to sinister influences, often succeed in acquiring by the Press a greater influence than most responsible statesmen. They constitute themselves the mouthpiece and the representatives of the nation, and they are often accepted as such throughout Europe. They make it their task to select, classify, and colour the information, and to supply the opinions of their readers; and as comparatively few men have the wish or the time or the power to compare evidence and weigh arguments, they dictate absolutely the conclusions of thousands. If they cannot altogether make opinion, they can at least exaggerate, bias, and inflame it. They can give its particular forms a wholly factitious importance; and while there are very few fields of labour in which the prolonged exercise of brilliant talent produces so little personal reputation, there are also very few in which exceedingly moderate abilities may exercise so wide an influence. Few things to a reflecting mind are more curious than the extraordinary weight which is attached to the anonymous expression of political opinion. Partly by the illusion of the imagination, which magnifies the hidden representative of a great corporation—partly by the weight of emphatic assertion, a plural pronoun, conspicuous type, and continual repetition, unknown men, who would probably be unable to induce any constituency to return them to Parliament, are able, without exciting any surprise or sense of incongruity, to assume the language of the accredited representatives of the nation, and to rebuke, patronise, or insult its leading men with a tone of authority which would not be tolerated from the foremost statesmen of their time. It was the theory of the more sanguine among the early free-traders that under the system of unrestricted competition all things would rank according to their real merits. In that case the power and popularity of a newspaper would depend mainly upon the accuracy and amount of its information, the force of its arguments, the fidelity with which it represented the dominant opinion of the nation. But anyone who will impartially examine the newspapers that have acquired the greatest circulation and influence in Europe and in America, may easily convince himself of the falseness of this theory. A knack of clever writing, great enterprise in bringing together the kind of information which amuses or interests the public, tact in catching and following the first symptoms of change of opinions, a skilful pandering to popular prejudice; malevolent gossip, sensational falsehood, coarse descriptions, vindictive attacks on individuals, nations, or classes, are the elements of which many great newspaper ascendencies have been mainly built. Newspaper writing is one of the most open of all professions, but some of the qualities that are most successful in it do not give the smallest presumption either of moral worth or of political competence or integrity.

It is a strange thing, though custom has made it very familiar, that so large a part of the formation and representation of political opinion should be a commercial speculation. Many papers have no doubt been set up solely to advocate particular causes and interests, and have discharged their task with admirable disinterestedness and integrity. But these are not usually the papers which have acquired the widest popularity and success. A newspaper, as such, is and must be a commercial speculation, with interests in many respects coincident, in some respects directly clashing with the true interests of the nation. Considered commercially, its popularity is the condition and the measure of its success, and it is a matter of perfect indifference from what source that popularity is derived. It must write down to the level of its readers. Its business is not to improve them but to please them. If a vicious style, if coarse, vulgar, or immoral descriptions, if personal slander or class attacks are widely popular, it is the commercial interest of the newspaper to gratify the taste, and by gratifying, it immeasurably increases it. Day after day, week after week, the impression is deepened, the taste is strengthened. No such powerful instrument as a corrupt Press has ever been discovered for vulgarising the national mind, for lowering the moral sense, for deepening, stimulating, and perpetuating class hatreds or national animosities. Most modern wars may be ultimately traced to national antipathies which have been largely created by newspaper invectives and by the gross partiality of newspaper representations. As the writers have no part in the dangers, while, by the increased circulation of their papers, they reap a large harvest from the excitement of war, they have a direct interest in producing it. Wherever there is some vicious spot, some old class hatred, some lingering provincial antipathy, a newspaper will arise to represent and to inflame it. In countries where class animosities are deep and savage, or where the form of government is still unsettled and contested, it is extremely difficult to reconcile an unshackled Press with national stability and security. The most plausible argument of the opponents of national education is the fact that in many countries it is tolerably certain that one of the chief forms of reading of the poor will consist of newspapers written for the express purpose of playing upon their most odious passions.

It was one of the felicities of English history that the Press only rose to great political importance when the troubles of a disputed succession had completely subsided; and although it is impossible to feel much respect for those who conducted it in the days of Wilkes and of Junius, they undoubtedly rendered a most important service to their country. In the early years of George III., and especially about the year 1770, there was grave danger that under the system of parliamentary government the Crown would regain all, or nearly all, the power it had lost by the Revolution. The Opposition was broken, divided, defeated. The King and the King's friends had succeeded in disintegrating the old parties in the State, in sapping the aristocratical power which was once the most formidable barrier to their designs, in disposing for their own objects of the vast fields of Government patronage, in forming a great permanent interest and acquiring an overwhelming majority in both Houses of Parliament. The Scotch, the bishops, the numerous members of both Houses who held Court offices, steadily voted together, and the ranks of the King's friends were speedily recruited by place-hunters drawn from the different connections. The elective system was so corrupt, the influence of the Treasury on the boroughs was so great, the Government patronage was so vast and so redundant, that there seemed every prospect of the continuance of their power. The immediate causes of their defeat are to be found chiefly in the growth of a free Press, which gave a new strength and energy to the popular movement for reform, and in the overwhelming discredit which the disastrous termination of the American War threw upon the ministry which had conducted it. The earlier phases of the American movement I have already very cursorily indicated. I shall now proceed to examine that movement in some detail, and to estimate its vast and various influence upon the fortunes of England.

CHAPTER XII.

AMERICA, 1763–1776.

AT the time of the Peace of Paris in 1763, the thirteen American colonies which were afterwards detached from the English Crown contained, according to the best computation, about a million and a half freemen, and their number probably slightly exceeded two millions at the time of the Declaration of Independence. No part of the British Empire had gained so largely by the late war and by the ministry of Pitt. The expulsion of the French from Canada and of the Spaniards from Florida, by removing for ever the danger of foreign interference, had left the colonists almost absolute masters of their destinies, and had dispelled the one dark cloud which hung over their future. No serious danger any longer menaced them. No limits could be assigned to their expansion. Their exultation was unbounded, and it showed itself in an outburst of genuine loyalty. The name of Pittsburg given to the fortress erected where Fort Duquesne had once stood attested the gratitude of America to the minister to whom she owed so much. Massachusetts, the foremost of the New England States, voted a costly monument in Westminster Abbey to Lord Howe, who had fallen in the conquest of Canada. The Assembly of the same State in a congratulatory address to the Governor declared that without the assistance of the parent State they must have fallen a prey to the power of France, that without the compensation granted to them by Parliament the burdens of the war would have been insupportable, that without the provisions of the treaty of peace all their successes would have been delusive. In an address to the King they repeated the same acknowledgment, and pledged themselves, in terms to which later events gave a strange significance, to demonstrate their gratitude by every possible testimony of duty and loyalty.[1]

Several acute observers had already predicted that the triumph of England would be soon followed by the revolt of her colonies. I have quoted in a former chapter the remarkable passage in which the Swedish traveller, Kalm, contended in 1748 that the presence of the French in Canada, by making the English colonists depend for their security on the support of the mother-country, was the main cause of the submission of the colonies. In his 'Notes upon England,' which were probably written about 1730, Montesquieu had dilated upon the restrictive character of the English commercial code, and had expressed his belief that England would be the first nation abandoned by her colonies. A few years later, Argenson, who has left some of the most striking political predictions upon record, foretold in his Memoirs that the English colonies in America would one day rise against the mother-country, that they would form themselves into a republic, and that they would astonish the world by their prosperity. In a discourse delivered before the Sorbonne in 1750 Turgot compared colonies to fruits which only remain on the stem till they have reached the period of maturity, and he prophesied that America would some day detach herself from the parent tree. The French ministers consoled themselves for the Peace of Paris by the reflection that the loss of Canada was a sure prelude to the independence of the colonies; and Vergennes, the sagacious French ambassador at Constantinople, predicted to an English traveller, with striking accuracy, the events that would occur. 'England,' he said, 'will soon repent of having removed the only check that could keep her colonies in awe. They stand no longer in need of her protection. She will call on them to contribute towards supporting the burdens they have helped to bring on her, and they will answer by striking off all dependence.'[2]

It is not to be supposed that Englishmen were wholly blind to this danger. One of the ablest advocates of the retention of Canada was the old Lord Bath, who published a pamphlet on

---

[1] Grahame's *Hist. of the United States*, iv. 94, 95. Hutchinson's *Hist. of Massachusetts Bay from 1749 to* 1774, p. 101.
[2] Bancroft's *Hist. of the United States*, i. 525.

the subject which had a very wide influence and circulation;[1] but there were a few politicians who maintained that it would be wiser to restore Canada and to retain Guadaloupe, with perhaps Martinico and St. Lucia. This view was supported with distinguished talent in an anonymous reply to Lord Bath, which is said to have been written by William Burke, the friend and kinsman of the great orator. Canada, this writer argued, was not one of the original objects of the war, and we had no original right to it. The acquisition of a vast, barren, and almost uninhabited country, lying in an inhospitable climate, and with no commerce except that of furs and skins, was economically far less valuable to England than the acquisition of Guadaloupe, which was one of the most important of the sugar islands. Before the war France had a real superiority in the West Indies, and the English Caribbean islands were far more endangered by the French possession of Guadaloupe, than the English American colonies by the French possession of Canada. The latter danger was, indeed, never great, and by a slight modification of territory and the erection of a few forts it might be reduced to insignificance. England in America was both a far greater continental and a far greater naval Power than France, and she had an immense superiority both in population and position. But in addition to these considerations, it was urged, an island colony is more advantageous than a continental one, for it is necessarily more dependent upon the mother-country. In the New England provinces there are already colleges and academies where the American youth can receive their education. America produces, or can easily produce, almost everything she wants. Her population and her wealth are rapidly increasing; and as the colonies recede more and more from the sea, the necessity for their connection with England will steadily diminish. 'They will have nothing to expect, they must live wholly by their own labour, and in process of time will know little, inquire little, and care little about the mother-country. If the people of our colonies find no check from Canada they will extend themselves almost without bounds into the inland parts. . . . What the consequence will be to have a numerous, hardy, independent

[1] *Letter to Two Great Men on the Prospect of Peace.*

people possessed of a strong country, communicating little or not at all with England, I leave to your own reflections. . . . By eagerly grasping at extensive territory we may run the risk, and that perhaps in no very distant period, of losing what we now possess. The possession of Canada, far from being necessary to our safety, may in its consequences be even dangerous. A neighbour that keeps us in some awe is not always the worst of neighbours. So far from sacrificing Guadaloupe to Canada, perhaps if we might have Canada without any sacrifice, we ought not to desire it. . . . There is a balance of power in America as well as in Europe.'[1]

These views are said to have been countenanced by Lord Hardwicke,[2] but the tide of opinion ran strongly in the opposite direction. Mauduit as well as Bath wrote in favour of the retention of Canada, and their arguments were supported by Franklin, who in a remarkable pamphlet sketched the great undeveloped capabilities of the colonies, and ridiculed the 'visionary fear' that they could ever be combined against England.[3] Pitt was strongly on the same side. The nation had learned to look with pride and sympathy upon that greater England which was growing up beyond the Atlantic, and there was a desire which was not ungenerous or ignoble to remove at any risk the one obstacle to its future happiness. It was felt that the colonists who had contributed so largely to the conquest of Cape Breton had been shamefully sacrificed at the Peace of Aix-la-Chapelle, when that province was restored to France; and that the expulsion of the French from Canada was essential, not only

---

[1] *Remarks on the Letter Addressed to Two Great Men*, pp. 30, 31.

[2] Hutchinson's *History of Massachusetts Bay, from 1749 to 1774*, p. 100. Hardwicke, however, is said to have been governed exclusively by commercial considerations.

[3] 'Their jealousy of each other is so great, that however necessary a union of the colonies has long been for their common defence and security against their enemies, and how sensible soever each colony has been of that necessity, yet they have never been able to effect such a union among themselves, nor even to agree in requesting the mother-country to establish it for them. Nothing but the immediate command of the Crown has been able to produce even the imperfect union but lately seen there of the forces of some colonies. If they could not agree to unite for their defence against the French and Indians . . . can it reasonably be supposed there is any danger of their uniting against their own nation, which protects and encourages them, with which they have so many connections and ties of blood, interest, and affection, and which it is well known, they all love much more than they love one another?'—Canada Pamphlet, Franklin's *Works*, iv. 41, 42.

to the political and commercial prosperity of the Northern colonists, but also to the security of their homes. The Indian tribes clustered thickly around the disputed frontier, and the French being numerically very inferior to the English, had taken great pains to conciliate them, and at the same time to incite them against the English. Six times within eighty-five years the horrors of Indian war had devastated the northern and eastern frontier.[1] The Peace of Paris, by depriving the Indians of French support, was one of the most important steps to their subjection.

To any statesman who looked upon the question without passion and without illusion it must have appeared evident that if the English colonies resolved to sever themselves from the British Empire, it would be impossible to prevent them. Their population is said to have doubled in twenty-five years. They were separated from the mother-country by three thousand miles of water. Their seaboard extended for more than one thousand miles. Their territory was almost boundless in its extent and in its resources, and the greater part of it was still untraversed and unexplored. To conquer such a country would be a task of great difficulty, and of ruinous expense. To hold it in opposition to the general wish of the people would be impossible. England by her command of the sea might easily destroy its commerce, disturb its fisheries, bombard its seaboard towns, and deprive it of many of the luxuries of life, but she could strike no vital blow. The colonists were chiefly small and independent freeholders, hardy backwoodsmen and hunters, universally acquainted with the use of arms, and with all the resources and energies which life in a new country seldom fails to develop. They had representative assemblies to levy taxes and organise resistance. They had militias which in some colonies included all adult freemen between the ages of sixteen or eighteen and fifty or sixty;[2] and in addition to the Indian raids, they had the

---

[1] Hildreth's *History of the United States,* ii. 496.

[2] Burnaby's *Travels in North America.* Pinkerton's *Voyages,* xiii. 725, 728, 749. Gerard Hamilton, in a letter written in 1767, said, 'There are in the different provinces above a million of people of which we may suppose at least 200,000 men able to bear arms; and not only able to bear arms, but having arms in their possession unrestrained by any iniquitous game Act. In the Massachusetts Government particularly there is an express law by which every man is obliged to have a musket, a pound of

military experience of two great wars. The capture of Louisburg in 1749 had been mainly their work, and although at the beginning of the following war they exhibited but little alacrity, Pitt, by promising that the expenses should be reimbursed by the British Parliament, had speedily called them to arms. In the latter stages of the war more than 20,000 colonial troops, 10,000 of them from New England alone, had been continually in the field, and more than 400 privateers had been fitted out in the colonial harbours.[1] The colonial troops were, it is true, only enlisted for a single campaign, and they therefore never attained the steadiness and discipline of English veterans; but they had co-operated honourably in the conquest of Canada, and even in the expeditions against Havannah and Martinique, and they contained many skilful officers quite capable of conducting a war.

Under such circumstances, with the most moderate heroism, and even without foreign assistance, a united rebellion of the English colonies must have been successful, and their connection with the mother-country depended mainly upon their disposition towards her and towards each other. For some years before the English Revolution, and for several years after the accession of William, the relations of the colonies to England had been extremely tense; but in the long period of unbroken Whig rule which followed, most of the elements of discontent had subsided. The wise neglect of Walpole and Newcastle was eminently conducive to colonial interests. The substitution in several colonies of royal for proprietary governments was very popular. It was found that the direct rule of the Sovereign was much more equitable and liberal than that of private companies or individuals. Pennsylvania, Maryland, and Delaware alone retained the proprietary form, and in the first two at least, a large party desired that the proprietors should be compensated, and that the colonies should be placed directly under the Crown.[2] There were slight differences in the colonial forms of government,

---

powder, and a pound of bullets always by him, so there is nothing wanting but knapsacks (or old stockings, which will do as well) to equip an army for marching.'—*Chatham Correspondence*, iii. 203.

[1] Ramsay's *Hist. of the American Revolution*, i. 40. Hildreth, ii. 486.

Grahame, iv. 94.

[2] See a very remarkable pamphlet of Franklin, called *Cool Thoughts on the Present Situation* (1764), advocating the abolition of the proprietary government in Pennsylvania. *Franklin's Works*, iv. 78–93.

but everywhere the colonists paid their governors and their other officials. The lower chamber in each province was elected freely by the people, and in nearly every respect they governed themselves under the shadow of the British dominion with a liberty which was hardly equalled in any other portion of the civilised globe. Political power was incomparably more diffused, and the representative system was incomparably less corrupt than at home, and real constitutional liberty was flourishing in the English colonies when nearly all European countries and all other colonies were despotically governed. Material prosperity was at the same time advancing with giant strides, and religious liberty was steadily maintained. Whatever might be her policy nearer home, in the colonies the English Government in the eighteenth century uniformly opposed the efforts of any one sect to oppress the others.[1]

The circumstances and traditions of the colonists had made them extremely impatient of every kind of authority, but there is no reason for doubting that they were animated by a real attachment to England. Their commercial intercourse, under the restrictions of the Navigation Law, was mainly with her. Their institutions, their culture, their religion, their ideas were derived from English sources. They had a direct interest in the English war against France and Spain. They were proud of their English lineage, of English greatness, and of English liberty, and, in the words of Franklin, they had 'not only a respect but an affection for Great Britain; . . . to be an Old England man was of itself a character of some respect, and gave a kind of rank among them.'[2] Hutchinson, the Governor of Massachusetts, who was one of the strongest supporters of the royal authority, acknowledges that when George III. mounted the throne, if speculative men sometimes figured in their minds an American Empire, it was only 'in such distant ages that nobody then

---

[1] In Carolina a law had been passed depriving the Dissenters of their political privileges, but it was repealed by the King in Council. Franklin's *Works*, iv. 84. Franklin adds, 'Nor is there existing in any of the American colonies any test imposed by Great Britain to exclude Dissenters from office. In some colonies, indeed, where the Episcopalians, and in others the Dissenters, have been predominant, they have made partial laws in favour of their respective sects, and laid some difficulties on the others, but those laws have been generally, on complaint, repealed at home.' P. 88.

[2] See his evidence before Parliament in 1766. Franklin's *Works*, iv. 169.

living could expect to see it;' and he adds that the rapid growth of colonial power had as yet produced no 'plan or even desire of independency,' and that 'the greatest hope from the reduction of Canada, as far as could be judged from the public prayers of the clergy as well as from the conversation of people in general, was 'to sit quiet under their own vines and fig-trees, and to have none to make them afraid.'[1] The great career of Pitt, which had intensified patriotic feelings throughout the Empire, was nowhere more appreciated than in America, and the Peace of Paris, however distasteful to Englishmen, might at least have been expected to strengthen the loyalty of the colonies. It had been made by men who were wholly beyond the range of their influence, yet they had gained incomparably more by it than any other portion of the Empire.

The patriotism of the colonies indeed attracted them far more to England than to each other. Small groups of colonies were no doubt drawn together by a natural affinity, but there was no common colonial government, and they were in general, at least as jealous of each other as of England. One of the chief excuses for imposing by parliamentary authority imperial taxation on the colonies was the extreme difficulty of inducing them to co-operate cordially for military purposes.[2] Soon after the Revolution William had proposed a plan for general defence against the French forces in Canada by which each colony was to contribute a contingent proportionate to its numbers, but all the colonial Assemblies rejected it, and the States which were most remote from the danger absolutely refused to participate in the

---

[1] Hutchinson's *Hist. of Massachusetts Bay,* 84, 85.

[2] The Swedish traveller Kalm, who visited North America in 1749 and 1750, was much struck with this dislike to co-operation. He says, 'Each English colony in North America is independent of the other.... From hence it happens that in time of war things go on very slowly and irregularly here; for not only the sense of one province is sometimes directly opposite to that of another, but frequently the views of the governor and those of the Assembly of the same province are quite different.... It has commonly happened that while some provinces have been suffering from their enemies, the neighbouring ones were quiet and inactive and as if it did not in the least concern them. They have frequently taken up two or three years in considering whether they should give assistance to an oppressed sister colony, and sometimes they have expressly declared themselves against it. There are instances of provinces who were not only neuter in these circumstances, but who even carried on a great trade with the Power which at that very time was attacking and laying waste some other provinces.'—Pinkerton's *Voyages,* xiii 460, 461.

expense.¹ In 1754, when another great war was impending, a Congress of Commissioners from the different colonies assembled at Albany, at the summons of the Lords of Trade, for the purpose of concerting together and with the friendly Indians upon measures of defence. Benjamin Franklin was one of the Commissioners for Pennsylvania, and he brought forward a plan for uniting the colonies for defence and for some other purposes of general utility into a single Federal State, administered by a President-General appointed by the Crown, and by a general council elected by the colonial Assemblies; but the plan was equally repudiated by the colonial Legislatures as likely to abridge their authority, and by the Board of Trade as likely to foster colonial independence.² In the war that ensued it was therefore left to the colonial legislatures to act independently in raising troops and money, and while the Northern colonies which lay nearest Canada more than fulfilled their part, some of the Southern ones refused to take any considerable share of the burden. The management of Indian affairs gradually passed with general approval from the different colonial legislatures to the Crown, as it was found impossible to induce the former to act together on any settled plan.³ The history of the colonies during the twenty or thirty years preceding the Declaration of Independence is full of intestine or inter-colonial disputes. There were angry discussions about boundaries between Massachusetts on the one hand, and Rhode Island, New Hampshire, and Connecticut on the other. Albany was long accused of trafficking largely with the Indians for the spoils they had obtained in their raids upon New England. New York quarrelled fiercely with Virginia about the responsibility for the failure of a military expedition, and with New Hampshire about the government of the territory which was subsequently known as Vermont. In Pennsylvania and Maryland the Assemblies were in continual hostility with their proprietaries, and the mother-country was compelled to decide a violent dispute about salaries between the Virginian laity and clergy. Great bodies of Dutch, Germans, French, Swedes, Scotch,

¹ Grahame, iii 13.   ² Franklin's *Works*, i. 177.
³ Grahame, iv. 145–147.

and Irish, scattered among the descendants of the English, contributed to the heterogeneous character of the colonies, and they comprised so many varieties of government, religious belief, commercial interest, and social type, that their union appeared to many incredible on the very eve of the Revolution.[1] The movement which at last arrayed them in a united front against England was not a blind instinctive patriotism or community of sentiment, like that which animates old countries. It was the deliberate calculation of intelligent men, who perceived that by such union alone could they attain the objects of their desire.

New England, which was the centre of the resistance, was then divided into the four States of Massachusetts Bay, Connecticut, New Hampshire, and Rhode Island, and it was, in proportion to its size, by far the most populous portion of British America. It comprised about a third part of its whole population,[2] and Massachusetts alone had, during a great part of the last war, maintained 7,000 men under arms. The descendants of the old Puritans, the New Englanders were still chiefly Congregationalists or Presbyterians, and there might be found among them an austerity of manners and of belief which was hardly exceeded in Scotland. It was, however, gradually declining under many influences. Time, increas-

---

[1] The following is the judgment of that usually very acute observer, Burnaby, who travelled through the colonies in 1759 and 1760. 'Fire and water are not more heterogeneous than the different colonies in North America. Nothing can exceed the jealousy and emulation which they possess in regard to each other. The inhabitants of Pennsylvania and New York have an inexhaustible source of animosity in their jealousy for the trade of the Jerseys. Massachusetts Bay and Rhode Island are not less interested in that of Connecticut. The West Indies are a common subject of emulation to them all. Even the limits and boundaries of each colony are a constant source of litigation. In short, such is the difference of character, of manners, of religion, of interest of the different colonies, that I think if I am not wholly ignorant of the human mind, were they left to themselves, there would soon be a civil war from one end of the continent to the other; while the Indians and negroes would with better reason impatiently watch the opportunity of exterminating them altogether.'—Pinkerton, xiii. 752. Otis, one of the earliest and most considerable of the American patriots, wrote in 1765, 'God forbid these colonies should ever prove undutiful to their mother-country. Whenever such a day shall come it will be the beginning of a terrible scene. Were these colonies left to themselves to-morrow, America would be a mere shambles of blood and confusion before little petty states could be settled.'—*Answer to the Halifax Libel*, p. 16.

[2] According to Grahame (iv. 125) in 1763 it contained upwards of 500,000 persons. The *North American Gazetteer* (2nd edit. 1778) estimates its population at upwards of 600,000.

ing wealth, the intellectual atmosphere of the eighteenth century, the disorders and changes produced by a state of war, contact with large bodies of European soldiers, and also the demoralising influence of a great smuggling trade with the French West Indies, had all in their different ways impaired the old types of character. The Governments of three of the colonies were exceedingly democratic. In Massachusetts the Council or Upper Chamber, instead of being, as in most provinces, appointed by the Sovereign, was elected annually by the Lower Chamber; every town officer was annually chosen; all town affairs were decided in public meetings; the clergy were selected by their congregations, and, with the exception of a few Custom-house officers, the Crown officers were paid by the State. The Governor was appointed by the Crown, and he possessed a right of veto upon laws, and also upon the appointment of Councillors; but as his own salary and that of the whole Executive depended on the popular vote, and as the Council emanated directly from the representative body, his actual power was extremely small. The civil list allowed by the Assembly was precarious and was cut down to the narrowest limits. The Governor usually received 1,000*l*. English currency a year, but obtained some additional occasional grants. The Lieutenant-Governor received no salary as such, except during the absence of the Governor, and the office was therefore usually combined with some other. The judges had each only about 120*l*. sterling a year, with the addition of some fees, which were said not to have been sufficient to cover their travelling expenses.[1] The Attorney-General received no salary from the Assembly, as the Governor refused to recognise its claim to have a voice in his appointment. Rhode Island and Connecticut were even more democratic than Massachusetts. By the charters conceded to these colonies, the freemen elected all their officers from the highest to the lowest, and they were not obliged to communicate the acts of their local legislatures to the King. Such a system had naturally led to grave abuses, and in Rhode Island especially there were loud complaints of the scandalous par-

---

[1] *Reports of the Board of Trade on the Establishments in America* (1766). American Papers, MSS., Record Office. See too a letter of Hutchinson in the *American Remembrancer*, 1776, part i. 159.

tiality of the judges and of the low prevailing tone of honesty and statesmanship.[1]

One of the most remarkable recent changes in New England manners was the extraordinary increase of litigation and the rapid growth in numbers and importance of the legal class. For a century and a half of colonial days there were but two lay presidents of Harvard College; nearly half the students were intended for some church ministry, and the profession of a lawyer was looked upon as in some degree dishonest and disreputable. It was rapidly rising, however, in New England as elsewhere, and it contributed more than any other profession to the Revolution.[2] Jefferson, Adams, Otis, Dickenson, and many other minor agents in the struggle were lawyers. Another influence which did much to lower the New England character was the abundance of depreciated paper money. In 1750 the British Parliament granted a sum of money to reimburse Massachusetts for what it had expended more than its proportion towards the general expense of the war, and the Legislature of the province determined to redeem their paper, but to do so at a depreciated value, and only an ounce of silver was given for 50s. of paper, though the bills themselves promised an ounce for 6s. 8d. In 1751 the mother-country was obliged to interpose to prevent the New Englanders from cheating their English creditors by making paper legal tender.[3]

---

[1] See the very unfavourable picture given by Burnaby; Pinkerton, xiii. 742, 743. Winterbotham's *Present Situation of the United States* (1795), ii. 236. Burke's *European Settlements in America*, ii. 300.

[2] See a curious passage in the Life of Adams prefixed to his *Familiar Letters to his Wife*, pp. x. xiv. Tucker says of America, 'In no country perhaps in the world are there so many lawsuits.'—*Letter to Burke*, p. 26. So too Burke, 'In no country perhaps in the world is the law so general a study. The profession itself is numerous and powerful, and in most provinces it takes the lead. The greater number of the deputies sent to Congress were lawyers. . . . I have been told by an eminent bookseller that in no branch of his business, after tracts of popular devotion, were so many books as those on the law exported to the plantations.'—*Speech on Conciliation with America*. See too Burke's *European Settlements in America*, ii. 304. The passion for the law steadily increased, and in 1787 Noah Webster wrote, 'Never was such a rage for the study of law. From one end of the continent to the other the students of this science are multiplying without number. An infallible proof that the business is lucrative.'—Webster's *Essays*, p. 116.

[3] 24 Geo. II. c. 53. Another law to facilitate recovery of debts from America was made in 1732 (5 Geo. II. c. 7). See on this subject Tucker's *Letter to Burke*, pp. 29-31. Bolles' *Financial History of the United States*, pp. 29, 30.

Still with every drawback the bulk of the New Englanders were a people of strong fibre and high morals. Strictly Sabbatarian, rigidly orthodox, averse to extravagance, to gambling, and to effeminate amusements, capable of great efforts of self-sacrifice, hard, stubborn, and indomitably intractable, they had most of the qualities of a ruling race. The revival of Jonathan Edwards, the later preaching of Whitefield, and the numerous days of fasting or thanksgiving, had done something to sustain their fanaticism. A severe climate and long struggles with the French and the Indians had indurated their characters, and the common schools which had been established in the middle of the seventeenth century in every village had made a certain level of education universal. Their essentially republican religion, the traditions of their republican origin, and the republican tone of their manners, had all conspired to maintain among them a spirit of fierce and jealous independence. They had few manufactures. Slavery, being unsuited to their soil and climate, had taken but little root, and there was said to be no other portion of the globe in which there was so little either of wealth or of poverty.[1] The bulk of the population were small freeholders cultivating their own land. By a somewhat singular anomaly, the democratic colony of Rhode Island, during nearly the whole of its colonial history, adopted the English law of real property with its system of entail and primogeniture; but in the other New England colonies the law favoured equal division, reserving, however, in the case of intestacy, a double portion for the elder son.[2] Extreme poverty was unknown; yet Burke, who was admirably acquainted with American life, questioned whether there were two persons either in Massachusetts or Connecticut who could afford to spend 1,000l. a year at a distance from their estates.[3] Boston, at the time of the Peace of Paris, contained 18,000 or 20,000 inhabitants.[4] It was the great intellectual centre of

---

[1] Winterbotham's *View of the United States*, ii. 3, 4.
[2] Story's *Constitution of the United States*, i. 90, 166.
[3] *Observations on the State of the Nation.*
[4] Burnaby in 1759 reckons the population of Boston at from 18,000 to 20,000. Pinkerton, xiii. 744. Adams in his Diary, *Works* ii. 213, estimates it at 16,000. Winterbotham, some years after the Revolution, reckons it at 18,038. In the *North American Gazetteer*, it is placed as high as 30,000, but this is certainly an exaggeration.

the colonies, and five printing presses were in constant employment within its walls. It contained the chief distilleries in America; it was noted for its commerce, its ship-building, and its cod-fishery; and in 1763 no less than eighty New England vessels were employed in the whale fishery at the mouth of the St. Lawrence.[1] Boston, however, unlike most American towns, appears for a long time to have been almost stationary. The rise of New York, Philadelphia, and other towns had diminished its prosperity, and the New England States were burdened by considerable natural disadvantages, and by the great weight of debt bequeathed from the war.

Among the Middle States the two provinces of New York and New Jersey still contained many families descended from the old Dutch settlers; but they were being rapidly lost in a very miscellaneous population. Twenty-one years before New York, or, as it was then called, New Amsterdam, fell into the hands of the English, it was computed that no less than eighteen different languages were spoken in or near the town,[2] and it continued under English rule to be one of the chief centres of foreign immigration. It was noticed during the War of Independence, that the political indifference of these colonies formed a curious contrast to the vehemence of New England,[3] and New York fluctuated more violently in its political attitude than any other colony in America. The town at the Peace of Paris was little more than half the size of Boston, but it was rapidly advancing in commercial prosperity, and large fortunes were being accumulated. In the country districts much of the simplicity and frugality of the old Dutch settlers survived; but the tone of manners in the town was less severe and more luxurious than in New England. There were but few signs of the theological intolerance so conspicuous in some of the older States, and very many religions, representing very many nationalities, subsisted side by side in apparent harmony. There was little intellectual life; education was very backward, and the pursuit of wealth appears to have been the absorbing passion. The letters written by the Governor and Lieutenant-Governor to the home authorities in

---

[1] Grahame's *Hist.* iv. 129, 130. Burke's *European Settlements*, ii. 183.
[2] Tyler's *Hist. of American Literature*, ii. 206.
[3] Chastellux (Eng. trans.), *Travels in North America in 1780–1782*, ii. 180.

1765 and the two following years give a curious, though perhaps somewhat overcharged picture, of the less favourable aspects of New York life. The most opulent men in the State had risen within a single generation from the lowest class. Few persons except lawyers had any tincture of literature, and lawyers under these circumstances had attained a greater power in this province than in any other part of the King's dominions. They had formed an association for the purpose of directing political affairs. In an Assembly where the majority of the members were ignorant and simple-minded farmers, they had acquired a controlling power; they knew the secrets of every family. They were the chief writers in a singularly violent press. They organised and directed every opposition to the Governor, and they had attained an influence not less than that of the priesthood in a bigoted Catholic country. There was a long and bitter quarrel about the position of the judges, one party wishing that they should hold their office during good behaviour, and should thus be beyond the control of the Executive or Home Government; the other party wishing that they should receive fixed and adequate salaries, instead of being dependent on the annual vote of the Assembly. The utmost annual sum the Assembly would vote for its Chief Justice was 300l. of New York currency, which was much less valuable than the currency of England. Legal decisions are said to have been given with great and manifest partiality. 'In the present state of our courts of justice,' wrote the Lieutenant-Governor, 'all private property for some years past, as well as the rights and authority of the King, are more precarious than can be easily imagined.' On one occasion the Chief Justice gave a judgment against a member of the Assembly; by the influence of that member his salary was reduced by 50l. In cases affecting the Revenue Acts or the property rights of the Crown, the law was almost impotent, and the Governor vainly tried to obtain the right of appeal to an English court. Cases under 5l. in value were decided by the local magistrates; and as it was the custom for each member of the Assembly to have the nomination to all civil and military offices in his own county, the Commission of the Peace was the usual reward of electioneering services. Nothing was more common than to find petty cases decided in public-houses by magistrates who were selected from the meanest and least respectable tradesmen, and who were sometimes so ignorant that they were obliged to put a mark instead of a signature to their warrants.[1]

By far the most important of the Middle States was the great industrial colony of Pennsylvania. A fertile soil, a great abundance of mineral wealth, a situation singularly favourable to commercial intercourse, and a population admirably energetic and industrious, had contributed to develop it, and it far surpassed all the other colonies in the perfection of its agriculture, and in the variety, magnitude, and prosperity of its manufactures. Its population at the time of the Declaration of Independence appears to have been about 350,000. The Quakers, who were its first colonists, now formed about a fifth part of the population, and still exercised the greatest power in the Assembly. Pennsylvania, however, rivalled or surpassed New York in its attraction to foreign immigrants, and few countries have contained so great a mixture of nationalities. The Germans were so numerous that they for some time returned 15 out of the 69 members of the Assembly.[2] Nearly 12,000 had landed in the single summer of 1749, and in the middle of the century a German weekly paper was published at Philadelphia.[3] There was also a large colony of Irish Presbyterians, who lived chiefly along the western frontier, and who had established a prosperous linen manufacture; and Swedes, Scotch, Welsh, and a few Dutch might be found among the inhabitants. The law of real property was nearly the same as in Massachusetts. There was perfect liberty, and the prevailing spirit was gentle, humane, pacific, and keenly money-

[1] *Documents relating to the Colonial History of New York procured in Holland, England, and France,* vii. 500, 705, 760, 774, 796, 797, 908, 979. New York is described by most of the writers on America I have already quoted. J. Adams gives a very unfavourable picture of the manners of its inhabitants. He writes, 'With all the opulence and splendour of this city [New York] there is very little good breeding to be found. We have been treated with an assiduous respect, but I have not seen one real gentleman, one well-bred man, since I came to town. At their entertainments there is no conversation that is agreeable; there is no modesty; no attention to one another. They talk very loud, very fast, and all together. If they ask you a question, before you can utter three words of your answer they will break out upon you again and talk away.'—Adams' Diary, 1774. *Works,* ii. 353. On the condition of education in New York, see Tyler's *Hist. of American Literature,* ii. 206, 207.

[2] Winterbotham, ii. 439.

[3] Kalm's *Travels in North America.* Pinkerton, xiii. 395, 396.

making. The Quakers, though their distinctive character was very clearly imprinted on the colony, had found that some departure from their original principles was indispensable. A section of them, in flagrant opposition to the original tenet of their sect, contended that war was not criminal when it was strictly defensive. A long line of cannon defended the old Quaker capital against the French and Spanish privateers; and the Pennsylvanian Assembly, in which the Quakers predominated, repeatedly voted military aids to the Crown during the French wars, disguising their act by voting the money only 'for the King's use,' and on one occasion ' for the purchase of bread, flour, wheat, *or other grain*,' the latter being understood to be gunpowder.[1]

Philadelphia was probably at this time the most beautiful and attractive city in the American colonies; famous for its shipbuilding, for the great variety of its commerce, and for its very numerous institutions of benevolence and instruction. Burnaby, who visited it in 1759, was filled 'with wonder and admiration' at the noble city which had grown up where, eighty years before, the deer and the buffalo had ranged. He dilates upon the admirable lighting and paving of the streets, upon its stately town hall, upon its two public libraries; upon its numerous churches, almshouses, and schools; upon its market, which was 'almost equal to that of Leadenhall;' upon the crowd of ships that thronged its harbour. He estimated its population at 18,000 or 20,000, and he tells us that about twenty-five ships were annually built in its docks, and that many of its houses were let for what was then the very large sum of 100*l*. a year. It contained an opulent and brilliant, if somewhat exclusive society, with all the luxury of a European city. The gay profusion of flowers that were scattered through the houses, the rich orchards extending to the very verge of the town, and encircling every important dwelling; the aspect of well-being which was displayed in every class; the use of tea, which as early as 1750 was universal in every farmer's house;[2] the mul-

---

[1] Franklin's *Life*, pp. 148–155. Kalm's *Travels*. Pinkerton, xiii. 391. As early as 1741, the Quaker, Thomas Chalkley, had lamented the falling away of Pennsylvanian Quakers in this respect. See his curious *Life, Travels, and Christian Experiences* (ed. 1850), pp. 362, 363.

[2] Kalm's *Travels*. Pinkerton, xiii. 494.

tiplication of country seats; the taste for lighter and more cheerful manners, which had sprung from contact with the English officers during the war; the periodical assemblies of gentlemen and ladies of the best society to pass the summer days in fishing upon the Schuylkill, diversified with music and with dancing—all bring before us the picture of a State which was far removed from the simplicity, the poverty, and the austerity of its Quaker founders.[1] To a European, however, or at least to a French taste, the tone of manners appeared formal and cumbrous. A brilliant Frenchman who visited Philadelphia during the War of Independence, complained with some humour that dancing, which in other countries was regarded as an emblem of gaiety and love, was treated in America as an emblem of legislation and marriage; that every detail of a ball was regulated beforehand with the most minute precision, and carried out with a stern severity; that each dancer was restricted to the same partner for the whole evening;[2] and that the almost endless succession of toasts that were rigidly enforced, made an American entertainment nearly intolerable to a stranger. He noticed, too, the significant manner in which, in the absence of titles, precedence had come to be determined by wealth.[3] A curious relic of a standard of commercial integrity which had long since passed away, survived in the middle of the century in the custom of 'marriage in the shift.' When a man died leaving debts which his widow was unable to pay, she was obliged, if she contracted a second marriage, to leave her clothes in the hands of the creditors, and to go through the ceremony in her shift. Gradually, however, the ceremony was mitigated by the bridegroom lending her clothes for the occasion.[4] The conflicts with the proprietary

---

[1] Burnaby's *Travels*. See too Kalm's *Travels*, ten years earlier, and the *North American Gazetteer*, arts. 'Pennsylvania' and 'Philadelphia.' There is a very graphic description of Philadelphia, evidently by an eye-witness, in that curious book, the *Life of Bampfylde Moore Carew*, published in 1749, 1750.

[2] The same custom, however, appears to have prevailed in England. Junius, in one of his private letters to Wilkes, alludes to it. 'I appeal to Miss Wilkes, whose judgment I hear highly commended, would she think herself much indebted to her favourite admirer if he forced a most disagreeable partner upon her, for a long winter's night, because he would not dance with her himself?' See on this custom the remarks of Twisleton, Twisleton and Chabot's *Handwriting of Junius*, p. 235.

[3] Chastellux's *Travels*, i. 278.

[4] Kalm. Pinkerton, xiii. 512.

government turned chiefly upon the question of how far the proprietary estates might be submitted to taxation, and the decision of the mother-country was given in favour of the colonists. The conflict was especially violent on account of the peculiarity of the Pennsylvanian Government, which consisted only of two parts, a governor and a representative chamber, while in the other colonies the council or upper chamber acted the part of a mediator or umpire. A Council existed, it is true, in Pennsylvania, but it had no legislative power, and was restricted to the function of advising the Executive. The proprietary government was both weak and unpopular; and Pennsylvania, like most other colonies, was disturbed by many outbreaks of lawless violence.

The only other colony which it is necessary particularly to notice on account of the part which it played in the Revolution, is Virginia, the oldest of the charter colonies—the colony of Washington, Jefferson, Patrick Henry, the Randolphs, and the Lees. At the Peace of Paris, in 1763, it appears to have contained about 200,000 inhabitants, the large majority being slaves,[1] and its character was wholly different from the Puritan type of New England and from the industrial type of Pennsylvania. The Church of England was here the dominant religion, and it was established by law. There was a fixed revenue for the support of the civil establishments, derived partly from Crown quit rents, and partly from a duty on tobacco, which had been granted for ever. A system of entails subsisted which was even stricter than that in England, and it concurred with the conditions of slave labour and with the nature of the soil to produce a much more unequal distribution of property than in the Northern colonies. The Ulster Presbyterians, who had penetrated largely into Massachusetts, Pennsylvania, Maryland, and North Carolina, had formed a considerable settlement on the northern and western frontiers of Virginia, and a few French refugees were also established in the colony, but over the greater part of it the English element was in the free population almost unmixed. Education in general was very backward. There were scarcely any manufactures, and

[1] Compare, on the population of Virginia, Burnaby; Pinkerton, xiii. p. 711; Grahame, iv. 122; Winterbotham.

there was but little town life. Wheat was produced in abundance, and the tobacco of Virginia and of the adjoining colony of Maryland was long esteemed the finest in the world. Four great navigable rivers enabled the planters to load their ships before their own doors at distances of more than eighty miles from the sea; and in 1758, 70,000 hogsheads of tobacco were exported from Virginia.[1] After this time the tobacco culture seems to have somewhat dwindled, under the rising competition of Georgia and of the western country along the Mississippi. The management of the colony was chiefly in the hands of great planters, some of them descended from Cavaliers who had emigrated during the troubles of the Commonwealth. They were a high-spirited and haughty class, extremely tenacious of social rank, hospitable, convivial, full of energy and courage, and as essentially aristocratic in their feelings, if not in their manners, as the proudest nobility of Europe. They resented bitterly the entry during the Revolution war of new families into power, and it was noticed that the popular or democratic party in this province showed more zeal in breaking down precedence than in combating the English.[2] A great portion of the colony was absolutely uncultivated and uncleared,[3] but large landed properties gave so much social consequence that they were rarely broken up, though they were usually very heavily encumbered by debts. In Virginia, as in the other colonies, there were some yeomen, but this class can never flourish where slavery exists, and there was an idle, dissipated, indebted, and impoverished population, descended in a great degree from younger sons of planters, who looked with contempt on manual labour, and who were quite ready to throw themselves into any military enterprise. A traveller from Europe, after passing through the greater part of the colonies, noticed that in Virginia, for the first time, he saw evidence of real poverty among the whites.[4] The upper classes were keen huntsmen; among all classes there was much gambling and an intense

---

[1] Winterbotham, iii. 112.
[2] Chastellux, ii. 189.
[3] Noah Webster, who was one of the best of the early economists of America, wrote in 1790: 'In Virginia and Maryland I should question whether a tenth of the land is yet cultivated. In New England more than half the whole is cultivated, and in Connecticut scarcely a tenth remains in a wild state.' Webster's *Essays*, p. 365.
[4] Chastellux, ii. 190.

passion for horse-racing, and even in districts where there were no public conveyances and no tolerable inns, great crowds from distances of thirty or forty miles were easily collected by a cock-fight.[1] Among the lower class of whites there was a great brutality of manners, and they were especially noted for their habit of 'gouging' out each other's eyes in boxing matches and quarrels.[2] 'Indians and negroes,' a traveller observed, 'they scarcely consider as of the human species.' Acts of violence, and even murder, of which they were the victims, were never or scarcely ever punished, and no negro was suffered to give evidence in a court of law except at the trial of a slave for a capital offence.[3] Virginia, however, was a great breeding country for negroes, and chiefly, perhaps, for this reason they are said to have been treated there with somewhat less habitual cruelty than in the West Indies.[4]

Burke has very truly said that slave-owners are often of all men the most jealous of their freedom, for they regard it not only as an enjoyment but as a kind of rank; and it may be added that slavery, when it does not coexist with a thoroughly enervating climate, is exceedingly favourable to the military qualities, for by the stigma which it attaches to labour it diverts men from most peaceful and industrial pursuits. Both of these truths were exemplified in Virginia, which produced a very large proportion of the most prominent advocates of independence, while it was early noted for the efficiency of its militia.[5] Virginia always claimed to be the leading as well as the oldest colony in America, and though its people were much more dissipated and extravagant than those of the Northern colonies, the natural advantages of the province were so great, and the tobacco crop raised by the negroes was so valuable, that in the ten years preceding 1770 the average value of the exports from Virginia and Maryland exceeded by considerably more than a third the united exports of the New England colonies, New York and Pennsylvania.[6] A large number of the planters appear to

---

[1] Chastellux, pp. 28, 29.
[2] Ibid. pp. 192, 193.
[3] Burnaby. Pinkerton's *Voyages*, xiii. 714, 715.
[4] Chastellux, ii. 193-195. There is an excellent description of Virginian society in Wirt's *Life of Patrick Henry*.
See too Grahame, iv. 122-124. Webster's *Essays*, pp. 361-364. Story's *Constitution of the United States*, i. 29-33.
[5] Sparks' *Life of Washington*. Washington's *Works*, i. 133.
[6] Hildreth, ii. 559.

have been warmly attached to England, but much discontent was produced by the interference of the mother-country in the quarrel, to which I have already referred, between the laity and the clergy of this State. The sixty or seventy clergymen of the Established Church received, in addition to a house and to some glebe lands, an annual stipend in the form of tobacco, which was delivered to them packed in hogsheads for exportation at the nearest warehouse. In a year when the tobacco crop failed, the Assembly passed a law obliging the clergy to receive their stipends in money instead of tobacco, and enforced it without waiting for the royal assent. The clergy complained that no allowance having been made for the low price of tobacco in good years, it was unfair that they should be deprived of the benefit of its high price in a bad year, and they sent over an agent to England and induced the English Government to disallow the law. Actions were brought by the clergy to recover the sums out of which they had been defrauded, but although the law was indisputably on their side they found it impossible to obtain verdicts from Virginian juries. It was in pleading against them that Patrick Henry, the greatest of American orators, first exhibited his eloquence and his antipathy to England. He had been successively a storekeeper, a farmer, and a shopkeeper, but had failed in all these pursuits, had become bankrupt, and at last, with a very tarnished reputation, had entered the law courts, where he soon displayed a power of popular eloquence which had never yet been equalled, or perhaps approached, in America. He openly told the juries that the act of the English Government in disallowing the proceedings of the Virginian Assembly was an instance of tyranny and misgovernment that dissolved the political compact, and speaking in a popular cause he created so fierce a spirit in the colony that the clergy gave up all attempts to obtain what was due to them.[1] In addition to this passing quarrel, there was a more chronic source of anti-English feeling in Virginia in the commercial restrictions which prevented the planters from sending their tobacco to foreign countries.

It is not necessary to pursue further a description of the Southern colonies. Maryland in soil, produce, and social con-

---

[1] Burnaby. Pinkerton, xiii. 712–714. Wirt's *Life of Henry*.

dition greatly resembled Virginia, but properties were smaller; a few rich Roman Catholics might still be found among the landowners,[1] and the colony was full of convicts, who were brought there in great numbers from England, and sold as slaves to the planters. In Maryland the same law of real property prevailed as in Massachusetts and Pennsylvania, but in all the other Southern colonies the English law, with its tendency to favour great agglomerations of land, was maintained.[2] In the vast provinces of Carolina the climate was more enervating and the proportion of negroes was much larger than in Virginia, and there were greater contrasts of wealth and poverty than in any other parts of British America. Georgia and Florida were too undeveloped to have much political or intellectual influence. Through the whole of the Southern colonies there was much less severity of religious orthodoxy, less energy and moral fibre, less industrial, political, and intellectual activity than in the North, and a much greater tendency both to idleness and to amusement. Charleston is said, of all the American towns, to have approached most nearly to the social refinement of a great European capital.

In general, however, the American colonies had attained to great prosperity and to a high level of civilisation. Burnaby noticed that in a journey of 1,200 miles through the Northern and Central colonies he had not met with a single beggar.[3] Domestic wages were much higher,[4] and farmers and farm-

[1] Adams mentions in 1774 a Catholic gentleman named Carroll (one of the signers of the Declaration of Independence) who lived at Annapolis, in Maryland, as a man of the first fortune in America. 'His income is 10,000*l.* a year now, will be 14,000*l.* in two or three years they say; besides, his father has a vast estate which will be his.'—Adams' *Works*, ii. 380.

[2] Story's *Constitution of the United States*, i. 165, 166. In 1777 Adams writes that in Maryland 'they have but few merchants. They are chiefly planters and farmers; the planters are those who raise tobacco, and the farmers such as raise wheat, &c. The lands are cultivated and all sorts of trades are exercised by negroes or by transported convicts, which has occasioned the planters and farmers to assume the title of gentlemen, and they hold their negroes and convicts—that is, all labouring people and tradesmen—in such contempt, that they think themselves a distinct order of beings. Hence they never will suffer their sons to labour or learn any trade, but they bring them up in idleness or, what is worse, in horse-racing, cock-fighting, and card-playing. . . . The object of the men of property here, the planters, &c., is universally wealth. Every way in the world is sought to get and save money; land jobbers, speculators in land; little generosity to the public, little public spirit.'—Adams' *Works*, ii. 436.

[3] Pinkerton's *Voyages*, xiii. 750.

[4] Ibid. xiii. 500. It must be remembered, however, that the slaves in America were not only negroes and

labourers incomparably more prosperous than in England or in any other part of Europe. 'The Northern yeomanry,' wrote an American economist at a time when America can have done little more than recover from the losses of the War of Independence, 'not only require more clothing than the Southern, but they live on expensive food and drinks. Every man, even the poorest, makes use of tea, sugar, spirits, and a multitude of articles which are not consumed by the labourers of any other country.... Most of the labouring people in New England eat meat twice a day, and as much as their appetites demand.' Owing to the admirable parish libraries, there were New England parishes 'where almost every householder has read the works of Addison, Sherlock, Atterbury, Watts, Young, and other similar writings, and will converse handsomely on the subjects of which they treat;'[1] and Boston, New York, Philadelphia, and Charleston, would in almost all the elements of civilisation have ranked high among the provincial towns of Europe. When Kalm visited Canada in 1750, he found that there was not a single printing press in the whole territory possessed by the French,[2] but before that time most of the more important British colonies possessed a newspaper, and by the close of 1765 at least forty-three newspapers are said to have been established in America.[3] There were seven important colleges,[4] and there were at least four literary magazines.[5]

In New England, education was always conducted at home, but in the Southern and some of the Middle colonies the rich planters were accustomed to send their sons for education to England.[6] In these States education was almost a monopoly of the rich; schoolmasters were despised, and schools were extremely rare. Martin, the last royal governor in North Carolina, stated that in his time there were only two schools in the whole colony.[7] In the first thirty years of the eighteenth century there was but one grammar school, in the next forty years there

convicts—many of the poor emigrants from Europe sold themselves to the planters for a term of years, and sometimes in this way paid their passage.

[1] Webster's *Essays*, pp. 339, 366. This was published in 1790.

[2] Pinkerton, xiii. 660.

[3] Tyler's *Hist. of American Literature*, ii. 304. Miller, however, gives a much lower estimate (*Retrospect of the Eighteenth Century*, iii. 90–92).

[4] Harvard, William and Mary, Yale, New Jersey, King's, Philadelphia, and Rhode Island.

[5] Tyler, ii. 305, 306.

[6] Miller, iii. 191, 192, 194.

[7] See Sabine's *American Loyalists*, p. 35.

were but three in the great province of South Carolina.¹ Noah Webster mentions that he once saw a copy of instructions given to a representative of Maryland by his constituents, and he found that out of more than a hundred names that were subscribed, 'three-fifths were marked by a cross because the men could not write.' He ascertained in 1785 that the circulation of newspapers in the single New England State of Connecticut was equal to that in the whole American territory south of Pennsylvania,² and he has recorded the extraordinary fact that in some parts of the colonies the education of the young was frequently confided to the care of purchased convicts.³ All the great seminaries of learning lay in the Northern and Middle colonies and in Virginia, and the English education of the rich planters of the South had greatly coloured their political opinions. At the same time they formed the more important part of the very small leisure class which existed in America; and it is a remarkable fact that the Southern colonies, though in general far behind the Northern ones, produced no less than five out of the first seven presidents of the United States.

In the Northern colonies, on the contrary, education was both very widely diffused and very equal. The average was exceedingly high, but there were no eminences. The men were early devoted to money-making, but it was noticed that there was a general ambition to educate women above their fortunes, and that in some towns there were three times as many 'genteelly bred' women as men.⁴ The absence of any considerable leisure class, the difficulty of procuring books,⁵ and especially

---

¹ Miller's *Retrospect*, iii. 230.
² Webster's *Essays*, 338, 360.
³ 'The most important business in civil society is in many parts of America committed to the most worthless characters. . . . Education is sunk to a level with the most menial services. . . . Will it be denied that before the war it was a frequent practice for gentlemen to purchase convicts who had been transported for their crimes and employ them as private tutors in their families?'—Ibid. pp. 17-19. See too pp. 55, 338.
⁴ Ibid. p. 30.
⁵ In that curious book, the *Life of Bampfylde Moore Carew*, which was published in 1749, and which shows great personal knowledge of America, it is said, 'There are five printing houses [in Boston], at one of which the *Boston Gazette* is printed, and comes out twice a week. The presses here are generally full of work, which is in a great measure owing to the colleges and schools for useful learning in New England, whereas at New York there is but one little bookseller's shop, and none at all in Virginia, Maryland, Carolina, Barbadoes, or any of the sugar islands,' p. 199. As late as 1760 it is said that 'there were no Greek types in the country, or if there were that no printer knew how to set them.'—Tudor's *Life of Otis*, p. 16.

the intensely commercial and money-making character of the colonists, were fatal to original literature; and, except for a few theological works, American literary history before the middle of the eighteenth century would be almost a blank. Berkeley wrote his 'Alciphron and his 'Minute Philosopher' in Rhode Island; but the first native writer of real eminence was Jonathan Edwards, who was born in 1703. He was soon followed by Benjamin Franklin, who in literature, as in science, took a place among the greatest of his contemporaries. Rittenhouse, who was born near Philadelphia in 1732, attained some distinction in astronomy; and among the Americans who sought a home in England were the painters Copley and West, and the grammarian Lindley Murray. Several of those noble public libraries which are now one of the great glories of America had already arisen; the first circulating library was established at Philadelphia in 1731,[1] and between 1763 and 1770 a medical school was founded in the same city, and courses of lectures were for the first time given on anatomy, on the institutes of medicine, on the Linnæan system of botany, and on the discoveries of Lavoisier in chemistry.[2]

The moral and political aspect of the country presented a much more blended and doubtful picture, and must have greatly perplexed those who tried to cast the horoscope of America. Nations are essentially what their circumstances make them, and the circumstances of the American colonists were exceedingly peculiar. A country where so large a proportion of the inhabitants were recent immigrants, drawn from different nations and professing various creeds; where, owing to the vast extent of territory and the imperfection of the means of communication, they were thrown very slightly in contact with one another, and where the money-making spirit was peculiarly intense, was not likely to produce much patriotism or community of feeling. On the other hand, the same circumstances had developed to an almost unprecedented degree energy, variety of resource, independence of character, capacity

---

[1] Franklin's *Life*, p. 99.
[2] Miller's *Retrospect of the Eighteenth Century*, iii. 236, 237, 282. This book contains an admirable account of the early intellectual history of the colonies. See too Hildreth's *Hist. of the United States*, ii. 513.

for self-government. In a simple and laborious society many of the seed-plots of European vice were unknown. Small freeholders cultivating their own lands were placed under conditions very favourable to moral development, and the wild life of the explorer, the pioneer, and the huntsman gave an unbounded scope to those superfluous energies which become so dangerous when they are repressed or misdirected. Beliefs that had long been waning in Europe retained much vigour in the colonies, and there were little sects or societies which represented the fervour and purity of the early Christians perhaps as perfectly as anything upon earth. Travellers noticed that, except where slavery had exercised its demoralising influence, the intercourse between the sexes was singularly free and at the same time singularly pure.[1] There was a great simplicity and freshness of character, a spirit of warm hospitality, a strong domestic feeling. Political corruption, which was the great cancer of English life, was almost unknown, though there were serious scandals connected with the law courts, and though the level of commercial integrity was probably lower than in England. A large proportion of the men who played a conspicuous part in the events to be recorded, were men of high private morals, simple, domestic, honourable, and religious. When the conflict with England became inevitable, one of the first proceedings of the different States was to appoint days of humiliation and prayer, and Washington notes in his private diary how on this occasion he 'went to church and fasted all day.' The most stringent rules were made in the American camp to suppress all games of chance and to punish all profane language. John Adams, recounting week after week in his diary the texts of the sermons he had heard, and his estimate of the comparative merits of the preachers, when he was leading the popular party in the very agony of the struggle for the independence of America, is a typical example of a class of politicians strangely unlike the revolutionists of Europe.

The most serious evil of the colonies was the number and force of the influences which were impelling large classes to

---

[1] Chastellux, i. 153, 154. *Mémoires de Lafayette*, i. p. 25. See too the very engaging picture of Pennsylvanian morals and manners in the *Mémoires du Comte de Ségur*.

violence and anarchy, brutalising them by accustoming them to an unrestrained exercise of power, and breaking down among them that salutary respect for authority which lies at the root of all true national greatness. The influence of negro slavery in this respect can hardly be overrated, and in the slave States a master could commit any act of violence and outrage on a negro with practical impunity. The relations of the colonists to the Indian tribes were scarcely less demoralising. White men planted among savages and removed from the control of European opinion seldom fail to contract the worst vices of tyrants.

The voluminous and very copious despatches of Sir W. Johnson and of Mr. Stuart, who during many years had the management of Indian affairs, are, on the whole, extremely creditable to the writers. They show that the Government laboured with great humanity, equity, and vigilance to protect the rights of the Indians, but they also show that they had to encounter insuperable difficulties in their task. The Executive was miserably weak. There were usually no troops within reach. Juries in Indian cases could never be trusted, and public opinion on the frontier looked upon Indians as little better than wild beasts. The French had in this respect succeeded much better. The strong Executive of Canada guarded the Indians effectually from depredations, restricted commercial dealings with them to the better class of traders, and attached them by a warm feeling of gratitude. But the despatches of Johnson and Stuart are full of accounts of how the English settlers continually encroached on the territory which was allotted by treaty to the Indians; how the rules that had been established for the regulation of the Indian trade were systematically violated; how traders of the lowest kind went among the savages, keeping them in a state of continual drunkenness till they had induced them to surrender their land; how the goods that were sold to Indians were of the most fraudulent description; how many traders deliberately excited outrages against their rivals; how great numbers of Indians who were perfectly peaceful, and loyal to the English, were murdered without a shadow of provocation; and how these crimes were perpetrated without punishment and almost without blame.[1] A few voices were no doubt raised in the colonies on their behalf. Franklin wrote with honest indignation denouncing some horrible murders that had been perpetrated in Pennsylvania. The Quakers were usually noted for their righteous dealing with the Indians. John Eliot in the seventeenth century, and Brainerd in the eighteenth century, had laboured with admirable zeal for the conversion of the Indians, and the Society for the Propagation of the Gospel had planted several missionary stations among them. In general, however, the French missionaries were far more successful. This was partly, no doubt, owing to their creed, for Catholicism, being a highly pictorial, authoritative, and material religion, is much more suited than Protestantism to influence savages and idolaters; but much also depended on the great superiority of the Catholic missionaries in organisation, education, and even character. The strange spectacle was often shown of Presbyterians, Baptists, and Anglicans contending in rivalry for converts. New England Puritans tried to persuade their converts that their dances, their rejoicings at marriages, and their most innocent amusements were wrong. Many missionaries were absolutely unacquainted with the language of those to whom they preached, and they had no interpreters except ignorant backwoodsmen.[2] It is a significant fact that in the French war the Indians were usually on the side of the French, and in the War of Independence on the side of the Government, and the explanation is probably chiefly to be found in the constant and atrocious outrages which they endured from the American traders.

To these elements of anarchy must be added the enormous extent of smuggling along the American coast, and also the

---

[1] Letters on Indian affairs form a very large proportion of the papers (Plantations, General) on America in the Record Office. The most valuable have been printed in the admirable collection of *Documents relative to the Colonial History of New York*, published by order of the Legislature of that State. See *e.g.* vol. vii. 602, 637–641, 837, 838, 946–948, 953–977.

[2] Ibid. vii. 969, 970. Sir W. Johnson mentions that he was himself present when one of the missionaries, preaching to the Indians, 'delivered as his text, "For God is no respecter of persons," and desired it to be explained to them; the interpreter (though the best in that country) told the Indians that "God had no love for such people as them," on which I immediately stopped him and explained the text, as I did the rest of his discourse, to prevent farther mistakes; had I not been present the error must have passed, and many more might have been committed in the course of the sermon.'

extreme weakness of the Government, which made it impossible to enforce any unpopular law or repress any riot. There was no standing army, and the position of the governors was in several States one of the most humiliating dependence. In the four New England States, in New Jersey, and in New York, all the executive and judicial authorities depended mainly or entirely for their salaries upon an annual vote of the Assembly, which was at all times liable to be withdrawn or diminished. It was not possible under such circumstances that any strong feeling of respect for authority could subsist, and the absence of any great superiority either in rank or in genius contributed to foster a spirit of unbounded self-confidence among the people.

The relation of this great, rising, and civilised community to the parent State was a question of transcendent importance to the future of the Empire. The general principle which was adopted was, that each colony should regulate with perfect freedom its local affairs, but that matters of imperial concern, and especially the commercial system, should remain under the control of the Imperial Parliament. The common law and the statute law, as far as they existed before the colonisation, were extended to the colonies, but the relation of the colonial legislatures to the Government at home was not very accurately defined. The original charters, while authorising them to levy taxes and make laws for the colonies, had declared that the colonists should be deemed natural-born English subjects, and should enjoy all the privileges and immunities thereof; that the laws of England, in so far as they were applicable to their circumstances, should be in force in the colonies, and that no law should be made in the colonies which was repugnant or did not, 'as near as may be conveniently,' conform to the laws of England. A statute of William provided that all colonial laws which were repugnant to laws made in England, ' so far as such law shall relate to and mention the said plantations, are illegal, null, and void.'[1]

These restrictions are of a very vague description, and, as is often the case in English law, the meaning was determined more by a course of precedents than by express definition. Great

[1] 7 and 8 William III. cap. 22. Story's *Constitution of the United States* i. 130, 147–149.

remedial measures, guaranteeing the rights of subjects, such as the Great Charter or the Habeas Corpus Act, were in full force in the colonies; but the colonial legislatures, with the entire assent of the Home Government, assumed the right of modifying almost every portion both of the common and of the statute law, with a view to their special circumstances. The laws relating to real property, the penal code, and the laws relating to religious belief, were freely dealt with, and it became a recognised principle that the colonies might legislate for themselves as they pleased, provided they left untouched allegiance to the Crown and Acts of the English Parliament in which they were expressly mentioned.

The scope of the Act of William establishing this latter restriction was also determined by precedent. The theory of the English Government was, that Parliament had by right an absolute and unrestricted power of legislation over the dependencies of England. The colonies were of the nature of corporations which lay within its supreme dominion, but which were entrusted with certain corporate powers of self-government. In an early period of colonial history this theory had been contested in the colonies, and especially in Massachusetts; and it had been contended that the colonies, having been founded in most instances without any assistance from the Home Government, and having received their charters from the Sovereign, and not from the Parliament, were in the position of Scotland before the Union, bound in allegiance to the King, but altogether independent of the English Parliament. This theory, however, was inconsistent with the whole course of English legislation about the colonies, with the terms of the charters, and with the claims of the colonists to rights that were derived exclusively from English law. It was not within the prerogative of the Sovereign either to emancipate English subjects by charter from the dominion of Parliament, or to confer upon aliens the character of Englishmen. The claim to be beyond the jurisdiction of Parliament was accordingly soon dropped by the colonists; and, although it revived at the era of the Revolution, we find Massachusetts in 1757, 1761, and 1768, acknowledging, in the most explicit and emphatic terms, the right of the English Parliament to bind the colonies by its

Acts.[1] The only modern Acts of Parliament, however, which were esteemed binding were those in which the colonies were expressly mentioned; and these Acts dealt with them, not as separate units, but as integral parts of one connected Empire. It was the recognised right of Parliament to establish a uniform commercial system, extending over the whole Empire, and binding every portion of it. There were also some matters which were mainly, if not exclusively, of colonial interest, on which Parliament undertook to legislate, and its authority was submitted to, though not without some protest and remonstrance. It was sometimes necessary to establish a general regulation binding on all the colonies; and as there existed no general or central colonial government, it devolved upon the Imperial Parliament to enforce it. On this principle Parliament introduced the English Post-office system into the colonies, determined the rates of postage, regulated the currency, created new facilities for the collection of debts, established a uniform law of naturalisation, and even legislated about joint-stock companies.[2]

The relation of the colonial governments to the Crown varied in some degree in the different colonies. As a general rule the Governor and the Council represented the royal authority, and, except in the case of the three colonies of Connecticut, Rhode Island, and Maryland, the Crown had a right of disallowing laws which had passed through all their stages in America.[3] The royal veto had fallen into complete disuse in England, but in the case of colonial legislation it was still not unfrequently employed. With the exception, however, of measures relating to commerce, colonial Acts were rarely or never annulled, except when they tended to injure or oppress some class of colonists. As the Governor was usually paid by an annual vote of the Assembly, and as he had very little patronage to dispose of, the Executive in the colonies was extremely weak, and the colonists, in spite of the occasional exercise of the royal veto, had probably a much more real control over legislation than the people of England. Trial by jury, both in civil and criminal cases, was as universal as in England; but an appeal

---

[1] Story's *Constitution of the United States*, i. 174.
[2] Hildreth, ii. 517. [3] Story, i. 158.

lay from all the highest courts of judicature in the colonies to the King in Council.

There were assuredly no other colonies in the world so favourably situated. They had, however, before the passing of the Stamp Act, one real and genuine grievance, which was already preparing the way to the disruption of the Empire. I have already in a former volume enumerated the chief restrictions of the commercial code; but it is so important that the true extent of colonial grievances should be clearly understood, that I trust the reader will excuse some repetition in my narrative. The colonies were not, like Ireland, excluded from the Navigation Act, and they had no special reason to complain that their trade was restricted to vessels built either in England or in the plantations, and manned to the extent of two-thirds of their crew by British subjects. In this respect they were on an exact level with the mother-country, and the arrangement was supposed to be very beneficial to both. It was, however, undoubtedly a great evil that the colonists were confined to the British dominions for a market for their tobacco, cotton, silk, coffee, indigo, naval stores, skins, sugar, and rice,[1] as well as many less important articles; that they were prohibited from carrying any goods from Europe to America which had not first been landed in England, and that every form of colonial manufacture which could possibly compete with the manufactures of England was deliberately crushed. In the interest of the English wool manufacture they were forbidden to export their own woollen goods to any country whatever, or even to send them from colony to colony. In the interests of English iron merchants they were forbidden to set up any steel furnaces or slitting mills in the colonies. In the interest of English hatters they were forbidden to export their hats, or even to send them from one colony to another, and serious obstacles were thrown in the way of those who sought to establish a manufacture for purely home consumption. In the interest of the English sugar colonies, the importation of sugar, molasses, and rum from the French West Indian islands, which was of extreme importance to the New England colonies, was virtually

---

[1] The law about the last three articles varied. They were sometimes among the enumerated, sometimes among the unenumerated articles.

forbidden. Every act of the colonial legislatures which sought to encourage a native or discourage an English branch of trade, was watched with jealous scrutiny. Thus in 1761 the Assembly of South Carolina, being sensible of the great social and political danger arising from the enormous multiplication of negroes in the colony, passed a law imposing a heavy duty upon the importation of slaves; but as the slave trade was one of the most lucrative branches of English commerce, the law was rescinded by the Crown. In the same year instructions were sent to the Governor of New Hampshire to refuse his assent to any law imposing duties on negroes imported into the colonies.[1]

There is, no doubt, much to be said in palliation of the conduct of England. If Virginia was prohibited from sending her tobacco to any European country except England, Englishmen were also prohibited from purchasing any tobacco except that which came from America or Bermuda. If many of the trades and manufactures in which the colonies were naturally most fitted to excel were restricted or crushed by law, the cultivation of indigo, and the importation into England of pitch, tar, hemp, flax, and ship-timber from America were encouraged by English bounties, and several articles of American produce obtained a virtual monopoly of the English market by their exemption from the duties which were imposed on similar articles imported from foreign countries. If the commercial system diminished very seriously the area of profitable commerce that was open to the colonies, it at least left them the elements of a great national prosperity. The trade with England and the trade with the English West Indies were large and lucrative, and the export trade to foreign countries was only prohibited in the case of those articles which were enumerated in the Navigation Act. Among the non-enumerated articles were some of the chief productions of the colonies—grain of all kinds, salted provisions, timber, fish, and rum; and in all these articles the colonists were suffered to trade with foreign nations without any other restriction than that of sending them in ships built and chiefly manned by British subjects. They were, however, forbidden, in the ordinary state of the law, to send salted provisions or any kind of grain except rice to Eng-

[1] Grahame, iv. 79.

land. The prohibition of the extremely important trade with the French West Indies was allowed, with the tacit connivance of the Government, to become for a long time little more than a dead letter. The provision which prevented the colonists from receiving any European goods except direct from England was much mitigated before 1763, and to some extent after that date, by the system of drawbacks freeing these goods from the greater part of the duties that would have been paid in England, so that many Continental goods were actually sold more cheaply in America than in England. It was a great grievance and absurdity that, for the sake of a few Portugal merchants in London who charged a commission on the goods that passed through their hands, the colonists were forbidden to import directly wine, oil, and fruit from Portugal, and were obliged to send them the long journey to England, to be landed there, and then reshipped for America. But in practice this rule was somewhat mitigated, and American ships carrying fish to Portugal were tacitly allowed to bring back small quantities of wine and fruit as ship stores.[1] It is a gross and flagrant misrepresentation to describe the commercial policy of England as exceptionally tyrannical. As Adam Smith truly said, 'Every European nation had endeavoured more or less to monopolise to itself the commerce of its colonies, and upon that account had prohibited the ships of foreign nations from trading to them, and had prohibited them from importing European goods from any foreign nation;' and 'though the policy of Great Britain with regard to the trade of her colonies has been dictated by the same mercantile spirit as that of other nations, it has, upon the whole, been less illiberal and oppressive than that of any of them.'[2] Even France, which was

---

[1] *Letters of Governor Bernard on the Trade and Government of America*, p. 4. See too Franklin's *Causes of American Discontents before 1768. Works,* iv. 250, 251. *Wealth of Nations,* book iv. ch. iv., vii.

[2] *Wealth of Nations,* book iv. ch. vii. See too Gentz *On the State of Europe before and after the French Revolution* (English trans.), pp. 295 308. 'Ever since the discovery of America,' says Dean Tucker, 'it has been the system of every European Power which had colonies in that part of the world, to confine (as far as laws can confine) the trade of the colonies to the mother-country. . . . Thus the trade of the Spanish colonies is confined by law to Old Spain, the trade of the Brazils to Portugal, the trade of Martinico and the other French colonies to Old France, and the trade of Curaçoa and Surinam to Holland. But in one instance the Hollanders make an exception (perhaps a wise one), viz. in the case of Eustatia, which is open to all the world.'— Tucker's *Four Tracts,* p. 133.

by far the most liberal of Continental nations in her dealings with her colonies, imposed commercial restrictions more severe than those of England. Not only was the trade of French Canada, like that of British America, a monopoly of the mother-country; it was not even open without restriction to Frenchmen and to Canadians, for the important trade in beavers belonged exclusively to a company in France, and could only be exercised under its authorisation.[1]

Still, when every allowance has been made, it is undoubtedly true that the commercial policy of England had established a real opposition of interest between the mother-country and her colonies; and, if the policy which was the proximate cause of the American Revolution was chiefly due to the King and to the landed gentry, the ultimate cause may be mainly traced to the great influence which the commercial classes possessed in British legislation. The expulsion of the French from Canada made it possible for the Americans to dispense with English protection. The commercial restrictions alone made it their interest to do so. If the 'Wealth of Nations' had been published a century earlier, and if its principles had passed into legislation, it is quite possible that the separation of England and her colonies might have been indefinitely adjourned. A false theory of commerce, then universally accepted, had involved both the mother-country and her colonies in a web of restrictions which greatly retarded their development, and had provided a perpetual subject of irritation and dissension. The Custom-house and revenue officers, unlike other officials in America, were not paid by the local legislatures. They were appointed directly by the Crown or by the governors, and in America as in England cases of revenue fraud might by means of the Admiralty Court be tried without the intervention of a jury. Smuggling was very lucrative, and therefore very popular, and any attempt to interfere with it was greatly resented.

The attention of the British Government was urgently called to it during the war. At a time when Great Britain was straining every nerve to conquer Canada from the French, when the security of British America was one of the first objects of

[1] Kalm. Pinkerton's *Voyages*, xiii. 700.

English policy, and when large sums were remitted from England to pay the colonies for fighting in their own cause, it was found that the French fleets, the French garrisons, and the French West India islands, were systematically supplied with large quantities of provisions by the New England colonies. The trade was carried on partly by ordinary smuggling and partly under the cover of flags of truce, granted ostensibly for the exchange of prisoners, and large numbers of persons, some of them, it is said, high in official life, connived and participated in it. Pitt, who still directed affairs, wrote with great indignation that this trade must at all hazards be suppressed; but the whole mercantile community of the New England seaports appears to have favoured or partaken in it, and great difficulties were found in putting the law into execution. The smuggling was even defended with a wonderful cynicism on the ground that it was good policy to make as much money as possible out of the enemy. Some papers seized in the possession of Frenchmen at New York, showed clearly how extensive and well-organised was the plan of the French for obtaining their supplies from New England. Amherst wrote to Massachusetts, Rhode Island, and Connecticut to lay an embargo on all but transports engaged in Government employ, and this measure was actually taken, but it was removed in little more than a month.[1] In order to detect if possible the smuggled goods, the Custom-house officers in 1761 applied to the Superior Court in Massachusetts to grant them 'writs of assistance.' These writs, which were frequently employed in England, and occasionally in the colonies, bore a great resemblance to the general warrants which soon after became so obnoxious in England. They were general writs authorising Custom-house officers to search any house they pleased for smuggled goods, and they were said to have been sometimes used for purposes of private annoyance. They appear, however, to have been perfectly legal, and if their employment was ever justifiable, it was in an attempt to put down a smuggling trade with the enemy in time of war. The issue of the warrants was resisted, though unsuccessfully,

---

[1] Hildreth, ii. 498. Macpherson's *Annals of Commerce*, iii. 330. Arnold's *Hist. of Rhode Island*, ii. 227, 235, 236.

by the Boston merchants, and a young lawyer of some talent named James Otis, whose father had just been disappointed in his hopes of obtaining a seat upon the bench, signalised himself by an impassioned attack on the whole commercial code and on the alleged oppression of Parliament, which excited great enthusiasm in the colonies, and was afterwards regarded by John Adams and some others as the first step towards the Revolution.[1]

There were indeed already on all sides symptoms by which a careful observer might have foreseen that dangers were approaching. The country was full of restless military adventurers called into prominence by the war. The rapid rise of an ambitious legal profession and the great development of the Press made it certain that there would be abundant mouthpieces of discontent, and there was so much in the legal relations of England to her colonies that was anomalous, unsettled, or undefined, that causes of quarrel were sure to arise. The revenue laws were habitually violated. There was, in the Northern colonies at least, an extreme impatience of every form of control, and the Executive was almost powerless. The Government would gladly have secured for the judges in Massachusetts a permanent provision, which would place them in some degree beyond the control of the Assembly, but it found it impossible to carry it. The Assemblies of North Carolina and New York would gladly have secured for their judges a tenure of office during good behaviour, as in England, instead of at the King's pleasure, but the Home Government, fearing that this would still further weaken the Executive, gave orders that no such measure should receive the assent of the governors, and in New York the Assembly having refused on any other condition to vote the salaries of the judges, they were paid out of the royal quitrents.[2] There were frequent quarrels between the governors and the Assemblies, and much violent language was employed.

---

[1] Otis tells a story of a man who possessed one of these writs, being summoned by a judge for Sabbath-breaking and swearing, and avenging himself by searching the house of the judge from top to bottom.—Tudor's *Life of Otis*, p. 67. A very full abstract of the great speech of Otis against the writs of assistance will be found in this work—a remarkable book from which I have derived much assistance. See too Adams' *Works*, i. 57, 58, ii. 524, 525.

[2] Bancroft, i. 502, 503. Grahame, iv. 87, 88.

In 1762, on the arrival of some French ships off Newfoundland, the inhabitants of Massachusetts, who were largely employed in the fishery, petitioned the governor that a ship and sloop belonging to the province should be fitted out to protect their fishing boats. The governor and council complied with their request, and in order that the sloop should obtain rapidly its full complement of men he offered a bounty for enlistment. The whole expense of the bounty did not exceed 400*l*. The proceeding might be justified by many precedents, and it certainly wore no appearance of tyranny; but Otis, who had been made one of the representatives of Boston as a reward for his incendiary speech about the writs of assistance, saw an opportunity of gaining fresh laurels. He induced the House to vote a remonstrance to the governor, declaring that he had invaded 'their most darling privilege, the right of originating taxes,' and that 'it would be of little consequence to the people whether they were subject to George the King of Great Britain or Lewis the French king if both were arbitrary, as both would be if both could levy taxes without Parliament.' It was with some difficulty that the governor prevailed on the House to expunge the passage in which the King's name was so disloyally introduced.[1]

The immense advantages which the colonists obtained by the Peace of Paris had no doubt produced even in the New England colonies an outburst of loyal gratitude, but the prospect was again speedily overclouded. The direction of colonial affairs passed into the hands of George Grenville, and that unhappy course of policy was begun which in a few years deprived England of the noblest fruits of the administration of Pitt.

Up to this time the North American colonies had in time of peace been in general almost outside the cognisance of the Government. As their affairs had no influence on party politics Parliament took no interest in them, and Newcastle, during his long administration, had left them in almost every respect absolutely to themselves. It was afterwards said by a Treasury official, who was intimately acquainted with the management of affairs, that 'Grenville lost America because he read the American despatches, which none of his predecessors had done.'

[1] Hutchinson, pp. 97, 98. Tudor's *Life of Otis*, pp. 118–122.

The ignorance and neglect of all colonial matters can indeed hardly be exaggerated, and it is stated by a very considerable American authority, that letters had repeatedly arrived from the Secretary of State who was officially entrusted with the administration of the colonies, addressed 'to the Governor of the Island of New England.'[1] America owed much to this ignorance and to this neglect; and England was so rich, and the colonies were long looked upon as so poor, that there was no disposition to seek anything more from America than was derived from a partial monopoly of her trade. But the position of England, as well as of America, was now wholly changed. Her empire had been raised by Pitt to an unprecedented height of greatness, but she was reeling under a national debt of nearly 140 millions. Taxation was greatly increased. Poverty and distress were very general, and it had become necessary to introduce a spirit of economy into all parts of the administration, to foster every form of revenue, and if possible, to diffuse over the gigantic empire a military burden which was too great for one small island. There is reason to believe that in the ministry of Bute, Charles Townshend and his colleagues had already contemplated a change in the colonial system, that they desired to reduce the colonial governments to a more uniform system, to plant an army in America, and to support it by colonial taxes levied by the British Parliament, and that it was only the briefness of their tenure of office that prevented their scheme from coming to maturity.[2] When Grenville succeeded to power on the fall of Bute, he took up the design, and his thorough knowledge of all the details of office, his impatience of any kind of neglect, abuse, and illegality, as well as his complete want of that political tact which teaches statesmen how far they may safely press their views, foreshadowed a great change in colonial affairs. He resolved to enforce strictly the trade laws, to establish permanently in America a portion of the British army, and to raise by parliamentary taxation of America at least a part of the money which was necessary for its support.

---

[1] Otis, *Rights of the British Colonies asserted* (3rd ed. 1766), p. 37.
[2] See Knox's *Extra-official Papers*, ii. 29. Almon's *Biographical Anecdotes*, ii. 81–83. Bedford Correspondence, iii. 210. Walpole's *George III.* iii. 32. Mr. Bancroft has collected with great industry all the extant evidence of this plan.

These three measures produced the American Revolution, and they are well worthy of a careful and dispassionate examination The enormous extent of American smuggling had been brought into clear relief during the war, when it had assumed a very considerable military importance, and as early as 1762 there were loud complaints in Parliament of the administration of the Custom-house patronage. Grenville found on examination that the whole revenue derived by England from the custom-houses in America amounted to between 1,000*l.* and 2,000*l.* a year; that for the purpose of collecting this revenue the English Exchequer paid annually between 7,000*l.* and 8,000*l.*, and that the chief custom-house officers appointed by the Crown had treated their offices as sinecures, and by leave of the Treasury resided habitually in England.[1] Great portions of the trade laws had been systematically violated. Thus, for example, the colonists were allowed by law to import no tea except from the mother-country, and it was computed that of a million and a half pounds of tea which they annually consumed, not more than a tenth part came from England.[2] This neglect Grenville resolved to terminate. The Commissioners of Customs were ordered at once to their posts. Several new revenue officers were appointed with more rigid rules for the discharge of their duties. The Board of Trade issued a circular to the colonies representing that the revenue had not kept pace with the increasing commerce, and did not yield more than one-quarter of the cost of collection, and requiring that illicit commerce should be suppressed, and that proper support should be given to the Custom-house officials. English ships of war were at the same time stationed off the American coast for the purpose of intercepting smugglers.[3]

In 1764 new measures of great severity were taken. The trade with the French West India islands and with the Spanish settlements, for molasses and sugar, had been one of the most lucrative branches of New England commerce. New

---

[1] *Grenville Papers,* ii. 114.
[2] Bancroft, ii. 178. See too *Massachusettensis,* Letter iii. According to Sabine, 'Nine-tenths probably of all the tea, wine and fruit, sugar and molasses, consumed in the colonies, were smuggled.'—Sabine's *American Loyalists,* i. p. 12.
[3] Arnold's *Hist. of Rhode Island,* ii. 246.

England found in the French islands a market for her timber, and she obtained in return an abundant supply of the molasses required for her distilleries. The French West India islands were nearer than those of England. They were in extreme need of the timber of which New England furnished an inexhaustible supply, and they were in no less need of a market for their molasses, which had been excluded from France as interfering with French brandies, and of which enormous quantities were bought by the New England colonies. In 1763, 14,500 hogsheads of molasses were imported into New England from the French and Spanish settlements; it was largely paid for by timber which would otherwise have rotted uselessly on the ground, and the possibility of selling this timber at a profit gave a great impulse to the necessary work of clearing land in New England. No trade could have been more clearly beneficial to both parties, and the New Englanders maintained that it was the foundation of their whole system of commerce. The distilleries of Boston, and of other parts of New England, had acquired a great magnitude. Rum was sent in large quantities to the Newfoundland fisheries and to the Indians, and it is a circumstance of peculiar and melancholy interest that it was the main article which the Americans sent to Africa in exchange for negro slaves. In the trade with the Spanish settlements the colonists obtained the greater part of the gold and silver with which they purchased English commodities, and this fact was the more important because an English Act of Parliament had recently restrained the colonists from issuing paper money.[1]

In the interest of the English sugar colonies, which desired to obtain a monopoly for their molasses and their sugar, and which at the same time were quite incapable of furnishing a sufficient market for the superfluous articles of American commerce, a law had been passed in 1733 which imposed upon molasses a prohibitory duty of sixpence a gallon and on sugar a duty of five shillings per cwt. if they were imported into any of the British plantations from any foreign colonies. No portion of the commercial code was so deeply resented in America,

---

[1] Macpherson's *Annals of Commerce*, iii. 171–177, 192. Bancroft. Grahame. Letters of Governor Bernard.

and its effects would have been ruinous, had not the law been systematically eluded with the connivance of the revenue officers, and had not smuggling almost assumed the dimensions and the character of a branch of regular commerce. After several renewals the Act expired in 1763, and the colonies urgently petitioned that it should not be renewed.

Bernard, the Governor, and Hutchinson, the Lieutenant-Governor of Massachusetts, strongly condemned the policy of the Act, and dwelt upon the impossibility of enforcing it. Grenville, however, refused to relinquish what might be made a source of revenue, and the old law was renewed with several important modifications. The duty on molasses was reduced by one-half, but new duties were imposed on coffee, pimento, French and East India goods, white sugar and indigo from foreign colonies, Spanish and Portuguese wine, and wine from Madeira and the Azores, and the most stringent measures were taken to enforce the law. Bonds were exacted from every merchant who exported lumber or iron; the jurisdiction of the Courts of Admiralty, which tried smuggling cases without a jury, was strengthened and enlarged, and all the officers of ships of war stationed on the coasts of America were made to take the Custom-house oaths and act as revenue officers. In addition, therefore, to the old race of experienced but conniving revenue officers, the repression of smuggling became the business of a multitude of rough and zealous sailors, who entered into the work with real keenness, with no respect of persons, and sometimes with not a little unnecessary or excessive violence. The measure was one of the most serious blows that could be administered to the somewhat waning prosperity of Boston, and it was the more obnoxious on account of its preamble, which announced as a reason for imposing additional duties that 'it is just and necessary that a revenue be raised in your Majesty's dominions in America for defraying the expenses of defending, protecting, and securing the same.' In order to diminish the severity of these restrictions, bounties were in the same year given to the cultivation of hemp and flax in the colonies. South Carolina and Georgia were allowed to export the rice which was their chief product to the French West India islands; and the whale fishery, which was one of the most profitable industries of New England, was relieved of a duty which had hitherto alone prevented it from completely superseding or eclipsing the whale fishery of England.[1]

Judging by the mere letter of the law, the commercial policy of Grenville can hardly be said to have aggravated the severity of the commercial code, for the new restrictions that were imposed were balanced by the new indulgences that were conferred. In truth, however, the severe enforcement of rules which had been allowed to become nearly obsolete was a most serious injury to the prosperity of New England. A trade which was in the highest degree natural and beneficial, and which had long been pursued with scarcely any hindrance, was impeded, and the avowed object of raising by imperial authority a revenue to defray the expense of defending the colonies, created a constitutional question of the gravest kind.

It was closely connected with the intention to place rather more than 10,000 soldiers permanently in America. This scheme was also much objected to. The colonists retained in its full force the dread of a standing army, which had been so powerful in England at the time of the Revolution. In time of war, they said, they had always shown themselves willing to raise troops at the requisition of the governor. Parliament, in the last war, had repeatedly acknowledged the alacrity which they had shown, and they asked why the country might not, as heretofore, be protected in time of peace by its own militias, which were organised and paid without any assistance from the mother-country. It was urged that the expulsion of the French from Canada had greatly diminished its foreign dangers, and it was asked whether the army was really intended to guard against foreigners.

It is possible, and indeed very probable, that a desire to strengthen the feeble Executive, and to prevent the systematic violation of the revenue laws, was a motive with those who recommended the establishment of an army in America; but the primary object was, no doubt, the defence of the colonies and the maintenance of imperial interests. In the earlier stages of colonial history, little had been done in the way of protection,

---

[1] 4 Geo. III. 15, 26, 27, 29. Macpherson's *Hist. of Commerce*, iii. 395–401. Grahame, iv. 169–176. Tudor's *Life of Otis*, p. 165.

because these poor and scattered communities appeared of little value either to England or to her enemies. British America, however, was now a great and prosperous country. When we remember its vast extent, its great wealth, and its distance from the mother-country; when we remember also that a great part of it had been but just annexed to the Crown, and that its most prosperous provinces were fringed by tribes of wild Indians, the permanent maintenance in it of a small army appears evidently expedient. The dangers from Indians in the north had been no doubt diminished by the conquest of Canada, but a terrible lesson had very recently shown how formidable Indian warfare might still become. In June 1763, a confederation including several Indian tribes had suddenly and unexpectedly swept over the whole western frontier of Pennsylvania and Virginia, had murdered almost all the English settlers who were scattered beyond the mountains, had surprised and captured every British fort between the Ohio and Lake Erie, and had closely blockaded Fort Detroit and Pittsburg. In no previous war had the Indians shown such skill, tenacity, and concert; and had there not been British troops in the country, the whole of Pennsylvania, Virginia, and Maryland would probably have been overrun. In spite of every effort, a long line of country twenty miles in breadth was completely desolated, and presented one hideous scene of plunder, massacre, and torture. It was only after much desperate fighting, after some losses, and several reverses, that the troops of Amherst succeeded in repelling the invaders and securing the three great fortresses of Niagara, Detroit, and Pittsburg.

The war lasted for fourteen months; but during the first six months, when the danger was at its height, the hard fighting appears to have been mainly done by English troops, though a considerable body of the militia of the Southern colonies were in the field. At last Amherst called upon the New England colonies to assist their brethren, but his request was almost disregarded. Massachusetts, being beyond the zone of immediate danger, and fatigued with the burden of the late war, would give no help; and Connecticut with great reluctance sent 250 men. After a war of extreme horror, peace was signed in September 1764. In a large degree by the efforts of English soldiers, the Indian territory was again rolled back, and one more great service was rendered by England to her colonies.[1]

This event was surely a sufficient justification of the policy of establishing a small army in the colonies. But it was not alone against the Indians that it was required. It was a general belief in America that if another war broke out, France would endeavour to regain Canada, and that she might be aided by an insurrection of her former subjects.[2] It was almost certain that the next French war would extend to the West Indies, and in that case America would be a post of vital importance both for defence and for attack. It was plainly unwise that such a position should be left wholly denuded of troops, and dependent for its protection upon the precarious favour of the winds.

These considerations appear to me to justify fully the policy of the ministers in desiring to place a small army permanently in the colonies. We must next inquire whether it was unreasonable to expect the colonists to support it. The position of England after the Peace of Paris was wholly different from her position in the preceding century. She was no longer a small, compact, and essentially European country, with a few outlying possessions of comparatively little value. By the conquests of Clive in Hindostan, by the great development of the colonies of British America, by the acquisition of Florida and Canada and of the important islands which had recently been annexed, she had become the centre of an empire unrivalled since that of Charles V. and pregnant with the possibilities of almost unbounded progress. It devolved upon the English statesmen who obtained power after the Peace of Paris to legislate for these new conditions of national greatness, and to secure, as far as human sagacity could do so, the permanence of that great Empire which had been built up by so much genius and with so much blood, and which might be made the instrument of such incalculable benefits to mankind. The burden of the naval protection they proposed to leave exclusively with the mother-country, but the burden of the military protection they proposed to divide. They maintained that it was wholly impossible that 8,000,000 Englishmen, weighed down with debt

---

[1] Trumbull's *Hist. of the United States*, pp. 455-467. Hildreth, Grahame, Hutchinson.
[2] Otis, *Rights of the Colonies*, p. 97

and with taxation, and with a strong traditional hostility to standing armies, could alone undertake the military protection of an empire so vast, so various, and in many of its parts so distant. Two subsidiary armies had already been created. The East India Company had its own forces for the defence of India, and Ireland supported a large force both for its own defence and for the general service of the Empire. Townshend and Grenville resolved to plant a third army in the colonies.

The case of Ireland is here worthy of special notice. If North America was the part of the British Empire where well-being was most widely diffused, Ireland was probably the part where there was most poverty and wretchedness. Her population exceeded that of British America by barely half a million; her natural resources were infinitely less. By her exclusion from the Navigation Act she had been shut out from all direct trade with the British dependencies, while her most important manufactures had been suppressed by law. The great majority of her population had been reduced to extreme degradation by the penal code. She was burdened by a tithe system supporting an alien Church. Her social system was disorganised by repeated confiscations and by the emigration of her most energetic classes, and she was drained of her little wealth by absenteeism, by a heavy pension list, and by an exaggerated establishment in Church and State, in which the chief offices were reserved for Englishmen. Yet Ireland from Irish revenues supported an army of 12,000 men, which was raised in 1769 to 15,000.

I have no wish to deny that the Stamp Act was a grievance to the Americans, but it is due to the truth of history that the gross exaggerations which have been repeated on the subject should be dispelled, and that the nature of the alleged tyranny of England should be clearly defined. It cannot be too distinctly stated that there is not a fragment of evidence that any English statesman, or any class of the English people, desired to raise anything by direct taxation from the colonies for purposes that were purely English. They asked them to contribute nothing to the support of the navy which protected their coast, nothing to the interest of the English debt. At the close of a war which had left England overwhelmed with additional burdens, in which the whole resources of the British Empire had been strained for the extension and security of the British territory in America, by which the American colonists had gained incomparably more than any other of the subjects of the Crown, the colonies were asked to bear their share in the burden of the Empire by contributing a third part—they would no doubt ultimately have been asked to contribute the whole—of what was required for the maintenance of an army of 10,000 men, intended primarily for their own defence. 100,000*l.* was the highest estimate of what the Stamp Act would annually produce, and it was rather less than a third part of the expense of the new army. This was what England asked from the most prosperous portion of her Empire. Every farthing which it was intended to raise in America, it was intended also to spend there.

The great grievance was of course that the sum was to be raised by imperial taxation, and that it was therefore a departure from the old system of government in the colonies. Hitherto the distinction between external and internal taxation had been the leading principle of colonial administration. Parliament exercised a recognised right when it determined the commercial system of the colonies by the imposition of duties which produced indeed some small revenue, but which were not intended for that purpose, but solely for the purpose of commercial regulation. But taxes intended for the purpose of revenue had only been imposed by the colonial assemblies. Twice already in the eighteenth century the imposition of imperial taxation for military purposes had been contemplated. In 1739 a body of American merchants under the leadership of Sir W. Keith, the Governor of Pennsylvania, had proposed the establishment of a body of troops along the western frontier of the British settlements, and had suggested a parliamentary duty on stamped paper and parchments as a means of defraying the expense; but Walpole had wisely declined to accede to the proposition. In 1754, when it was necessary to make preparations for the great war with France, and when the scheme for uniting the colonies for military purposes had failed, the Government proposed that the governors of the several provinces should meet together, and with some members of the general councils should concert measures for the defence of the colonies. It was proposed that the English Treasury should advance such sums as they deemed necessary for this purpose, and that it should be reimbursed by a tax imposed on all the colonies by the Imperial Parliament. The extreme difficulty of obtaining any simultaneous military action of the colonies, and the impossibility of inducing the colonies which were remote from the immediate danger to contribute their quota to the common cause, were the reasons alleged; and in order that the grievance should be as small as possible, it was intended that Parliament should only determine the proportion to be paid by each colony, leaving it to each colonial assembly to raise that sum as it pleased. Franklin, who was consulted about the scheme, wrote some able letters to Shirley, the Governor of Massachusetts, protesting against it, and Pitt refused to adopt it.[1]

The constitutional competence of Parliament to tax the colonies is a question of great difficulty, upon which the highest legal authorities have been divided, though the decided preponderance of legal opinion has been in favour of the right. Parliament repeatedly claimed and exercised a general right of legislating for the colonies, and it is not possible to show by the distinct letter of the law that this did not include the right to make laws imposing taxes. It was admitted by the Americans that it might impose trade duties which produced revenue, though they were not primarily intended for that purpose; and it is certain that the Charter of Pennsylvania, though of that colony alone, expressly reserved to Parliament the right of taxation.[2] To an accurate thinker, indeed, it must appear evident that every law which in the interest of English manufacturers prohibited the Americans from pursuing a form of manufacture, or buying a particular class of goods from foreigners, was in reality a tax. The effect of the monopoly was that the Americans paid more for these goods than

---

[1] See on this negotiation Franklin's letters to Shirley, with the prefatory note.—*Franklin's Works*, iii. 56-58. Thackeray's *Life of Chatham*, ii. 56, 57. *The Controversy between Great Britain and her Colonies Reviewed* (1769), pp. 194-198. Bancroft, i. 195-198.

[2] By the Charter the Sovereign engaged never to levy any tax in Pennsylvania, 'unless the same be with the consent of the proprietors or chief governor or Assembly, or by Act of Parliament in England.'

if they had produced them or bought them from foreigners, and this excess was a sum levied from the Americans for the benefit of England. If the Virginian planters were obliged by restrictive laws to send their tobacco to England alone, and if a tax was imposed on all tobacco in England for the purpose of revenue, it is clear that at least a portion of that tax was really paid by the producer in Virginia. It is also not evident in the nature of things why the general defence of the Empire should be esteemed less an imperial concern than the regulation of commerce; and why, if Parliament might bind the colonies and raise money for the regulation of their commercial system, she might not also both determine and enforce their military obligations. The general opinion of English lawyers appears to have been that the distinction between internal and external taxation had no basis in law or in fact, and that the right of the English Legislature was supreme over the colonies, however impolitic it might be to exercise it. In 1724 the law officers of the Crown, one of whom was Sir Philip Yorke, had given their opinion that 'a colony of English subjects cannot be taxed but by some representative body of their own or by the Parliament of England;' and a similar opinion was given in 1744 by Murray, afterwards Lord Mansfield. Mansfield was subsequently one of the strongest advocates of the Stamp Act, and the most vehement opponent of its repeal. In a few years the colonial lawyers appear to have agreed substantially with those of England, for they maintained that, in order to establish by argument the sole right of the Assemblies to tax the colonies, it was necessary to deny that the Imperial Parliament had any power of legislating for them.

It was admitted that it was a new thing to impose internal taxation on the colonies. The Post Office revenue, which was often alleged as an example, might be regarded merely as a payment exacted for the performance of a service of general utility, and the propriety of imposing this new burden on the colonies was defended on the ground that the circumstances both of the colonies and of England had radically changed.[1] The idea, however, of supporting an American army by im-

---

[1] As Dr. Johnson wittily though somewhat offensively wrote: 'We do not put a calf into the plough; we wait till it is an ox.'

perial taxation of America was, as we have seen, not new, and some of the best judges of American affairs appeared to regard it as feasible. When the question of establishing a general fund during the war was under discussion in 1754 and 1755, Governor Shirley gave his opinion 'that the several assemblies within the colonies will not agree among themselves upon such a fund; that consequently it must be done in England, and that the only effectual way of doing it there will be by an Act of Parliament, in which I have great reason to think the people will readily acquiesce, and that the success of any other method will be doubtful.'[1]

This passage implies what was probably the strongest argument weighing upon the Ministers. It was the absolute impossibility of inducing America to support her own army unless the English Parliament intervened. There was no central colonial government. There was no body, like the Irish Parliament, competent to tax the several provinces. In order to raise the money for the support of an American army with the assent of the colonies, it was necessary to have the assent of no less than seventeen colonial assemblies. The hopelessness of attempting to fulfil this condition was very manifest. If in the agonies of a great war it had been found impossible to induce the colonies to act together; if the Southern colonies long refused to assist the Northern ones in their struggle against France because they were far from the danger; if South Carolina, when reluctantly raising troops for the war, stipulated that they should act only within their own province; if New England would give little or no assistance while the Indians were carrying desolation over Virginia and Pennsylvania; what chance was there that all these colonies would agree in time of peace to impose uniform and proportionate taxation upon themselves for the support of an English army?[2] It seemed evident, as a matter of practical statesmanship, that

---

[1] *The Controversy between Great Britain and her Colonies,* pp. 196, 197.

[2] See a very able statement of the dissension among the colonies in *The Controversy between Great Britain and her Colonies,* pp. 93-97. Governor Franklin (the son of Benjamin Franklin) in a speech to the Assembly of New Jersey in 1775, said, 'The necessity of some supreme judge [to determine the quota of each province to the general expense] is evident from the very nature of the case, as otherwise some of the colonies might not contribute their due proportion. During the last war I well remember it

it would be impossible, without the assistance of Parliament, to support an American army by American taxation, unless the provinces could be induced to confide the power of taxation to a single colonial assembly, and unless England could induce that assembly, by the promise of commercial relaxations, to vote a subsidy. To both parts of this scheme the difficulties were enormous, and probably insuperable. Extreme jealousy of England, of the Executive, and of each other, animated the colonies, while a spirit of intense commercial monopoly was dominant in England. Under these conditions the problem might well have appeared a hopeless one.

It would have been far wiser, under such circumstances, to have abandoned the project of making the Americans pay for their army, and to have thrown the burden on the mother-country. Heavily as the English were at this time taxed, grievous as was the discontent that was manifested among the people, the support of an American army of 10,000 men would not have been overwhelming, while a conflict with the colonists on the question could lead to no issue that was not disastrous. There was indeed one method which might possibly have been successful. Fresh duties imposed on American goods might have raised the required sum in a manner mischievous and wasteful indeed both to England and the colonies, but not wholly inconsistent with the usual tenor of their government, and in the opinion of Franklin such a measure might have been acquiesced in. In the beginning of 1764 that very shrewd observer wrote a letter urging the necessity of converting the Government of Pennsylvania from a proprietary into a royal one, in which there occurs a passage which is singularly curious when read in the light of the author's subsequent career. 'That we shall have a standing army to maintain,' he says, 'is another bugbear raised to

---

was ardently wished by some of the colonies that others, who were thought to be delinquent, might be compelled by Act of Parliament to bear an equal share of the public burdens. . . . When the Assembly in 1764 was called upon to make provision for raising some troops on account of the Indian war, they declined doing it for some time but on condition a majority of the eastern colonies so far as to include Massachusetts Bay should come into his Majesty's requisition on the occasion. But as none of the Assemblies of the New England Governments thought themselves nearly concerned, nothing was granted by them, and the whole burden of the expedition then carried on fell on Great Britain and three or four of the middle colonies.'—See *Tucker's Letter to Burke*, pp. 49, 50.

terrify us from endeavouring to obtain a king's government. It is very possible that the Crown may think it necessary to keep troops in America henceforward, to maintain its conquests and defend the colonies, and that the Parliament may establish some revenue arising out of the American trade to be applied towards supporting these troops. It is possible too that we may, after a few years' experience, be generally very well satisfied with that measure, from the steady protection it will afford us against foreign enemies and the security of internal peace among ourselves without the expense and trouble of a militia.'[1]

Grenville adopted another course, but he acted with evident reluctance and hesitation. In March 1764, at the same time as the commercial measure I have already described, he brought forward and carried a resolution asserting that 'for further defraying the expense of protecting the colonies it may be proper to charge certain stamp duties in the said colonies.' Further measures were postponed for a year, in order to ascertain fully the sentiments of the colonies, and also to give them an opportunity, if they chose to avail themselves of it, either of suggesting some other tax or of preventing the action of Parliament by themselves raising the sum which was required.[2]

At the close of this session the agents of the different colonies went in a body to Grenville to ask him if it was still his intention to bring in the threatened Bill. Grenville replied positively in the affirmative, and he defended his determination by arguments which he had already used both in private and in the House of Commons. The interview was described by Mauduit, the agent of Massachusetts, in a letter to his colony, and his accuracy was fully attested by Montagu, the agent for Virginia. Grenville, according to these reporters, urged 'that the late war had found us 70 millions and had left us more than 140 millions in debt. He knew that all men wished not to be taxed, but in these unhappy circumstances it was his duty as a steward for the public to make use of every just means of improving the public revenue. He never meant, however, to charge the colonies with any part of the interest of the national debt. But, besides that public debt, the nation had incurred a great annual expense in the maintaining of the several new

[1] Franklin's Works, iv, 89, 90. [2] Almon's Biographical Anecdotes, ii. 88–92.

conquests which we had made during the war, and by which the colonies were so much benefited. The American civil and military establishment, after the Peace of Aix-la-Chapelle, was only 70,000*l.* per annum. It was now 350,000*l.* This was a great additional expense incurred upon American account, and he thought therefore that America ought to contribute towards it. He did not expect that the colonies should raise the whole; but some part of it he thought they ought to raise, and a stamp duty was intended for that purpose.' He then proceeded to defend the particular tax which he had selected. It was the easiest. It was the most equitable. It would fall exclusively on property. It could be collected by very few officers. It would be equally spread over America and the West Indies. 'I am not, however,' he continued, 'set upon this tax. If the Americans dislike it, and prefer any other method of raising the money themselves, I shall be content. Write therefore to your several colonies, and if they choose any other mode I shall be satisfied, provided the money be but raised.'[1] He hinted

---

[1] Almon's *Biographical Anecdotes*, ii. 82-92. In the reply of the Massachusetts Assembly to Mauduit, the following passage occurs : ' The actual laying the stamp duty, you say, is deferred till next year, Mr. Grenville being willing to give the provinces their option to raise that or some equivalent tax, "desirous," as he was pleased to express himself, "to consult the ease, and quiet, and the goodwill of the colonies."' 'This suspension,' the letter adds, 'amounts to no more than this, that if the colonies will not tax themselves as they may be directed, the Parliament will tax them.'—Mauduit's *View of the New England Colonies*, pp. 95-100. In *The Controversy between Great Britain and her Colonies*, which was perhaps the ablest statement of the case against the colonies, and which was written by Knox, the Under-Secretary of State, and one of Grenville's confidential writers, it is said, ' Mr. Grenville, indeed, went so far as to desire the agents to acquaint the colonies that if they could not agree among themselves upon raising a revenue by their own Assemblies, yet if they all, or any of them, disliked stamp duties, and would propose any other sort of tax which would carry the appearance of equal efficacy, he would adopt it. But he warmly recommended to them the making grants by their own Assemblies as the most expedient method for themselves.'—P. 199. Burke, however, states that Grenville in the many debates on the Stamp Act never made this apology for himself, that he always expressed his dislike to the system of raising money by requisitions to the colonial Assemblies, and his preference for parliamentary taxation, and that it is therefore impossible he can have recommended the colonies to tax themselves, though he may have urged them to agree upon the tax which they would wish Parliament to propose (Speech on American Taxation). It appears, however, evident from the Massachusetts letter that although Grenville was inexorable about the right of Parliament to tax the colonies, the colonists understood him to have intentionally left it open to them to prevent the exercise of that right by raising the money themselves. All that politicians in England really wanted was an American contribution to the defence of the Empire. See too the

that by agreeing to the tax the Americans could make a precedent for their being always consulted by the ministry before they were taxed by Parliament.[1]

Grenville has been much blamed for not having made a formal requisition to each colonial Assembly, as was usual in time of war, requesting them to raise a sum for the support of the army; but it is almost certain that such a requisition would in most, if not all, cases have been refused, and the demand would have been made use of as a proof that Parliament had no right to impose the required tax. It is evident, however, that if the colonies were anxious to avoid what they regarded as the oppression of parliamentary taxation, by themselves making the provision for the required army, they had ample time and opportunity to do so. They were, however, quite resolved not to contribute to the army in any form. They had not asked for it. They disliked and dreaded it as strengthening the English Government. Their own taxes were much increased by burdens inherited from the war, a great part of the country was still suffering from recent devastations by the Indians, and the irritation caused by the measures against smuggling was very strong. The proposed tax was discussed in every provincial Assembly, and the result was a long series of resolutions and addresses to Parliament denying in the most emphatic terms the right of Parliament to tax America, and asserting that if the scheme of the Minister were carried into effect, 'it would establish the melancholy truth that the inhabitants of the colonies are the slaves of the Britons from whom they are descended.'[2] The Pennsylvanians alone made some advance in the direction of compromise by resolving that, 'as they always had thought, so they always shall think it their duty to grant aid to the Crown, according to their abilities, whenever required of them in the usual constitutional manner,' but they took no measure to carry their resolution into effect. In New England the doctrine that Parliament had no right whatever to legislate for America was now loudly proclaimed, and Otis was as usual active in fanning resistance to the Government.

---

statement of Garth, the Agent of South Carolina; Bancroft, ii. 211; and that of Franklin, Works, i. 291, 292; iv. 194.

[1] *Annual Register*, 1765, p. 33.
[2] See the Virginian Address, Grahame, iv. 180.

It was obvious that a very dangerous spirit was arising in the colonies. A few voices were raised in favour of the admission of American representatives into Parliament; but this plan, which was advocated by Otis and supported by the great names of Franklin and of Adam Smith, would have encountered enormous practical difficulties, and it found few friends in either country. Grenville himself, however, appears to have for a time seriously contemplated it. As he was accustomed to say to his friends, he had never entertained the smallest design against American liberty, and the sole object of his colonial policy was to induce or oblige America to contribute to the expense of her own defence in the same manner as Ireland. He had consulted the colonial agents in order that the colonies might themselves suggest the form of the contribution, and establish the precedent of being always in such cases consulted. He had deferred the Stamp Act for a whole year in order that the colonies might, if they chose, make imperial taxation unnecessary; and if the Americans thought that their liberties would become more secure by the introduction of American representatives into the British Parliament, he was quite ready to support such a scheme.[1] He would probably, however, have found it not easy to carry in England, and it was soon after utterly repudiated in America. At the same time, after the open denial of the competence of Parliament to tax the colonies, it was especially difficult to recede, and Grenville had some reason to think that the colonial addresses exaggerated the sentiments of the people. When the project was first laid before the agents of the colonies, the Agent for Rhode Island was the only one who unequivocally repudiated it.[2] The form of the tax was not one which would naturally attract much attention, and it might be hoped that public opinion would soon look upon it as of the same nature as the

---

[1] See Knox's *Extra-official Papers*, ii. 24, 25, 31–33. Hutchinson's *Hist. of Massachusetts*, p. 112. In his *Notes on the United States*, Sir Augustus Foster, who was English Secretary of Legation at Washington, 1804–1806, mentions that both Jefferson and his successor in the Presidency, Madison, expressed their belief that 'the timely concession of a few seats in the Upper as well as the Lower House would have set at rest the whole question.' Lord Liverpool was accustomed to say that no serious resistance to the Stamp Act would have been made, if Grenville had carried it at once without leaving a year for discussion. See *Quarterly Review*, No. cxxxv, p. 37.

[2] See Grahame, iv. 188.

postal revenue which the Imperial Parliament had long levied in the colonies.

In February 1765 the agents of several of the colonies had an interview with Grenville, and made one last effort to dissuade him from introducing the measure. Grenville, in his reply, expressed his sincere regret if he was exciting resentments in America, but, he said, 'it is the duty of my office to manage the revenue. I have really been made to believe that, considering the whole circumstances of the mother-country and the colonies, the latter can and ought to pay something to the public cause. I know of no better way than that now pursuing to lay such a tax. If you can tell of a better I will adopt it.' Benjamin Franklin, who had shortly before come over as Agent for Philadelphia, presented the resolution of the Assembly of his province, and urged that the demand for money should be made in the old constitutional way to the Assembly of each province in the form of a requisition by the governor. 'Can you agree,' rejoined Grenville, ' on the proportions each colony should raise?' The question touched the heart of the difficulty; the agents were obliged to answer in the negative, and the interview speedily closed. A few days later the fatal Bill was introduced into a nearly empty House, and it passed through all its stages almost unopposed. It made it necessary for all bills, bonds, leases, policies of insurance, newspapers, broadsides, and legal documents of all kinds to be written on stamped paper, to be sold by public officers at varying prices prescribed by the law. The proceeds were to be paid into his Majesty's treasury, and they were to be applied, under the direction of the Parliament, exclusively to the protection and defence of the colonies.[1] Offences against the Stamp Act were to be cognisable in America as in England by the Courts of Admiralty, and without the intervention of juries. In order to soften the opposition, and to consult, to the utmost of his power, the wishes of the colonists, Grenville informed the colonial agents that the distribution of the stamps should be confided not to Englishmen but to Americans, and he requested them to name such persons in their respective provinces as they thought best qualified for the purpose and most

---

[1] 5 Geo. III. c. 12.

acceptable to the inhabitants. They all complied with the request, and Franklin named one of his intimate friends as stamp distributor for Pennsylvania.

The Stamp Act, when its ultimate consequences are considered, must be deemed one of the most momentous legislative Acts in the history of mankind; but in England it passed almost completely unnoticed. The Wilkes excitement absorbed public attention, and no English politician appears to have realised the importance of the measure. It is scarcely mentioned in the contemporary correspondence of Horace Walpole, of Grenville, or of Pitt. Burke, who was not yet a member of the House of Commons, afterwards declared that he had followed the debate from the gallery, and that he had never heard a more languid one in the House; that not more than two or three gentlemen spoke against the Bill; that there was but one division in the whole course of the discussion, and that the minority in that division was not more than thirty-nine or forty. In the House of Lords he could not remember that there had been either a debate or division, and he was certain that there was no protest.[1] Pitt was at this time confined to his bed by illness, and Conway, Beckford, and Barré appear to have been almost the only opponents of the measure. The latter, whose American experience during the Canadian war had given him considerable weight, described the colonists, in a fine piece of declamation, as 'sons of liberty' planted in America by the oppression and strengthened by the neglect of England, and he predicted that the same love of freedom which had led them into an uncultivated and inhospitable country, and had supported them through so many hardships and so many dangers, would accompany them still, and would inspire them with an indomitable resolution to vindicate their violated liberty. His words appear to have excited no attention in England, and were not even reported in the contemporary parliamentary history;

---

[1] Burke's speech on American taxation, April 1774. The following is Horace Walpole's sole notice of the measure: 'There has been nothing of note in Parliament but one slight day on the American taxes, which Charles Townshend supporting, received a pretty heavy thump from Barré, who is the present Pitt and the dread of all the vociferous Norths and Rigbys, on whose lungs depended so much of Mr. Grenville's power.' Walpole to Hertford, Feb. 12, 1765. Beckford, some years later, mentioned that he had opposed the Stamp Act.—*Cavendish Debates*, i. 41.

but they were at once transmitted to America by the Agent for Connecticut, who had been present in the gallery, and they contributed not a little to stimulate the flame. The 'sons of liberty' became from this time the favourite designation of the American associations against the Stamp Act.

In truth, the measure, although it was by no means as unjust or as unreasonable as has been alleged, and although it might perhaps in some periods of colonial history have passed almost unperceived, did unquestionably infringe upon a principle which the English race both at home and abroad have always regarded with a peculiar jealousy. The doctrine that taxation and representation are in free nations inseparably connected, that constitutional government is closely connected with the rights of property, and that no people can be legitimately taxed except by themselves or their representatives, lay at the very root of the English conception of political liberty. The same principle that had led the English people to provide so carefully in the Great Charter, in a well-known statute of Edward I., and in the Bill of Rights, that no taxation should be drawn from them except by the English Parliament; the same principle which had gradually invested the representative branch of the Legislature with the special and peculiar function of granting supplies, led the colonists to maintain that their liberty would be destroyed if they were taxed by a Legislature in which they had no representatives, and which sat 3,000 miles from their shore. It was a principle which had been respected by Henry VIII. and Elizabeth in the most arbitrary moments of their reigns, and its violation by Charles I. was one of the chief causes of the Rebellion. The principle which led Hampden to refuse to pay 20s. of ship money was substantially the same as that which inspired the resistance to the Stamp Act. It might be impossible to show by the letter of the law that there was any generical distinction between taxing and other legislative Acts; but in the constitutional traditions of the English people a broad line did undoubtedly exist. As Burke truly said, 'the great contests for freedom in this country were from the earliest times chiefly on the question of taxing.' The English people have always held that as long as their representatives retain the power of the purse they will be able at last to check every extravagance of tyranny, but that whenever this is given up the whole fabric of their liberty is undermined. The English Parliament had always abstained from imposing taxes on Wales until Welsh members sat among them. When the right of self-taxation was withdrawn from Convocation, the clergy at once assumed and exercised the privilege of voting for Members of Parliament in virtue of their ecclesiastical freeholds. The English Parliament repeatedly asserted its authority over the Parliament of Ireland, and it often exerted it in a manner which was grossly tyrannical; but it never imposed any direct tax upon the Irish people. The weighty language of Henry Cromwell, who governed Ireland in one of the darkest periods of her history, was remembered: 'I am glad,' he wrote, 'to hear that as well non-legal as contra-legal ways of raising money are not hearkened to. . . . Errors in raising money are the compendious ways to cause a general discontent; for whereas other things are but the concernments of some, this is of all. Wherefore, I hope God will in His mercy not lead us into temptation.'[1]

It is quite true that this theory, like that of the social contract which has also borne a great part in the history of political liberty, will not bear a severe and philosophical examination. The opponents of the American claims were able to reply, with undoubted truth, that at least nine-tenths of the English people had no votes; that the great manufacturing towns, which contributed so largely to the public burdens, were for the most part wholly unrepresented; that the minority in Parliament voted only in order to be systematically overruled; and that, in a country where the constituencies were as unequal as in England, that minority often represented the large majority of the voters. It was easy to show that the financial system of the country consisted chiefly of a number of particular taxes imposed on particular classes and industries, and that in the great majority of cases these taxes were levied not only without the consent but in spite of the strenuous opposition of the representatives of those who paid them. The doctrine that 'whatever a man has honestly acquired is abso-

[1] H. Cromwell to Thurloe, February 24, 1657. *Thurloe State Papers*, vi. 820.

lutely his own, and cannot without robbery be taken from him, except by his own consent,' if it were applied rigidly to taxation, would reduce every society to anarchy; for there is no tax which on such principles a large proportion of the taxpayers would not be authorised in resisting. It was a first principle of the Constitution that a Member of Parliament was the representative not merely of his own constituency, but also of the whole empire. Men connected with, or at least specially interested in the colonies, always found their way into Parliament; and the very fact that the colonial arguments were maintained with transcendent power within its walls was sufficient to show that the colonies were virtually represented.

Such arguments gave an easy dialectic victory to the supporters of the Stamp Act; but in the eyes of a true statesman they are very insufficient. Severe accuracy of definition, refinement and precision of reasoning, are for the most part wholly out of place in practical politics. It might be true that there was a line where internal and external taxation, taxation for purposes of commerce and taxation for purposes of revenue, faded imperceptibly into one another; but still there was a broad, rough distinction between the two provinces which was sufficiently palpable to form the basis of a colonial policy. The theory connecting representation with taxation was susceptible of a similar justification. A Parliament elected by a considerable part of the English people, drawn from the English people, sitting in the midst of them, and exposed to their social and intellectual influence, was assumed to represent the whole nation, and the decision of its majority was assumed to be the decision of the whole. If it be asked how these assumptions could be defended, it can only be answered that they had rendered possible a form of government which had arrested the incursions of the royal prerogative, had given England a longer period and a larger measure of self-government than was enjoyed by any other great European nation, and had created a public spirit sufficiently powerful to defend the liberties that had been won. Such arguments, however worthless they might appear to a lawyer or a theorist, ought to be very sufficient to a statesman. Manchester and Sheffield had no more direct representation in Parliament than Boston or Philadelphia; but the relations of unrepresented Englishmen and of colonists to the English Parliament were very different. Parliament could never long neglect the fierce beatings of the waves of popular discontent around its walls. It might long continue perfectly indifferent to the wishes of a population 3,000 miles from the English shore. When Parliament taxed the English people, the taxing body itself felt the weight of the burden it imposed; but Parliament felt no part of the weight of colonial taxation, and had therefore a direct interest in increasing it. The English people might justly complain that they were taxed by a body in which they were very imperfectly represented; but this was a widely different thing from being taxed by the Legislature of another country. To adopt the powerful language of an Irish writer, no free people will ever admit 'that persons distant from them 1,000 leagues are to tax them to what amount they please, without their consent, without knowing them or their concerns, without any sympathy of affection or interest, without even sharing themselves in the taxes they impose—on the contrary, diminishing their own burdens exactly in the degree they increase theirs.' [1]

The Stamp Act received the royal assent on March 22, 1765, and it was to come into operation on the 1st of November following. It was accompanied by a measure granting the colonies bounties for the import of their timber into England, permitting them to export it freely to Ireland, Madeira, the Azores, and any part of Europe south of Cape Finisterre; and in some other ways slightly relaxing the trade restrictions.[2] A measure was also passed which obliged the colonists to provide the British troops stationed among them with quarters, and also with fire, candles, beds, vinegar, and salt. Neither of these measures, however, at the time excited much attention, and public interest in the colonies was wholly concentrated upon the Stamp Act. The long delay, which English statesmen had hoped would have led to some proposal of compromise from America, had been sedulously employed by skilful agitators in stimulating the excitement; and when the news

---

[1] *Considerations on the Dependencies of Great Britain* (by Sir Hercules Langrishe), Dublin, 1769, p. 75.
[2] 5 Geo. III. c. 45.

arrived that the Stamp Act had been carried, the train was fully laid, and the indignation of the colonies rose at once into a flame. Virginia set the example by a series of resolutions which were termed 'the alarum bell to the disaffected,' and which were speedily copied in the other provinces. They declared that the colonists were entitled by charter to all the liberties and privileges of natural-born subjects; 'that the taxation of the people by themselves, or by persons chosen by themselves to represent them, . . . is the distinguishing characteristic of British freedom, without which the ancient constitution cannot exist,' and that this inestimable right had always been recognised by the King and people of Great Britain as undoubtedly belonging to the colonies. A congress of representatives of nine States was held at New York, and in an extremely able State paper they drew up the case of the colonies. They acknowledged that they owed allegiance to the Crown, and 'all due subordination to that august body, the Parliament of Great Britain;' but they maintained that they were entitled to all the inherent rights and liberties of natural-born subjects; 'that it is inseparably essential to the freedom of a people, and the undoubted right of Englishmen, that no taxes be imposed on them but with their own consent, given personally or by their representatives;' that the colonists 'are not, and from their local circumstances cannot be, represented in the House of Commons of Great Britain;' that the only representatives of the colonies, and therefore the only persons constitutionally competent to tax them, were the members chosen in the colonies by themselves; and 'that all supplies of the Crown being free gifts from the people, it is unreasonable and inconsistent with the principles and spirit of the British Constitution for the people of Great Britain to grant to his Majesty the property of the colonies.' A petition to the King and memorials to both Houses of Parliament were drawn up embodying these views.[1]

It was not, however, only by such legal measures that the opposition was shown. A furious outburst of popular violence speedily showed that it would be impossible to enforce the Act. In Boston, Oliver, the secretary of the province, who had ac-

[1] See Story's *Constitution of the United States*, i. 175, 176.

cepted the office of stamp distributor, was hung in effigy on a tree in the main street of the town. The building which had been erected as a Stamp Office was levelled with the dust; the house of Oliver was attacked, plundered, and wrecked, and he was compelled by the mob to resign his office and to swear beneath the tree on which his effigy had been so ignominiously hung, that he never would resume it. A few nights later the riots recommenced with redoubled fury. The houses of two of the leading officials connected with the Admiralty Court and with the Custom-house were attacked and rifled, and the files and records of the Admiralty Court were burnt. The mob, intoxicated with the liquors which they had found in one of the cellars they had plundered, next turned to the house of Hutchinson, the Lieutenant-Governor and Chief Justice of the province. Hutchinson was not only the second person in rank in the colony, he was also a man who had personal claims of the highest kind upon his countrymen. He was an American, a Calvinist, a member of one of the oldest colonial families, and in a country where literary enterprise was very uncommon he had devoted a great part of his life to investigating the history of his native province. His rare ability, his stainless private character, and his great charm of manner were universally recognised;[1] he had at one time been one of the most popular men in the colony, and he had been selected by the great majority of the Assembly as their agent to oppose in England the restrictive commercial laws of Grenville. Bernard, however, considering this position incompatible with the office of Lieutenant-Governor, which Hutchinson had held since 1758, induced him to decline it; and although Hutchinson was opposed to the policy of the Stamp Act, the determination with which he acted as Chief Justice in supporting the law soon made him obnoxious to the mob. He had barely time to escape with his family, when his house, which was the finest in Boston, was attacked and destroyed. His plate, his furniture, his pictures, the public documents in his possession, and a noble library which he had spent thirty years in collecting, were plundered and burnt. Resolutions were afterwards carried in the town for suppressing riots, but nothing was done, and it was evident

---

[1] See Tudor's *Life of Otis*, pp. 121-133.

that the prevailing feeling was with the rioters. Mayhew, one of the most popular preachers of Boston, had just before denounced the Stamp Act from the pulpit, preaching from the text, 'I would that they were even cut off which trouble you.' A leading tradesman who had been notoriously a ringleader was apprehended by the sheriffs, but he was released without inquiry in consequence of a large portion of the civic guard having threatened to disband themselves if he were committed to prison. Eight or ten persons of inferior note were actually imprisoned, but the mob compelled the jailer to surrender the keys and released them, and not a single person was really punished.[1]

The flame rapidly spread. In the newly annexed provinces, indeed, and in most of the West Indian islands, the Act was received without difficulty, but in nearly every American colony those who had consented to be stamp distributors were hung and burnt in effigy, and compelled by mob violence to resign their posts. The houses of many who were known to be supporters of the Act or sympathisers with the Government were attacked and plundered. Some were compelled to fly from the colonies, and the authority of the Home Government was exposed to every kind of insult. In New York the effigy of the Governor was paraded with that of the devil round the town and then publicly burnt, and threatening letters were circulated menacing the lives of those who distributed stamps.[2] The merchants of the chief towns entered into agreements to order no more goods from England, to cancel all orders already given, in some cases even to send no remittances to England in payment of their debts, till the Stamp Act was repealed. The lawyers combined to make no use of the stamped papers. In order that the colonies might be able to dispense with assistance from England, great efforts were made to promote manufactures. The richest citizens set the example of dressing in old or homespun clothes rather than wear new clothes imported from England; and in order to supply the deficiency of wool, a general agreement was made to abstain from eating lamb.

When the 1st of November arrived, the bells were tolled as

---

[1] Holmes' *Annals of America*, 1765. Grahame's *Hist.* iv. *Annual Register*, 1765. Adams' Diary, *Works*, ii. 156.

[2] *Documents relating to the Colonial Hist. of New York*, vii. pp. 770-775.

for the funeral of a nation. The flags were hung half-mast high. The shops were shut, and the Stamp Act was hawked about with the inscription, 'The folly of England and the ruin of America.' The newspapers were obliged by the new law to bear the stamp, which probably contributed much to the extreme virulence of their opposition, and many of them now appeared with a death's head in the place where the stamp should have been. It was found not only impossible to distribute stamps, but even impossible to keep them in the colonies, for the mob seized on every box which was brought from England and committed it to the flames. Stamps were required for the validity of every legal document, yet in most of the colonies not a single sheet of stamped paper could be found. The law courts were for a time closed, and almost all business was suspended. At last the governors, considering the impossibility of carrying on public business or protecting property under these conditions, took the law into their own hands, and issued letters authorising non-compliance with the Act on the ground that it was absolutely impossible to procure the requisite stamps in the colony.

The determination of the opponents of the Act was all the greater because in the interval between its enactment and the period in which it was to come into operation a change had taken place in the Administration at home. The Grenville Ministry had fallen in July, and had been succeeded by that of Rockingham; and Conway, who had been one of the few opponents of the Stamp Act, was now Secretary of State for the Colonies.

Up to this time colonial affairs had scarcely excited any attention in the English political world. The Duke of Cumberland, in a long and detailed memorial,[1] has recounted the negotiations he was instructed to carry on with Pitt in April and May 1765, with a view to inducing that statesman to combine with the Rockingham party in a new ministry, and it is very remarkable that in this memorial there is not a word relating to the colonies. The general political condition of the country was carefully reviewed. Much was said about the Regency Bill, the Cyder Bill, the dismissal of officers on account of their

[1] Albemarle's *Life of Rockingham*, i. 185-203.

votes, the illegality of general warrants, the abuses of military patronage, the growing power of the House of Bourbon, the propriety of attempting a new alliance with Prussia; but there is not the smallest evidence that either Pitt or Cumberland, or any of the other statesmen who were concerned in the negotiation, were conscious that any serious question was impending in America. The Stamp Act had contributed nothing to the downfall of Grenville; it attracted so little attention that it was only in the last days of 1765 or the first days of 1766 that the new ministers learnt the views of Pitt upon the subject; it was probably a complete surprise to them to learn that it had brought the colonies to the verge of rebellion, and in the first months of their power they appear to have been quite uncertain what policy they would pursue. One of the first persons in England who fully realised the magnitude of the question was the King. On December 5, 1765, he wrote to Conway: 'I am more and more grieved at the accounts of America. Where this spirit will end is not to be said. It is undoubtedly the most serious matter that ever came before Parliament; it requires more deliberation, candour, and temper than I fear it will meet with.'[2]

The Ministers would gladly have left the question of American taxation undecided, but this was no longer possible. Parliament had almost unanimously asserted its right, and the colonial Assemblies had defiantly denied it. The servants of the Crown had in nearly every colony been insulted or plundered, and the honour of England and of the Parliament was deeply touched. The Ministry was very weak; Pitt had refused to join it; the King disliked and distrusted it, and he was strongly in favour of the coercion of America. On the other hand, it was clear that the Act could not be enforced without war, and the merchants all over England were suffering seriously from the suspension of the American trade. Petitions were presented from the traders of London, Bristol, Liverpool, and other towns, stating that the colonists were indebted to the merchants of this country to the amount of several millions sterling for English goods which had been exported to America; that the colonists had hitherto faithfully

[1] Albemarle's *Life of Rockingham*, i. 269.   [2] Ibid. i. 256.

made good their engagements, but that they now declared their inability to do so; that they would neither give orders for new goods nor pay for those which they had actually received; and that unless Parliament speedily retraced its steps, multitudes of English manufacturers would be reduced to bankruptcy. In Manchester, Nottingham, Leeds, and many other towns, thousands of artisans had been thrown out of employment. Glasgow complained that the Stamp Act was threatening it with absolute ruin, for its trade was principally with America, and not less than half a million of money was due by the colonists of Maryland and Virginia alone, to Glasgow merchants.[1]

Parliament met on December 17, 1765, and the attitude of the different parties was speedily disclosed. A powerful Opposition, led by Grenville and Bedford, strenuously urged that no relaxation or indulgence should be granted to the colonists. In two successive sessions the policy of taxing America had been deliberately affirmed, and if Parliament now suffered itself to be defied or intimidated its authority would be for ever at an end. The method of reasoning by which the Americans maintained that they could not be taxed by a Parliament in which they were not represented, might be applied with equal plausibility to the Navigation Act and to every other branch of imperial legislation for the colonies, and it led directly to the disintegration of the Empire. The supreme authority of Parliament chiefly held the different parts of that Empire together. The right of taxation was an essential part of the sovereign power. The colonial constitutions were created by royal charter, and it could not be admitted that the King, while retaining his own sovereignty over certain portions of his dominions, could by a mere exercise of his prerogative withdraw them wholly or in part from the authority of the British Parliament. It was the right and the duty of the Imperial Legislature to determine in what proportions the different parts of the Empire should contribute to the defence of the whole, and to see that no one part evaded its obligations and unjustly transferred its share to the others. The conduct of the colonies, in the eyes of these politicians, admitted of no excuse or palliation. The disputed

---

[1] *Parl. Hist.* xvi. 133-137; Walpole's *Memoirs*, ii. 296; *Burke's Correspondence*, i. 100.

right of taxation was established by a long series of legal authorities, and there was no real distinction between internal and external taxation. It now suited the Americans to describe themselves as apostles of liberty, and to denounce England as an oppressor. It was a simple truth that England governed her colonies more liberally than any other country in the world. They were the only existing colonies which enjoyed real political liberty. Their commercial system was more liberal than that of any other colonies. They had attained, under British rule, to a degree of prosperity which was surpassed in no quarter of the globe. England had loaded herself with debt in order to remove the one great danger to their future; she cheerfully bore the whole burden of their protection by sea. At the Peace of Paris she had made their interests the very first object of her policy, and she only asked them in return to bear a portion of the cost of their own defence. Somewhat more than eight millions of Englishmen were burdened with a national debt of 140,000,000*l.* The united debt of about two millions of Americans was now less than 800,000*l.* The annual sum the colonists were asked to contribute in the form of stamp duties was less than 100,000*l.*, with an express provision that no part of that sum should be devoted to any other purpose than the defence and protection of the colonies. And the country which refused to bear this small tax was so rich that in the space of three years it had paid off 1,755,000*l.* of its debt. No demand could be more moderate and equitable than that of England; and amid all the high-sounding declamations that were wafted across the Atlantic, it was not difficult to perceive that the true motive of the resistance was of the vulgarest kind. It was a desire to pay as little as possible; to throw as much as possible upon the mother-country. Nor was the mode of resistance more respectable—the plunder of private houses and custom-houses; mob violence connived at by all classes and perfectly unpunished; agreements of merchants to refuse to pay their private debts in order to attain political ends. If this was the attitude of America within two years of the Peace of Paris, if these were the firstfruits of the new sense of security which British triumphs in Canada had given, could it be doubted that concessions would only be the prelude to new demands?

Already the Custom-house officers were attacked by the mobs almost as fiercely as the stamp distributors. Already Otis, the most popular advocate of the American cause, was ridiculing the distinction between internal and external taxation, and denying that the British Legislature possessed any rightful authority in America. Already a highly seditious press had grown up in the colonies, and to talk scarcely disguised treason had become the best passport to popular favour. It would be impossible for Parliament, if it now receded, to retain permanently any legislative authority over the colonies; and if this too were given up, the unity of the Empire would be but a name, and America would in reality contribute nothing to its strength. If ministers now repealed the Stamp Act they would be guilty of treachery to England. They would abdicate a vital portion of the sovereignty which England rightfully possessed. They would humiliate the British Parliament before the Empire and before the world. They would establish the fatal principle that it must never again ask any of the distant portions of the Empire to contribute to the burden of their own permanent defence. They would establish the still more fatal precedent, that the best way of inducing Parliament to repeal an obnoxious tax was to refuse to pay it, and to hound on mobs against those who were entrusted with its collection.

These were the chief arguments on the side of the late ministers. Pitt, on the other hand, rose from his sick-bed, and in speeches of extraordinary eloquence, and which produced an amazing effect on both sides of the Atlantic, he justified the resistance of the colonists. He stood apart from all parties, and, while he declared that 'every capital measure' of the late ministry was wrong, he ostentatiously refused to give his confidence to their successors. He maintained in the strongest terms the doctrine that self-taxation is the essential and discriminating circumstance of political freedom. His opinion on the great question at issue cannot be better expressed than in his own terse and luminous sentences. 'It is my opinion,' he said, 'that this kingdom has no right to lay a tax upon the colonies. At the same time I assert the authority of this kingdom over the colonies to be sovereign and supreme in every circumstance of government and legislation whatsoever. . . .

Taxation is no part of the governing or legislative power. The taxes are a voluntary gift and grant of the Commons alone. In legislation the three estates of the realm are alike concerned; but the concurrence of the peers and the Crown to a tax is only necessary to close with the form of a law. The gift and grant is of the Commons alone. . . . The distinction between legislation and taxation is essentially necessary to liberty. . . . The Commons of America, represented in their several Assemblies, have ever been in possession of the exercise of this, their constitutional right of giving and granting their own money. They would have been slaves if they had not enjoyed it. At the same time this kingdom, as the supreme governing and legislative power, has always bound the colonies . . . in everything, except that of taking their money out of their pockets without their consent.' In his reply to Grenville he reiterated these principles with still stronger emphasis. 'I rejoice,' he said, 'that America has resisted. Three millions of people, so dead to all the feelings of liberty as voluntarily to submit to be slaves, would have been fit instruments to make slaves of the rest. . . . In such a cause your success would be hazardous. America, if she fell, would fall like the strong man with his arms around the pillars of the Constitution. . . . When two countries are connected together like England and her colonies without being incorporated, the one must necessarily govern; the greater must rule the less, but so rule it as not to contradict the fundamental principles that are common to both. If the gentleman does not understand the difference between external and internal taxes, I cannot help it; but there is a plain distinction between taxes levied for the purpose of raising a revenue, and duties imposed for the regulation of trade for the accommodation of the subject; although in the consequences some revenue might incidentally arise from the latter. . . . I will be bold to affirm that the profits to Great Britain from the trade of the colonies through all its branches is two millions a year. This is the fund that carried you triumphantly through the last war. . . . This is the price America pays for her protection. . . . I dare not say how much higher these profits may be augmented. . . . The Americans have not acted in all things with prudence and temper. They have been driven to madness by injustice. Will you punish them for the madness you have occasioned? Rather let prudence and temper come first from this side. I will undertake for America that she will follow the example. . . . Upon the whole I will beg leave to tell the House what is really my opinion. It is that the Stamp Act should be repealed absolutely, totally, and immediately; that the reason for the repeal should be assigned, because it was founded on an erroneous principle. At the same time let the sovereign authority of this country over the colonies be asserted in as strong terms as can be devised, and be made to extend to every point of legislation whatsoever; that we may bind their trade, confine their manufactures, and exercise every power whatsoever—except that of taking their money out of their pockets without their consent.'[1]

These views were defended in the strongest terms by Lord Camden, who pledged his great legal reputation to the doctrine that taxation is not included under the general right of legislation, and that taxation and representation are morally inseparable. 'This position,' he very rashly affirmed, 'is founded on the laws of nature; nay, more, it is itself an eternal law of nature. For whatever is a man's own is absolutely his own. No man has a right to take it from him without his consent, either expressed by himself or representative. Whoever attempts to do it attempts an injury. Whoever does it commits a robbery.'[2]

The task of the ministers in dealing with this question was extremely difficult. The great majority of them desired ardently the repeal of the Stamp Act; but the wishes of the King, the abstention of Pitt, and the divided condition of parties had compelled Rockingham to include in his Government Charles Townshend, Barrington, and Northington, who were all strong advocates of the taxation of America, and Northington took an early opportunity of delivering an invective against the colonies which seemed specially intended to prolong the exasperation. 'If they withdraw allegiance,' he concluded, 'you must withdraw protection, and then the little State of

---

[1] *Chatham Correspondence*, ii. 363-372. Rockingham next day wrote to the King, 'The events of yesterday in the House of Commons have shown the amazing power and influence which Mr. Pitt has whenever he takes part in debate.'—Albemarle's *Life of Rockingham*, i. 270.
[2] *Parl. Hist.* xvi. 178.

Genoa or the king of the of Sweden may soon overrun them.' The King himself, though he was prepared to see the Stamp Act altered in some of its provisions, was decidedly hostile to the repeal. When the measure was first contemplated, two partisans of Bute came to the King offering to resign their places, as they meant to oppose the repeal, but they were at once told that they might keep their places and vote as they pleased. The hint was taken, and the King's friends were among the most active, though not the most conspicuous, opponents of the ministers.[1] And in addition to all these difficulties the ministers had to deal with the exasperation which was produced in Parliament by the continual outrages and insults to which all who represented the English Government in America were exposed.

Their policy consisted of two parts. They asserted in the strongest and most unrestricted form the sovereignty of the British Legislature, first of all by resolutions and then by a Declaratory Act affirming the right of Parliament to make laws binding the British colonies 'in all cases whatsoever,' and condemning as unlawful the votes of the colonial Assemblies which had denied to Parliament the right of taxing them. Side by side with this measure they brought in a Bill repealing the Stamp Act.[2] It was advocated both in its preamble and in the speeches of its supporters on the ground of simple expediency. The Stamp Act had already produced evils far outweighing any benefits that could flow from it. To enforce it over a vast and thinly populated country, and in the face of the universal and vehement opposition of the people, had proved hitherto impossible, and would always be difficult, dangerous, and disastrous. It might produce rebellion. It would certainly produce permanent and general disaffection, great derangement of commercial relations, a smothered resistance which could only be overcome by a costly and extensive system of coercion. It could not be wise to convert the Americans into a nation of rebels who were only waiting for a European war to throw off their allegiance. Yet this would be the natural and almost inevitable consequence of persisting in the policy

---

[1] *Grenville Papers*, iii. 353, 362, 365. Albemarle's *Life of Rockingham*
[2] 6 Geo. III. c. 11, 12.

of Grenville. The chief interests of England in her colonies were commercial, and these had been profoundly injured by the Stamp Act. As long as it continued, the Americans were resolved to make it their main effort to abstain as much as possible from English goods, and the English commercial classes were unanimous in favour of the repeal. The right of the country was affirmed and the honour of Parliament vindicated by the Declaratory Act. It now remained only—if possible without idle recrimination—to pursue the course which was most conducive to the interests of England. And that course was plainly to retire from a position which had become utterly untenable.

The debates on this theme were among the fiercest and longest ever known in Parliament. The former ministers opposed the repeal at every stage, and most of those who were under the direct influence of the King plotted busily against it. Nearly a dozen members of the King's household, nearly all the bishops, nearly all the Scotch, nearly all the Tories voted against the ministry, and in the very agony of the contest Lord Strange spread abroad the report that he had heard from the King's own lips that the King was opposed to the repeal. Rockingham acted with great decision. He insisted on accompanying Lord Strange into the King's presence, and in obtaining from the King a written paper stating that he was in favour of the repeal rather than the enforcement of the Act, though he would have preferred its modification to either course. The great and manifest desire of the commercial classes throughout England had much weight; the repeal was carried through the House of Commons, brought up by no less than 200 members to the Lords, and finally carried amid the strongest expressions of public joy. Burke described it as 'an event that caused more universal joy throughout the British dominions than perhaps any other that can be remembered.'[1]

Of these two measures the repeal of the Stamp Act was that which was most violently denounced at the time; but the Declaratory Act, which passed almost unopposed, is the one which now requires defence. It has been represented as the

---

[1] Albemarle's *Life of Rockingham*, i. 250, 292, 299-302, 314, 321. *Annual Register*, 1766. *Grenville Papers*, iii 353-370.

source indemnifying those that ensued, for as long as the right of Parliament to tax America was asserted, the liberty of the colonies was precarious. I have already stated my opinion that no just blame attaches to the ministry on this matter. It would no doubt have been better if the question of the right of taxation had never been raised, and no one asserted this more constantly than Burke, who largely inspired the policy of the Government. But the ministers had no alternative. Parliament had already twice asserted its right to tax. With the exception of Lord Camden, the first legal authorities in the country unanimously maintained it. The Americans had openly denied it, and they had aggravated their denial by treating an Act of Parliament and those who were appointed to administer it with the grossest outrage. It was quite impossible that Parliament with any regard to its own dignity could acquiesce tamely in these proceedings. It was quite impossible that a weak ministry, divided on this very question and undermined by the Court, could have carried the repeal if it had been unaccompanied by an assertion of parliamentary authority on the matter that was in dispute. All accounts concur in showing that the proceedings of the Americans had produced a violent and very natural irritation,[1] and every mail brought news which was only too well fitted to aggravate it. The judgment on this subject of Sir George Savile, who was one of the most sagacious members of the Rockingham party, is of great weight. In a letter addressed to the Americans he wrote: 'You should know that the great obstacle in the way of the ministers has been unhappily thrown in by yourselves— I mean the intemperate proceedings of various ranks of people on your side the water—and that the difficulties of the repeal would have been nothing if you had not by your violence in word and action awakened the honour of Parliament, and thereby involved every friend of the repeal in the imputation

---

[1] Thus Shelburne reported to Pitt, December 21, 1765. 'The prejudice against the Americans on the whole seemed very great, and no very decided opinion in favour of the ministry.'— *Chatham Correspondence,* ii.

355. Walpole says, 'As the accounts from America grew every day worse, the ministers, who at first were inclined to repeal the Act, were borne down by the flagrancy of the provocation.'—*Memoirs of George III.* ii. 221.

of betraying the dignity of Parliament, you;land in her ue that the Act would certainly not have been repealed if men's minds had not been in some measure satisfied with the Declaration of Right.'[1]

Franklin, in the very remarkable evidence which he at this time gave before a committee of the House of Commons about the political condition and prospects of America, having been asked whether he thought the Americans would be contented with a repeal of the Stamp Act even if it were accompanied by an assertion of the right of Parliament to tax them, answered, 'I think the resolutions of right will give them very little concern, if they are never attempted to be carried into practice.'[2] There can be little doubt that this judgment was a just one. All testimony concurs in showing that the repeal of the Stamp Act produced, for a time at least, a complete pacification of America. As Adams, who was watching the current of American feeling with great keenness, wrote, 'The repeal of the Stamp Act has hushed into silence almost every popular clamour, and composed every wave of popular disorder into a smooth and peaceful calm.'[3]

In addition to these measures, the colonial Governors were instructed to ask the Assemblies to compensate those whose property had been destroyed in the late riots. An Act was

---

[1] Albemarle's *Life of Rockingham*, i. 305. Charles Fox, in a speech which he made on December 10, 1777, fully corroborated this assertion, and declared that 'it was not the inclination of Lord Rockingham, but the necessity of his situation, which was the cause of the Declaratory Act.'—*Parl. Hist.* xix. 563. The Duke of Richmond, who on all American questions was one of the most prominent members of the Rockingham party, said in 1778, 'that with respect to the Declaratory Act any reason that ever weighed with him in favour of that Act was to obtain the repeal of the Stamp Act. Many people of high principles would never, in his opinion, have been brought to repeal the Stamp Act without it; the number of those who opposed that repeal, even as it was, were very numerous.'—*Chatham Correspondence*, iv. 501, 502.

[2] Franklin's *Works*, iv. 176.

[3] Adams' Diary. *Works*, ii. 203. Adams' biographer says the colonists 'received the repeal of the Stamp Act with transports of joy, and disregarded the mere empty declaration of a right which they flattered themselves was never to be exercised. The spirit of resistance immediately subsided, and a general tranquillity prevailed until the project of levying internal taxes upon the people of the colonies by Act of Parliament was resumed in England.' *Ibid.* i. 81, 82. Burke in his great speech in 1774 on the American question, speaking of the repeal of the Stamp Act, said: 'I am bold to say, so sudden a calm, recovered after so violent a storm, is without parallel in history.' The testimony of Hutchinson is equally decisive. 'The Act which accompanied it [the repeal of the Stamp Act] with the title of "Securing the Dependency of the Colonies," caused no allay of the joy, and was considered as mere naked form.' *Hist. of Massachusetts Bay*, p. 147.

carried indemnifying those who had violated the Stamp Act, and some considerable changes were made in that commercial system which was by far the most real of the grievances of America. It was impossible for a Government which had just won a great victory for the Americans, by the assistance of the commercial and manufacturing classes, to touch either the laws prohibiting some of the chief forms of manufacture in the colonies or the general principle of colonial monopoly; and the favourite argument of the opponents of the Stamp Act was that the trade advantages arising from that monopoly were the real contribution of America to the defence and prosperity of the Empire. Within these limits, however, much remained to be done. The restrictions imposed upon the trade with the French West India islands, and especially upon the importation of molasses, had been, as we have seen, the main practical grievance of the commercial system. The prohibition of manufactures, however unreasonable and unjust, was of no great consequence to a country where agriculture, fisheries, and commerce were naturally the most lucrative forms of enterprise; but an abundant supply of molasses was essential to the great distilleries at Boston. The duty when it was 1s. a gallon had been a mere dead letter. When Grenville reduced it to 6d. a gallon, the most violent measures had still been unable to suppress a great smuggling trade, and the duty only yielded 2,000l. a year. The Rockingham Government lowered it to 1d., and this small duty, being no longer a grievance, produced no less than 17,000l. The duties imposed on coffee and pimento from the British plantations, and on foreign cambrics and lawns, imported into America, were at the same time lowered; and the British West India islands, in whose favour the colonial trade with the French islands had been restricted, were compensated by the opening in them of some free ports and by some other commercial favours.[1]

'The Americans,' said Chatham a few years later, when describing this period, 'had almost forgot, in their excess of gratitude for the repeal of the Stamp Act, any interest but that of the mother-country; there seemed an emulation among the different provinces who should be most dutiful and forward

[1] Macpherson's *Annals of Commerce*, iii. 446, 447.

in their expressions of loyalty.'[1] The Rockingham Ministry had undoubtedly, under circumstances of very great difficulty, restored confidence to America, and concluded for the present a contest which would probably have ended in a war. In most of the provincial Assemblies and in many public meetings of citizens, addresses of thanks were carried to the King, to the ministry, to Pitt, Camden, and Barré; and in more than one province statues were raised to the King and to Pitt. The shrewd Philadelphian Quakers passed a characteristic resolution, 'that to demonstrate our zeal to Great Britain, and our gratitude for the repeal of the Stamp Act, each of us will on the 4th of June next, being the birthday of our gracious Sovereign, dress ourselves in a new suit of the manufactures of England, and give what homespun clothes we have to the poor.'[2] A feeling of real and genuine loyalty to the mother-country appears to have at this time existed in the colonies, though it required much skill to maintain it.

The Americans had in truth won a great victory, which inspired them with unbounded confidence in their strength. They had gone through all the excitement of a violent and brilliantly successful political campaign; they had realised for a time the union which appeared formerly so chimerical; they had found their natural leaders in the struggle, and had discovered the weakness of the mother-country. Many writers and speakers had arisen who had learnt the lesson that a defiance of English authority was one of the easiest and safest paths to popular favour, and the speeches of Pitt had kindled a fierce enthusiasm of liberty through the colonies. There was no want of men who regretted that the agitation had ceased, who would gladly have pressed on the struggle to new issues, and who were ready to take advantage of the first occasion for quarrel. It was not easy for an ambitious man in these distant colonies to make his name known to the world; but if events ever led to a collision, a great field of ambition would be suddenly opened. Besides this, principles of a far-reaching and revolutionary character had become familiar to the people. It is a dangerous thing when nations begin to scrutinise too closely the foundations of political authority, the possible results to

---

[1] Thackeray's *Life of Chatham*, ii. 263   [2] *Annual Register*, 1766, p. 114.

which political principles may logically lead, the exact limits by which the different powers of a heterogeneous and prescriptive government must be confined. The theory of English lawyers that a Parliament in which the Americans were unrepresented might fetter their commerce in all its parts, and exact in taxation the last shilling of their fortunes, and that their whole representative system existed only by the indulgence of England, would, if fully acted on, have reduced the colonies to absolute slavery. On the other hand, Otis and other agitators were vehemently urging that the principles of Chatham and Camden would authorise the Americans to repudiate all parliamentary restrictions on American trade. No objection seems indeed to have been felt to the bounties which England conferred upon it, or to the protection of their coasts by English vessels; but in all other respects parliamentary interference was profoundly disliked. Lawyers had assumed during the late troubles a great prominence in colonial politics, and a litigious, captious, and defining spirit was abroad.

It was noticed that in the addresses to the King and to the Government thanking them for the repeal of the Stamp Act, as little as possible was said about the supremacy of Parliament, and in the most exuberant moments of colonial gratitude there were no signs of any disposition, in any province, to undertake, under proper guarantees and limitation, the task of supporting such English troops as might be stationed in America. Had the colonies been before willing to contribute this small service to the support of the Empire, the constitutional question might never have been raised; had they now offered to do so, it would probably never have been revived. The requisitions to the colonial Assemblies to compensate the sufferers in the late riots were very unpopular. In one or two provinces the money was, it is true, frankly and promptly voted; but in most cases there was much delay. Massachusetts, where the most scandalous riots took place, rebelled violently against the too peremptory terms of the requisition; refused at first to pass any vote of compensation; yielded at last, after a long delay, and by a small majority, but accompanied its grant by a clause indemnifying the rioters, which was afterwards annulled by the King. Bernard, who since the beginning of 1760 had been

Governor of Massachusetts, had of late become extremely unpopular, and his name has been pursued with untiring virulence to the present day. His letters are those of an honest and rather able, but injudicious and disputatious man, who was trying, under circumstances of extreme difficulty, to do his duty both to the Government and the people, but who was profoundly discontented with the constitution of the province. In 1763 and 1764 he exerted all his influence to procure the lowering or the abolition of the duties in the Sugar Act, and in general a larger amount of free trade for the colonies. In 1765 he opposed the Stamp Act as inexpedient, though he maintained that Parliament had the right of taxing the colonies, provided those taxes were exclusively applied for the benefit of those who paid them. Up to this time he appears to have been generally liked and esteemed;[1] but he was now called upon to take the most prominent part in maintaining the policy of the English Government, and his letters give a vivid picture of the difficulties he encountered. He describes himself as placed 'in the midst of those who first stirred up these disturbances, without a force to protect my person, without a council to advise me, watched by every eye, and misrepresented or condemned for everything I do on the King's behalf.' He laments that the governments of the colonies 'were weak and impotent to an amazing degree,' that 'the governors and officers of the Crown were in several of the chief provinces entirely dependent upon the people for subsistence,' that 'the persons of the governors and Crown officers are quite defenceless and exposed to the violence of the people, without any possible resort for protection,' and he continually urged that as long as the Council, which was the natural support of the Executive, was elected annually by the Assembly, and as long as almost all the civil officers were mainly dependent for their salaries on an annual vote of the Assembly, it would be impossible to enforce in Massachusetts any unpopular law or to punish any outrage which was supported by popular favour. It was his leading doctrine that if British rule was to be perpetuated in America, and if a period of complete anarchy was to be averted, it was necessary to put an end to the ob-

[1] See Hutchinson, p. 251.

scurity which rested upon the relations of the colonies to the Home Government; to establish finally and decisively the legislative ascendency of the British Parliament, and to remodel the constitutions of the colonies on a uniform type. He proposed that the Assemblies should, as at present, remain completely representative; but that the democratic element in the Constitution should be always balanced by a council consisting of a kind of life peers, appointed directly by the King, and that there should be a fixed civil list from which the King's officers should derive a certain provision. As such changes were wholly incompatible with the charters of the more democratic colonies, he proposed that American representatives should be temporarily summoned to the British Parliament, and that Parliament should then authoritatively settle the colonial system.[1]

These views were of course at first only communicated confidentially to the Government, but in the open acts of Bernard there was much that was offensive to the people. His addresses were often very injudicious; he had a bad habit of entering into elaborate arguments with the Assembly, and he was accused of straining the small amount of prerogative which he possessed. The Assembly, shortly after the repeal of the Stamp Act, showed its gratitude by electing Otis, the most violent assailant of the whole legislative authority of England, as its Speaker, and Bernard negatived the choice. The Assembly, contrary to immemorial usage, refused to elect Hutchinson, the Lieutenant-Governor, Oliver, the Secretary of the Province, and the other chief officers of the Crown, members of the Council. Bernard remonstrated strongly against the exclusion; he himself negatived six 'friends of the people' who had been elected, and he countenanced a claim of Hutchinson to take his seat in his capacity of Lieutenant-Governor among the councillors. The relations between the Executive and the Assembly were thus extremely tense, while the inhabitants of Boston were very naturally and very pardonably intoxicated with the triumph they had obtained. The little town, which was probably hardly known even by name in Europe outside

[1] He proposed that thirty representatives should be sent from the continental colonies, and fifteen from the islands.—*Letters of George Bernard*, p. 34.

commercial circles, had bearded the Government of England, and it was deeply sensible of the heroism it had displayed. Not only were the rioters never punished, not only were they the objects of general sympathy—the 'sons of liberty' resolved to meet annually to commemorate their resistance to the Stamp Act, and to express their admiration for one another. Attempts to enforce the revenue Acts were continually resisted. It was observed that the phrase, 'No representation, no taxation!' which had been the popular watch-cry, was beginning to be replaced by the phrase, 'No representation, no legislation!' and many 'patriots' whose names are emblazoned in American history, with unbounded applause and with the most perfect security were hurling highly rhetorical defiances at the British Government.

The clause in the Mutiny Act requiring the colonists to supply English troops with some of the first necessaries of life, was another grievance. Boston, as usual, disputed it at every point with the Governor; and New York positively refused to obey. In a very able book called 'The Farmer's Letters,' written by a lawyer named Dickinson, which appeared about this time, it was maintained that if the British Legislature has the right of ordering the colonies to provide a single article for British troops, it has a right to tax: 'An Act of Parliament commanding to do a certain thing, if it has any validity, is a tax upon us for the expense that accrues in complying with it.'

It is evident that great wisdom, moderation, and tact were needed if healthy relations were to be established between England and her colonies, and unfortunately these qualities were conspicuously absent from English councils. The downfall of the Rockingham Ministry, and the formation of a ministry of which Grafton was the nominal and Pitt the real head, seemed on the whole a favourable event. The influence and popularity of Pitt were even greater in America than in England. His acceptance of the title of Earl of Chatham, which injured him so deeply in English opinion, was a matter of indifference to the colonists; and he possessed far beyond all other English statesmen the power of attracting or conciliating great bodies of men, and firing them with the enthusiasm of loyalty or patriotism. Camden, who next to Chatham was the chief

English advocate of the colonial cause, was Chancellor. Conway, who moved the repeal of the Stamp Act, was one of the Secretaries of State; and Shelburne, who at the age of twenty-nine was placed over American affairs, had on the question of taxing America been on the side of Chatham and Camden. Illness, however, speedily withdrew Chatham from public affairs, and in the scene of anarchy which ensued it was left for the strongest man to seize the helm. Unfortunately, in the absence of Chatham, that man was unquestionably the Chancellor of the Exchequer, Charles Townshend.

From this time the English government of America is little more than a series of deplorable blunders. A feeling of great irritation against the colonies had begun to prevail in English political circles. The Court party continually repeated that England had been humiliated by the repeal of the Stamp Act.[1] Grenville maintained that if that Act had been enforced with common firmness, the stamp duties in America would soon have been collected with as little difficulty as the land tax in England; and he pointed to the recent news as a conclusive proof that the policy of conciliation had failed; and that through the vacillation or encouragement of English statesmen, the spirit of rebellion and of anarchy was steadily growing beyond the Atlantic. There was a general feeling that it was perfectly equitable that America should support an army for her own defence, and for that of the neighbouring islands; and also, that this had become a matter of vital and pressing importance to the British Empire. The political correspondence of the time teems with intimations of the incessant activity with which France and Spain were intriguing to regain the position they had lost in the late war. The dispute about the Manilla ransom and the annexation of Corsica were the most conspicuous, but they were not the most significant, signs of the attitude of those Powers. Plans for the invasion of England had been carefully elaborated. French spies had surveyed the English coast. In 1764 and 1765 an agent of Choiseul had minutely studied the American colonies, and had reported to his master

---

[1] 'The whole body of courtiers drove him [Charles Townshend] onwards. They always talked as if the King stood in a sort of humiliated state until something of the kind should be done.'—Burke's Speech on American Taxation (1774).

that the English troops were so few and scattered that they could be of no real service, and that democratic and provincial jealousy had prevented the erection of a single citadel in all New England.[1] The King fully agreed with his wisest ministers that the army was wholly insufficient to protect the Empire, and the scheme of Chatham for averting the rapidly growing dangers from France by a new alliance with Prussia had signally failed. England was beginning to learn the lesson that in the crisis of her fate she could rely on herself alone, and that in political life gratitude is of all ties the frailest and the most precarious. At the same time, the country gentlemen who remembered the days of Walpole, when England was more prosperous though less great, murmured at the heavy land tax in time of peace, and had begun to complain bitterly that the whole expense of the defence of wealthy colonies was thrown on them. The factious vote, in which the partisans of Grenville and most of the partisans of Rockingham, with the notable exception of Burke, concurred, which reduced the land tax proposed by the Government from 4s. to 3s. in the pound, made it necessary to seek some other source of revenue.[2] Shelburne himself fully adopted the view that America should support her own army, and he imagined that if it were reduced to the smallest proportions the required sum might be gradually raised by enforcing strictly the quit rents of the Crown, which appear to have fallen into very general neglect, and by turning the grants of land to real benefit.[3] Townshend, however, had other schemes, and he lost little time in forcing them upon Parliament.

On January 26, 1767, in a debate on the army, George Grenville moved that America, like Ireland, should support an establishment of her own; and in the course of the discussion which followed, Townshend took occasion to declare himself a firm advocate of the principle of the Stamp Act. He described

---

[1] Bancroft, iii. 28. Fitzmaurice's *Life of Shelburne*, ii. 3-5.
[2] See p. 117.
[3] 'The forming of an American fund to support the exigencies of government in the same manner as is done in Ireland, is what is so highly reasonable that it must take place sooner or later. The most obvious manner of laying a foundation for such a fund seems to be by taking proper care of the quit lands, and by turning the grants of land to real benefit.'—Fitzmaurice's *Life of Shelburne*, ii. 35.

the distinction between external and internal taxes as ridiculous, in the opinion of every one except the Americans; and he pledged himself to find a revenue in America nearly sufficient for the purposes that were required.[1] His colleagues listened in blank astonishment to a pledge which was perfectly unauthorised by the Cabinet, and indeed contrary to the known decision of all its members; but, as the Duke of Grafton afterwards wrote, no one in the ministry had sufficient authority in the absence of Chatham to advise the dismissal of Townshend, and this measure alone could have arrested his policy. Shelburne, who was the official chief of the colonies, wrote to Chatham, who was then an almost helpless invalid, relating the circumstances and expressing his complete ignorance of the intentions of his colleague. The news had just arrived that New York had openly repudiated an Act of Parliament by refusing to furnish troops with the first necessaries of life; and it produced an indignation in Parliament which Chatham himself appears fully to have shared. 'America,' he wrote confidentially to Shelburne, 'affords a gloomy prospect. A spirit of infatuation has taken possession of New York. Their disobedience to the Mutiny Act will justly create a great ferment here, open a fair field to the arraigners of America, and leave no room to any to say a word in their defence. I foresee confusion will ensue. The petition of the merchants of New York is highly improper; . . . they are doing the work of their worst enemies themselves. The torrent of indignation in Parliament will, I apprehend, become irresistible.'[2] In a letter written a few days later he says, 'The advices from America afford unpleasing views. New York has drunk the deepest of the baneful cup of infatuation, but none seem to be quite sober and in full possession of reason. It is a literal truth to say that the Stamp Act of most unhappy memory has frightened those irritable and umbrageous people quite out of their senses.'[3] Letters from colonial governors

---

[1] There are two accounts of this speech: the first in a letter from Lord Charlemont to Flood (Jan. 29), *Chatham Correspondence,* iii. 178, 179; the other in a letter from Shelburne to Chatham (Feb. 1), ibid. iii. 182–188. See too *Grenville Papers,* iv. 211, 222, and the extracts from the Duke of Grafton's Memoirs in Lord Stanhope's *History,* v. App. xvii. xviii.

[2] *Chatham Correspondence,* iii. 188, 189.

[3] Ibid. p. 193.

painted the state of feeling in the darkest colours. At every election, in the bestowal of every kind of popular favour, to have opposed parliamentary authority in America was now the first title to success; to have supported it, the most fatal of disqualifications. The pulpit, the press, the lawyers, the 'sons of liberty'—all those classes who subsist or flourish by popularity—were busy in inflaming the jealousy against England, and in extending the field of conflict. There was a general concurrence of opinion among American officials that, even apart from the necessity of providing for the defence of the colonies, it was indispensable, if any Act of Parliament was henceforth to be obeyed, that a small army should be permanently established in America, and that the Executive should be strengthened by making at least the governor, who represented the English Crown, and the judges, who represented English law, independent of the favour of the Assemblies. It is remarkable that among the officials who advocated these views was the son of Benjamin Franklin, who had been appointed Crown Governor of New Jersey. It was urged, too, that the more democratic constitutions among the colonies must be remodelled; that, while the Assembly should always be the legitimate and unfettered representative of the people, the Council must always be chosen by the Governor.

Very strong arguments might be urged in favour of these changes; but there was one still stronger against them—that it was absolutely impossible to effect them. On May 13, 1767, however, when Chatham was completely incapacitated, and when all other statesmen had sunk before the ascendency of Townshend, the Chancellor of the Exchequer brought in his measure. With that brilliancy of eloquence which never failed to charm the House, he dilated upon the spirit of insubordination that was growing up in all the colonies, upon the open defiance of an Act of Parliament by New York, and upon the absolute necessity of asserting with dignity and decision the legal ascendency of Parliament. The measures which he ultimately brought forward and carried were of three kinds: By one Act of Parliament the legislative functions of the New York Assembly were suspended, and the Governor was forbidden to give his sanction to any local law in that province till the terms of the Mutiny Act had been complied with.[1] By another Act a Board of Commissioners of the Customs with large powers was established in America for the purpose of superintending the execution of the laws relating to trade.[2] By a third Act the proposal of taxing America was resumed. Townshend explained that the distinction between internal and external taxation was in his eyes entirely worthless; but in the discussions on the Stamp Act the Americans had taken their stand upon it. They had represented it as transcendently important, and had professed to be quite willing that Parliament should regulate their trade by duties, provided it raised no internal revenue. This distinction Townshend said he would observe. He would raise a revenue, but he would do so only by a port duty imposed upon glass, red and white lead, painters' colours, paper, and tea, imported into the colonies. The charge on the last-named article was to be 3d. in the pound. The whole annual revenue expected from these duties amounted to less than 40,000l.,[3] and it was to be employed in giving a civil list to the Crown. Out of that civil list, salaries were to be paid to the governors and judges in America; and in the very improbable event of there being any surplus, it was to go towards defraying the expense of protecting the colonies. In order to assist in the enforcement of the law, writs of assistance were formally legalised. Coffee and cocoa exported from England to the colonies were at the same time freed from the duty which they had previously paid on importation into England. Tea exported to the colonies obtained a similar indulgence for five years, but the drawback on the export of china earthenware to America was withdrawn.[4]

It is a strange instance of the fallibility of political foresight if Townshend imagined that America would acquiesce in these measures, that England possessed any adequate means of enforcing them, or that she could a second time recede from her demands and yet maintain her authority over the colonies. It is mournful to notice how the field of controversy had widened and deepened, and how a quarrel which might at one time have

---

[1] 7 Geo. III. c. 59.
[2] Ibid. c. 41.
[3] Walpole's *Memoirs of George III.* iii. 28.
[4] 7 Geo. III. c. 46, 56.

been appeased by slight mutual concessions was leading inevitably to the disruption of the Empire. England was originally quite right in her contention that it was the duty of the colonies to contribute something to the support of the army which defended the unity of the Empire. She was quite right in her belief that in some of the colonial constitutions the Executive was far too feeble, that the line which divides liberty from anarchy was often passed, and that the result was profoundly and permanently injurious to the American character. She was also, I think, quite right in ascribing a great part of the resistance of America to the disposition, so common and so natural in dependencies, to shrink as much as possible from any expense that could possibly be thrown on the mother-country, and in forming a very low estimate of the character and motives of a large proportion of those ambitious lawyers, newspaper writers, preachers, and pamphleteers who, in New England at least, were labouring with untiring assiduity to win popular applause by sowing dissension between England and her colonies. But the Americans were only too well justified in asserting that the suppression of several of their industries and the monopoly by England of some of the chief branches of their trade, if they did not benefit the mother-country, at least imposed sacrifices on her colonies fully equivalent to a considerable tax.[1] They were also quite justified in contending that the power of taxation was essential to the importance of their Assemblies, and that an extreme jealousy of any encroachment on this prerogative was in perfect accordance with the traditions of English liberty. They had before their eyes the hereditary revenue, the scandalous pension list, the monstrous abuses of patronage, in Ireland, and they were quite resolved not to suffer similar abuses in America.[2] The judges only held their seats during the royal pleasure. Ministerial patronage in the colonies, as elsewhere, was often grossly corrupt,[3] and in the eyes of the

---

[1] See the 'Cause of American Discontents before 1768.'—Franklin's *Works*, iv. 250, 251.

[2] See a powerful statement of the abuses in Ireland in the *Farmer's Letters*, No. 10.

[3] In a private letter written by General Huske, a prominent American who was residing in England in 1758, there is an extraordinary, though probably somewhat overcharged, account of English appointments in America. 'For many years past . . . most of the places in the gift of the Crown have been filled with broken Members of Parliament, of bad if any principles,

colonists the annual grant was the one efficient control upon maladministration.

A period of wild and feverish confusion followed. Counsels of the most violent kind were freely circulated, and for a time it seemed as if the appointment of the new Board of Commissioners would be resisted by force; but Otis and some of the other popular leaders held back from the conflict, and in several colonies a clear sense of the serious nature of the struggle that was impending exercised a sobering influence. Georgia, which had been inclined to follow the example of New York, was brought to reason by the prospect of being left without the protection of English troops in the midst of the negroes and the Indians.[1] The central and southern colonies hesitated for some time to follow the lead of New England. Hutchinson wrote to the Government at home that Boston would probably find no other town to follow her in her career of violence; and De Kalb, the secret agent of Choiseul, who was busily employed in fomenting rebellion in the colonies, appears for a time to have thought it would all end in words, and that England, by keeping her taxes within very moderate limits, would maintain her authority.[2] Massachusetts, however, had thrown herself with fierce energy into the conflict, and she soon carried the other provinces in her wake. Non-importation agreements binding all the inhabitants to abstain from English manufactures, and especially from every article on which duties were levied in England, spread from colony to colony, and the Assembly of Massachusetts issued a circular addressed to all the other colonial Assemblies denouncing the new laws as unconstitutional, and inviting the different Assemblies to take united measures for their repeal.

pimps, valets de chambre, electioneering scoundrels, and even livery servants. In one word, America has been for many years made the hospital of Great Britain for her decayed courtiers, and abandoned, worn-out dependants. I can point you out a chief justice of a province appointed from home for no other reason than publicly prostituting his honour and conscience at an election; a livery servant that is secretary of a province, appointed from hence; a pimp, collector of a whole province, who got this place of the man in power for prostituting his handsome wife to his embraces and procuring him other means of gratifying his lust. Innumerable are instances of this sort in places of great trust.'—Phillimore's *Life of Lyttelton*, ii. 604. In Parliament Captain Phipps, speaking of America, said, 'Individuals have been taken from the gaols to preside in the seat of justice; offices have been given to men who had never seen America.'—*Cavendish Debates*, i. 91.

[1] Hildreth, ii. 540.
[2] Bancroft, iii. 116, 140.

The Assembly at the same time drew up a petition to the King and addresses to the leading English supporters of the American cause.[1] These addresses, which were intended to act upon English opinion, were composed with great ability and moderation; and while expressing the firm resolution of the Americans to resist every attempt at parliamentary taxation, they acknowledged fully the general legislative authority of Parliament, and disclaimed in the strongest language any wish for independence. In America itself the language commonly used was less decorous. One of the Boston newspapers dilated furiously upon the 'obstinate malice, diabolical thirst for mischief, effrontery, guileful treachery, and wickedness' of the Governor[2] in such terms that the paper was brought before the Assembly, but that body would take no notice of it, and the grand jury refused to find a true bill against its publisher. The Commissioners of the revenue found that it was idle to attempt to enforce the Revenue Acts without the presence of British troops. Riots were perfectly unpunished, for no jury would convict the rioters. Bernard wrote that his position was one of utter and humiliating impotence, and that the first condition of the maintenance of English authority in Massachusetts was to quarter a powerful military force at Boston.

While these things were happening in America, the composition of the Ministry at home was rapidly changing. On September 4, 1767, after a short fever, Charles Townshend died, leaving to his successors the legacy of his disastrous policy in America, but having achieved absolutely nothing to justify the extraordinary reputation he possessed among his contemporaries.

---

[1] In their petition to the King they say, 'With great sincerity permit us to assure your Majesty that your subjects of this province ever have, and still continue to acknowledge your Majesty's High Court of Parliament, the supreme legislative power of the whole Empire, the superintending authority of which is clearly admitted in all cases that can consist with the fundamental rights of nature and the Constitution.' 'Your lordship,' they wrote to Shelburne, 'is too candid and just in your sentiments to suppose that the House have the most distant thought of independency of Great Britain.' 'So sensible are the members of this House,' they wrote to Rockingham, 'of their happiness and safety in their union with and dependence upon the mother-country, that they would by no means be inclined to accept of an independency if offered to them.'—*The true Sentiments of America, as contained in a Collection of Letters sent from the House of Representatives of Massachusetts Bay to several Persons of High Rank in this Kingdom.* London, 1768.

[2] Bancroft. Hutchinson.

Nothing of the smallest value remains of an eloquence which some of the best judges placed above that of Burke and only second to that of Chatham,[1] and the two or three pamphlets which are ascribed to his pen hardly surpass the average of the political literature of the time. Exuberant animal spirits, a brilliant and ever ready wit, boundless facility of repartee, a clear, rapid, and spontaneous eloquence, a gift of mimicry which is said to have been not inferior to that of Garrick and of Foote, great charm of manner, and an unrivalled skill in adapting himself to the moods and tempers of those who were about him, had made him the delight of every circle in which he moved, the spoilt child of the House of Commons. He died when only forty-two, but he had already much experience of official life. He had been made a Lord of the Admiralty in 1754, Treasurer of the Chamber and member of the Privy Council in 1756, Secretary of War in 1761, President of the Board of Trade in 1763, Paymaster-General in 1765, Chancellor of the Exchequer in 1766. The extraordinary quickness of apprehension which was his most remarkable intellectual gift, soon made him a perfect master of official business, and no man knew so well how to apply his knowledge to the exigencies of debate, and how to pursue every topic to the exact line which pleased and convinced without tiring the House. Had he possessed any earnestness of character, any settled convictions, any power of acting with fidelity to his colleagues, or any self-control, he might have won a great name in English politics. He sought, however, only to sparkle and to please, and was ever ready to sacrifice any principle or any connection for the excitement and the vanity of a momentary triumph. In the absence of Chatham, whom he disliked and feared, he had been rapidly rising to the foremost place. He had obtained a peerage for his wife, and

---

[1] Flood, in a letter to Charlemont, describing a debate in which almost all the chief speakers in Parliament had exerted themselves, says that 'Burke acquitted himself very honourably,' but there was 'no one person near Townshend. He is an orator. The rest are speakers.'—*Original Letters to Flood,* p. 27. Walpole in his numerous allusions to his speeches describes him as greatly superior to Burke in brilliancy and spontaneity of wit, to Chatham in solid sense, and to every other speaker in histrionic power.—*Memoirs of George III.* See especially, ii. 275; iii. 23-27. Sir George Colebrooke said that 'Nobody excepting Mr. Pitt possessed a style of oratory so perfectly suited to the House' (Walpole's *George III.* iii. 102). And Thurlow described him as 'the most delightful speaker he ever knew.'—Nicholls' *George III.* p. 26.

the post of Lord-Lieutenant of Ireland for his brother; he had won the favour of the King, and was the idol of the House of Commons, and had forced the Government into a line of policy which was wholly opposed to that of Camden, Grafton, and Shelburne. In a few months, or perhaps weeks, he would probably have been the head of a new ministry. Death called him away in the full flush of his triumph and his powers, and he obeyed the summons with the same good-humoured levity which he had shown in so many periods of his brief and agitated career.[1]

He was replaced by Lord North, the favourite minister of the King, and one of the strongest advocates of American taxation, and in the course of the next few months nearly all those who were favourable to America disappeared from the Government. Conway, Shelburne, and Chatham successively resigned, and though Camden remained for a time in office he restricted himself exclusively to his judicial duties, and took no part in politics. Lord Hillsborough was entrusted as Secretary of State with the special care of the colonies, and the Bedford party, who now joined and in a great measure controlled the Government, were strenuous supporters of the policy of coercing America.

The circular of the Massachusetts Assembly calling the other provincial Assemblies to assist in obtaining the repeal of the recent Act was first adverted to. Hillsborough, in an angry circular addressed to the governors of the different provinces, urged them to exert their influence to prevent the Assemblies of their respective provinces from taking any notice of it, and he characterised it in severe terms as 'a flagitious attempt to disturb the public peace' by 'promoting an unwarrantable combination and exhibiting an open opposition to and denial

---

[1] Townshend is now chiefly remembered by the singularly beautiful character of him in Burke's speech on American taxation. Horace Walpole says of him, 'He had almost every great talent and every little quality. ... With such a capacity he must have been the greatest man of this age, and perhaps inferior to no man in any age, had his faults been only in a moderate proportion.'—*Memoirs of George III.* iii. 100. See too, Sir G. Colebrooke's character of him. Ibid. pp. 100–102. In an able paper in the *North Briton* (No. 20) it is said of him, 'He joins to an infinite fire of imagination and brilliancy of wit, a cool and solid judgment, a wonderful capacity for business of every kind, the most intense application to it, and a consummate knowledge of the great commercial interests of this country, which I never heard were before united in the same person.'

of the authority of Parliament.' He at the same time called on the Massachusetts Assembly to rescind its proceedings on the subject. After an animated debate the Assembly, in the summer of 1768, refused by 92 votes to 17. It was at once dissolved, and no new Chamber was summoned till the following year. The Assembly of Virginia was dissolved on account of resolutions condemning the whole recent policy of England, and in the course of a few months a similar step was taken in Maryland, Georgia, North Carolina, and New York. It was a useless measure, for the new Assemblies which were summoned in obedience to the charter were very similar to their predecessors. In the meantime, two regiments escorted by seven ships of war were sent to Boston to strengthen the Government. More energetic attempts were made to enforce the revenue laws, and several collisions took place. Thus the sloop 'Liberty,' belonging to Hancock, a leading merchant of the patriot party, arrived at Boston in June 1768, laden with wines from Madeira, and a Custom-house officer went on board to inspect the cargo. He was seized by the crew and detained for several hours while the cargo was landed, and a few pipes of wine were entered on oath at the Custom-house as if they had been the whole. On the liberation of the officer the vessel was seized for a false entry, and in order to prevent the possibility of a rescue it was removed from the wharf under the guns of a man-of-war. A great riot followed, and the Custom-house officers were obliged to fly to a ship of war, and afterwards to the barracks, for protection.[1] On another occasion a cargo of smuggled Madeira was ostentatiously carried through the streets of Boston with an escort of thirty or forty strong men armed with bludgeons, and the Custom-house officers were so intimidated that they did not dare to interfere.[2] At Newport an inhabitant of the town was killed in an affray with some midshipmen of a ship of war,[3] and a few months later a revenue cutter which was lying at the wharf was attacked and burnt.[4] At Providence, an active Custom-house officer was tarred and feathered.[5] Effigies

---

[1] Holmes' *American Annals*, 1768. Hutchinson's *Hist. of Massachusetts Bay*, pp. 189, 190.
[2] Ibid. p. 188.
[3] Arnold's *Hist. of Rhode Island*, ii. 288.
[4] Ibid. p. 297.
[5] Ibid. p. 294.

of the new Commissioners were hung on the liberty tree at Boston. The Governor and other officials were insulted by the mob, and new non-importation engagements were largely subscribed.

The first troops from England arrived in Massachusetts between the dissolution of the old and the election of the new Assembly, but shortly before their arrival the inhabitants of Boston gathered together in an immense meeting and voted that a standing army could not be kept in the province without its consent. Much was said about Brutus, Cassius, Oliver Cromwell, and Paoli; the arms belonging to the town were brought out, and Otis declared that if an attempt was made against the liberties of the people they would be distributed. A day of prayer and fasting was appointed; a very significant resolution was carried by an immense majority, calling upon all the inhabitants to provide themselves with arms and ammunition, and no one was deceived by the transparent pretext that they might be wanted against the French. Open treason was freely talked, and many of the addresses to the Governor were models of grave and studied insolence.

These documents were chiefly composed by Samuel Adams, a very remarkable man who had now begun to exercise a dominant influence in Boston politics, and who was one of the chief authors of the American Revolution. He had an hereditary antipathy to the British Government, for his father seems to have been ruined by the restrictions the English Parliament imposed on the circulation of paper money, and a bank in which his father was largely concerned had been dissolved by Act of Parliament, leaving debts which seventeen years later were still unpaid. It appears that Hutchinson was a leading person in dissolving the bank. Samuel Adams had taken part in various occupations. He was at one time a small brewer and at another a tax-gatherer, but in the last capacity he entirely failed, for a large sum of money which ought to have passed into the Exchequer was not forthcoming. It seems, however, that no more serious charge could be substantiated against him than that of unbusiness-like habits and an insufficient stringency in levying the public dues; the best judges appear to have been fully convinced of his integrity in money matters, and it is strongly confirmed by the austere and simple tenor of his whole later life.[1] He early became one of the most active writers in the American Press, and was the soul of every agitation against the Government. It was noticed that he had a special skill in discovering young men of promise and brilliancy, and that, without himself possessing any dazzling qualities, he seldom failed by the force of his character and the intense energy of his convictions in obtaining an ascendency over their minds, and in inspiring them with hostility to the British Government. It was only in 1765, when Adams was already forty-three, that he obtained a seat in the Assembly, when, with Otis and two or three others, he took a chief part in organising opposition to the Government. In the lax moral atmosphere of the eighteenth century he exhibited in perfection the fierce and sombre type of the seventeenth-century Covenanter. Poor, simple, ostentatiously austere and indomitably courageous, the blended influence of Calvinistic theology and of republican principles had permeated and indurated his whole character, and he carried into politics all the fervour of an apostle and all the narrowness of a sectarian. Hating with a fierce hatred, monarchy and the English Church, and all privileged classes and all who were invested with dignity and rank; utterly incapable of seeing any good thing in an opponent, or of accepting any form of political compromise, he advocated on all occasions the strongest measures, and appears to have been one of the first both to foresee and to desire an armed struggle. He had some literary talent, and his firm will and clearly defined principles gave him for a time a greater influence than abler men. He now maintained openly that any British troops which landed should be treated as enemies, attacked, and, if possible, destroyed. More moderate counsels prevailed; yet measures verging on revolution were adopted. As the Governor alone could summon or prorogue the Assembly, a convention was held at Boston when it was not sitting, to which almost every town and every district of the province sent its delegate, and it assumed all the semblance of a legislative body.

The Assembly itself, when it met, pronounced the establish-

---

[1] The life of S. Adams has been written with great elaboration and unqualified eulogy by W. V. Wells, and Bancroft adopts a very similar view of his character. Several facts relating to him will be found in Hutchinson's *Hist. of Massachusetts Bay*, pp. 294, 295.

ment of a standing army in the colony in time of peace to be an invasion of natural rights and a violation of the Constitution, and it positively refused to provide quarters for the troops on the ground that the barracks in an island three miles from the town, though within the municipal circle of Boston, were not yet full. The plea was ingenious and strictly legal, and the troops were accordingly quartered as well as paid at the expense of the Crown. The simple presence among the colonists of English soldiers was, however, now treated as an intolerable grievance; the regiments were absurdly called 'an unlawful assembly,' and they were invariably spoken of as if they were foreign invaders. The old distinction between internal and external taxation, the old acquiescence in commercial restrictions, and the old acknowledgment of the general legislative authority of Parliament, had completely disappeared from Boston politics. The treatise which, half a century earlier, Molyneux had written on the rights of the Irish Parliament now became a text-book in the colonies, and it was the received doctrine that they owed allegiance indeed to the King, but were wholly independent of the English Parliament. They scornfully repudiated at the same time the notion of maintaining like Ireland a military establishment for the general defence of the Empire. It is also remarkable that the project of a legislative union with Great Britain, which was at this time advocated by Pownall in England, was absolutely repudiated in America. Pownall wished the colonial Assemblies to continue, but to send representatives to the English Parliament, which would thus possess the right of taxing the colonists. But this scheme found no favour in America. It was pronounced impracticable and dangerous. It was said that the colonial representatives would speedily be corrupted, that the colonists could never hope to obtain a representation adequate to their importance, and that inadequate representation was even a greater grievance than taxation without representation. Bernard now strongly advocated the permanent admission of American representatives into the British Parliament as the only possible solution, but he acknowledged that the idea was unpopular, and he alleged that the true reason was that if the colonies were represented in Parliament they could have no pretext for disobeying it.¹ It was evident that every path of compromise was closing, and that disaffection was steadily rising to the height of revolution. Foreign observers saw that the catastrophe was fast approaching, and Choiseul noticed that the English had no cavalry and scarcely 10,000 infantry in America, while the colonial militia numbered 400,000 men, including several cavalry regiments. It was not difficult, he concluded, to predict that if America could only find a Cromwell she would speedily cease to form a part of the British Empire.²

For the present, except a few revenue riots, resistance was purely passive. The Massachusetts Assembly petitioned for the removal of the troops and for the removal of the Governor. Acute lawyers contested every legal point that could possibly be raised against the Government. The grand juries being elected by the townships were wholly on the side of the people, and they systematically refused to present persons guilty of libel, riot, or sedition. Non-importation agreements spread rapidly from town to town, and had a serious effect upon English commerce. The troops had little to do as there was no open resistance, but they found themselves treated as pariahs and excluded from every kind of society, and they had even much difficulty in procuring the necessaries of life.

The English Parliament in December 1768 and January 1769 greatly aggravated the contest. Both Houses passed resolutions condemning the disloyal spirit of Massachusetts, the non-importation agreements, and the Boston convention; and addresses were carried thanking the Sovereign for the measures he had taken to maintain the authority of England; promising a full support to future measures taken with that end, and suggesting that the names of the most active agitators should be transmitted to one of the Secretaries of State, and that a long disused law of Henry VIII. which empowered the Governor to bring to England for trial, persons accused of treason outside England, should be put in force.³ This last measure was due to the Duke of Bedford, and although it was certainly not unprovoked, it excited a fierce and legitimate indignation in America, and added a new and very serious item to the long

¹ Letters of Governor Bernard, pp. 55–60.   ² Bancroft.
³ Parl. Hist. xvi. 477–487.   Cavendish Debates, i. 192–194.

list of colonial grievances. Already, the colonial advocates were accustomed to say, a Parliament in which the colonies were wholly unrepresented, claimed an absolute power of restricting their commerce, of taxing them, and even, as in the case of New York, of suspending their legislative assemblies. British troops were planted among them to coerce them. Their governors and judges were to be made independent of their Assemblies, and now the protection of a native jury, which alone remained, was to be destroyed. By virtue of an obsolete law, passed in one of the darkest periods of English history and at a time when England possessed not a single colony, any colonist who was designated by the Governor as a traitor might be carried three thousand miles from his home, from his witnesses, from the scene of his alleged crime, from all those who were acquainted with the general tenor of his life, to be tried by strangers of the very nation against whom he was supposed to have offended. Combine all these measures, it was said, and what trace of political freedom would be left in the colonies?

This measure was apparently intended only to intimidate the more violent agitators, and it was never put in action. The Cabinet were much divided about their American policy, and signs of weakness speedily appeared. Townshend's Act had brought America to the verge of revolution, and had entailed great expense on the country, but it had hitherto produced no appreciable revenue, and there was little or no prospect of improvement. It was stated that the total produce of the new taxes for the first year was less than 16,000*l.*, that the net proceeds of the Crown revenue in America were only about 295*l.*, and that extraordinary military expenses amounting to 170,000*l.* had in the same period been incurred.[1] Pownall, who had preceded Bernard as Governor of Massachusetts, strongly urged in Parliament the repeal of the new duties, and a considerable section of the Cabinet supported his view. After much discussion it was resolved to adopt a policy of compromise [2]—to repeal

---

[1] Hildreth, ii. 553.
[2] The Massachusetts Agent, De Berdt, wrote to the Assembly in July 1768, describing an interview with Hillsborough. 'He assured me, before the warm measures taken on your side had come to their knowledge he had settled the repeal of those Acts [for the taxation or coercion of America] with Lord North the Chancellor, but

the duties on glass, paper, and painters' colours, and to retain that on tea for the purpose of keeping up the right. Less than 300*l.* had hitherto been obtained by this charge; but the King, the Bedford section of the Cabinet, and Lord North determined, in opposition to Grafton and Camden, to retain it, and they carried their point in the Cabinet by a majority of one vote. A circular intimating the intention of the Government was despatched in the course of 1769 to the governors of the different colonies, and in this circular Lord Hillsborough officially informed them that the Cabinet 'entertained no design to propose to Parliament to lay any further taxes on America for the purpose of raising a revenue.'[1] Governor Bernard, whose relations with the Assembly and Council of Massachusetts had long been as hostile as possible, was rewarded for his services to the Crown by a baronetcy, but in the August of 1769 he was recalled to England amid a storm of insult and rejoicing from the people he had governed; and after about a year, Hutchinson, who, though equally devoted to the Government, was somewhat less unpopular with the colonists, was promoted to the ungrateful post. Some slight signs of improvement were visible. New York submitted to the Mutiny Act, and its Assembly accordingly regained its normal powers. The non-importation agreements had for some time been very imperfectly observed, and it was soon noticed that a good deal of tea was imported in small quantities, and that the port duty was paid without difficulty.[2]

Hitherto, though the townspeople of Boston had done everything in their power to provoke and irritate the soldiers who were quartered among them, there had been no serious collision. The condition of the town, however, was such that it was scarcely possible that any severity of discipline could long avert it. There was a perfect reign of terror directed against all who supported the revenue Acts and who sympathised with authority. Soldiers could scarcely appear in the streets without being the objects of the grossest insult. A Press eminently scurrilous and vindictive was ceaselessly employed in abusing

---

the opposition you had made rendered it absolutely necessary to support the authority of Parliament.'—*Massachusetts State Papers*, p. 161.

[1] Grahame, iv. 297.
[2] See Hutchinson's *Hist. of Massachusetts Bay*, pp. 350, 351, 422, 423.

them: they had become, as Samuel Adams boasted, 'the objects of the contempt even of women and children.' Every offence they committed was maliciously exaggerated and vindictively prosecuted, while in the absence of martial law they were obliged to look on upon the most flagrant insults to authority. At one time the 'sons of liberty' in a procession a mile and a half long marched round the State House to commemorate their riots against the Stamp Act, and met in the open fields to chant their liberty song and drink 'strong halters, firm blocks, and sharp axes to such as deserve them.' At another an informer who was found guilty of giving information to revenue officers was seized by a great multitude, tarred and feathered, and led through the streets of Boston, which were illuminated in honour of the achievement. A printer who had dared to caricature the champions of freedom was obliged to fly from his house, to take refuge among the soldiers, and ultimately to escape from Boston in disguise. Merchants who had ventured to import goods from England were compelled by mob violence to give them up to be destroyed or to be re-embarked. A shopkeeper who sold some English goods found a post planted in the ground with a hand pointing to his door, and when a friend tried to remove it he was stoned by a fierce mob through the streets. A popular minister delighted his congregation by publicly praying that the Almighty would remove from Boston the English soldiers. It was said that they corrupted the morals of the town, that their drums and fifes were heard upon the Sabbath-day, that their language was often violent, threatening, or profane, that on several occasions they had struck citizens who insulted them.[1] On March 2, 1770, there was a scuffle at a ropewalk between some soldiers and the ropemakers, and on the night of the 5th there occurred the tragedy which, in the somewhat grandiloquent phrase of John Adams, 'laid the foundation of American independence.' A false alarm of fire had called a crowd into the streets, and a mob of boys and

---

[1] Holmes. Bancroft. One of the later accusations against the English soldiers was, that they impaired the purity of the American pronunciation of English. Noah Webster, in his curious essay on the 'Manners of the United States' (1787), says, 'I presume we may safely say that our language has suffered more injurious changes in America since the British army landed on our shores than it had suffered before, in the period of three centuries.'—*Webster's Essays*, p. 96.

men amused themselves by surrounding and insulting a solitary sentinel who was on guard before one of the public buildings. He called for rescue, and a party consisting of a corporal and six common soldiers, under the command of Captain Preston, appeared with loaded muskets upon the scene. The mob, however, refused to give way. Some forty or fifty men—many of them armed with sticks—surrounded the little band of soldiers, shouting, 'Rascals, lobsters, bloody backs!'[1] and defying them to use their arms. They soon proceeded to violence. Snowballs and, according to some testimony, stones were thrown. The crowd pressed violently on the soldiers, and it was afterwards alleged that one of the soldiers was struck by a club. Whether it was panic or resentment, or the mere necessity of self-defence, was never clearly established, but a soldier fired, and in another moment seven muskets, each loaded with two balls, were discharged with deadly effect into the crowd. Five men fell dead or dying, and six others were wounded.

There are many dreadful massacres recorded in the page of history—the massacre of the Danes by the Saxons, the massacre of the Sicilian Vespers, the massacre of St. Bartholomew—but it may be questioned whether any of them had produced such torrents of indignant eloquence as the affray which I have described. The 'Boston massacre,' or, as the Americans, desiring to distinguish it from the minor tragedies of history, loved to call it, 'the bloody massacre,' at once kindled the colonies into a flame. The terrible tale of how the bloody and brutal myrmidons of England had shot down the inoffensive citizens in the streets of Boston raised an indignation which was never suffered to flag. In Boston, as soon as the tidings of the tragedy were spread abroad, the church bells rang, the drums beat to call the people to arms, and next day an immense meeting of the citizens resolved that the soldiers must no longer remain in the town. Samuel Adams and the other leading agitators, as the representatives of the people, rushed into the presence of Hutchinson, and rather commanded than asked for their removal. Hutchinson hesitated much. He was not yet governor. Bernard was in England. Hutchinson had himself asked for the troops to be sent to Boston. He knew that their removal

---

[1] In allusion to the British custom of flogging soldiers.

would, under the circumstances, be a great humiliation to the Government and a great encouragement to the mob, and that if once removed it would be extremely difficult to recall them. On the other hand, if they remained it was only too probable that in a few hours the streets of Boston would run with blood. He consulted the council, and found it as usual an echo of the public voice. He yielded at last, and the troops were removed to Fort William, on an island three miles from Boston, and the wish of the townsmen was thus at last accomplished. An immense crowd accompanied the bodies of the 'martyred' citizens to their last resting-place. An annual celebration was at once resolved upon, and for several years the citizens were accustomed on every anniversary to meet in the chief towns of America in chapels hung with crape, while the most popular orators described the horrors of the Boston massacre, the tyranny of England, and the ferocious character of standing armies.[1]

Few things contributed more to the American revolution than this unfortunate affray. Skilful agitators perceived the advantage it gave them, and the most fantastic exaggerations were dexterously diffused. The incident had, however, a sequel which is extremely creditable to the American people. It was determined to try the soldiers for their lives, and public feeling ran so fiercely against them that it seemed as if their fate was sealed. The trial, however, was delayed for seven months, till the excitement had in some degree subsided. Captain Preston very judiciously appealed to John Adams, who was rapidly rising to the first place both among the lawyers and the popular patriots of Boston, to undertake his defence. Adams knew well how much he was risking by espousing so unpopular a cause, but he knew also his professional duty, and, though violently opposed to the British Government, he was an eminently honest, brave, and humane man. In conjunction with Josiah Quincy, a young lawyer who was also of the patriotic party, he undertook the invidious task, and he discharged it with consummate ability. It was clearly shown that the popular account which had been printed in Boston and circulated

---

[1] The commemoration was kept up till 1783, after which it was replaced by that of the 4th of July, Tudor's *Life of Otis*, p. 462.

assiduously through the colonies, representing the affair as a deliberate and premeditated massacre of unoffending citizens, was grossly untrue. As was natural in the case of a confused scuffle in the dark, there was much conflict of testimony about the exact circumstances of the affair, but there was no sufficient evidence that Captain Preston had given an order to fire; and although no soldier was seriously injured, there was abundant evidence that the soldiers had endured gross provocation and some violence. If the trial had been the prosecution of a smuggler or a seditious writer, the jury would probably have decided against evidence, but they had no disposition to shed innocent blood. Judges, counsel, and jurymen acted bravely and honourably. All the soldiers were acquitted, except two, who were found guilty of manslaughter, and who escaped with very slight punishment.

It is very remarkable that after Adams had accepted the task of defending the incriminated soldiers, he was elected by the people of Boston as their representative in the Assembly, and the public opinion of the province appears to have fully acquiesced in the verdict.[1] In truth, although no people have indulged more largely than the Americans in violent, reckless, and unscrupulous language, no people have at every period of their history been more signally free from the thirst for blood, which in moments of great political excitement has been often shown both in England and France. It is a characteristic fact that one of the first protests against the excessive multiplication of capital offences in the English legislation of the eighteenth century was made by the Assembly of Massachusetts, which in 1762 objected to death as a punishment for forgery on the ground that 'the House are very averse to capital punishment in any case where the interest of the Government does

[1] See on this episode, Adams' *Works*, i. 97-114, ii. 229-233; Hutchinson's *Hist. of Massachusetts Bay*; Hutchinson's letters to Bernard, and the histories of Hildreth and Bancroft. Mr. Bancroft in his account of this transaction appears to me to exhibit even more strongly than usual that violent partisanship which so greatly impairs the value of his very learned history. Outside Boston the verdict seems to have given much satisfaction. Hutchinson wrote (Dec. 1770): 'The reception which has been given to the late verdicts everywhere except in Boston has been favourable beyond my hopes. I expected that the court and jury would be censured, but they are generally applauded.'— *American Remembrancer*, 1776, part i. p. 159.

not absolutely require it,' and where some other punishment will be sufficiently deterrent.[1] In the long period of anarchy, riot, and excitement which preceded the American revolution there was scarcely any bloodshed and no political assassination, and the essential humanity of American public opinion which was shown so conspicuously during the trial of the soldiers at Boston, was afterwards displayed on a far wider field and in still more trying circumstances during the fierce passions of the Revolutionary war, and still more remarkably in the triumph of the North in the War of Secession.

While these things were taking place in America, Lord North carried through Parliament his measure repealing all the duties imposed by Townshend's Act, with the exception of that on tea,[2] which he maintained in spite of a very able opposition led by Pownall. His defence of the distinction was by no means destitute of plausibility or even of real force. The other duties, he said, were imposed on articles of English manufacture imported into America, and such duties were both unprecedented and economically inexpedient, as calculated to injure English industry. The duty on tea, however, was of another kind, and it was in perfect accordance with commercial precedents. The Americans had themselves drawn a broad distinction between external and internal taxation. No less than thirty-two Acts binding their trade had been imposed and submitted to, and the power of Parliament to impose port duties had, till the last two years, been unquestioned.[3] Whatever might be said of the Stamp Act, the tea duty was certainly not a grievance to America, for Parliament had relieved the colonies of a duty of nearly 12d. in the pound, which had hitherto been levied in England, and the colonists were only asked in compensation to pay a duty of 3d. in the pound on the arrival of the tea in America. The measure was, therefore, not an act of oppression but of relief, making the price of tea in the colonies positively cheaper than it had been before.[4] It was coupled with the

---

[1] Tudor's *Life of Otis*, p. 113. According to Dr. Price (*On Civil Liberty*, p. 101), not more than one execution had taken place in Massachusetts Bay in eighteen years. The annual average of executions in London alone for twenty-three years before 1772 was from twenty-nine to thirty.—Howard *On Prisons*, p 9.

[2] 10 Geo. III. 17.

[3] See *Cavendish Debates*, i. 198, 222.

[4] Stedman, i. 74. Hutchinson says: 'By taking off 12d., which used to be

circular of Lord Hillsborough pledging the English Government to raise no further revenue from America. At the same time the quartering Act, which had been so much objected to, was allowed silently to expire.[1]

It will probably strike the reader that every argument which showed that the tea duty was not a grievance to the colonies, was equally powerful to show that it was perfectly useless as a means of obtaining a revenue from them. It would be difficult, indeed, to find a more curious instance of legislative incapacity than the whole transaction displayed. The repeal of the greater part of Townshend's Act had given the agitators in America a signal triumph; the maintenance of the tea duty for the avowed purpose of obtaining a colonial revenue left them their old pretext for agitation, and at the same time that duty could not possibly attain the end for which it was ostensibly intended, and the Government by the circular of Lord Hillsborough had precluded themselves from increasing it. Hutchinson, whose judgment of American opinion is entitled to the highest respect, has expressed his firm conviction that the Government might have raised the whole revenue they expected from Townshend's Act without the smallest difficulty, if they had simply adopted the expedient of levying the duty on goods exported to America in England instead of in the colonies.[2]

The object of maintaining the tea duty was, of course, to assert the right of Parliament to impose port duties, and this assertion was thought necessary on account of the recent conduct and language of the Americans.[3] At the same time North,

paid in England, and substituting 3*d*. only, payable in the colonies, tea was cheaper than it had ever been sold by the illicit traders, and the poor people in America drank the same tea in quality at 3*s*. the lb. which the people in England drank at 6*s*.'—*Hist. of Massachusetts Bay*, p. 351.

[1] *Parl. Hist.* xvi. 852–874; *Cavendish Debates*, i. 484–500.

[2] 'If these duties [those in Townshend's Act] had been paid upon exportation from England and applied to the purpose proposed, there would not have been any opposition made to the Act. It would have been a favour to the colonies The saving upon tea would have been more than the whole paid on the other articles. The consumer in America would have paid the duty just as much as if it had been paid upon importation.'—*Hist. of Massachusetts Bay*, p. 179. I have already quoted the opinion of Franklin to much the same effect.

[3] See Lord North's strong statement of the reluctance with which he maintained any part of the duties. *Parl. Hist.* xvi. 854; *Cavendish Debates*, i. 485, 486. The speech of George Grenville in this debate, as reported by Cavendish, is particularly worthy of attention.

like Grenville, continually maintained that the plan of obliging America to pay for her own army might have been easily and peaceably carried out had the condition of English parties rendered possible any steady, systematic, and united policy. It was the changes, vacillation, divisions, and weaknesses of English ministries, the utter disintegration of English parties, the rapid alternations of severity and indulgence, the existence in Parliament of a powerful section who had at every step of the struggle actively supported the Americans and encouraged them to resist, the existence outside Parliament of a still more democratic party mainly occupied with political agitation—it was these things which had chiefly lured the colonies to their present state of anarchy, had rendered all resistance to authority a popular thing, and had introduced the habit of questioning the validity of Acts of Parliament. The evil, however, was accomplished. The plan of making America pay for her defence was virtually abandoned, and the ministers were only trying feebly and ineffectively to uphold the doctrine of the Declaratory Act, that Parliament had a right to draw a revenue from America, by maintaining a duty which was in full accordance with American precedents and which was a positive boon to the American people.

The policy was not quite unsuccessful. The non-importation agreements had lately been so formidable that the English exports to America, which amounted to 2,378,000*l.* in 1768, amounted only to 1,634,000*l.* in 1769;[1] but the merchants in the colonies, after some hesitation, now resolved to abandon these agreements, and commerce with England resumed its old activity. An exception, however, was still made in the case of tea, and associations were formed binding all classes to abstain from that beverage, or at least to drink only what was smuggled. The next two or three years of colonial history were somewhat less eventful, though it was evident that the spirit of insubordination and anarchy was extending. In North Carolina in 1771, some 1,500 men, complaining of extortions and oppressions of their local courts, rose to arms, and refused to pay taxes, and the colony was rapidly dividing into a civil war. The Governor, however, at the head of rather more than 1,000

[1] *Parl. Hist.* xvi 855.

militia, completely defeated the insurgents in a pitched battle. Some hundreds were killed or wounded, and six were afterwards hung for high treason. In Massachusetts the troops were not again brought into Boston, but Castle William, which commanded the harbour, and to which the Boston patriots had once been so anxious to relegate them, was placed under martial law, and the provincial garrison was withdrawn. There were long and acrimonious disputes between Hutchinson and the Massachusetts Assembly about the right of the former to convene the latter at Cambridge instead of Boston; about the extent to which the salaries of Crown officers should be exempted from taxation; about the refusal of the governor to ratify the grant of certain sums of money to the colonial agents in England. In 1772, Hutchinson, to the great indignation of the colony, informed the Assembly that, as his salary would henceforth be paid by the Crown, no appropriation would be required for that purpose. Otis, who had long been the most fiery of the Boston demagogues, had now nearly lost his intellect as well as his influence; and John Adams, who was a far abler man, had for a time retired from agitation, and devoted himself to his profession. Samuel Adams, however, still retained his influence in the Assembly, and he was unwearied in his efforts to excite ill-feeling against England, and to push the colony into rebellion.

In Rhode Island a revenue outrage of more than common daring took place. A ship of war, called the 'Gaspee,' commanded by Lieutenant Duddingston, and carrying eight guns, was employed under the royal commission in enforcing the revenue Acts along the coast, and the commander is said to have discharged his duty with a zeal that often outran both discretion and law. He stopped and searched every ship that entered Narraganset Bay, compelled all ships to salute his flag; sent a captured cargo of smuggled rum, contrary to law, out of the colony to Boston on the ground that it could not be safely detained in Newport; seized more than one vessel upon insufficient evidence; searched for smuggled goods with what was considered unnecessary violence, and made himself extremely obnoxious to the colony, in which smuggling was one of the most flourishing and most popular of trades. The Chief

Justice gave an opinion that the commander of one of his Majesty's ships could exercise no authority in the colony without having previously applied to the Governor, and shown him his warrant. Duddingston appealed to the Admiral at Boston, who fully justified his conduct, and an angry altercation ensued between the civil and naval authorities. On June 9, 1772, the 'Gaspee,' when chasing a suspected vessel, ran aground on a shoal in the river some miles from Providence, and the ship which had escaped brought the news to that town. Soon after a drum was beat through the streets, and all persons who were disposed to assist in the destruction of the King's ship were summoned to meet at the house of a prominent citizen. There appears to have been no concealment or disguise, and shortly after ten at night eight boats, full of armed men, started with muffled oars on the expedition. They reached the stranded vessel in the deep darkness of the early morning. Twice the sentinel on board vainly hailed them, when Duddingston himself appeared in his shirt upon the gunwale and asked who it was that approached. The leader of the party answered with a profusion of oaths that he was the sheriff of the county come to arrest him, and while he was speaking one of his men deliberately shot the lieutenant, who fell badly wounded on the deck. In another minute the 'Gaspee' was boarded. The crew were soon overpowered, bound, and placed upon the shore. Duddingston, his wounds having been dressed, was landed at a neighbouring house; the party then set fire to the 'Gaspee,' and while its flames announced to the whole country the success of their expedition, they returned in the broad daylight to Providence. Large rewards were offered by the British Government for their detection; but, though they were universally known, no evidence could be obtained, and the outrage was entirely unpunished.[1] An American historian complains that this event, though due to a mere 'sudden impulse,' inspired at least one English statesman with a deep hostility to the charter of the colony, according to which Governor, Assembly, and Council were all elected directly by the people.[2]

[1] A full account of this transaction will be found in Mr. Arnold's very interesting *History of Rhode Island*, ii. 309-320. Mr. Arnold has given a curious letter describing it, by Ephraim Bowen, one of the party who captured the 'Gaspee.'
[2] Bancroft, iii 461

It is a curious coincidence that, just before this outrage took place, the British Parliament had passed an Act for the protection of his Majesty's ships, dockyards, and naval stores, by which their destruction was made a felony, and the Ministry were empowered, if they pleased, to try those who were accused of such acts in England.[1] This law, though it applied to the colonies, was not made with any special reference to them, but it became one of their great grievances. Perhaps the state of feeling disclosed in the town of Providence at the time of the destruction of the 'Gaspee,' may be regarded as the strongest argument in its defence.

A considerable step towards uniting the colonies was taken in this year and in 1773 by the appointment in Massachusetts, Virginia, and some other colonies of committees specially charged with the task of collecting and publishing colonial grievances, maintaining a correspondence between the different provinces, and procuring authentic intelligence of all the acts of the British Parliament or Ministry relating to them. In England they were already represented by agents of great ability, the most prominent being Benjamin Franklin, who at this time possessed a greater reputation than any living American.

He was born in 1706, and was therefore now in the decline of life. A younger son in a large and poor family, ill-treated by his elder brother, and little favoured by casual good fortune, he had risen by his own energies from a humble journeyman printer at Boston and Philadelphia to a foremost place among his countrymen; and he enjoyed a reputation which the lapse of a century has scarcely dimmed. Franklin is, indeed, one of the very small class of men who can be said to have added something of real value to the art of living. Very few writers have left so many profound and original observations on the causes of success in life, and on the best means of cultivating the intellect and the character. To extract from surrounding circumstances the largest possible amount of comfort and rational enjoyment, was the ideal he placed before himself and others, and he brought to its attainment one of the shrewdest and most inventive of human intellects, one of the calmest and

[1] 12 Geo. III. c. 24.

best balanced of human characters. 'It is hard,' he once wrote, 'for an empty sack to stand upright;' and it was his leading principle that a certain amount of material prosperity is the almost indispensable condition as well as the chief reward of integrity of character. He had no religious fervour, and no sympathy with those who appeal to strong passions or heroic self-abnegation; but his busy and somewhat pedestrian intellect was ceaselessly employed in devising useful schemes for the benefit of mankind. He founded societies for mutual improvement, established the first circulating library in America, introduced new methods for extinguishing fires, warming rooms, paving and lighting the streets, gave a great impulse to education in Pennsylvania, took part in many schemes for strengthening the defences and improving the police of the colony, and was the soul of more than one enterprise of public charity. 'Poor Richard's Almanac,' which he began in 1732, and which he continued for twenty-five years, attained an annual circulation of near 10,000, and he made it a vehicle for diffusing through the colonies a vast amount of practical knowledge and homely wisdom. His brother printed the fourth newspaper which ever appeared in America, and Franklin wrote in it when still a boy. He had afterwards a newspaper of his own, and there were few questions of local politics in which he did not take an active part. He was very ambitious of literary success, and within certain limits he has rarely been surpassed. How completely blind he was to the sublime and the poetical in literature, he indeed conclusively showed when he tried to improve the majestic language of the Book of Job or the Lord's Prayer by translating them into ordinary eighteenth century phraseology; but on his own subjects no one wrote better. His style was always terse, luminous, simple, pregnant with meaning, eminently persuasive. There is scarcely an obscure or involved or superfluous sentence, scarcely an ambiguous term in his works, and not a trace of that false and inflated rhetoric which has spoilt much American writing, and from which the addresses of Washington himself are not quite free. He was a most skilful and plausible reasoner, abounding in ingenious illustration, and with a happy gift of carrying into difficult and intricate subjects that transparent simplicity of style which is, perhaps, the highest reach of art. At the same time his researches and writings on electricity gave him a wide reputation in the scientific world, and in 1752 his great discovery of the lightning conductor made his name universally known through Europe. It was indeed pre-eminently fitted to strike the imagination; and it was a strange freak of fortune that one of the most sublime and poetic of scientific discoveries should have fallen to the lot of one of the most prosaic of great men.

In every phase of the struggle with England he took a prominent part; and it may be safely asserted that if he had been able to guide American opinion, it would never have ended in revolution. During a great portion of the struggle he always professed a warm attachment for England and the English Constitution. In conversation with Burke he expressed the greatest concern at the impending separation of the two countries; predicted that 'America would never again see such happy days as she had passed under the protection of England, and observed that ours was the only instance of a great empire in which the most distant parts and members had been as well governed as the metropolis and its vicinage.'[1] A man so eminently wise and temperate must have clearly seen that colonies situated 3,000 miles from the mother-country, doubling their population every twenty-five years, possessing representative institutions of the freest and most democratic type, and inhabited by a people who, from their circumstances and their religion, carried the sentiment of independence to the highest point, were never in any real danger of political servitude, and that there was no difference between America and England which reasonable men might not easily have compromised. Personally, no one had less sympathy than Franklin with anarchy, violence, and declamation, and in some respects his natural leaning was towards the Tories. It is remarkable that when he was in England at the time of the Middlesex election, his sympathies ran strongly against Wilkes, he spoke with indignation of the punishment that must await a people 'who are ungratefully abusing the best Constitution and the best King

---

[1] Burke's 'Appeal from the New to the Old Whigs.' *Works*, vi. 122. See too Franklin's *Works*, i. 413, 414

any nation was ever blessed with;'[1] and he fully adopted the Tory maxim that the whole political power of a nation belongs of right to the freeholders.[2] He held under the Government the position of Postmaster-General for America. He was once thought of as Under-Secretary of State for the Colonies under Lord Hillsborough, and his son was royal Governor of New Jersey.

His writings are full of suggestions which, if they had been acted on, might have averted the disruption. As we have already seen, he had advocated an union of the Colonies for defensive purposes as early as 1754, and in 1764 had regarded with great equanimity, and even approval, the possible establishment of an English army in America, paid for by duties imposed on the colonies. He opposed the Stamp Act; but it is quite evident, from his conduct, that he neither expected nor desired that it should be resisted. In one of his writings, he very wisely suggested that England should give up her trade monopoly, and that America should in return agree to pay a fixed annual sum for the military purposes of the Empire. In another, he advocated a legislative union, which would have enabled the English Parliament, without injustice, to tax America. He strongly maintained the reality of the distinction between internal and external taxation, and asserted with great truth that 'the real grievance is not that Britain puts duties upon her own manufactures exported to us, but that she forbids us to buy like manufactures from any other country.' He was agent for Pennsylvania at the time of the Stamp Act, and, in his examination soon after, before the House of Commons, he defended the colonial cause with an ability, a presence of mind, and a moderation that produced a great impression upon Parliament. His many tracts in defence of their cause, though they are very far from a fair or candid statement even of the facts of the case, were undoubtedly the ablest and most plausible arguments advanced on the American side. In 1767 he mentioned the assiduity with which the French ambassador

---

[1] Franklin's *Works*, vii. 399-404.
[2] 'All the land in England is in fact represented. . . . As to those who have no landed property in a county, the allowing them to vote for legislators is an impropriety.'—'Political Observations,' Franklin's *Works*, iv. 221.

was courting him, and he added, 'I fancy that intriguing nation would like very well to meddle on occasion and blow up the coals between Britain and her colonies; but I hope we shall give them no opportunity.'[1] In his confidential correspondence with American politicians, he constantly advocated moderation and patience. 'Our great security,' he wrote in 1773, 'lies in our growing strength both in numbers and wealth, that creates an increasing ability of assisting this nation in its wars, which will make us more respectable, our friendship more valued, and our enmity feared . . . . In confidence of this coming change in our favour, I think our prudence is, meanwhile, to be quiet, only holding up our rights and claims on all occasions . . . but bearing patiently the little present notice that is taken of them. They will all have their weight in time, and that time is at no great distance.'[2] 'There seems to be among us some violent spirits who are for an immediate rupture; but I trust the general prudence of our country will see that by our growing strength we advance fast to a situation in which our claims must be allowed; that by a premature struggle we may be crippled and kept down another age . . . that between governed and governing every mistake in government, every encroachment on right, is not worth a rebellion . . . remembering withal that this Protestant country (our mother, though lately an unkind one) is worth preserving, and that her weight in the scale of Europe, and her safety in a great degree, may depend on our union with her.'[3]

In addition to his position of agent for Pennsylvania, he became agent for New Jersey, for Georgia, and in 1770 for Massachusetts. His relations, however, with the latter colony were not always absolutely cordial. His religious scepticism, his known hatred of war, his personal relations to the British Government, his dislike to violent counsels, and to that exaggerated and declamatory rhetoric which was peculiarly popular at Boston, all placed him somewhat out of harmony with his constituents; and although they were justly proud of his Euro-

---

[1] Franklin's *Works*, vii. 357.
[2] Ibid. viii. pp. 30, 31. After the Stamp Act, Franklin expressed his opinion in a pithy sentence to Ingersoll, who was then returning to America. 'Go home and tell your countrymen to get children as fast as they can.'
[3] Ibid. pp. 78, 79.

pean reputation, even this was sometimes a cause of suspicion. They felt that he, and he alone, of living Americans, by his own unassisted merit, had won a great position in England, and they doubted whether he could be as devoted to their cause as men whose reputation was purely provincial. In 1771, Arthur Lee, of Virginia, who was fully identified with the extreme party, was appointed his colleague, and there were several other symptoms that Franklin was looked on with some distrust. The suspicions of his sincerity were, however, wholly groundless. His heart was warmly in the American cause, and although he would have gladly moderated the policy of his countrymen, he was by no means disposed to suffer himself to be stranded and distanced. His views became more extensive, and his language more emphatic; he now maintained with great ability the position that the colonies, like Hanover, or like Scotland before the Union, though they were subject to the English king, were wholly independent of the British Legislature; and in 1773 he was concerned in a transaction which placed him at open war with English opinion.

It had been for a long time the habit of Hutchinson, the Governor-General of Massachusetts; of Oliver, who was now Lieutenant-Governor; and of some other politicians of the province who were attached to the Crown, to carry on a strictly private and confidential correspondence about the state of the colonies with Whately, who had formerly been private secretary to George Grenville. In June 1772 Whately died, and in December, by some person and some means that have never been certainly disclosed, the letters of his American correspondents were stolen and carried to Franklin. The letters of Hutchinson had, with one exception, been written before his appointment as Governor, but at a time when he held high office in the colony, and they were written with the perfect freedom of confidential intercourse. Whately, though peculiarly conversant with colonial matters, held at this time no office under the Crown, and was a simple member of the Opposition. Hutchinson, in writing to him, dilated upon the turbulent and rebellious disposition of Boston, the factious character of the local agitators, the weakness of the Executive, the necessity of a military force to support the Government, and the excessive predominance of the democratic element in the constitution of Massachusetts. 'I never think,' he wrote in the letter which was afterwards most violently attacked, 'of the measures necessary for the peace and good order of the colonies without pain. There must be an abridgment of what are called English liberties. . . . I doubt whether it is possible to project a system of government in which a colony 3,000 miles distant from the parent State shall enjoy all the liberty of the parent State. . . . I wish the good of the colony when I wish to see some further restraint of liberty rather than the connection with the parent State should be broken, for I am sure such a breach must prove the ruin of the colony.' Oliver argued with more detail that the Council or Upper Chamber should consist exclusively of landed proprietors, that the Crown officers should have salaries independent of popular favour, that the popular election of grand juries should be abolished, and that there should be a colonial representation in the English Parliament. All this appears to have been most honestly written, but it was written without the reserve and the caution which would have been maintained in letters intended to be published. Both Hutchinson and Oliver impressed on their correspondent their desire that these letters should be deemed strictly confidential.[1] They were brought to Franklin as political information for his perusal. He at once perceived the advantage they would give to the popular party, and he asked and obtained permission to send them to Massachusetts on condition that they should not be printed or copied; that they should be shown only to a few of the leading people, that they should be eventually returned, and that the source from which they were obtained should be concealed.

The letters were accordingly sent to Thomas Cushing, the Speaker of the Assembly of Massachusetts, and, as might have been expected, they soon created a general ferment. As Franklin acutely wrote, 'there was no restraint proposed to talking of them, but only to copying.' They were shown to many of the leading agitators. John Adams was suffered to take them with him on his judicial circuit, and they were finally brought before the Assembly in a secret sitting. The

[1] See the letters of Oct. 26, 1769, and May 7, 1767.

Assembly at once carried resolutions censuring them as designed to sow discord and encourage the oppressive acts of the British Government, to introduce arbitrary power into the province and subvert its constitution, and with the concurrence of the Council it petitioned the King to remove Hutchinson and Oliver from the Government. The letters were soon generally known. The sole obstacle to their diffusion was the promise that they should not be copied or printed, and it was not likely that this would be observed. According to one account,[1] copies were produced which were falsely said to have come by the last mail from England, and which were therefore not included under the original promise. According to another account[2] Hancock, one of the leading patriots, took 'advantage of the implied permission of Hutchinson' to have copies made. Hutchinson had indeed been challenged with the letters, and been asked for copies of them and of such others as he should think proper to communicate. After some delay, he answered evasively, 'If you desire copies with a view to make them public, the originals are more proper for the purpose than the copies,' and this sentence appears to have been considered a sufficient authorisation. The letters were accordingly printed and scattered broadcast over the colonies.

When the printed copies arrived in England, they excited great astonishment, and William Whately, the brother and executor of the late Secretary, was filled with a very natural consternation at a theft which was likely to have such important consequences, and for which public opinion was inclined to make him responsible. He, in his turn, suspected a certain Mr. Temple, who had been allowed to look through the papers of his deceased brother, for the purpose of perusing one relating to the colonies, and a duel ensued, in which Whately was wounded. Franklin then, for the first time, in a letter to a newspaper, disclosed the part he had taken. He stated that he, and he alone, had obtained and transmitted to Boston the letters in question, that they had never passed into the hands of William Whately, and that it was therefore impossible either that Whately could have communicated them or that Temple could have taken them from his papers. There is some reason

---

[1] Sparks' *Continuation of Franklin's Life*.   [2] Bancroft.

to believe that the original owner had left them carelessly in a public office, from whence they had been abstracted, but the mystery was never decisively solved.

Franklin always maintained that in all this matter he had simply done his duty, and that his conduct was perfectly honourable. The letters, he said, 'were written by public officers to persons in public stations, on public affairs, and intended to procure public measures.' They were brought to him as the Agent for Massachusetts, and it was his duty as such to communicate to his constituents intelligence that was of such vital importance to their affairs. He even urged, more ingeniously than plausibly, that he was animated by a virtuous desire to lessen the breach between England and the colonies. Like most Americans, he said, he had viewed with indignation the coercive measures which emanated, as he supposed, from the British Government, but his feelings were much changed when it was proved that their real origin might be traced to Americans holding high offices in their native country. It was to convince him of this truth that the letters had been originally brought to him. It was to spread a similar conviction among his countrymen that he had sent them across the Atlantic. With more force his apologists have urged that the sanctity of private correspondence was not then regarded as it is regarded now, and that the Government itself continually tampered with it for political purposes.[1] In 1766 the Duke of Bedford discovered, to his great indignation, that a letter which he had written to the Duke of Grafton had been opened; and among the items of secret-service money during the administration of Grenville was a sum to a Post Office official 'for engraving the many seals we are obliged to make use of.'[2] If Government was not ashamed to resort to such methods, was it reasonable to expect that an agent who was endeavouring in a hostile country and against overwhelming obstacles to maintain the interests of his colony would be more scrupulous? Letters of Franklin himself, written to the colony, had been opened, and their contents had been employed for political purposes. Hutchinson had been concerned in this proceeding, and could

[1] See p 75. Burke's *Works*, ix. 148.
[2] *Grenville Papers*, iii. 99, 311, 312.

therefore hardly complain that his own weapons were turned against himself.[1]

These considerations, no doubt, palliate the conduct of Franklin. Whether they do more than palliate it, must be left to the judgment of the reader. In England that conduct was judged with the utmost severity. For the purpose of ruining honourable officials, it was said, their most confidential letters, written several years before to a private Member of Parliament who had at that time no connection with the Government, had been deliberately stolen; and although the original thief was undiscovered, the full weight of the guilt and of the dishonour rested upon Franklin. He was perfectly aware that the letters had been written in the strictest confidence, that they had been dishonestly obtained without the knowledge either of the person who received them or of the persons who wrote them, and that their exposure would be a deadly injury to the writers. Under these circumstances he procured them. Under these circumstances he sent them to a small group of politicians whom he knew to be the bitterest enemies of the Governor, and one of the consequences of his conduct was a duel in which the brother of the man whose private papers had been stolen was nearly killed. Any man of high and sensitive honour, it was said, would sooner have put his hand in the fire than have been concerned in such a transaction. When the petition for the removal of Hutchinson and Oliver arrived, the Government referred it to the Committee of the Privy Council, that the allegations might be publicly examined with counsel on either side, and the case excited an interest which had been rarely paralleled. No less than thirty-five Privy Councillors attended. Among the distinguished strangers who crowded the Bar were Burke, Priestley, and Jeremy Bentham. Dunning and Lee, who spoke for the petitioners, appear to have made no impression; while on the other side, Wedderburn, the Solicitor-General, made one of his most brilliant but most virulent speeches. After a brief but eloquent eulogy of the character and services of Hutchinson, he passed to the manner in which the letters were procured, and turning to Franklin, who stood

---

[1] See Franklin's own vindication of his proceedings, with the accompanying notes. *Works*, iv. 404-455.

before him, he delivered an invective which appears to have electrified his audience. 'How the letters came into the possession of anyone but the right owners,' he said, 'is still a mystery for Dr. Franklin to explain. He was not the rightful owner, and they could not have come into his hands by fair means. Nothing will acquit Dr. Franklin of the charge of obtaining them by fraudulent or corrupt means for the most malignant of purposes, unless he stole them from the person who stole them. I hope, my Lords, you will brand this man for the honour of this country, of Europe, and of mankind. . . . Into what country will the fabricator of this iniquity hereafter go with unembarrassed face? Men will watch him with a jealous eye. They will hide their papers from him, and lock up their escritoires. Having hitherto aspired after fame by his writings, he will henceforth esteem it a libel to be called a man of letters—*homo trium literarum*.[1] But he not only took away those papers from one brother—he kept himself concealed till he nearly occasioned the murder of another. It is impossible to read his account, expressive of the coolest and most deliberate malice, without horror. Amid these tragical events, of one person nearly murdered, of another answerable for the issue, of a worthy Governor hurt in his dearest interests, the fate of America in suspense—here is a man who, with the utmost insensibility of remorse, stands up and avows himself the author of all. I can compare him only to Zanga in Dr. Young's Revenge:'

> Know then, 'twas I—
> I forged the letter. I disposed the picture,
> I hated, I despised, and I destroy.

I ask, my Lords, whether the revengeful temper attributed by poetic fiction only to the bloody African, is not surpassed by the coolness and apathy of the wily American?'

The scene was a very strange one, and it is well suited to the brush of an historical painter. Franklin was now an old man of sixty-seven, the greatest writer, the greatest philosopher America had produced, a member of some of the chief scientific societies in Europe, the accredited representative of the most important of the colonies of America, and for nearly an

---

[1] For a thief.

hour and in the midst of the most distinguished of living Englishmen he was compelled to hear himself denounced as a thief or the accomplice of thieves. He stood there conspicuous and erect, and without moving a muscle, amid the torrent of invective, but his apparent composure was shared by few who were about him. With the single exception of Lord North, the Privy Councillors who were present lost all dignity and all self-respect. They laughed aloud at each sarcastic sally of Wedderburn. 'The indecency of their behaviour,' in the words of Shelburne, 'exceeded, as is agreed on all hands, that of any committee of elections;' and Fox, in a speech which he made as late as 1803, reminded the House how on that memorable occasion 'all men tossed up their hats and clapped their hands in boundless delight at Mr. Wedderburn's speech.' The Committee at once voted that the petition of the Massachusetts Assembly was 'false, groundless, and scandalous, and calculated only for the seditious purpose of keeping up a spirit of clamour and discontent in the province.' The King in Council confirmed the report, and Franklin was ignominiously dismissed from his office of Postmaster. It was an office which had yielded no revenue before he had received it, but which his admirable organisation had made lucrative and important. The colonists accepted the insults directed against their great representative as directed against themselves,[1] and from this time the most sagacious of American leaders had a deep personal grudge against the British Government.[2]

In the meantime a serious attempt was made to make the tea duty a reality. About seventeen million pounds of tea lay unsold in the warehouses of the East India Company. The Company was at this time in extreme financial embarrassment, almost amounting to bankruptcy, and in order to assist it the whole duty which had formerly been imposed on the exportation to America was remitted.[3] Hitherto the Company had been obliged to send their tea to England, where it was sold by public sale to merchants and dealers, and by them exported to the colo-

---

[1] On the extraordinary popularity of Franklin at this time, see the letter of Dr. Rush, quoted in Sparks' *Continuation to the Life of Franklin*.

[2] *Life of Franklin*. Campbell's *Lives of the Chancellors*, viii. 14–19. *Chatham Correspondence*, iv. 322, 323.

[3] By the previous law (12 Geo. III. c. 60) a drawback of three-fifths of the duty had been allowed.

nies. The Company were now permitted to export tea direct from their warehouses on their own account on obtaining a licence from the Treasury,[1] and they accordingly selected their own agents in the different colonies. As the East India Company had of late been brought to a great extent under the direction of the Government, the consignees were such as favoured the Administration, and in Boston they included the two sons of Hutchinson. Several ships freighted with tea were sent to the colonies, and the Government hoped, and the 'sons of liberty' feared, that if it were once landed it would probably find purchasers, for owing to the drawback of the duty on exportation it could be sold much cheaper than in England itself, and cheaper than tea imported from any other country. The colonies at once entered into a conspiracy to prevent the tea being landed, and a long series of violent measures were taken for the purpose of intimidating those who were concerned in receiving it. At last, in December 1773, three ships laden with tea arrived at Boston, and on the 16th of that month forty or fifty men disguised as Mohawk Indians, and under the direct superintendence of Samuel Adams, Hancock,[2] and other leading patriots, boarded them, and posting sentinels to keep all agents of authority at a distance, they flung the whole cargo, consisting of 342 chests, into the sea. In the course of the violent proceedings at Boston in this year, the Council, the militia, the corps of cadets had been vainly asked to assist in maintaining the law. The sheriff of the town was grossly insulted. The magistrates would do nothing, and, as usual, the crowning outrage of the destruction of the tea was accomplished with perfect impunity, and not a single person engaged in it was in any way molested. At Charleston a ship arrived with tea, but the consignees were intimidated into resignation, and the tea was stored in cellars where it ultimately perished. At New York and Philadelphia the inhabitants obliged the captains of the tea ships at once to sail back with their cargoes to the Thames.

[1] 13 George III. c. 44.
[2] Hutchinson notices that Hancock's uncle had made his large fortune chiefly by smuggling tea from St. Eustatia. *Hist. of Massachusetts Bay,* p. 297. See too Sabine's *American Loyalists,* i. 9.

While the law was thus openly defied, the popular party were inflexibly opposed to the project of granting the judges fixed salaries from the Crown, and thus making them in some degree independent of the Assemblies. In Massachusetts the Assembly declared all judges who received salaries from the Crown instead of the people unworthy of public confidence, and it threatened to impeach them before the Council and the Governor. In February 1774, proceedings of this kind were actually instituted against Oliver, the Chief Justice of the province, because he had accepted an annual stipend from the Crown. Out of 100 members who voted, no less than 92 supported the impeachment. Hutchinson of course refused to concur in the measure, and on March 30 he prorogued the House, and at the same time accused it of having been guilty of proceedings which 'strike directly at the honour and authority of the King and Parliament.'

The news of these events convinced most intelligent Englishmen that war was imminent, and that the taxation of America could only be enforced by the sword. Several distinct lines of policy were during the next two or three years advocated in England. Tucker, the Dean of Gloucester, a bitter Tory, but one of the best living writers on all questions of trade, maintained a theory which was then esteemed visionary and almost childish, but which will now be very differently regarded. He had no respect for the Americans; he dissected with unsparing severity the many weaknesses in their arguments, and the declamatory and rhetorical character of much of their patriotism; but he contended that matters had now come to such a point that the only real remedy was separation. Colonies which would do nothing for their own defence, which were in a condition of smothered rebellion, and which were continually waiting for the difficulties of the mother-country in order to assert their power, were a source of political weakness and not of political strength, and the trade advantages which were supposed to spring from the connection were of the most delusive kind. Trade, as he showed, will always ultimately flow in the most lucrative channels. The most stringent laws had been unable to prevent the Americans from trading with foreign countries if they could do so with advantage, and in case of separation the Americans would still resort to England for most of their goods, for the simple reason that England could supply them more cheaply than any other nation. The supremacy of English industry did not rest upon political causes. 'The trade of the world is carried on in a great measure by British capital. British capital is greater than that of any other country in the world, and as long as this superiority lasts it is morally impossible that the trade of the British nation can suffer any very great or alarming diminution.' No single fact is more clearly established by history than that the bitterest political animosity is insufficient to prevent nations from ultimately resorting to the markets that are most advantageous to them, and as long as England maintained the conditions of her industrial supremacy unimpaired she was in this respect perfectly secure. But nothing impairs these conditions so much as war, which wastes capital unproductively and burdens industry with a great additional weight of debt, military establishments, and taxation. The war which began about the Spanish right of search had cost sixty millions, and had scarcely produced any benefit to England. The last war cost ninety millions, and its most important result had been, by securing the Americans from French aggression, to render possible their present rebellion. Let England, then, be wise in time, and before she draws the sword let her calculate what possible advantage she could derive commensurate with the permanent evils which would inevitably follow. The Americans have refused to submit to the authority and legislation of the Supreme Legislature, or to bear their part in supporting the burden of the Empire. Let them, then, cease to be fellow-members of that Empire. Let them go their way to form their own destinies. Let England free herself from the cost, the responsibility, and the danger of defending them, retaining, like other nations, the right of connecting herself with them by treaties of commerce or of alliance.[1]

The views of Adam Smith, though less strongly expressed, are not very different from those of Tucker. The 'Wealth of Nations' appeared in 1776, and although it at first attracted no great attention and had little political influence for at least a generation after its appearance, it has ultimately proved

[1] Tucker's *Political Tracts*.

one of the most important events in the economical, and indeed in the intellectual, history of modern Europe. No part of it is more remarkable than the chapters devoted to the colonies. Adam Smith showed by an exhaustive examination that the liberty of commerce which England allowed to her colonies, though greatly and variously restricted, was at least more extensive than that which any other nation conceded to its dependencies, and that it was sufficient to give them a large and increasing measure of prosperity. The laws, however, preventing them from employing their industry in manufactures for themselves, he described as 'a manifest violation of the most sacred rights of mankind,' and likely 'in a more advanced state' to prove 'really oppressive and insupportable.' Hitherto, however, these laws, though they were 'badges of slavery imposed without any sufficient reason,' had been of little practical importance; for, owing to the great cheapness of land and the great dearness of labour in the colonies, it was obviously the most economical course for the Americans to devote themselves to agriculture and fisheries, and to import manufactured goods. His chief contention, however, was that the system of trade monopoly which, with many exceptions and qualifications, was maintained in the colonies for the benefit of England, was essentially vicious; that the colonies were profoundly injured by the restrictions which confined them to the English market, and that these restrictions were not beneficial, but were indeed positively injurious to England herself. These positions were maintained in a long, complicated, but singularly luminous argument, and it followed that the very keystone of English colonial policy was a delusion. 'The maintenance of this monopoly has hitherto been the principal, or, more properly, perhaps, the sole end and purpose of the dominion which Great Britain assumes over the colonies.' The burden of a great peace establishment by land and sea, maintained almost exclusively from English revenue, two great wars which had arisen chiefly from colonial questions, and the risk and probability of many others, were all supposed to be counterbalanced by the great advantage which the mother-country derived from the monopoly of the colonial trade. The truth, however, is that 'the monopoly of the colony trade depresses the industry of all other countries, but chiefly that of the colonies, without in the least increasing, but, on the contrary, diminishing, that of the country in whose favour it is established.' 'Under the present system of management, therefore, Great Britain derives nothing but loss from the dominion which she assumes over the colonies.'

Like Tucker, Adam Smith would gladly have seen a peaceful separation. 'Great Britain,' he wrote, 'would not only be immediately freed from the whole annual expense of the peace establishment of the colonies, but might settle with them such a treaty of commerce as would effectually secure to her a free trade more advantageous to the great body of the people, though less so to the merchants, than the monopoly which she at present enjoys.' She would at the same time probably revive that good feeling between the two great branches of the English race which was now rapidly turning to hatred. Such a solution, however, though the best, must be put aside as manifestly impracticable. No serious politician would propose the voluntary and peaceful cession of the great dominion of England in America with any real hope of being listened to. ' Such a measure never was and never will be adopted by any nation in the world.'

Dismissing this solution, then, Adam Smith agreed with Grenville that every part of the British Empire should be obliged to support its own civil and military establishments, and to pay its proper proportion of the expense of the general government or defence of the British Empire. He also agreed with Grenville that it naturally devolved upon the British Parliament to determine the amount of the colonial contributions, though the colonial Legislatures might decide in what way those contributions should be raised. It was practically impossible to induce the colonial Legislatures of themselves to levy such taxation, or to agree upon its proportionate distribution. Moreover, a colonial Assembly, though, like the vestry of a parish, it is an admirable judge of the affairs of its own district, can have no proper means of determining what is necessary for the defence and support of the whole Empire. This ' can be judged of only by that Assembly which inspects and superintends the affairs of the whole nation.' 'The Parliament of England,' he added, ' has not upon any occasion shown the smallest disposition to overburden those parts of the Empire which are not represented in Parliament. The islands of Jersey and Guernsey ... are more lightly taxed than any parts of Great Britain. Parliament ... has never hitherto demanded of the colonies anything which even approached to a just proportion of what was paid by their fellow-subjects at home,' and the fear of an excessive taxation might be easily met by making the colonial contribution bear a fixed proportion to the English land tax. The colonists, however, almost unanimously refused to submit to taxation by a Parliament in which they were not represented. The only solution, then, was to give them a representation in it, and at the same time to open to them all the prizes of English politics. The colonists should ultimately be subjected to the same taxes as Englishmen, and should be admitted, in compensation, to the same freedom of trade and manufacture.

If we pass from the political philosophers to active politicians, we find that Chatham and Burke were substantially agreed upon the line they recommended. Burke, who had long shown a knowledge and a zeal on American questions which no other politician could rival, had in the preceding year accepted, with very doubtful propriety, the position of paid agent of New York; and in 1774 he made his great speech on American taxation. In the same year Chatham reappeared in the House of Lords, and took a prominent part in the American debates. Burke and Chatham continued to differ on the question of the abstract right of Parliament to tax America, but they agreed in maintaining that the union to the British Crown of a vast civilised and rapidly progressive country, evidently destined to take a foremost place in the history of the world, was a matter of vital importance to the future of the Empire. In the speeches and letters of Chatham especially, this doctrine is maintained in the most emphatic language. 'I fear the bond between us and America,' he wrote in 1774, 'will be cut off for ever. Devoted England will then have seen her best days, which nothing can restore again.'[1] 'Although I love the Americans as men prizing and setting a just value upon that inestimable blessing, liberty, yet if I could once persuade myself that they entertain the most distant intention of

[1] Thackeray's *Life of Chatham*, ii. 274.

throwing off the legislative supremacy and great constitutional superintending power and control of the British Legislature, I should myself be the very first person . . . to enforce that power by every exertion this country is capable of making.'[1]

In the speeches of Burke, no passages of equal emphasis will be found; but Burke, like Chatham, entirely refused at this time to contemplate the separation of the colonies from the Empire; and he maintained that the only good policy was a policy of conciliation, reverting to the condition of affairs which existed before the Stamp Act, and repealing all the coercive and aggressive laws which had since then been promulgated. This was what the Americans themselves asked. In presenting a petition from the Assembly of Massachusetts in August 1773 Franklin, their agent, had written 'that a sincere disposition prevails in the people there to be on good terms with the mother-country; that the Assembly have declared their desire only to be put into the situation they were in before the Stamp Act. They aim at no revolution.'[2] In this spirit Burke urged their claims. 'Revert to your old principles . . . leave America, if she has taxable matter in her, to tax herself. I am not here going into a distinction of rights, nor attempting to mark their boundaries. I do not enter into these metaphysical distinctions. I hate the very sound of them. Leave the Americans as they anciently stood, and these distinctions, born of our unhappy contest, will die along with it. . . . Let the memory of all actions in contradiction to that good old mode, on both sides be extinguished for ever. Be content to bind America by laws of trade; you have always done it. Let this be your reason for binding their trade. Do not burthen them with taxes; you were not used to do so from the beginning. Let this be your reason for not taxing. These are the arguments of states and kingdoms. Leave the rest to the schools; for there only they may be discussed with safety. If intemperately, unwisely, fatally, you sophisticate and poison the very source of government by urging subtle deductions and consequences odious to those you govern, from the unlimited and illimitable nature of supreme sovereignty, you will teach them by these means to call that sovereignty itself in question.'

[1] Thackeray's *Life of Chatham*, ii. 279.   [2] Franklin's *Works*, iv. 432.

The duty on tea should especially be at once repealed. It was said that it was an external tax such as the Americans had always professed themselves ready to pay; that port duties had been imposed by Grenville as late as 1764 without exciting any protest, and that it was therefore evident that the claims of the Americans were extending. But the American distinction had always been that they would acknowledge external taxes, which were intended only to regulate trade; but not internal taxes, which were intended to raise revenue. Townshend, with unhappy ingenuity, proved that an external tax could be made to raise revenue like an internal tax, and this purpose was expressly stated in the preamble of the Act. 'It was just and necessary,' the preamble said, ' that a revenue should be raised there;' and again, the Commons 'being desirous to make some provision in the present Session of Parliament towards raising the said revenue.' It would also be difficult to conceive a more absurd position than that of the Ministry which retained the tea duty. It was an intelligible policy to force the Americans to support an army for the defence of the Empire; but it was calculated that the duty would at the utmost produce 16,000l. a year, and the Ministry had precluded themselves from the possibility of increasing the revenue. Townshend no doubt had meant to do so; but Lord North had authorised Lord Hillsborough to assure the colonial Governors, in his letter of May 1769, 'that his Majesty's present Administration have at no time entertained a design to propose to Parliament to lay any further taxes upon America for the purpose of raising a revenue.' 16,000l. a year was therefore the utmost the Ministers expected from a policy which had led England to the brink of an almost inevitable war. But even this was not all. In order to impose this unhappy port duty of 3d. in the pound on the Americans, Parliament had actually withdrawn a duty of 1s. in the pound which had hitherto been paid without question and without difficulty upon exportation from England, and which necessarily fell chiefly, if not wholly, upon those who purchased the tea. 'Incredible as it may seem, you have deliberately thrown away a large duty which you held secure and quiet in your hands, for the vain hope of getting three-fourths less, through every hazard, through certain litigation, and possibly through war.'[1] It was said that the duty was merely an assertion of right, like the Declaratory Act of 1766. The answer is to be found in the very preamble of the new Act, which asserted not merely the justice, but also the expediency, of taxing the colonies. A simple repeal was the one possible form of conciliation, for a legislative union between countries 3,000 miles apart was wholly impracticable, and it was absolutely repudiated by the colonies. On the subject of the restrictive trade laws, Burke wisely said as little as possible. He knew that the question could not be raised without dividing the friends of America, and probably without alienating the commercial classes, who were the chief English opponents of American taxation.

Whether the policy of Burke and Chatham would have succeeded is very doubtful. After so much agitation and violence, after the promulgation of so many subversive doctrines in America, and the exhibition of so much weakness and vacillation in England, it could scarcely be expected that the tempest would have been calmed, and that the race of active agitators would have retired peaceably into obscurity. Philosophers in their studies might draw out reasonable plans of conciliation, but pure reason plays but a small part in politics, and the difficulty of carrying these plans into execution was enormous. Party animosities, divisions, and subdivisions; the personal interests of statesmen who wanted to climb into office, and of agitators who wanted to retain or increase their power; the obstinacy of the Court, which was opposed to all concession to the colonies, and no less opposed to a consolidation of parties at home; the spirit of commercial monopoly, which made one class averse to all trade concessions; the heavy weight of the land tax, which made another class peculiarly indignant at the refusal of the colonists to bear the burden of their own defence; the natural pride of Parliament, which had been repeatedly insulted and defied; the anger, the jealousy, and the suspicion which recent events had created on both sides

---

[1] The East India Company had clearly seen the absurdity of the transaction, and offered that the Government should retain a duty of sixpence in the pound on exportation, provided it consented to repeal the duty of threepence in the pound paid in America. *Parl. Hist.* xviii 178.

of the Atlantic; the doubts which existed in England about the extent to which the disloyal spirit of New England had permeated the other colonies; the doubts which existed in America about which of the many sections of English public opinion would ultimately obtain an ascendency; and, finally, the weak characters, the divided opinions, the imperfect information, and the extremely ordinary capacities of the English Ministers, must all be taken into account. Had Chatham been at the head of affairs and in the full force of his powers, conciliation might have been possible; but such a policy required a firm hand, an eagle eye, a great personal ascendency. Popular opinion in England, which had supported the repeal of the Stamp Act, and had acquiesced in the repeal of the greater part of Townshend's Act, was now opposed to further concession. England, it was said, had sufficiently humiliated herself. The claims and the language of the colonial agitators excited profound and not unnatural indignation, and every mail from America brought news that New England at least was in a condition of virtual rebellion; that Acts of Parliament were defied and disobeyed with the most perfect impunity; that the representatives of the British Government were habitually exposed to the grossest insult, and reduced to the most humiliating impotence. The utility of colonies to the mother-country was becoming a doubtful question to some. Ministers, it was said, admitted in Parliament that 'it might be a great question whether the colonies should not be given up.'[1] England, indeed, was plainly staggering under the weight of her empire. In 1774, on the very eve of its gigantic struggle, Parliament resounded with complaints of the magnitude of the peace establishment, and there were loud cries for reduction. It was noticed that the land tax was 1s. higher than in any previous peace establishment; that the Three per Cents., which some

---

[1] *Annual Register*, 1774, p. 62. The King himself wrote (Nov. 1774): 'We must either master them [the colonies] or totally leave them to themselves, and treat them as aliens.' —*Correspondence of George III.* i. 216. As early as Jan. 1769 Hussey, the Attorney-General to the Queen, said in Parliament: 'I have my doubts whether there should ever be a strict union between the colonies and the mother-country; I have doubts whether they are a real service or a burthen to us; but I never had a doubt as to our right to lay an internal tax upon them.'—*Cavendish Debates*, i. 197.

years ago were above 90, had now fallen to about 86; that the land and malt taxes were almost entirely absorbed by the increased expenditure required for the navy.[1] All this rendered the attitude of the colonies peculiarly irritating. The publication of the letters of Hutchinson produced great indignation among English politicians; and the burning of the 'Gaspee,' the destruction of tea in Boston harbour, and the manifest connivance of the whole population in the outrage, raised that indignation to the highest point. The time for temporising, it was said, was over. It was necessary to show that England possessed some real power of executing her laws and protecting her officers, and the Ministers were probably supported by a large majority of the English people when they resolved to throw away the scabbard, and to exert all the powers of Parliament to reduce Massachusetts to obedience.

The measures that were taken were very stringent. By one Act the harbour of Boston was legally closed. The Customhouse officers were removed to Salem. All landing, lading, and shipping of merchandise in Boston harbour was forbidden, and English men-of-war were appointed to maintain the blockade. The town, which owed its whole prosperity to its commercial activity, was debarred from all commerce by sea, and was to continue under this ban till it had made compensation to the East India Company for the tea which had been destroyed, and had satisfied the Crown that trade would for the future be safely carried on in Boston, property protected, laws obeyed, and duties regularly paid.[2]

By another Act, Parliament exercised the power which, as the supreme legislative body of the Empire, Mansfield and other lawyers ascribed to it, of remodelling by its own authority the Charter of Massachusetts. The General Assembly, which was esteemed the legitimate representative of the democratic element in the Constitution, was left entirely untouched; but the Council, or Upper Chamber, which had been hitherto elected by the Assembly, was now to be appointed, as in most of the other colonies of America, by the Crown, and the whole executive power was to cease to emanate from the people. The judges and magistrates of all kinds, including

[1] *Annual Register*, 1774, p. 53.   [2] 14 George III. c. 19.

the sheriffs, were to be appointed by the royal governor, and were to be revocable at pleasure. Jurymen, instead of being chosen by popular election, were to be summoned by the sheriffs. The right of public meeting, which had lately been much employed in inciting the populace against the Government, was seriously abridged. No meeting except election meetings might henceforth be held, and no subject discussed, without the permission of the governor.[1]

It was more than probable that such grave changes would be resisted by force, that blood would be shed, and that English soldiers would again be tried for their lives before a civil tribunal. The conduct of the Boston judges and of the Boston jury at the trial of Captain Preston and his soldiers had redounded to their immortal honour; but Government was resolved that no such risk should be again incurred, and that soldiers who were brought to trial for enforcing the law against the inhabitants of Boston, should never again be tried by a Boston jury. To remove the trial of prisoners from a district where popular feeling was so violent that a fair trial was not likely to be obtained, was a practice not wholly unknown to English law. Scotch juries were not suffered to try rebels, or Sussex juries smugglers; and an Act was now passed 'for the impartial administration of justice,' which provided that if any person in the province of Massachusetts were indicted for murder or any other capital offence, and if it should appear to the governor that the incriminated act was committed in aiding the magistrates to suppress tumult and riot, and also that a fair trial cannot be had in the province, the prisoner should be sent for trial to any other colony, or to Great Britain.[2]

These were the three great coercive measures of 1774. It is not necessary to dilate upon them, for their character is transparently evident, and the provocation that produced them has been sufficiently explained. The colonial estimate of them was tersely stated in the remonstrance of the province. 'By the first,' they say, 'the property of unoffending thousands is arbitrarily taken away for the act of a few individuals; by the second our chartered liberties are annihilated, and by the third our lives may be destroyed with impunity.' General Gage,

---

[1] 14 George III. c. 45.   [2] Ibid: c. 39.

who had for some years been commander-in-chief of the whole English army in America, was appointed Governor of Massachusetts, and entrusted with the task of carrying out the coercive policy of Parliament; and in order to assist him, an Act was carried, quartering soldiers on the inhabitants.[1]

One other measure relating to the colonies was carried during this session, which met with great opposition, and which, though important in American history, is still more important in the history of religious liberty. It was the famous Quebec Act, for the purpose of ascertaining the limits and regulating the condition of the new province of Canada.[2] The great majority of the inhabitants of that province were French, who had been accustomed to live under an arbitrary government, and whose religious and social conditions differed widely from those of the English colonists. The Government resolved, as the event showed very wisely, that they would not subvert the ancient laws of the province, or introduce into them the democratic system which existed in New England. The English law with trial by jury was introduced in all criminal cases; but as all contracts and settlements had hitherto been made under French law, and as that law was most congenial to their tastes and habits and traditions, it was maintained.[3] In all civil cases, therefore, French law without trial by jury continued in force. A legislative Council, varying from seventeen to twenty-three members, open to men of both religions, and appointed by the Crown, managed all legislative business except taxation, which was expressly reserved. The territory of the province, determined by the proclamation of 1763, was enlarged so as to include some outlying districts, which were chiefly inhabited by French; and by a bold measure, which excited great indignation both among the Puritans of New England and among the Whigs at home, the Catholic religion, which was that of the great majority of the inhabitants, was virtually established. The Catholic clergy obtained a full parliamentary title to their

---

[1] 14 George III. c. 54.
[2] Ibid. c. 83.
[3] According to General Carleton, the Governor, Canada contained 150,000 Catholics, and less than 400 Protestants; and the French Catholics greatly preferred having their trials determined by judges to having them determined by juries, and had not the least desire for any popular assemblies —*Parl. Hist.* xvii. 1367, 1368.

old ecclesiastical estates, and to tithes paid by members of their own religion; but no Protestant was obliged to pay tithes.

The Quebec Act was little less distasteful to the colonists than the coercive measures that have been related. The existence upon their frontiers of an English state governed on a despotic principle was deemed a new danger to their liberties, while the establishment of Catholicism offended their deepest religious sentiment. Its toleration had indeed been provided for by the Peace of Paris, and on the death of the last French bishop the Government had agreed to recognise a resident Catholic bishop on the condition that he and his successors should be designated by itself, but the political position of the Catholics had been for some time undetermined. The Protestant grand jurors at Quebec had insisted that no Catholic should be admitted to grand or petty juries, and the party they represented would have gladly concentrated all civil and political power in the hands of an infinitesimal body of Protestant immigrants, degraded the Catholics into a servile caste, and reproduced in America in a greatly aggravated form the detestable social condition which existed in Ireland. At home the strength of the anti-Catholic feeling was a few years later abundantly shown, but, with the exception of some parts of Scotland, no portion of the British Islands was animated with the religious fervour of New England, and no sketch of the American Revolution is adequate which does not take this influence into account. In this as in many other respects these colonies presented a vivid image of an England which had long since passed away. Their democratic church government, according to which each congregation elected its own minister, their historical connection with those austere republicans who had abandoned their native country to worship God after their own fashion in a desert land, and the intensely Protestant type of their belief, had all conspired to strengthen the Puritan spirit, and in the absence of most forms of intellectual life the pulpit had acquired an almost unparalleled ascendency. The chief and almost the only popular celebration in Massachusetts before the struggle of the Revolution was that of the 5th of November.[1] In Boston, which

---

[1] See a curious account of this celebration in Tudor's *Life of Otis*, pp. 26–29. It degenerated into a violent contention between different parts of

was the chief centre of the political movement, the theological spirit was especially strong, for the population was unusually homogeneous both in race and in religion. The Congregationalists were three or four times as numerous as the Episcopalians, and other sects were as yet scarcely represented.[1]

The spirit of American puritanism was indeed so fierce and jealous that the American Episcopalians who were connected with the English Church were never suffered in the colonial period to have a bishop among them, but remained under the jurisdiction of the Bishop of London. Berkeley, Butler, and Secker had vainly represented how injurious this system was to the spiritual welfare of the American Episcopalians. Sherlock complained bitterly that he was made responsible for the religious welfare of a vast country which he had never seen, which he never would see, and over which he could exercise no real influence. Gibson tried to exercise some control over the colonial clergy, but found that he had no means of enforcing his will. Archbishop Tenison had even left a legacy for the endowment of two bishoprics in America. The Episcopalians themselves petitioned earnestly for a resident bishop, and stated in the clearest terms that they wished him to be only a spiritual functionary destitute of all temporal authority. 'The powers exercised in the consistory courts in England,' it was said, 'are not desired for bishops residing in America.' They were not to be supported by any tax; they were not to be placed either in New England or Pennsylvania, where non-episcopal forms of religion prevailed, or to be suffered in any colony to exercise any authority, except over the members of their own persuasion.[2] It was urged that those who were in communion with the Established Church of

---

Boston. When the Americans invaded Canada in 1775, Washington forbade the commemoration, lest it should irritate the Canadian Catholics. Sparks' *Washington*, iii. 144.

[1] Tudor's *Life of Otis*, pp. 446, 447.
[2] See the report of Bishop Sherlock to the King in Council, on the Church in the Colonies.—*Documents relating to the Colonial History of New York*, vol. vii. pp. 360–369. Much information about the condition of the Episcopalians in America will be found in the correspondence between Archbishop Secker and some American clergymen in the same volume.

According to Sherlock, the Episcopalian ministers in America were chiefly Scotch and Irish. A great number of them appear to have been educated in Dublin University. The Massachusetts Assembly, writing in 1768 to their agent in England, against the taxation of America by England, say: 'The revenue raised in America, for aught we can tell, may be as constitutionally applied towards the support of prelacy, as of soldiers and pensioners;' and they add, 'We hope in God such an establishment will never take place in America.'—Wells' *Life of S. Adams*, i. 200.

England were the only Christians in America who were deprived of what they believed to be the necessary means of religious discipline; that the rite of confirmation, which is so important in the Anglican system, was unknown among them; that it was an intolerable grievance and a fatal discouragement to their creed, that every candidate for ordination was obliged to travel 6,000 miles before he could become qualified to conduct public worship in his own village. By a very low computation, it was said, this necessity alone, imposed on each candidate an expenditure of 100*l*., and out of fifty-two candidates who, in 1767, crossed the sea from the Northern colonies, no less than ten had died on the voyage or from its results.[1] More than once the propriety of sending out one or two bishops to the colonies had been discussed, but the notion always produced such a storm of indignation in New England that it was speedily abandoned. It was not indeed a question on which the Ministers at all cared to provoke American opinion; and it is a curiously significant illustration of the theological indifference of the English Government that the first Anglican colonial bishop was the Bishop of Nova Scotia, who was only appointed in 1787; and that the first Anglican Indian bishop was the Bishop of Calcutta, who was appointed by the influence of Wilberforce in 1814.

It is easy to conceive how fiercely a Protestantism as jealous and sensitive as that of New England must have resented the establishment of Catholicism in Canada; and in these colonies at least the political influence exercised by the clergy was very great. Public meetings were held in the churches. Proclamations were read from the pulpit. The Episcopalianism of a large proportion of the Government officers contributed perceptibly to their unpopularity; political preaching was almost universal, and the sermons of Mayhew, Chauncey, and Samuel Cooper had much influence in stimulating resistance. The few clergymen who abstained from introducing politics into the pulpit were looked upon with great suspicion or dislike.[2] The fast days which were held in every important crisis diffused, intensified,

---

[1] Petition to Lord Hillsborough from the Anglican clergy of New York and New Jersey, Oct. 12, 1771. MSS. Record Office.

[2] This was one of the charges brought against Dr. Byles, a well-known Tory clergyman in Boston. He answered his accusers: 'I do not understand politics, and you all do. ... You have politics all the week: pray let one day in seven be devoted to religion. ... Give me any subject

and consecrated the spirit of resistance, and gave a semi-religious tone to the whole movement. There were a few prominent leaders, indeed, who were of a different character. Otis lamented bitterly that the profession of a saintly piety was in New England the best means of obtaining political power. Franklin was intensely secular in the character of his mind, and his theology was confined to an admiration for the pure moral teaching of the Evangelists, while Jefferson sympathised with the freethinkers of France; but such ways of thinking were not common in America, and the fervid Puritanism of New England had a very important bearing upon the character of the struggle.

It was soon evident that the Americans were not intimidated by the Coercion Acts, and that the hope of the Ministry that resistance would be confined to Massachusetts, and perhaps to Boston, was wholly deceptive. The closing of the port of Boston took place on the 1st of June, 1774, but before that time the sympathies of the other colonies had been clearly shown. The Assembly of Virginia, which was in session when the news of the intended measure arrived, of its own authority appointed the 1st of June to be set apart as a day of fasting, prayer, and humiliation, 'to implore the Divine interposition to avert the heavy calamity which threatened destruction to their civil rights, with the evils of civil war, and to give one heart and one mind to the people firmly to oppose every injury to the American rights.' The Governor at once dissolved the House, but its members reassembled, drew up a declaration expressing warm sympathy with Boston, and called upon all the colonies to support it. The example was speedily followed. Subscriptions poured in for the relief of the Boston poor who were thrown out of employment by the closing of the port. Virginia, South Carolina, and Maryland sent great quantities of corn and rice. Salem and Marblehead, which were expected to grow rich by the ruin of Boston, offered the Boston merchants the free use of their harbours, wharfs, and warehouses. Provincial, town, and

---

to preach on of more consequence than the truths I bring to you, and I will preach on it next Sabbath.' Lafayette mentions how, 'ayant taxé un ministre anglican de ne parler que du ciel,' he was much gratified on the following Sunday by hearing from the pulpit a denunciation of the 'execrable house of Hanover.'—*Mém. de Lafayette*, i. 38. See too on the use made of days of 'fasting and prayer' for the purpose of exciting the revolutionary feeling, Tucker's *Life of Jefferson*, i. 54, 55.

county meetings were held in every colony encouraging Boston to resist, and the 1st of June was generally observed throughout America as a day of fasting and prayer. The Assembly of Massachusetts was convoked by the new Governor, and soon after removed from Boston to Salem, and it showed its feelings by calling on him to appoint a day of general fasting and prayer, by recommending the assembly of a congress of representatives of all the colonies to take measures for the security of colonial liberty, by accusing the British Government of an evident design to destroy the free constitutions of America, and to erect in their place systems of tyranny and arbitrary sway, and by calling upon their constituents to obstruct the Government by every means in their power, and to give up every kind of intercourse with England till their wrongs were redressed. As was expected in Boston, the Assembly was at once dissolved, but the movement of resistance was unchecked. An attempt made by some loyalists to procure a resolution from a public meeting in favour of paying the East India Company for the tea which had been destroyed was defeated by a great majority. The system of committees charged in every district with organising resistance and keeping up correspondence between the colonies, which had been found so efficient in 1765 and 1767, was revived; the press and the pulpit all over America called on the people to unite; and a 'solemn league and covenant' was formed, binding the subscribers to abstain from all commercial intercourse with Great Britain till the obnoxious Acts were repealed. It was agreed that all delinquents should be held up in the newspapers to popular vengeance, and on the 5th of September, 1774, the delegates of the twelve States assembled in Congress at Philadelphia.

'The die is now cast,' wrote the King at this time; 'the colonies must either submit or triumph.' The war did not indeed yet break out, but both sides were rapidly preparing. Fresh ships of war and fresh troops were sent to Boston. General Gage fortified the neck of land which connected it with the continent; he took possession, amid fierce demonstrations of popular indignation, of the gunpowder in some of the arsenals of New England; he issued a proclamation describing the new 'league and covenant' as 'an illegal and traitorous combination,' but he was unable to obtain any prosecution. He tried to erect new barracks in Boston, but found it almost impossible to obtain builders. Most of the new councillors appointed by the Crown were obliged by mob violence to resign their posts, and the few who accepted the appointment were held up to execration as enemies of their country. Riots and outrages were of almost daily occurrence. Conspicuous Tories were tarred and feathered, or placed astride of rails, and carried in triumph through the streets of the chief towns. One man was fastened in the body of a dead ox which he had bought from an obnoxious loyalist, and thus carted for several miles between Plymouth and Kingston. Another was nearly suffocated by being confined in a room with a fire, while the chimney and all other apertures were carefully closed. Juries summoned under the new regulations refused to be sworn. Judges who accepted salaries from the Crown were prevented by armed mobs from going to their courts. Most of the courts of justice in Massachusetts were forcibly closed, and the judges of the Supreme Court informed General Gage that it was totally impossible for them to administer justice in the province, that no jurors could be obtained, and that the troops were altogether insufficient for their protection.

Conspicuous politicians, even members of the Congress, are said to have led the mobs. In Berkshire the mob actually forced the judges from the bench and shut up the court-house. At Worcester, about 5,000 persons, a large proportion of them being armed, having formed themselves in two files, compelled the judges, sheriffs, and gentlemen of the bar to pass between them with bare heads, and at least thirty times to read a paper promising to hold no courts under the new Acts of Parliament. At Springfield the judges and sheriffs were treated with the same ignominy. At Westminster, in the province of New York, the court-house and jail were captured by the mob, and the judges, sheriffs, and many loyalist inhabitants were locked up in prison. A judge in the same province had the courage to commit to prison a man who was employed in disarming the loyalists. The prisoner was at once rescued, and the judge carried, tarred and feathered, five or six miles through the country.[1] Great

[1] Moore's *Diary of the American Revolution*, vol. i. 37–52, 138. This

numbers of loyalists were driven from their estates or their business; and except under the very guns of British soldiers, they could find no safety in New England. As the Crown possessed scarcely any patronage in the colonies to reward its friends, all but the most courageous and devoted were reduced to silence, or hastened to identify themselves with the popular cause. 'Are not the bands of society,' wrote a very able loyalist at this time, 'cast asunder, and the sanctions that hold man to man trampled upon? Can any of us recover debts, or obtain compensation for an injury, by law? Are not many persons whom we once respected and revered driven from their homes and families, and forced to fly to the army for protection, for no other reason but their having accepted commissions under our King? Is not civil government dissolved? . . . What kind of offence is it for a number of men to assemble armed, and forcibly to obstruct the course of justice, even to prevent the King's courts from being held at their stated terms; to seize upon the King's provincial revenue, I mean the moneys collected by virtue of grants made to his Majesty for the support of his government within this province; to assemble without being called by authority, and to pass Governmental Acts; to take the militia out of the hands of the King's representative, or to form a new militia; to raise men and appoint officers for a public purpose without the order or permission of the King or his representative, or to take arms and march with a professed design of opposing the King's troops?' 'Committees not known in law . . . frequently elect themselves into a tribunal, where the same persons are at once legislator, accusers, witnesses, judges, and jurors, and the mob the executioners. The accused has no day in court, and the execution of the sentence is the first notice he receives. This is the channel through which liberty matters have been chiefly conducted the summer and fall past. . . . It is chiefly owing to these committees that so many respectable persons have been abused and forced to sign recantations and resignations; that so many persons, to avoid such reiterated

very interesting book is a collection of extracts from the contemporary newspapers on both sides of the question, and gives a vivid picture of the social condition of the colonies. See too Force's *American Archives* (4th series), i. 747, 748, 767–769, 795, 1260–1263.

insults as are more to be deprecated by a man of sentiment than death itself, have been obliged to quit their houses, families, and business, and fly to the army for protection; that husband has been separated from wife, father from son, brother from brother, the sweet intercourse of conjugal and natural affection interrupted, and the unfortunate refugee forced to abandon all the comforts of domestic life.'[1] Even in cases which had little or no connection with politics, mob violence was almost uncontrolled. Thus a custom-house officer named Malcolm, who in a street riot had struck or threatened to strike with a cutlass a person who insulted him, was dragged out of his house by the mob, stripped, tarred and feathered, then carted for several hours during an intense frost, and finally scourged, with a halter round his neck, through the streets of Boston, and all this was done in the presence of thousands of spectators, and with the most absolute impunity. At Marblehead the mob, believing that an hospital erected for the purpose of inoculation was spreading contagion, burnt it to the ground, and for several days the whole town was in their undisputed possession.[2]

Among many graver matters, an amusing indignation was about this time excited by a proclamation which General Gage, according to a usual custom, issued 'for the encouragement of piety and virtue, and the prevention of vice, profaneness, and immorality.' The General knew that the Boston preachers made it a favourite theme that the presence of British soldiers was fatal to the purity of New England morals, and he now for the first time inserted 'hypocrisy' in the list of the vices against which the people were warned. The vehemence with which this was resented as a studied insult to the clergy, convinced many impartial persons that the insinuation was not wholly undeserved.

---

[1] *Massachusettensis, or Letters on the Present Troubles of Massachusetts Bay,* Letters I, IV.
[2] Ibid. Letter III. These very remarkable letters were written by Leonard, one of his Majesty's Council. The author was himself driven from his house in Taunton, and bullets were fired into it.—Moore's *Diary,* i. 38. Among the numerous persons who were at this time driven into exile was Dr. Cooper, President of King's College in New York, and the most distinguished Episcopalian in America. He had written something on the loyalist side, and accordingly received a letter threatening his life, and was soon after compelled to fly half-dressed over the college fence, to take refuge in an English ship of war, and ultimately in England.— *Documents relating to the Colonial History of New York,* viii. 297.

The people were in the meantime rapidly arming. Guns were collected from all sides, the militia was assiduously drilled, and its organisation was improved; bodies of volunteers called 'minute men' were formed, who were bound to rise to arms at the shortest notice, and New England had all the aspect of a country at war. A false alarm was spread abroad—possibly in order to ascertain the number who would rise in case of insurrection—that the British troops and vessels were firing upon Boston, and in a few hours no less than 30,000 men from Massachusetts and Connecticut are said to have been in arms. The collision was happily averted, but the episode gave the popular party new confidence in their strength, and over the greater part of New England their ascendency was undisputed. The new seat of government at Salem was abandoned; the new councillors, and all or nearly all the officers connected with the revenue, fled for safety to Boston, and although the troops were not openly resisted they experienced on every side the animosity of the people. Farmers refused to sell them provisions. Straw which they had purchased was burnt. Carts with wood were overturned, boats with bricks were sunk, when it was discovered that they were for the King's service, and at the same time colonial agents were industriously tempting individual soldiers to desert.

The Congress which met in Philadelphia, though it had no legal authority, was obeyed as the supreme power in America. It consisted of delegates selected by the Provincial Assemblies which then were sitting, and, in cases where the Governor had refused to convoke them, by Provincial Congresses chosen by the people for that purpose. Except Georgia, all the colonies which existed before the peace of 1763 were represented. The number of delegates varied according to the magnitude of the States, but after much discussion it was determined that no colony should count for more than one in voting. The Congress in the first place expressed its full and unqualified approbation of the conduct of the inhabitants of Boston, exhorted them to continue unflinching in their opposition to the invasion of their Constitution, and invited the other colonies to contribute liberally to their assistance. It next drew up a series of extremely able State papers defining and enforcing the position of the Americans. After long debate and violent difference of opinion, it was resolved not to treat the commercial restrictions as a grievance, or to deny the general legislative authority of Parliament over America. Franklin, as we have seen, had recently contended that the colonies, though subject to the King, were by right wholly independent of the Parliament, and this doctrine had been formally maintained by the Assembly of Massachusetts in its addresses of 1773, but it was not the contention of the original opponents of the Stamp Act,[1] and it was not generally accepted in the other colonies.[2] The Congress, therefore, while asserting in the strongest terms the exclusive right of the provincial legislatures in all cases of taxation and internal policy, at last consented to add these remarkable words in their declaration of rights: 'From the necessity of the case and in regard to the mutual interests of both countries, we cheerfully consent to the operation of such Acts of the British Parliament as are *bonâ fide* restrained to the regulation of our external commerce for the purpose of securing the commercial advantages of the whole Empire to the mother-country and the commercial benefits of its respective members.' They enumerated, however, a long series of Acts carried during the present reign which were violations of their liberty, and which must be repealed if the two countries were to continue in amity. Among them were

---

[1] Even Otis, who had been the first to denounce the commercial restrictions as unconstitutional, and who repudiated writs of assistance as the creation of the English Parliament, maintained—not very consistently—that Parliament had a real legislative authority in America, and he deprecated in the strongest language any measure tending to separation. 'The supreme Legislative,' he wrote in 1765, 'represents the whole society or community, as well the dominions as the realm; and this is the true reason why the dominions are justly bound by such Acts of Parliament as name them. This is implied in the idea of a supreme sovereign power; and if the Parliament had not such authority the colonies would be independent, which none but rebels, fools, or madmen will contend for.'—*Answer to the Halifax Libel*, p. 16.

The same doctrine is laid down with equal emphasis in the *Farmer's Letters*: 'The Parliament unquestionably possesses a legal authority to regulate the trade of Great Britain and all its colonies. Such an authority is essential to the relation between a mother-country and its colonies.... We are but parts of a whole, and therefore there must exist a power somewhere to preside and preserve the connection in due order. This power is lodged in the Parliament.'—Letter II.

[2] Story's *Constitution of the United States*, i. 178, 179. Jefferson says that about the middle of 1774 he maintained that the relations of England to the colonies were similar to those of England with Scotland before the Union, or of England with Hanover at present, but he only found one person to agree with him.—*Autobiography*.

the Acts closing the harbour of Boston, changing the constitution of Massachusetts, establishing despotic government and the Popish religion in Canada, interfering with the right of public meeting, quartering British troops upon the colonists, and above all imposing taxation by Imperial authority.

They pronounced it unnecessary to maintain a standing army in the colonies in time of peace, and illegal to do so without the consent of the local legislatures. They complained also that their assemblies had been arbitrarily dissolved, that their governors had conspired against their liberty, and that in several cases they had been deprived of their constitutional right of trial by jury or at least by a 'jury of the vicinage.' The Court of Admiralty tried revenue cases without a jury, and the governor had power to send for trial out of the colony those who were accused of treason, of destroying the King's ships or naval stores, or of homicide committed in suppressing riot or rebellion. All this mass of legislation Parliament must speedily and absolutely repeal. For the present, however, the Congress resolved to resort only to peaceful means, and their weapon was a rigid non-importation, non-consumption, and non-exportation agreement, which was to be imposed by their authority upon all the colonies they represented and was to continue until their grievances had been fully redressed.

From December 1 following, the members of the Congress bound themselves and their constituents to import no goods from Great Britain, to purchase no slave imported after that date and no tea imported on account of the East India Company, and to extend the same prohibition to the chief products of the British plantations, to the wines of Madeira and the West India islands which were unloaded to pay duty in England, and to foreign indigo. On September 10, 1775, if the grievances were not yet redressed a new series of measures were to come into force, and no commodity whatever was to be exported from America to Great Britain, Ireland, or the West Indies, except rice to Europe; committees were to be appointed in every town and county to observe the conduct of all persons touching this association, and to publish in the 'Gazette' the name of anyone who had violated it; and all dealings with such persons and with any portion of the colonies which refused to join the association were forbidden. At the same time the Congress agreed for themselves and their constituents to do the utmost in their power to encourage frugality and promote manufactures, to suppress or suspend every form of gambling and expensive amusement, to abandon the custom of wearing any other mourning than a black ribbon or necklace for the dead, and to diminish the expenditure at funerals.

In addition to these measures, they issued very powerful addresses to the King and to the people of England professing their full loyalty to the Crown, but enumerating their grievances in emphatic terms. In the address to the people of England they skilfully appealed to the strong anti-Catholic feeling of the nation, denying the competence of the Legislature ' to establish a religion fraught with sanguinary and impious tenets,' ' a religion that has deluged your island in blood, and dispersed impiety, bigotry, persecution, murder, and rebellion through every part of the world;' and they predicted that if the Ministers succeeded in their designs, 'the taxes from America, the wealth and, we may add, the men, and particularly the Roman Catholics of this vast continent, will be in their power' to enslave the people of Great Britain. Their own attachment to Great Britain they emphatically affirmed. 'You have been told,' they said, ' that we are seditious, impatient of government, and desirous of independency. Be assured that these are not facts but calumnies. . . . Place us in the same situation that we were at the close of the last war, and our former harmony will be restored.' At the same time, in an ingenious address to the Canadians they endeavoured to alienate them from England, to persuade them that they were both oppressed, deceived, and insulted by the present Ministers, and to induce them to join with the other colonies in vindicating their common freedom. Difference of religion, they maintained, could be no bar to cooperation. 'We are too well acquainted,' they said, ' with the liberality of sentiment distinguishing your nation to imagine that difference of religion will prejudice you against a hearty amity with us,' and they referred to the example of the Swiss cantons, where Protestant and Catholic combined with the utmost concord to vindicate and guard their political liberty. Having issued these addresses, the Congress dissolved itself in less than eight weeks; but it determined that unless grievances were first redressed, another Congress should meet at Philadelphia on May 10 following, and it recommended all the colonies to choose deputies as soon as possible.[1]

Such were the proceedings of this memorable body, which laid the foundation of American independence. Perhaps the most perplexing question raised by its proceedings is the degree of sincerity that can be ascribed to the disclaimer of all wish for separation. That a considerable party in New England anticipated and desired an open breach with England appears to me undoubted, but it is equally certain that many of the leading agents in the Revolution expressed even to the last moment a strong desire to remain united to England. It was in August 1774, when the Americans were busily arming themselves for the struggle, that Franklin assured Chatham that there was no desire for independence in the colonies.[2] John Adams, who had not, like Franklin, the excuse of absence from his native country, wrote in March 1775, as I conceive, very untruly, of the people of Massachusetts, 'that there are any that pant after independence is the greatest slander on the province.' Jefferson declared that before the Declaration of Independence he had never heard a whisper of disposition to separate from Great Britain; and Washington himself, in the October of 1774, denied in the strongest terms that there was any wish for independence in any province in America.[3]

The truth seems to be that the more distinguished Americans were quite resolved to appeal to the sword rather than submit to parliamentary taxation and to the other oppressive laws that were complained of, but if they could restore the relations to the mother-country which subsisted before the Stamp Act, they had no desire whatever to sever the connection. In 1774 and during the greater part of 1775 very few Americans wished

---

[1] *Journal of the Proceedings of the Congress held at Philadelphia, Sept.* 1774. See too the account of the debates in Adams's *Diary.*

[2] He said to Chatham that, 'having more than once travelled almost from one end of the continent to the other, and kept a great variety of company—eating, drinking, and conversing with them freely, I have never heard in any conversation, from any person, drunk or sober, the least expression of a wish for a separation, or hint that such a thing would be advantageous to America.'—*Negotiations in London.* Franklin's *Works,* v. 7.

[3] See on this subject, Washington's *Works,* ii. 401, 496–502.

for independence, and long after this period many of those who took an active part in the Revolution would gladly have restored the connection if they could have done so on terms which they considered compatible with their freedom. The instructions of the chief colonies to their delegates in Congress are on this subject very unequivocal. Thus New Hampshire instructed its delegates to endeavour 'to restore that peace, harmony, and mutual confidence which once happily subsisted between the parent country and her colonies.' Massachusetts spoke of 'the restoration of union and harmony between Great Britain and the colonies most ardently desired by all good men.' Pennsylvania enjoined its representatives to aim not only at the redress of American grievances and the definition of American rights, but also at the establishment of 'that union and harmony between Great Britain and her colonies which is indispensably necessary to the welfare and the happiness of both.' Virginia aspired after 'the return of that harmony and union so beneficial to the whole Empire and so ardently desired by all British America,' and North and South Carolina adopted a similar language.[1] In 1775 the Convention of South Carolina assured their new governor that they adhered to the British Crown, though they had taken arms against British tyranny. The Virginian Convention in the same year declared 'before God and the world' that they bore their faith to the King, and would disband their forces whenever the liberties of America were restored; the Assembly of New Jersey, while their State was in open rebellion, rebuked their governor for supposing the Americans to be aiming at national independence;[2] and, lastly, the Provincial Congress of New York, when congratulating Washington on his appointment as commander-in-chief of the insurgent force, took care to add their assurance 'that whenever this important contest shall be decided by that fondest wish of each American soul, an accommodation with our mother-country, you will cheerfully resign the deposit committed into your hands.'[3]

Many other public documents might be cited showing that

[1] *Journal of the Proceedings of the Congress held at Philadelphia, Sept.* 5, 1774.
[2] See other instances in Grahame, iv. 392, 395.
[3] Ramsay, i. 220.

the Americans took up arms to redress grievances and not to establish independence, and that it was only very slowly and reluctantly that they became familiarised with the idea of a complete separation from England. Nor is there, I think, any reason to believe that this language was substantially untrue. In March 1776 General Reed, in confidential letters to Washington, lamented that the public mind in Virginia was violently opposed to the idea of independence.[1] Galloway, one of the ablest of the Pennyslvanian loyalists, afterwards expressed his belief before a committee of the House of Commons that at the time when the Americans took up arms less than a fifth part of them 'had independence in view;'[2] and John Adams when an old man related how, when he first went to the Congress at Philadelphia, the leading conspirators in that town said to him, 'You must not utter the word independence or give the least hint or insinuation of the idea either in congress or any private conversation; if you do you are undone, for the idea of independence is as unpopular in Pennsylvania and in all the Middle and Southern States as the Stamp Act itself.'[3] Adams tells how, when a letter which he had written in 1775 advocating independence was intercepted and published, he was 'avoided like a man infected with the leprosy,' and 'walked the streets of Philadelphia in solitude, borne down by the weight of care and unpopularity.'[4] Few men contributed more to hasten the separation between the two countries, yet he afterwards wrote these remarkable words, 'For my own part there was not a moment during the Revolution when I would not have given everything I possessed for a restoration to the state of things before the contest began, provided we could have a sufficient security for its continuance.'[5]

In 1774 also, it is evident that a large proportion of the most ardent patriots imagined that redress could be obtained

---

[1] March 3 and 15, 1776. See Washington's *Works*, iii. 347, 348.
[2] *Examination of Joseph Galloway*, p. 4.
[3] Adams' *Works*, ii. 512.
[4] Ibid. p. 513. In a confidential letter from New York, dated Aug. 7, 1775, Governor Tryon said: 'I should do great injustice to America were I to hold up an idea that the bulk of its inhabitants wishes an independency. I am satisfied (not to answer for our eastern neighbours) a very large majority, particularly in this province, are utter enemies to such a principle.'—*Documents relating to the Colonial History of New York*, viii. 603.
[5] See Washington's *Works*, ii. 501

without actual fighting, and that the Legislature of the greatest country in the world would repeal no less than eleven recent Acts of Parliament in obedience to a mere threat of resistance. They knew that numerous urgent petitions in favour of conciliation had been presented by English merchants, and that many of the most conspicuous English politicans, including Chatham, Camden, Shelburne, Conway, Barré, and Burke, were on their side, and they overrated greatly the strength of their friends, and especially the effect of the non-importation agreements upon English prosperity. 'England,' it was argued in the Congress, 'is already taxed as much as she can bear. She is compelled to raise ten millions in time of peace. Her whole foreign trade is but four and half millions, while the value of the importations to the colonies is probably little, if at all, less than three millions.' 'A total non-importation and non-exportation to Great Britain and the West Indies must produce a national bankruptcy in a very short space of time.'[1] Richard Henry Lee, one of the most prominent Virginian politicians, was so confident in the effect of non-importation that he declared himself 'absolutely certain that the same ship which carries home the resolution will bring back the redress.'[2] Washington was more doubtful, but he expressed his opinion privately that by a non-importation and a non-exportation agreement combined, America would win the day, though one alone would be insufficient. John Adams, Hawley, and Patrick Henry, however, were of opinion that the proceedings of the Congress were very useful in uniting the colonies, but that they were quite insufficient to coerce Great Britain, and that the question must ultimately be decided by the sword.[3]

In England, on the other hand, there was to the very last a great disbelief in the reality of a colonial union. Nearly all the rumours of violence and insubordination had come from two or three of the New England States and from Virginia, and it was supposed that in the moment of crisis the other States would hold aloof, and that even in the insurgent colonies a large party of active loyalists could be fully counted on.

[1] Speech of Chase. Adams' *Works*, ii. 383.
[2] Ibid. ii. 362.
[3] Tudor's *Life of Otis*, pp. 256, 257.

Provincial governors being surrounded by such men were naturally inclined to underrate the capacity or the sincerity of their opponents, and they thought that the wild talk of lawyers and demagogues and the demonstrations of mob violence would speedily collapse before firm action. Hutchinson, who lived in the centre of the disaffection, and who ought to have known the New England character as well as any man, predicted that the people of America would not attempt to resist a British army, and that if they did a few troops would be sufficient to quell them.[1] His opinion appears to have had considerable weight with George III., and greatly strengthened him in his determination to coerce.[2] General Gage for some time took the same view. He assured the King in the beginning of 1774 that the Americans 'will be lions while we are lambs, but if we take the resolute part they will undoubtedly prove very meek,' and he thought that 'four regiments, intended to relieve as many regiments in America, if sent to Boston' would be 'sufficient to prevent any disturbance.'[3] General Carleton, it is true, the Governor of Canada, and Tryon, the Governor of New York, though they had no doubt of the ability of England to crush insurrection, warned the Government that the task would be a very serious one, and would require much time and large armies,[4] but the prevailing English opinion was that any armed movement could be easily repressed. Soldiers spoke of the Americans with professional arrogance, as if volunteers and militias organised by skilful and experienced officers, consisting of men who were accustomed from childhood to the use of arms, and fighting with every advantage of numbers and situation, were likely to be as helpless before regular troops as a Middlesex mob. Unfortunately, this ignorant boasting was not confined to the mess-room, and Lord Sandwich, in March 1775, expressed the prevailing infatuation with reckless insolence in the House of Lords. He described the Americans as 'raw, undisciplined, cowardly men.' He said that the more they produced in the field, the easier would be their conquest. He

---

[1] Tudor's *Life of Otis*, p. 428.
[2] *Correspondence of George III. with Lord North*, vol. i. pp. 194, 195.
[3] Ibid. p. 164.
[4] See their opinions in Tudor's *Life of Otis*, p. 428.

accused them of having shown egregious cowardice at the siege of Louisburg, and he predicted that they would take to flight at the very sound of a cannon.¹ Whether, under the most favourable circumstances, the subjugation would produce any advantages commensurate with the cost; whether, assuming that England had conquered her colonies, she could permanently hold them contrary to their will; and whether other nations were likely to remain passive during the struggle, were questions which appear to have scarcely occurred to the ordinary English mind.

It was, however, quite true that in America there was much difference of opinion, and that large bodies were only dragged with extreme reluctance into war. In New York a powerful and wealthy party sympathised strongly with the Government, and they succeeded in June 1775 in inducing their Assembly to refuse its approbation to the proceedings of the Congress.² Even in New England a few meetings were held repudiating the proceedings at Philadelphia.³ Three out of the four delegates of South Carolina in the Congress declined to sign the non-importation agreements until a provision had been made to permit the exportation of rice to Europe.⁴ The Pennsylvanian Quakers recoiled with horror from the prospect of war, and the Convention of the province gave instructions to their delegates in the Congress, which were eminently marked by wisdom and moderation. They desired that England should repeal absolutely the obnoxious Acts; but, in order that such a measure should not be inconsistent with her dignity, they recommended an indemnity to the East India Company, promised obedience to the Act of Navigation, disowned with abhorrence all idea of independence, and declared their willingness of their own accord to settle an annual revenue on the King, subject to the approbation of Parliament. Virginia had been very prominent in hurrying the colonies into war, and its great orator, Patrick Henry, exerted all his powers in stimu-

¹ *Parl. Hist.* xviii. 446, 447. See too the very similar speech of Rigby. Walpole's *Last Journals,* i. 481.
² Ramsay, i. 143. See, on the remarkable loyalty shown by the New York Assembly at this time, a striking letter of Lieutenant-Governor Colden to Lord Dartmouth (Feb. 1, 1775) in the *Documents relating to the Colonial History of New York,* viii. 531, 532.
³ Adolphus, ii. 211.
⁴ Adams, ii. 385.

lating resistance; but even Virginia insisted, in opposition to John Adams and to other New Englanders, on limiting the list of grievances to Acts passed since 1763, in order that there might be some possibility of reconciliation.[1] Among the Episcopalians, and among the more wealthy and especially the older planters, the English party always predominated, and a large section of the mercantile class detested the measures which suspended their trade, and believed that America could not subsist without the molasses, sugar, and other products of the British dominions. There was a wide-spread dislike to the levelling principles of New England, to the arrogant, restless, and ambitious policy of its demagogues, to their manifest desire to invent or discover grievances, foment quarrels, and keep the wound open and festering.[2] There were brave and honest men in America who were proud of the great and free Empire to which they belonged, who had no desire to shrink from the burden of maintaining it, who remembered with gratitude all the English blood that had been shed around Quebec and Montreal, and who, with nothing to hope for from the Crown, were prepared to face the most brutal mob violence and the invectives of a scurrilous Press, to risk their fortunes, their reputations, and sometimes even their lives, in order to avert civil war and ultimate separation. Most of them ended their days in poverty and exile, and as the supporters of a beaten cause history has paid but a scanty tribute to their memory, but they comprised some of the best and ablest men America has ever produced, and they were contending for an ideal which was at least as worthy as that for which Washington fought. The maintenance of one free, industrial, and pacific empire, comprising the whole English race, holding the richest plains of Asia in subjection, blending all that was most venerable in an ancient civilisation with the redundant energies of a youthful society, and destined in a few generations to outstrip every competitor and acquire an indisputable ascendency on the globe, may have been a dream, but it was at least a noble one, and there were Americans who were prepared to make any personal sacrifices rather than assist in destroying it.

[1] Adams' *Works*, ii. 384.
[2] See a graphic account of the differences in Congress in Adams' *Works*, ii. 350, 410.

Conspicuous among these politicians was Galloway, one of the ablest delegates from Pennsylvania, who saw clearly that a change in the American Constitution was necessary if England was to remain united to her colonies. He proposed that a President-General appointed by the Crown should be placed over the whole group of American colonies; that a Grand Council, competent to tax the colonies and to legislate on all matters relating to more colonies than one, should be elected by the Provincial Assemblies; that Parliament should have the right of revising the Acts of this Grand Council, and that the Council should have the right of negative upon any parliamentary measure relating to the colonies.[1] The proposal at first met with considerable support in the Congress, and it was finally defeated by a majority of only one vote. Dickinson, whose 'Farmer's Letters' had been one of the ablest statements of the American case, shrank with horror from the idea of rebellion. He bitterly accused John Adams and the other New Englanders of opposing all measures of reconciliation, and declared that he and his friends would no longer co-operate with them, but would carry on the opposition in their own way.[2] The remarkable eloquence and the touching and manifest earnestness of the letters which appeared at Boston under the signature of 'Massachusettensis,' urging the people to shrink from the great calamity of civil war, had for a time some influence upon opinion. As usual, however, in such a crisis, the more energetic and determined men directed the movement, and the fierce spirit of New England substantially triumphed over all opposition. The Congress agreed, it is true, to profess its loyalty, to petition the King, and to limit its grievances to measures carried since 1763, but it offered no basis of compromise; it demanded only an unqualified submission, and it enumerated so long a list of laws that must be repealed that it was quite impossible that Parliament could comply. General Gage deemed the aspect of affairs so threatening that he suspended by proclamation the writs which he had issued summoning the Assembly of Massachusetts to meet at Salem in October 1774. But a provincial congress was at once convened. It was obeyed as if it had been

[1] Adams' *Works*, ii. 387–389. Galloway's *Examination*, pp. 47–49.
[2] Adams' *Works*, ii. 410, 419.

a regular branch of the Legislature, and it proceeded to organise the revolution. Measures were taken for enlisting soldiers for the defence of the province; general officers were selected. It was resolved to enroll as speedily as possible an army of 12,000 men within the province, and Rhode Island, New Hampshire, and Connecticut were asked to join to raise the number of men to 20,000. A committee was at the same time formed for corresponding with the people of Canada, and a circular was sent round to all the New England clergy asking them to use their influence in the cause.[1]

Before the end of the year intelligence arrived that a proclamation had been issued in England forbidding the exportation of military stores, and it was at once responded to by open violence. In Rhode Island, by order of the Provincial Assembly, forty cannon with a large amount of ammunition were removed from Fort George, which defended the harbour, and placed under a colonial guard at Providence. The captain of a King's ship which was stationed off the province demanded an explanation. The Governor replied that the cannon had been removed lest the King's officers should seize them, and that they would be used against any enemy of the colony. In New Hampshire a small fort called William and Mary, garrisoned by one officer and five private soldiers, was surprised and captured by a large body of armed colonists, and the military stores which it contained were carried away. Mills for manufacturing gunpowder and arms were set up in several provinces, and immediate orders were given for casting sixty heavy cannon.

Though no blood had yet been shed, it is no exaggeration to say that the war had already begun, and in England the indignation rose fierce and high. Parliament had been unexpectedly dissolved, and the new Parliament met on November 30, 1774, but no serious measure relating to America was taken till January 1775, when the House reassembled after the Christmas vacation. The Ministers had a large majority, and even apart from party interest the genuine feeling of both Houses ran strongly against the Americans. Yet at no previous period were they more powerfully defended. I have already noticed that Chatham, having returned to active politics after his long

[1] Ramsay, i. 130.

illness in 1774, had completely identified himself with the American cause, and had advocated with all his eloquence measures of conciliation. He reiterated on every occasion his old opinion that self-taxation is the essential condition of political freedom, described the conduct of the British Legislature in establishing Catholicism in Canada as not less outrageous than if it had repealed the Great Charter or the Bill of Rights,[1] and moved an address to the King praying that he would as soon as possible, 'in order to open the way towards a happy settlement of the dangerous troubles in America,' withdraw the British troops stationed in Boston. In the course of his speech he represented the question of American taxation as the root-cause of the whole division, and maintained that the only real basis of conciliation was to be found in a distinct recognition of the principle that 'taxation is theirs, and commercial regulation ours;' that England has a supreme right of regulating the commerce and navigation of America, and that the Americans have an inalienable right to their own property. He fully justified their resistance, predicted that all attempts to coerce them would fail, and eulogised the Congress at Philadelphia as worthy of the greatest periods of antiquity. Only eighteen peers voted for the address, while sixty-eight opposed it.

On February 1 he reappeared with an elaborate Bill for settling the troubles in America. It asserted in strong terms the right of Parliament to bind the colonies in all matters of imperial concern, and especially in all matters of commerce and navigation. It pronounced the new colonial doctrine that the Crown had no right to send British soldiers to the colonies without the assent of the Provincial Assemblies, dangerous and unconstitutional in the highest degree, but at the same time it recognised the sole right of the colonists to tax themselves, guaranteed the inviolability of their charters, and made the tenure of their judges the same as in England. It proposed to make the Congress which had met at Philadelphia an official and permanent body, and asked it to make a free grant for imperial purposes. England, in return, was to reduce the Admiralty Courts to their ancient limits, and to suspend for

---

[1] *Chatham Correspondence,* iv. 352.

the present the different Acts complained of by the colonists. The Bill was not even admitted to a second reading.

Several other propositions tending towards conciliation were made in this session. On March 22, 1775, Burke, in one of his greatest speeches, moved a series of resolutions recommending a repeal of the recent Acts complained of in America, reforming the Admiralty Court and the position of the judges, and leaving American taxation to the American Assemblies, without touching upon any question of abstract right. A few days later, Hartley moved a resolution calling upon the Government to make requisitions to the colonial Assemblies to provide of their own authority for their own defence; and Lord Camden in the House of Lords and Sir G. Savile in the House of Commons endeavoured to obtain a repeal of the Quebec Act. All these attempts, however, were defeated by enormous majorities. The petition of Congress to the King was referred to Parliament, which refused to receive it, and Franklin, after vain efforts to effect a reconciliation, returned from England to America. The Legislature of New York, separating from the other colonies, made a supreme effort to heal the wound by a remonstrance which was presented by Burke on May 15. Though strongly asserting the sole right of the colonies to tax themselves, and complaining of the many recent Acts inconsistent with their freedom, it was drawn up in terms that were studiously moderate and respectful. It disclaimed 'the most distant desire of independence of the parent kingdom.' It acknowledged fully the general superintending power of the English Parliament, and its right 'to regulate the trade of the colonies, so as to make it subservient to the interest of the mother-country,' and it expressed the readiness of New York to bear its 'full proportion of aids to the Crown for the public service,' though it made no allusion to the project of supporting an American army. The Government, however, induced the House of Commons to refuse to receive it, on the ground that it denied the complete legislative authority of Parliament in the colonies as it had been defined by the Declaratory Act.

Parliament at the same time took stringent measures to enforce obedience. It pronounced Massachusetts in a state of rebellion, and promised to lend the Ministers every aid in subjugating it. It voted about 6,000 additional men for the land and sea service; it answered the non-importation and non-exportation agreements of the colonies by an Act restraining the New England States from all trade with Great Britain, Ireland, and the West Indies, and from all participation in the Newfoundland fisheries, and it soon after, on the arrival of fresh intelligence from America, extended the same disabilities to Pennsylvania, New Jersey, Maryland, Virginia, and South Carolina. It was also resolved that the British force in Boston should be at once raised to 10,000 men, which it was vainly thought would be sufficient to enforce obedience.

At the same time North was careful to announce that these coercive measures would at once cease upon the submission of the colonies, and on February 20, 1775, he had, to the great surprise of Parliament, himself introduced a conciliatory resolution which was very unpalatable to many of his followers and very inconsistent with some of his own earlier speeches, but by which he hoped, if not to appease, at least to divide the Americans. His proposition was, that if and as long as any colony thought fit of its own accord to make such a contribution to the common defence of the Empire, and such a fixed provision for the support of the civil government and administration of justice, as met the approbation of Parliament, it should be exempted from all imperial taxation for the purpose of revenue.

The reception of this conciliatory measure was very remarkable. Hitherto Lord North had guided the House with an almost absolute sway, and on American questions the Opposition seldom could count upon 90 votes, while the Ministers had usually about 260. The disclosure, however, of the conciliatory resolution produced an immediate revolt in the ministerial ranks. Six times Lord North rose in vain efforts to appease the storm. The King's friends denounced him as betraying the cause. The Bedford faction was expected every moment to fly into open rebellion, and Chatham states that for about two hours it was the prevailing belief in the House of Commons that the Minister would be left in a small minority. The storm, however, had a sudden and most significant ending. Sir Gilbert Elliot, who was known to be in the intimate confidence of the King, declared for the Bill, and the old majority speedily rallied around the Minister.[1]

At an earlier stage of the dispute this resolution might have been accepted as a reasonable compromise, but in the midst of the coercive measures that had been adopted it pleased no one. Burke and the Whig party denounced it as not stating what sum the colonists were expected to pay, leaving them to bid against one another, and to bargain with the mother-country, and in the meantime holding them in duress with fleets and armies, like prisoners who had not yet paid their ransom. Barré assailed it with great bitterness, as intended for no other object than to excite divisions in America. The colonists themselves repudiated it as interfering with their absolute right of disposing as they pleased of their own property, and most later historians have treated it as wholly delusive.[2] With this view I am unable to concur. The proposition appears to me to have been a real and considerable step towards conciliation. It was accepted as such by Governor Pownall, who was one of the ablest and most moderate of the defenders of the colonies in Parliament,[3] and it was recommended to the Americans by Lord Dartmouth in language of much force and of evident sincerity. He argued that the colonies owed much of their greatness to English protection, that it was but justice that they should in their turn contribute according to their respective abilities to the common defence, and that their own welfare and interests demanded that their civil establishments should be supported with a becoming dignity. Parliament, he says, leaves each colony 'to judge of the ways and means of making due provision for these purposes, reserving to itself a discretionary power of approving or disapproving what shall be offered.' It determines nothing about the specific sum to be raised. The King trusts that adequate provision will be made by the colonies, and that it will be 'proposed in such a way as to increase or diminish according as the public burthens of this kingdom are from time to time augmented or reduced, in so far as those burthens consist of taxes and duties which are not a security

---

[1] *Chatham Correspondence*, iv. 403, 404. See too Gibbon to Holroyd, Feb. 25, *Annual Register*, 1775, pp. 95–98. Walpole's *Last Journals*, i. 463, 464.

[2] See e.g. Lord Russell's *Life of Fox*, i. 85, 86.

[3] See his very able speech, *Parl. Hist.* xviii. 322–329.

for the National Debt. By such a mode of contribution,' he adds, 'the colonies will have full security that they can never be required to tax themselves without Parliament taxing the subjects of this kingdom in a far greater proportion.' He assured them that any proposal of this nature from any colony would be received with every possible indulgence, provided it was unaccompanied by declarations inconsistent with parliamentary authority.[1]

The letter of Lord Dartmouth to the governors of the colonies was written in March. Little more than a month later the first blood was shed at Lexington. On the night of April 18, 1775, General Gage sent about 800 soldiers to capture a magazine of stores which had been collected for the use of the provincial army in the town of Concord, about eighteen miles from Boston. The road lay through the little village of Lexington, where, about five o'clock on the morning of the 19th, the advanced guard of the British found a party of sixty or seventy armed volunteers drawn up to oppose them, on a green beside the road. They refused when summoned to disperse, and the English at once fired a volley, which killed or wounded sixteen of their number. The detachment then proceeded to Concord, where it succeeded in spiking two cannon, casting into the river five hundred pounds of ball and sixty barrels of powder, and destroying a large quantity of flour, and it then prepared to return. The alarm had, however, now been given; the whole country was roused. Great bodies of yeomen and militia flocked in to the assistance of the provincials. From farmhouses and hedges and from the shelter of stone walls bullets poured upon the tired retreating troops, and a complete disaster would probably have occurred had they not been reinforced at Lexington by 900 men and two cannon under Lord Percy. As it was the British lost 65 killed, 180 wounded, and 28 made prisoners, while the American loss was less than 90 men.

The whole province was now in arms. The Massachusetts Congress at once resolved that the New England army should be raised to 30,000 men, and thousands of brave and ardent

---

[1] This letter is printed in the *Documents relating to the Colonial History of New York*, viii. 515-517. Force's *American Archives* (4th series), ii. 27, 28.

yeomen were being rapidly drilled into good soldiers. The American camp at Cambridge contained many experienced soldiers who had learnt their profession in the great French war, and very many others who in the ranks of the militia had already acquired the rudiments of military knowledge, and even when they had no previous training, the recruits were widely different from the rude peasants who filled the armies of England. As an American military writer truly said, the middle and lower classes in England, owing to the operation of the game laws and to the circumstances of their lives, were in general almost as ignorant of the use of a musket as of the use of a catapult. The New England yeomen were accustomed to firearms from their childhood; they were invariably skilful in the use of spade, hatchet, and pickaxe, so important in military operations; and their great natural quickness and the high level of intelligence which their excellent schools had produced, made it certain that they would not be long in mastering their military duties. The whole country was practically at their disposal. All who were suspected of Toryism were ordered to surrender their weapons. General Gage was blockaded in Boston, and he remained strictly on the defensive, waiting for reinforcements from England, which only arrived at the end of May. Even then, he for some time took no active measures, but contented himself with offering pardon to all insurgents who laid down their arms, except Samuel Adams and John Hancock, and with proclaiming martial law in Massachusetts. He at length, however, determined to extend his lines, so as to include and fortify a very important post, which by a strange negligence had been left hitherto unoccupied.

On a narrow peninsula to the north of Boston, but separated from it by rather less than half a mile of water, lay the little town of Charleston, behind which rose two small connected hills, which commanded a great part both of the town and harbour of Boston. Breed's Hill, which was nearest to Charleston, was about seventy-five feet, Bunker's Hill was about one hundred and ten feet, in height. The peninsula, which was little more than a mile long, was connected with the mainland by a narrow causeway. Cambridge, the head-quarters of the American forces, was by road about four miles from Bunker's

Hill, but much of the intervening space was occupied by American outposts. The possession, under these circumstances, of Bunker's Hill, was a matter of great military importance, and Gage determined to fortify it. The Americans learnt his intention, and determined to defeat it.

On the night of June 16, an American force under the command of Colonel Prescott, and accompanied by some skilful engineers and by a few field-guns, silently occupied Breed's Hill and threw up a strong redoubt before daylight revealed their presence to the British. Next day, after much unnecessary delay, a detachment under General Howe was sent from Boston to dislodge them. The Americans had in the meantime received some reinforcements from their camp, but the whole force upon the hill is said not to have exceeded 1,500 men. Most of them were inexperienced volunteers. Many of them were weary with a long night's toil, and they had been exposed for hours to a harassing though ineffectual fire from the ships in the harbour; but they were now strongly entrenched behind a redoubt and a breastwork. The British engaged on this memorable day consisted in all of between 2,000 and 3,000 regular troops, fresh from the barracks, and supported by artillery. The town of Charleston, having been occupied by some American riflemen, who poured their fire upon the English from the shelter of the houses, was burnt by order of General Howe, and its flames cast a ghastly splendour upon the scene. The English were foolishly encumbered by heavy knapsacks with three days' provisions. Instead of endeavouring to cut off the Americans by occupying the neck of land to the rear of Breed's Hill, they climbed the steep and difficult ascent in front of the battery, struggling through the long tangled grass beneath a burning sun, and exposed at every step to the fire of a sheltered enemy. The Americans waited till their assailants were within a few rods of the entrenchment, when they greeted them with a fire so deadly and so sustained that the British line twice recoiled, broken, intimidated, and disordered. The third attack was more successful. The position was carried at the point of the bayonet. The Americans were put to flight, and five out of their six cannon were taken. But the victory was dearly purchased. On the British side 1,054 men, including 89 commissioned officers, fell. The Americans only admitted a loss of 449 men; and they contended that, if they had been properly reinforced, and if their ammunition had not begun to fail, they would have held the position.[1]

The battle of Breed's, or, as it is commonly called, of Bunker's Hill, though extremely bloody in proportion to the number of men engaged, can hardly be said to present any very remarkable military character, and in a great European war it would have been almost unnoticed. Few battles, however, have had more important consequences. It roused at once the fierce instinct of combat in America, weakened seriously the only British army in New England, and dispelled for ever the almost superstitious belief in the impossibility of encountering regular troops with hastily levied volunteers. The ignoble taunts which had been directed against the Americans were for ever silenced. No one questioned the conspicuous gallantry with which the provincial troops had supported a long fire from the ships and awaited the charge of the enemy, and British soldiers had been twice driven back in disorder before their fire. From this time the best judges predicted the ultimate success of America.

On May 10 the new Continental Congress had met at Philadelphia, and it at once occupied itself, with an energy and an industry that few legislative bodies have ever equalled, in organising the war.[2] Like the former Congress, its debates were secret, and its decisions were ultimately unanimous. New York, which for a time had flinched, was now fully rallied to the cause, and before the close of the Congress, Georgia for the first time openly joined the twelve other colonies. The conciliatory offer of Lord North was emphatically rejected. The colonies, it was said, had the exclusive right, not only of granting their own money, but also of deliberating whether they will make any gift, for what purpose and to what amount;

---

[1] See General Gage's despatch. *American Remembrancer*, 1776, part ii., pp. 132, 133. Ramsay, Stedman, and Bancroft.

[2] John Adams, describing his life at Philadelphia to his wife, in December 1775, says: 'The whole Congress is taken up almost, in different committees, from seven to ten in the morning. From ten to four, or sometimes five, we are in Congress, and from six to ten in committees again. I don't mention this to make you think me a man of importance, because not I alone, but the whole Congress, is thus employed.—Adams' *Familiar Letters*, p. 127.

and 'it is not just that they should be required to oblige themselves to other contributions, while Great Britain possesses a monopoly of their trade.' Still professing to have no desire to separate from Great Britain, the Congress drew up another petition, expressing deep loyalty to the King, and addresses to the people of Great Britain, Ireland, and Canada, and to the Assembly of Jamaica, asserting that the British had been the aggressors at Lexington, and had destroyed every vestige of constitutional liberty in Massachusetts, and that America, in taking up arms, acted strictly in self-defence. It forbade the colonists to have any commercial intercourse with those ports of America which had not observed the non-importation agreement of the preceding year. It forbade them to furnish any provisions or other necessaries to British fishermen on their coast, or to anyone connected with the British army or navy. It at the same time ordered that ten companies of riflemen from Pennsylvania, Maryland, and Virginia, should be raised to reinforce the New England army at Cambridge; made rules for the regulation of the revolutionary army; determined upon an expedition to Canada; issued bills of credit to the amount of 3,000,000 Spanish dollars; established an American post-office with Franklin at its head; appointed a number of general officers, and, above all, selected George Washington as Commander-in-chief of the American army.

The unanimity with which these measures were decreed was due to the great forbearance of many members of the Congress, for the secret debates of that body were distracted by the bitterest divisions. As John Adams wrote, 'Every important step was opposed and carried by bare majorities,' and a large amount of jealousy and suspicion was displayed.[1] Adams, at the head of the New England party, maintained that America should at once declare her independence, form herself into a confederation, seize all the Crown officers as hostages, and enter into negotiations with France and Spain; and letters which he had written expressing these views fell into the hands of the British Government. Dickin-

---

[1] Autobiography. Adams' *Works*, ii. 503. 'It is almost impossible,' wrote Adams, 'to move anything but you instantly see private friendships and enmities, and provincial views and prejudices, intermingle in the consultation.—Ibid. ii. 448.

son, however, supported by Pennsylvania and by some of the other Middle States, insisted upon drawing up another petition to the King, and making a last effort towards reconciliation; and after a very angry resistance, Adams was obliged to yield. Zubly, a Swiss clergyman, who was prominent among the delegates of Georgia, appears to have gone still further. 'There are persons in America,' he complained, ' who wish to break off with Great Britain; a proposal has been made to apply to France and Spain; before I agree to it I will inform my constituents. I apprehend the man who should propose it would be torn to pieces, like De Witt.'[1] He objected strongly to the proposed invasion of Canada as an unjustifiable aggression, and to the non-importation and non-exportation agreements as certain to ruin America. He openly expressed his hope that the present winter would witness a reconciliation with the mother-country; and he declared his opinion that 'a republican government is little better than government of devils.'[2] The trade agreements were debated vehemently through several days, and a large proportion of the members appear to have held that the non-exportation agreement would render it impossible for the colonies to obtain the money which was necessary for carrying on the war. Negotiations with France and Spain were spoken of, but as yet there was great doubt about the disposition of these Powers. It is curious, amid the storm of invective which at this time was directed against English tyranny, to read the opinion of Gadsden, one of the representatives of South Carolina, who was most active in promoting the Revolution: 'France and Spain,' he said, 'would be glad to see Great Britain despotic in America. Our being in a better state than their colonies, occasions complaints among them, insurrections and rebellions. But these Powers would be glad we were an independent State.'[3]

Perhaps the most difficult question, however, was the appointment of a commander-in-chief; and on no other subject did the Congress exhibit more conspicuous wisdom. When only twenty-three, Washington had been appointed commander of the Virginian forces against the French; and in the late war, though he had met with one serious disaster, and had no op-

[1] Adams' *Works*, ii. 459.
[2] Ibid. ii. 466, 469, 472.
[3] Ibid. p. 474.

portunity of obtaining any very brilliant military reputation, he had always shown himself an eminently brave and skilful soldier. His great modesty and taciturnity kept him in the background, both in the Provincial Legislature and in the Continental Congress; but though his voice was scarcely ever heard in debate, his superiority was soon felt in the practical work of the committees. 'If you speak of solid information or sound judgment,' said Patrick Henry about this time, 'Colonel Washington is unquestionably the greatest man in the Congress.' He appeared in the Assembly in uniform, and in military matters his voice had an almost decisive weight. Several circumstances distinguished him from other officers, who in military service might have been his rivals. He was of an old American family. He was a planter of wealth and social position, and being a Virginian, his appointment was a great step towards enlisting that important colony cordially in the cause. The capital question now pending in America was, how far the other colonies would support New England in the struggle. In the preceding March, Patrick Henry had carried a resolution for embodying and reorganising the Virginia militia, and had openly proclaimed that an appeal to arms was inevitable; but as yet New England had borne almost the whole burden. The army at Cambridge was a New England army, and General Ward, who commanded it, had been appointed by Massachusetts. Even if Ward were superseded, there were many New England competitors for the post of commander; the army naturally desired a chief of their own province, and there were divisions and hostilities among the New England deputies.[1] The great personal merit of Washington and the great political importance of securing Virginia, determined the issue; and the New England deputies ultimately took a leading part in the appointment. The second place was given to General Ward, and the third to Charles Lee, an English soldier of fortune who had lately purchased land in Virginia and embraced the American cause with great passion. Lee had probably a wider military experience than any other officer in America, but he was a man of no settled principles, and his great talents were marred by a very irritable and capricious temper.

[1] See Adams' Diary. *Works*, ii. 415.

To the appointment of Washington, far more than to any other single circumstance, is due the ultimate success of the American Revolution, though in purely intellectual powers, Washington was certainly inferior to Franklin, and perhaps to two or three other of his colleagues. There is a theory which once received the countenance of some considerable physiologists, though it is now, I believe, completely discarded, that one of the great lines of division among men may be traced to the comparative development of the cerebrum and the cerebellum. To the first organ it was supposed belong those special gifts or powers which make men poets, orators, thinkers, artists, conquerors, or wits. To the second belong the superintending, restraining, discerning, and directing faculties which enable men to employ their several talents with sanity and wisdom, which maintain the balance and the proportion of intellect and character, and make sound judgments and well-regulated lives. The theory, however untrue in its physiological aspect, corresponds to a real distinction in human minds and characters, and it was especially in the second order of faculties that Washington excelled. His mind was not quick or remarkably original. His conversation had no brilliancy or wit. He was entirely without the gift of eloquence, and he had very few accomplishments. He knew no language but his own, and except for a rather strong turn for mathematics, he had no taste which can be called purely intellectual. There was nothing in him of the meteor or the cataract, nothing that either dazzled or overpowered. A courteous and hospitable country gentleman, a skilful farmer, a very keen sportsman, he probably differed little in tastes and habits from the better members of the class to which he belonged; and it was in a great degree in the administration of a large estate and in assiduous attention to county and provincial business that he acquired his rare skill in reading and managing men.

As a soldier the circumstances of his career brought him into the blaze not only of domestic, but of foreign criticism, and it was only very gradually that his superiority was fully recognised. Lee, who of all American soldiers had seen most service in the English army, and Conway, who had risen to great repute in the French army, were both accustomed to speak of his military talents with extreme disparagement; but personal jealousy and animosity undoubtedly coloured their judgments. Kalb, who had been trained in the best military schools of the Continent, at first pronounced him to be very deficient in the strength, decision, and promptitude of a general; and, although he soon learnt to form the highest estimate of his military capacity, he continued to lament that an excessive modesty led him too frequently to act upon the opinion of inferior men, rather than upon his own most excellent judgment.[1] In the army and the Congress more than one rival was opposed to him. He had his full share of disaster; the operations which he conducted, if compared with great European wars were on a very small scale; and he had the immense advantage of encountering in most cases generals of singular incapacity. It may, however, be truly said of him that his military reputation steadily rose through many successive campaigns, and before the end of the struggle he had outlived all rivalry, and almost all envy. He had a thorough knowledge of the technical part of his profession, a good eye for military combinations, an extraordinary gift of military administration. Punctual, methodical, and exact in the highest degree, he excelled in managing those minute details which are so essential to the efficiency of an army, and he possessed to an eminent degree not only the common courage of a soldier, but also that much rarer form of courage which can endure long-continued suspense, bear the weight of great responsibility, and encounter the risks of misrepresentation and unpopularity. For several years, and usually in the neighbourhood of superior forces, he commanded a perpetually fluctuating army, almost wholly destitute of discipline and respect for authority, torn by the most violent personal and provincial jealousies, wretchedly armed, wretchedly clothed, and sometimes in imminent danger of starvation. Unsupported for the most part by the population among whom he was quartered, and incessantly thwarted by the jealousy of Congress, he kept his army together by a combination of skill, firmness, patience, and judgment which has rarely been surpassed, and he led it at last to a signal triumph.

In civil as in military life, he was pre-eminent among his

[1] See Greene's *German Element in the American War*, pp. 142-144.

contemporaries for the clearness and soundness of his judgment, for his perfect moderation and self-control, for the quiet dignity and the indomitable firmness with which he pursued every path which he had deliberately chosen. Of all the great men in history he was the most invariably judicious, and there is scarcely a rash word or action or judgment recorded of him. Those who knew him well, noticed that he had keen sensibilities and strong passions; but his power of self-command never failed him, and no act of his public life can be traced to personal caprice, ambition, or resentment. In the despondency of long-continued failure, in the elation of sudden success, at times when his soldiers were deserting by hundreds and when malignant plots were formed against his reputation, amid the constant quarrels, rivalries, and jealousies of his subordinates, in the dark hour of national ingratitude, and in the midst of the most universal and intoxicating flattery, he was always the same calm, wise, just, and single-minded man, pursuing the course which he believed to be right, without fear or favour or fanaticism; equally free from the passions that spring from interest, and from the passions that spring from imagination. He never acted on the impulse of an absorbing or uncalculating enthusiasm, and he valued very highly fortune, position, and reputation; but at the command of duty he was ready to risk and sacrifice them all. He was in the highest sense of the words a gentleman and a man of honour, and he carried into public life the severest standard of private morals. It was at first the constant dread of large sections of the American people, that if the old Government were overthrown, they would fall into the hands of military adventurers, and undergo the yoke of military despotism. It was mainly the transparent integrity of the character of Washington that dispelled the fear. It was always known by his friends, and it was soon acknowledged by the whole nation and by the English themselves, that in Washington America had found a leader who could be induced by no earthly motive to tell a falsehood, or to break an engagement, or to commit any dishonourable act. Men of this moral type are happily not rare, and we have all met them in our experience; but there is scarcely another instance in history of such a man having reached and maintained the highest position in the convulsions of civil war and of a great popular agitation.

It is one of the great advantages of the long practice of free institutions, that it diffuses through the community a knowledge of character and a soundness of judgment which save it from the enormous mistakes that are almost always made by enslaved nations when suddenly called upon to choose their rulers. No fact shows so eminently the high intelligence of the men who managed the American Revolution as their selection of a leader whose qualities were so much more solid than brilliant, and who was so entirely free from all the characteristics of a demagogue. It was only slowly and very deliberately that Washington identified himself with the revolutionary cause. No man had a deeper admiration for the British Constitution, or a more sincere wish to preserve the connection and to put an end to the disputes between the two countries. In Virginia the revolutionary movement was preceded and prepared by a democratic movement of the yeomanry of the province, led by Patrick Henry, against the planter aristocracy,[1] and Washington was a conspicuous member of the latter. In tastes, manners, instincts, and sympathies he might have been taken as an admirable specimen of the better type of English country gentleman, and he had a great deal of the strong conservative feeling which is natural to the class. From the first promulgation of the Stamp Act, however, he adopted the conviction that a recognition of the sole right of the colonies to tax themselves was essential to their freedom, and as soon as it became evident that Parliament was resolved at all hazards to assert and exercise its authority of taxing America, he no longer hesitated. An interesting letter to his wife, however, shows clearly that he accepted the proffered command of the American forces with extreme diffidence and reluctance, and solely because he believed that it was impossible for him honourably to refuse it. He declined to accept from Congress any emoluments for his service beyond the simple payment of his expenses, of which he was accustomed to draw up most exact and methodical accounts.

The other military events of the year must be very briefly

[1] See Wirt's *Life of Patrick Henry*.

related. About three weeks after the skirmish at Lexington a party of colonists under Colonels Allen and Benedict Arnold had succeeded, without the loss of a man, in seizing the two very important forts of Ticonderoga and Crown Point, which commanded Lakes George and Champlain, and were indeed the key of Canada, but which had been left by the English in the charge of only sixty or seventy soldiers. In September, in obedience to the direction of the Congress, a colonial army invaded Canada. Washington was at this time organising the army in Massachusetts, but the Canadian expedition was entrusted to the joint command of Schuyler—who, however, was soon obliged through ill-health to return to Ticonderoga—and of Montgomery, a brave and skilful Irish soldier from Donegal, who had been for many years settled in the colonies, and had served with great distinction in the late French war. For some time the invasion was successful. Several parties of Indians joined the provincials.[1] General Carleton, who commanded the English in Canada, with 800 soldiers was driven back when attempting to cross the St. Lawrence. The small fort of Chamblée and the much more important fort of St. John were taken. Montreal was occupied in November, and in the beginning of December Montgomery laid siege to Quebec. He had been joined just before by Benedict Arnold, who had been sent by Washington at the head of an expedition to assist him, but their joint efforts were unsuccessful. The Canadians remained loyal to England. Their laws and their religion had been guaranteed. They had enjoyed under English rule much prosperity and happiness. The Catholic priests were strongly on the side of the English Government.[2] The contagion of New England republicanism had not penetrated to Canada, and the Canadians had no sympathy with the New England character or the New England creed. They were especially indignant, too, at the invasion, because on June 1, 1775, about four weeks before Congress secretly decided upon this step, that body had passed a resolution disclaiming any such intention, and had caused it to be widely disseminated through Canada.[3] Unsupported by the inhabitants, in the midst of a Canadian winter, without large

[1] Stedman, i. 133.
[2] See Adolphus, ii. 239. Ramsay, i. 238.
[3] Compare Lord Stanhope's *Hist.* vi. 76, and Bancroft, *Hist. of the United States*, viii. 176 177.

cannon or sufficient ammunition, Montgomery soon found his position a hopeless one. His troops deserted in such numbers that only 800 remained.¹ They were turbulent, insubordinate, and half-trained; and they had enlisted for so short a period and were so unwilling to renew their contract that it was necessary to press on operations as quickly as possible.² He fell on the last day of 1775 in a desperate but unsuccessful attempt to storm Quebec, and in the course of the following year the Americans evacuated Canada.

In most parts of the colonies the British government simply perished through the absence of British soldiers, but in Virginia Lord Dunmore, the Governor of the province, made desperate efforts to retain it. Having removed a store of gunpowder from Williamsburg, in order to secure it from the provincials, he was obliged to fly from the palace to a British man-of-war. There were no English soldiers in the province, but with the assistance of some British frigates, of some hundreds of loyalists who followed his fortunes, and of a few runaway negroes, he equipped a marine force which spread terror along the Virginian coast, and kept up a harassing, though almost useless, predatory war. Two incidents in the struggle excited deep resent-

---

¹ Bancroft.
² 'The New Englanders,' wrote Montgomery, 'are the worst stuff imaginable for soldiers. They are homesick. Their regiments are melted away, and yet not a man dead of any distemper. There is such an equality among them that the officers have no authority, and there are very few among them in whose spirit I have confidence. The privates are all generals, but not soldiers, and so jealous that it is impossible, though a man risk his person, to escape the imputation of treachery.'—Bancroft, *Hist. of the United States*, viii. p. 185. The day after the capitulation of Montreal, Montgomery wrote to General Schuyler: 'I am exceedingly sorry that Congress has not favoured me with a committee; it would have had great effect with the troops, who are exceedingly turbulent, and even mutinous. . . . I wish some method could be fallen upon of engaging gentlemen to serve. A point of honour and more knowledge of the world to be found in that class of men would greatly reform discipline, and render the troops much more tractable.'—Washington's *Works*, iii. 180, 181. Washington writes (Jan. 31, 1776): 'The account given of the behaviour of the men under General Montgomery is exactly consonant to the opinion I have formed of these people, and such as they will exhibit abundant proofs of in similar cases whenever called upon. Place them behind a parapet, a breastwork, stone wall, or anything that will afford them shelter, and from their knowledge of a firelock they will give a good account of the enemy; but I am as well convinced as if I had seen it, that they will not march boldly up to a work, nor stand exposed in a plain.'—Ibid. p. 277. See too p. 285. The failure and death of Montgomery, Washington ascribed to the system of short enlistments,' for had he not been apprehensive of the troops leaving him at so important a crisis, but continued the blockade of Quebec, a capitulation, from the best accounts I have been able to collect, must inevitably have followed.'—Ibid 278.

ment throughout America. The first was a proclamation by which freedom was promised to all slaves who took arms against the rebels. The second was the burning of the important town of Norfolk, which had been occupied by the provincials, had fired on the King's ships, and had refused to supply them with provisions. It was impossible, however, by such means to subdue the province. An attempt to raise a loyalist force in the back settlements of Virginia and the Carolinas was defeated by the arrest of its chief instigators in the summer of 1776, and soon after, Dunmore, being no longer able to obtain provisions for his ships, abandoned the colony. The unhappy negroes who had taken part with the loyalists are said to have almost universally perished.[1]

In the Southern provinces, and especially in the two Carolinas and in Georgia, there was a considerable loyalist party, but it was unsupported by any regular troops, and after a few spasmodic struggles it was easily crushed. Most of the governors took refuge in English men-of-war; a few were arrested and imprisoned. Provincial Congresses assumed the direction of affairs; except in the immediate neighbourhood of British soldiers the power of England had ceased, and there was no force in America competent to restore it. In the chief towns the stir of military preparation was incessant. When Franklin attended the Congress at Philadelphia in the September of 1775, he found companies of provincial soldiers drilled twice a day in the square of the Quaker capital, and the fortifications along the Delaware were rapidly advancing. Six powder mills were already designed, and two were just about to open. A manufactory of muskets had been established which was expected to complete twenty-five muskets a day. Suspected persons were constantly arrested, and the letter-bags systematically examined. Tories were either tarred and feathered or compelled to mount a cart and ask pardon of the crowd, and the ladies of the town were busily employed in scraping lint or making bandages for the wounded.[2]

Over the inland districts the revolutionary party was as yet supreme, but the whole coast was exposed, almost without defence, to the attacks of English ships of war, and all the

[1] Stedman. Bancroft. Ramsay, i. 252. [2] Parton's *Life of Franklin*, ii. 100.

chief towns in America were seaport. The Americans possessed a large population of seafaring men who were eminently fitted for maritime warfare, but they had as yet not a single ship of war. The Government made large offers to gunsmiths to induce them to abandon America for England [1] The manufacture of gunpowder was only slowly organised, and for many months the colonial forces were often in extreme danger in consequence of the scantiness of their supply. It was wisely determined to pay the provincial troops and to pay them well; but as all foreign commerce was arrested, and as most forms of industry were dislocated, there was very little money in the country, and paper was speedily depreciated. Some of the necessaries of life had hitherto been imported from England, and the great want of native woollen goods was especially felt in the rigour of the first winter of the war.

Though the negroes, who were so numerous in the Southern States, were a cause of great anxiety to the colonists,[2] they remained at this time, with few exceptions, perfectly passive; but one of the first consequences of the appeal to arms was to bring Indian tribes into the field. In the great French war they had been constantly employed by the French and frequently by the English, and it was not likely that so formidable a weapon would be long unused. Neither side, it is true, desired a general Indian rising. Neither side can be justly accused of the great crime of inciting the Indians to indiscriminate massacre or plunder, but both sides were ready to employ them as auxiliaries. Before the battle of Lexington the Provincial Congress of Massachusetts formed a company out of Stockbridge Indians residing in the colony.[3] In the beginning of April 1775 they issued an address to the Mohawk Indians exhorting them 'to whet the hatchet' for war against the English,[4]

---

[1] See a letter of Governor Tryon, *Documents relating to the Colonial History of New York*, viii. 647.

[2] Thus J. Adams in 1775 gives an account of an interview with some gentlemen from Georgia. 'These gentlemen give a melancholy account of the State of Georgia and South Carolina. They say that if 1,000 regular troops should land in Georgia, and their commander be provided with arms and clothes enough, and proclaim freedom to all the negroes who would join his camp, 20,000 negroes would join it from the two provinces in a fortnight.... Their only security is that all the King's friends and tools of Government have large plantations and property in negroes, so that the slaves of the Tories would be lost as well as those of the Whigs.—Adams' *Works*, ii. 428.

[3] Washington's *Works*, iii. 175.

[4] Force's *American Archives* (4th series), i. 1349, 1350.

and Indians were, as we have seen, employed by the Provincials in their invasion of Canada. In March 1775 Mr. Stuart, who managed Indian affairs for the Government in the Southern colonies, reported to the Government that General Gage had informed him 'that ill-affected people in those parts had been endeavouring to poison the minds of the Indians of the six nations and other tribes with jealousies, in order to alienate their affection from his Majesty,'[1] and New England missionaries appear to have been in this respect especially active.[2] Up to the middle of this year the English professed great reluctance to make use of savages. In July, Stuart wrote very emphatically to the Revolutionary Committee of Intelligence at Charleston, which had expressed suspicions on this subject. 'I never have received any orders from my superiors which by the most tortured construction could be interpreted to spirit up or employ the Indians to fall upon the frontier inhabitants, or to take any part in the disputes between Great Britain and her colonies,'[3] and both English and colonists exhorted the Indians as a body to remain neutral.[4] It is, however, certain that in the beginning of June 1775, Colonel Guy Johnson, who had succeeded Sir William Johnson in the direction of one great department of Indian affairs, had, in obedience to secret instructions from General Gage, induced a large body of Indians to undertake 'to assist his Majesty's troops in their operations in Canada,'[5] and in July this policy was openly

---

[1] March 28, 1775. MSS. Record Office (Plantations, General).

[2] *Documents relating to the Colonial History of New York*, viii. 656, 657. See too a letter of the Provincial Congress, dated April 4, 1775, to a New England missionary, urging him to use his influence to make the Indians take up arms against the English. Washington's *Works*, iii. 495.

[3] July 18, 1775. MSS. Record Office.

[4] In a speech to the Indians, August 30, 1775, Stuart said: 'There is a difference between the white people of England and the white people of America; this is a matter which does not concern you, they will decide it among themselves.'—MSS. Record Office (Plantations, General). In August 1775, the Commissioners sent by the twelve colonies had a long interview with the chiefs of the six nations, and gave them an elaborate account of the motives which had united them against England. They added, however: 'This is a family quarrel between us and Old England. You Indians are not concerned in it. We do not wish you to take up the hatchet against the King's troops. We desire you to remain at home and not join either side, but keep the hatchet buried deep.'— *Documents relating to the Colonial History of New York*, viii. 619. See too the *Secret Journals of Congress*, July 17, 1775.

[5] *Documents relating to the Colonial Hist. of New York*, viii. 636. See *Secret Journals of Congress*, June 27 1775.

avowed by Lord Dartmouth. It was defended on the ground that the Americans had themselves adopted it.[1]

Few things were more terrible to the Americans than the scourge of Indian war. As it had generally been the function of the Government to protect the savages against the rapacity and violence of the colonists, England could count largely upon their gratitude, and the horrors which never failed to multiply in their track gave a darker hue of animosity to the struggle.

But the greatest danger to the colonial cause was the half-heartedness of its supporters. It is difficult or impossible to form any safe conjecture of the number of real loyalists in America, but it is certain that it was very considerable. John Adams, who would naturally be inclined to overrate the preponderance in favour of independence, declared at the end of the war his belief that a third part of the whole population, more than a third part of the principal persons in America, were throughout opposed to the Revolution.[2] Massachusetts was of all the provinces the most revolutionary, but when General Gage evacuated Boston in 1776 he was accompanied

---

[1] July 24, 1775, Lord Dartmouth wrote to Colonel Johnson: 'The unnatural rebellion now raging in America calls for every effort to suppress it, and the intelligence his Majesty has received of the rebels having excited the Indians to take a part, and of their having actually engaged a body of them in arms to support their rebellion, justifies the resolution his Majesty has taken of requiring the assistance of his faithful adherents the six nations. It is, therefore, his Majesty's pleasure that you lose no time in taking such steps as may induce them to take up the hatchet against his Majesty's rebellious subjects.'—*Documents on the Colonial History of New York*, viii. 596. General Gage wrote to Stuart (September 12, 1775) telling him to hold a correspondence with the Indians, 'to make them take arms against his Majesty's enemies, and to distress them all in their power, for no terms are now to be kept with them.' 'The rebels,' he continues, 'have themselves opened the door. They have brought down all the savages they could against us here, who with their riflemen are continually firing on our advanced sentries.'—MSS. Record Office. On October 24, 1775, Stuart sent ammunition to the savages according to instructions, adding: 'You will understand that an indiscriminate attack upon the province is not meant, but to act in the execution of any concerted plan, and to assist his Majesty's troops or friends in distressing the rebels.'—Ibid. On November 20, 1775, Lord North said in Parliament: 'As to the means of conducting the war, he declared there was never any idea of employing the negroes or the Indians until the Americans themselves had first applied to them; that General Carleton did then apply to them, and that even then it was only for the defence of his own province.'—*Parl. Hist.* xviii. 994.

[2] Adams' *Works*, x. 87. Many particulars about the strength of the loyalist party will be found in Mr. Sabine's very interesting book, *The Loyalists of America*.

by more than 1,000 loyalists of that town and of the neighbouring country. Two-thirds of the property of New York was supposed to belong to Tories, and except in the city there appears to have been no serious disaffection.[1] In some of the Southern colonies they were believed to form nearly half the population, and there was no colony in which they were not largely represented. There were also great multitudes who, though they would never take up arms for the King, though they perhaps agreed with the constitutional doctrines of the Revolutionists, dissented on grounds of principle, policy, or interest from the course which they were adopting. There were those who wished to wait till the natural increase of the colonies made coercion manifestly impossible, who feared to stake acknowledged liberties on the doubtful issue of an armed struggle, who shrank from measures that would destroy their private fortunes, who determined to stand aloof till the event showed which side was likely to win, who still dreamed of the possibility of resisting the Parliament without casting off allegiance to the Crown. If America succeeded in throwing off the yoke of England, it could hardly be without the assistance of France, and many feared that France would thus acquire a power on the Continent far more dangerous than that of England to the liberties of the colonies. Was it not likely, too, that an independent America would degenerate, as so many of the best judges had predicted, into a multitude of petty, heterogeneous, feeble, and perhaps hostile States? Was it not certain that the cost of the struggle and the burden of independence would drain its purse of far more money than England was ever likely to ask for the defence of her Empire? Was it not possible that the lawless and anarchical spirit which had of late years been steadily growing, and which the patriotic party had actively encouraged, would gain the upper hand, and that the whole fabric of society would be dissolved? John Adams in his Diary relates the 'profound melancholy' which fell upon him in one of the most critical moments of the struggle, when a man whom he knew to be a horse-jockey and a cheat, and whom, as an advocate, he had often defended in the

---

[1] *Parl. Hist.* xviii. 123–129. Sparks' *Life of Washington*. Force's *American Archives* (4th series), i. 773, 957.

law courts, came to him and expressed the unbounded gratitude which he felt for the great things which Adams and his colleagues had done. 'We can never,' he said, 'be grateful enough to you. There are now no courts of justice in this province, and I hope there will never be another.' 'Is this the object,' Adams continued, 'for which I have been contending?' said I to myself. . . . Are these the sentiments of such people, and how many of them are there in the country? Half the nation, for what I know; for half the nation are debtors, if not more, and these have been in all countries the sentiments of debtors. If the power of the country should get into such hands—and there is great danger that it will—to what purpose have we sacrificed our time, health, and everything else?'[1]

Misgivings of this kind must have passed through many minds, and the older colonists were not of the stuff of which ardent soldiers are made. Among the poor, vagrant, adventurous immigrants who had lately poured in by thousands from Ireland and Scotland, there was indeed a keen military spirit, and it was these men who ultimately bore the chief part in the war of independence; but the older and more settled colonists were men of a very different type. Shrewd, prosperous, and well-educated farmers, industrious, money-loving, and eminently domestic, they were men who, if they were compelled to fight, would do so with courage and intelligence, but who cared little or nothing for military glory, and grudged every hour that separated them from their families and their farms. Such men were dragged very reluctantly into the struggle. The American Revolution, like most others, was the work of an energetic minority, who succeeded in committing an undecided and fluctuating majority to courses for which they had little love, and leading them step by step to a position from which it was impossible to recede.[2] To the last, however, we find

---

[1] Adams' *Works*, ii. 420.

[2] One of the most remarkable documents relating to the state of opinion in America is the examination of Galloway (late Speaker of the House of Assembly in Pennsylvania) by a Committee of the House of Commons, June 16, 1779. As a loyalist, his mind was no doubt biassed, but he was a very able and honest man, and he had much more than common means of forming a correct judgment. He says, 'I do not believe, from the best knowledge I have of that time [the beginning of the rebellion], that one-fifth of the people had independence in view. . . . Many of those who have appeared in support of the

vacillation, uncertainty, half-measures, and in large classes a great apparent apathy. In June 1775, the Provincial Congress of New York received two startling pieces of intelligence, that Washington was about to pass through their city on his way to Cambridge, and that Tryon, the royal governor, had just arrived in the harbour. The Congress, though it was an essentially Whig body, and had assumed an attitude which was virtually rebellion, still dreaded the necessity of declaring itself irrevocably on either side, and it ultimately ordered the colonel of militia to dispose of his troops so as to receive ' either the General or Governor Tryon, whichever should first arrive, and wait on both as well as circumstances would admit.'[1] The dominant Quaker party of Pennsylvania was at least as hostile to rebellion as to imperial taxation, and Chastellux justified the very democratic institutions which Franklin established in that province when the Revolution had begun, on the ground that ' it was necessary to employ a sort of seduction in order to conduct a timid and avaricious people to independence, who were besides so divided in their opinions that the Republican party was scarcely stronger than the other.'[2] In every Southern colony a similar division and a similar hesitation may be detected.

present rebellion have by a variety of means been compelled. . . . I think I may venture to say that many more than four-fifths of the people would prefer an union with Great Britain upon constitutional principles to that of independence.' Galloway was asked the following question: ' That part of the rebel army that enlisted in the service of the Congress—were they chiefly composed of natives of America, or were the greatest part of them English, Scotch, and Irish?' Galloway answered, ' The names and places of their nativity being taken down, I can answer the question with precision. There were scarcely one-fourth natives of America—about one-half Irish—the other fourth were English and Scotch.' This last answer, however, must be qualified by a subsequent answer, that he judged of the country of the troops by the deserters who came over to the number of between 2,000 and 3,000, at the time when Galloway was with Sir W. Howe at Philadelphia. I have no doubt that in the beginning of the war the proportion of pure Americans in the army was much larger, as it was chiefly recruited in New England, where the population was most unmixed. It is stated that more than a fourth part of the continental soldiers employed during the war were from Massachusetts. See Greene's *Historical View of the American Revolution*, p. 235. Galloway's very remarkable evidence was reprinted at Philadelphia in 1855. In his *Letters to a Nobleman on the Conduct of the War*, Galloway reiterates his assertion that ' three-fourths of the rebel army have been generally composed of English, Scotch, and Irish, while scarcely the small proportion of one-fourth are American, notwithstanding the severe and arbitrary laws to force them into the service.'—P. 25.

[1] See a curious note in Washington's *Works*, iii. 8.

[2] Chastellux, *Travels in North America*, Eng. trans. i. 332.

The result of all this was, that there was much less genuine military enthusiasm than might have been expected. When Washington arrived at Cambridge to command the army, he found that it nominally consisted of about 17,000 men, but that not more than 14,500 were actually available for service, and they had to guard a line extending for nearly twelve miles, in face of a force of at least 9,000 regular troops, besides seamen and loyalists. Urgent demands were made to the different colonies to send recruits, but they were very imperfectly responded to. Colonel Lee, in a remarkable letter on the military prospects of the Americans, estimated that in three or four months the colonists could easily have an efficient army of 100,000 infantry.[1] As a matter of fact, a month's recruiting during this most critical period produced only 5,000 men. There was abundant courage and energy among the soldiers, but there was very little subordination, discipline, or self-sacrifice. Each body of troops had been raised by the laws of its own colony, and it was reluctant to obey any other authority. Washington complained bitterly of 'the egregious want of public spirit' in his army. The Congress had made rules for its regulation. The troops positively refused to accept them, as they had not enlisted on those terms, and Washington was obliged to yield, except in the case of new recruits. The Congress had appointed a number of officers, but the troops rebelled violently against their choice, and it soon became evident that they would only remain at their post as long as they served under such officers as they pleased.[2] The absence of any social difference between officers and soldiers greatly aggravated the difficulty of enforcing discipline.[3] The local feeling was so strong that General Schuyler gave it as his deliberate opinion that 'troops from the colony of Connecticut will not bear with a general from another colony.'[4] The short period for which the troops had consented to enlist made it impossible to give them steadiness or discipline, to count upon the future, or to engage in enterprises of magnitude or continuity. What little subordination had been attained in the beginning of the period was

[1] *American Remembrancer*, 1776, part i. p. 25.
[2] Washington's *Works*, iii. 176.
[3] Ibid. p. 279.
[4] Ibid. p. 243; see too p. 151.

destroyed at the close, for the officers were obliged to connive at every kind of relaxation of discipline in order to persuade their soldiers to re-enlist.[1] Personal recriminations and jealousies, quarrels about rank and pay and service, were incessant. Great numbers held aloof from enlisting, imagining that the distress of their cause would oblige the Congress to offer large bounties,[2] no possible inducement could persuade a large proportion of the soldiers to re-enlist when their short time of service had expired, and there were instances of gross selfishness and misconduct among the disbanding soldiers.[3] The term for which the Connecticut troops had enlisted expired in December, and the whole body, amounting to some 5,000 men, absolutely refused to re-enlist. It was vainly represented to them that their desertion threatened the whole American cause with absolute ruin. The utmost that the most strenuous exertions could effect was, that they would delay their departure for ten days. There were bitter complaints that Congress granted no bounties, leaving this to the option of the several colonies, and also that the scale of pay, though very liberal, was lower than what they might have obtained in other employments. Great numbers pretended sickness, in order to escape from the service;[4] great numbers would only continue in the army on the condition of obtaining long furloughs at a time when every man was needed for the security of the lines.[5] There was a constant fear of concentrating too much power in military hands, and of building

---

[1] Washington's *Works*, iii. p. 280.
[2] Ibid. pp. 200, 201, 281.
[3] Ibid. pp. 240, 280.
[4] Ibid. p. 191.
[5] Washington's letters are full of complaints on the subject. I will quote a few lines from a letter of Nov. 28, 1775. 'Such a dearth of public spirit, and such want of virtue, such stockjobbing and fertility in all the low arts to obtain advantages of one kind or another in this great change of military arrangement, I never saw before, and pray God's mercy that I may never be witness to again. ... I have been obliged to allow furloughs as far as fifty men to a regiment, and the officers, I am persuaded, indulge as many more ... Such a mercenary spirit pervades the whole that I should not be at all surprised at any disaster that may happen. ... Could I have foreseen what I have experienced, and am likely to experience, no consideration upon earth should have induced me to accept this command.' (Washington's *Works*, iii. 178, 179.) 'No troops,' he writes in another letter, 'were ever better provided or higher paid, yet their backwardness to enlist for another year is amazing. It grieves me to see so little of that patriotic spirit which I was taught to believe was characteristic of this people.' (Ibid. p. 181.) 'The present soldiery are in expectation of drawing from the landed interest and farmers a bounty equal to that given at the commencement of this army and therefore they keep aloof.' Ibid. p. 188.

up a system of despotism, and there was a general belief among the soldiers that unquestioning obedience to their officers was derogatory to their dignity and inconsistent with their freedom.

The truth is, that although the circumstances of the New Englanders had developed to a very high degree many of the qualities that are essential to a soldier, they had been very unfavourable to others. To obey, to act together, to sacrifice private judgment to any authority, to acknowledge any superior, was wholly alien to their temperament,[1] and they had nothing of that passionate and all-absorbing enthusiasm which transforms the character, and raises men to an heroic height of patriotic self-devotion. Such a spirit is never evoked by mere money disputes. The question whether the Supreme Legislature of the Empire had or had not the right of obliging the colonies to contribute something to the support of the imperial army, was well fitted to produce constitutional agitation, eloquence, riots, and even organised armed resistance; but it was not one of those questions which touch the deeper springs of human feeling or action. Any nation might be proud of the shrewd, brave, prosperous, and highly intelligent yeomen who flocked to the American camp; but they were very different men from those who defended the walls of Leyden, or immortalised the field of Bannockburn. Few of the great pages of history are less marked by the stamp of heroism than the American Revolution; and perhaps the most formidable of the difficulties which Washington had to encounter were in his own camp.

Had there been a general of any enterprise or genius at the head of the British army, the Americans could scarcely have escaped a great disaster; but at this period, and indeed during all the earlier period of the Revolutionary War, the English

[1] General Trumbull wrote to Washington, Dec. 1775: 'The late extraordinary and reprehensible conduct of some of the troops of this colony impresses me and the minds of many of our people with grief, surprise, and indignation. . . . There is great difficulty to support liberty, to exercise government, to maintain subordination, and at the same time to prevent the operation of licentious and levelling principles, which many very easily imbibe. The pulse of a New England man beats high for liberty; his engagement in the service he thinks purely voluntary, therefore when the time of enlistment is out he thinks himself not holden without further engagement. This was the case in the last war. I greatly fear its operation amongst the soldiers of the other colonies, as I am sensible that it is the genius and spirit of our people.' Ibid. p. 183.

exhibited an utter absence of all military capacity. That spirit of enterprise and daring which had characterised every branch of the service during the administration of Chatham, had absolutely disappeared. Every week was of vital importance at a time when undisciplined yeomen were being drilled into regular troops, and the different provincial contingents were being slowly and painfully organised into a compact army. But week after week, month after month, passed away, while the British lay inactively behind their trenches. After the first reinforcements had arrived at the end of May 1775, General Gage had upwards of 11,000 men at his disposal, including seamen and loyalists; yet even then weeks of inactivity followed. At Bunker's Hill more than 1,000 men were lost in capturing a position which during several months might have been occupied any day without resistance. Gage knew that the town which he held was bitterly hostile; that the Americans greatly outnumbered him; that they occupied strong and fortified positions; that he was himself secure through his command of the sea; that his army was the sole support of the British Empire in New England. A very large proportion of his soldiers were incapacitated by illness.[1] He considered those who remained too few to be divided with safety; and he maintained that, in the absence of sufficient means of transport, it would be both rash and useless to attempt to penetrate into the country, and that success would only drive the Americans out of one stronghold into another.

He probably feared, also, by energetic measures, to commit the country irrevocably to a war which might still be possibly avoided, and to produce in an undecided and divided people an outburst of military enthusiasm. There was a wide-spread expectation that the resistance would fall to pieces through the divisions of the Americans, through the stress of the blockade, or in consequence of the conciliatory propositions of North. Gage would risk nothing. His information was miserably im-

[1] According to Bancroft, Gage had never more than 6,500 effective troops, though his nominal force, including sailors and loyalists, was estimated at 11,500 men. Washington at this time had nominally 17,000 men, but never more than 14,500 fit for duty. (Bancroft, *Hist. of the United States*, viii. pp. 42–44.) Still the British troops were regular soldiers, admirably provided with all munitions of war, while the Americans were almost undisciplined and singularly destitute of all that was required.

perfect, and he was probably very indifferently informed of the extreme weakness of the Americans. The Provincials had as yet no cavalry. They had scarcely any bayonets. Their ammunition was so deplorably scanty that in the beginning of August it was discovered that there were only nine rounds of ammunition for each man, and a fortnight passed before they received additional supplies, and in this condition they succeeded in blockading, almost without resistance, a powerful English army. Nor was Gage more successful in conciliating than in fighting. He had made an agreement with the inhabitants of Boston that, on delivering up their arms, they might depart with their effects; but he soon after repented, and though the people had complied, he refused to fulfil his promise. Many, indeed, were allowed to depart, but they were obliged to leave their effects behind as a security for their loyalty.

At length, in October, he was recalled, and General Howe assumed the command; but the spirit of indecision and incapacity still presided over the British forces. In November and December, the time for which the American troops enlisted having ended, most of them insisted on disbanding, and a new army had to be formed in the presence of the enemy. On the last day of December, 1775, when the old army had been disbanded, only 9,650 men had been enlisted to supply their place, and more than 1,000 of these were on furlough, which it had been necessary to grant in order to persuade them to enlist.[1] Yet not a single attempt appears to have been made to break the American lines. 'It is not in the page of history, perhaps,' wrote Washington, ' to furnish a case like ours: to maintain a post within musket-shot of the enemy for six months together without powder, and at the same time to disband our army and recruit another within that distance of twenty odd British regiments.'[2] 'My situation,' he wrote in February 1776, ' has been such that I have been obliged to use art to conceal it from my own officers,' and he expressed his emphatic astonishment that Howe had not obliged him,

---

[1] Washington's *Works*, i. 164.   [2] Ibid. iii. 221, 222.

under very disadvantageous circumstances, to defend the lines he had occupied.[1]

The negligence and delay of the British probably saved the American cause, and great efforts were made to recruit the provincial army. Before many weeks the army around Boston had considerably increased, and before the middle of the year it was pretended, though probably with great exaggeration, that the Americans had altogether 80,000 men in arms.[2] In April the Congress voted about 1,300,000*l.* for the support of the army, and in June it offered a bounty of ten dollars for every man who would enlist for three years. Large numbers of cannon were cast in New York, and great exertions were made to fit out a fleet. A hardy seafaring population, scattered over a long seaboard, accustomed from childhood both to smuggling and to distant commercial enterprises, formed an admirable material for the new navy. The old privateersmen of the last war resumed their occupation, and the number of British merchant vessels that were captured brought a rich return to the American sailors. The want of ammunition was the most serious deficiency, but it was gradually supplied. Manufactories of arms and gunpowder were set up in different provinces. The Americans succeeded in purchasing powder in Africa, in the Bahama Islands, and in Ireland. A few daring men sailed from Charleston to East Florida, which had never joined in opposition to the Government, and surprised and captured near St. Augustine a ship containing 15,000 lbs. of powder. A cargo, which was but little less considerable, was seized by the people of Georgia immediately on its arrival from England; and several ships, carrying military stores to Boston, were intercepted before the British appear to have been aware that American privateers were upon the sea. The news from Canada was extremely discouraging, but it was counterbalanced by a great triumph in Massachusetts. The blockade of Boston became more severe; sickness disabled many of the British soldiers; swarms of privateers made it very difficult to obtain provisions; and at last, on the night of March 4, 1776,

---

[1] Washington's *Works*, iii. 285.
[2] *American Remembrancer*, 1776, part ii. p. 281. It is evident from Washington's letters that the estimates in the *American Remembrancer* greatly exceeded the truth.

the Americans obtained possession of Dorchester heights, which commanded the harbour. The town was now no longer tenable. On March 17, Howe, with the remainder of his army, consisting of about 7,600 men, sailed for Halifax, and Washington marched in triumph into the capital of Massachusetts

At the same time public opinion in the colonies began to run strongly in the direction of independence. Great stress has been placed on the effect of an anonymous pamphlet called 'Common Sense,' advocating complete separation from England, which appeared at Philadelphia in January 1776.[1] It was the first considerable work of the notorious Thomas Paine, who had only a few months before come over from England, and had at once thrown himself, with the true instinct of a revolutionist, into hostility to his country. Like all his works, this pamphlet was written in clear, racy, vivid English, and with much power of popular reasoning; and, like most of his works, it was shallow, violent, and scurrilous. Much of it consists of attacks upon monarchy in general, and hereditary monarchy in particular; of very crude schemes for the establishment of democratic forms of government in America, and of violent denunciations of the English King and people. England is described as 'that barbarous and hellish power which hath stirred up the Indians and negroes to destroy us.' The lingering attachment to her is ridiculed as mere local prejudice. Not one-third part of the inhabitants even of Pennsylvania, it is said, are of English descent; and the Americans are recommended to put to death as traitors all their countrymen who were taken in arms for the King. At the same time the arguments showing that America was capable of subsisting as an independent Power, and that, as a part of the British Empire, she could only be a secondary object in the system of British politics, were stated with great force. The present moment, it was urged, was eminently opportune for complete separation. Reunion could only be purchased by concessions that would be fatal to American liberty. Cordial reconciliation was no longer possible, and America had now the inestimable advantage of the military experience of the last war, which had filled the country with veteran soldiers. If the struggle were

[1] See the *American Remembrancer*, 1776, part i. pp. 238–241.

adjourned for forty or fifty years, the Americans would no doubt be more numerous, but they would probably be less united, and it was quite possible that there would not be a general or skilful military officer among them.

It is said that not less than 100,000 copies of this pamphlet were sold; and Washington himself, not long after its appearance, described it as 'working a powerful change in the minds of many men.'[1] As is usually, however, the case with very popular political writings, its success was mainly due to extraneous circumstances. It fell in with the prevailing tendency of the time, and gave an expression to sentiments which were rising in countless minds. The position of men who were professing unbounded devotion to their Sovereign, and were at the same time imprisoning his governors, waging a fierce war against his armies, and invading a peaceful province which was subject to his rule, was manifestly untenable. When blood was once shed, amid the deepening excitement of the contest the figments of lawyers disappeared, and the struggle assumed a new character of earnestness and animosity. Several acts of war had already been committed, of which Americans might justly complain, and others were grossly exaggerated or misrepresented. The conduct of the British troops in the beginning of the war in firing upon the Provincials at Lexington, was absurdly described as a wanton massacre. The conduct of Gage to the inhabitants of Boston, and the burning of Charleston during the battle of Bunker's Hill to prevent it from being a shelter for American soldiers, were more justly objected to; while the proceedings of Lord Dunmore in Virginia raised the indignation of the colonists to the highest point. When the news of the burning of Norfolk arrived, Washington expressed his hope that it would 'unite the whole country in one indissoluble band against a nation which seems to be lost to every sense of virtue and those feelings which distinguish a civilised people from the most barbarous savages.'[2] If such language could be employed by such a man, it is easy to conceive how fierce a spirit must have been abroad. In the dissolution of all government, mob intimidation had a great power over

---

[1] Washington's *Works*, iii. 276, 347.
[2] *Life and Correspondence of Joseph Reed*, i. 148

politicians, and mobs are always in favour of the strongest measures; and the adoption of the policy of armed resistance had naturally given an increased power to those who had been the first to advocate it. Every step which was taken in England added to the exasperation. Already the Americans had been proclaimed rebels; and all commercial intercourse with them had been forbidden. The petition of Congress to the King, which was the last serious effort of America for pacification, was duly taken over to England; but, after a short delay, Lord Dartmouth informed the delegates that 'no answer would be given to it.' An Act of Parliament was passed authorising the confiscation of all American ships and cargoes, and of all vessels of other nations trading with the American ports; and by a clause of especial atrocity, the commanders of the British ships of war were empowered to seize the crews of all American vessels, and compel them, under pain of being treated as mutineers, to serve against their countrymen.[1]

All these things contributed to sever the colonies from amicable connection with England, and to make the prospect of reconciliation appear strange and remote. Separation, it was plausibly said, was the act of the British Parliament itself, which had thrown the thirteen colonies out of the protection of the Crown. But another and more practical consideration concurred with the foregoing in producing the Declaration of Independence. One of the gravest of the questions which were agitating the Revolutionary party was the expediency of asking for foreign, and especially for French, assistance. France had hitherto been regarded in America, even more than in England, as a natural enemy. She was a despotic Power, and could not therefore have much real sympathy with a struggle for constitutional liberty. Her expulsion from America had been for generations one of the first objects of American patriots; and if she again mixed in American affairs, it was natural that she should seek to regain the province she had so lately lost. If America was destined to be an independent Republic, nothing could be more dangerous than to have a military and aggressive colony belonging to the most powerful despotism in Europe planted on her frontiers. But, on the other hand, it

[1] 16 Geo. III. c. 5

appeared more than probable that the intervention or non-intervention of France would determine the result of the present struggle. If America were cordially united in her resistance to England, it would be impossible to subdue her; but it was quite evident to serious men that America was not united; that outside New England there was scarcely an approach to unanimity; that powerful minorities in almost every province were ardently attached to England; and that, of the remainder of the population, a very large proportion were vacillating, selfish, or indifferent, ready, if the occasion could be found, to be reconciled with England, and altogether unprepared to make any long or strenuous sacrifices in the cause. Under these circumstances the Revolutionary leaders had much to fear. There was a party in the Congress, among whom Patrick Henry was conspicuous, who desired to purchase French assistance by large territorial cessions in America;[1] but this view found little favour. Apart from all considerations of territorial aggrandisement, it was the evident interest of France to promote the independence of America. She could thus obtain for herself a share in that vast field of commerce from which she had hitherto been excluded by the Navigation Act. The humiliation of the loss of Canada would be amply avenged if the thirteen old colonies were separated from England. A formidable if not fatal blow would be given to that maritime supremacy against which France had so long and so vainly struggled; and the French West India islands, which were now in time of war completely at the mercy of England, would become comparatively secure if the harbours of the neighbouring continent were held by a neutral or a friendly Power. Ever since the Peace of Paris, a feeling of deep humiliation and discontent had brooded over French society; and even in Europe the influence of France appeared to have diminished. The recent appearance of Russia as an active and formidable agent in the European system, and the recent growth of Prussia into the dimensions of a first-class Power, had profoundly altered the European equilibrium. Both of these Powers lay in a great degree beyond the influence of France; and although one school of French politicians maintained that the rise of Prussia

[1] Adams' Life, *Works*, i. 201.

was beneficial, as establishing a balance of power in Germany, and checking the preponderance of Austria, another school looked upon it as seriously affecting both French ascendency and French security. Great indignation was felt in Paris at the passive attitude of the Government at the time of the first partition of Poland in 1772, and during the war that ended in the treaty of Kainardji in 1774, when Russia succeeded in extending her territory southwards, in separating the Crimea from the Turkish Empire, and in acquiring a right of protectorate over Christians in Constantinople. As long as the old King lived, there seemed little chance of a more active policy; but in May 1774, Lewis XV. died, and a new and more adventurous spirit was ruling at the Tuileries. Under such circumstances it appeared to Adams, and to the more sagacious of his supporters, that it would be possible to obtain from France such a measure of assistance as would insure the independence of America without involving her future in European complications. But the first condition of this policy was a declaration by the colonies that they were finally and for ever detached from Great Britain. France had no possible interest in their constitutional liberties. She had a vital interest in their independence. It was idle to suppose that she would risk a war with England for rebels who might at any time be converted by constitutional concessions into loyal subjects, and enemies of the enemies of England.

The questions of a French alliance and of a declaration of independence were thus indissolubly connected. In the autumn of 1775 a motion was made in Congress, and strongly supported by John Adams, to send ambassadors to France. But Congress still shrank from so formidable a step, though it agreed, after long debates and hesitation, to form a secret committee 'to correspond with friends in Great Britain, Ireland, and other parts of the world.'[1] But the conduct of England herself soon dispelled the hesitation of America. England found herself at this time confronted with a military problem which she was utterly unable by her own unassisted efforts to solve. The same pressure of financial distress, the same reluctance to increase the army estimates, which had made the English

[1] Adams' Life, Works, i. 200-203.

Ministers so anxious to throw upon America the burden of supporting her own army, had prevented the maintenance of any considerable army at home. Public opinion had never yet fully accepted the fact that the forces which were very adequate under Walpole were wholly insufficient after the Peace of Paris. The King, indeed, had for many years steadily maintained that military economy in England had been carried to a fatal point, and that the army was much below what the security of the Empire required; but his warnings had been disregarded.[1] The feeling of the country, the feeling of the House of Commons, against large standing armies was so strong that it was impossible to resist it. As late as December 1774, the seamen had been reduced from 20,000 to 16,000, and the land forces had been fixed at 17,547 effective men.[2] In the following year, when the war became inevitable, Parliament voted 28,000 seamen and 55,000 land forces, but even this was utterly inadequate for the conquest of America, and as yet it only existed upon paper. Most of the troops that could be safely spared had been already sent, and the result had been the formation of two armies, one of which was not more than sufficient for the protection of Canada, while the other had been for months confined within the town of Boston. It was quite evident that much larger forces were required if America was to be subdued, and Howe strongly urged that he could make no aggressive movement with any prospect of success unless he had at least 20,000 men. To raise the required troops at short notice was very difficult. In January 1776, Lord Barrington warned the King that Scotland had never yet been so bare of troops, and

---

[1] As early as Aug. 11, 1765, the King had written to Conway: 'The only method that at present occurs to me by which the French can be prevented settling on the coast of Newfoundland would be the having a greater military force in that island; but the economical, and I may say injudicious, ideas of this country in time of peace, make it not very practicable, for a corps ought on purpose to be raised for that service, we having more places to garrison than we have troops to supply.' He adds that we are 'very unable to draw the sword.'—*British Museum. Eg. MSS.*

982.

On August 26, 1775, he wrote to Lord North, 'The misfortune is, that at the beginning of this American business there has been an unwillingness to augment the army and navy. I proposed early in the summer the sending beating orders to Ireland; this was objected to in the Cabinet; if it had then been adopted, the army would have been at least 2,000 or 3,000 men stronger at this hour.'— *Correspondence of George III. and Lord North*, vol. i. 265, 266.

[2] Adolphus, ii. 159.

that those in England were too few for the security of the country.[1] The land tax for 1776 was raised to four shillings in the pound. New duties were imposed; new bounties were offered. Recruiting agents traversed the Highlands of Scotland, and the most remote districts of Ireland, and the poor Catholics of Munster and Connaught, who had been so long excluded from the English army, were gladly welcomed. Recruits, however, came in very slowly. There was no enthusiasm for a war with English settlers. The pressgangs met with an unusual resistance. No measure short of a conscription could raise at once the necessary army in England, and to propose a conscription would be fatal to any Government.

The difficulties of subduing America by land operations, even under the most favourable circumstances, were enormous. Except on the sea-coast there were no fixed points, no fortified places of such importance that their possession could give a permanent command of any large tract of territory; the vast distances and the difficulties of transport made it easy for insurgents to avoid decisive combats; and in a hostile and very thinly populated country, the army must derive its supplies almost exclusively from England.[2] The magnitude, the ruinous expense of such an enterprise, and the almost absolute impossibility of carrying the war into distant inland quarters, ought to have been manifest to all, and no less a person than Lord Barrington, the Secretary for War, held from the beginning that it would be impossible for England to subdue America by an army, though he thought it might be subdued by a fleet which blockaded its seaport towns and destroyed its commerce. But Barrington was one of the most devoted of the King's friends, and he was a conspicuous instance of the demoralising influence of the system of politics which had lately prevailed

---

[1] *The Political Life of Lord Barrington*, pp. 162–164.

[2] General Lloyd, who was one of the best English writers on the art of war, maintained that England, in consequence of her possession of Canada, might have completely crushed the four provinces of New England by operating vigorously on the line of country (about 150 miles) extending from Boston to Albany, or to some other point on the Hudson river; and he thought that, in the existing condition of opinion in America, if New England were subdued, the rest of the colonies would all submit. The impossibility, however, of subduing them by land measures, if they did not, he clearly showed. See a remarkable chapter on the American war in his 'Reflections on the Principles of War,' appended to his *History of the Seven Years' War*.

in England. Already, at the close of 1774, he informed his colleagues in the clearest and most decisive manner of his disapproval of the policy they were pursuing, and he repeatedly begged the King to accept his resignation. 'I am summoned to meetings' of the Ministers, he complained, 'when I sometimes think it my duty to declare my opinions openly before perhaps twenty or thirty persons, and the next day I am forced either to vote contrary to them or to vote with an Opposition which I abhor.' He wished to retire both from the Ministry and from Parliament, but he had declared that he would remain in both as long as his Majesty thought fit, and he accordingly continued year after year one of the responsible Ministers of the Crown, though he believed that the policy of the Government was mistaken and disastrous. It was only in December 1778 that his resignation was accepted.[1] The King was the real director of the Administration, and he was determined to relinquish no part of his dominions. He was accordingly reduced to the humiliating necessity of asking for foreign assistance to subdue his own subjects. It was sought from many quarters. He himself, as Elector of Hanover, agreed to lend 2,355 men of his Electoral army to garrison Minorca and Gibraltar, and thus to release some British soldiers for the American war. The Dutch had for a long time maintained a Scotch brigade in their service, and the Government wished to take it into English pay, but the States-General refused to consent. Russia had just concluded her war with the Turks, and it was hoped that she might sell some 20,000 of her spare troops to the English service, but Catherine sternly refused. The little sovereigns of Germany were less chary, and were quite ready to sell their subjects to England to fight in a quarrel with which they had no possible concern. The Duke of Brunswick, the Landgrave of Hesse Cassel, the Hereditary Prince of Hesse Cassel, and the Prince of Waldeck were the chief persons engaged in this white slave trade, and they agreed for a liberal payment to supply 17,742 men to serve under English officers in America.[2]

---

[1] *Political Life of Lord Barrington*, pp. 146-186.
[2] See on the terms of this bargain, *Correspondence of George III. and Lord North*, i. 258-260, 266, 267, 294, 295. Frederick the Great is said to have marked his opinion of the transaction by claiming to levy on the hired troops which passed through his dominions the same duty as on so many head of cattle.

The German princelets acted after their kind, and the contempt and indignation which they inspired were probably unmixed with any feeling of surprise. The conduct, however, of England in hiring German mercenaries to subdue the essentially English population beyond the Atlantic, made reconciliation hopeless and the Declaration of Independence inevitable. It was idle for the Americans to have any further scruples about calling in foreigners to assist them when England had herself set the example. It was necessary that they should do so if they were successfully to resist the powerful reinforcement which was thus brought against them.

It belongs rather to the historian of America than to the historian of England to recount in detail the various steps that led immediately to the Declaration of Independence. It will here be sufficient to indicate very briefly the main forces that were at work. Even after the enlistment of foreign mercenaries by Great Britain, the difficulty of carrying the Declaration was very great. As late as March 1776, John Adams, who was the chief advocate of the measure, described the terror and disgust with which it was regarded by a large section of the Congress, and he clearly shows the nature of the opposition. 'All our misfortunes,' he added, 'arise from the reluctance of the Southern colonies to republican government,' and he complains bitterly that 'popular principles and axioms' are 'abhorrent to the inclinations of the barons of the South and the proprietary interests in the Middle States, as well as to that avarice of land which has made on this continent so many votaries to Mammon.' It was necessary, in the first place, to mould the governments of the Southern and Middle States into a purely popular form, destroying altogether the proprietary system and those institutions which gave the more wealthy planters, if not a preponderance, at least a special weight in the management of affairs. The Congress recommended the colonists 'where no government sufficient to the exigencies of their affairs hath hitherto been established' to adopt a new form of government, and it pronounced it necessary that the whole proprietary system should be dissolved.[1] The Revolution was speedily

---

[1] Adams' *Works*, i. 207, 208, 217, 218; Story's *Constitution of the* *United States*, book ii. ch. i.; Jay's *Life*, by his Son, i. 43.

accomplished, and the tide of democratic feeling ran strongly towards independence. Virginia, now wholly in the hands of the revolutionary party, concurred fully with Massachusetts, and the influence of these two leading colonies overpowered the rest. In Pennsylvania, in New Jersey, in Maryland, in Delaware, in New York, in South Carolina, there was powerful opposition, but the strongest pressure was applied to overcome it. New Jersey and Maryland first dropped off and accepted the Resolution of Independence, but South Carolina and Pennsylvania opposed it almost to the last, while Delaware was divided and New York abstained. John Adams was now the most powerful advocate, while John Dinkinson was the chief opponent of independence. At last, however, it was resolved not to show any appearance of dissension to the world. The arrival of a new delegate from Delaware, and the abstention of two delegates of Pennsylvania, gave the party of independence the control of the votes of these provinces. South Carolina, for the sake of preserving unity, changed sides. New York still abstained, and on July 2 the twelve colonies resolved that ' these united colonies are, and of right ought to be, free and independent States; that they are absolved from all allegiance to the British Crown, and that all political connection between them and the State of Great Britain is, and ought to be, totally dissolved.' Thomas Jefferson, of Virginia, whose literary power had been shown in many able State papers, had already drawn up the Declaration of Independence, which having been revised by Franklin and by John Adams, was now submitted to the examination of Congress, and was voted after some slight changes on the evening of the 4th. It proclaimed that a new nation had arisen in the world, and that the political unity of the English race was for ever at an end.

CHAPTER XIII.

The importance of the American question during the few years that preceded the Declaration of Independence was so transcendently great that I have thought it advisable to devote the last chapter exclusively to its development, and have endeavoured to preserve the unity and clearness of my narrative by omitting several matters of domestic policy which I shall now proceed to relate.

The Government from the accession of Lord North to the foremost place had continued steadily to increase in parliamentary authority, and the long period of anarchy and rapid political fluctuation which marked the beginning of the reign had completely ceased. The Court was now closely united with the Ministers. The King disposed personally of nearly all the ecclesiastical, and most of the other departments of patronage. He prescribed in a great measure the policy of his Government. His friends in Parliament steadily supported it; the most important of the old followers of Grenville had joined it; it was strengthened by the personal popularity of North, by the eclipse of Chatham, and by the dissension between his followers and those of Rockingham, and it commanded overwhelming majorities in both Houses. The democratic movement which followed the Middlesex election had gradually subsided. The City opposition was broken into small and hostile fragments, and a great political apathy prevailed in the nation.

But while the course of events appeared thus eminently favourable to the designs of the Court, a long series of disgraces and calamities had cast a dark shadow around the throne. In 1770 the Duke of Cumberland, one of the brothers of the King, had been compelled to appear as defendant in an action for criminal conversation on account of his adultery with Lady Grosvenor, and to pay 10,000*l.* in damages. He then formed a new and notorious connection with another married woman, and soon after the King learnt with bitter indignation that in October 1771 he had secretly married Mrs. Horton, the widow of an undistinguished Derbyshire gentleman. The new Duchess was daughter of Lord Irnham, and, as Junius and the other satirists of the Court noticed with ferocious pleasure, she was sister to that Colonel Luttrell who had been so lately put forward in opposition to Wilkes as the champion of the Court. Immediately after this marriage had been announced, the Duke of Gloucester, the favourite brother of the King, confessed that he had several years before contracted a secret marriage with the Dowager Countess of Waldegrave, an illegitimate daughter of Sir Edward Walpole, and granddaughter of the great statesman of the last reign. Very soon after, news arrived from Copenhagen of the disgrace of the King's sister, the Queen of Denmark, who had been arrested by the command of her husband on a charge of adultery with Count Struensee, the Prime Minister of Denmark, and had been thrown into prison. Struensee was executed with circumstances of peculiar horror, but the Queen after four months of confinement was suffered to retire to Hanover, where a few years later she died. The Princess Dowager, the mother of the King, was in the meantime slowly dying of cancer, and ten days after the news of her daughter's disgrace arrived in England, she ended her stormy and unhappy life. There is no evidence whatever that for several years before her death she had exercised any political power; but the belief in her influence had never ceased, and neither her sex nor her sorrows nor her munificent charities could screen her from the most brutal insults, which pursued her to the very end of her life. Wilkes, Horne, Junius, and a crowd of nameless libellers and caricaturists, and especially the infamous papers called the 'Whisperer' and the 'Parliamentary Spy,' vied with each other in insulting her; and in March 1771, when the Princess was stricken down with her mortal illness, Alderman Townshend made a furious attack upon her in the House of Commons, declaring that for ten years England had been governed by a woman, that he considered the Princess Dowager of Wales to be the cause of all the calamities of the country, and that an inquiry should be made into her conduct.[1] The Princess died on February 8, 1772, and her body was a few days later carried to the tomb amid the shouts and rejoicings of the mob.[2]

In the same month, and in consequence of the scandals connected with the Dukes of Cumberland and Gloucester, a King's message was brought to Parliament urging both Houses to take into consideration measures for making more effectual the right which had always, it was stated, belonged to the kings of this nation of approving of all marriages in the royal family, and it was followed by the Royal Marriage Bill, which more than any other measure in 1772 divided opinion both in Parliament and in the country. The object of this Bill was to prevent the great dangers which might arise from clandestine or improper marriages in the royal family. It was possible that in consequence of such marriages the title of the successor to the throne might become a matter of doubt and of dispute, and it was very probable that connections might be formed, and disgraceful elements introduced into the royal family, which would greatly lower the authority of the monarchy in the country. To guard against these dangers, the Marriage Bill prohibited any descendant of the late King except those who were the issue of princesses married into foreign houses, from contracting marriage before the age of twenty-five without the assent of the King signified under the Great Seal. After that age they might marry without the royal consent, but only if they had given notice of their intention to the Privy Council twelve months before the ceremony was performed, and if the two Houses of Parliament did not signify their disapprobation. All marriages contracted in defiance of this Act were to be null, and all who celebrated them or assisted at them were to be subject to the penalties of præmunire.[3]

This Bill was fiercely and persistently opposed. Its adversaries emphatically denied that the King possessed either by law or by prerogative any control over the marriages of his family other than that which every parent or guardian possesses over

---

[1] *Chatham Correspondence,* iv. 134, 135. *Cavendish Debates,* ii. 447. *Parl Hist.* xvii. 122.
[2] Walpole's *Last Journals,* i. 17.
[3] 12 Geo. III. c. xi.

his children or his wards when they are minors. They dilated upon the great number of persons far removed from the throne who would ultimately be brought under the provisions of the law, and deprived during their whole lives of their natural and inherent right of marrying according to their inclination; and they urged that while no immorality was so pernicious to the community as the immorality of those who occupied an eminent position in the eyes of men, the moral effects of a Bill imposing such formidable restraints upon marriage must be in the highest degree injurious. To treat the whole royal family as a separate caste, and to make intermarriage between its members and subjects almost impossible, was no doubt very congenial to the sentiments of a German court, but it was a slur upon the English nobility, it was utterly inconsistent with English traditions, and it claimed for a German family reigning by a parliamentary title a position which had not been claimed either by the Plantagenets, the Tudors, or the Stuarts. The principle that a marriage which was valid in the eyes of God and of the Church could be pronounced by the civil law to be not only criminal and irregular, but null and void, had indeed been introduced into English legislation in the last reign, but it was a principle which was contrary to religion, and would never be fully recognised by opinion. Nor was the Bill likely to fulfil its objects. It was intended to prevent improper persons from sitting on the throne, but it imposed no restraint on the imprudent or profligate marriage of the reigning prince. It was intended to prevent the possibility of disputed successions; but it would almost certainly multiply clandestine marriages, and call into being two classes of heirs; those who were legitimate in the eyes of God, of the Church, and perhaps of public opinion, and those whose legitimacy depended on an Act of Parliament.

Arguments of this kind made the Bill exceedingly unpopular outside Parliament, and in the House of Commons itself the feeling against it was so strong that an amendment limiting it to the reign of George III. and three years longer was only rejected by a majority of 18.[1] The measure was

[1] *Correspondence of George III. with Lord North,* i. 99, 100. *Parl. Hist.* xvii. 423.

generally understood to emanate especially from the King, and his influence was employed to the utmost to carry it. 'I do expect,' he wrote to Lord North, 'every nerve to be strained to carry the Bill through both Houses with a becoming firmness, for it is not a question that immediately relates to administration, but personally to myself, and therefore I have a right to expect a hearty support from everyone in my service, and shall remember defaulters.'[1]

The Bill was carried by large majorities, and it still remains on the Statute Book; and, although it may be justly regarded as oppressive by the collateral branches of the House of Brunswick, who are too far from the throne to have any reasonable prospect of succeeding to it, it cannot be said to have hitherto produced any of the public dangers that were foretold. The discussions on the measure are especially interesting as marking the first appearance in opposition to the Government of Charles James Fox, a man whose name during the next thirty years occupies a foremost place in English history, and whose character and early life it will now be necessary to sketch.

He was the third son of the first Lord Holland, the old rival of Pitt. He had entered Parliament irregularly and illegally in November 1768, when he had not yet completed his twentieth year, and in February 1770 he had been made a Lord of the Admiralty in the Government of Lord North. The last political connection of Lord Holland had been with Bute, and his son appears to have accepted the heritage of his Tory principles without inquiry or reluctance. His early life was in the highest degree discreditable, and gave very little promise of greatness. His vehement and passionate temperament threw him speedily into the wildest dissipation, and the almost insane indulgence of his father gratified his every whim. When he was only fourteen Lord Holland had brought him to the gambling table at Spa,[2] and, at a time when he had hardly reached manhood, he was one of the most desperate gamblers of his day. Lord Holland died in 1774, but before his death he is said to have paid no less than 140,000*l*. in extricating his son from gambling debts. The death of his mother and the death of his elder brother in the same year brought him a considerable fortune, including

[1] *Correspondence of George III. with Lord North,* i. 91.
[2] Russell's *Life of Fox,* i. 4.

an estate in the Isle of Thanet and the sinecure office of Clerk of the Pells in Ireland, which was worth 2,300*l.* a year; but in a short time he was obliged to sell or mortgage everything he possessed. He himself nicknamed his ante-chamber the Jerusalem Chamber from the multitude of Jews who haunted it. Lord Carlisle was at one time security for him to the extent of 15,000*l.* or 16,000*l.* During one of the most critical debates in 1781 his house was in the occupation of the sheriffs. He was even debtor for small sums to chairmen and to waiters at Brooks's; and although in the latter part of his life he was partly relieved by a large subscription raised by his friends, he never appears to have wholly emerged from the money difficulties in which his gambling tastes had involved him. Nor was this his only vice. With some men the passion for gambling is an irresistible moral monomania, the single morbid taint in a nature otherwise faultless and pure. With Fox it was but one of many forms of an insatiable appetite for vicious excitement, which continued with little abatement during many years of his public career. In 1777, during a long visit to Paris, he lived much in the society of Madame du Deffand, and that very acute judge of character formed an opinion of him which was, on the whole, very unfavourable. He has much talent, she said, much goodness of heart and natural truthfulness, but he is absolutely without principle, he has a contempt for everyone who has principle, he lives in a perpetual intoxication of excitement, he never gives a thought to the morrow, he is a man eminently fitted to corrupt youth.[1] In 1779, when he was already one of the foremost politicians in England, he was one night drinking at Almack's with Lord Derby, Major Stanley, and a few other young men of rank, when they determined at three in the morning to make a tour through the streets, and amused themselves by instigating a mob to break the windows of the chief members of the Government.[2] His profligacy with women during a great part of his life was

---

[1] Mdme. du Deffand to H. Walpole. See *Correspondence of Fox,* i. p. 149.

[2] Ibid. i. 224, 225. Fox appears, however, to have drunk less, or to have borne drink better, than several of his leading contemporaries. Sir Gilbert Elliot, in a letter to his wife, says, 'Fox drinks what I should call a great deal, though he is not reckoned to do so by his companions; Sheridan excessively, and Grey more than any of them. . . . Pitt, I am told, drinks as much as anybody, generally more than any of his company, and that he is a pleasant, con-

notorious, though he appears at last to have confined himself to his connection with Mrs. Armitstead, whom he secretly married in September 1795.[1] He was the soul of a group of brilliant and profligate spendthrifts, who did much to dazzle and corrupt the fashionable youth of the time; and in judging the intense animosity with which George III. always regarded him, it must not be forgotten that his example and his friendship had probably a considerable influence in encouraging the Prince of Wales in those vicious habits and in that undutiful course of conduct which produced so much misery in the palace and so much evil in the nation.[2] One of the friends of Charles Fox summed up his whole career in a few significant sentences. 'He had three passions—women, play, and politics. Yet he never formed a creditable connection with a woman. He squandered all his means at the gaming table, and, except for eleven months, he was invariably in opposition.'

That a man of whom all this can be truly said should have taken a high and honourable place in English history, and should have won for himself the perennial love and loyalty of some of the best Englishmen of his time, is not a little surprising, for a life such as I have described would with most men have destroyed every fibre of intellectual energy and of moral worth. But in truth there are some characters which nature has so happily compounded that even vice is unable wholly to degrade them, and there is a charm of manner and of temper which sometimes accompanies the excesses of a strong animal nature that wins more popularity in the world than the purest and the most self-denying virtue. Of this truth Fox was an eminent example. With a herculean frame, with iron nerves, with that happy vividness and buoyancy of temperament that can ever throw itself passionately into the pursuits and the impressions of the hour, and can then cast them aside without an effort, he combined one of the sweetest of human tempers, one of the warmest of human hearts. Nothing in his career is more remarkable than the spell which he cast over men who in character and principles were as unlike as possible to himself.

---

vivial man at table.'—Lady Minto's *Life of Sir G. Elliot*, i. 189.

[1] Russell's *Life of Fox*, iii. 78.

[2] See Walpole's *Last Journals*, ii. 480, 502, 503, 598, 599.

'He is a man,' said Burke, 'made to be loved, of the most artless, candid, open, and benevolent disposition; disinterested in the extreme, of a temper mild and placable to a fault, without one drop of gall in his whole constitution.' 'The power of a superior man,' said Gibbon, 'was blended in his attractive character with the softness and simplicity of a child. Perhaps no human being was ever more perfectly exempt from the taint of malevolence, vanity, or falsehood.' 'He possessed,' said Erskine, 'above all men I ever knew, the most gentle, and yet the most ardent spirit.' He retained amid all his vices a capacity for warm and steady friendship, a capacity for struggling passionately and persistently in opposition, for an unpopular cause; a purity of taste and a love of literature which made him, with the exception of Burke, the foremost scholar among the leading members of the House of Commons; an earnestness, disinterestedness, and simplicity of character which was admitted and admired even by his political opponents.

He resembled Bolingbroke in his power of passing at once from scenes of dissipation into the House of Commons, and in retaining in public affairs during the most disorderly periods of his private life all his soundness of judgment and all his force of eloquence and of decision. Gibbon described how he 'prepared himself' for one important debate by spending twenty-two previous hours at the hazard table and losing 11,000*l*. Walpole extols the extraordinary brilliancy of the speech which he made on another occasion, when he had but just arrived from Newmarket and had been sitting up drinking the whole of the preceding night, and he states that in the early period of his brilliant opposition to the American policy of North he was rarely in bed before five in the morning, or out of it before two in the afternoon.[1] Yet like Bolingbroke he never lost the taste and passion for study even at the time when he was most immersed in a life of pleasure. At Eton and Oxford he had been a very earnest student, and few of his contemporaries can have had a wider knowledge of the imaginative literatures of Greece, Italy, or France. He was passionately fond of poetry, and a singularly delicate and discriminating critic; but he always looked upon literature chiefly from its

[1] Walpole's *Last Journals*, ii. 4.

ornamental and imaginative side. Incomparably the most important book relating to the art of government which appeared during his lifetime was the 'Wealth of Nations,' but Fox once owned that he had never read it, and the history which was his one serious composition added nothing to his reputation. In books, however, he found an unfailing solace in trouble and disappointment. One morning, when one of his friends having heard that Fox on the previous night had been completely ruined at the gaming table, went to visit and console him, he found him tranquilly reading Herodotus in the original. 'What,' he said, 'would you have a man do who has lost his last shilling?'

His merits as a politician can only be allowed with great deductions and qualifications. But little stress should indeed be laid on the sudden and violent change in his political principles, which was faintly foreshadowed in 1772 and fully accomplished in 1774, though that change did undoubtedly synchronise with his personal quarrel with Lord North. Changes of principle and policy, which at forty or fifty would indicate great instability of character, are very venial at twenty-four or twenty-five, and from the time when Fox joined the Whig party his career through long years of adversity and of trial was singularly consistent. I cannot, however, regard a politician either as a great statesman or a great party leader who left so very little of permanent value behind him, who offended so frequently and so bitterly the national feelings of his countrymen, who on two memorable occasions reduced his party to the lowest stage of depression, and who failed so signally during a long public life in winning the confidence of the nation. His failure is the more remarkable as one of the features most conspicuous both in his speeches and his letters is the general soundness of his judgment, and his opinions during the greater part of his life were singularly free from every kind of violence, exaggeration, and eccentricity. Much of it was due to his private life, much to his divergence from popular opinion on the American question and on the question of the French Revolution, and much also to an extraordinary deficiency in the art of party management, and to the frequent employment of language which, though eminently adapted to the immediate purposes of debate, was certain from its injudicious energy to be afterwards quoted against him. Like more than one great master of words, he was trammelled and injured at every stage of his career by his own speeches. The extreme shock which the disastrous coalition of 1784 gave to the public opinion of England was largely, if not mainly, due to the outrageous violence of the language with which Fox had in the preceding years denounced Lord North, and a similar violence made his breach with the Court irrevocable, and greatly aggravated his difference with the nation on the question of the French Revolution.

But if his rank as a statesman and as a party leader is by no means of the highest order, he stood, by the concurrent testimony of all his contemporaries, in the very first line, if not in the very first place, among English parliamentary debaters. He threw the whole energy of his character into his career, and he practised it continually till he attained a dexterity in debate which to his contemporaries appeared little less than miraculous. 'During five whole sessions,' he once said, 'I spoke every night but one, and I regret only that I did not speak on that night.' With a delivery that in the beginning of his speeches was somewhat slow and hesitating, with little method, with great repetition, with no grace of gesture, with an utter indifference to the mere oratory of display, thinking of nothing but how to convince and persuade the audience who were immediately before him, never for a moment forgetting the vital issue, never employing an argument which was not completely level with the apprehensions of his audience, he possessed to the very highest degree the debating qualities which an educated political assembly of Englishmen most highly value. The masculine vigour and strong common sense of his arguments, his unfailing lucidity, his power of grasping in a moment the essential issue of a debate, his skill in hitting blots and throwing the arguments on his own side into the most vivid and various lights, his marvellous memory in catching up the scattered threads of a debate, the rare combination in his speeches of the most glowing vehemence of style with the closest and most transparent reasoning, and the air of intense conviction which he threw into every discussion, had never been surpassed. He was one of the fairest of debaters, and it was said that the arguments of his opponents were very rarely stated with such masterly power as by Fox himself before he proceeded to grapple with, and to overthrow them.[1] He possessed to the highest degree what Walpole called the power of 'declaiming argument,' and that combination of rapidity and soundness of judgment which is the first quality of a debater. 'Others,' said Sir George Savile, 'may have had more stock, but Fox had more ready money about him than any of his party.' 'I believe,' said Lord Carlisle, 'there never was a person yet created who had the faculty of reasoning like him.' 'Nature,' said Horace Walpole, 'had made him the most powerful reasoner of the age.' 'He possessed beyond all moderns,' wrote Mackintosh, 'that union of reason, simplicity, and vehemence which formed the prince of orators.' 'Had he been bred to the bar,' wrote Philip Francis, 'he would in my judgment have made himself in a shorter time, and with much less application than any other man, the most powerful litigant that ever appeared there.' 'He rose by slow degrees,' said Burke, 'to be the most brilliant and accomplished debater the world ever saw.' His finest speeches were wholly unpremeditated, and the complete subordination in them of all rhetorical and philosophical ambition to the immediate purpose of the debate has greatly impaired their permanent value; but even in the imperfect fragments that remain, the essential qualities of his eloquence may be plainly seen.

At the period, however, we are now examining, his talent was yet far from its maturity, and the statesman who became one of the steadiest and most consistent of Whigs was still one of the most ardent of Tories. Almost the first speech he ever made was in favour of the expulsion of Wilkes, and he was one of the ablest advocates of the election of Luttrell, one of the fiercest vituperators of the City democrats. Very few politicians were so unpopular in the City, and in the great riot of 1771 his chariot was shattered by the mob, he was dragged through the mud, and his life was in some danger.[2] He defended the Nullum Tempus Act, which was one of the harshest measures of the early period of the reign, and resisted the attempt of Sir W. Meredith in 1771 to procure its repeal. He opposed the law which punished by disfranchisement the gross corrup-

[1] Butler's *Reminiscences*, i. 159.
[2] See the admirable description of this riot in Mr. Trevelyan's noble *Life of Fox*.

tion of the electors of Shoreham. He opposed the law making the Grenville Election Act perpetual. He opposed the motion for relieving clergymen of their subscription to the Thirty-nine Articles, though he expressed a strong wish that the obligation should be no longer extended to students at the Universities.[1] It is curious to find Lord Holland congratulating himself on the close connection of his son with Lord North, and anticipating that the young statesman would infuse a new energy into his chief in the struggle with the Whigs that followed the resignation of Grafton,[2] and it is not less curious to read the judgment of the future historian of James II. upon the history of Clarendon. 'I think the style bad, and that he has a great deal of the old woman in his way of thinking, but hate the opposite party so much that it gives me a kind of partiality for him.'[3]

The resignation of Fox in February 1772 was not due to any general opposition to the policy of North, but to his opposition to the Royal Marriage Bill, and to his unsuccessful effort to amend that Marriage Act of Lord Hardwicke which his father had so ably and so bitterly opposed. It appears, however, from a letter addressed by Lord Holland to Lord Ossory that Fox considered that he 'had reason to be dissatisfied,' and to think that 'Lord North did not treat him with the confidence and attention he used to do,' and also that his father considered that he 'had been too hasty in a step of this consequence.' Fox himself probably soon adopted a similar view, for he spoke of North in a tone of marked moderation and compliment, expressed in strong terms his general concurrence with his political principles, and clearly intimated his desire not to go into general opposition.[4] North met his overtures in the same spirit, and towards the close of 1772 the first quarrel of Fox with the Tory party was ended. A new disposition of places was made expressly to open a place for him, and he became one of the Commissioners of the Treasury.

The most engrossing subject of parliamentary discussion in 1772 and the following year was the affairs of the East

---

[1] *Parl. Hist.* xvii. 293.
[2] *Correspondence of Fox,* i. 63, 64.
[3] Jesse's *Life of Selwyn,* iii. 11.
[4] *Correspondence of Fox,* i. 70–87. Russell's *Life of Fox,* i. 33–38.

India Company, and in order to understand them it will be necessary to resume in a few pages the narrative which was broken off in a former volume. The period of Indian history during the five years that followed the return of Clive to England in February, 1760, though it is not the most tragical, is perhaps the most shameful in its whole annals. The victories of Clive had filled the natives with an abject terror of the English name, and had given Englishmen an almost absolute ascendency in Bengal. But this power was not in the hands of the responsible government of England. It was not even in the hands of the great commercial Company which nominally ruled the British possessions in Hindostan. It was practically monopolised by a great multitude of isolated officials, scattered over vast and remote districts, dominating in the native Courts, far removed from all control, and commanding great bodies of disciplined Sepoys. Most of them had left England when little more than schoolboys, and at a time when their characters were wholly unformed. Some of them were desperate adventurers of broken fortunes and tarnished honour, and they had gone to the East at a time when very few even of the best Europeans would have considered themselves bound to apply the whole moral law to men of a pagan creed and of a colour differing from their own. The government of the Company was too weak, too divided, and too distant to exercise any real control upon their conduct; and they found themselves wholly beyond the range and influence of European opinion, and in a country where all the traditions, habits, and examples of government were violent and despotic. The Company had regulated the salaries of its servants according to a European scale, and they were utterly insufficient to support them in the East. By the strictest economy they could barely live upon their pay, while they had unlimited opportunities of acquiring by illicit means enormous wealth. Nowhere in Europe, nowhere else, perhaps, in the world, were large fortunes so easily amassed. Clive himself had gone out a penniless clerk; when he returned to England, at thirty-four, he had acquired a fortune of more than 40,000*l.* a year, besides giving 50,000*l.* to his relatives;[1] and he afterwards declared that when he remem-

[1] Malcolm's *Life of Clive*, ii. 187.

bered what he might have obtained he was astonished at his moderation. It was a common thing for young men who had gone out without a penny to return, in ten or twelve years, with fortunes that enabled them to rival or eclipse the oldest families in their counties.

It needs but little knowledge of human nature to perceive that such a combination of circumstances must have led to the grossest abuses. The English officials began everywhere to trade on their own account, and to exercise their enormous power in order to drive all competitors from the field. A chief part of the native revenues consisted of duties imposed on the transit of goods; but the servants of the Company insisted on exempting themselves from paying them. Sometimes they sold for large sums a similar exemption to native traders. They defied, displaced, or intimidated all native functionaries who attempted to resist them. They refused to permit any other traders to sell the goods in which they dealt. They even descended upon the villages, and forced the inhabitants, by flogging and confinement, to purchase their goods at exorbitant prices, or to sell what they desired to purchase, at prices far below the market value. They exacted heavy sums, as fines, from those who refused to yield; disorganised the whole system of taxation in the native states by the exemptions they claimed; seized, bound, and beat the agents of the native governments; openly defied the commands of the Nabob, and speedily undermined all authority in Bengal except their own. Monopolising the trade in some of the first necessaries of life, to the utter ruin of thousands of native traders, and selling those necessaries at famine prices to a half-starving population, they reduced those who came under their influence to a wretchedness they had never known before. The native rulers had often swept like some fierce monsoon over great districts, spreading devastation and ruin in their path; but the oppression of the English was of a new and wholly different kind. Never before had the natives experienced a tyranny which was at once so skilful, so searching, and so strong. Every Sepoy in the service of the Company felt himself invested with the power of his masters. Whole districts which had once been populous and flourishing were at last utterly depopulated, and it was noticed that on the appearance of a party of English merchants the villages were at once deserted, and the shops shut, and the roads thronged with panic-stricken fugitives.

There were other means by which the vast fortunes of the upper servants of the Company were accumulated. The Company had not adopted the plan of governing the country directly. It ruled mainly by its influence over the native authorities, and its chief servants exercised an almost unlimited power of promoting or degrading. They became the centre of a vast web of intrigue, countless native officials competing for their support, and purchasing it by gifts wrung from an impoverished people. More than one native ruler struggled against the tyranny, and there was much mutiny and disorder among the British; but in critical moments they always displayed a skill, a courage, and a discipline that enabled them to crush all opposition. The Emperor had been murdered in 1760, and his successor, having made the Nabob of Oude his Viceroy, attempted to restore the Imperial ascendency in Bengal; but, after two severe defeats, he was compelled to retreat. Meer Jaffier, whom the English had made Nabob of Bengal after the battle of Plassy, was deposed by them, and his son-in-law, Meer Cossim, was raised to the vacant seat. He proved, however, to be a man of energy and capacity. He resented bitterly the trade privileges of the English, and he attempted to place the English traders on a level with his own subjects. The English, finding him recalcitrant, soon resolved to depose him. The struggle was long and desperate; 150 English were deliberately massacred by the Nabob at Patna. The Nabob of Oude joined his forces with those of Meer Cossim; but the prowess of the English proved again victorious. Meer Jaffier was once more made Nabob of Bengal, and the total defeat of the Nabob of Oude in the battle of Buxar, on September 15, 1764, destroyed the power of the only great Mogul chief remaining, and placed the Emperor himself under the protection of the English. In Madras the English influence was extended by the subjugation of some independent chiefs. Mohammed Ali, the Nabob of that province, was wholly subservient to the English; and the Company obtained the grant of a great part of the revenues of the Carnatic. In

January 1765, Meer Jaffier died, and the succession to his throne lay between his surviving son, who was a youth of twenty, and an infant who was the son of his eldest deceased son. The choice legally rested with the Emperor; but he was not even consulted. The Company made Nujum-ad-dowla, the son of Meer Jaffier, Nabob; but he purchased the dignity both by large money gifts and by conditions which marked another step in the subjugation of Bengal to the English. The new Nabob was compelled to leave the whole military defence of the province to the English, keeping only as many troops as were necessary for purposes of parade and for the administration of justice and the collection of the revenue. The civil administration was hardly less effectually transferred by a provision placing it in the hands of a Vicegerent, who was to be chosen by the Nabob by the advice of the Governor and Council, and who might not be removed without their consent. The large revenues the Company already received from Bengal were confirmed and increased; the Company's servants obtained a formal concession of the privilege of trading within the country without paying the duties exacted from native traders, provided they paid two and a half per cent. on the single article of salt, and the accountants of the Revenue were not to be appointed except with their approbation.

At every turn of the wheel, at every change in the system or the personality of the Government, vast sums were drawn from the native treasury, and most steps of promotion were purchased by gifts to the English. A great part of these gifts, going to minor servants for procuring minor promotions, have never been traced; but the Select Committee of 1773 published a detailed account of such sums as had been proved and acknowledged to have been distributed by the princes and other natives of Bengal from the year 1757 to 1766, both included. Omitting the great grant which had been made to Clive after the battle of Plassy, these sums amounted to no less than 5,940,498*l.*

Rumours of these abuses had begun to come to England. The Indian adventurer, or, as he was popularly called, the Nabob, was now a conspicuous and a very unpopular figure in Parliament, and the feeling of discontent was greatly strengthened by the impoverished and embarrassed condition of the Company. While numbers of its servants were returning to England laden with enormous wealth, the great corporation itself seemed on the verge of bankruptcy. The pay of its troops was in arrears, and the treasury at Calcutta was empty; heavy bills had been drawn in Bengal, and it was with the utmost difficulty they could be met.[1] Vansittart, who had succeeded Clive in the government of Bengal, though a man of good intentions and of some ability, was utterly unable to control his servants, and he was often paralysed by resistance in his own Council. Orders were sent out from England, in 1764, forbidding the servants of the Company from engaging on their own account in the inland trade, and enjoining that all presents exceeding 4,000 rupees received by them should be paid to their masters; but these orders were completely disregarded. It was felt by the Directors that if the Company was to be saved, a stronger hand was needed in India. After several stormy debates and much division of opinion, Clive was again made Governor and Commander-in-Chief of Bengal, and was invested with extraordinary powers; and in May, 1765, he arrived at Calcutta.

His administration lasted only for eighteen months, but it was one of the most memorable in Indian history. He found, in his own emphatic words, 'that every spring of the Government was smeared with corruption; that principles of rapacity and oppression universally prevailed, and that every spark of sentiment and public spirit was lost and extinguished in the unbounded lust of unmerited wealth.' The condition of affairs, he informed the Directors, was 'nearly desperate,' and, he added, 'in a country where money is plenty, where fear is the principle of government, and where your arms are ever victorious, it is no wonder that the lust of riches should readily embrace the proffered means of its gratification, and that the instruments of your power should avail themselves of your authority and proceed even to extortion in those cases where simple corruption could not keep pace with their rapacity. Examples of this sort set by superiors could not fail of being followed in a proportionate degree by inferiors. The evil was

[1] Mill, book iv. ch. v.

contagious, and spread among the civil and military down to the writer, the ensign, and the free merchant.'[1]

The scheme of policy which he adopted shows clear traces of a powerful and organising mind. Though himself the greatest conqueror in the Indian service, he strongly censured the spirit of aggrandisement and adventure that had passed into the Company, and he declared that they never could expect good finances till they recognised their own position as a purely commercial body, put a check to the incessant military expeditions in which they had engaged, and resolved to restrict their influence and their possessions to Bengal, Orissa, and Behar.[2] But the relations of the English with the Emperor and with the Nabob of Bengal were both changed. The Emperor and his Vizier, the Nabob of Oude, were still in a state of hostility to the Company, but they were thoroughly broken and humiliated, and the war had for some time languished. Clive now concluded a definite peace with them. The Nabob of Oude received back all his territory on paying a large sum in compensation, with the exception of Allahabad and Corah, which were reserved for the Emperor. The financial relations between the Emperor and Bengal were much modified, and one change was made which was of capital importance in the future Government of India. The 'Dewannee,' or right of collecting, receiving, and administering the revenue of Bengal, Orissa, and Behar, was granted to the English. They thus became practically the sovereigns of the country. The Nabob of Bengal received a large pension from the Government, but he was deprived of all real power, though, by the advice of Clive, he was still retained as a nominal ruler, in order that in case of any complication with European Powers the English might be able, under the fiction of a native prince, to preserve a somewhat greater liberty of action in declaring or in declining hostilities.

He at the same time made great efforts to cure the abuses of the administration. The difficulties he had here to encounter were enormous, for he had not only to struggle with the opposition of the civil servants in India, but also with very serious obstacles raised by the Directors at home. In spite of the orders of the Directors enormous presents had passed to

[1] Malcolm's *Life of Clive* ii. 335-338.   [2] Mill, iv. 7.

their chief servants in India on the accession of Nujum-ad-dowla, and on the appointment of his vicegerent the inland trade had been expressly recognised and encouraged by the treaty with the new Nabob. At the same time the Directors positively refused to raise the salaries of their servants, and until such a step was taken it was impossible that the inland trade could be suppressed. Some compromise was evidently necessary, and that which was adopted by Clive, though it was in direct disobedience to the instructions of his superiors at home, and though he was accused, apparently with good reason, of having in the course of the transaction speculated largely for his own interest,[1] was probably one of the best that could have been devised. A peremptory order was issued forbidding the infamous practice of forcing the natives to buy and sell at such prices as the servants of the Company chose to prescribe, and the inland trade and presents from natives were in general terms prohibited. Clive resolved, however, to maintain for the Company a strict monopoly of the salt trade, which was probably the most lucrative in Bengal, and to assign the profits of that trade in specified proportions to the Governor, the Councillors, and the senior civil and military officers. The shares of the trade were granted to the civil servants as low down as factors, and to the military servants as low down as majors, and the chaplains and surgeons were included in the arrangement. 35 per cent. was allowed as a tax to the Company. According to the estimate of Clive, the profits from this source of a councillor or colonel would be at least 7,000*l.* a year; those of a major or factor, 2,000*l.*[2]

These measures and several others of detailed reform were carried amid storms of unpopularity. When some of the Bengal functionaries refused to act under him, he sent to Madras for substitutes. On one day 200 officers resigned, and but for the fidelity of the Sepoys the whole military organisation of the Company might have fallen to the ground. But the iron will of Clive was never diverted from its object. He encountered the animosities of those whose illicit gains he disturbed with the same calm courage which he had displayed at Fort William,

---

[1] Mill, book iv., chap. vii.; see too chap. v.
[2] Malcolm's *Clive*, iii. 101–103.

at Plassy, and at Chinsurah; and when at last, in January 1767, his broken health obliged him to return to England, he had undoubtedly left the state of India much better than he had found it. Had the lines of his policy been steadily maintained, the affairs of the Company might never have passed under the hostile notice of Parliament.

The Directors, however, refused to confirm the provisions he had made about the salt trade, and on the removal of Clive the old trade abuses grew up again, though in a somewhat mitigated form. The belief in the enormous wealth of India had greatly increased, and the proprietors of the Company began to clamour loudly for an augmented dividend. In spite of the great debts of the Company, in spite of the strong opposition of the Directors, the proprietors insisted on raising the dividend in 1766 from 6 to 10 per cent., and in 1767 to $12\frac{1}{2}$ per cent.

It was about this time that the great question of the justice and propriety of a parliamentary interference with the government of India first came into practical importance. We have seen in a former chapter that Chatham strongly maintained that it was both the right and the duty of the Crown to take the government of India under its direct control; that no subjects could acquire the sovereignty of any territory for themselves, but only for the nation to which they belonged; that while the trading privileges of the Company should be preserved as long as its charter was in force, its territorial revenue belonged of right to the nation; and that the gross corruption and oppression that existed in India loudly called for parliamentary interference. These views were maintained with equal emphasis by Shelburne; but in the Cabinet of Chatham himself Charles Townshend strongly urged that the question should not be brought before the House of Commons, and the whole Rockingham section of the Whigs maintained the sole right of the Company under the terms of its charters to the government and revenues of India. As no reservation of territorial revenue to the Crown had been made when these charters were purchased by the Company, granted by the Crown, and confirmed by Parliament, they contended that the claims now put forward on the part of the Government were utterly inconsistent with good faith or respect for property. In November

1766, however, Parliament appointed a committee to inquire into and to publish the state of the Company's revenue and other affairs, its relations to the Indian princes, the expenses the Government had incurred on its account, and even the correspondence of the Company with its servants in India. It was with difficulty that the Company procured an exemption of the confidential portion of that correspondence from the general publicity. In 1767 a law was passed which introduced several new regulations into the manner of voting and declaring dividends in public companies;[1] it was immediately followed by an Act which, in defiance of the late resolution of the Court of Proprietors raising the dividend of the East India Company to 12½ per cent., limited it till the next Session of Parliament to 10 per cent.,[2] and the Company, terrified by the action of the Government, then entered into an agreement, by which it purchased the extension of its territorial revenue, and also a temporary exemption from a duty which had been imposed upon some kinds of tea, by binding itself to pay 400,000l. a year into the public exchequer for two years from February 1, 1767.[3]

The question of right which was thus raised was a very grave one. The enactment of a law restraining a trading company from granting such dividends as were voted and declared by those who were legally entrusted with the power of doing so, was opposed by all sections of the Opposition as a gross violation of the rights of property, and as inconsistent with the security of every commercial corporation in the country. Counsel were heard against the Bill. On the third reading in the House of Lords a minority of forty-four divided against a majority of fifty-nine, and nineteen peers signed a protest against the measure.[4] The principle, however, was maintained and extended. In 1768 the restraint on the dividend was continued for another year, and in 1769 a new agreement was made by Parliament with the East India Company for five years, during which time the Company was guaranteed its territorial revenues, but was bound to pay an annuity of 400,000l.,

---

[1] 7 Geo. III. c. 48.
[2] Ibid. c. 49.
[3] Ibid. c. 56, 57. See Macpherson's *Annals of Commerce*, iii. 463–466.
[4] Adolphus, i. 301, 302.

and to export a specified quantity of British goods. It was at liberty to increase its dividend during that time to 12½ per cent. providing the increase in any one year did not exceed 1 per cent. If, however, the dividend should fall below 10 per cent. the sum to be paid to the Government was to be proportionately reduced. If it sank to 6 per cent. the payment to the Government was to cease. In case the finances of the Company enabled it to pay off some specified debts, it was to lend some money to the public at 2 per cent.[1]

It is obvious that this law rested upon the supposition that the Company possessed an enormous surplus revenue, and a large section of politicians regarded the exaction of the annuity as a simple extortion, which was wholly unwarranted by the terms of the charter. It soon became evident that the Company was totally unable to pay it. Its debts were already estimated at more than six millions sterling.[2] It supported an army of about 30,000 men. It paid about one million sterling a year in the form of tributes, pensions, or compensations to the Emperor, the Nabob of Bengal, and other great native personages.[3] Its incessant wars, though they had hitherto been always successful, were always expensive, and a large proportion of the wealth which should have passed into the general exchequer was still diverted to the private accounts of its servants. At this critical period, too, the Company was engaged in a desperate and calamitous struggle with Hyder Ali, the ruler of Mysore, who was by far the ablest and most daring native enemy the English had yet encountered in Hindostan. The war had begun in 1767, when Hyder Ali succeeded in inducing the Nizam of Deccan to join him against the English; but although it had become evident from the beginning that an enemy had arisen who was widely different in skill and courage from those whom the Company had as yet encountered, it seemed as if English discipline was likely to be as usual completely victorious. After several vicissitudes of fortune Hyder Ali was defeated in a great battle near Amboor. The Nizam fell away from him and made peace with the English. Mangalore, one of Hyder Ali's principal seaports, was captured by

---

[1] 9 Geo. III. c. 24. [2] *Wealth of Nations*, book v. ch. i. part 3
[3] *Annual Register*, 1773, p. 65.

a squadron from Bombay. Colonel Smith pursued the defeated chieftain into his own country, and although he was unable to force him to give battle, he penetrated far into Mysore and captured several fortresses. But towards the close of 1768 a great turn took place in the fortunes of the war. Hyder Ali reconquered everything that had been taken. With 14,000 horsemen and a large force of Sepoys, he swept almost without resistance over the southern division of the Carnatic, reducing a once fertile land to utter ruin; and soon after, having by a series of artful manœuvres succeeded in drawing the English army far from Madras, he, at the head of 6,000 cavalry, traversed 120 miles in three days, and appeared unexpectedly in the immediate neighbourhood of the English capital. He at once proposed a peace; and, as the open town and the rich country round Madras were at his mercy, the English agreed to negotiate. In April 1769 a treaty was signed, providing for a mutual restitution of conquests and an alliance.

It was the first instance in which a victorious native Power had almost dictated terms to the English, and its effects on the fortunes of the Company were immediate. The price of East India Stock fell 60 per cent., the credit of the Company sank, and as the revenues from India began to fail, and the shadow of unpopularity fell more darkly upon the Corporation, the old complaints of the abuses that were practised grew louder Three supervisors were sent out to India by the Directors in 1769, with authority to investigate every department of the service; but the ship in which they sailed never reached its destination. In 1770 Bengal was desolated by perhaps the most terrible of the many terrible famines that have darkened its history, and it was estimated that more than a third part of its inhabitants perished. Yet in spite of all these calamities, in spite of the rapidly accumulating evidence of the inadequacy of the Indian revenues, the rapacity of the proprietors at home prevailed, and dividends of 12 and 12½ per cent., as permitted by the last Act, were declared. The result of all this could hardly be doubtful. In July 1772, the Directors were obliged to confess that the sum required for the necessary payments of the next three months was deficient to the extent of no less than 1,293,000*l.*, and in August the Chairman and Deputy

Chairman waited on the Minister to inform him that nothing short of a loan of at least one million from the public could save the Company from ruin.

The whole system of Indian government had thus for a time broken down. The division between the Directors and a large part of the proprietors, and between the authorities of the Company in England and those in India, the private and selfish interests of its servants in India, and of its proprietors at home, the continual oscillation between a policy of conquest and a policy of trade, and the great want in the whole organisation of any adequate power of command and of restraint, had fatally weakened the great corporation. In England the conviction was rapidly growing that the whole system of governing a great country by a commercial company was radically and incurably false. The arguments on the subject cannot be better stated than they were a few years later by Adam Smith. The first interest, he said, of the Sovereign of a people is that its wealth should increase as much as possible; and this is especially the case in a country like Bengal, where the revenue is chiefly derived from land rent. But a company of merchants exercising sovereign power will always treat their character of sovereigns as a mere appendix to their character of merchants, will make all government subservient to the maintenance of trade monopoly, and will employ it to stunt or distort the economical development of the people over whom they rule. In the Spice Islands the Dutch were said to burn all spiceries which a fertile season produces beyond what they expected to be able to dispose of in Europe with such profit as they deemed sufficient. In British India, Government officials had been known to compel a peasant to plough up a rich field of poppies, for no other reason than that they might be able to sell their own opium at a higher price. As sovereigns it was the plain interest of the Company that their subjects should buy European goods as cheaply, and should sell their own goods as profitably, as possible. As merchants possessing the sole right of trading between India and Europe, it was their interest to compel the Indians to buy what the Company supplied at the dearest rate, and sell what the Company purchased for the European market at the cheapest rate. The first object of sovereign merchant companies is always to exclude competitors from the markets of the country they rule, and consequently to reduce some part at least of the surplus produce of that country to what they themselves require or can dispose of at the profit they consider reasonable. Insensibly but invariably, on all ordinary occasions, they will prefer the little and transitory profit of the monopolist to the great and permanent revenues of a sovereign. And the public trade monopoly of the Company is but a small part of the evil. This, at least, extends only to the trade with Europe. But the private trade of the servants of the Company extended to a far greater number of articles, to every article in which they chose to deal, to articles of the first necessity intended for home consumption. It is idle to suppose that the clerks of a great counting house, 10,000 miles distant from their masters, will abstain from a trade which is at once so lucrative and so easy, and it is no less idle to doubt that this trade will become a ruinous form of oppression. The Company has, at least, a connection with India, and has, therefore, a strong interest in not ruining it. Its servants have gone out for a few years to make their fortunes, and when they have left the country they are absolutely indifferent to its fate. If their wishes are attended to, they will establish the same legal monopoly for their private trade as the Company possesses for its public trade. If they are not suffered to do so, they will attain the same end by other means, by perverting the authority of Government and the administration of justice, in order to harass and to ruin all rival traders.[1]

The subject was discussed in Parliament, in 1772, at great length, and with much acrimony. Several propositions were put forward by the Directors, but rejected by the Parliament; and Parliament, under the influence of Lord North, and in spite of the strenuous and passionate opposition of Burke, asserted in unequivocal terms its right to the territorial revenues of the Company. A Select Committee, consisting of thirty-one members, was appointed by Parliament to make a full inquiry into the affairs of the Company. It was not, however, till 1773 that decisive measures were taken. The

---

[1] *Wealth of Nations*, book iv. ch. vii.

Company was at this time absolutely helpless. Lord North commanded an overwhelming majority in both Houses, and on Indian questions he was supported by a portion of the Opposition. The Company was on the brink of ruin, unable to pay its tribute to the Government, unable to meet the bills which were becoming due in Bengal. The publication, in 1773, of the report of the Select Committee, revealed a scene of maladministration, oppression, and fraud which aroused a widespread indignation through England; and the Government was able without difficulty, in spite of the provisions of the charter, to exercise a complete controlling and regulating power over the affairs of the Company. A new Committee—this time sitting in secret—was appointed by the Government to investigate its affairs, and Parliament took the decisive step of preventing by law the Company from sending out to India a Commission of Supervision which it had appointed, on the ground that it would throw a heavy additional expenditure on its tottering finances.[1]

A very earnest opposition was made to this measure by a few members, among whom Burke was pre-eminent. The part which Burke took in the contest is a curious illustration of the strong natural conservatism of his intellect, and a curious contrast to his later speeches on Indian affairs; and few persons who follow his speeches as they appear in the parliamentary reports will fail to be struck with the ungovernable violence of language, and the glaring faults of taste, temper, and tact which they display.[2] His arguments, however, when reduced to their simplest expression, were very forcible. He contended that to violate a royal charter, repeatedly confirmed by Act of Parliament, was to strike at the security of every trading corporation, and, indeed, of all private property, in the kingdom, and that it was a clear violation of the charter of a self-governed Company to prevent it, by Act of Parliament, from managing its own affairs and exercising a supervision and control over its own servants. Every additional proof of the abuses in India

---

[1] 13 Geo. III. c. 9. *Annual Register*, 1773, pp. 73-76.

[2] See *Parl. Hist.* xvii. It is curious to contrast the wild language of these speeches with the admirable summary of the arguments against the Government proposal in the *Annual Register* and in the protests of the dissentient peers, which were probably all written by Burke.

was an additional argument for permitting the Company to send out a committee of supervision, and the simple postponement of such a step would necessarily aggravate the evils that were complained of. It was true that the financial condition of the Company was deplorable; but its embarrassments were partly due to transient and exceptional causes, and mainly to the conduct of the Government itself. Without a shadow of authority in the terms of the charter or in the letter of the law, the ministers had raised a distinction between the territorial revenue and the trade revenue of the Company. By threatening the former they had extorted, in addition to the legitimate duties which had been paid into the Imperial exchequer, no less than 400,000*l*. a year, at a time when the finances of the Company were altogether unable to bear the exaction. This tribute, which was the true origin of the bankruptcy of the Company,[1] was purely extortionate. In one form or another it was computed that little less than two millions sterling had of late passed annually from the Company to the Government.[2] The interference of Parliament with the affairs of the Company had been going on since 1767, and had produced nothing but unmixed disaster. Not a single abuse had been in reality removed. Government had shaken the credit of the Company; had introduced a fatal element of uncertainty into all its calculations; had imposed upon it a tribute which reduced it to bankruptcy; had paralysed its efforts to control the abuses of its own servants. Nor was there the smallest reason to believe that the withdrawal of the chief patronage of India from the Company, and the transfer of an almost boundless fund of corruption to the servants of the Crown, would prove beneficial either to England or to India. In the eyes of the law Parliament may, no doubt, be regarded as omnipotent; but its power does not equitably extend to the violation of compacts and the subversion of privileges which had been duly purchased. Yet this was the course which Parliament was now taking when it virtually cancelled the charter it had granted.

These arguments, however, proved of no avail. A large number of proprietors of the Company supported the Govern-

[1] *Parl. Hist.* xvii. 567.   [2] *Ann. Reg.* 1773 p. 76.

ment. Clive himself, who was in violent opposition to the predominating party among the Directors, was usually on their side.[1] The public mind was at last keenly sensible of the enormity of the abuses in India, and it was felt that an empire already exceeding in magnitude every European country except France and Russia, with a gross revenue of four millions, and a trade in proportion,[2] should not any longer be left uncontrolled by Parliament. The Company was obliged to come to Parliament for assistance, and the ministers resolved to avail themselves of the situation to reorganise its whole constitution. By enormous majorities two measures were passed through Parliament in 1773, which mark the commencement of a new epoch in the history of the East India Company. By one Act, the ministers met its financial embarrassments by a loan of 1,400,000*l*. at an interest of 4 per cent., and agreed to forego the claim of 400,000*l*. till this loan had been discharged. The Company was restricted from declaring any dividend above 6 per cent. till the new loan had been discharged, and above 7 per cent. till its bond-debt was reduced to 1,500,000*l*. It was obliged to submit its accounts every half-year to the Lords of the Treasury; it was restricted from accepting bills drawn by its servants in India for above 300,000*l*. a year, and it was obliged to export to the British settlements within its limits British goods of a specified value. By another Act, the whole constitution of the Company was changed, and the great centre of authority and power was transferred to the Crown. The qualification to vote in the Court of Proprietors was raised from 500*l*. to 1,000*l*., and restricted to those who had held their stock for twelve months; and by this measure 1,246 voters were at once disfranchised. The Directors, instead of being, as heretofore, annually elected, were to sit for four years, a quarter of the number being annually renewed. The Mayor's Court at Calcutta was to be restricted to small mercantile cases, and all the more important matters of jurisdiction in India were to be submitted to a new court, consisting of a Chief Justice and three puisne judges appointed by the Crown. A Governor-General of Bengal, Behar, and Orissa, was to be appointed at a salary of 25,000*l*. a year, with four Councillors, at salaries of

[1] Malcolm's *Life of Clive*, iii. 313-316.   [2] *Ibid.* 289.

8,000*l.* a year, and the other presidencies were made subordinate to Bengal. The first Governor-General and Councillors were to be nominated, not by the East India Company, but by Parliament; they were to be named in the Act, and to hold their offices for five years; after that period the appointments reverted to the Directors, but were subject to the approbation of the Crown. Everything in the Company's correspondence with India relating to civil and military affairs was to be laid before the Government. No person in the service of the King or of the Company might receive presents, and the Governor-General, the Councillors, and the judges were excluded from all commercial profits and pursuits.[1]

By this memorable Act the charter of the East India Company was completely subverted, and the government of India passed mainly into the hands of the ministers of the Crown The chief management of affairs was vested in persons in whose appointment or removal the Company had no voice or share, who might govern without its approbation or sanction, but who nevertheless drew, by authority of an Act of Parliament, large salaries from its exchequer. Such a measure could be justified only by extreme necessity and by brilliant success, and it was obviously open to the gravest objections from many sides. The direct appointment by the legislative body of great executive officers was especially denounced as at once unprecedented and unconstitutional; for it freed ministers from the responsibility, while it left them the advantages, of the patronage, and thus, in the words of the protest of the Rockingham peers, 'defeated the wise design of the Constitution, which placed the nomination of all offices either immediately or derivatively in the Crown, while it committed the check upon improper nominations to Parliament.' Some of the names then selected were afterwards very prominent in English and Indian history. Warren Hastings was the first Governor-General: Barwell, Clavering, Monson, and Philip Francis were the four Councillors.

In a future chapter of this history it will be my task to describe the results of this great change and experiment in govern-

---

[1] 13 Geo. III. ch. 63, 64; *Parl. Hist.* xvii. 928, 929; *Annual Register* 1773, 95-105; Mill's *History of British India,* book iv. ch. ix.

ment which makes the year 1773 so memorable in the history of British administration in India. The overwhelming majorities by which the measure was carried, in spite of the opposition of the Company, of the City of London, and of the Rockingham Whigs, show that it obtained something more than a mere party support; and Lord North, having attained his end, was anxious as much as possible to alleviate the stroke. Seventeen millions of pounds of tea were lying in the warehouses of the Company, and by permitting the direct export of this tea to the Colonies, North hoped to grant a great boon to India, and did not foresee that he was taking a great step toward the loss of America.

Another subject which now attracted general attention was the charges that were brought against Clive. He complained bitterly that he had been examined before the Select Committee as if he had been a sheep-stealer. The report of the Committee unveiled the many acts of violence and rapacity he had committed during his earlier administration; the great reforms which he had undertaken during his later administration had mortally offended many corrupt interests; he had bitter enemies among the Directors; he was the most prominent and most wealthy representative of a class of men who were very unpopular in the country; and as he had attached himself to the Grenville connection in politics, and had not after the death of Grenville fully identified himself with North, his position in Parliament was somewhat isolated. General Burgoyne, when presenting one of the reports of the Select Committee, declared that it contained an account of crimes shocking to human nature; and a few days later he brought on a vote of censure directed personally against Clive. Having enumerated the disgraceful circumstances attending the deposition of Surajah Dowlah in 1757, the fictitious treaty drawn up by Clive in order to elude the payment that had been promised to Omichund, the forgery by Clive of the name of Admiral Watson, and the enormous gifts which Clive had received as a reward for the elevation of Meer Jaffier, he moved that Clive did at that time, 'through the influence of powers with which he was entrusted,' obtain, under various authorities, sums amounting to 234,000*l*., and in so doing abused those powers. The debates that followed were very remarkable for the confusion of parties and persons they displayed. Clive defended himself with great ability and power, and his chief advocate was Wedderburne, the Solicitor-General, while one of his chief assailants was Thurlow, the Attorney-General. Lord North voted with his enemies. The Court party were divided;[1] and the bulk of the Opposition supported Clive. Fox and Barré agreed in attacking him, while Lord G. Germaine powerfully defended him. Burke was also among his defenders. He always drew a broad distinction between the career of Clive and the career of Hastings, and maintained that though the former had committed great crimes, his serious attempts in his last administration to purify the government of India, and especially his prohibition of presents from the natives, had done much to atone for them.[2] The facts that were alleged against him could not, indeed, be disputed; but the danger of the crisis, and the universal habits of Indian life, were strong circumstances of palliation. It was remembered that fifteen years had passed since the incriminated acts were committed; that Clive had performed services of transcendent value to the Empire; that in his last administration, with every opportunity of enormously increasing his fortune, he had refrained from doing so; and that the animosity against him was quite as much due to his merits as to his crimes. The resolution of Burgoyne was divided into two parts. The first part, asserting that Clive had accepted 234,000*l.*, was carried without a division; but the latter part, censuring his conduct, was rejected after a long debate, and, on the motion of Wedderburne, the House unanimously resolved 'that Robert Clive did at the same time render great and meritorious services to this country.'[3]

He did not long survive the triumph. The excitement of the conflict and the storm of invective that was directed against him

---

[1] The King himself was very hostile to Clive. He wrote to North, May 22, 1773: 'I own I am amazed that private interest could make so many individuals forget what they owe to their country, and come to a resolution that seems to approve of Lord Clive's rapine.' *Correspondence of George III. with Lord North.* See, too, Fox's *Correspondence,* i. 92.

[2] See Burke's *Works*, xiii. 141-146.
[3] See *Annual Register*, 1773, p. 107. Malcolm's *Memoirs of Clive*, iii. 359, 360. The account in the *Parl. Hist.* xvii. 881, 882, represents the motion of censure as having been carried, but this appears to be an error. Walpole (*Last Journals*, i. 243-245) mentions several speeches which are not given in the *Parl. Hist.*

contributed to unhinge his mind, which had always been subject to a dark, constitutional melancholy; and a painful disease, and a dangerous narcotic taken to alleviate it, aggravated the evil. In November 1774, he died by his own hand, when but just forty-nine; and in this manner, about two years before the outbreak of the American War, England lost the greatest general she had produced since the death of Marlborough.[1]

Another group of measures of considerable importance, which occupied at this time the attention of the public and of Parliament related to religious liberty. The spirit of intolerance, as we have seen in the last volume, had been for a long time steadily declining in England, and there was no disposition in the higher ranks of the Government and among the leaders of either of the great parties in the State to make legislation subservient to religious fanaticism. Prosecutions for religious heterodoxy had almost wholly ceased. The only case, I believe, of the punishment of a freethinker for his writings in the early years of George III. was that of Peter Anet, who was sentenced in 1762 to stand twice in the pillory, and to be imprisoned for a year in Bridewell with hard labour, for a very violent and scurrilous attack upon Christianity.[2] The Methodist movement, however, contributed to strengthen a spirit of fanaticism among the classes who were influenced by it, and, on the other hand, as we have already seen, it was encountered by explosions of mob violence which often amounted to a high degree of persecution, and which were sometimes in a very shameful manner connived at, countenanced, or even instigated by local magistrates and by clergymen. Isolated incidents occasionally occurred which seemed to show that the spirit of persecution was rather dormant than dead;[3] and the law, though mildly administered, contained many things that were repugnant to true religious liberty.

---

[1] See Malcolm's *Memoirs of Clive*. Mill's *Hist. of British India*, Parl. *Debates*, vol. xvii., and the admirable account of Indian affairs in the *Annual Register*.

[2] *Annual Register*, 1762, p. 113.

[3] Thus in 1769 Abel Proffer was convicted at the Monmouth Assizes for barbarous treatment of a Jew. He had placed him before a large fire with his hands tied behind him, to roast, and then stuffed hot bacon down his throat.—*Ann. Reg.* 1769, p. 93. In the same year we read that 'On Saturday morning a Methodist preacher, who had disturbed the peace of the city of Gloucester with his enthusiastic rant, was flogged through the streets by order of the mayor.'—*Ib.* p. 108.

The Ecclesiastical Courts still retained a jurisdiction which was in many respects oppressive and anomalous, and there were frequent complaints of their expensive, vexatious, and dilatory proceedings. Their conflict with the temporal courts dates from a period long anterior to the Reformation, and the temporal courts had early assumed, and exercised with much severity, a superintending influence over the spiritual ones, defining their sphere of action, and arresting by 'writs of prohibition' their attempts to extend their authority. The Ecclesiastical Courts retained, however, a power of taking cognisance of acts of private immorality, heresy, and neglect of religious observances, and some large departments of wrong lay within their jurisdiction. The withholding of tithes and other ecclesiastical dues and fees from the parson or vicar, injuries done by one clergyman to another, questions of spoliation and dilapidation of churches or parsonages, matrimonial cases, and also, by a peculiarity of English law, testamentary cases and cases of intestacy, passed under their control.

The tendency of English law, however, was gradually to abridge their sphere. The strange power they originally possessed of compelling an accused person to criminate himself, by tendering to him what was termed an *ex-officio* oath relating to the matter in dispute, would probably have been abolished under Elizabeth but for the direct intervention of the Queen.[1] It was finally taken away under Charles II.[2] and the jurisdiction of the Ecclesiastical Courts in cases of tithes and other pecuniary dues was greatly limited. When a question of disputed right was raised, the trial passed at once from the Ecclesiastical to the Civil Court, and this rule applied to all tithe cases in which the defendant pleaded any custom, modus, or composition. The Ecclesiastical Court had, therefore, only to enforce an undisputed right, and in cases of dues or tithes under the value of 40s. a law of William III. provided a summary process by which they might be recovered before a justice of the peace.[3] The discipline the Spiritual Courts exercised in cases of immorality, and especially in cases of non-attendance at church, gradually faded away, from the impossibility of enforcing it.

---

[1] Hallam's *Hist. of England*, ch. iv. [2] 13 Car. II. st. i. c. 12.
[3] Blackstone, book iii. ch. vii.

The only place where in the eighteenth century the discipline of the Anglican Church appears to have been habitually and severely enforced was in the Isle of Man under the Episcopate of Bishop Wilson.

Already in the seventeenth century it had become customary to commute these penances for a money payment,[1] and such payments in cases which were mainly *pro salute animi* gradually ceased. Archbishop Secker in 1753 complained bitterly of the difficulty of enforcing any kind of ecclesiastical discipline. Yet occasionally in some country parishes, even in the closing years of the eighteenth century, the spectacle might be seen of some poor woman arrayed in a white sheet doing public penance for her fault.[2]

In cases, however, of the wrongs which I have enumerated, and also in cases of defamation, the Ecclesiastical Courts retained all their vigour, and there were bitter complaints of their abuses and of the excessive expense of their procedure. They possessed also a peculiar weapon of terrible force. The sentence of excommunication might be imposed by them for many offences; but it was most commonly employed as a punishment for contempt of the Ecclesiastical Court in not appearing before it, or not obeying its decrees, or not paying its fees or costs. An excommunicated person in England was placed almost wholly beyond the protection of the law. He could not be a witness or a juryman. He could not bring an action to secure or recover his property. If he died without the removal of his sentence he had no right to Christian burial.[3] Nor was this all. After forty days' contumacy he might be arrested by the writ 'De excommunicato capiendo,' issued by the Court of Chancery, and imprisoned till he was reconciled to the Church.

It is a singular fact that such a tremendous power, which

---

[1] Blackstone, book iv. ch. xv, xix. In the debate about Ecclesiastical Courts in 1813, one of the speakers mentions a case of defamation in which 'the defendant had been acquitted before the Commissary Court of Surrey, but was afterwards found guilty in the Court of Arches and condemned to do penance, and then came a dispensation from performance, for which he had to pay 95*l*.'— *An. Reg.* 1813, p. 56.

[2] Several curious particulars about Church discipline in England in the eighteenth century will be found in Abbey and Overton's very interesting work on *The English Church in the Eighteenth Century*, ii. 52-54, 506-509.

[3] See Jacob's *Law Dictionary*, art. 'Excommunication.' Tomlins' *Law Dict.* art. 'Excommunication.'

in theory at least, might extend even to perpetual imprisonment, should during the whole of the eighteenth century have been lodged with an Ecclesiastical Court, and that it might be applied to men who had committed such trivial offences as the non-payment of fees or costs. Nor was it by any means a dead letter. Howard, in the course of his visits to the English gaols, mentions that in Rothwell gaol, in Yorkshire, he found a weaver named William Carr, who, 'having given a bad name to a woman who was said not to deserve a very good one,' was cited before the Ecclesiastical Court and imprisoned 'until he shall have made satisfaction to the Holy Church as well for the contempt as for the injury by him done unto it.' He lay in prison from May 1774 to July 1776, when he was released by an insolvent Act which forgave that class of debtors their fees.[1] In 1787 two women were committed to Northampton gaol by virtue of the writ 'De excommunicato capiendo,' 'because they had wickedly contemned the power of the keys.'[2] In this year, however, an Act was carried limiting the time of commencing suits in these Courts for different offences to six or eight months.[3] But the most serious abuses connected with them continued to the present century. In 1812 Lord Folkestone brought forward the subject when presenting a petition from a young woman who had lain for two years in Bristol gaol as an excommunicated person. She had neglected to perform a penance imposed on her by the Ecclesiastical Court; had been excommunicated and imprisoned in consequence; and, as she was too poor to pay the fees that had been incurred, she was unable to obtain her release. Lord Folkestone related six or seven other cases of a similar kind, and in about half of them the excommunicated person had been at least three years in prison.[4] In 1813 an important Act was passed regulating the Ecclesiastical Courts. The power of excommunication for contempt and non-payment of fees was taken away. The penalty was reserved only for certain expressly defined offences, and no civil penalty or disability, except im-

---

[1] *Howard on Prisons* (3rd ed.), p. 416.
[2] Disney's *Life of Sykes*, 199, 200, 373, 374.
[3] 27 Geo. III. c. 44.
[4] *Parl. Debates*, xxi. 99, 100, 295-303.

prisonment not exceeding six months, could any longer attach to excommunication.[1]

A very scandalous form of persecution, in which, however, religious motives had no part, was practised in the last years of George II. and the early years of George III. by no less a body than the Corporation of the City of London. In 1748 that Corporation made a bye-law imposing a fine of 400*l.* and 20 marks on any person who, being nominated by the Lord Mayor for the office of Sheriff, refused to stand the election of the Common Hall, and 600*l.* on anyone who, being elected, refused to serve. The proceeds of these fines were to be employed in building the New Mansion House, which had just been begun. But the office of Sheriff was one of those in which no one could serve who had not previously taken the Sacrament according to the Anglican rite, and it was, therefore, one of those from which Dissenters were excluded. It would appear almost incredible, if the facts were not amply attested, that under these circumstances the City of London systematically elected wealthy Dissenters to the office in order that they should be objected to and fined, and that in this manner it extorted no less than 15,000*l.* The electors appointed these Dissenters with a clear knowledge that they would not serve, and with the sole purpose of extorting money. One of those whom they selected was blind; another was bedridden. Sometimes the victims appealed against the sentence, but the case was brought in the first instance before a City court, which always gave verdicts for the Corporation, and the cost of appeals against the whole weight of the City influence was so great that few men were rich enough or determined enough to encounter it. At last a gentleman named Evans, who had been elected Sheriff, determined to fight the battle to the end. For no less than ten years the case was before the Courts. It was contended on the part of the Corporation that the Toleration Act did nothing more than suspend the penalties for attending the Nonconformist, and neglecting the Anglican, service; that it left the Dissenters liable to every other penalty and inconvenience to which they had been previously subject, and that they might, therefore, be legally fined for refusing to serve in

[1] 53 Geo. III. c. 127.

an office which they could not legally fill without going through a ceremony repugnant to their conscience. This doctrine was at last finally overthrown in 1767 by a judgment of the House of Lords. After consultation with the judges, and after one of the most admirable of the many admirable speeches of Lord Mansfield, the House decided that the Toleration Act took away the crime as well as the penalty of Nonconformity, and that no fine could be legally imposed on Nonconformists who refused to serve in offices to which conscientious Dissenters were ineligible by law.[1]

The next important question relating to religious liberty was one to which I have already adverted in another connection. The movement for abolishing the subscription to the Thirty-nine Articles was defended mainly on the principles of Locke and of Hoadly. Though not absolutely coextensive, it was at least closely connected with the growth of the Arian school of which Clarke, Sykes, Clayton, and Lindsey were prominent representatives, and it received a great impulse in 1766 from the publication and the popularity of the 'Confessional' of Archdeacon Blackburne. In 1771 a society called the Feather's Tavern Association was formed for the purpose of applying to the Legislature for relief. Blackburne and Lindsey were its most active members, and in February 1772 a petition, drawn up by Blackburne and signed by 250 persons, was presented to the House of Commons by Sir W. Meredith. Of those who signed it about 200 were clergymen, and the remainder were lawyers and doctors, who protested especially against the custom which prevailed at the universities of obliging students who came up for matriculation, at the age of sixteen or even earlier,[2] and who were not intended for the Church, to subscribe their consent to the Articles. It was remarked that Oxford was strongly opposed to the movement, while a powerful party at Cambridge supported it. Watson, who was afterwards Bishop of Llandaff, and who was at this time Professor of Divinity at Cambridge, published two letters in favour of it, under the signature of 'A Christian Whig,' which were presented to every Member of Par-

---

[1] See the noble speech of Lord Mansfield, *Parl. Hist.* xvi. 313–327. Campbell's *Chief Justices*, ii. 511–514. Stephens on the *Constitution*, pp. 337, 338.
[2] *Parl. Hist.* xvii. 250.

liament the day before the petition was taken into consideration.[1] Paley, who was then rising to prominence as a lecturer at Cambridge, refused to sign the petition on the characteristic ground that he was 'too poor to keep a conscience,' but he fully concurred in it, and he wrote anonymously in its support.[2] It was signed by Jebb and John Law, who were prominent tutors at Cambridge, and it was countenanced by the Bishop of Carlisle, who was father of John Law, and also it is said in some degree by Bishop Lowth.[3]

Lord North was anxious that the petition should be received and silently laid aside; but Sir Roger Newdigate, who was violently opposed to it, insisted upon moving its rejection, and a very interesting debate ensued. On the side of the petitioners the chief topics were the obscurities, the absurdities, and inconsistencies of the Articles, the manifest severity with which they pressed upon many clerical consciences, the folly of asking schoolboys of sixteen to declare their assent to a long series of complicated dogmatic assertions, the individual right and duty of every Protestant to interpret Scripture freely for himself, the essentially Popish character of all attempts to prescribe religious opinions by human formularies, the danger and the immorality of holding out temptations to dissimulation and prevarication by annexing rewards or punishments to particular opinions, the duty of opening the Church as wide as possible to all conscientious men. The petitioners were quite ready to assent to Scripture as the inspired Word of God, and to abjure all popish tendencies, but they refused to be bound by any merely human formularies. Among the arguments on the other side may be mentioned the appearance, perhaps for the first time, of two political doctrines which were afterwards destined in connection with Irish politics, and with the Roman Catholic question, to attain a great importance. It was contended that the Corona-

---

[1] Watson's *Autobiography*, i. 65, 66.

[2] Meadley's *Life of Paley*, pp. 47–50, Append. 3–46. In his *Moral Philosophy*, book iii. ch. xxii., Paley justified subscription, but strongly denied that it bound the subscriber to believe every proposition contained in the Articles, or all the theological opinions of their compilers. The Articles, he maintained, were intended by the Legislature to exclude abettors of Popery, Anabaptists, and members of sects hostile to episcopacy, and the intention of the Legislature is the measure of the obligation of the subscriber.

[3] Walpole's *Last Journals*, i. 7–13.

tion Oath made it unlawful for the Sovereign to give his assent to any law which changed the form or character of the Established Church, and that a similar incapacity was imposed upon Parliament by the articles of the Scotch Union, which enacted the permanent maintenance of the then existing Church establishments in the two countries.[1] It is remarkable that Burke, while strongly opposing the petition, took great pains to disclaim all sympathy with these arguments, and asserted that the Coronation Oath only bound the Sovereign to respect the religion which his Parliament had sanctioned, and that the Act of Union was no bar to the right of the united Parliament to revise and modify the ecclesiastical conditions of the country.[2]

The King was very strongly opposed to the prayer of the petitioners,[3] and Lord North, in a temperate speech, opposed it as disturbing what was now quiet, and as likely to introduce anarchy, confusion, and dissension into the Church. The petition was supported among others by Lord George Germaine, Sir George Savile, and Thomas Pitt, the nephew of Chatham, who belonged to different political connections, and its advocates appear to have been chiefly Whigs. Dowdeswell, however, and Burke on this question severed themselves from their friends,[4] and the speech of Burke was by far the ablest in the debate. He urged the great danger of religious alterations, which usually pave the way to religious tumults and shake one of the capital pillars of the State. He dwelt upon the complete indifference of the great majority of the people to the subject, and he laid down very emphatically the principle which always governed his own attitude and that of the section of the Whig party which he inspired, towards proposed reforms. 'The ground for a legislative alteration of a legal establishment is this and this only; that you find the inclinations of the majority of the people, concurring with your own sense of the intolerable nature of the abuse, are in favour of a change.' No such desire existed

---

[1] See both of these arguments in the speech of Sir Roger Newdigate, *Parl. Hist.* xvii. 255, 256.
[2] Ibid. 276–279.
[3] *Correspondence of George III. with Lord North*, i. 89; ii. 378.
[4] Burke, in a letter to Lady Huntingdon, promising to oppose the petition, says, 'My sentiments in regard to the petition of the clergy praying to be relieved from subscription to the 39 Articles, are in opposition to the opinions of nearly all my own party.'—*Life of the Countess of Huntingdon*, ii. 287.

in the present case. While strongly asserting the right of every man to follow his own convictions in religion, he as strongly maintained the undoubted right of the Legislature 'to annex its own conditions to benefits artificially created,' and 'to take a security that a tax raised on the people shall be applied only to those who profess such doctrines and follow such a mode of worship as the Legislature representing the people has thought most agreeable to their general sense, binding as usual the minority not to an assent to the doctrines, but to a payment of the tax.' The present question, he said, is not a question of the rights of private conscience, but of the title to public emoluments. He drew a vivid picture of the utter unsuitability of the Bible to be treated as a bond of union or a summary of faith,[1] and he dilated upon the impossibility of maintaining a religious organisation without any fixed code of belief, and the confusion and anarchy which an abolition of subscription would probably produce. By a majority of 217 to 71 the House refused to receive the petition.[2]

The question was again introduced in 1773 and 1774, but it made no progress either in the House or in the country, though the subscription of students at Cambridge was soon after modified. Several of the leaders of the movement seceded from the Church of England to Unitarianism, and the school of Hoadly was in its decadence, and a new spirit was arising in the Church. It was a significant fact that the Methodists, and the section of the Anglican clergy who were most imbued with their principles, were the most ardent opponents of the relaxation of subscription,[3] and the strongly dogmatic character of

---

[1] 'What is that Scripture to which they are content to subscribe? They do not think that a book becomes of Divine authority because it is bound in blue morocco, and is printed by John Basket and his assigns? The Bible is a vast collection of different treatises. A man who holds the Divine authority of one may consider the other as merely human. . . . There are some who reject the Canticles—others six of the Epistles. The Apocalypse has been suspected even as heretical, and was doubted of for many ages. . . . The Scripture is no one summary of doctrines regularly digested, in which a man could not mistake his way. It is a most venerable but most multifarious collection of the records of the Divine economy, a collection of an infinite variety of cosmogony, theology, history, prophecy, psalmody, morality, apologue, allegory, legislation, ethics, carried through different books, by different authors, at different ages, for different ends and purposes.'—Burke's *Works*, x. 20, 21.

[2] *Parl. Hist.* xvii. 246-296. Burke's *Works*, x. 3-21.

[3] *Life of the Countess of Huntingdon*, ii. 285-288. Walpole's *Last Journals*, i. 376.

the Evangelical school, and the Calvinistic theology which soon became dominant within it, tended to attach its members to the Articles. The opposition to them soon died away, and when it was next revived it was by the school which was beyond all others the most opposed to that of Hoadly, by the school of Newman and Keble, who justly looked upon the Articles as the stronghold of that Protestant faith which they desired to extirpate from the Church.

In the course of the debates on the subscription, Lord North said that if the application for relief had come from Dissenting ministers, who received no emoluments from the Establishment, he could see no objection to it, and this remark encouraged the Dissenters to apply for a relief from their subscription. As we have seen, their ministers, schoolmasters, and tutors were compelled by the Toleration Act to assent to thirty-five and a half of the Thirty-nine Articles of the Church of England. No such subscription had been exacted in the Irish Toleration Act of 1719, which legalised the position of the Irish Protestant Dissenters, and it was on various grounds unpopular among the Dissenters in England. Many had drifted far from the orthodoxy of their fathers, many had adopted the views of Hoadly, that all subscriptions to human formularies were wrong, and many others who cordially believed the doctrinal articles, regarded the subscription to them as a humiliating act of homage to a rival Church. The law indeed appears to have been very rarely enforced, and there was a party among the more orthodox Dissenters who desired its maintenance, and even petitioned against the abolition of the subscription to the Anglican Articles as tending to encourage the growth of Arianism.[1] The prevailing Dissenting opinion, however, was on the other side, and the relief Bill was extremely well received in the House of Commons. The ministers, though they did not take it under their own charge, appear to have favoured it, or at least to have been divided on the subject. On the side of the Opposition, Burke spoke strongly in its favour, and the great body of the Whigs supported it. It was carried through the House of Commons by large majorities in 1772 and 1773, but the bishops—strongly countenanced by the King, and ap-

[1] *Parl. Hist.* xvii 441, 443, 770-772, 786-790.

parently at his orders by the ministry[1]—opposed it in the Lords, and in spite of the warm support of Chatham it was defeated in that House. In 1779, however, it was brought in with more success, and by the concurrence of both parties Dissenting ministers and tutors were admitted to the benefits of the Toleration Act without a subscription to the Articles, provided they declared themselves Christians and Protestants, and believers in the Old and New Testaments.[2] In the same year the Irish Parliament relieved the Irish Nonconformists from the Test Act.

On these questions the tendency of the Whigs was somewhat more decidedly towards religious liberty than that of the Tories. This was, however, in some degree due to the greater freedom of an Opposition, and in some degree to the old alliance of the Dissenters with the Whigs; and each party was much divided, and the prevailing temper of Lord North was far removed from intolerance. In one most important measure, which marks an epoch in the history of religious liberty, the Government, as we have already seen, represented the liberal, and the Opposition the intolerant side. The Quebec Act of 1774, establishing Catholicism in Canada, would a generation earlier have been impossible, and it was justly considered a remarkable sign of the altered condition of opinion that such a law should be enacted by a British Parliament, and should have created no serious disturbances in the country. The Church party was at this time closely allied with the Court against the Americans. The bishops were on nearly all questions steady supporters of Lord North, and only one of them actively opposed the Quebec Bill. The Whig party and the City politicians were fiercely hostile to the measure. Chatham denounced it as 'a breach of the Reformation, of the Revolution, and of the King's Coronation Oath,' 'a gross violation of the Protestant religion.' The City of London presented an address to the King petitioning him not to give his assent to a Bill which was inconsistent with his Coronation Oath and with his position as protector of the Protestant religion. When the King went down to the House of Lords to give his assent to

---

[1] *Correspondence of George III. with Lord North*, i. 101.

[2] 19 Geo. III. c. 44. See Belsham's *Life of Lindsey*, pp. 66 67

the Bill, he was met by cries of 'No Popery!' from an angry mob,[1] and the Sovereign who in his later years was justly regarded as the bitterest enemy of his Catholic subjects in Ireland, was now described as leaning more strongly to Popery than any English monarch since the Stuarts. It was customary to compare George III. in this respect to Charles I.[2] When Burke, in 1775, moved his famous scheme for conciliating America, Horace Walpole commented upon it in these terms: 'It is remarkable that in his proposed repeal he did not mention the Quebec Bill—another symptom of his old Popery.'[3]

The success of the Quebec Act led Parliament, a few years later, to undertake the relief of the Catholics at home from some part of the atrocious penal laws to which they were still subject. The absurdity of maintaining such laws suspended over the heads of a small and peaceful fraction of the nation, in an age of general enlightenment and toleration, was now keenly felt, and it was the more conspicuous on account of the marked change which had passed over the spirit of the chief Catholic Governments of Europe. Religion had everywhere ceased to be a guiding motive in politics. Nearly all the Catholic governments of Europe were animated by a purely secular spirit, and were completely emancipated from clerical influence. Pombal in Portugal; Choiseul, Malesherbes, and Turgot in France; Aranda and Grimaldi in Spain, however much they may have differed on other points, were in this perfectly agreed. If Austria, under Maria Theresa, formed a partial exception, the accession to the empire of Joseph II. in 1764 had already given a new bias to its policy. The Jesuits, who represented especially the intolerance and aggressiveness of Catholicism, had, for many years, lost all credit and almost all

---

[1] Walpole's *Last Journals*, i. 374–379.

[2] 'James II. lost his crown for such enormities. The prince that wears it to the prejudice of that family is authorised by a free Parliament to do what James was expelled for doing! A prince cried up like Charles I. for his piety is as favourable to Papists as Charles was, and has a bench of bishops as unjust to the Presbyterians, as propitious to Papists, as Charles had. And George III. has an army, which Charles had not.'—Walpole's *Last Journals*, i. 378. The poet Cowper wrote (Feb. 13, 1780) about the resemblance of the reigns of George III. and of Charles I., 'especially the suspicion that obtains of a fixed design of Government to favour the growth of Popery.'—See Albemarle's *Life of Rockingham*, ii. 393.

[3] Walpole's *Last Journals*, i. 511.

power. They had been expelled from Portugal in 1759, from France in 1764, from Bohemia and Denmark in 1766, from Spain, the Spanish colonies in America, Venice and Genoa in 1767, from Malta, Naples, and Parma in 1768, and, at last, in 1773 Clement XIV. had been induced to issue his famous bull suppressing the order. In nearly all Catholic countries, the tendency was to enlarge the bounds of religious liberty, to secularise the Government, and to restrict the power of the Church. Charles III. had almost completely fettered the Inquisition of Spain. In the course of a few years, stringent laws were made reducing the power of the clergy in Venice, Austrian Lombardy, Piedmont, Parma, and the Two Sicilies. An imperial edict in 1776 had abolished some of the worst forms of persecution in Austria and Hungary, and in the same year Necker, though an austere Calvinist, obtained a foremost place among the ministers of France.

All these things made the legal position of the English Catholics appear especially shameful, and the laws against them manifestly reflected the passions and the intolerance of another age. In considering, however, the real working of these laws, we must remember the curious conservatism of English legislators, who have continually preferred to allow a bad or an unpopular law to become dormant rather than repeal it. The Statute-book is by no means a true reflex of contemporary opinion and practice, for it is full of strange survivals of other ages. Thus a law of Henry V. which provided that all members of counties and boroughs must be residents in the constituencies they represented, and that no non-resident could be a voter, was suffered to be completely obsolete for centuries, and was at last removed from the Statute-book in 1774.[1] I have already referred to the law for slowly pressing to death prisoners who refused to plead, which was only repealed in 1772,[2] and to the law for punishing Irish witches with death, which was only repealed in 1821,[3] and several other almost equally striking instances may be adduced. Shortly before the Restoration, thirteen gipsies were executed at one Suffolk assize, under a law of Elizabeth, which made all gipsies found

---

[1] It was repealed by 14 Geo. III. c. 58. See for much information on this subject, Creasy's *Hist. of the Constitution*, 257–260.
[2] 12 Geo. III. c. 20.
[3] 1 & 2 Geo. IV. c. 18.

in England liable to death,[1] and this law, though censured by a committee of the House of Commons in 1772,[2] was not repealed till 1783.[3] The mediæval 'appeal of murder,' which enabled the heir of the deceased person to challenge the alleged murderer to battle, after his acquittal by a jury, and which took away from the Crown all power of pardoning the accused if he were defeated, was recognised by English law during the whole of the eighteenth century. It was eulogised in Parliament by Dunning in 1774,[4] and it was only abolished in 1819 on account of an appellee having, in the previous year, thrown down his glove in the Court of King's Bench and demanded his legal right of trial by battle.[5] The 'wager of law,' according to which a man who was charged with a debt was released from it if he denied the obligation, and obtained eleven neighbours to swear, from a general knowledge of his character, that they believed him, existed in English law till 1833.[6] From time to time an ingenious man exhumed some obsolete and forgotten law for the purpose of extorting money or gratifying revenge. Thus, in 1761, we find a lady tried at Westminster to recover a penalty of 20l., under a law of Elizabeth, because she had not attended any authorised place of worship for a month previously, and acquitted by the jury on the ground of her ill-health.[7] In 1772, a vicar was fined 10l. and his curate 5l. for not having read in church an old Act against cursing and swearing. The vicar, it appears, had dismissed his curate, and the sons of the latter having discovered the existence of this long-forgotten law, brought the action in revenge, not knowing that their father would be involved in the condemnation.[8] In 1774, a gentleman was indicted at the Chester Assizes for having broken the law of Elizabeth, which, in order to prevent the increase of the poor, made it penal to erect any detached cottage without accompanying it with four acres of freehold land.[9] The judges expressed great indignation at the proceeding, and at their representation the statute

---

[1] Blackstone, book iv. c. 13.
[2] Parl. Hist. xvii. 448-450.
[3] 23 Geo. III. c. 51.
[4] Parl. Hist. xvii. 1291-1297. See, too, Campbell's *Lives of the Chancellors*, viii. 22-24.
[5] 3 & 4 William IV. c. 42.
[6] British Chronicle, Feb. 23, 1761.
[7] Gentleman's Magazine, 1772, p. 339.
[8] 21 Eliz. c. 7. See Blackstone, book iv. c. 13.

was repealed in the following session.[1] Two statutes of Charles II. requiring that the dead should be buried in woollen, and imposing a penalty of 5*l*. on clergymen who neglected to certify to the churchwarden any instances in which the Act was not complied with, were only repealed in 1814, on account of a number of actions being brought by a common informer to recover the penalties.[2]

In all, or nearly all of these cases, the prosecutions were due to private motives of revenge or avarice, and similar motives, no doubt, inspired most of those directed against Catholics. The Act still subsisted which gave a reward of 100*l*. to any informer who procured the conviction of a Catholic priest performing his functions in England, and there were occasional prosecutions, though the judges strained the law to the utmost in order to defeat them, and insisted upon a rigour and fulness of proof that would not have been exacted in any other case. In 1767, a priest named John Baptist Malony was tried at Croydon on the charge of having administered the sacrament to a sick person, was found guilty and was condemned to perpetual imprisonment. He lay for some years[3] in confinement, and was then banished from England. In the same year, a mass-house in Southwark was suppressed, but the priest succeeded in escaping by a back-door. Two priests, named Webb and Talbot— the latter a brother of Lord Shrewsbury— were prosecuted in 1768 and 1769, but were acquitted through a defect in the evidence establishing their orders. Malony

---

[1] *Observations on a Scheme for the Maintenance of the Poor, in a Letter to Thomas Gilbert* (Chester, 1776), pp. 21, 22. The law was repealed by 15 Geo. III. c. 32.

[2] Phillimore's *Hist. of Geo. III.* p. 68. 54 Geo. III. c. 108.

[3] According to Burke (speech at Bristol in 1780), two or three years. Burke's *Works*, iii. 389. Oliver says his imprisonment lasted four years. (*Collections illustrating the Hist. of the Catholic Religion in Cornwall, Devon, Dorset, &c.* pp. 14, 15.) Lord Shelburne alluded to this case in a speech in 1778. 'Mr. Malony, a priest of the Roman Catholic persuasion, had been apprehended and brought to trial by the lowest and most despicable of mankind, a common informing constable of the City of London. He was convicted of being a popish priest, and the Court were reluctantly obliged to condemn him (shocking as the idea was) to perpetual imprisonment. His Lordship was then in office, and though every method was taken by the Privy Council to give a legal discharge to the prisoner, neither the laws then in force would allow of it, nor dared the King himself to grant him a pardon. He, however, with his colleagues in office, was so perfectly persuaded of the impolicy and inhumanity of the law, that they ventured to give him his liberty at every hazard.'—*Parl. Hist.* xix. 1145.

was, I believe, the only priest actually convicted during the reign of George III., but prosecutions were sufficiently frequent to make their position exceedingly precarious. Mrs. Lingard, the mother of the historian, who died in 1824 at the age of 92, is said to have remembered the time when her family had to go in a cart at night to hear mass, the priest wearing a round frock to resemble a poor man.[1]

Mansfield and Camden, who differed on most questions, agreed cordially in discountenancing legal measures against Catholics. One priest appears to have escaped conviction mainly through the extraordinary ingenuity with which Mansfield from the bench suggested doubts and difficulties in the evidence of a very clear case, and thus gave the jury a pretext for acquitting the prisoner.[2] Sir William Stanley, of Hooton, was indicted in 1770 for refusing to part with his four coach-horses when a 20l. note was tendered to him, but he was acquitted upon the ground that a bank-note was not legal tender.[3] In another case, the owner of an estate in the north of England endeavoured to reduce a lady, who was a near relative of his own, to utter poverty by depriving her of her jointure, which was in the form of a rent-charge on his estate, on the plea that being a Catholic she could take no estate or interest in land. Lord Camden took up her case with great zeal, and finding that there was no remedy in the existing law, he took the extreme step of bringing in and carrying a special Act of Parliament for her relief.[4] The position of Catholics, however, and especially of Catholic landowners, was always one of

---

[1] Oliver's *Collections illustrating the History of the Catholic Religion*, p. 33. *Gentleman's Magazine*, 1767, pp. 141, 142. Butler's *Memorials of the English Catholics*. Butler states (ii. 64) that in 1780 he ascertained that a single house of attorneys in Gray's Inn had defended more than twenty priests under prosecution for their religion, and had defended them in most cases gratuitously. Butler does not say over how long a period these prosecutions were diffused. I suspect the time must have included at least the whole reign of George III., and that the defence of all the Catholic cases must have fallen to this firm.

[2] See his very curious charge in Campbell's *Chief Justices*, ii. 514–516. In 1776 Dunning moved in the Court of King's Bench for informations against two Middlesex justices of the peace, who had refused to compel two persons charged with being Roman Catholics, to take the oaths. Mansfield refused the injunction, and at the same time expressed his disapproval of the attempt to revive the severities of the penal code.—*Annual Register*, 1776, p. 191.

[3] Oliver, p. 15.

[4] Burke's *Works*, iii. 389. Butler's *Memorials of the English Catholics*, ii. 72, 73.

extreme precariousness. They were still subject to a double land-tax. They were at the mercy of their Protestant relatives, who might easily deprive them of their land ; at the mercy of common informers ; at the mercy of any two justices who might at any time tender to them the oath of supremacy. They were virtually outlaws in their own country, doomed to a life of secrecy and retirement, and sometimes obliged to purchase by regular contributions an exemption from prosecution.

Several of their largest landowners had recently taken the oath, and the English Catholics were a small body with no power in the State. A Catholic writer, in 1781, estimated that in that year they counted 7 peers, 22 baronets, and about 150 other gentlemen of landed property. Several of the peers and three or four of the baronets were men of great estates, but the landed properties of the remaining commoners did not average more than 1,000*l.* a year, and not more than two or three Catholics held prominent positions in the mercantile world.[1]

The worst part of the persecution of Catholics was based upon a law of William III., and in 1778 Sir George Savile introduced a Bill to repeal those portions of this Act which related to the apprehending of Popish bishops, priests, and Jesuits, which subjected these and also Papists keeping a school to perpetual imprisonment, and which disabled all Papists from inheriting or purchasing land. In order to obtain the benefits of the law, it was necessary that the Catholics should take a special oath abjuring the Pretender, the temporal jurisdiction and deposing power of the Pope, and the doctrine that faith should not be kept with heretics, and that heretics, as such, may be lawfully put to death.[2]

It is an honourable fact that this Relief Bill was carried without a division in either House, without any serious opposition from the bench of bishops, and with the concurrence of both parties in the State. The law applied to England only, but the Lord Advocate promised, in the ensuing session, to introduce a similar measure for Scotland.

It was hoped that a measure which was so manifestly mode-

---

[1] *State and Behaviour of English Catholics from the Reformation to the Year* 1781, pp. 121, 122. [2] 18 Geo. III. c. 60.

rate and equitable, and which was carried with such unanimity through Parliament, would have passed almost unnoticed in the country; but fiercer elements of fanaticism than politicians perceived were still smouldering in the nation. The first signs of the coming storm were seen among the Presbyterians of Scotland. The General Assembly of the Scotch Established Church was sitting when the English Relief Bill was pending, and it rejected by a large majority a motion for a remonstrance to Parliament against it. But in a few months an agitation of the most dangerous description spread swiftly through the Lowlands. It was stimulated by many incendiary resolutions of provincial synods, by pamphlets, handbills, newspapers, and sermons, and a 'Committee for the Protestant Interests' was formed at Edinburgh to direct it. The Scotch Catholics were exceedingly alarmed, and they endeavoured to avert the danger which they feared by signing and publishing, in the beginning of 1779, a letter to Lord North, entreating him to forego his intention of putting them in the same position as their brethren in England, as any such attempt would arouse a spirit of fanaticism in Scotland that would endanger their lives and property. But it was now too late. Furious riots broke out in January 1779, both in Edinburgh and Glasgow. Several houses in which Catholics lived, or the Catholic worship was celebrated, were burnt to the ground. The shops of Catholic tradesmen were wrecked, and their goods scattered, plundered, or destroyed. Catholic ladies were compelled to take refuge in Edinburgh Castle. The houses of many Protestants who were believed to sympathise with the Relief Bill were attacked, and among the number was that of Robertson the historian. The troops were called out to suppress the riot, but they were resisted and pelted, and not suffered to fire in their defence; and the fears or sympathies of the Edinburgh magistrates were clearly shown in the almost grotesque servility of the proclamation which they issued to the rioters. 'To remove the fears and apprehensions,' they wrote, 'which had distressed the minds of many well-meaning people in the metropolis, with regard to the repeal of the penal statutes against Papists, the public are informed that the Act of Parliament passed for that purpose was totally laid aside, and therefore it was expected that all peaceable subjects would carefully avoid connecting themselves with any tumultuous assembly for the future.'[1]

The flame soon spread southwards. For some years letters on the increase of Popery had been frequently appearing in the London newspapers.[2] Many murmurs had been heard at the enactment of the Quebec Act, and many striking instances in the last ten years had shown how easily the spirit of riot could be aroused, and how impotent the ordinary watchmen were to cope with it. Great discontent had undoubtedly been produced in large sections of the population by the Relief Bill in 1778; the success of the Scotch riots in preventing the introduction of a similar measure for Scotland encouraged the hopes of procuring its repeal; and the fanatical party had unfortunately acquired an unscrupulous leader in the person of Lord George Gordon, whose name now attained a melancholy celebrity. He was a young man of thirty, of very ordinary talents, and with nothing to recommend him but his connection with the ducal house of Gordon, and his position as a member of Parliament, and he had for some time distinguished himself by coarse, violent, and eminently absurd speeches on the enormities of Popery, which only excited ridicule in the House of Commons, but which found admirers beyond its walls. He was a Scotchman, and appears to have been honestly fanatical, but his fanaticism was mixed with something of the vanity and ambition of a demagogue, and with a vein of recklessness and eccentricity closely akin to insanity. A 'Protestant Association,' consisting of the worst agitators and fanatics, was formed, and at a great meeting held on May 29, 1780, and presided over by Lord George Gordon, it was determined that 20,000 men should march to the Parliament House to present a petition for the repeal of the Relief Act.

It was about half-past two on the afternoon of Friday, June 2, that three great bodies, consisting of many thousands of men, wearing blue cockades, and carrying a petition which was said to have been signed by near 120,000 persons, arrived by different

---

[1] Campbell's *Chief Justices*, ii. 516.
[2] Several curious letters on this subject will be found in the *St. James's Chronicle* for 1765. The alarm at the alleged increase of Popery led the House of Lords in the next year to pass a motion requesting the bishops in their several dioceses to obtain from their clergy an account of the Catholics in each parish. See *Gent. Mag.* 1767 p. 429.

roads at the Parliament House. Their first design appears to have been only to intimidate, but they very soon proceeded to actual violence. The two Houses were just meeting, and the scene that ensued resembled on a large scale and in an aggravated form the great riot which had taken place around the Parliament House in Dublin during the administration of the Duke of Bedford. The members were seized, insulted, compelled to put blue cockades in their hats, to shout 'No Popery!' and to swear that they would vote for the repeal; and many of them, but especially the members of the House of Lords, were exposed to the grossest indignities. Lord Mansfield, who was now in his 76th year, was particularly obnoxious to the mob on account of the recent acquittal of a Popish priest by his influence. The windows of his carriage were broken, the panels were forced in, and he was in great danger of being torn to pieces, when the Archbishop of York succeeded with much courage in extricating him from the grasp of his assailants. The Chancellor, Lord Thurlow, who was equally unpopular, was not present, but the mob speedily recognised his brother, the Bishop of Lincoln. In a few moments a wheel of his carriage was wrenched off, and the bishop was for a time in extreme danger, when a law student succeeded in dragging him, half fainting, into a neighbouring house, where he disguised himself and then escaped over the roofs. The carriage of Lord Stormont was shattered to pieces, and he was for half an hour in the hands of the mob. Bathurst, Boston, Townshend, Hillsborough, and many other peers underwent the grossest ill-usage. The Duke of Richmond was that day bringing in a motion—to which the insensate proceedings of the mob furnished a ghastly commentary—in favour of putting all power in the hands of the populace by granting them universal suffrage and annual parliaments. But no serious discussion was possible. Pale, bruised, and agitated, with their wigs torn off, their hair dishevelled, their clothes torn and bespattered with mud, the peers of England sat listening to the frantic yells of the multitude who already thronged the lobbies. In the Commons Lord George Gordon presented the petition, and demanded its instant consideration. The House behaved with much courage, and after a hurried debate it was decided by 192 to 7 to adjourn its consideration till the 6th. Lord George Gordon several times appeared on the stairs of the gallery, and addressed the crowd, denouncing by name those who opposed him, and especially Burke and North; but Conway rebuked him in the sight and hearing of the mob, and Colonel Gordon, one of his own relatives, declared that the moment the first man of the mob entered the House he would plunge his sword into the body of Lord George. The doors were locked. The strangers' gallery was empty, but only a few doorkeepers and a few other ordinary officials protected the House, while the mob is said at first to have numbered not less than 60,000 men. Lord North succeeded in sending a messenger for the Guards, but many anxious hours passed before they arrived. Twice attempts were made to force the doors. At one time the danger seemed so imminent that Colonel Luttrell proposed that they should be thrown open, and that the members should, with their drawn swords, endeavour to cut their way through the mob. Happily, however, the crowd, though it contained some desperate fanatics, and some desperate criminals, consisted chiefly of idle, purposeless ruffians of the lowest class, bent only on mischief and amusement, but animated by no very bitter animosity, by no means desirous of carrying matters to extremity, and content with having kept the two Houses of Parliament for several hours blockaded and imprisoned. The stifling heat of the day caused many to drop away. Lord Mahon harangued the crowd with some effect from the window of a neighbouring coffee-house; Alderman Sawbridge and the Assistant Chaplain expostulated with them, but without much success, and at last about nine o'clock the troops appeared, and the crowd, without resisting, agreed to disperse.

A great part of them, however, were bent on further outrages. They attacked the Sardinian Minister's chapel in Duke Street, Lincoln's Inn Fields. They broke it open, carried away the silver lamps and other furniture, burnt the benches in the street, and flung the burning brands into the chapel. The Bavarian Minister's chapel in Warwick Street Golden Square was next attacked, plundered, and burnt before the soldiers could intervene. They at last appeared upon the scene, and some slight scuffling ensued, and thirteen of the rioters were captured

It was hoped that the riot had expended its force, for Saturday and the greater part of Sunday passed with little disturbance, but on Sunday afternoon new outrages began in Moorfields, where a considerable Catholic population resided. Several houses were attacked and plundered, and the chapels utterly ruined. The mob tore up altars, pulpits, pews and benches, and made large fires of them. Nothing but the bare walls remained, and even these sometimes fell before the heat. The soldiers were called in, but only when it was too late, and they were not suffered to fire. Authority seemed completely paralysed. The impunity that had hitherto attended the outrages, the hope of gigantic plunder, the madness which every hour became stronger and more contagious, the desperation of men who had already compromised themselves beyond return, all added to the flame. The mob were fast finding their leaders; and as their confidence in themselves increased, they loudly boasted that they would root out Popery from the land, release the prisoners who had been confined in Newgate for the outrages on Friday, and take signal vengeance on the magistrates who had committed them, and on all who had given evidence against them.

Monday, June 5, was the anniversary of the King's birthday, and the signs of official rejoicing contrasted strangely with the panic that was abroad. The military preparations were still miserably inadequate. A proclamation was issued promising a reward of 500*l.* for the detection of those who were concerned in plundering the Sardinian and Bavarian chapels, but the rioters were as far as possible from being intimidated. One party, carrying spoils of the chapels they had plundered, marched in triumph to Lord George Gordon's house in Welbeck Street, and then burnt them in the adjoining fields. Another party went to Virginia Lane, Wapping, and a third to Nightingale Lane, and in each of these places a Catholic chapel was soon in a blaze. A Catholic school at Hoxton was next destroyed. They then attacked the houses and shops of those who had given evidence against the rioters, burnt them, and plundered their contents. Sir George Savile's house in Leicester Square underwent the same fate. As the proposer of the Relief Bill, he was especially obnoxious to the fanatical portion of the rioters, and he had prudently taken the precaution of secretly removing his plate and some other valuables. The house, however, was completely wrecked, and when the evening closed in, it was little more than a ruin. The iron rails that surrounded it were torn up, and became formidable weapons in the hands of the mob.

All this was done with complete impunity, and as a natural consequence the spirits of the rioters rose higher and higher. On Tuesday, June 6, more daring enterprises were attempted. All the troops in London were concentrated on a few points, such as the Tower, the Houses of Parliament, St. James's Palace, and St. George's-in-the-Fields, and great districts were almost wholly unprotected. No Catholic house was any longer secure. No one knew how many were implicated in or sympathised with the rioters, for the most peaceful subjects now wore blue cockades as a protection from the mob. The two Houses met under strong military protection, but, in spite of that protection, Lord Sandwich, on his way to Parliament, was torn out of his carriage, which was broken in pieces, his face was cut, and he was rescued with difficulty by the Horse-guards. An attack was made on the house of Lord North, but it was successfully defended by a party of light horse, who with drawn swords charged the mob and trampled several men under their horses' hoofs. At six in the evening a party went to the house of Justice Hyde, near Leicester Fields, which in less than half an hour was utterly wrecked; while another party, consisting of many thousands of desperate men, passed rapidly through Long Acre, and down Holborn, till they arrived at Newgate. They summoned Mr. Akerman, the keeper, to release their comrades, and on his refusal they at once besieged the gaol. It had been lately built at an expense of 40,000*l.*, and was esteemed the strongest in England. The mob, however, were under the direction of men who well knew what they had undertaken, and they had provided themselves with sledge hammers and pickaxes to batter down the door, and long ladders to scale the walls. For a time the great iron gate resisted their efforts, and no gunpowder appears to have been employed. But another and not less formidable means of assault was speedily discovered. The house of the chief keeper, which adjoined the gaol, was easily broken open, and great masses of furniture were flung down through the windows, piled against the prison door, and then ignited. New combustibles were brought in from all sides, and a furious blaze was kindled, till the door was red-hot and tottering upon its hinges. In the meantime the keeper's house was set on fire, and the prison chapel caught the flames, while men, climbing on high ladders, flung burning brands through the grated orifices, and soon ignited the woodwork of the prison. The fire spread far and fast, casting its red and fluctuating glare upon the dense and savage crowd half-mad with drink and with excitement. One hundred constables endeavoured to disperse them, but the rioters closed around them and overpowered them, and flung their staves into the flames, and sentinels kept watch at every street to guard the depredators against surprise. About 300 prisoners, four of whom were under sentence of death, were confined in Newgate. They were divided between the hope of escape and the still more pressing fear of being burnt alive or smothered by the dense volumes of smoke that already rolled through the prison, and their piercing cries were clearly heard above the tumult. At length the iron door gave way beneath the heat and the repeated blows. The crowd rushed in; some climbed to the roof, and made a hole through the rafters; others penetrated through a gap made by the burning chapel. The cells were broken open, and the prisoners dragged out. All seem to have been saved except some intoxicated rioters, who sank down stupified with drink, and perished in the fall of the burning rafters. In a short time little but blackened walls remained of the greatest prison in London, and a new contingent of desperate malefactors was added to the rioters.

The mob had triumphed, but they did not pause in their career of crime. Parties were at once told off for different enterprises. One party attacked the Catholics in Devonshire Street, Red Lion Square; another destroyed the house of Justice Cox, in Great Queen Street; a third broke open the new prison in Clerkenwell, and released all the prisoners; a fourth attacked and wrecked the house of Sir John Fielding, who, as the most active magistrate in London, was especially obnoxious to them; a fifth, shortly after midnight, attacked the great house of Lord Mansfield in Bloomsbury Square.

Lord and Lady Mansfield had but just time to escape through the back when it was broken open, and in a few minutes the furniture was thrown out of the windows, and kindled into a blaze before the door. A collection of precious pictures, a noble law library, many priceless manuscripts from the pen of Mansfield himself, many important legal papers which were in his care, were thrown in to feed the flames. The wine cellars were broken open, and the crowd was soon mad with drink. A party of guards arrived when the ruin was almost accomplished, and, the Riot Act having been read, the magistrates ordered them to fire, and six men and a woman were killed, and several wounded; but the passions of the mob had risen too high for fear. It was remembered that Lord Mansfield possessed a country house between Highgate and Hampstead, and a party was sent to burn it; but they were anticipated and repelled by a party of horse. Eleven or twelve private houses were, however, that night in a blaze, and the conflagration mingled with the splendour of a general illumination; for the mob compelled every householder to illuminate in honour of their triumph.

Wednesday, June 7, long known in London by the name of 'Black Wednesday,' witnessed a spectacle such as London had never before seen. The long tension, the succession of sleepless nights, the complete triumph of the mob during four days, the proved incapacity of the City authorities to keep the peace, the knowledge that the worst criminals from the gaols were at large, the threatening warnings sent out by the mob that they would destroy the Bank, the prisons, and the palaces, had utterly cowed the people. A camp was formed and cannon were drawn out in Hyde Park. The Berkshire Militia, and soon after the Northumberland Militia, arrived to reinforce the regular troops. Strong guards were stationed at the chief public buildings, at the houses of the ministers, at Devonshire House and Rockingham House, and every important dwelling was barricaded as in a siege, and guarded by armed men. But a great section of London was completely in the hands of the mob. The Lord Mayor and the City magistrates seemed paralysed with fear. Many magistrates had fled from London; the houses of the few who were really active had been plundered or burnt, and all spirit of self-reliance and resistance appeared for the moment to have been extinguished. Fanaticism had but little part in the proceedings of this day; it was outrage and plunder in their most naked forms. Richard Burke, in a letter dated from 'What was London,' gives us a vivid picture of the abject terror that was prevailing. 'This is the fourth day,' he writes, 'that the metropolis of England (once of the world) is possessed by an enraged, furious, and numerous enemy. Their outrages are beyond description, and meet with no resistance. . . . What this night will produce is known only to the Great Disposer of things. . . . If one could in decency laugh, must one not laugh to see what I saw: a single boy, of fifteen years at most, in Queen Street, mounted on a pent-house demolishing a house with great zeal, but much at his ease, and throwing the pieces to two boys still younger, who burnt them for their amusement, no one daring to obstruct them? Children are plundering at noonday the City of London.'[1] Three boys, armed with iron bars torn up from Lord Mansfield's house, went down Holborn in the middle of the day shouting 'No Popery!' and extorting money from every shop, and they met with no opposition. Small parties of the same kind levied contributions in almost every district, no one daring to resist them, lest the mob should be called down upon their houses. One man on horseback was especially noticed who refused to take anything but gold. Dr. Johnson walked on that day to visit the ruins of Newgate, and he passed a party plundering the sessions house of Old Bailey. They consisted, as he observed, of less than 100 men, and 'they did their work at leisure, in full security, without sentinels, without trepidation, as men lawfully employed in full day.'[2] In the afternoon the shops were shut. 'No Popery!' was chalked upon the shutters, and bits of blue silk were hung out from almost every house. Rumours of the most terrible kind were circulated through the town. It was reported that the mob had threatened to let loose the lunatics from Bedlam and the lions from the Tower; that the French had organised the whole movement in order that the destruction of London, and especially of the Bank, might produce a national bankruptcy; that the soldiers had been tampered with,

[1] Burke's *Correspondence*, ii. 350, 351.   [2] Croker's *Boswell*, p. 648.

and would refuse to fire on the people. The Duke of Grafton gives a curious illustration of the universality of the alarm, in the fact that even the servants of the Secretary of State wore blue cockades to conciliate the mob. In the evening, scenes more terrible than any that had yet been witnessed took place. The King's Bench prison, the Fleet prison, the new Bridewell, the watchhouses in Kent Street near St. George's Church, the toll-gates on Blackfriars Bridge, and a great number of private houses, were simultaneously in flames. From a single point thirty-six distinct conflagrations were counted. The tall pinnacles of fire rising like volcanoes in the air, the shouts of the populace, the blaze reflected in the waters of the Thames, the shrieks of women, mingling with the crackling of the flames, with the crash of falling buildings, and, from time to time, with the sound of musketry as the troops fired in platoons into the crowd, all combined to form, in the words of an eye-witness, a perfect 'picture of a city sacked and abandoned to a ferocious enemy.' The rioters had seized large supplies of arms in the artillery grounds, and the great number of felons who were now in their ranks gave an additional desperation to the conflict. It was noticed that a brewer's boy, riding on a horse strangely decorated with chains from Newgate, led the most daring party. Under his guidance they attempted to capture and burn the Bank of England; but a strong body of soldiers, under the command of Colonel Holroyd, repelled them with the loss of many lives, and they were in like manner defeated in an attempt upon the Pay Office.

The riots were fortunately localised. The worst conflagrations were in Queen Street, Little Russell Street, Bloomsbury, and Holborn. Chains drawn across the Strand and Holborn, and protected by lines of soldiers, prevented the mob from passing westwards; but Charing Cross, the Haymarket, and Piccadilly were illuminated through fear. Strange to say, in the unmolested parts of the town the ordinary amusements still went on, and Horace Walpole notices that on this dreadful night Lady Ailesbury was at the play in the Haymarket, and that his four nieces were with the Duke of Gloucester at Ranelagh.[1] The night was fortunately very calm, and the sky

[1] *Letters to the Countess of Ossory,* June 7, 1780.

was clear, and glowing with the reflected flames, save where dark volumes of ascending smoke from time to time overspread it. The streets in the quarters where the riot was at its height were thronged with idle spectators—many of them women with infants in their arms—gazing on the scene, and mixing with terror-stricken fugitives who were endeavouring to save some portion of their property. Spectators were, in most places, in little danger; for the rioters were busily engaged, and they might be distinctly seen by the glare of the flames pursuing their work of plunder and demolition, for the most part entirely undisturbed, in the midst of the burning houses. Wraxall went through a great part of the disturbed district on foot, without the smallest hindrance, and he noticed that as he stood with his companions by the wall of St. Andrew's churchyard, near the spot where the fiercest conflagration was raging, a watchman with a lantern in his hand passed by, calling the hour as in a time of profound tranquillity.

The resistance was confined to a few points. Some attempts were made to extinguish the flames, but they were baffled by the mob. A large engine was brought to play upon the Fleet prison; but, in spite of the presence of soldiers, the rioters cut off its pipes and flung it into the flames. At Blackfriars Bridge, when the toll-gates were plundered, the soldiers fired with considerable effect. Many rioters were killed; one man was noticed to run thirty or forty yards, when pierced by a bullet, before he dropped dead; and several, when dead or dying, are said to have been thrown by their comrades into the Thames. Others were killed in the attack on the King's Bench prison; but the greater number fell in the unsuccessful attacks on the Bank and on the Pay Office. The most terrible scene, however, took place near the decline of Holborn Hill, in front of St. Andrew's Church, where the buildings of a great Catholic distiller, named Langdale, were attacked and burnt. Immense casks of unrectified spirits, still wholly unfit for human consumption, were staved in, and the spirits flowed in great streams along the road, while men, women, and children gathered it up in pails or lapped it with their hands. Such a scene of drunken madness had perhaps never been before exhibited in England. Numbers, both of men and women, killed themselves by drinking the poisonous draught. Women with infants in their arms were seen lying insensible along the road. Soon the fire reached the spirits, and it leapt forth, with a tenfold fury, in the midst of the reeling and dizzy crowd who were plundering the house. Numbers fell into the burning ruins, or into the midst of the liquid fire. Eight or nine wretched creatures were dragged out when half-burnt, but most of those who fell perished by one of the most horrible of deaths.

The night of June 7 was the end of all that was serious in the Gordon riots. The defeat of the attacks upon the Bank and the Pay Office, and the terrible scene on Holborn Hill, had broken the spirits and power of the rioters, while the introduction into London of large bodies of regular troops and of militia had made further resistance impossible. In addition to the permanent debility and indeed impotence of the London police force, and to the incompetence of the Lord Mayor and of several of the City magistrates, other causes combined to paralyse the civil power. The military forces at the disposal of the Crown were diminished by the exigencies of the great war which was raging in America. The Ministry of Lord North was already tottering to its fall, and its weakness enfeebled every branch of the Executive, while the recollection of the furious outbursts of popular indignation which had been aroused against those who employed soldiers in suppressing the Wilkes riots in 1769 made both magistrates and ministers extremely timid.[1] As Lord Mansfield once said with profound truth, 'It is the highest humanity to check the infancy of tumults, and a well-directed volley on the first day of the riots, though it would have exposed the Government to much foolish declamation, would probably have prevented all the horrible scenes that ensued. It is a curious fact that Wilkes, who had been the instigator or the pretext of the last great riots in London, took, as alderman, a distinguished and courageous part in suppressing the Gordon riots, in defending the Bank, and in protecting the Catholics, and he received the special thanks

---

[1] In 1776—four years before the Gordon riots—Dr. Johnson had said, 'The characteristic of our own Government at present is imbecility. The magistrates dare not call the Guards for fear of being hanged. The Guards will not come for fear of being given up to the blind rage of popular juries.' —Croker's *Boswell*, p. 509.

of the Privy Council for his services. No one, however, in this trying period appeared in a more honourable light than the King. The calm courage which he never failed to show, and his extreme tenacity of purpose, which in civil affairs often proved very mischievous, were in the moments of crisis peculiarly valuable. Many lives and a vast amount of property had been sacrificed because no officer dared to allow his soldiers to fire except by the direction of a magistrate, and after the Riot Act had been read and a whole hour had elapsed. Such an interpretation of the law made the display of soldiers in the midst of burning houses and in the agonies of a great struggle little more than a mockery, and the King strongly contested it. On the 7th he called of his own accord a meeting of the Privy Council, and obtained from Wedderburn, the Attorney-General, an opinion that, if a mob were committing a felony, such as burning down a house, and could not be prevented by any other means, the military might and ought to fire on them at once, and that the reading of the Riot Act under such circumstances was wholly unnecessary. Much hesitation appears to have been shown in the Council, but the King, declaring that at least one magistrate would do his duty, announced his intention of acting on his own responsibility, on the opinion of Wedderburn, and his readiness, if any difficulty were shown, to lead his guards in person. The Council at length agreed with the opinion, and a discretionary power was given to the soldiers, which, though it was much complained of by some constitutional pedants, was manifestly necessary, and was the chief means of suppressing the riots.[1]

In the course of the four days during which the riots were at their height no less than seventy-two private houses and four gaols were destroyed.[2] Of the number of the rioters who were killed it is impossible to speak with accuracy. No account was made of those who died of drink, who perished in the ruins or in the burning spirits, who were thrown into the Thames, or who were carried away when wounded and concealed in their own homes. Excluding these, it appears from a report issued by

[1] See Campbell's *Chancellors*, viii. 41–43. Jesse's *Memoirs of Geo. III.*, ii. 276–279.
[2] See Lord Loughborough's Charge, *Ann. Reg.* 1780, p. 281.

Amherst shortly after the suppression of the riots, that 285 had been killed or had died of their wounds, and that 173 wounded prisoners were still in his hands. In the opinion of the most competent judges the whole city had been in imminent danger of destruction, and owed its escape mainly to the fact that the mob at the time when it would have been impossible to have resisted them, wasted their strength upon chapels and private buildings, instead of at once attacking the Bank and the public offices, and also to the happy accident that on the night of the 7th there was scarcely a breath of wind to spread the flames. 135 prisoners were soon after brought to trial, and 59 were capitally convicted, of whom 21 were executed. Lord George Gordon was thrown into the Tower, and was tried before Lord Mansfield on the charge of high treason for levying war upon the Crown. The charge was what is termed by lawyers 'constructive treason.' It rested upon the assertion that the agitation which he had created and led was the originating cause of the outrages that had taken place. As there was no evidence that Lord George Gordon had anticipated these outrages, as he had taken no part in them, and had even offered his services to the Government to assist in their suppression, the accusation was one which, if it had been maintained, would have had consequences very dangerous to public liberty. After one of the greatest speeches of Erskine, Lord George Gordon was acquitted, and he still retained such a hold over large classes that thanksgivings were publicly offered up in several churches and chapels. He was many years after thrown into prison for a libel upon Marie Antoinette, and he died in Newgate in 1793. Before the close of his life he startled his theological admirers by his conversion to Judaism.[1]

[1] The three most detailed contemporary accounts of these riots are: the *Narrative of the Late Disturbances in London and Westminster*, by William Vincent, of Gray's Inn (the real writer of this, which is the fullest account of the riots, was Thomas Holcroft); the *Annual Register* of 1780, which also contains reports of the trials of the chief rioters; and an anonymous *Narrative of the Proceedings of Lord George Gordon and the Persons assembled under the Denomination of the Protestant Association* (London, 1780). The poet Crabbe witnessed some of the scenes, and especially the capture of Newgate, and he describes them in a letter in his biography, which is unfortunately imperfect. Horace Walpole and Wraxall were both witnesses of the scenes on Black Wednesday. The first has described them very fully in his letters to Lord Strafford and to the Countess of Ossory; and the second in his *Memoirs*. See also a

In the House of Commons a series of resolutions were introduced by Burke with the concurrence of the Government, vindicating the recent Relief Bill, and condemning the misrepresentations which had led to the tumults. An attempt was made to allay the fears of the more fanatical Protestants by a Bill introduced by Sir George Savile forbidding Catholics from taking any part in the education of Protestants; but though it passed the Commons, it miscarried in the Lords.

The riots of 1780 do not properly belong to the period of time with which the present chapter is occupied; but it is the plan of this book to prefer the order of subjects to the order of chronology, and these disturbances were the immediate consequence of the religious legislation under Lord North. Making every allowance for the amount of ordinary crime which entered into them, and considering how infinitesimal was the provocation that produced them, they display a depth and intensity of fanaticism we should scarcely have expected in the eighteenth century; and similar disturbances, though on a much smaller scale, took place at Hull, Bristol, and Bath. The disgrace was keenly felt both at home and abroad.[1] Secret negotiations for peace were at this time going on with Spain, and it was noticed that the reports of the riots in London greatly interfered with them, for the no-Popery fanaticism in London irritated the public opinion of Spain, while the success of the rioters was thought clearly to prove the weakness of the Government.[2] 'Our danger,' wrote Gibbon shortly after the suppression, 'is at an end, but our disgrace will be lasting, and the month of June 1780 will ever be marked by a dark and diabolical fanaticism which I had supposed to be extinct.'[3]

---

letter from Dr. Warner in Jesse's *Life of Selwyn*, iv. 327–335, and the interesting journal of the Moravian, James Hutton.—Benham's *Life of Hutton*, pp. 530–536. I need scarcely refer to the admirable narrative of Dickens, in *Barnaby Rudge*, based upon Holcroft, Walpole, and the *Annual Register*.

[1] See e.g. the two well-known poems of Cowper on the burning of Lord Mansfield's library.

[2] See Cumberland's *Memoirs*, ii. 35–36, 48.

[3] *Miscellaneous Works*, ii. 241. 'Rien,' wrote Madame Du Deffand, 'n'est plus affreux que tout ce qui arrive chez vous. Votre liberté ne me séduit point. Cette liberté tant vantée me paraît bien plus onéreuse que notre esclavage.'—Walpole's *Letters*, vi. 88. In one of the letters of Maria Theresa to Marie Antoinette (June 30, 1780) she speaks with great dislike of a contemplated visit of the Emperor to England: 'Surtout après la terrible émeute, inouïe entre les puissances civilisées qui vient de se

To a writer of the nineteenth century, however, the lesson to be derived from the narrative is not altogether a gloomy one. Whatever judgment may be formed in other respects in the old controversy between those who regard the history of modern England as a history of unqualified progress, and those who regard it in its most essential features as a history of decay, there is at least one fact which no serious student of the eighteenth century will dispute. It is, that the immense changes which have taken place in the past century in the enlargement of personal and political liberty, and in the mitigation of the penal code, have been accompanied by an at least equal progress in the maintenance of public order and in the security of private property in England.

The Government of Lord North during the period preceding the great outbreak of the American War was almost wholly occupied with domestic, Indian, and colonial questions, and neither exercised nor aspired to exercise any considerable influence on the affairs of other nations. The Revolution, which in 1772 changed the Constitution of Sweden, breaking the power of the aristocracy and aggrandising that of the Crown, was effected, in a great measure, under French instigation, and England had no voice in the infamous treaty which in the same year sanctioned the first partition of Poland, or in the treaty of Kainardji in 1774, by which Russia made the Crimea a separate khanate, and greatly extended both her own frontier and her influence in Turkey. In 1772 the Government had to contend with a keen commercial crisis and a period of acute and general distress. In many parts of England there were desperate food riots. Several banks broke, and a widespread panic prevailed.[1] But in Parliament the Government continued for some years invincibly strong, and its Indian policy and the earlier parts of its American policy appear to have been generally regarded either with approval or with indifference.

passer. Voilà cette liberté tant prônée—cette législation unique. Sans religion, sans mœurs, rien ne se soutient.' — Arneth, *Correspondance secrète de Marie Thérèse et Marie Antoinette*, iii. 444. Hillsborough, in a private letter to Buckinghamshire, the Lord-Lieutenant of Ireland, speaks of 'the dreadful and unaccountable insurrection which for four days together has made such devastation in this town, and threatened not less than a total destruction of it.'—June 10, 1780. MSS. Record Office.

[1] Walpole's *Last Journals*, i. 88, 122, 128. *Ann. Reg.* 1772, 90, 91, 109, 110.

In 1774 Parliament was dissolved shortly before the natural period of its existence had expired; and the American measures of the Government, if they had been seriously unpopular in the constituencies, would certainly have affected the elections. The election, however, fully confirmed the ministerial majority.[1] In the first important party division on an American question that followed the dissolution the ministers counted 264 votes to 73.[2] The Reform spirit appeared to have almost died away. Grenville's Act for the trial of disputed elections was, it is true, renewed and made perpetual in 1774, in spite of the opposition of Lord North; but different motions for shortening the duration of Parliament, and for making its constitution more popular, were rejected without difficulty, and appear to have excited no interest. The city of Westminster supported the ministers, and the democratic fervour of the City of London had greatly subsided. Wilkes found rivals and bitter enemies in Horne and Townshend; but at last, after two disappointments, he became Lord Mayor of London in 1774, and in the election of the same year he without opposition regained his seat as member for Middlesex; but though he made some good speeches against the policy of the Government in America, his position in Parliament was never a distinguished one, and he soon abandoned the character and the practices of an agitator. All the worst measures of American coercion that preceded the Declaration of Independence were carried by enormous majorities in Parliament. The Act for closing Boston harbour passed its chief stages without even a division. The Act for subverting the charter of Massachusetts was finally carried in the House of Commons by 239 to 64, in the House of Lords by 92 to 20.

---

[1] Lord Russell thinks that 'the abrupt dissolution prevented any influence being exercised by American affairs on the temper of the elections,' and he quotes a speech of Lord Suffolk, who said he advised the dissolution, foreseeing that if it were delayed the Americans would take steps 'to influence the general election by creating jealousies, fears, and prejudices among the mercantile and trading part of the nation.'—Russell's *Life of Fox*, i. 70, 71. According to Walpole one reason of the premature dissolution was, that 'the advices from America, though industriously concealed, were so bad that great clamour was feared from the American merchants and trading towns'—*Last Journals*, i. 399. At the same time the American Coercion Acts were among the most conspicuous acts of the Government in the late Parliament, and they must necessarily have had a considerable part in determining the votes of the electors.

[2] Walpole's *Last Journals*, i. 436.

The Act for enabling the Governor of Massachusetts to send colonists accused on capital charges to be tried in England, was ultimately carried in the Commons by 127 to 24, in the Lords by 43 to 12. The motion for repealing the tea duty, which was supported by one of the greatest speeches of Burke, was rejected by 182 to 49. In February 1775 the address moved by Lord North, pledging Parliament to support the Government in crushing the resistance in America, was carried by 296 to 106, and an amendment of Fox, censuring the American policy of the ministers, was rejected by 304 to 105. In March the conciliatory propositions of Burke were defeated by the previous question, which was carried by 270 to 78. In May the very respectful remonstrance of the General Assembly of New York, which was one of the last efforts of conciliation by the moderate party in America, was censured by the House of Commons, as 'inconsistent with the legislative authority of Parliament,' by 186 to 67. The Duke of Grafton had urged in the Cabinet the repeal of the tea duty, but had been outvoted. He still remained for some time in the ministry, trying in vain to modify its policy in the direction of conciliation. In August 1775 he wrote a strong remonstrance to Lord North on the subject. Seven weeks later he resigned the Privy Seal and went into opposition, declaring in Parliament that he had hitherto 'concurred when he could not approve, from a hope that in proportion to the strength of the Government would be the probability of amicable adjustment,' and recommending the repeal of all Acts relating to America which had been carried since 1763. But although Grafton had very lately been Prime Minister of England, he did not, according to Walpole, carry six votes with him in his secession.[1] The resignation of Conway, which immediately followed, proved even less important. Dartmouth, who had hitherto directed American affairs, obtained the Privy Seal, and he was replaced by Lord George Germaine, better known under the name of Lord George Sackville, who had never overcome the stigma which his conduct at Minden had left upon his reputation, but

---

[1] Walpole's *Last Journals*, iii. 3. Donne's *Correspondence of George III.* i. 281, 282. Thackeray's *Chatham*, ii. 307, 308.

who was an able administrator, and a still more able debater. He speedily infused a new energy into the direction of American affairs, and the enlistment of the German troops appears to have been principally due to him. The Opposition in the beginning of 1776 was almost contemptible in numbers, and at the same time divided and discredited. The Duke of Richmond in one House, and Burke in the other, were the steadiest and most powerful opponents of the American policy of the Government, and they had now found an ally, who excelled them both as a parliamentary debater, in Charles Fox, who, having been dismissed from the Government in February 1774, at once threw himself with a passionate vehemence into the Opposition.

His secession, like most acts of his early life, was very discreditable in its circumstances. A libel on the Speaker, written by Horne, had been brought under the notice of the House of Commons. Lord North, with his usual moderation, would gladly have suffered the matter to drop; but one of the members insisted on Woodfall, the printer, appearing before the House, and it was moved, upon his apology, that he should be committed to the Sergeant-at-Arms. North, after some hesitation, agreed to this course; but Charles Fox, who was at this time a Commissioner of the Treasury, in opposition to the known wishes of his chief moved that Woodfall should be committed to Newgate, declared that he selected this gaol in defiance of the City and Sheriffs, in whose jurisdiction it lay, and insisted on carrying his motion to a division. Lord North, perplexed, irresolute, and embarrassed by a previous speech in which he had leaned towards severity, voted with his turbulent subordinate; but most of the ministerial party were on the other side, and the motion of Fox was rejected by 152 to 68. Such an act of glaring insubordination could not be passed over. The King wrote next day, with much indignation, 'I am greatly incensed at the presumption of Charles Fox in obliging you to vote with him last night, but approve much of your making your friends vote in the majority; indeed, that young man has so thoroughly cast off every principle of common honour and honesty that he must become as contemptible as he is odious, and I hope you will let him know that you are not insensible of his conduct towards you.'[1] About ten days later Lord North curtly dismissed Fox, who thus, at the age of twenty-five, was finally severed from the Tories.

He did not for some years formally attach himself to any section of the Whigs;[2] but he passed at once from an extreme Tory into virulent and unqualified opposition to his former chief, and he was conspicuous beyond all other speakers for his attacks upon the American policy of the Government. It must be acknowledged, however, that he never appears when in office to have taken any active part in defending the American policy of the Government, that this policy only attained its full distinctness and prominence after his dismissal, and that his father had from the first disapproved of the taxation of America.[3] From an early period of his life, Fox seems to have had some intimacy with Burke,[4] and the conversation of that extraordinary man profoundly influenced his opinions. The sincerity of his opposition to the American War never appears to have been seriously questioned, and it is confirmed by the great sacrifices of popularity he made in the cause, and by the strong internal evidence of his speeches and letters. The circumstances of his secession, his extreme youth, and the extravagant dissipation in which he at this time indulged,[5] deprived him of all the weight that attaches to character; but his extraordinary debating skill developed rapidly in opposition, and Grattan, who had heard him speak in many periods of his career, considered his speeches during the American war the most brilliant he ever delivered.[6]

The division of opinion in the country upon the American question was probably much more equal than in Parliament, and it is also much more difficult to estimate with accuracy; but it appears to me evident that in 1775 and in 1776 the preponderating opinion, or at least the opinion of the most powerful and most intelligent classes in the community, was on American questions with the King and with his ministers. In February 1775, Lord Camden wrote, 'I am grieved to observe that the landed interest is almost altogether anti-

---

[1] *Correspondence of George III. and Lord North,* i. 170.
[2] See *Correspondence of Fox,* i. 223.
[3] Ibid. i. 122, 123.
[4] Ibid. p. 26.
[5] Walpole's *Last Journals,* ii. 4.
[6] *Correspondence of Fox,* i. 298.

American, though the common people hold the war in abhorrence, and the merchants and tradesmen, for obvious reasons, are likewise against it.'[1] The Established Church was strenuously anti-American, and the Bishops voted steadily for the measures of coercion.[2] The two Universities presented addresses on the same side, and the addresses from the great towns in favour of the Government were both more numerous and more largely signed than those which opposed it. Manchester, which was still, as in 1745, a great centre of English Toryism, led the way;[3] while on the other hand, 'the majority of the inhabitants of the great trading cities of London and Bristol still wished and struggled to have matters restored to their ancient state.'[4] It was said, however, with some truth, that the opposition of the merchants was mainly an opposition of interest, and the opposition of the City an opposition of faction, and it was acknowledged by the warmest advocates of the Americans that the trading classes on this question were greatly divided, and the bulk of them exceedingly languid in their opposition. The cessation of the Turkish war and of the troubles in Poland had revived trade, and the loss of American commerce was not yet sensibly felt, while the supply of the army in America and the equipment of new ships of war had given a sudden stimulus to the transport trade and to many branches of English industry.[5] The stress of legal opinion in every stage of the controversy appears to have been hostile to the Americans, and, in 1776, Horace Walpole emphatically declared that 'the Court have now at their devotion the three great bodies of the clergy, army, and law.'[6] The general English opinion, which at the time of the repeal of the Stamp Act had been very favourable to the colonists, appears to have turned.

[1] Chatham's *Correspondence*, iv. 401.
[2] As Franklin wrote, 'Sixteen Scotch peers and twenty-four bishops, with all the Lords in possession or expectation of places, when they vote together unanimously, as they generally do for ministerial measures, make a dead majority that renders all debating ridiculous.'—Franklin's *Works*, v. 46.
[3] See a valuable note by Mr. Donne in the *Correspondence of George III. and Lord North*, i. 267–271.
[4] See the very remarkable and impartial analysis of English opinion (very probably written by Burke) in the *Annual Register*, 1776, pp. 38, 39.
[5] Ibid. p. 38. See, too, on the apathy of the trading classes at this time, Walpole's *Last Journals*, ii. 6; Burke's *Correspondence*, ii. 50; *Correspondence of George III. and Lord North*, i. 235, 236, 272, 273.
[6] Walpole's *Last Journals*, ii. 90, 91.

There was a strong feeling of indignation at the recent proceedings in America; a general belief that, as a matter of patriotism, Government ought now to be supported, even though some of its past acts had been culpable; a widespread anticipation that by a little decision all resistance might be overcome, that the civil war might still be averted, or that at least it might be terminated in a single campaign.

The great strength of the Opposition lay in the Nonconformist bodies, who were in general earnestly and steadily in favour of the Americans. The 'Essay on Liberty,' by Dr. Price, which was published in 1775, was a powerful defence of their cause, and it identified it very skilfully with the cause of constitutional liberty and of parliamentary reform at home. In two years it passed through eight editions, and in the judgment of Walpole it was 'the first publication on that side that made any impression.'[1] But though the majority of the old Dissenters were staunch supporters of the Americans, even in their ranks there was some languor and division,[2] while a large section of the Methodists, as we have already seen, took the other side. The tract of John Wesley against the American pretensions had an enormous circulation. Lord Dartmouth was one of the most conspicuous laymen in the Evangelical religious world; and Cowper, the great poet of the movement, believed that the King would be committing a sin if he acknowledged the independence of America. Literary opinion was, on the whole, anti-American. The views of Junius, of Adam Smith, and of Dean Tucker have been already given. Dr. Johnson was a leading pamphleteer in support of the Government. Gibbon in Parliament steadily supported Lord North, and Robertson, though somewhat timidly, leaned to the same side. Hume, however, though in most of his sympathies a decided Tory, was one of the very few men who as early as 1775 agreed cordially with Burke that the attempt to coerce America could lead to nothing but disaster and ruin.[3]

---

[1] *Last Journals,* ii. 22, 23.
[2] Walpole in one place even asserts that the Presbyterians and other Dissenters in England 'were entirely passive,' being bribed or sold by their leaders, though those in Ireland were active on the American side' (Ibid. 84, 85); and in another place he says, the Dissenters, though on the whole American, 'were yet kept quiet by pensions to their chiefs.'—Ibid. pp. 323, 324.
[3] See Donne's notes to the *Corre-*

The confidential letters of Burke throw much valuable light on the condition of English opinion on the American question, and they are full of bitter complaints of the languor or alienation even of the natural supporters of the Whig party. In January 1775, describing the failure of his friends to arrest the American measures of the ministry, he says: 'The mercantile interest, which ought to have supported with efficacy and power the opposition to the fatal cause of all this mischief, was pleaded against us, and we were obliged to stoop under the accumulated weight of all the interests in this kingdom. I never remember the opposition so totally abandoned as on that occasion.'[1] In the August of the same year, he writes with great bitterness to Rockingham: 'As to the good people of England, they seem to partake every day more and more of the character of that administration which they have been induced to tolerate. I am satisfied that within a few years there has been a great change in the national character. We seem no longer that eager, inquisitive, jealous, fiery people which we have been formerly. . . . No man commends the measures which have been pursued, or expects any good from those which are in preparation, but it is a cold, languid opinion, like what men discover in affairs that do not concern them. . . . The merchants are gone from us and from themselves. . . . The leading men among them are kept full fed with contracts and remittances and jobs of all descriptions, and are indefatigable in their endeavours to keep the others quiet. . . . They all, or the greatest number of them, begin to snuff the cadaverous *haut goût* of lucrative war. War is indeed become a sort of substitute for commerce. The freighting business never was so lively on account of the prodigious taking up for transport service. Great orders for provisions and stores of all kinds . . . keep up the spirits of the mercantile world, and induce them to consider the American war not so much their calamity as their resource in an inevitable distress.'[2] 'The real fact,' he wrote a month later, 'is that the generality of the people of England are now led away by the misrepresentations and arts of the Ministry, the Court and their abettors, so that the violent

---

[1] *spondence of George III. and Lord North*, i. 279, 280; ii. 401.

[2] Burke's *Correspondence*, ii. 2. Ibid. ii. 48–50.

measures towards America are fairly adopted and countenanced by a majority of individuals of all ranks, professions, or occupations in this country,' and he complains that the Opposition were compelled 'to face a torrent not merely of ministerial and Court power, but also of almost general opinion.'[1]

The party in England, however, that favoured the Americans, though it could not shatter the Government, was quite sufficiently strong to encourage the colonists, and many of its members threw themselves into their cause with the most passionate ardour. It is easy to imagine the effect that must have been produced on the excited minds beyond the Atlantic by the language of Chatham in his great speech in January 1775. 'The spirit which resists your taxation in America,' he said, ' is the same that formerly opposed loans, benevolences, and ship-money in England. . . . This glorious spirit of Whiggism animates three millions in America who prefer poverty with liberty to gilded chains and sordid affluence, and who will die in defence of their rights as freemen. . . . For myself, I must declare that in all my reading and observation—and history has been my favourite study—I have read Thucydides, and have studied and admired the master states of the world—that for solidity of reasoning, force of sagacity, and wisdom of conclusion under such a complication of difficult circumstances, no nation or body of men can stand in preference to the General Congress at Philadelphia. . . . All attempts to impose servitude upon such men, to establish despotism over such a mighty continental nation, must be vain, must be fatal. We shall be forced ultimately to retract. Let us retract while we can, not when we must.' In accordance with these sentiments he withdrew his eldest son from the army rather than suffer him to be engaged in the war.[2] Lord Effingham for the same reason threw up his commission, and Amherst is said to have refused the command against the Americans.[3] In 1775 the question was openly debated in Parliament whether British officers ought to serve their sovereign against the Americans, and no less a person than General Conway leaned decidedly to the negative, and compared the case to that of French officers who were em-

---

[1] Burke's *Correspondence*, ii. 68, 69. [2] Chatham *Correspondence*, iv. 420.
[3] Walpole's *Last Journals*, i. 459

ployed in the massacre of St. Bartholomew.[1] The Duke of Richmond, after the battle of Bunker's Hill, declared in Parliament that 'he did not think that the Americans were in rebellion, but that they were resisting acts of the most unexampled cruelty and oppression.'[2] The Corporation of London in 1775 drew up an address strongly approving of their resistance,[3] and the addresses of several other towns expressed similar views. A great meeting in London, and also the guild of merchants in Dublin, returned thanks to Lord Effingham for his recent conduct, and in 1776 the freedom of the City was conferred on Dr. Price, on account of his defence of the Americans.[4] An English subscription—though a very small one—was raised for the relief of the Americans who were wounded at Lexington, and for the relatives of those who had been killed,[5] and in 1777 Horne was sentenced to a year's imprisonment and to a fine of 200*l*. for publishing an advertisement of the Constitutional Society, accusing the English troops in that battle, of murder.[6] When Montgomery fell at the head of the American troops in the invasion of Canada, he was eulogised in the British Parliament as if he had been the most devoted servant of the Crown.[7]

With scarcely an exception the whole political representation of Scotland in both Houses of Parliament supported Lord North, and was bitterly hostile to the Americans. Scotland, however, is one of the very few instances in history, of a nation whose political representation was so grossly defective as not merely to distort but absolutely to conceal its opinions. It was habitually looked upon as the most servile and corrupt portion of the British Empire; and the eminent liberalism and the very superior political qualities of its people seem to have been scarcely suspected to the very eve of the Reform

---

[1] *Parl. Hist.* xviii. 998. Cartwright, who in the next generation became so prominent as a parliamentary reformer, refused a naval appointment at this time because it would imply service against the Americans. *Life and Correspondence of Major Cartwright*, i. 75, 81.
[2] *Parl. Hist.* xviii. 1076.
[3] Adolphus, ii. 253. *Annual Reg.*
1776, p. 41.
[4] *Annual Register*, 1776, pp. 41–43, 126. Walpole's *Last Journals*, i. 502, 503; ii. 23.
[5] Franklin's *Life*, p. 401.
[6] *Annual Register*, 1777, p. 211.
[7] *Annual Register*, 1776, p 15. Fox's *Correspondence*, i. 142. Adolphus, ii. 241.

Bill of 1832. That something of that liberalism for which Scotland is now so distinguished, existed at the outbreak of the American War, may, I think, be inferred from the very significant fact that the Government were unable to obtain addresses in their favour either from Edinburgh or Glasgow.[1] The country, however, was judged mainly by its representatives, and it was regarded as far more hostile to the American cause than either England or Ireland. A very able observer, when complaining of the apathy and lassitude with which the American policy of the Government was generally regarded, adds, 'We must except from all these observations the people of North Britain, who almost to a man, so far as they could be described or distinguished under any particular denomination, not only applauded, but proffered life and fortune in support of the present measures.'[2]

'In Ireland,' says the same writer, 'though those in office and the principal nobility and gentry declared against America, by far the majority of the Protestant inhabitants there, who are strenuous and declared Whigs, strongly leaned to the cause of the colonies.'[3] 'There are three million Whigs in America,' said Chatham, in 1775, 'and all Ireland is Whig, and many in England.'[4] Protestant Ireland was indeed far more earnestly enlisted on the side of the Americans than any other portion of the Empire. Emigrants from Ulster formed a great part of the American army, and the constitutional question of the independence of the Irish Parliament was closely connected with the American question. The movement of opinion, however, was confined to the Protestants. The Catholic gentry, on this as on all other occasions of national danger, presented addresses to the King attesting in strong terms their loyalty,

[1] *Correspondence of Geo. III.* i. 269.
[2] *Annual Register*, 1776, p. 39. The same character seems to have extended to the Scotch in America. 'The Irish in America,' it was said, 'with a few exceptions were attached to independence. . . . The Scotch, on the other hand, though they had formerly sacrificed much to liberty in their own country, were generally disposed to support the claims of Great Britain.'—Ramsay's *History of the American Revolution,* ii. 311. Ramsay adds, however, that 'the army and the Congress ranked among their best officers and most valuable members some individuals of that nation.'—*Ibid.* Adams notices the strong opposition of the Scotch, who were settled in Virginia, to the measures taken by the Congress in 1775.—Adams' Diary, *Works*, ii. 431.
[3] *Annual Register*, 1776, p. 39.
[4] Walpole's *Last Journals*, i. 446. Thackeray's *Chatham*, ii. 286.

but the mass of the Catholic population were politically dead, and can hardly be said to have contributed anything to the public opinion of the country.

One remarkable fact, however, was noticed both in England and Ireland. There was a complete absence of alacrity and enthusiasm in enlisting for the army and navy.[1] This was one of the chief reasons why Germans were so largely enlisted, and it is the more remarkable because Irish Catholics were now freely admitted into the service. For a long time the system of enrolling soldiers, and still more the system of enrolling sailors, had excited much discontent, and the legality of press-gangs had very lately been brought into question. The impressing for the navy rested rather on immemorial custom than on positive law, and it was pronounced by lawyers to be a part of the common law.[2] The impressing for the army was more rarely resorted to, but a statute of Anne authorised magistrates within their specified limits to impress for the army such able-bodied men as did not follow any lawful calling and had not some other support, and several subsequent Acts continued the system for limited periods. A special clause exempted such as had votes for members of Parliament from liability to impressment.[3] In 1757, a gentleman of property having been pressed and confined in the Savoy, his friends applied for an immediate writ of Habeas Corpus, under the well-known Act of Charles II. The question was not determined, as the gentleman was released by order of the Secretary of War; but the judges who were consulted all pronounced that this Act only applied to those who had committed or were accused of committing a criminal offence, and that a man accused of no crime could not claim its protection. A Bill was introduced in the beginning of 1758 to remedy this strange anomaly, but it was thrown out by the instrumentality of Lord Hardwicke,[4] and this extension of the Habeas Corpus Act was only granted in 1816.[5]

The enormous cruelty and injustice of the impressment for the navy, as it was actually carried on, can hardly be exag-

---

[1] See *Annual Register*, 1776, p. 39.
[2] Blackstone, book i. c. 13.
[3] 2 & 3 Anne, c. 19. *Parl. Hist.* xv. 875; Clode's *Military Forces of the Crown*, ii. 15-19. The last Act for impressment for the army appears to have expired in 1780.
[4] *Parl. Hist.* xv. 875-923.
[5] 56 Geo. III. c. 100.

gerated, and it seemed doubly extraordinary in a country which was so proud of its freedom. 'Impressment,' as has been truly said, 'is the arbitrary and capricious seizure of individuals from the general body of citizens. It differs from conscription as a particular confiscation differs from a general tax.'[1] Voltaire was much struck with this feature of English life, and he drew a vivid picture of a boatman on the Thames boasting to him one day of the glories of English freedom and declaring that he would sooner be a sailor in England than an archbishop in France, the next day with irons on his feet, begging money through the gratings of the prison into which he had been thrown without the imputation of any crime, and where he must remain till the ship was ready which was to carry him to the Baltic. In a system so violent and so arbitrary, all kinds of abuses were practised. As we have already seen, the press-gang was often employed to drag Methodist teachers from a work which the magistrates disliked. It was sometimes employed to avenge private grudges. It was thus that Fielding represents Lord Fellamar endeavouring to get rid of his rival by employing a lieutenant to press him. On one occasion in 1770 a marriage ceremony in St. Olave's, Southwark, was interrupted by a press-gang, who burst into the church, struck the clergyman, and tried to carry away the bridegroom.[2] As merchant ships came in from America, and the sailors looked forward, after their long voyage, to see once more their wives and children, a danger more terrible than that of the sea awaited them, for it was a common thing for ships of war to lie in wait for the returning vessels, in order to board them and to press their sailors before they landed.[3] Often the press-gang went down to some great sea-port and boarded all the merchant-ships lying at anchor, in order to collect sailors for the royal navy.[4] They were sometimes fiercely resisted. On one occasion in 1770, 110 impressed seamen who were being carried down the Thames in a tender, broke open the hatches, overpowered the officers and crew, ran the tender aground

---

[1] May's *Const. Hist. of England.* Hume, in his Essay 'On some remarkable Customs,' called attention to the great anomaly of impressment in a free country.

[2] *Annual Register*, 1770, p. 161.
[3] See the *Life of Bampfylde Moore Carew* (1749), pp. 128–130.
[4] *Annual Register*, 1770, p. 147.

on the coast of Essex, and thus succeeded in escaping.[1] On another, when the sailors of a merchant vessel, which was lying off Gravesend, saw the boat of a ship-of-war approaching, they seized all the arms on board and drove off their assailants with a loss of one man killed and of several dangerously wounded.[2] In 1779 a man was hung at Stafford for killing one of those who were endeavouring to press him, and a party of sailors were tried at Ipswich for the murder of a publican in whose house they were impressing sailors, but were acquitted on account of the impossibility of ascertaining who struck the blow.[3] Of the vast sum of private misery produced by the system it is difficult to form an adequate estimate. One case—which was probably but one of many—happened to attract considerable attention on account of its being mentioned in Parliament by Sir William Meredith, in 1777. A sailor had been taken in the press that followed the alarm about the Falkland Islands, and carried away, leaving a wife who was then not nineteen, with two infant children. The breadwinner being gone, his goods were seized for an old debt, and his wife was driven into the streets to beg. At last, in despair she stole a piece of coarse linen from a linendraper's shop. Her defence, which was fully corroborated, was that 'she had lived in credit and wanted for nothing till a press-gang came and stole her husband from her, but since then she had no bed to lie on, nothing to give her children to eat, and they were almost naked. She might have done something wrong, for she hardly knew what she did.' The lawyers declared that shop-lifting being a common offence, she must be executed, and she was driven to Tyburn with a child still suckling at her breast.[4]

Even worse than the authorised system was the illicit pressing for the East India Company. Great numbers of young men were inveigled or kidnapped by crimps in its service, confined often for long periods, and with circumstances of the most aggravated cruelty, in secret depôts which existed in the heart of London, and at last, in the dead of night, shipped for Hindostan. Several cases of this kind were detected in the latter part of the eighteenth century by the escape of

---

[1] *Annual Register*, 1770, p. 147.
[2] Ibid. p. 149.
[3] Ibid. 1779, pp. 204, 215, 216.
[4] *Parl. Hist.* xix. 238.

prisoners, and it was evident that the system was practised on a large scale.¹

The regular press-gang was not confined to England, and it formed one of the gravest and most justifiable grievances of the American colonists. As early as 1747, one of the most terrible riots ever known in New England was produced by the seizure of some Boston sailors by the press-gang of Admiral Knowles. An English vessel was burnt. English officers were seized and imprisoned by the crowd. The Governor was obliged to take refuge in the Castle. The sub-sheriff was impounded in the stocks, the militia refused to act against the people, and the Admiral was ultimately obliged to release his captives.² A similar resistance was shown to many subsequent attempts to impress in New England,³ and one of the first and ablest writers against the system was Benjamin Franklin. In England a great opposition was raised in the City of London in 1770 and 1771, at the time of the great press for seamen which was made when a war with Spain about the Falkland Islands appeared imminent. Press warrants in the City were only legal when backed by an alderman, and Crosby the Lord Mayor, and most of the aldermen refused to back them. Wilkes and Sawbridge, in their capacity of aldermen, dismissed some men who had been pressed in the City. A press-gang, which was beating a drum through the City, was brought before the Lord Mayor and reprimanded; and at a great meeting in Westminster Hall, at which both Wilkes and Sawbridge spoke, impressment was denounced as a violation of the Constitution.⁴ The agitation, however, did not spread. The attempts which had been made more than once since the Revolution to make impressing unnecessary, by a system of additional bounties and pensions, and by the formation of a reserve,⁵ had

---

¹ See several instances of the kind in Andrews' *XVIII. Cent.* p. 209–212. Phillimore's *Hist. of Geo. III.* pp. 60, 61. *Annual Register*, 1767, p. 82.
² Grahame's *History of the United States*, iii. 295–300.
³ Arnold's *Hist. of New England*, ii. 255, 256. See, too, on the pressing in New England, the very curious *Journal* of Thomas Chalkley from 1697 to 1741 (ed. 1850), pp. 313, 314, and Hutchinson's *Hist. of Massachusetts Bay*, p. 231.
⁴ *Annual Register*, 1770, pp. 157, 161, 162, 169, 174; 1771, pp. 16, 67, 68, 70.
⁵ See vol. i. p. 504. In 1770, in order to escape the necessity of pressing, several of the chief towns subscribed additional bounties for sailors who enlisted voluntarily. *Annual Register*, 1770, pp. 150, 163.

not succeeded, and it is remarkable that the legality and absolute necessity of impressment were at this time strongly asserted by three such different authorities as Chatham, Mansfield, and Junius.[1]

In the great difficulty of obtaining voluntary recruits for the American War, the press for sailors was very largely resorted to, and in 1776 it was especially fierce. In less than a month 800 men were seized in London alone, and several lives were lost in the scuffles that took place.[2]

While these means were employed for recruiting the navy, others of an equally questionable kind were found necessary for filling the vacancies in the army. I have noticed in a former chapter that it had been a common thing for press-gangs for the navy to hang about the prison-gates and seize criminals whose sentences had just expired, and this was not the only way in which the gaols were made to furnish their contingent for the defence of the country. Two or three Acts in favour of insolvent debtors had been passed, granting them their liberty on condition of enlisting in the army or navy, and in 1702 a system had begun which continued up to the time of the Peninsular War, of permitting criminals, who were undergoing their sentence, to pass into the army.[3] In the beginning of the American War, this system appears to have been much extended. The usual manner of disposing of criminals under sentence of transportation had hitherto been to send them to America, where they were sold as slaves to the planters; but the war that had just broken out rendered this course impossible. For a time the Government was in great perplexity. The gaols were crowded with prisoners whose sentence it was impossible to execute. The governors of the African colonies protested against the introduction of a criminal element among them. An Act was, it is true, passed, authorising the punish-

---

[1] Walpole's *Memoirs of Geo. III.* iv. 181. *Chatham Correspondence*, iii. 480, 481; iv. 22, 43. Adolphus, i. 459. Junius' *Letters* (signature Philo-Junius). Campbell's *Chief Justices*, ii. p. 419. Chatham said, 'I believe every man who knows anything of the British navy will acknowledge that, without impressing, it is impossible to equip a respectable fleet within the time in which such armaments are usually wanted.'—Thackeray's *Chatham*, ii. 217.

[2] Walpole's *Last Journals*, ii. 75 77, 81.

[3] Clode's *Military Forces of the Crown*, ii. 12-15

ment of hard labour in England as a substitute for transportation to 'any of his Majesty's colonies and plantations,' and galleys were set up in the Thames where criminals, under sentence of transportation, were employed in hard labour.[1] But it soon occurred to the Government that able-bodied criminals might be more usefully employed in the coercion of the revolted colonists,[2] and there is reason to believe that large numbers of criminals, of all but the worst category, passed at this time into the English army and navy. In estimating the light in which British soldiers were regarded in America, and in estimating the violence and misconduct of which British soldiers were sometimes guilty, this fact must not be forgotten. It is indeed a curious thing to notice how large a part of the reputation of England in the world rests upon the achievements of a force which was formed mainly out of the very dregs of her population, and to some considerable extent even out of her criminal classes.[3]

The difficulty of procuring voluntary recruits for the army and navy seems to show that, if the bulk of the poorer population of the country did not actively sympathise with the Americans, a war with a people of their own race and language

---

[1] 16 Geo. III. c. 43. Walpole's *Last Journals*, ii. 38. *Annual Register*, 1776, p. 163.

[2] My knowledge of this subject is derived from the 'Government Correspondence' in the Irish State Paper Office. On March 30, 1776, Lord Harcourt, the Lord-Lieutenant of Ireland, wrote to the Secretary of State, Lord Weymouth, complaining that the gaols in Ireland were full of convicts under sentence of transportation, 'as no merchant will contract to convoy them to America whilst the present rebellion subsists.' He proposed, therefore, to pardon such of them as were fit and serviceable men, 'on condition of their entering into his Majesty's land and sea service, as I shall direct.' Weymouth answered (April 23, 1776), 'The measure proposed by your Excellency for granting pardons to prisoners who may be found, on proper examination, to be fit for the sea or the land service, has been of late in many instances pursued here, and his Majesty approves of your granting pardons to prisoners in the several gaols of Ireland under these circumstances. But it will occur to your Excellency how necessary it is, that the enlisting officers should, in the strongest manner, be enjoined to examine and report, before the pardon shall be granted, whether the prisoners are really fit for service, as a discharge cannot so properly be granted. It should also be observed that when they are engaged, particular care should be taken to secure this kind of recruits, and that they be considered rather in a different light from those who enter voluntarily.'

[3] It does not appear to have been only the British troops who were recruited from the prisons. Speaking of the Germans in the British service, Goltz wrote to Frederick (March 13, 1777), 'Les recrues hessoises sont en grande partie des malfaiteurs détachés de la chaine.'—*Circourt, Action Commune de la France et de l'Amérique*, iii. 81.

had at least no popularity among them. In concluding this review of the condition of English opinion in 1776, a few words must be added about the relations of the American contest to English party principles. Chatham, as we have seen, invariably maintained that the American cause was essentially the cause of the Whigs. In his great speech in the beginning of 1775 he asserted that 'the great fundamental maxim' of the British Constitution is, 'that no subject of England shall be taxed but by his own consent,' and that 'to maintain this principle is the common cause of the Whigs on the other side of the Atlantic and on this.' In December 1777, when the war had been long declared, he extolled the Americans as 'Whigs in principle and heroes in conduct,' and he openly expressed his wish for their success. Like the Whigs the Americans made the full development of civil liberty, and especially the defence of the great Whig principle that taxation and representation are inseparably connected, the main object of their policy, and the highly democratic character of their political constitutions lay at the root of their resistance. Public meetings, instructions to members, all the forms of political agitation that had of late years grown up in England, were employed by the popular party in America. On the other hand, all who esteemed licentiousness rather than despotism the great danger of England, all who disliked the development of the popular element in the Constitution, all whose natural leaning was towards authority, repression, and prerogative, gravitated to the anti-American side. In America the supporters of the English Government were invariably called Tories. In England the King, the followers of Bute, and the whole body of Tories, were ultimately enlisted against the Americans, while the support of their cause became more and more the bond of union between the Whigs who followed Chatham and the Whigs who followed Rockingham. By a true political instinct the clergy of the Established Church and the country gentry, who were the natural supporters of Toryism, were generally ranged on one side, and the Dissenters and the commercial classes on the other.

So far the party lines of the American question appear very clear; but on the other hand, Grenville, who began the policy of taxing America, always called himself a Whig, he defended his measure by Whig arguments, and he strenuously maintained that the bulk of the party, in supporting the Americans, had deserted the orthodox traditions of their policy. The Whigs were the hereditary champions of the rights of Parliament, and it was the power of Parliament that was in question. The Whigs had made it one of their first objects to make the Sovereign dependent on Parliament for his supplies, and they were therefore bound to look with peculiar jealousy on a theory according to which supplies might be raised by requisition from the Crown, and for other than local purposes, by Assemblies over which Parliament had no control. The Whigs were the natural opponents of all extensions of the royal prerogative, and they could not with any consistency admit that the King could withdraw by charter a portion of his dominions from the full authority of Parliament. Much of the language and some of the arguments of the Americans were undoubtedly drawn from the Tory arsenal. As Lord North truly said, it was the colonists who appealed to the King's prerogative. It was the ministers who upheld the authority of Parliament. The Americans delighted in contrasting their devotion to the Sovereign with their repudiation of parliamentary control, and they dilated, in language which seemed an echo of that of the early Tories, upon the unconstitutional enlargement of the dominion of Parliament. With the deep-seated conservatism of the English character, the Whigs had always pretended that the Revolution had made no real change in the relative position of the great powers of the State; that it had only arrested encroachments by the Sovereign, and defined, asserted, and protected the ancient liberties of the people. The Americans, on the other hand, maintained with great reason that Parliament, since the Revolution, or at least since the Rebellion, had acquired a wholly new place in the British Empire, and that the arguments of English lawyers about the necessary subordination of all parts of the British Empire to the Supreme Legislature, and about the impossibility of the Sovereign withdrawing British subjects by charter from parliamentary control, were based upon a state of things which at the time when the colonies were founded existed neither in law nor in fact. 'At present,' Franklin wrote, 'the colonies consent and submit to the supremacy of the Legislature for the regulations of general commerce, but a submission to Acts of Parliament was no part of their original Constitution. Our former kings governed their colonies as they had governed their dominions in France, without the participation of British Parliaments. The Parliament of England never presumed to interfere in that prerogative till the time of the great Rebellion, when they usurped the government of all the King's other dominions, Ireland, Scotland, &c.'[1]

But although the arguments by which the followers of Grenville and Bedford maintained that their policy was a legitimate outcome of the principles of the Whig party were by no means without plausibility, or even without real force, the main current of Whig sentiment flowed irresistibly in the opposite direction. As the conflict deepened, the line of division corresponded closely with the division of parties. The whole body of the Tories, headed by the King, steadily supported a policy of coercion, while the Whigs made the cause of the colonists their own, though they defended it, as we have seen, by different arguments and in different degrees. Chatham could never tolerate the idea of an independent America, though he foresaw the danger at a very early stage of the conflict. He treated the whole question as one of the right of every free people to be taxed only by their own representatives. He strongly asserted the right and policy of the parliamentary restrictions of American commerce, and with Shelburne he emphatically protested against the new American doctrine that the Sovereign could not place his troops in any part of his dominions that he chose.[2] The Rockingham Whigs, on the other hand, while they regarded the surrender of the parliamentary power of taxation as a matter not of right but of policy, were prepared to make wide concessions in other

---

[1] Letter of B. Franklin, Nov. 29, 1769. *American Remembrancer*, 1775, p. 52. In a speech in 1775 Lord North said, 'If he understood the meaning of the words Whig and Tory, he conceived that it was the characteristic of Whiggism to gain as much for the people as possible, while the aim of Toryism was to increase the prerogative. In the present case, Administration contended for the right of Parliament, while the Americans talked of their belonging to the Crown. Their language, therefore, was that of Toryism.'—*Parl. Hist.* xviii. 771.

[2] Adolphus, ii. 309.

directions; and some members of the party, almost from the beginning of the struggle, were willing to consent to a final surrender of English dominion over the colonies. Of this section the Duke of Richmond was the most conspicuous. As early as 1776 he argued that America never could be subdued except at a ruinous expense; that by continuing the war, she would be forced into alliance with our natural enemy France; that if subdued, she would take the first opportunity of revolting, and that this opportunity would probably be when England was engaged in a deadly struggle, and when an American revolt might prove her ruin. If, then, he contended, America can no longer be kept amicably dependent, it is better to acknowledge her independence at once, to save further expenditure, to enter while it is still possible into close alliance with her, and thus to avert the great danger of her alliance with France.[1]

One other consideration weighed greatly with the Whig statesmen. It was the firm conviction of many, if not of all of them, that the triumph of the English in America would give such an ascendency to the Tory party and to the power of the Crown, that it would be fatal to English liberty. Such an opinion was more than once implied in the speeches of Chatham. It was the opinion of Fox[2] and of Horace Walpole,[3] and many years after the struggle had terminated it was deliberately reaffirmed by Burke.[4] We have a curious picture of the tone of thought prevailing among some of the Whig leaders

---

[1] These views were privately expressed by the Duke of Richmond to his brother-in-law, Mr. Connolly, in a remarkable letter dated Nov. 1776, now in the possession of Sir Charles Bunbury, who has kindly allowed me to make use of it. In Jan. 1778, Richmond declared in Parliament his readiness to acknowledge American independence. (Walpole's *Last Journals*, ii. 182.)

[2] Fox's *Correspondence*, i. 142–147.

[3] In March 1778, he writes, 'I had as little doubt but if the conquest of America should be achieved, the moment of the victorious army's return would be that of the destruction of our liberty.'—Walpole's *Last Journals*, ii. 241.

[4] In defending his conduct on the American question, he says, 'He certainly never could, and never did, wish the colonists to be subdued by arms. He was fully persuaded that if such should be the event, they must be held in that subdued state by a great body of standing forces, and perhaps of foreign forces. He was strongly of opinion that such armies, first victorious over Englishmen, in a conflict for English constitutional rights and privileges, and afterwards habituated (though in America) to keep an English people in a state of abject subjection, would prove fatal in the end to the liberties of England itself.'—'Appeal from the New to the Old Whigs,' Burke's *Works*, vi. 124.

in the beginning of the American contest, in a letter which was written by the Duke of Richmond to Burke from Paris in the August of 1776. Richmond had gone to France to prosecute his claim to an old French peerage, and he declares that the political condition of England was one reason why he was anxious to obtain it. England, he believed, was on the verge of despotism, and it would be a despotism more oppressive than that of France, for it would be less tempered by habit and manners. He himself was likely to be among the proscribed, and in that case, ' if America be not open to receive us, France is some retreat, and a peerage here is something.'[1]

Under all these circumstances, England entered into the ill-omened conflict in which she was engaged, profoundly divided. A party, small indeed in numbers, but powerful from its traditions, its connections, and its abilities, had identified itself completely with the cause of the insurgents, opposed and embarrassed the Government in every effort to augment its forces and to subsidise allies, openly rejoiced in the victories of the Americans, and exerted all its eloquence to justify and to encourage them. We must now pass to the other side of the Atlantic, and examine the movements of public opinion in America and the measures of the American Congress to organise the war.

[1] Burke's *Correspondence*, ii. 112-120.

www.ingramcontent.com/pod-product-compliance
Lightning Source LLC
Chambersburg PA
CBHW031940290426
44108CB00011B/630